# Assessment of Children and Youth with Special Needs

## SECOND EDITION

**Libby G. Cohen**

*The Spurwink Institute*

**Loraine J. Spenciner**

*University of Maine at Farmington*

Boston   New York   San Francisco
Mexico City   Montreal   Toronto   London   Madrid   Munich   Paris
Hong Kong   Singapore   Tokyo   Cape Town   Sydney

**Editor-in-Chief:** *Paul Smith*
**Executive Editor:** *Virginia Lanigan*
**Series Editorial Assistant:** *Robert Champagne*
**Marketing Manager:** *Amy Cronin*
**Composition Buyer:** *Linda Cox*
**Manufacturing Buyer:** *JoAnne Sweeney*
**Editorial-Production Administrator:** *Karen Mason*
**Editorial-Production Service:** *Denise Botelho, Colophon Production Service*
**Photo Researcher:** *Katharine S. Cook*
**Cover Designer:** *Kristina Mose-Libon*

For related titles and support materials, visit our online catalog at www.ablongman.com.

**Library of Congress Cataloging-in-Publication Data**
Cohen, Libby G.
    Assessment of children and youth with special needs / Libby G. Cohen, Loraine J. Spenciner.—2nd ed.
      p.  cm.
    Rev. ed. of: Assessment of children and youth.
    Includes bibliographical references and index.
    ISBN 0-205-37203-1 (alk. paper)
    1. Psychological tests for children. 2. Child development—Testing. 3. Youth—Psychological testing. 4. Adolescence. 5. Behavioral assessment of children. 6. Behavioral assessment of teenagers. 7. Educational tests and measurements. I. Spenciner, Loraine J. II. Cohen, Libby G. Assessment of children and youth. III. Title.

BF722 .C638 2002
371.26—dc21

                                                    2002024652

*See photo and permissions credits on page 544.*

# Contents

**7** *Performance-Based, Authentic, and Portfolio Assessments* **164**

**8** *Reading* **193**

## 17   *Youth in Transition*    459

# *Preface*

The purpose of this book is to provide future and experienced educators and other professionals with a fundamental understanding of traditional and contemporary perspectives on the assessment of children and youth, ages 3 through 21. New developments in cognitive psychology and school reform and research on teaching and learning have had an impact on current thinking about assessment. The changing composition of our society has also influenced assessment practices. The traditional family unit now includes a much broader definition of "family." In the twenty-first century, individuals in the United States represent increasingly diverse cultural and linguistic backgrounds.

## *Features*

This book features broad coverage of traditional and contemporary assessment approaches. The text discusses individual tests at length and explains various assessment approaches in detail. A format for evaluating traditional and contemporary approaches is included. Snapshots (case studies) illustrate the use of tests and assessment approaches.

Major topics this revised book covers are:

- Individuals with Disabilities Education Act
- description of professional standards
- the role of families in the assessment process
- issues of diversity
- assessment of the physical, learning, and social environments
- observation techniques

- functional behavioral assessment
- performance-based, authentic, and portfolio assessment
- standardized instruments, with recent updates
- criterion-referenced testing
- curriculum-based assessment
- informal assessment
- contemporary approaches to the assessment of mathematics and literacy
- transition assessment
- assessment of sensory and motor abilities
- the role of technology in gathering, synthesizing, interpreting, and reporting information
- interpreting tests and writing reports
- program evaluation

## *Organization*

Several themes are common throughout the book. Each chapter begins with a set of objectives. We hope that the reader will use these objectives as guideposts in learning. Most chapters include a section titled "What Shapes Our Views." This section links the topic of the chapter to one or more theoretical perspectives. Each assessment area includes a description of assessment questions, purposes, and approaches. Diversity is addressed in most chapters in a section titled "Responding to Diversity." The book observes the physical, learning, and social environments of students in discussions throughout the book. Each chapter includes case studies and a section called "Preferred Practices" in which we summarize key points from the chapter and highlight best professional practices. Finally, at the end of each chapter, we offer a group of questions for reflection called "Extending Learning."

## Companion Website

This text is accompanied by a website (http://www.ablongman.com/cohen2e) that provides students and instructors with numerous activities and ideas to extend learning along with information about the book and its authors. The site consists of a student area and an instructor area.

In the student area, students can select Web-based activities and links, locate chapter objectives, and check word meanings in the glossary. These Web-based activities:

- relate to each chapter of the textbook,
- describe problems for individuals or small group of students to solve by finding information on the Web,
- provide students with opportunities to apply concepts discussed in the text, and to locate assessment information related to actual questions that might arise in the classroom.

In the links area, students can continue to build Web-based resources by following links related to individual chapters or through awareness activities designed by the instructor.

The instructor area provides a place for instructors to post a course syllabus, quizzes, and tests.

## Acknowledgments

We dedicate this book to current and future teachers—we admire and respect you for your dedication to improving the lives of children and youth. We extend our sincere appreciation to the many people who helped and supported us in the development of this book. We extend a very special thank you to Donna Benjamin, Cindy Carroll, Linda Davis, Donna Dwyer, Viki Hellgren, Jody Hill, Adrienne Parson, and Deb Twitchell.

We extend grateful appreciation to the manuscript reviewers who provided us with thoughtful and insightful reviews for this edition: Betty N. Higdon, University of Alabama at Birmingham; Ming-Gon John Lian, Illinois State University; Nancy Marchand-Martella, Eastern Washington University; Jane Pemberton, University of North Texas; and Marilyn K. Urquhart, University of South Dakota; and for the previous editions: Mary R. Adair, Slippery Rock University; Paul Beare, Moorhead State University; V. K. Constenbader, Rochester Institute of Technology; Laurie U. deBettencourt, University of North Carolina at Greensboro; Bill Evans, University of West Florida; Dan Fennerty, Central Washington University; Janice Ferguson, Western Kentucky University; James E. Gilliam, University of Texas at Austin; Ted Gloeckler, University of Akron; Robert G. Harrington, University of Kansas; Randy Kamphaus, University of Georgia; Nancy E. Marchand-Martella, Eastern Washington University; Martha J. Meyer, Butler University; Clyde Shepherd, Keene State College; and Robert J. Wright, Widener University.

Finally, we are especially grateful to our families, Les, Seth, Jay, Amy, Dave, and Dina—we appreciate your continued support and good humor.

*Libby G. Cohen*
*Loraine J. Spenciner*

# 1

## *Looking at Assessment*

## *Overview*

A teacher shares concerns with another teacher about a new student in the classroom. A mother calls to discuss questions that were raised during a meeting about her child. Teachers and other professionals who work with students with disabilities not only raise questions but must work with others to respond to concerns and make decisions about students. They must be able to observe, collect, record, and interpret information about students with disabilities. As members of a school team, they plan, monitor, and evaluate individualized education programs.

This chapter begins with a discussion of federal law that relates to the assessment of children and youth with disabilities. Federal legislation has had profound effects on assessment practices. Since this is an area that continues to change, we will examine resources that regularly provide updated information.

Next, the chapter introduces assessment questions that guide the process of collecting information and the steps and purposes of the assessment process. Selecting assessment approaches begins with a careful consideration of the assessment questions and purposes. Throughout the chapters in this book, you will find detailed discussions of specific assessment questions, purposes, and approaches.

Discussions of professional standards and ethical considerations developed by the American Psychological Association, the Council for Exceptional Children, and the National Association for the Education of Young Children provide a foundation for assessment later in this chapter. These standards will serve to guide your work with students and their families.

Finally, sections of this chapter begin themes that you will see throughout this book. You will find in the section "What Shapes Our Views" a discussion of the theories, perspectives, and conceptual frameworks; in "Assessment Questions, Purposes, and Approaches" an examination of the assessment questions and appropriate assessment approaches; and in "Responding to Diversity" a probing of issues in sensitivity and responsiveness to students and the uniqueness of their families.

## Chapter Objectives

After completing this chapter, you should be able to:

- Explain the general requirements for assessment as mandated by federal laws.
- Provide a rationale for the participation of families in the assessment process.
- Explain the requirements for confidentiality and for family rights.
- Identify assessment questions and describe the different steps and purposes for assessment.

- Describe how to administer an assessment instrument.
- Discuss issues related to assessing students who come from diverse cultural, ethnic, racial, and linguistic backgrounds; geographic regions of origin; economic groups; and according to disability and gender.
- Apply professional standards and ethical considerations.

## What Shapes Our Views

Assessment is an integral aspect of instruction. Assessment enables educators to gather and interpret information about students and to make decisions. Assessment provides information about what individual students can and cannot do, know and do not know. School-wide assessments help administrators and school board members determine the success of school programs.

Assessment is a major focal point in education reform. In addition to quizzes, tests, and exams, teachers use other assessment approaches such as portfolios or authentic assessments to provide regular feedback to students regarding their performance and to give them

opportunities to improve. Teachers connect instruction with assessment and use this information to change or modify teaching and learning activities.

Teachers also use assessment approaches to answer questions regarding student achievement, abilities, behavior, development, and skills. Is there a possibility that the student has a disability? Should the student be referred for further assessment? By observing, collecting, and recording information, classroom teachers work with other educators and school personnel to interpret the information, answer questions, and make decisions about students. Some of these students may have disabilities.

Questions about students with disabilities bring assessment to another level. Assessment in the field of special education involves not only these general assessment aspects but legal aspects as well. Does the student have a disability? Federal and state laws specify assessment requirements that must be followed. Special educators and other personnel working with students with disabilities must comply with these requirements.

In the following section, we will examine the federal mandates regarding assessment practices. These mandates address the assessment process that will be conducted. The term **assessment approach** describes the way information is collected for making an educational decision.

## Federal Mandates Regarding Assessment Practices

Children and youth with disabilities have been able to receive special education services in their local schools since the passage of federal legislation (PL 94–142) in 1975, PL 94–142 has been reauthorized and updated several times. In 1990, the reauthorization (PL 101–476) was known as the **Individuals with Disabilities Education Act,** or **IDEA.**

Since then, IDEA has been revised and reauthorized several times. The revised law provides new emphasis on improving results for students with disabilities. IDEA specifies special education services for children and youth ages 3 through 21 and early intervention services for infants and toddlers, birth through age 2. IDEA includes mandated requirements relating to the assessment process that teachers and test examiners must know and understand. These requirements form the legal basis for identifying and providing services to children and youth with disabilities.

### Locating Children and Youth

Identifying children and youth who need early intervention or special education services is a collaborative effort among teachers in the schools and personnel who work in agencies that serve children and families.

***Child Find.*** **Child Find** is an identification process for locating and evaluating children with disabilities. As part of Child Find activities, public schools and other state and local agencies alert parents of preschool children to the availability of screening services in their community.

### Children and Youth Who Are Eligible for Special Education

IDEA guarantees that children and youth with disabilities have the right to a **free, appropriate public education (FAPE).** Children and youth receive support in their education program from special education services if their disability adversely affects their educational performance and if these special services would allow them to benefit from the education program. Figure 1.1 describes the areas of eligibility according to IDEA.

***Special Considerations for Young Children.*** The Division for Early Childhood of the Council for Exceptional Children (2000) and other professional organizations have voiced concerns over (1) the potential detrimental effects of labeling a child at a young age, (2) the lack of adequate assessment tools for young children, and (3) the belief that some of the disability categories used with older children may not be appropriate (Figure 1.1). IDEA allows state personnel to include the term **developmental delay** in state regulations so that children ages 3 through 9 can receive education and related services without being labeled according to specific disability category (Figure 1.2). The term *developmental delay* refers to a delay in one or more areas of development including: physical, cognitive, communication, social or emotional, or adaptive development.

Although young children vary greatly in their rate of development, this term intentionally reflects a significant delay in development. The term refers to:

a condition which represents a significant delay in the process of development. It does not

## FIGURE 1.1   *Children and Youth Who Are Eligible for Special Education and Related Services*

**Autism:** A child with autism has a developmental disability that significantly affects verbal and nonverbal communication and social interaction, typically observed before age 3, and that adversely affects the child's educational performance. (If a child manifests characteristics of autism after the age of 3, the child can still be eligible for services under this definition if these criteria are satisfied.) Other characteristics that are often associated with autism include: engagement in repetitive activities and stereotyped movements, resistance to change in the environment or during daily routines, and unusual responses to sensory experiences. The term does not apply if a child's educational performance is adversely affected primarily due to a serious emotional disturbance.

**Deaf-blindness:** A child with deaf-blindness exhibits concomitant visual and hearing impairments that together cause such severe communication and other developmental and educational problems that they cannot be accommodated in special education programs solely for children with deafness or children with blindness.

**Deafness:** A child who is deaf has a hearing loss so severe that with or without amplification the child is unable to process language through hearing. The condition adversely affects the child's educational performance.

**Hearing impairment:** A child has a hearing impairment, whether permanent or fluctuating, if it adversely affects the child's educational performance but is not included under the definition of deafness.

**Mental retardation:** A child with mental retardation functions significantly below average in intellectual functioning concurrently with deficits in adaptive behavior that are manifested during the developmental period. The child's educational performance is adversely affected.

**Multiple disabilities:** A child has multiple disabilities (e.g., mental retardation–blindness, or mental retardation–orthopedic impairment), the combination of which causes such severe educational problems that they cannot be accommodated in special education programs solely for one of the impairments. This term does not include deaf-blindness.

**Orthopedic impairment:** A child has a severe orthopedic impairment that adversely affects educational performance. The term includes impairments caused by congenital anomaly (e.g., clubfoot or absence of some member), impairments caused by disease (e.g., poliomyelitis or bone tuberculosis), and impairments from other causes (e.g., cerebral palsy, amputations, and fractures or burns that cause contractures).

**Other health impairment:** A child with a health impairment shows limited strength, vitality, or alertness due to chronic or acute health problems such as heart condition, tuberculosis, rheumatic fever, nephritis, asthma, sickle cell anemia, hemophilia, epilepsy, lead poisoning, leukemia, or diabetes that adversely affect a child's educational performance.

**Serious emotional disturbance:** A child with a serious emotional disturbance exhibits one or more of the following characteristics over a long period of time and to a marked degree that adversely affects a child's educational performance:

1. an inability to learn that cannot be explained by intellectual, sensory, or health factors;
2. an inability to build or maintain satisfactory interpersonal relationships with peers and teachers;
3. inappropriate types of behavior or feelings under normal circumstances;
4. a general pervasive mood of unhappiness or depression;
5. a tendency to develop physical symptoms or fears associated with personal or school problems.

The term includes schizophrenia. The term does not apply to children who are socially maladjusted, unless it is determined that they have a serious emotional disturbance.

**Specific learning disability:** A child with a specific learning disability exhibits a disorder in one or more of the basic psychological processes involved in understanding or in using language, spoken or written, that may manifest itself in an imperfect ability to listen, think, speak, read, write, spell, or to do mathematic calculations. The term includes such conditions as perceptual disabilities, brain injury, minimal brain dysfunction, dyslexia, and developmental aphasia. The term does not apply to children who have learning problems that are primarily the result of visual, hearing, or motor disabilities, of mental retardation, of emotional disturbance, or of environmental, cultural, or economic disadvantage.

**Speech or language impairment:** A child with a speech or language impairment has a communication disorder such as stuttering, impaired articulation, a language impairment, or a voice impairment that adversely affects the child's educational performance.

**Traumatic brain injury:** A child with traumatic brain injury has an acquired injury to the brain that was caused by an external physical force resulting in total or partial functional disability or psychosocial impairment, or both, that adversely affects a child's educational performance. The term applies to open or closed head injuries resulting in impairments in one or more areas, such as cognition; language; memory; attention; reasoning; abstract thinking; judgment; problem solving; sensory, perceptual and motor abilities; psychosocial behavior; physical functions; information processing; and speech. The term does not apply to brain injuries that are congenital or degenerative, or to brain injuries induced by birth trauma.

**Visual impairment including blindness:** A child has an impairment in vision if, even with correction, it adversely affects the child's educational performance. The term includes both partial sight and blindness.

*Source:* Federal Register, 1999, Sec. 300.7(c).

---

**FIGURE 1.2** *Definition of Developmental Delay*

A developmental delay is a delay in one or more of the following:
- Physical development including fine and gross motor
- Cognitive development
- Communication development
- Social or emotional development
- Adaptive development

*Source: Federal Register*, 1999, sec. 300.7(b)(1).

refer to a condition in which a child is slightly or momentarily lagging in development. The presence of developmental delay is an indication that the process of development is significantly affected and that without special intervention, it is likely that educational performance at school age will be affected. (McLean, Smith, McCormick, Schakel, and McEvoy, 1991, p. 2)

Developmental delay is also used with infants and toddlers in determining eligibility for early intervention services.

## Procedures for Ensuring the Rights of Students and Families

IDEA specifies procedures that ensure the protection of parents' and children's rights during the assessment process and the delivery of services. These procedures, called **due process** requirements, specify that:

- Parents must receive written notice whenever there is a proposal to initiate or change the identification, evaluation, or educational placement of their child.
- Parents have the right to review their child's records regarding the assessment and educational placement.
- Parents may obtain an independent evaluation of their child by a qualified examiner who is not employed by the school. The evaluation is at no cost to the parent and is paid for by the public school.
- Due process also ensures that parents, schools, or agencies have a right to an impartial hearing conducted by a hearing officer when disagreements occur. A hearing can be requested by either a parent or a school district.

## Multidisciplinary Teams

***The IEP Team.*** Teachers and other professionals who assess children and youth with disabilities represent various disciplines, depending on the needs of the student. For example, individuals may come from the fields of medicine, occupational therapy, physical therapy, psychology, social work, speech-language pathology, or therapeutic recreation in addition to general education and special education. When the student's **IEP team** meets, there must be an individual who can interpret the instructional implications of assessment results (*Federal Register*, 1999, sec. 300.344). Professionals involved in the assessment of students with disabilities should be knowledgeable of the general requirements of assessment (Figure 1.3).

***The Early Childhood Team.*** The **early childhood team** is a **multidisciplinary team** that includes parents, the family service coordinator, and other team members from various disciplines. This team assesses, implements, and evaluates early childhood intervention services. Early childhood teams focus on children with disabilities from birth through age 2. In some states, early childhood teams cover children from birth to school-age 5.

The general assessment requirements differ for young children and school-age students in several main areas (Table 1.1). Some differences involve the emphasis and focus of the assessment. Other requirements involve differences in time lines.

## The Individualized Education Program

Each child or youth who receives services must have an **individualized education program (IEP)**. An IEP team develops the written document from a comprehensive assessment. Figure

**FIGURE 1.3**    *General Requirements of Assessment*

Assessment procedures must be fair and equitable for all children and youth:

- Tests and other evaluation materials used to assess a child are selected and administered so as not to be discriminatory on a racial or cultural basis.
- Tests are administered in the student's native language or other mode of communication, unless it is clearly not feasible to do so.
- A variety of assessment tools and strategies are used to gather relevant functional and developmental information about the child, including information provided by the parent, and information related to enabling the child to be involved in and progress in the general curriculum (or for a preschool child, to participate in appropriate activities), that may assist in determining whether the child has a disability and the content of the child's IEP.
- Any standardized test should be validated for the purpose that it is being used.
- The test should be administered by trained personnel in conformance with instructions from the test publisher.
- If an assessment is not conducted under standard conditions, a description of the extent to which it varied from standard conditions (for example, the method of test administration) must be included in the assessment report.
- Tests and other evaluation materials include those tailored to assess specific areas of educa-

tional need and are not merely a single general intelligence quotient.

- The assessment of students with impaired sensory, manual, or speaking skills is completed with tests that are selected and administered to reflect the student's aptitude or achievement level (or other factor) accurately. The tests should not reflect the student's impaired sensory, manual, or speaking skills (except where these skills are the factors that are being measured).
- No single procedure is used to determine a student's eligibility for special education services and in determining an appropriate educational program for the student.
- The student is assessed in all areas related to the suspected disability, including, where appropriate, health, vision, hearing, social and emotional status, general intelligence, academic performance, communicative status, and motor abilities.
- The evaluation is comprehensive so that all of the child's special education and related services needs are identified.
- Technically sound instruments are used that may assess the relative contribution of cognitive and behavioral factors, in addition to physical or developmental factors.
- Assessment tools and strategies provide relevant information that directly assists persons in determining the educational needs of the child.

*Source: Federal Register,* 1999, sec. 300.532.

1.4 on page 8 describes the specific assessment information required in the IEP.

The IEP team conducts a reevaluation at least every three years by first reviewing existing assessment information. Using the review and input from the parents, the team determines what additional assessment is needed.

### The Individualized Family Service Plan

The early childhood team writes an **individualized family service plan (IFSP)** for children

age birth through age 2. Children who are 3 through 5 years of age may have an IFSP rather than an IEP as long as (1) the IFSP is consistent with state policy, and (2) the parents concur (*Federal Register,* 1999, sec. 300.342[c]). Similar to an IEP, the Individualized Family Service Plan includes information about the child's level of functioning, the goals or outcomes for the child, and the services they will receive. The services described in the plan can include some for the family as well as for the child. Figure 1.5 on page 8 lists the required components of the IFSP related to assessment.

**TABLE 1.1** *Assessment for Young Children and School-Age Students and Youth*

| Federal Requirement | Children Birth through Age 2 and Preschoolers Who Receive Services under an IFSP | Children and Youth Ages 3 through 21 Who Receive Services under an IEP |
| --- | --- | --- |
| Emphasis | Child and family focus | Student focus |
| Assessment team | Early childhood team | IEP team or student assistance team (for prereferral model) |
| Prereferral (optional) | None | Student assistance team (SAT) develops interventions and strategies before referral to the IEP team |
| Referral | Parent, practitioner, or teacher identifies questions and concerns | Parent, practitioner, teacher, or student identifies questions and concerns |
| Assessment focus | Adaptive, cognitive, communication, physical, and social emotional development | Academic performance, adaptive skills, general intelligence, health, motor ability, communication, social-emotional status, transitional assessment, and vision or hearing |
| Parent permission for assessment | Required before all assessments | Required before most assessments |
| Plan for services | Individualized Family Service Plan | Individualized Education Program |
| Parent permission for services | Required before child participates in early intervention or special education services | Required before student participates in special education services |
| Review of service plan | 6 months | 12 months |
| Reevaluation | 1 year | 3 years (based on IEP team's determination) |

Team members must complete the assessment of each child (including the needs identified by the family) within 45 calendar days from the time the child is referred to them. The law also provides that the team, with the consent of the parents, can begin early intervention services before completion of the assessment if the team writes an interim IFSP.

## Transition Services

When a student reaches the teen years, the IEP team must consider not only education but transition needs for postsecondary education, employment, and community living. Beginning at age 14 (or younger, if determined appropriate by the IEP team), the team writes a statement of transition service needs. Transition needs are based on the individual student, taking into account the student's preferences and interests. They describe the services that the student needs during the transition from school to adulthood as determined by the IEP team. **Transition services** means a coordinated set of activities for a student, designed within an outcome-oriented process, that promotes movement from school

**FIGURE 1.4**    *Assessment Information Required in the IEP*

Assessment information required in the IEP includes:

- The student's current level of education performance including how the disability affects the child's involvement and progress in the general curriculum
- Measurable annual goals including benchmarks or short-term objectives
- A statement regarding the specific special education and related services to be provided and the extent to which the student will be able to participate in the regular education program
- A statement of any individual modifications in the administration of state or districtwide assessments
- The projected dates for the beginning of services and the anticipated length of services
- Information as to how the student's progress will be measured and how the child's parents will be informed

*Source: Federal Register*, 1999, sec. 300.347(a).

to post-school activities, including postsecondary education, vocational training, integrated employment (including supported employment) continuing and adult education, adult services, independent living, and community participation. These services could include instruction, related services, community experiences, the development of employment and other post-school adult

**FIGURE 1.5**    *Assessment Information Required in the IFSP*

1. A statement of the child's present level of development, including physical, cognitive, communication, social-emotional, and adaptive (self-help skills) descriptions, based on acceptable objective criteria.
2. An optional statement of the family's concerns, resources, and priorities related to enhancing their child's development. This information, called family-directed assessment, is gathered only with parental permission.
3. A statement of the major outcomes expected to be achieved for the child and family, and the criteria, procedures, and time lines used to document progress.
4. A statement of specific early intervention services necessary to meet the needs of the child and family, including the frequency, intensity, and method of delivering services.
5. A statement of the natural environments in which early intervention services will be provided.
6. The projected dates for the beginning of services and the anticipated duration.
7. The name of the family service coordinator who will be responsible for the implementation of the plan and coordination with other agencies and persons.
8. The date for periodic review of the IFSP (usually at 6-month intervals or more frequently when appropriate) and the date for reevaluation (at 12 months or more frequently when appropriate).
9. The steps to be taken supporting the transition of the toddler to preschool or into other appropriate placement(s) if the child is no longer eligible for intervention services. (In some states there is a difference between the eligibility criteria for toddlers and for preschoolers.)
10. The contents of the plan will be fully explained to the parents or guardian, who must give written consent prior to provision of services described in the plan. If consent is not provided with respect to a particular early intervention service, then early intervention services to which consent is given will be provided.

*Source: EDLAW*, 1991.

living objectives (*Federal Register*, 1999, sec. 300.29[a]). Transition assessment is described in Chapter 17.

## Accommodations and Modifications

Another function of the IEP team is to determine if the child or youth needs accommodations or modifications to be successfully involved and make progress in the general curriculum and to achieve IEP goals. **Accommodations** are changes to the education program that do not substantially alter the instructional level, the content of the curriculum, or the assessment criteria. Accommodations to an activity or lesson may consist of changes in the format of materials, such as using a laptop computer with word prediction features to take classroom notes or providing choices for students to respond orally or by writing the answers. Accommodations also include changes to the classroom arrangement or other setting for the activity, scheduling, or timing; for example, giving a student extra time to complete the assignment. On the other hand, **modifications** refer to changes or adaptations made to the education program that alter the level, content, and or assessment criteria. For example, a modification to an assignment might include reading a condensed version of the assigned book or completing half of the assigned examples. In Chapter 4 we will look more closely at different types of accommodations and modifications used in assessing students.

## Confidentiality and Informed Consent

Professionals who are involved with the gathering of information about a student have both a legal and an ethical responsibility to maintain the information and use it appropriately. These individuals need to agree that the shared information is for the purposes of enabling the family and assisting the student through individualized educational services. Teachers and other practitioners should discuss a particular

student and family only with those professionals who have a legitimate interest in the information and with whom the family has consented to share information.

## Family Educational Rights and Privacy Act

The **Family Educational Rights and Privacy Act (FERPA)** of 1974 (PL 93–380), commonly referred to as the "Buckley amendment," states that no educational agency may release student information without written consent from the student's parents. This consent specifies which records to release, the reasons for such release, and to whom. The agency should then send a copy of the released records to the student's parents.

FERPA allows families and students over 18 years of age access to and the right to inspect any of their records from any education institution, including preschool, elementary and secondary schools, community colleges, and colleges and universities that accept federal money. Parents also have the right to challenge and correct any information contained in these records. Professionals will want to ensure that they file only materials relevant to the student in the student's folder. Irrelevant information about the personal lives of families or information that is at best subjective and impressionistic has no place in a family's record.

## Assessment Questions, Purposes, and Approaches

### Assessment Questions

**Assessment** is a global term for observing, gathering, recording, and interpreting information to answer questions and make legal and instructional decisions about students. What types of questions do teachers and parents have? Teachers of young children and parents wonder if the child is developing typically in one or more of the following developmental areas:

*Communication development.* Should Jaleh be talking more now that she is 4 years old?

*Cognitive development.* Is Katie experiencing difficulty performing many activities that the other children can do quite easily?

*Physical development.* Does Sammy have difficulty seeing? Hearing? Does he have problems with fine and gross motor activities?

*Adaptive development.* Should Luis be able to feed himself and take care of toileting needs?

*Social-emotional development.* Sonia has difficulty getting along with other children. Will she "outgrow" this?

Teachers and parents of older children frequently have questions about a student's achievement, ability, or skills in one or more areas:

*Academic area.* Does Elliot have a reading problem?

*Overall achievement.* Why isn't Bill doing better in school?

*General intelligence.* Will Joy be able to learn how to compute a math problem?

*Social-emotional status.* Daryle has difficulty making friends. How can he be helped? Sabrina seems sad and depressed. What is causing this behavior?

*Vision, hearing, or motor ability.* Can Norweeta hear students speaking during class discussions? Joey frequently walks on tiptoes. Does this indicate a problem?

*Communication.* Bradley can hear the speaker but doesn't seem to understand. What could be the cause of his difficulty?

## Assessment Steps and Purposes

In working with students with disabilities or who may have disabilities, professionals need to ask specific questions and make specific decisions during each of the assessment steps: screening, referral, determining eligibility, program planning, program monitoring, and program evaluation (Figure 1.6 on pages 12 and 13).

As Figure 1.6 illustrates, the steps are sequential and progressive. Decision points allow the team to use the information to make decisions regarding the needs of the student.

## Assessment Approaches

Educators use a variety of assessment approaches to gather information about the student and about the classroom environment. A teacher may administer a test that consists of a set of questions to a student to determine the individual's knowledge or skill(s). The teacher reports the results in one or more types of scores. However, **testing** of students is only one approach. Some approaches can answer many different questions about a student, while other approaches are useful for gathering information for a specific purpose (Table 1.2 on pages 14 and 15). Be sure that the approach will yield the type of information that you need.

Table 1.2 illustrates the assessment questions, steps and purposes, and approaches. The assessment questions guide each of the steps and purposes during the assessment process. Various assessment approaches can be used to gather information.

IDEA specifies that information the parent provides is included in the assessment (*Federal Register*, 1999, sec. 300.532[b]). Best practice suggests that team members encourage parents to participate in the assessment to the degree that they choose to be involved. Team members can suggest assessment approaches for parents to use. Table 1.3 on page 16 illustrates some of the questions that parents have and the tools that they can use in helping to answer assessment questions.

## Assessment Steps and Purposes
### Step 1. Screening

The assessment question focuses on "Is there a possibility that the student may have a disability?" The purpose of **screening** is to determine whether students may have disabilities and to refer them for further assessment. Screening is designed to assess large numbers of students efficiently and economically. Based on the information collected during screening, evaluators decide whether to refer the student to the team for further assessment. Screening approaches differ, depending on whether the student is a preschooler or of school age.

*Preschool Children.* In many communities, children under age 6 come to the assessment process as a result of Child Find activities. Child Find directs parents to screening services in their community that are open to infants, toddlers, and preschoolers and that are free of charge.

Comprehensive screening of young children includes several components: parent concerns; medical history (often given through parental reports or completed by parents using a checklist); vision and hearing tests; and the use of commercial screening instruments and observation reports in the areas of general development, abilities, and skills. Screening instruments are generally inexpensive and are designed so they may be completed in a short amount of time, 30 minutes or less. Chapter 12 discusses specific screening instruments.

*School-Age Students.* Children who are entering public school for the first time or transferring to a new school require screening. One or more individuals such as the special education or general education teacher conduct the screening, which involves various approaches. An educator often begins by reviewing past work and test scores of the incoming student, or by asking the new student a set of questions. In the classroom, teachers observe and collect information about the student's work and performance. Teachers may observe that the student is having trouble seeing a computer screen, understanding and following directions, working with others, reading and comprehending. Parents utilize screening approaches too. They may have concerns about

their child when they see their child in relation to other children in the neighborhood or when they compare their child to their knowledge about growth and development.

School personnel conduct a variety of other screening activities. The school nurse arranges for students to have a regular vision and hearing screening. Educators review student attendance records and follow up on students who are not attending school on a regular basis. Classroom teachers administer group tests of school achievement, and screen student scores to identify those students who show they are having difficulty. When young children or school-age students are identified by the screening process as needing further assessment, the evaluator, teacher, or parent completes a referral form.

### Step 2. Making a Referral

Teachers or parents identify their questions and concerns and request further assessment by completing a written **referral** (Figure 1.7 on page 17). For example, during the beginning of the school year a fifth-grade teacher began to worry about one of her students, Cory, who was experiencing some difficulties in attention and organization. The Snapshot about Cory discusses the steps that his teacher took in addressing her concerns.

The route that the written referral travels differs, depending on school policy. Some schools have a policy in which the written referral goes directly to the IEP team (Referral Decision). Other schools use a prereferral step before sending the referral to this team (Prereferral Decision) (Figure 1.6).

*Prereferral Decisions.* Questions about a student are referred to an **assistance team,** which usually comprises regular classroom teachers and special educators in the school building. The team may be a student assistance team (SAT), teacher assistance team, or intervention assistance team. In addition to questions about individual student behaviors or academic work, this team enables teachers, both regular and special education, to help one another with general academic

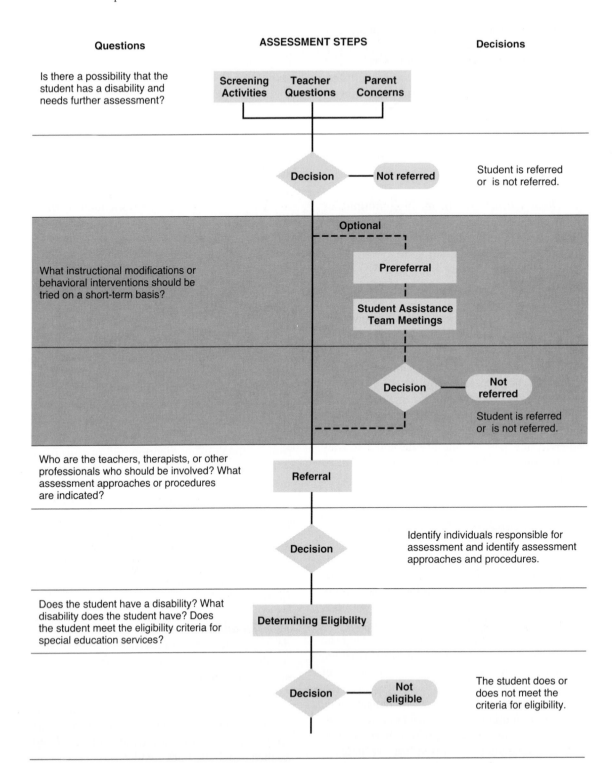

**FIGURE 1.6**   *The Steps in the Assessment Process*

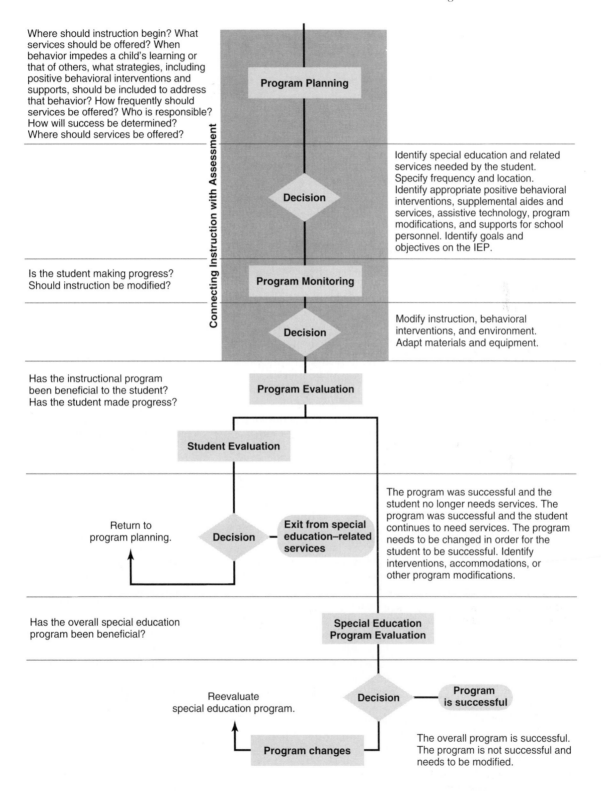

Where should instruction begin? What services should be offered? When behavior impedes a child's learning or that of others, what strategies, including positive behavioral interventions and supports, should be included to address that behavior? How frequently should services be offered? Who is responsible? How will success be determined? Where should services be offered?

**Connecting Instruction with Assessment**

**Program Planning**

**Decision**

Identify special education and related services needed by the student. Specify frequency and location. Identify appropriate positive behavioral interventions, supplemental aides and services, assistive technology, program modifications, and supports for school personnel. Identify goals and objectives on the IEP.

Is the student making progress? Should instruction be modified?

**Program Monitoring**

**Decision**

Modify instruction, behavioral interventions, and environment. Adapt materials and equipment.

Has the instructional program been beneficial to the student? Has the student made progress?

**Program Evaluation**

**Student Evaluation**

Return to program planning.

**Decision**

**Exit from special education–related services**

The program was successful and the student no longer needs services. The program was successful and the student continues to need services. The program needs to be changed in order for the student to be successful. Identify interventions, accommodations, or other program modifications.

Has the overall special education program been beneficial?

**Special Education Program Evaluation**

Reevaluate special education program.

**Decision**

**Program is successful**

**Program changes**

The overall program is successful. The program is not successful and needs to be modified.

**TABLE 1.2**   *Assessment Questions, Purposes, and Approaches*

| Assessment Questions | Steps and Purposes | Approaches |
|---|---|---|
| Is there a possibility of a disability? | **Screening**<br>To determine whether students *may* have a disability and should be referred for further assessment | Norm-referenced instruments<br>Curriculum-based assessments<br>Criterion-referenced assessments<br>Observations<br>Checklists |
| Who are the teachers, therapists, or other professionals who should be involved?<br>What approaches are indicated? | **Referral**<br>To determine the professionals who should be involved and the assessment approaches that are indicated | |
| Does the student have a disability?<br>What disability does the student have?<br>Does the student meet the criteria for services?<br>What are the strengths and weaknesses?<br>What is the student having trouble doing?<br>What does the student understand? | **Eligibility**<br>To determine if there is a disability<br>To determine the need for special education and related services<br>To compare the student's performance with the performance of the peer group<br>To determine specific strengths and weaknesses<br>To understand why the student is having difficulty | Norm-referenced instruments<br>Curriculum-based assessments<br>Criterion-referenced assessments<br>Observations<br>Probes<br>Error analysis<br>Interviews<br>Checklists<br>Student, parent, and/or teacher conferences<br>Performance assessments |

*Connecting Instruction with Assessment*

| | | |
|---|---|---|
| What types of special education and related services should be provided?<br>What classroom modifications and adaptations should be implemented?<br>What does the student not understand?<br>Where should instruction begin? | **Program Planning**<br>To determine the locations and type of service(s) to be received<br>To assess the physical, learning, and social classroom environments<br>To understand what the student knows and does not know<br>To determine where instruction should begin<br>To plan the student's program<br>To determine instructional approaches | Norm-referenced instruments<br>Curriculum-based assessments<br>Criterion-referenced assessments<br>Observations<br>Probes<br>Error analysis<br>Interviews<br>Checklists<br>Student, parent, and/or teacher conferences<br>Performance assessments |

**TABLE 1.2** *Continued*

| Assessment Questions | Steps and Purposes | Approaches |
|---|---|---|
| | *Connecting Instruction with Assessment* | |
| | **Program Monitoring** | |
| Once instruction begins, is the student making progress? Should the instruction be modified? | To understand the pace of instruction<br>To understand what the student knows prior to and after instruction<br>To understand the strategies and concepts the student uses<br>To monitor the student's program | Curriculum-based assessments<br>Criterion-referenced assessments<br>Observations<br>Probes<br>Error analysis<br>Interviews<br>Checklists<br>Student, parent, and/or teacher conferences<br>Portfolios<br>Exhibitions<br>Journals<br>Written descriptions<br>Oral descriptions |
| | **Program Evaluation** | |
| Has the student met the goals of the IEP?<br>Has the instructional program been successful for the student?<br>Has the student made progress?<br>Has the instructional program achieved its goals? | To determine whether the IEP goals have been met<br>To determine whether the goals of the program have been met<br>To evaluate program effectiveness | Curriculum-based assessments<br>Criterion-referenced assessments<br>Observations<br>Probes<br>Error analysis<br>Interviews<br>Checklists<br>Student, parent, and/or teacher conferences<br>Portfolios<br>Exhibitions<br>Journals<br>Written descriptions<br>Oral descriptions<br>Surveys |

or discipline concerns including making accommodations to the classroom setting or to the curriculum. Although the law does not require **prereferral** procedures, they represent good professional practice.

***Referral Decisions.*** The IEP team, which is different from the assistance team, receives the written referral form. Based on the referral in-

formation about the student, the team may recommend specific assessment approaches or assessment instruments to be used in **determining eligibility.**

## *Step 3. Determining Eligibility*

The assessment questions focus on "Does the student have a disability? What disability does

TABLE 1.3    *Parent Involvement in the Assessment Process*

| Assessment Step | Questions Parents May Raise | Assessment Tools Used by Parents |
|---|---|---|
| Screening | Is Juan developing like other children? | Parent report form<br>Parent observation |
| Prereferral | What can we do?<br>Will Jimmy fall behind his class? | Observation sheet<br>Monitoring sheet |
| Eligibility | Does Alexandra's behavior indicate a need for special services? | Parent historical report of student's behavior<br>Parent observation |
| Program Planning | What are our priorities for Elaina?*<br>Where would be the most appropriate setting for services?<br>How will we evaluate the services?<br>Who will coordinate the services? | Parent report form |
| Program Monitoring | How is the plan working? | Parent-made video or audiotape |
| Evaluation of Student | Do we feel that our child has made progress? | Parent questionnaire<br>Parent-made videotape |
| Evaluation of Student's Program | Does the program meet our child's needs? | Parent questionnaire |

*Children who have an IFSP.

the student have? Does the student meet the criteria for services?" The purpose of this step is to examine the assessment information to make a determination regarding the student's eligibility for special education and related services according to state and federal (IDEA) guidelines for children and youth ages 3 through 21 or early intervention for infants and toddlers.

As specified in IDEA, a multidisciplinary team conducts assessment for the purposes of eligibility. Thus, a student's assessment covers all areas related to the suspected disability including, if appropriate, health, vision, hearing, social and emotional status, general intelligence, academic performance, communication, and motor abilities. For example, a student who is nonver-

bal may have a multidisciplinary evaluation that includes meeting with (1) an audiologist to determine the extent, if any, of a hearing loss; (2) a speech and language pathologist to assess understanding of language (receptive language) and communication skills; (3) a special educator to assess academic and functional skills; (4) a vocational rehabilitation counselor to identify interests and abilities; and (5) a psychologist to determine intellectual functioning. The team will use various approaches, including, for example, observations, norm-referenced instruments, and performance assessments. The team will ask the student's parent(s) to provide information too. All of these individuals work together to view and analyze the assessment information, with all

## SNAPSHOT ■ *Cory*

Cory is a fifth-grade student at Memorial School. Although he has never been referred for special education services, Cory has had considerable difficulty in school. This year, his teacher, Joanne Leslie, has become increasingly concerned about his lack of academic progress and his difficulty in organizing his work. Cory is very distractible in class and has a short attention span. Because his reading and math skills are weak, he has difficulty in keeping up with assignments.

Ms. Leslie decided to examine Cory's records determine what accommodations last year helped him be more successful. She found that Cory had sat near the teacher to help with attention difficulties and that a teacher assistant had worked with him in spelling. His previous teacher had noted that Cory still had problems completing assignments and the teacher assistant was not always available. Miss Leslie examined his most recent achievement scores. Compared to other students in fifth grade, Cory's reading and math scores were low. After consulting with Cory's parents, she completed a referral form for special education servi (see Figure 1.7).

---

**MEMORIAL SCHOOL**

**Referral Form**

Student's Name: __Cory Young__                     Date of Birth: __9/7/xx__

Grade: __5__                                                     Teacher: __Ms. Leslie__

Parent/Guardian: __Joseph Davis__

Address: __Harris Lane__
__Columbia__

Source of referral: __Joanne Leslie, classroom teacher__

Designated school official accepting referral: __Ralph Townsend, principal__

Reason for referral: __Cory has a lot of difficulty organizing his work. His reading and math skills are below grade level. He is highly distractible. His written work is weak— mechanics, story line, and topic development below average.__

Procedures, tests, records or reports used as a basis for the referral:
__Iowa Tests of Basic Skills: reading 3.0, language/writing 2.8, spelling 2.5, math 3.1. Even with alternative seating, Cory gets little accomplished.__

Other relevant factors involving the referral:
__He wears glasses inconsistently. Cory's family is proud of their Native American heritage and speaks their native language in the home.__

---

**FIGURE 1.7** *A Teacher's Referral Form*

*A special educator conducts an educational assessment to later assist the team in determining whether the student has a disability.*

contributing expertise from their respective disciplines.

Team members share the assessment information during the IEP meeting and determine the student's eligibility to receive special education and related services.

Because the team bases its decisions on assessment information, they must choose and use appropriate assessment approaches carefully. Evaluators must have appropriate training, take responsibility in evaluating the adequacy of the approach, follow professional standards and ethical principles, and be knowledgeable about the limitations of specific approaches. In the chapters that follow we will discuss these approaches in more detail.

## Step 4. Program Planning

In **program planning,** the assessment questions focus on "What should be included in the stu-

dent's individualized program? If behavior impedes learning, what strategies, including positive behavioral interventions, should the team write in the plan? What supplemental aides, services, and assistive technology does the student need? What types of accommodations and/or modifications should team members make to the curriculum? Where should instruction begin? What supports for school personnel does the student need?" The purposes are to: (1) determine the student's current level of functioning, and (2) plan the instructional program. Much of the information gathered in Step 4 will be useful in planning the instruction and developing realistic goals.

### What Should Program Planning Include?
Program planning includes assessing the student's current level of functioning and determining where instruction should begin. Members of the IEP team identify the special education and related services they will include in the student's

program. The team plans accommodations and/ or modifications to the curriculum and to the classroom environment. Team members utilize commercially published norm-referenced and criterion-referenced tests, checklists, observations, or curriculum-based assessments, as well as other assessment approaches.

***Connecting Assessment with Instruction.*** Connecting assessment with instruction is part of program planning and Step 5, **monitoring individual progress.** Connecting assessment with instruction provides rich information about a student's current level of achievement, which allows the teacher to make informed decisions regarding the student's instructional program. A teacher uses this type of assessment in planning daily teaching and learning activities to address the special needs of students. "Good classroom assessment tells us more than 'Knows it; doesn't know it.' It also tells us why" (Shepard, 1996). Connecting assessment with instruction is one of the most important aspects of the assessment process. In later chapters we will examine a variety of assessment approaches that link instruction with assessment.

## Step 5. Monitoring Individual Progress

The purposes of this step are to determine: (1) if the student is making progress and (2) whether to modify instruction if the student is not making progress. Teachers should assess the student's progress frequently. Teachers use several different approaches to gather information; these are described in the following chapters. Information from this assessment step allows the IEP team members to modify interventions, teaching procedures, or materials if the student's progress is lagging.

## Step 6. Evaluating the Program

Evaluating the program consists of several types of questions. One type focuses on the student's program described in the IEP. The emphasis is on whether the student is making progress and meeting the goals of the individualized education program.

Another type addresses the overall evaluation of special education services. These questions focus on the progress, as a group, of student participants in the program; the degree of satisfaction with the program as expressed by teachers, administrators, and parents; and the effectiveness of the program. The following section examines these two types of evaluation questions in more detail.

***Student Evaluation.*** This type of assessment helps evaluators make decisions about the success of the instructional program for individual students. IDEA requires a reevaluation of the student's performance and educational needs at least every three years, or more frequently if conditions warrant a reevaluation or if the child's parent or teacher requests a reevaluation. For children receiving services under an IFSP, family and evaluators must review the program every six months (or more frequently, if appropriate), and conduct the full evaluation annually.

**1.** *Annual review.* The purpose of the review is to determine whether or not the IEP/ IFSP goals have been met. Teachers may use a variety of assessment approaches to answer questions about the success of the individualized program.

**2.** *Reevaluation.* The team reviews existing assessment information and considers the following questions: Does the student continue to need special education and related services? What is the student's present level of performance and educational need? On the basis of the review, and with input from the student's parents, the team decides what additional information they need and what assessment approaches to use.

***Program Evaluation.*** Program evaluation involves evaluating the overall services provided to groups of students or programs. Educators need to examine the success of programs offered to students, to replicate strong programs, and to refine or change programs that are not effective. Evaluation questions include: Is the program successful? Are goals being met? Do parents feel satisfied with the services? Information is collected in a variety of ways including: aggregating assessment results of students who participate or have participated in the program; asking teachers, students, and parents to complete checklists or rating scales; interviewing current students in the program and their parents; or asking graduates of the school or program and their employers to complete questionnaires. We will study program evaluation in more detail in Chapter 19.

## Preparing to Administer an Assessment Instrument

Preparing to administer an assessment instrument begins with careful planning.

### Before the Testing Begins

Before the testing session begins, the examiner should:

1. Understand the purpose(s) of the assessment (as stated in the test manual).
2. Read the test manual thoroughly.
3. Carefully review the test items.
4. Know the administrative procedures. Some examiners find that it is helpful to mark the different sections in the manual with a paper clip or self-stick note for easy reference.
5. Organize the necessary materials and check to see that none are missing.
6. Reexamine the scoring procedures to verify that answers can be recorded correctly. Recording student responses accurately will ensure a reliable test administration.

### When the Student Arrives

When the student arrives, the examiner should:

1. Establish and maintain rapport. Some students may be nervous and anxious about the testing; other students may have little motivation to participate or to do their best. Plan to spend enough time in making the student feel comfortable before beginning the session.
2. Convey a sense of confidence about the student's performance and avoid statements such as, "This is going to be a difficult test." The examiner can say, for example, "This test may have some items that you will find easy and some items that will be more difficult."
3. Be aware of changes in lighting or noise level once the testing begins. Watch for signs of student fatigue or hunger. Some students may need a test break or an additional test session.
4. Maintain neutrality during the testing. Be careful about providing the student with information about the correctness of responses. Remember that not only words but facial expressions and other body language convey information. Students might ask if an answer is correct. Phrases such as "I see that you are trying hard" provide encouragement to students without violating testing procedures.
5. Carefully record student responses in the appropriate spaces on the test form.
6. Be sensitive to the needs of the student. Some students may need more time to explore test materials or share an interesting thought that has nothing to do with the test items!

### After the Testing Is Completed

After the testing session is ended:

1. Thank the student for participating.
2. Finish recording any additional information. Note any observations of the student.
3. Compute scores.

4. Interpret results.
5. Write reports.

Chapters 3 and 18 discuss calculating scores, analyzing results, and report writing in detail.

## *Responding to Diversity*

Students and their families have diverse cultural, ethnic, racial, and linguistic backgrounds, and come from different geographic regions of origin and from different gender, disability, and economic groups. They bring with them various perspectives, values, knowledge of native languages, and attitudes about the roles and responsibilities of the family, society, education, and professionals. The perspectives and values that students bring to the assessment situation can affect the student's attitudes toward the testing environment and performance, the examiner, and the purposes of the assessment (Sattler, 2001).

Sometimes perspectives and school expectations work in opposing directions. For example, educational expectations of the classroom developed by members of the majority culture tend to focus on the individual work of the student and competitiveness between students; whereas, the educational expectations held by some families place an importance on group affiliation rather than individual accomplishment. These diverse perspectives may conflict with aspects of special education services and assessment practices in which assessment focuses on building student independence and individualizing intervention services.

### *Sensitivity*

Sensitivity involves concern and respect for others; it begins by learning about yourself, your beliefs, and your family heritage. Sensitivity grows by meeting other peoples, listening to who they are, and discovering their traditions, beliefs, and values. In working with families, there should be a balance between knowledge and an appreciation for that particular family, their experience of culture, their levels of acculturation, and the changing nature of culture itself (Dennis and Giangreco, 1996).

## *Avoiding Assessment Bias*

Assessment approaches are considered biased if they ". . . project only predominant values and attitudes and do not reflect the linguistic and cultural experiences of minority groups" (Padilla and Medina, 1996, p. 6). For example, students from nondominant groups may be less familiar with testing and less test-wise than other students. There may be a lack of motivation to participate in certain assessment approaches, and that lack of motivation prevents the student from performing to the best ability.

There are special considerations for students whose primary language is not English. IDEA specifies assessment requirements to ensure that assessment procedures are fair for children who are English language learners (Table 1.4). Teachers and other professionals should be aware that translating a test into another language does not mean that its content, difficulty, reliability, and validity are the same. A word in one language can have a different meaning, a different frequency of use, and a different difficulty level when translated into another language (American Educational Research Association, American Psychological Association, and National Council on Measurement in Education, 1999).

## *Professional Standards and Ethical Considerations*

Individuals who conduct assessments must know and understand professional standards. According to authorities in the field (American Educational Research Association et al., 1999; Bredekamp and Rosegrant, 1995), educators and test examiners who administer tests should have the training and experience necessary and

**TABLE 1.4**  *Assessment Requirements for an English Language Learner Who Has a Disability or Is Suspected of Having a Disability*

---

*Planning the Assessment*

What is the student's native language? Native language refers to the language normally used by the student, or, in the case of a child, the language normally used by the parents of the child.

*During the Assessment Procedure*

Assessment materials or procedures are selected and administered in the child's native language or other mode of communication, unless it is clearly not feasible to do so. No single procedure should be the sole criterion for determining an appropriate educational program for a child. Any standardized tests that the child takes must:

  (i)  have been validated for the specific purpose for which they are used;
  (ii)  be administered by trained and knowledgeable personnel; and

  (iii)  be administered in accordance with any instructions provided by the producer of such tests.

Materials and procedures used to assess a child with limited English proficiency are selected and administered to ensure that they measure the extent to which the child has a disability and needs special education, rather than measuring the child's English language skills.

*IEP Meeting*

The IEP Team must consider the language needs of the student as those needs relate to the child's IEP.

The school must take whatever action is necessary to ensure that the parent understands the proceedings at the IEP meeting, including arranging for an interpreter for parents who are deaf or whose native language is other than English.

---

*Source: Federal Register*, 1999, sec. 300.19, 300.532.

should follow professional standards and ethical procedures. Educators and examiners should not attempt to evaluate students whose age, disability, linguistic, or cultural backgrounds are outside the range of their academic training or supervised experience.

The Council for Educational Diagnostic Services (1995), a division of the Council for Exceptional Children, has published a list of minimal competencies for educational diagnosticians (Table 1.5).

## Preferred Practices

Assessing students involves preparation and a variety of skills on the part of the teachers and other examiners. These individuals should be knowledgeable regarding federal mandates and the requirements for assessing students with disabilities. The examiner needs to understand a variety of assessment approaches and must be able to select those approaches that are appropriate for

each of the purposes in the assessment process. The examiner must use only those approaches in which the examiner has received thorough training in administering and interpreting and must follow ethical procedures, adhering to the highest professional standards.

An examiner must develop good interpersonal skills for working with students and their families. These skills include being sensitive and responsive to diversity. Some of these skills will be in areas that an examiner needs to develop; other skills may come more naturally for the examiner because of previous experience.

An examiner must be aware of and sensitive to the family's feelings about their child's academic performance or problem behaviors. Family members have much information about their child and may wish to share this knowledge. The examiner should recognize and appreciate individual preferences. One family is comfortable with a minimal level of involvement, whereas another family would like to be involved fully with the process.

**TABLE 1.5** *Minimum Standards for Educational Diagnosticians*

*The Educational Diagnostician Must Have Knowledge of:*

1. Laws, regulations, and policies, including those at the federal, state/provincial, and local levels related to diagnosis, assessment, placement, and due process;
2. Ethical issues and standards of professional practice, including confidentiality, training standards for particular instruments and procedures, limitations of one's own competence, and a willingness to pursue continuous professional development;
3. The criteria for technical adequacy of instruments as well as the limitations and appropriate use of each type of assessment procedure.

*The Educational Diagnostician Must Have Knowledge of and Skills in:*

4. Collection of assessment data, including the selection, administration and accurate scoring of instruments and procedures appropriate to the areas of concern, such as basic academic skills, perception, language, adaptive behavior, and classroom behavior. Knowledge and skill in a wide variety of observation techniques is also essential. Throughout the process, an educational diagnostician must conduct these procedures in a manner that demonstrates respect for the individual;
5. Assessment strategies for culturally diverse groups that include a selection of approaches that encourage nonbiased assessment and take into consideration the influence of English as a second language;
6. Appropriate use of assessment information to make classification and instructional planning recommendations;
7. Communication, both oral and written, including development of assessment reports that convey results to parents and other professionals in a manner that is understandable, conveys the importance of the assessment process, and includes any reservations regarding the assessment procedures.

*Source:* Adapted from Council for Educational Diagnostic Services (1995). Knowledge and Skills Needed by Educational Diagnosticians: A Policy Statement. *CEDS Communique* 23(1, Fall), 2.

As a member of a multidisciplinary team, an examiner can differ from other team members in philosophy and in amount and type of training. Teams often comprise members of various agencies and programs with different job responsibilities and schedules. The way in which team members work together affects the success of the assessment process.

## Extending Learning

1. You have been asked to make a presentation to the new members of the school board regarding the requirements for assessment as mandated by IDEA. Prepare an outline for your talk.
2. What are the purposes of assessment and how do they differ from one another?
3. Make a list of various assessment approaches that you have experienced. Which approaches were the most effective for you? Why?
4. Make arrangements to visit two different school districts and discuss the process used in screening new students and in referring students for further assessment. What types of forms do they use? Compare and contrast the approaches.
5. The Family Educational Rights and Privacy Act (FERPA) applies to any student who attends a school that receives federal funds. How do these regulations apply to your college or university?
6. Contact your State Department of Education. What information resources does it provide on assessment of students with disabilities?
7. Being responsive to diversity begins with sensitivity to others. Make a list of ways that

have been helpful to you in developing sensitivity toward others and identify the ways that have been most effective. Share your list and discuss your findings with the class.

8. Review the referral form (Figure 1.7) on Cory Young. If you were a member of Cory's IEP team, what considerations would be important when planning assessment for an English language learner?

## References

American Educational Research Association, American Psychological Association, and National Council on Measurement in Education (1999). *Standards for educational and psychological testing.* Washington, DC: American Educational Research Association.

Bredekamp, S., and T. Rosegrant, eds. (1995). *Reaching potentials: Transforming early childhood curriculum and assessment.* Vol. 2. Washington, DC: National Association for the Education of Young Children.

Council for Educational Diagnostic Services (1995). Knowledge and skills needed by educational diagnosticians: A policy statement. *CEDS Communique* 23(1, Fall), 2.

Dennis, R. E., and M. F. Giangreco (1996). Creating conversation: Reflections on cultural sensitivity in family interviewing. *Exceptional Children* 63(1), 103–116.

Division for Early Childhood (2000). Developmental delay as an eligibility category: A position statement of the Division for Early Childhood of the Council for Exceptional Children. Retrieved May 16, 2001, from www.dec-sped.org/positions/devdelayposition.html.

EDLAW. (1991). "Individuals with disabilities education act as amended by Pub. L. 101–476." Potomac, MD: Author.

*Federal Register* (Vol. 64, No. 48, pp. 12418–12536). Washington, DC: U.S. Government Printing Office, March 12, 1999.

McLean, M., B. J. Smith, K. McCormick, J. Schakel, and M. McEvoy (1991). *Developmental delay: Establishing parameters for a preschool category of exceptionality.* CEC Position Paper. Reston, VA: Council for Exceptional Children.

Padilla, A. M., and A. Medina (1996). Cross-cultural sensitivity in assessment: Using tests in culturally appropriate ways. In *Handbook of multicultural assessment*, edited by L. A. Suzuki, P. J. Meller, and J. G. Ponterotto. San Francisco: Jossey-Bass.

Sattler, J. (2001). *Assessment of children: Cognitive applications.* 4th ed. La Mesa, CA: Jerome M. Sattler.

Shepard, L. (1996). Classroom testing and external accountability. Paper presented at the annual meeting of the American Educational Research Association, April, New York, New York.

# Involving Families and Being Responsive to Diversity

## Overview

Educators work closely with family members in identifying student strengths and needs, in planning the education program, and in assessing progress. Within each family, adult members may have similar or very different priorities for their children. They may wish to be involved in their child's program in a variety of ways. Family members are often at different points in their understanding and acceptance of their child's disability. For example, one parent wants to assist the team by sharing medical reports and discussing the child's diagnosis; another parent looks to team members for help and explanations. In working with families, you will need to identify the extent to which families wish to be involved in their child's assessment process and in the development of the individualized plan as well as the preferred methods of home and school communication.

Working with diverse family groups involves many skills: listening carefully, understanding and being responsive to various perspectives, sharing meaningful information, and planning together to develop an appropriate education program.

Each family unit is unique. The uniqueness of families includes such diverse aspects as culture, disability, economic status, ethnicity, gender, geographic region of origin, language, and race. Professionals who work with families must be sensitive to and responsive to all elements of diversity. This chapter will give you a foundation in these skills.

## Chapter Objectives

After completing this chapter, you should be able to:

- Define the term *family* and describe areas that are important to consider in working with families.
- Identify the important issues in being responsive to family diversity.
- Discuss special considerations for working with families of very young children from birth through age 2.
- Identify areas important for working with families of children and youth ages 3 through 21.

- Describe the role of families in the assessment process as outlined by federal law.
- Discuss the ways families are involved in each of the various assessment steps.
- Compare assessment tools designed for parent use.
- Use techniques for listening to and understanding parents.
- Discuss important components of conferencing with parents.

## What Shapes Our Views

Our definition of the term **family** continues to undergo changes. Today, the term reflects our understanding of the increasing diversity of family patterns and structures. Although there continues to be much debate regarding the definition, many agree that a family consists of two or more individuals who may or may not be related but who have extended commitments to each other.

Although families can include many or only a few members, each family unit is affected by four major factors. Turnbull and Turnbull (1997) developed a family systems model, consisting of four components, to assist in organizing concepts about these important factors:

1. a family's interaction system
2. family functions
3. family characteristics
4. a family's life cycle

The first component, a family's interaction system, is the center of the model and involves the interactions of individual family members on a daily and weekly basis. There are four major subsystems of interaction: adult and adult; parent and child; child and child; and extended family, friends, neighbors, and professionals.

The second component, family functions, or the needs of the family, is met by tasks that fall into seven broad categories:

1. economic considerations
2. daily care
3. recreation
4. socialization
5. affection
6. self-definition
7. educational/vocational considerations

Certain functions or needs are more important to some families than to other families because of personal desires or cultural traditions.

The third component, family characteristics, includes not only the individual characteristics of family members but the characteristics of the family unit as well. For example, the number of family members, their cultural background(s), and their socioeconomic status all affect family characteristics. A child's disability, including any special challenges the child's disability presents, affects family characteristics as well.

Finally, families, like individuals, have life cycles. Progressing through a lifetime, an individual experiences a series of transitions during stages of growth. These stages of the life cycle may be characterized by changing interests and needs. Similarly, all families go through periods of transition during growth stages as the family unit's needs and interests change. For example, a young family's immediate needs may be finding a job and a place to live. The family may be coping with any number of related problems, including poverty, illiteracy, and lack of job skills. Young children make many demands, both physical and emotional, just when parents would rather spend time finding friends for themselves or perhaps someone to assist with child care.

As children grow older, the role of parents shifts from one of meeting children's needs to one of assisting them to become independent. Families in this stage become more involved in their child's schooling and in planning for their future. Families of various backgrounds approach these roles differently. Family traditions can become an issue as parents develop an understanding of their own roles and adjust their dreams for their children. As children move into adulthood, families will experience other challenges and needs, such as accepting decisions of adult children and encouraging them in their chosen vocations.

For families that include a child with a disability, there will be additional considerations at each of these stages. Young families with an infant with special needs frequently must adjust a dream about their child's future. The child they envisioned running and skipping may never walk, hear, or speak. Grandparents who had looked forward to the birth of a grandchild may also need help in their acceptance of the infant with special needs. Later on, families with a preteenager find that they have to arrange for continued supervised child care. They will need to find time to attend team meetings at school and to meet with their child's teacher. Eventually, families with a young adult must make decisions regarding independent housing and moving from the familiar education system to a new service system. Rehabilitative services, which often have different criteria for eligibility, will replace educational services. Families eventually need information about guardianship, estate planning, and wills.

Thus, while in many ways, the basic life-cycle experience is common, whether or not the family unit includes a child with special needs, the challenges that the disability presents create additional demands. Furthermore, different expectations for the child and different concerns during the family life cycle frame different perspectives for families who have recently moved to this country, who come from poverty, who speak a home language different from the majority group, or who represent a nondominant group.

## Responding to Diversity

Educators, therapists, and other service providers who work with families and children with disabilities begin their work by developing an understanding of the family's culture, economic status, ethnicity, geographic region of origin, language, and race. These professionals know that assumptions by members of the dominant group may not be appropriate or relevant to members of less dominant groups. For example, the birth of a child with an hereditary disorder does not deter an Amish couple from having more children. A child with a disability is accepted as "God's will," and genetic counseling is inappropriate for an Amish family (Waltman, 1996). Individuals working with this family will need to accept and respect the family's decisions and to reassure them that professionals can work cooperatively with the family and not in opposition.

Often, professionals assume that because a family has lived in this country for many years they have become acculturated. Some families deliberately avoid adopting the "American way" in an effort to retain their cultural uniqueness. Thus, several generations may grow up not holding the values of the dominant culture.

Cultural heritages, values, and beliefs may dramatically affect the family's perception of and participation in the assessment process (Haney and Knox, 1995; Hanson, Lynch, and Wayman, 1990), development of the intervention, and plans for the future. Other aspects of diversity may affect a family's cooperation. Table 2.1 summarizes the important considerations in working with families and developing a sensitivity to diversity.

## Aspirations

A family's hopes for their child may range from appropriate to elevated or depressed expectations. Family aspirations have an impact on the levels of involvement that families choose: from making the referral for assessment, to participating in the assessment process, to helping develop a plan for services. Certain cultural or regional expectations can also influence family aspirations. For example, residents in some regions place a high value on family and community. A family from this region may hope that after completing school their child will join the family business.

## Assistance

The family may actively seek help from others, or the family may view its needs and problems as private matters to be addressed only within the family. For example, residents in some rural areas place a high value on personal independence and self-sufficiency. They may be reluctant to ask for additional assistance.

## Authority of the School

Cultural beliefs, such as feelings about school authority in decision making (Turnbull and Turnbull, 1990) or respect of authority (Alper, Schloss, and Schloss, 1994), often affect the level and type of involvement family members choose. Some families have difficulty with the joint decision-making process of parents and professionals working together. They consider professionals authority figures to be respected and obeyed. Such family members may try to avoid confrontation in discussions, or they may reject school authority altogether.

## Child Rearing

Families approach child rearing from various perspectives too. In some families there is much close physical contact between mother and child, and communication is characterized more by touch than by vocal stimulation. Other families spend much time talking and singing to their children. Some families do not encourage their child to participate in gross motor activities for safety concerns. Other families of young children promote independent exploration and travel.

## Communication

Communication involves active listening and responding to both verbal and nonverbal communication. Being sensitive and responsive to family diversity includes appreciating that family groups may have unique communication patterns. For example, some regional and cultural groups support and value assertiveness in making needs and wishes known to others; some groups view assertiveness as rude and avoidable.

Communication styles can help or hinder family members' efforts to seek services. For example, to receive services, family members have to make an initial referral, make follow-up phone calls, complete paperwork, and deal with a service system with various requirements and

**TABLE 2.1** *Considerations in Responding to Family Diversity*

| Area of Consideration | Issues in Being Responsive to Diversity |
| --- | --- |
| Aspirations | A family's hopes for their child may range from appropriate aspirations to elevated or depressed expectations. |
| | Family aspirations affect the level of involvement families choose in making the referral, in participating in the assessment process, and in helping to develop a plan of services. Family aspirations are influenced by culture, economic status, gender, or geographic regional expectations. |
| Assistance | Family members may actively seek help or they may view needs and concerns as private matters. Family views are influenced by one or more aspects of diversity. |
| Authority of the school | Some families wish to participate in parent professional partnerships. Families from some cultural communities naturally defer to authority. |
| Child rearing | Families approach child rearing from various perspectives, including independence, communication, and physical contact. |
| Communication | Some families use an assertive style in their verbal communication that assists them in referring their child and in entering the service system. Other families naturally defer to authority figures and do not pursue issues. |
| | Some families use nonverbal communication, including eye gaze and gestures to communicate important wants or needs. |
| | Communicating takes on a special significance to some groups. Finishing a conversation is more important than being on time. |
| | Communication that involves technology may be a barrier for some families. |
| Disability | A disability may be viewed as shameful, or the person with a disability may be viewed as having a second-class status. |
| | A disability can present social or physical barriers. These barriers may be perceived, or they may be actual barriers of access. |
| | Issues of acceptance involve one or more of the following groups: parents, extended family, community. |
| Legal status | Families may lack knowledge of their rights. |
| | Families with illegal status often fear government authorities or school officials. |
| Literacy and language | Family members may not have literacy skills in their own language or in English. |
| | Information and materials are seldom available in the family's native language. |
| | Translators may not be available. |
| | Standardized instruments often lack a representative norming sample. |
| | Examiners may not be familiar with aspects of diversity. |
| Medical practices | Medical practices differ and can cause misinterpretation between families and school personnel. |
| Meetings and support groups | The format of group discussions can cause difficulty for families of some communities. |
| Parental roles | In many cultures, the person who makes the decisions is the principal male family member. |
| Transient status | Families that are homeless or move frequently have difficulty entering the service system. |

eligibility procedures. The variety of communication and interpersonal skills needed to negotiate the service system can create barriers for some families in obtaining services.

Some family groups have unique nonverbal communication patterns; for example, avoiding eye contact with elders to signify respect. The art of communication may take on a special significance to some groups. For instance, a focus on relationships rather than on tasks can mean it is more important to continue a conversation with a friend than it is to be on time for an appointment to discuss a child's assessment.

For families newly arrived in this country, communication that involves technologies can create additional barriers. For example, families may not be acquainted with the procedure of operating a phone to negotiate a computer-assisted telephone call or using voice mail.

## Disability

Perceptions of disability encompass a range of emotions for family members: embarrassment and shame, guilt and blame, grief and acceptance. Some groups may view a person with a disability as having second-class status. Family members may believe that there are social or physical barriers because their child has a visible disability. Parents may lack knowledge about their child's disability and have difficulty in locating information to develop realistic expectations. Various issues relating to the acceptance of the disability involve the parents, the extended family, and the community. The extended family's perceptions and the cultural community's acceptance of the disability often play a critical role for the immediate family.

## Legal Status

Families may lack knowledge of their rights regarding services for their children. Parents who have an illegal status commonly fear government and school officials and are reluctant to have their child assessed.

## Literacy and Language

Some family members may not have the ability to speak, read, or write English. Other family members may have poor literacy skills in their native language. Even families who have strong literacy skills may be limited by the availability of materials in their native languages or dialects.

Identifying translators and their availability is critical for families so that they can participate in the assessment process. The challenge of translating exact meanings between two languages is often difficult. For families who speak a dialect different from the translator's, this challenge sometimes becomes a barrier.

Few standardized assessment instruments are written in languages other than English. Many standardized instruments do not include representative samples from cultural, racial, ethnic, and linguistic groups. To compound the problem, examiners can lack familiarity with family diversity.

## Medical Practices

Medical practices differ across cultures and can cause misinterpretation by school personnel.

> One example of a traditional practice that has led to misunderstandings in the American culture is the use of coin rubbing. This massage treatment is utilized by the Vietnamese community to treat disorders such as headaches and colds. Coin treatment, or *Cao Gio*, literally translates to "scratching the (bad) wind out of the body." The treatment involves the massaging of chest and back with a medicated substance, like Ben-Gay, and the striking or scratching of the skin with a coin or spoon. This process leaves superficial bruises and, when spotted by professionals who are unaware of the techniques, has often resulted in a referral for child abuse. This practice provides a clear example of differences and also dramatically underscores the issues in diagnosis and interpretation when the various cultures meet. (Hanson et al., p. 122)

## Meetings and Support Groups

Support groups are often helpful for family members who would like assistance; yet, the group discussion format is more difficult for some individuals than others. Shapiro (1994) describes how problems can be overcome in support groups among Latino families. Approaches that are beneficial include the development of ethnically competent group facilitators (who have a familiarity with Latino ethnic history and culture), the involvement of community leaders, outreach using the Latino media, repeated personal contact, attention to making the group culturally relevant, and meeting in a neutral or culturally significant location.

## Parental Roles

In many cultures, the person who makes the decisions is the principal male family member. This could be the father, grandfather, uncle, or brother-in-law. Although the mother or other female family representative might attend all meetings regarding the child, she may refuse to make any decisions or sign any papers. The male figure may never attend any of the meetings; yet the decisions are his to make. This decision-making process can be frustrating to the team; however, if the team has knowledge of the parental roles beforehand, additional attempts can be made to accommodate the male family member's schedule.

## Transient Status

Some families move frequently from one residence to another, and some can be homeless for periods of time. Locating children and providing services is challenging when families move from one service area to another.

Understanding and being responsive to diversity is a complex process. The skills involved require you to be thoughtful and reflective in practice. You must exercise care not to promote stereotypes by making generalities about cultural groups. A key point to remember in working with families is to *ask*. Asking families to determine preferences and needs avoids stereotypical assumptions as well as careless regard for family heritage.

## Federal Legislation and the Role of Parents

Federal legislation that regulates the provision of services to children and youth with disabilities has long recognized the role of the parents. One of the most important aspects of this legislation is the defining of parent and guardian rights. IDEA describes these rights under the broad term due process. Due process refers to the legal safeguards professionals must follow during the assessment process and the delivery of services. These safeguards protect the rights of families and their children.

## Guaranteed Rights

School personnel must notify the child's parent(s) or guardian of any assessment procedure (*right of notice*) and provide consent (*right of consent*) for the assessment of their child. Before the assessment process begins, school personnel must send the parents a written form that describes the types of assessments to be conducted. The parent provides consent by signing and returning the form. However, the parent can revoke consent at any time during the assessment process by notifying the school. The parent can request that a full assessment of all areas associated with the disability be completed. This assessment must include multiple measures, must be conducted by a multidisciplinary team, and, for children ages 3 through 21, must be completed within 60 days of referral. Sixty days is the maximum number of days; some states have passed legislation that specifies a 45-day maximum. Teachers and examiners should check with state department of education personnel to determine the laws in a specific state.

Infants and toddlers ages birth through 2 and preschoolers who will have an individualized family service plan must have assessment procedures completed 45 days after the initial referral (*right of evaluation*). Parents may request a reevaluation or obtain an independent evaluation if there are any questions or concerns regarding the evaluation (*right to an independent evaluation*). Table 2.2 describes these and other important rights.

## The Assessment Process for Families of Young Children

In this section we will examine some of the questions and decisions that parents make concerning the assessment of young children. Many teachers and other professionals who work with families of young children from birth through 2 and, in some states, children ages 3 through 5 provide services within the context of a **family-**

**TABLE 2.2**    *The Rights of Parents and Guardians According to IDEA*

| Right of Parents and Guardians | Definition |
| --- | --- |
| *Beginning the Assessment Process* | |
| Right of notice | The parent must receive a notification of the proposed assessment in the family's native language or principle mode of communication. |
| Right of consent | The parent must give consent before the child is assessed to determine eligibility for special education services. |
| Right of evaluation | The assessment must include multiple measures, be conducted by a multidisciplinary team, and be completed within 60 days of referral for special services. For young children who will have an IFSP, the assessment must be completed within 45 days of the initial referral. |
| Right to an independent evaluation | The parent has a right to request an evaluation by an independent evaluator if there are questions or concerns regarding the child's evaluation conducted by school personnel. |
| *Using the Assessment Information* | |
| Right of participation | The parent must be invited to participate in the writing of the child's educational plan (an individualized family service plan or an individualized educational program). |
| Right of notice | The parent must receive a notification of the proposed changes in the education program, which must be in the family's native language or principle mode of communication. |
| Right of access | The parent must be allowed access to all educational records. |
| Right to confidentiality | The educational records are confidential. The parent must give consent to have the child's records released to other institutions or agencies. The parent has the right to refuse disclosure of information contained in the records to other professionals or agencies. |
| Right to hearing | The parent has the right to a hearing with an impartial hearing officer. The parent has a right to present evidence and to cross-examine school staff. |
| Right to mediation | The parent has the right to a process, called mediation, which attempts to resolve differences with school personnel before going to a hearing. |
| Right to resolve differences | If the parent is not satisfied with the decision of the hearing officer, a second step, the right to appeal to the state court system, can be implemented. |

**focused philosophy.** A family-focused philosophy requires that teachers and therapists attempt to create opportunities for families to acquire the knowledge and skills necessary to strengthen the functioning of the family. A family-focused philosophy supports the belief that families need to be able to choose the services that will benefit them. Thus, families are not merely recipients of services but rather active participants in the assessment, implementation, and evaluation of special services.

Parents of young children have questions about their child's development; parents of school-age children have academic concerns. Some parents have questions about their child's behavior. Addressing the concerns of parents of infants and toddlers and parents of children enrolled in school involves two distinct processes. First, we will examine the process for children before their enrollment in school. This process includes the questions parents may have, the answers through assessment to these questions, and the procedure for making decisions.

## Initial Questions and Decisions

During the early years of a child's growth, parents and other family members may develop concerns about their child's development. In fact, parents are often the first to question or to observe areas of difficulty for their child, such as happened in the Snapshot of Juan and his family. Parents sometimes share their concerns with someone close to their child, such as a teacher or child care provider.

Teachers and child care personnel should listen to parents and encourage discussions about their children. They should inform parents about neighborhood screening activities and encourage them to have their children screened periodically. Assisting parents and other adults to become aware of screenings, programs, and services for children with special needs is called Child Find. Preschool teachers, public health nurses, social workers, and doctors are some of the professionals involved with Child Find. Personnel from state agencies who work with children and families conduct a variety of Child Find activities throughout the year. For example, radio and television announcements or newspaper articles describe community screenings and dates screenings will be held. Brochures distributed in public places explain ways to observe a young child's development and list common questions that arise for parents. These printed materials also contain information about community screenings. Families with questions about their child may decide to take advantage of these free screenings, or families may decide to discuss their concerns with their primary medical provider.

## Screening Questions for Families

Parents can share their observations and concerns during screening. A social worker, nurse

---

**SNAPSHOT ■** *Questions Concerning Juan's Physical Development*

Juan was born $3\frac{1}{2}$ months premature and is now 4 years old. He lives at home with his mother, father, maternal grandmother, and two younger brothers. Every day his grandmother takes him for a ride in his red wagon when she goes down to the corner store. He enjoys watching the activities at a construction site along the way. His grandmother and his father have some concerns about Juan's development. He was slow to walk and talk, and his speech is still difficult to understand. He prefers to play alone or to watch cartoons on television.

His grandmother shared her concerns with a neighbor who works at the community child care center. The staff at the center had recently completed an in-service workshop on child development. The neighbor listened sympathetically and then suggested that the grandmother could take Juan to the child center for a free community screening on the first Monday of the month.

**TABLE 2.3**   *Selected Standardized Screening Instruments that Incorporate a Parent Report*

| Screening Instrument | Age Range of Child | Parent Involvement | Scoring |
|---|---|---|---|
| *AGS Early Screening Profiles* (Harrison, Kaufman, Kaufman, Bruininks, Rynders, Ilmer, Sparrow, & Cicchetti, 1990) | 2 years through 6 years, 11 months | Home survey<br><br><br>Health survey<br><br><br><br>Self-help/social profile | Descriptive categories of above average, average, below average.<br>Information is not scored but integrated into the recommendations.<br>Percentile ranks. |
| *Ages & Stages Questionnaires (ASQ)* (Bricker & Squires, 1999) | 4 months through 60 months | Parent-completed child monitoring system | Descriptive categories of yes, sometimes, and not yet. |
| *BRIGANCE® Preschool Screen* (Brigance, 1998) | 3 years through 4 years | Parent rating form | Categories of yes, no, uncertain. Parents may include explanations in writing. |
| *DIAL–3* (Mardell-Czudnowski & Goldenberg, 1998) | 3 years through 6 years | Parent questionnaire | Open-ended questions on personal and medical background, rating scale on adaptive skills and social skill development. |
| *Early Screening Inventory–Revised* (Meisels, Marsden, Wiske, & Henderson, 1997). | 3 years through 4 years, 6 months (ESI–P)<br>4 years, 6 months through 6 years (ESI–K) | Parent questionnaire | Not scored; assists in providing an overview of the child's development. |
| *FirstSTEP* (Miller, 1993) | 2 years, 9 months through 6 years, 2 months | Parent/teacher scale | Descriptive categories of always/usually, some of the time, rarely or never. Raw scores are converted to scaled scores. Information is integrated into child's record form. |

practitioner, or educator usually meets with the parent(s) to discuss their questions and concerns and to record information about their child's development. The assessment question is: Does this child have a problem that requires further assessment?

Parents can complete a checklist or parent report form concerning various milestones in their child's development. Many standardized screening tools provide a parent report form as an integral part of the screening profile (Table 2.3).

**FIGURE 2.1**   *Selected Items from the Ages and Stages Questionnaire (ASQ) Second Edition*

**Problem Solving**   *Be sure to try each activity with your child*

| | Yes | Sometimes | Not Yet |
|---|---|---|---|

1. While your child watches, line up four objects like blocks or cars in a row. Does your child copy or imitate you and line up *four* objects in a row? (You can also use spools of thread, small boxes, or other toys.)

2. If your child wants something he cannot reach, does he find a chair or box to stand on to reach it?

3. When you point to the figure and ask your child, "What is this?" does your child say a word that means a person? Responses like "snowman," "boy," "man," "girl," and "Daddy" are correct.

   Please write your child's response here:

*Source:* Bricker, D., Squires, J. (1999). *Ages and stages questionnaires: A parent-completed, child-monitoring system* (2nd ed.) (p. 5). Baltimore: Paul H. Brookes Publishing Co.

One example of a standardized screening tool, the *Ages & Stages Questionnaires (ASQ)* 2nd ed. (Bricker and Squires, 1999) consists of comprehensive parent questionnaires (Figure 2.1). As Box 2.1 shows, these questionnaires are designed to provide information in five developmental areas: communication, gross motor, fine motor, problem solving, and personal-social skills. The parent rates whether or not the child does different activities within each of these five areas by indicating "yes," "sometimes," and "not yet."

### Screening Decisions for Families

If there are concerns after collecting all the information about the child, the screening team forwards the results to a team of professionals known as the early childhood team. This team

**BOX 2.1**   *Ages and Stages Questionnaires (ASQ) Second Edition*

- *Publication Date:* 1999
- *Purposes:* A parent-completed first level screening test that measures the following areas of development: communication, gross motor, fine motor, problem solving, and personal-social. The *Ages & Stages Questionnaires* are also available in Spanish. A set of intervention activities is included in the ASQ User's Guide and these may be photocopied for parents.
- *Age/Grade Level:* Ages 4 months through 60 months.
- *Time to Complete:* 5 minutes.
- *Technical Adequacy:* The instrument has undergone extensive development and reliability and validity are adequate.
- *Suggested Use:* May be used as part of an overall screening procedure.

will invite the child's parent(s) to participate and, together, they decide what additional assessment information is necessary.

## Questions Regarding Eligibility

As members of the early childhood team, parents have the opportunity to identify their concerns and participate in the team process in determining whether or not their child is eligible for special services. Parents can provide valuable information based on their child's developmental history or their observations of their child at home. The key question the team must address is, "Does this child meet eligibility

requirements for special services?" In Chapter 1 we describe this process in detail and how IDEA defines these areas of eligibility.

## Decisions Regarding Eligibility

Evaluators base decisions regarding eligibility on observations and other multiple-assessment measures. However, parents add valuable information to this decision by taking an active role during the assessment process. For example, parents can provide information informally through discussions or they can complete a parent report form from a standardized instrument (Table 2.4). Parents of young children often

**TABLE 2.4**    *Selected Standardized Instruments That Incorporate a Parent Report*

| Areas of Concern | Instrument | Age | Reliability | Validity |
|---|---|---|---|---|
| Behavior | *Behavior Rating Profile, Second Edition* (Brown & Hammill, 1990) | 6 years, 6 months to 18 years 6 months | Adequate | Not adequate for eligibility decisions |
| Behavior | *Child Behavior Checklist for Ages 1½–5* (Achenbach & Rescorla, 2000) | 1 year, 6 months through 5 years | Adequate | Adequate |
| Behavior | *Child Behavior Checklist for Ages 6–18* (Achenbach, 2001) | 6 years through 18 years | Adequate | Adequate |
| Behavior | *Conners' Parent Rating Scales* (Conners, 1990) | 3 years to 17 years | Adequate | Adequate |
| Behavior | *Revised Behavior Problem Checklist* (Quay & Peterson, 1987) | 5 years to 18 years | Adequate | Adequate |
| Concept comprehension | *Boehm–3 Preschool* (Boehm, 2001) | 3 years to 6 years | Adequate | Adequate |
| Development | *Bayley Scales of Infant Development II* (Bayley, 1993) | birth to 42 months | Adequate | Adequate |
| Development | *Child Development Inventory* (Ireton, 1992) | 15 months to 72 months | Adequate for younger | Not adequate for eligibility decisions |

choose to be present in the room so they can add their observations of their child's behavior. They may be able to provide feedback regarding whether or not the skills that their child demonstrates are typical of what they feel their child can do. Parents can supplement information about their child. For example, they may offer to share a videotape of their child in different settings.

For young children, assessment procedures focus on one or more of the following developmental domains: adaptive, such as self-help; cognitive; communication; physical, including gross and fine motor skills; and social-emotional. Early childhood team members should remember to complete each child's assessment (including the needs identified by the family) within 45 calendar days from the time the child is referred to the team.

## Questions and Decisions in Planning the Program

If the team decides that the child is eligible for special services, the next step involves questions and decisions regarding the child's program. What are the family's priorities and resources? **Family-directed assessment** focuses on information that family members choose to share with other team members regarding family resources, priorities, and concerns. Family-directed assess-

ment relates to children ages birth through 2 and, in some states, to children ages 3 through 5. The law does not require families to participate in family-directed assessment but families must be given the opportunity. Table 2.5 lists the assessment areas in family-directed assessment and illustrates information that a family may share. Thus, parents not only participate in the process of identifying child-related strengths and needs, but they may exchange information with practitioners regarding family-based needs. The focus of family-directed assessment is on the process that encourages families to identify needed services rather than on the assessment of families to determine which services to deliver.

A teacher or other professional may support family-directed assessment by assisting the family in identifying information or by helping the family complete a written form, rating scale, or other standard procedure. The *Family Interest Survey* (Cripe and Bricker, 1993) (Figure 2.2) is an example of an instrument used in family-directed assessment. This information aids the early childhood team in the development of the IFSP or IEP.

What are the outcomes, or goals, that the team believes that the child should accomplish? What type(s) of special services will help the child achieve the outcome(s)? Table 2.6 lists the types of special services available to the child and family *Interest Survey* (Cripe and Bricker, 1993).

**TABLE 2.5**   *Family-Directed Assessment: Hearing the Family's Concerns, Resources, and Priorities*

| Areas That Comprise Family-Directed Assessment | Sample Comments by Family Members during a Family-Directed Assessment |
|---|---|
| Family concerns | "How can I learn more about my child's disability?" |
| | "How will my child get along in school?" |
| Family resources | "We have reliable transportation." |
| | "Our child's relatives live nearby." |
| Family priorities | "We want to know how to communicate with our child." |
| | "We would like some help with toilet training." |

**FIGURE 2.2**   *Selected Items from the Family Interest Survey*

| For each date used, check one box in each row. | Date: _____ | | | Date: _____ | | |
|---|---|---|---|---|---|---|
| **Child's Interests** *I am interested in . . .* | Priority interest | Interest but not a current priority | Not an interest at this time | Priority interest | Interest but not a current priority | Not an interest at this time |
| Knowing more about my child's current strengths and needs | | | | | | |
| Learning about services and programs for my child | | | | | | |
| Knowing more about my child's condition/disability | | | | | | |
| Making plans for future services and programs | | | | | | |
| Knowing how my child grows and learns (such as social, motor, self-care) | | | | | | |
| Learning ways to care for and help my child (such as positioning, diet, health) | | | | | | |
| Learning about laws that affect my child, my rights, and how to advocate for my child | | | | | | |
| **Family's Interests** *I am interested in . . .* | Priority interest | Interest but not a current priority | Not an interest at this time | Priority interest | Interest but not a current priority | Not an interest at this time |
| Explaining my child's special needs to siblings, grandparents, and friends | | | | | | |
| Gaining support for my child's brothers and sisters | | | | | | |
| Involving family and friends in my child's care or free time | | | | | | |
| Counseling for my family | | | | | | |
| Learning to solve family problems ourselves | | | | | | |

*Source:* Cripe, J., & Bricker, D. (1993). AEPS™ family interest survey (pp. 4–5). Baltimore, MD: Paul H. Brookes Publishing Co.

**TABLE 2.6** *Related Services for the Child and Family According to IDEA*

| | |
|---|---|
| Audiology | This service includes identifying the hearing loss, determining the need for amplification, and providing auditory training, aural rehabilitation, speech reading, and other services. Guidance and counseling for children, parents, and teachers is included. |
| Counseling | Social workers, psychologists, guidance counselors, and other trained personnel assist the family in understanding the special needs of the child and enhancing the child's development. |
| Early identification and assessment of disabilities in children | These services include identifying a disability as early as possible in a child's life. |
| Medical | Medical services are provided by a licensed physician to determine a child's medically related disability. |
| Occupational therapy | These services are designed to improve, develop, or restore the child's functional ability. |
| Orientation and mobility services | Students who are blind or visually impaired can receive these services to attain systematic orientation and safe movement within the school, home, and community environments. |
| Parent counseling and training | These services are designed to assist parents in understanding the special needs of their child, provide parents with information about child development, and help parents to acquire the necessary skills to support their child's IEP or IFSP. |
| Physical therapy | These services promote sensorimotor function. |
| Psychological services | These services include:<br>• Administering psychological and educational tests and other assessment procedures;<br>• Interpreting assessment results;<br>• Obtaining, integrating, and interpreting information about behavior and conditions relating to learning;<br>• Consulting with other staff members in planning school programs;<br>• Providing psychological counseling to children and parents; and<br>• Assisting in developing positive behavioral intervention strategies. |
| Recreation | These services include: assessment of leisure function, therapeutic recreation services, recreation programs, and leisure education. |
| Rehabilitation counseling | Group or individual sessions focus on career development, employment preparation, achieving independence, and integration in the workplace and community. |
| School health | These services are provided by the school nurse. |
| Social work | These services include:<br>• Preparing a social or developmental history on the child;<br>• Counseling with the child and family;<br>• Working with parents and others on those problems in the home, school, and community that affect the child's adjustment to school;<br>• Mobilizing school and community resources to enable the child to learn as effectively as possible; and<br>• Assisting in developing positive behavioral intervention strategies. |
| Speech-language pathology | This area includes identifying children with speech or language impairments, diagnosis, referral for medical or other professional attention, provision of speech and language services, counseling and guidance of parents, children, and teachers regarding speech and language impairments. |
| Transportation | These services consist of travel to and from school and between schools, travel in and around school buildings, specialized equipment, such as lifts, ramps, and so on. |

*Source: Federal Register,* 1999, sec. 300.24.

The team must decide where to provide the services and how frequently. Young children and families can receive services in their home, a clinic, a child care center, a nursery school or Head Start Center, or a school-based program. Family members are important team participants in these decisions. A professional who is responsive to diversity understands that some families prefer to have services in their home while other families prefer to take their child outside the home for services.

The child's individualized plan contains a description of the services. Infants and toddlers (birth through 2 years of age) have an Individualized Family Service Plan (IFSP). Children who are 3 through 5 years of age may have an IFSP rather than an individualized education program (IEP) as long as: (1) the IFSP is consistent with state policy, and (2) the parents concur.

## Questions and Decisions in Monitoring the Special Services

Once the IFSP is implemented, teachers, therapists, other service providers, and parents monitor the program. The monitoring questions should relate to the measurable goals. Team members check the plan on a regular basis, noting progress or lack of progress.

## Questions and Decisions in Evaluating Special Services

Evaluating special services that are provided to young children with disabilities has two different aspects: first, evaluation of the child's progress; and second, evaluation of the program. Parents should have the opportunity to assist in both of these types of evaluations.

### Evaluating Progress: The 6-Month Review.
At the end of 6 months, or sooner if indicated, the team must meet to discuss progress and review the IFSP. Parents must receive written

notification of the IFSP meeting. Parents participate in the evaluation by completing checklists, providing videotapes and parent reports, and making observations. Let's examine some specific examples of information that family members share during team meetings:

- An aunt provides a list of information regarding what her nephew can do independently around the house.
- A grandfather makes a videotape of his granddaughter reading to her stuffed animals.
- A father completes the parent checklist on a recently standardized instrument.

If the information collected during the assessment process indicates that there is little progress, then the team will examine whether or not they believe that the program needs to be modified. Changes to the IFSP are based on team decision making.

### Reevaluation: The Annual Review.
Young children who receive special services must be reevaluated each year, or more often if the team feels it is necessary. Again, parents must be sent a notification of the reevaluation and they are invited to the team meeting to discuss the assessment results and write the new IFSP. If the information collected during the assessment process indicates that there are substantial gains, then the team will discuss whether the child still requires special services. If the team decides that the child and family continue to be eligible for services, then the next step is to write the new IFSP.

### Evaluating the Program.
Does the program address the family's needs? Through the use of informal assessment approaches, parents are asked to provide feedback. For example, a letter sent to all families participating in an early childhood special education play group serves as an effective informal evaluation instrument. Included in the letter is a postcard with several questions for families to answer and return by mail.

SNAPSHOT  ■  *Questions about Alexandra's General Academic Work*

Mrs. Balinsky is worried about her daughter's grades. She remembers with pride how Alexandra put a puzzle together when she was only 2 years old. Later, in elementary school, she always brought home report cards with As. But now, in ninth grade, Alexandra seems to have lost interest in schoolwork and good grades. She barely passed English and math last year. Why could there be such a change in Alexandra? Mrs. Balinsky decides to contact the school with her questions and concerns.

Teachers and other school staff may decide to use commercial program evaluations in soliciting parent feedback, many of which focus on the evaluation of early education programs. Commercial program evaluations should provide information regarding the standardization and technical characteristics of the instrument.

## How Parents of Children and Youth Are Involved in the Assessment Process

### Screening Questions and Decisions

The law mandates screening for all students enrolling in school for the first time and for students who move into a new school district. During the child's school career, teachers will contact parents regarding their concerns or parents can contact school personnel with their questions as the Snapshot of Alexandra illustrates. Physicians, too, refer a student for evaluation.

Teachers should encourage parents to discuss any questions or concerns that they have throughout the school year. Teachers can assist parents by asking informal questions such as, "What would be helpful for me to know about Alexandra?" or leading questions such as, "Tell me what Alexandra likes to do at home."

School staff handle parent questions and concerns in different ways. Some schools may use a prereferral model; others may not. IDEA does not mandate the prereferral model, but many schools find this model helpful in addressing questions and concerns.

### Prereferral Model: Addressing Parent Questions and Concerns

In Chapter 1 we discuss a prereferral system for special education services. In this model an assistance team consisting of regular classroom teachers and special educators in the school building meets to discuss parent or teacher concerns about a student's behavior or academic work and, following a problem-solving approach, plans a process for gathering information.

The team also develops intervention strategies. During the implementation of the intervention, the teacher or, when appropriate, the parent carefully records its effectiveness. If the first intervention is not successful, the team will develop and implement additional interventions and record the results. Although these prereferral procedures are not required by law, they can be helpful in addressing some questions and concerns. The Snapshot of Jimmy illustrates the concern that Jimmy's mother discussed with his teacher.

Using the prereferral model, Jimmy's teacher contacted other educators who make up the Bennington Middle School Student Assistance Team (the SAT) and met with his mother to discuss concerns and to devise a plan. Some examples of strategies that they discussed included teaching Jimmy a self-monitoring strategy when doing his homework and creating a list of incentives. Figure 2.3 shows an example of one of the materials, a parent-student monitoring sheet that Jimmy, his teacher, and his mother developed.

As a result of their discussions, Jimmy's mother agreed to let him work at the kitchen

Fourteen-year-old Jimmy, a ninth grader at Bennington Middle School, seems to struggle with completing his homework. After supper, he looks forward to watching his favorite television program before beginning his algebra and English assignments. After the program finishes, Jimmy sits down to work on the couch; yet, his mother has noticed that he usually gets up frequently and wanders around the house to find an assignment, a pencil, or a book. He becomes distracted easily and often forgets what he has set out to find. He rarely finishes his work before bedtime.

table because other family members usually watch television in the living room each evening. She agreed to remind him of the time they have set for evening homework. Jimmy's teacher suggested she can assist Jimmy in organizing his materials. The SAT agreed that she will help him decide where to keep school supplies such as pencils, dictionary, and paper. During the homework hour, Jimmy agreed to record his progress on the monitoring sheet. If he receives six checks out of a possible seven areas, he can choose a previously agreed-upon reward.

Perhaps for Jimmy these interventions will address the problem, and the assessment process will end. However, when assistance team members think that a student requires more extensive remediation, they provide a formal referral to the special services team.

## Referral

When questions about a student persist, the student assistance team completes a written referral form and forwards the referral to the coordinator of the special services team. This team consists of the student's parents, school personnel, and the student, when possible. The team may be known as the IEP team or child study team.

---

**JIMMY'S DAILY HOMEWORK CHECK**

September 13
Six checks for extra hour of TV

| | Parent checks | Comments |
|---|---|---|
| Quiet area for homework | _____ | |
| Study hour starts at 7:30 P.M. | _____ | |
| School supplies available | _____ | |
| | Jimmy checks | Comments |
| Working on homework 1 to 15 minutes | _____ | |
| Working on homework 16 to 30 minutes | _____ | |
| Working on homework 31 to 45 minutes | _____ | |
| Working on homework 46 to 60 minutes | _____ | |

---

**FIGURE 2.3**   *Parent-Student Monitoring Sheet*

***Decisions for the Team.***   The special services team receives the formal referral delineating questions about the student, which comes directly from the child's parents, teachers, student assistance team, or the student, who may self-refer. The special services team makes decisions regarding assessment procedures and develops an assessment plan. This plan describes questions the team is trying to answer about the student's special needs, the tests and procedures the team will use, and the individuals who will complete the assessments. The parent or guardian must sign a written permission before the assessment process begins. As team members, parents contribute information to this process. They may provide copies of medical records and/or educational reports. Parents frequently add observations of the student at home and in the community. They also assist the team in gathering information by using informal tools such as checklists, rating scales, or video recordings.

## Eligibility Questions and Decisions

In this step of the assessment process the team addresses the following question: Does the student meet the criteria for a disability? Does the student need special education to learn and to develop? Parents and other team members must decide if the student's special needs meet the eligibility requirements as described in IDEA and discussed in Chapter 1.

The IEP team plans an individual assessment to determine if the child has a disability and to determine what the educational needs of the child are. The child is assessed in all areas related to the suspected disability including, if appropriate,

- health
- vision
- hearing
- social and emotional status
- general intelligence
- academic performance
- communication
- motor abilities

The information collected during the assessment process determines the decisions regarding eligibility. Parents provide helpful information and a unique perspective; for example, in the Snapshot about Elaina, her mother shares information regarding her behavior at home and in the community. Furthermore, she is the only team member who can provide an historical perspective. In Alexandra's case, this information is necessary to develop a more comprehensive picture of the assessment questions.

Parents can provide information informally through discussions or contribute information on a standardized instrument. There are numerous instruments that solicit parent information as part of the profile. An example of one of these instruments, the *Child Behavior Checklist* (Achenbach, 2001), is illustrated in Figure 2.4.

---

**SNAPSHOT   ■   *Questions about Elaina's Behavior***

Elaina's mother is discouraged. Some days, Elaina seems to argue constantly with her sisters and neighborhood friends. She comes running into the house, slams the screen door, and screams that she hates everyone. Her mother has tried to talk with her, but Elaina usually ends up crying and locking herself in the bedroom. Her mother feels that the other children are becoming resentful and don't want to include Elaina in their plans.

Elaina's mother contacts the school and arranges to meet with Elaina's teacher and guidance counselor. During the meetings, the guidance counselor suggests several strategies to try at home. Elaina's teacher agrees to follow up in the classroom. However, as the months go by, the mother becomes more concerned with the lack of progress. She again contacts the school and fills out the referral form.

**FIGURE 2.4** *Sample Items from the Child Behavior Checklist (Ages 6–18)*

Below is a list of items that describe children and youths. For each item that describes your child **now or within the past 6 months** please circle the **2** if the item is **very true or often true** of your child. Circle the **1** if the item is **somewhat or sometimes true** of your child. If the item is **not true** of your child, circle the **0**. Please answer all items as well as you can, even if some do not seem to apply to your child.

**0 = Not True (as far as you know)    1 = Somewhat or Sometimes True    2 = Very True or Often True**

| | |
|---|---|
| 0 1 2    1. Acts too young for his/her age | 0 1 2    32. Feels he/she has to be perfect |
| 0 1 2    2. Drinks alcohol without parents' approval (describe): _____ | 0 1 2    33. Feels or complains that no one loves him/her |
| | 0 1 2    34. Feels others are out to get him/her |
| 0 1 2    3. Argues a lot | 0 1 2    35. Feels worthless or inferior |
| 0 1 2    4. Fails to finish things he/she starts | 0 1 2    36. Gets hurt a lot, accident-prone |
| 0 1 2    5. There is very little he/she enjoys | 0 1 2    37. Gets in many fights |
| 0 1 2    6. Bowel movements outside toilet | 0 1 2    38. Gets teased a lot |
| 0 1 2    7. Bragging, boasting | 0 1 2    39. Hangs around with others who get in trouble |
| 0 1 2    8. Can't concentrate, can't pay attention for long | 0 1 2    40. Hears sound or voices that aren't there (describe): _____ |
| 0 1 2    9. Can't get his/her mind off certain thoughts; obsessions (describe): _____ | |
| | 0 1 2    41. Impulsive or acts without thinking |
| 0 1 2    10. Can't sit still, restless, or hyperactive | 0 1 2    42. Would rather be alone than with others |
| 0 1 2    11. Clings to adults or too dependent | |
| 0 1 2    12. Complains of loneliness | 0 1 2    43. Lying or cheating |
| 0 1 2    13. Confused or seems to be in a fog | 0 1 2    44. Bites fingernails |
| 0 1 2    14. Cries a lot | 0 1 2    45. Nervous, highstrung, or tense |
| 0 1 2    15. Cruel to animals | 0 1 2    46. Nervous movements or twitching (describe): _____ |
| 0 1 2    16. Cruelty, bullying, or meanness to others | |
| 0 1 2    17. Daydreams or gets lost in his/her thoughts | 0 1 2    47. Nightmares |
| | 0 1 2    48. Not liked by other kids |
| 0 1 2    18. Deliberately harms self or attempts suicide | 0 1 2    49. Constipated, doesn't move bowels |
| | 0 1 2    50. Too fearful or anxious |
| 0 1 2    19. Demands a lot of attention | 0 1 2    51. Feels dizzy or lighthearted |
| 0 1 2    20. Destroys his/her own things | 0 1 2    52. Feels too guilty |
| 0 1 2    21. Destroys things belonging to his/her family or others | 0 1 2    53. Overeating |
| | 0 1 2    54. Overtired without good reason |
| 0 1 2    22. Disobedient at home | 0 1 2    55. Overweight |
| 0 1 2    23. Disobedient at school | 56. Physical problems *without known medical cause:* |
| 0 1 2    24. Doesn't eat well | |
| 0 1 2    25. Doesn't get along with other kids | 0 1 2    a. Aches or pains (*not* stomach or headaches) |
| 0 1 2    26. Doesn't seem to feel guilty after misbehaving | 0 1 2    b. Headaches |
| | 0 1 2    c. Nausea, feels sick |
| 0 1 2    27. Easily jealous | 0 1 2    d. Problems with eyes (*not* if corrected by glasses) (describe): _____ |
| 0 1 2    28. Breaks rules at home, school, or elsewhere | |
| 0 1 2    29. Fears certain animals, situations, or places, other than school (describe): | |
| | 0 1 2    e. Rashes or other skin problems. |
| | 0 1 2    f. Stomachaches |
| 0 1 2    30. Fears going to school | 0 1 2    g. Vomiting, throwing up |
| 0 1 2    31. Fears he/she might think or do something bad | 0 1 2    h. Other (describe): _____ |

*Source:* Copyright T. M. Achenbach. Reproduced by permission.

## Questions and Decisions in Planning Services

If the team decides that the student is eligible for special services, the next step involves questions and decisions regarding the student's program and writing the IEP. One of the rights of parents is to participate with other team members in planning the special education services that their child will receive. During the IEP meeting, the team addresses several questions: What types of special education does the student need? Where should the student receive the services? How should planners coordinate and evaluate the services?

Team members may decide to place the student in the regular classroom with the special education teacher providing consulting services. On the other hand, some parents may question whether or not their child will receive as much support in the regular classroom as in the resource room. Parents and other team members will need to discuss these difficult questions and make decisions based on the assessment process. The IEP team has 30 days to complete the writing of the IEP after the student qualifies for special education.

## Questions and Decisions in Monitoring Services

Once the plan is in place, communication between home and school is very important in monitoring services. The assessment questions during this step include: Is the student making progress? Does the program need to be modified? Teachers and parents will monitor student progress by observing the student's work and behavior or by completing informal assessments. For example, parents, as well as the student's teachers, can use a log book to enter comments about daily or weekly progress. Figure 2.5 illustrates information provided by the parent. These informal tools that parents utilize are helpful to the team in monitoring the student's individualized program.

## Questions and Decisions in Evaluating Services

Evaluating the special education services that students with disabilities receive involves two types of decision making: first, the team addresses questions regarding the student; and second, school personnel focus on questions

---

October 5

Jenny had an appointment with the doctor this afternoon. The doctor told us that she wants to change the dosage of her medication. This morning Jenny began the increased amount. The doctor said it may take her a few days to adjust.

Mrs. Williams

---

**FIGURE 2.5** *Entry from a Traveling Log Book*

regarding the overall program. Parents should have the opportunity to assist in both types of evaluations.

***Evaluating Student Gains Annually.*** At least once a year, the team must meet to review the student's current program and develop a new IEP. Parents or school personnel can request IEP meetings at other times, if needed. Parents must receive written notification of the IEP meeting. The team will address questions regarding whether or not the student is making gains or if the program needs changing. The part of the IEP form that lists the annual goals and objectives and the evaluation procedures will assist the team in these decisions. Teams will need to consider whether or not the student still requires special service(s) to benefit from the education program. Parents may actively participate in the evaluation of student gains by completing checklists, videotapes, and parent reports, or other recording sheets. Let's examine some specific examples of information that parents share during team meetings:

- A father shares information with the team regarding his son's behavior after school and on the weekend, while the teacher shares information regarding her observations of the student in the lunch room and on the playground.
- A grandmother records by audiotape information about homework habits and other behaviors at home.
- A mother and special education teacher report information that they have, together, compiled using observations of the student.

***The Three-Year Review.*** The IEP team must reevaluate students every three years, or more often if the parent(s) or school personnel believes it is necessary. The IEP team meets to review existing evaluation data and identifies what additional data is needed. Once team members gather additional assessment information, they reconvene to discuss the results. Based on the reevaluation assessment information, team members make a decision about the student's eligibil-

ity for special education. If the team makes the decision that the student is no longer eligible, then the student exits the special services system. If the team makes the decision that the student continues to be eligible for special services, then the next step is to write the new IEP.

***Evaluating the Education Program.*** As consumers, parents can contribute valuable information in this assessment step because they are most familiar with the day-to-day operation of the program. Parents commonly provide feedback to school personnel through the use of informal instruments, such as the teacher-made questionnaire illustrated in Figure 2.6.

To improve education programs, state departments of education and local school districts develop Web-based program evaluation questionnaires that parents complete. Figure 2.7 on page 48 illustrates a form that is designed for parents to provide feedback regarding their child's education program. We will study program evaluation in more detail in Chapter 19.

## Techniques for Listening to and Understanding Parent Perspectives

Parents and other family members have a wealth of knowledge about their child. Some people are more comfortable in sharing this information by filling out a form or checklist. Others prefer a more personal approach. Interviews and family stories allow families who are comfortable in talking to others to share valuable information.

In using these techniques, the first step is to acknowledge that you want to hear what parents are saying (Cohen and Spenciner, 1994). Careful listening ensures that your own biases do not overshadow what parents are relating to you. Listening to families requires complex skills, including sensitivity and respect.

### Interviews

The interview format allows different family members to talk and to share their individual

May 15

Dear Parent,

We are evaluating your child's reading program this spring, and we would appreciate your help. Please take a few minutes to answer the following questions. If possible, could you please return this letter in the enclosed stamped envelope by Friday.

Thank you,
Sandy Files
W. G. Willard School

|  | Yes | Sometimes | No |
|---|---|---|---|
| 1. My child brings home books from the school library. | _____ | _____ | _____ |
| 2. My child likes to read out loud to other family members. | _____ | _____ | _____ |
| 3. My child enjoys reading activities at school. | _____ | _____ | _____ |
| 4. I feel that my child is making progress in reading. | _____ | _____ | _____ |
| 5. My child completes homework assignments in a reasonable amount of time. | _____ | _____ | _____ |

6. Please add additional comments or suggestions:

Thank you for your help!

**FIGURE 2.6** *A Teacher-Developed Program Evaluation Form*

perspectives. An interview that is a face-to-face meeting is usually much more conducive to sharing information than an interview conducted over the telephone. Like other forms of assessment, the interview should be responsive to diversity. Create a positive tone by your respect, acceptance, support, and warmth. Set aside your own beliefs and judgments. You will need to focus on listening carefully and not let personal bias be a source of error.

Be sensitive in your probing. Respect parents' right to share only the information that they wish. Some parents are not ready to discuss some areas initially, or they do not want to confront a topic at certain periods of time.

Conducting an interview with the family (Dunst, Trivette, and Deal, 1988) includes sev-

eral steps: planning the interview, meeting the family, and completing the interview.

***Planning the Interview.*** When you contact the family, be sure to state the purpose of your visit. For example, "I'd like to visit with you and Alexandra's father to talk further about your concerns."

Decide on a mutually convenient place and time. Some families prefer a meeting in their home where they feel more comfortable in talking about their concerns in familiar surroundings. Other families prefer meeting in the home due to a strong sense of duty or cultural tradition to entertain a guest in their home. Some families are more comfortable meeting in a

**FIGURE 2.7**   *School Program Evaluation Questionnaire for Parents—Selected Items*

## PARENT QUESTIONNAIRE

**Use a pencil to completely fill in the circle next to your choice.**

*Indicate how much you agree or disagree with each statement by filling in one of the circles.*

| Strongly Disagree | Disagree | Neutral | Agree | Strongly Agree | |
|---|---|---|---|---|---|
| ○ | ○ | ○ | ○ | ○ | 23. The way they teach at this school works well with my child. |
| ○ | ○ | ○ | ○ | ○ | 24. My child is given a fair chance to succeed at school. |
| ○ | ○ | ○ | ○ | ○ | 25. There are good learning materials at my child's school. |
| ○ | ○ | ○ | ○ | ○ | 26. My child likes attending this school. |
| ○ | ○ | ○ | ○ | ○ | 27. I can talk with my child's teachers or principal whenever I need. |
| ○ | ○ | ○ | ○ | ○ | 28. My child's school is a good place to learn. |
| ○ | ○ | ○ | ○ | ○ | 29. My child uses computers effectively at school. |
| ○ | ○ | ○ | ○ | ○ | 30. I know how well my child is doing in class. |
| ○ | ○ | ○ | ○ | ○ | 31. I feel my child is safe at school. |
| ○ | ○ | ○ | ○ | ○ | 32. I am welcome to discuss my child's education needs with the school. |
| ○ | ○ | ○ | ○ | ○ | 33. My child's school building is in good condition. |
| ○ | ○ | ○ | ○ | ○ | 34. The community provides enough money to the schools to do a good job. |
| ○ | ○ | ○ | ○ | ○ | 35. Discipline in my child's school is handled fairly. |
| ○ | ○ | ○ | ○ | ○ | 36. If I could, I would send my child to a different school. |
| ○ | ○ | ○ | ○ | ○ | 37. In our community people tend to trust each other. |
| ○ | ○ | ○ | ○ | ○ | 38. The school encourages parents to be involved. |
| ○ | ○ | ○ | ○ | ○ | 39. The school board listens to parents' concerns. |
| ○ | ○ | ○ | ○ | ○ | 40. It is important for students to have access to computers at school. |
| ○ | ○ | ○ | ○ | ○ | 41. My child has been taught in school about respect for other cultures. |

*Source: Data Analysis for Comprehensive Schoolwide Improvement* by Victoria Bernhardt, published by Eye On Education, 6 Depot Way West, Larchmont, NY, 10538, (914) 833-0551, www.eyeoneducation.com.

community setting, perhaps a quiet coffee shop or at the school.

Many professionals find it helpful to prepare a few questions in advance. Prepared questions can help family members in "getting started." As you think about the types of questions that would be helpful, consider the wording of the questions and the type of answer that might result.

For example, a question such as, "Could you tell me about some of the difficult times during the day for Alexandra?" encourages an extended response. Leading questions such as, "Tell me more about . . ." are helpful too. Asking "What time of day is most difficult for Alexandra?" will likely lead to a word or phrase response, whereas "Is getting ready for school in the morning a difficult time for Alexandra?" will probably result in a minimal response (yes or no). These latter types of questions serve to stop or limit discussion.

***Meeting the Family.*** Four important aspects help ensure that the interview will go well. The first is to acknowledge each family member who is present and to thank each person for taking the time to be there. Next, establish rapport with family members by showing a genuine interest in what they have to say. Repeat the purpose of the visit. "I know that you have some concerns about Alexandra and I hope that from our visit I can better understand them." Finally, help family members clarify important points by asking questions and rephrasing statements.

***Completing the Interview.*** Remember that family members have many obligations and that they have probably made special arrangements to be present. Generally, interviews should not exceed an hour in length. Conclude the interview by summarizing the discussion and by thanking each of the family members present.

## Family Stories

Sharing a "family story" can be the easiest and the least intimidating assessment technique for family members. Family stories represent events and people that are important to the family. Family stories often include valuable information regarding how others in the household relate to the child with special needs. By listening to family stories, you learn about the family's cultural values and practices, attitudes, habits, and behaviors. Family stories give us a good idea of how families see themselves and how they want others to see them.

In preparing to conduct a family story, the following guidelines have been developed based on work by Robert Atkinson (1992).

1. Choose an appropriate setting: The setting should be quiet and comfortable.
2. Explain the purpose of the family story: Family members should understand that the information to be shared is valuable and will help you in understanding the child and in developing the education program.
3. Use open-ended interview techniques. Questions that encourage extended responses will assist the storyteller. Encourage family members to remember stories and events. Try to focus your questions around certain areas:
   a. The child
      1. How would you describe your child's growth and development?
      2. What do you think your child inherited from you?
      3. Who are the important family members or people in the community?
   b. Family traditions
      1. What beliefs or ideals do you want to pass on to your child?
      2. What holidays or celebrations are important to your family?
   c. Social factors
      1. How does your family like to spend free time together?
      2. What does your child like to do during these times?
   d. Education
      1. What do you hope your child will learn in school?

2. How would you like me to contact you . . . by telephone . . . by mail . . . by e-mail . . . or . . . ?

Photographs, drawings, and other materials are helpful in assisting the storyteller.

4. Be a good listener: Build trust and show that you care about what is being shared. At times you will want to ask follow-up questions, probe for details, and be responsive.

5. Look for connections: Family stories frequently provide useful information about the child's early years and present skills and competencies. Family stories are especially helpful in learning about family diversity in your classroom. Storytellers may become classroom resources to assist you in planning special events or celebrations.

The Snapshot of La Donna Harris illustrates the importance of "family" to the Comanche people as told by this family story. After reading this snapshot, consider the following questions: What are some important themes in this family story? How might these themes affect the assessment process?

## Planning Parent Conferences

Parent-teacher conferences can be effective ways to share information with parents and to learn more about the student from the parent's perspective. In addition to sharing and receiving information, parents and professionals can develop a rapport and a better ability to cooperate in preventing and solving problems (Turnbull and Turnbull, 1997). However, the key to successful conferences is planning. During parent-teacher conferences, the teacher typically has a limited amount of time scheduled for meetings. Parents, too, often have made several special arrangements to come to the school at the scheduled conference time.

---

**SNAPSHOT** ■ *La Donna Harris, a Comanche Woman*

---

(This snapshot includes excerpts from her speech, given a few years ago at the first Comanche training session [Harris, n.d.].)

I am the daughter of Lily Tabbytite, the granddaughter of Wakeah, and the great-granddaughter of Kotsepeah, who was the daughter of Maria, a Spanish captive. My grandfather was Tabbytite, son of Hohwah and Tsa-ee.

I do this so that you will know how we are related; if not by blood, then by extended family, the "Indian Way." It not only shows our relationship, but it shows me how I should behave toward you. Tribal governments and tribal societies were built on relationships and kinships; how you were related showed you the etiquette of how you should behave to one another. In a tribal society, one would never openly criticize a relative. There were other ways of doing it. There were only certain people that could do the criticism or the correcting—not necessarily criticism—but they could show you the way to be-

have properly. When we try to make tribal societies work like Western societies, sometimes it doesn't fit and creates a lot of stress in our community.

The first time that I went to tribal council, I remember Edgar Monetachi. Because he was such an eloquent speaker, people would ask him to speak for them, even if they disagreed with his position. He had a responsibility to those relatives and talked for them because he had the power and medicine to be able to be a good speaker.

It was always amazing to me when kaku and papa would go downtown to Walters and we would run into an old Comanche lady. The old lady would call me sister or daughter and they would chat for a while. Afterward, I'd say, "I didn't know that we were related to her" and kaku would trace it back to some wonderful thing that happened between families that made us kin—not between her and that other old lady, but between families. Those relationships made me feel strong and gave me a feeling of belonging to everybody. . . .

*During the parent conference, a teacher shares samples of the student's work with the parents.*

***Planning the Conference.***   Planning the conference consists of notifying the parent(s) and preparing the conference agenda. Notify the parents of the date and purpose of the conference. Many schools routinely schedule conference days at the beginning of the year and send written notices. If the meeting is to be an IEP conference, a written notice must be sent prior to the meeting.

Families generally appreciate a follow-up telephone call. However, be sure to ask the parent whether you have called at a convenient time. If not, ask when a better time would be for you to call back. The telephone conversation allows the parent to ask questions about the conference and to decide on which family members should attend. Families may want to decide whether or not the student with a disability should be present at the conference.

Planning the conference also includes identifying the agenda items. Notify other professionals who are working with the student and who may not be aware of the scheduled conference. For example, the speech therapist, occu-

pational therapist, or physical therapist may want to be present.

Review the student's folder and gather samples of the student's work. Plan a tentative agenda of areas or items to be covered. Consider where you will be meeting. Several chairs placed at a small round table look inviting and less threatening than chairs placed around your desk.

***Conference Time.***   To establish rapport, talk informally with parents and other family members before beginning the conference. Express your gratitude to family members for making arrangements to attend the conference. Have an interpreter or translator present for family members, if needed.

Begin with the student's accomplishments. Provide examples of student work or share classroom anecdotes. Discuss areas of growth and areas of concern. Encourage parents to ask questions or to make comments. Ask for clarification when you are unsure of the information that family members have shared. Use good communication skills, including jargon-free language. Remember, body posture and head nods, as well as the words you speak, are important ways of showing your interest in what family members have to say.

At the close of the conference, summarize the important points. End the meeting on a positive note and thank family members again for coming.

***Completing Postconference Activities.*** After the conference is over, there are two activities that need attention. First, teachers should record a brief summary of the conference as soon as possible after the meeting. These notes should include the date, the participants, highlights of the meeting, and any decisions made. These notes are particularly important if there is a due process hearing at some future time. If the conference were an IEP or IFSP meeting, teachers must mail a copy of the minutes of the meeting to the parents.

Next, whether or not the student attended the conference, set aside time to talk about the meeting with the student. Briefly summarize the meeting and any decisions that were made. Answer any questions the student may have about the conference.

## Preferred Practices

Parents have an important role in the assessment process. If their child will receive services under an IFSP, the focus of the assessment will be on the child and family. If their child will receive services under an IEP, then the focus of the assessment will be directed to their child. Family priorities will probably change over time. Always check to see if family members feel that the information they have provided in the past is current.

Involve families to the extent that they wish to be involved in the assessment process and accept the wishes of family members as to their levels of participation. Individual family members can differ in their preferences: one member will be more comfortable in just talking; another family member will prefer to provide information by completing a questionnaire or a rating scale.

Be open to issues in working with families different from your own. Family diversity can include issues of culture, disability, economic status, gender, geographic region or origin, and race. Avoid stereotypical assumptions. Work to become familiar with families in your community. When in doubt, ask families to determine preferences and needs.

## Extending Learning

1. Think about your own family based on the concepts identified by a family systems model. How does this help you in understanding the complexity of the family unit?
2. Obtain two or more of the commercial instruments described in this chapter to preview and compare. Which one would you choose to use? Why?
3. Interview a family with a child. In thinking about your conversation, did the family identify family needs and priorities for their child? Did they mention resources important to the functioning of their family? Which interview questions were most helpful? What questions might you include in another interview?
4. Using one of the Snapshots in this chapter, develop a simulation of a parent-teacher conference. Students can take on the roles of parent, teacher, and administrator. Assign one student the role of observer. The observer should be prepared to report observations made during the simulation.
5. Begin a list of resources to help you become responsive to diversity. What books would you include? What journals regularly publish helpful articles? What websites would you recommend? What families in your area would be willing to be a resource?
6. Attend a meeting of a parent organization. What were some of the issues discussed? In what ways was the meeting informative?

# *References*

Achenbach, T. M. (2001). *Child behavior checklist for ages 6–18*. Burlington, VT: ASEBA™.

Achenbach, T. M., and L. A. Rescorla (2000). *Child behavior checklist for ages 1½–5*. Burlington, VT: ASEBA™.

Alper, S. K., P. J. Schloss, and C. N. Schloss (1994). *Families of students with disabilities*. Boston: Allyn & Bacon.

Atkinson, R. (1992). *The life story book from autobiography to personal myth*. Gorham, ME: University of Southern Maine, Center for the Study of Lives.

Bayley, N. (1993). *Bayley scales of infant development*. 2d ed. San Antonio, TX: The Psychological Corporation.

Bernhardt, V. (1998). *Data analysis for comprehensive school-wide improvement*. Larchmont, NY: Eye on Education.

Boehm, A. E. (2001). *Boehm test of basic concepts, third edition—preschool (Boehm-3 preschool)*. San Antonio, TX: The Psychological Corporation.

Bricker, D., and J. Squires (1999). *Ages & Stages Questionnaires: A parent-completed child monitoring system*. (2d ed.) (p. 5). Baltimore, MD: Paul H. Brookes Publishing Co.

Brigance, A. H. (1998). *BRIGANCE® preschool screen for three- and four-year-old children*. No. Billerica, MA: Curriculum Associates.

Brown, L., and D. D. Hammill (1990). *Behavior rating profile (BRP-2)*. Austin, TX: PRO-ED.

Cohen, L. G., and L. J. Spenciner (1994). *Assessment of young children*. White Plains, NY: Longman.

Conners, C. K. (1990). *Conners' rating scales manual*. North Tonawanda, NY: Multi-Health Systems.

Cripe, J., and D. Bricker (1993). *AEPS™ Family interest survey*. Baltimore, MD: Paul H. Brookes.

Dunst, C., C. Trivette, and A. Deal (1988). *Enabling and empowering families*. Cambridge, MA: Brookline.

*Federal Register* (Vol. 64, No. 48, pp. 12423–12424). Washington, DC: U.S. Government Printing Office, March 12, 1999.

Haney, M., and V. Knox (1995). *Project unidos para el bienestar de los ninos y de su famila* (Project UBNF). Paper presented at the Zero to Three Conference, December, Atlanta, Georgia.

Hanson, M. J., E. W. Lynch, and K. I. Wayman (1990). Honoring the cultural diversity of families when gathering data. In *Topics in Early Childhood Special Education* 10(1): 112–131.

Harris, L. (n.d.). Summarized version of the speech given by La Donna Harris at the first Comanche training session. Unpublished manuscript.

Harrison, P. L., A. S. Kaufman, N. L. Kaufman, R. H. Bruininks, J. Rynders, S. Ilmer, S. S. Sparrow, and D. V. Cicchetti (1990). *AGS Early screening profiles*. Circle Pines, MN: American Guidance Service.

Ireton, H. R. (1992). *Child development inventory*. Minneapolis, MN: Behavior Science Systems.

Mardell-Czudnowski, C., and D. S. Goldenberg (1998). *Developmental Indicators for the Assessment of Learning (DIAL-3)*. 3d ed. Circle Pines, MN: American Guidance Service.

Meisels, S. J., D. B. Marsden, M. S. Wiske, and L. W. Henderson (1997). *Early Screening Inventory–Revised (ESI–R)*. Ann Arbor, MI: Rebus.

Miller, L. J. (1993). *FirstSTEP™: Screening test for evaluating preschoolers*. San Antonio, TX: The Psychological Corporation, Harcourt Brace.

Quay, H. C., and D. R. Peterson (1987). *Revised behavior problem checklist*. Odessa, FL: Psychological Assessment Resources.

Shapiro, J. (1994). Educational/support group for Latino families of children with Down syndrome. *Mental Retardation*, 32(6): 403–415.

Turnbull, A. P., and H. R. Turnbull, III (1997). *Families, professionals, and exceptionality: A special partnership*. 3d ed. Columbus, OH: Merrill.

Waltman, G. H. (1996). Amish health care beliefs and practices. In *Multicultural awareness in the health care professions*, ed. M. C. Julia, Boston: Allyn & Bacon.

# 3

# Norms and Test Scores

## Overview

This chapter initiates a discussion of scoring, interpreting, and reporting test performance and describes standardized assessment tests, scores, scoring procedures, and norms. Because it is up to the test user to evaluate the usefulness of a test, we will also discuss how you can determine whether a test is worthwhile. In the following chapters we will return to this discussion as we present assessment approaches.

## Chapter Objectives

After completing this chapter you should be able to:

- Describe norm-referenced assessment.
- Compare different ways of presenting and interpreting test scores.

- Discuss the advantages and disadvantages of using different types of test scores when interpreting test performance.

- Compare the application of the concepts of standard error of measurement and confidence intervals.

- Describe how to evaluate the usefulness of tests.
- Use test scoring procedures.

## Standardized Tests

Tests in which a test manual prescribes administration, scoring, and interpretation procedures that the test examiner must strictly follow are known as **standardized tests.** Standardized tests are usually norm-referenced. The characteristics of norm-referenced tests are discussed later in this chapter. Examiners must follow exact administration procedures when using standardized tests. Failure to follow these procedures compromises the reliability, validity, and interpretation of the test results. Standardized norm-referenced tests can be both individual and group administered. Examples of standardized norm-referenced tests include the *Iowa Tests of Educational Development, Terra Nova*®, and the *Stanford Achievement Test Series.*

## Standardization Sample

When a norm-referenced test is administered to a student, the teacher can compare the performance of that student with the scores obtained by the sample of students who participated in the normative sample during the development of the test. A **standardization sample** is a subgroup of a large group that is representative of the large group. When test publishers develop a test, it is this subgroup that is actually tested. The **population** is the larger group from which the sample of individuals is selected and to which individual comparisons are made regarding test performance. *Normative sample* or *norm sample* are other terms for the standardization sample.

The standardization sample must represent the population of students who will be taking the test. The standardization sample should include, in appropriate proportion, students from various geographic regions of the country, males and females, students who represent various racial,

ethnic, cultural, and linguistic populations, and students from various economic strata. Information may even include the occupational categories and educational levels of the parents of the students. The best way for a test publisher to determine the appropriate proportions of representative groups (e.g., males, females, race, ethnicity, native language, etc.) that should be included in the standardization sample is to refer to the most recent census data and base the selection of the standardization sample on those percentages. For example, a test that is to be used with students from Cambodia or from Central America should include appropriate samples of these student groups in the standardization group. If they intend to administer the test to students who are nonnative speakers of English and who come from various backgrounds, the test publisher must provide appropriate information concerning the administration and interpretation of test performance (American Educational Research Association, American Psychological Association, and National Council on Measurement in Education, 1999). Figure 3.1 shows how one test publisher illustrated the communities in the United States that participated in a national standardization of the test.

## Norm-Referenced Tests

A **norm-referenced test** is a test that compares a student's test performance with that of a sample of similar students who have taken the same test. After constructing a test, the test developers administer it to a standardization sample of students using the same administration and scoring procedures for all students. This makes the administration and scoring "standardized." The test scores of the standardization sample are called **norms,** which include a variety of types of scores. Norms are the

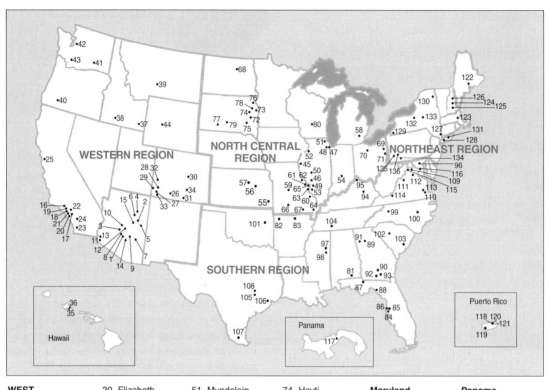

**WEST**

**Arizona**
1. Casa Grande
2. Dilkon
3. Glendale
4. Greasewood
5. Holbrook
6. Indian Wells
7. Mammoth
8. Maricopa
9. Mesa
10. Phoenix
11. San Luis
12. Scottsdale
13. Somerton
14. Stanfield
15. Teesto

**California**
16. Granada Hills
17. LaMirada
18. Los Angeles
19. North Hills
20. Norwalk
21. Paramount
22. Rosemead
23. San Diego
24. San Jacinto
25. Stockton

**Colorado**
26. Alamosa
27. Cortez
28. Dolores
29. Dove Creek

30. Elizabeth
31. La Veta
32. Norwood
33. Towaoc
34. Walsenburg

**Hawaii**
35. Honolulu
36. Kaneohe

**Idaho**
37. McCammon
38. Twin Falls

**Montana**
39. Laurel

**Oregon**
40. Klamath Falls

**Washington**
41. Mattawa
42. Seattle
43. Vancouver

**Wyoming**
44. Ft. Washakie

**NORTH CENTRAL**

**Illinois**
45. Biggsville
46. Brighton
47. Chicago
48. Cicero
49. Freeburg
50. Jacksonville

51. Mundelein
52. Orion
53. Waterloo

**Indiana**
54. Bedford

**Kansas**
55. Pittsburg
56. Topeka
57. Wamego

**Michigan**
58. Birmingham

**Missouri**
59. Boonville
60. Cadet
61. Florissant
62. Hannibal
63. Maplewood
64. Puxico
65. St. Louis
66. Springfield
67. Van Buren

**North Dakota**
68. Fort Totten

**Ohio**
69. Boardman
70. Fremont
71. Poland

**South Dakota**
72. Brookings
73. Clear Lake

74. Hayti
75. Madison
76. Milbank
77. Norris
78. Watertown
79. White River

**Wisconsin**
80. Portage

**SOUTH**

**Alabama**
81. Slocomb

**Arkansas**
82. Bentonville
83. Mountain Home

**Florida**
84. Bradenton
85. Clearwater
86. Dunedin
87. Greensboro
88. Perry

**Georgia**
89. Atlanta
90. Hahira
91. Lithia Springs
92. Quitman
93. Valdosta

**Kentucky**
94. Owingsville
95. Wilder

**Maryland**
96. Randallstown

**Mississippi**
97. Brooksville
98. Macon

**North Carolina**
99. Hickory
100. Snow Hill

**Oklahoma**
101. Sapulpa

**South Carolina**
102. Columbia
103. St. George

**Tennessee**
104. Savannah

**Texas**
105. Austin
106. Houston
107. Pharr
108. Round Rock

**Virginia**
109. Berryville
110. Hampton
111. Madison
112. New Baltimore
113. Newport News
114. Rocky Gap
115. Winchester

**District of Columbia**
116. Washington

**Panama**
117. Panama City

**Puerto Rico**
118. Condado
119. Mayagüez
120. Rio Piedras
121. San Juan

**NORTHEAST**

**Maine**
122. Bucksport

**Massachusetts**
123. Jamaica Plain

**New Hampshire**
124. Center Barnstead
125. Concord
126. North Conway

**New York**
127. Bronx
128. East Meadow
129. Jamestown
130. Plattsburgh
131. Smithtown
132. Syracuse
133. Utica

**Pennsylvania**
134. Bradenville
135. Latrobe
136. New Derry

**FIGURE 3.1** *Map of a Standardization Sample*

*Source: Developmental Indicators for the Assessment of Learning-Third Edition (DIAL-3)* Figure 6.1 from p 65 of the Manual by Carol Mardell-Czudnowski and Dorothea S. Goldenerg © 1998 American Guidance Service, Inc., 4201 Woodland Road, Circle Pines, Minnesota 55014-1796. Reproduced with permission of publisher. All rights reserved. www.agsnet.com

scores obtained by the standardization sample. Norms are the scores to which students are compared when they are administered a test.

Once test developers standardize a norm-referenced test, examiners can administer it to students with similar characteristics to the norm group, and can compare the scores of these students with those of the norm group. Norm-referenced standardized tests can use local, state, or national norms as a base. Because of the comparison of scores between a norm group and other groups of students, a norm-referenced test provides information on the relative standing of students.

When assessing students with disabilities, evaluators should employ caution before making comparisons or interpretations stemming from established norms. It is possible to use typical norms when making interpretations that draw from the relative performance of the students with disabilities and from the general population of students. However, when making comparisons or interpretations that use level or degree of disability, normative data should come from the sample population to which comparisons are made. Test manuals should provide sufficient details about the normative group so that test users can make informed judgments about the appropriateness of the norm sample (American Educational Research Association, American Psychological Association, and National Council on Measurement in Education, 1999).

### Criterion-Referenced Tests

Instead of comparing a student's performance to a norm group, **criterion-referenced tests** measure a student's performance with respect to a well-defined domain such as reading or mathematics. While norm-referenced tests discriminate between the performance of individual students on specific test items, criterion-referenced tests provide a description of a student's knowledge, skills, or behavior in a specific range of test items. This specific range is referred to as a **domain.** Test items on criterion-referenced tests frequently correspond to well-defined instructional objectives. Criterion-referenced tests, instead of using norms, provide information on the performance of a student with respect to specific test items. The results of criterion-referenced tests are not dependent on the performance of other students, as are norm-referenced tests. An example of a criterion-referenced test is the *BRIGANCE® Diagnostic Inventory of Essential Skills–Revised.*

### Distinguishing Norm-Referenced Tests from Criterion-Referenced Tests

There are several characteristics that distinguish norm-referenced tests from criterion-referenced tests. Performance on a criterion-referenced test provides information on whether the student has attained a predetermined achievement, behavioral, or social criterion. While it is possible for a test to be both norm-referenced and criterion-referenced, professionals must use caution when interpreting the results of these tests, because it is difficult to combine both types of tests in one instrument.

Another distinction is the breadth of the content domain the test covers (Mehrens and Lehmann, 1991). Typical norm-referenced tests survey a broad domain, while criterion-referenced tests usually have fewer domains but more items in each domain. Criterion-referenced tests typically sample the domain more thoroughly than norm-referenced tests (Mehrens and Lehmann, 1991).

Criterion-referenced tests are very helpful in making instructional planning decisions. Since criterion-referenced tests frequently cover a more restricted range of content than norm-referenced tests, they can provide more information about a student's level of performance.

### Scales of Measurement

Evaluators can estimate student performance using test scores based on different types of measurement scales. The description of a student's performance depends on the test's measurement scale. There are four different measurement scales: nominal, ordinal, interval, and ratio.

## Nominal Scale

A **nominal scale** represents the lowest level of measurement. It is a naming scale. Each value on the scale is a name, and the name does not have any innate or inherent value. Hair color, students' names, and numbers on football jerseys are all examples of nominal scales. Although there are numerals on football uniforms, there is no inherent rank or value to the numerals. A numeral is just associated with the name of the football player. A teacher may use a nominal scale to distinguish between groups 1, 2, and 3. The numbers 1, 2, and 3 have no intrinsic value; they are simply labels for the groups. Because nominal scales merely represent names, they have limited usefulness. They cannot be added, subtracted, multiplied, or divided. They are rarely used in reporting test performance.

## Ordinal Scale

An **ordinal scale** is the next level of measurement. An ordinal scale orders items in a scale or

**TABLE 3.1**    *Ordinal Scale*

| Student | Rank |
|---------|------|
| Jean | 10 |
| Mia | 9 |
| Mura | 8 |
| Melissa | 7 |
| Chris | 6 |
| Ruth | 5 |
| Lisa | 4 |
| Mei | 3 |
| Dan | 2 |
| David | 1 |

continuum. Ordering students according to class rank is an example of an ordinal scale (Table 3.1). The Snapshot "Activity Levels" also provides an example of an ordinal scale.

## Interval Scale

An **interval scale** is similar to an ordinal scale but it has several important advantages. Interval scales order items on a scale or continuum, as do ordinal scales, but unlike ordinal scales, the distance between the items is equal. Because of this characteristic, interval scales can be added, subtracted, multiplied, and divided.

**SNAPSHOT ■ *Activity Levels***

Suppose a teacher is observing a student with a high activity level. The teacher wants to rank the activity level of the student from 1 to 10, with 10 being the most active and 1 the least active, like this:

| Activity level | 1 | 2 | 3 | 4 | 5 | 6 | 7 | 8 | 9 | 10 |
|----------------|---|---|---|---|---|---|---|---|---|----|
| Classroom | | | | | | | | | | |
| Playground | | | | | | | | | | |

The distance between each of the ranks 1, 2, 3, and so forth is not equal. That is, the same increase in activity may not be required, in the teacher's judgment, to raise a ranking from 3 to 4 as from 7 to 8. Because of this limitation, ordinal scales cannot be added, subtracted, multiplied, or divided.

Interval scales have another interesting characteristic. Interval scales may include a zero point but do not have a true or rational zero. For example, a Fahrenheit scale is an equal interval scale; there is an equal distance between the degrees of temperature. The zero point, however, was arbitrarily established by Daniel Fahrenheit when he developed the temperature scale. Intelligence quotient tests also base their scores on equal interval scales. Although there is an equal distance between the scores, an IQ of zero cannot be measured. Another example of a test that uses an interval scale is the *Scholastic Aptitude Test* (SAT). SAT scores range from 200 to 800 points. There is no zero!

### Ratio Scale

A **ratio scale** has all the characteristics of ordinal and interval scales and, in addition, it has an absolute zero. Height and weight measurements are examples of ratio scales. Teacher-developed tests, such as classroom spelling or arithmetic tests, frequently use the ratio scale as a base. The total number of test items that a student answers correctly, or the raw score, is based on a ratio scale. Some observation and rating scales are also ratio scales. Because the ratio scale has an absolute zero, the scores adapt to mathematical operations. If we are recording the number of times students raise their hands, we may conclude that one student exhibits this behavior two or three times more than another student.

### Frequency Distribution and Normal Curve

#### Frequency Distribution

A **frequency distribution** is a way of organizing test scores according to how often they occur. To create a frequency distribution, arrange the test scores in a column from high to low. Next to each test score, record the number of students who obtained that score, then add the frequencies to find the total number of students

**TABLE 3.2** *Frequency Distribution*

| Score | Frequency |
| --- | --- |
| 100 | 3 |
| 90 | 2 |
| 80 | 5 |
| 70 | 4 |
| 60 | 6 |
| 50 | 5 |
| 40 | 2 |
| 30 | 1 |

Total number of students: 28

who took the test (Table 3.2). Next, construct a graph (Figure 3.2).

#### Normal Curve

Frequency distributions can have different shapes. The shape represents groupings of students' scores. In a **normal curve** most scores fall in the middle, and fewer scores occur at the ends of the distribution. The normal curve is a symmetrical, bell-shaped curve (Figure 3.3).

#### Normal Distribution

There has been considerable debate about whether human characteristics distribute in a normal curve. While there is some evidence that physical characteristics such as height and

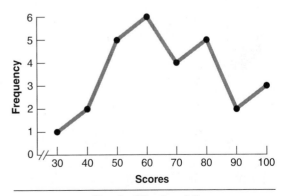

**FIGURE 3.2** *Graph of Students' Scores*

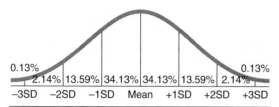

**FIGURE 3.3**   *Normal Distribution*

weight distribute normally, there has been active discussion about whether other characteristics, such as intelligence, development, and achievement, are normally distributed. While it is less likely that the performance of small groups of children will distribute normally on a specific characteristic, the test results from large norm samples will probably be more normal in appearance (Mehrens and Lehmann, 1991).

### Skewed Distributions

Sometimes, the majority of scores occur at one end of the curve. These scores show **skewed distribution.** Positively skewed distributions contain only a few high scores, with the majority of scores occurring at the low end. Negatively

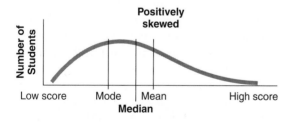

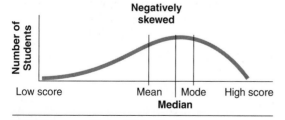

**FIGURE 3.4**   *Skewed Distributions*

skewed distributions have few scores at the low end and a majority of scores at the high end. When distributions are either positively or negatively skewed, the measures of central tendency—that is, the mean, median, and mode—shift. Figure 3.4 shows the placement of the mean, median, and mode in skewed distributions.

## Measures of Central Tendency

Measures of central tendency describe the typical test performance of a group of students using a single number. The number that results from the calculation of a measure of central tendency represents the typical score obtained by the group of students. The mean, mode, and median are measures of central tendency. In the Snapshot, teachers Brendan Strout and Ken Brown decide when to use measures of central tendency.

### Mean

The **mean,** or the average score, is the most frequently used measure of central tendency. To compute the mean, add all of the scores and divide by the total number of scores (Table 3.3). Because all the scores in a distribution are taken into account when the mean is calculated, extreme scores affect the mean.

### Median

Another measure of central tendency is the **median.** It is the point on a scale above which and below which 50 percent of the cases occur. The median is an excellent measure of central tendency when most of the scores cluster together but a few scores lie at the extreme ends of a distribution. The median score in Table 3.3 is 70.

### Mode

The mode is the score that occurs most frequently in a list of scores. In a distribution of

## SNAPSHOT ■ *Deciding When to Use Measures of Central Tendency*

Brendan Strout, the special education consultant at Washington School, was preparing to meet with Ken Brown, the sixth-grade classroom teacher. Brendan was examining the test scores of a group of students from Ken's classroom. Brendan wanted to be able to describe the performance of the students in order to assist Ken in making instructional decisions. Here are the scores of Ken's students:

90
82
81
80
79
75
75
75
20

Brendan summarized the scores in three ways.

1. He calculated the mean, or average, by adding up all of the scores and dividing by 9, the total number of scores.

90
82
81
80
79   Median
75 ⎫
75 ⎬ Mode
75 ⎭
20

$657 \div 9 = 73$. This is the mean, or average score.

2. Next, Brendan arranged the scores from high to low and found the score that separates the top 50 percent of students who took the test from the bottom 50 percent of students. This score is 79 and is the median.

3. Finally, Brendan found the score that occurred the most often in the group of scores. This score is 75 and is the mode.

Which measure of central tendency—the mean, median, or mode—should Brendan use in his discussion with Ken? (The answer can be found at the end of the "Extending Learning" section at the conclusion of this chapter.)

---

**TABLE 3.3**   *Finding the Average (Mean)*

| Score | Frequency | Frequency × Score |
|-------|-----------|-------------------|
| 100 | 1 | 100 |
| 98 | 2 | 196 |
| 90 | 2 | 180 |
| 85 | 4 | 340 |
| 70 | 6 | 420 |
| 50 | 5 | 250 |
| 42 | 3 | 126 |
| 30 | 2 | 60 |
| 25 | 1 | 25 |
| Number of scores: 26 | | Sum of scores: 1697 |

$$\frac{\text{Sum of scores}}{\text{Number of scores}} = \text{Mean} \qquad \frac{1697}{26} = 65.26$$

$$\text{Mean} = 65.26$$

scores, the mode is the most commonly occurring score. However, a distribution of test scores can have more than one mode. If a teacher wanted to know which test or test item students most frequently answered correctly, the teacher would look at the mode. However, educators use the mode infrequently because it is not very helpful when describing the performance of an individual child or of a group of students. In a normal distribution, the mean, median, and mode all occur at the same point (Figure 3.3).

### Standard Deviation

The **standard deviation (SD)** tells the degree to which various scores deviate from the mean.

It is a unit of measurement, just as an inch and a foot are units of measurement. Scores can be expressed by the number of standard deviation units that they deviate from the mean.

The standard deviation is useful when comparing several sets of scores. It can be helpful when interpreting the test performance of one student or a group of students. When comparing scores, the larger the standard deviation, the more variable is the performance; the smaller the standard deviation, the less variable is the performance of the students.

In a normal distribution, the percentage of scores that can be expected to fall within the first, second, and third standard deviations above or below the mean are shown in Figure 3.3. For example, when a group of scores distributes normally, 34.13 percent of the scores can be expected to occur between the mean and the +1 SD, and 34.13 percent of the scores also occur between the mean and –1 SD. Approximately 13.59 percent of the scores fall between the +1 SD and +2 SD, and 13.59 percent of the scores fall between the –1 SD and –2 SD. Just over 2 percent (2.14) of the scores occur between the second and third standard deviations and 0.13 percent of the scores occur beyond the third standard deviation.

For most tests, publishers provide information about the mean and the standard deviation in test manuals. You will not have to calculate the standard deviation. For example, the manual for the third edition of the *Wechsler Intelligence Scale for Children–III (WISC–III)* reports that this test has a mean of 100 and a standard deviation of 15. This represents that approximately 34.13 percent of students have intelligence quotients (IQs) between 100 and 115. Similarly, approximately 68.26 percent of students have IQs between 85 and 115. Many states mandate specific guidelines for identification and placement of students. For example, some states may require that school-age students who are labeled with mental retardation have IQs that are at least two standard deviations below the mean. In this example, you will have to subtract 30 (2 times the standard deviation of 15) from 100 to obtain an IQ of 70.

## Types of Scores

There are many ways of reporting test performance. A variety of scores can be used when interpreting students' test performance.

### Raw Scores

The **raw score** is the number of items a student answers correctly without adjustment for guessing. For example, if there are 15 problems on an arithmetic test, and a student answers 11 correctly, then the raw score is 11. Raw scores, however, do not provide us with enough information to describe student performance.

### Percentage Scores

A **percentage score** is the percent of test items answered correctly. These scores can be useful when describing a student's performance on a teacher-made test or on a criterion-referenced test. However, percentage scores have a major disadvantage: we have no way of comparing the percentage correct on one test with the percentage correct on another test. Suppose a child earned a score of 85 percent correct on one test and 55 percent correct on another test. The interpretation of the score is related to the difficulty level of the test items on each test. Because each test has a different or unique level of difficulty, we have no common way to interpret these scores; there is no frame of reference.

To interpret raw scores and percentage-correct scores, it is necessary to change the raw or percentage score to a different type of score in order to make comparisons. Evaluators rarely use raw scores and percentage-correct scores when interpreting performance because it is difficult to compare one student's scores on several tests or the performance of several students on several tests.

### Derived Scores

**Derived scores** are a family of scores that allow us to make comparisons between test scores. Raw scores are transformed to derived scores. Developmental scores and scores of relative standing are two types of derived scores. Scores of relative standing include percentiles, standard scores, and stanines.

***Developmental Scores.*** Sometimes called age and grade equivalents, **developmental scores** are scores that have been transformed from raw scores and reflect the average performance at age and grade levels. Thus, the student's raw score (number of items correct) is the same as the average raw score for students of a specific age or grade. Age equivalents are written with a hyphen between years and months (e.g., 12-4 means that the age equivalent is 12 years, 4 months old). A decimal point is used between the grade and month in grade equivalents (e.g., 1.2 is the first grade, second month).

Developmental scores can be useful (McLean, Bailey, and Wolery, 1996; Sattler, 2001). Parents and professionals easily interpret them and place the performance of students within a context. Because of the ease of misinterpretation of these scores, parents and professionals should approach them with extreme caution. There are a number of reasons for criticizing these scores.

For a student who is 6 years old and in the first grade, grade and age equivalents presume that for each month of first grade an equal amount of learning occurs. But, from our knowledge of child growth and development and theories about learning, we know that neither growth nor learning occurs in equal monthly intervals. Age and grade equivalents do not take into consideration the variation in individual growth and learning.

Teachers should not expect that students will gain a grade equivalent or age equivalent of one year for each year that they are in school. For example, suppose a child earned a grade equivalent of 1.5, first grade, fifth month, at the end of first grade. To assume that at the end of second grade the child should obtain a grade equivalent of 2.5, second grade, fifth month, is not good practice. This assumption is incorrect for two reasons: (1) the grade and age equivalent norms should not be confused with performance standards; and (2) a gain of 1.0 grade

equivalent is representative only of students who are in the average range for their grade. Students who are above average will gain more than 1.0 grade equivalent a year, and students who are below average will progress less than 1.0 grade equivalent a year (Gronlund and Linn, 1990).

A second criticism of developmental scores is the underlying idea that because two students obtain the same score on a test they are comparable and will display the same thinking, behavior, and skill patterns. For example, a student who is in second grade earned a grade equivalent score of 4.6 on a test of reading achievement. This does not mean that the second grader understands the reading process as it is taught in the fourth grade. Rather, this student just performed at a superior level for a student who is in second grade. It is incorrect to compare the second grader to a child who is in fourth grade; the comparison should be made to other students who are in second grade (Sattler, 2001).

A third criticism of developmental scores is that age and grade equivalents encourage the use of false standards. A second-grade teacher should not expect all students in the class to perform at the second-grade level on a reading test. Differences between students within a grade mean that the range of achievement actually spans several grades. In addition, developmental scores are calculated so that half of the scores fall below the median, and half fall above the median. Age and grade equivalents are not standards of performance.

A fourth criticism of age and grade equivalents is that they promote typological thinking. The use of age and grade equivalents causes us to think in terms of a typical kindergartner or a typical 10-year-old. In reality, students vary in their abilities and levels of performance. Developmental scores do not take these variations into account.

A fifth criticism is that most developmental scores are interpolated and extrapolated. A normed test includes students of *specific* ages and grades—not *all* ages and grades—in the norming sample. **Interpolation** is the process of estimating the scores of students within the ages and grades of the norming sample. **Extrapolation** is the process of estimating the performance of students outside the ages and grades of the normative sample.

### Developmental Quotient.   A **developmental quotient** is an estimate of the rate of development. If we know a student's developmental age and chronological age, it is possible to calculate a developmental quotient. For example, suppose a student's developmental age is 12 years (12 years × 12 months in a year = 144 months) and the chronological age is also 12 years, or 144 months. Then, using the following formula, we arrive at a developmental quotient of 100.

$$\frac{\text{Developmental age } 144 \text{ months}}{\text{Chronological age } 144 \text{ months}} \times 100 = 100$$

$$\frac{144}{144} \times 100 =$$

$$\frac{1}{1} \times 100 =$$

$$1 \times 100 = 100$$

But, suppose another student's chronological age is also 144 months and that the developmental age is 108 months. Using the formula, this student would have a developmental quotient of 75.

$$\frac{\text{Developmental age } 108 \text{ months}}{\text{Chronological age } 144 \text{ months}} \times 100 = 75$$

$$\frac{108}{144} \times 100 =$$

$$0.75 \times 100 = 75$$

Developmental quotients have all of the drawbacks associated with age and grade equivalents. In addition, they may be misleading because developmental age may not keep pace with chronological age as the individual gets older. Consequently, the gap between developmental age and chronological age is larger as the student gets older.

### Scores of Relative Standing.

*Percentile Ranks.*   A **percentile rank** is the point in a distribution at or below which the scores of a given percentage of students fall. Percentage correct refers to the percent of test items answered correctly. Percentiles provide information about the relative standing of students when compared with the standardization sample. Look at the following test scores and their corresponding percentile ranks.

| Student | Score | Percentile Rank |
|---------|-------|-----------------|
| Delia | 96 | 84 |
| Jana | 93 | 81 |
| Pete | 90 | 79 |
| Marcus | 86 | 75 |

Jana's score of 93 has a percentile rank of 81. This means that 81 percent of the students who took the test scored 93 or lower. Said another way, Jana scored as well as or better than 81 percent of the students who took the test.

A percentile rank of 50 represents average performance. In a normal distribution, both the mean and the median fall at the 50th percentile. Half the students fall above the 50th percentile and half fall below. Percentiles can be divided into quartiles. A *quartile* contains 25 percentiles or 25 percent of the scores in a distribution. The 25th and the 75th percentiles are the first and the third quartiles. In addition, percentiles can be divided into groups of 10 known as deciles. A *decile* contains 10 percentiles. Beginning at the bottom of a group of students, the first 10 percent are known as the first decile, the second 10 percent are known as the second decile, and so on.

The position of percentiles in a normal curve is shown in Figure 3.5. Despite their ease of interpretation, percentiles have several problems. First, the intervals they represent are unequal, especially at the lower and upper ends of the distribution. A difference of a few percentile points at the extreme ends of the distribution is more serious than a difference of a few points in the middle of the distribution. Second, percentiles do not apply to mathematical calculations

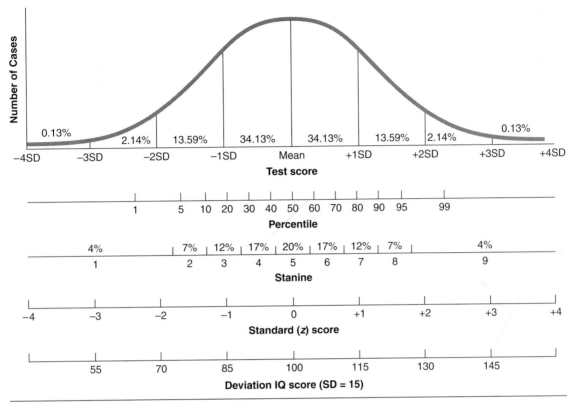

**FIGURE 3.5** *Normal Curve with Types of Scores*

(Gronlund and Linn, 1990). Lastly, percentile scores are reported in one hundredths. But, because of errors associated with measurement, they are only accurate to the nearest 0.06 (six one-hundredths) (Rudner, Conoley, and Plake, 1989). These limitations require the use of caution when interpreting percentile ranks. Confidence intervals, which are discussed later in this chapter, are useful when interpreting percentile scores.

*Standard Scores.* Another type of derived score is a **standard score.** Standard score is the name given to a group or category of scores. Each specific type of standard score within this group has the same mean and the same standard deviation. Because each type of standard score has the same mean and the same standard deviation, standard scores are an excellent way of representing a child's performance. Standard scores allow us to compare a child's performance on several tests and to compare one child's performance to the performance of other students. Unlike percentile scores, standard scores function in mathematical operations. For instance, standard scores can be averaged. In the Snapshot, teachers Lincoln Bates and Sari Andrews discuss test scores.

Figure 3.5 compares standard scores with the other types of scores we have discussed. As is apparent, standard scores are equal interval scores. The different types of standard scores, some of which we discuss in the following subsections, are:

1. *z-scores:* have a mean of 0 and a standard deviation of 1.
2. *T-scores:* have a mean of 50 and a standard deviation of 10.

## SNAPSHOT ■ *A Conversation between Lincoln Bates and Sari Andrews*

Just after school started in September, Lincoln Bates, a seventh-grade teacher of mathematics, reviewed last spring's test results for Karen Anderson, one of his students. He noticed that the results were reported using several types of scores:

**Student's Name:** Karen Anderson
**Age:** 13 years, 5 months
**Teacher:** J. Plante
**Grade:** 6

| Subtest | Grade Equivalent | Age Equivalent | Percentile Rank |
|---|---|---|---|
| Mathematics | 4.1 | 9-6 | 9 |
| Reading Comprehension | 10.2 | 13-0 | 75 |
| Spelling | 6.4 | 12-0 | 45 |

Lincoln was unsure how to interpret Karen's scores on the mathematics achievement subtest. He decided to ask Sari Andrews, the school's test examiner. Lincoln said, "I'm not sure how to interpret the age equivalent and grade equivalent scores. Even though I used to teach fourth grade, I don't think that Karen approaches mathematics in the same way that a typical fourth grader does."

Sari explained, "Just because Karen earned a grade equivalent of 4.1 in mathematics does not mean that her thinking, behavior, and skill patterns are the same as other students who are in the fourth grade. The same holds true for her age equivalent score of 9-6. Age and grade equivalent scores can be misleading. I prefer to use percentile rank or standard scores as a way of interpreting her performance." What do you think?

3. *Deviation IQ scores:* have a mean of 100 and a standard deviation of 15 or 16.
4. *Normal curve equivalents:* have a mean of 50 and a standard deviation of 21.06.
5. *Stanines:* standard score bands divide a distribution of scores into nine parts.
6. *Percentile ranks:* point in a distribution at or below which the scores of a given percentage of students fall.

*Deviation IQ Scores.* **Deviation IQ scores** are frequently used to report the performance of students on norm-referenced standardized tests. The deviation scores of the *Wechsler Intelligence Scale for Children–III,* and the *Wechsler Individual Achievement Test–II* have a mean of 100 and a standard deviation of 15, while the *Stanford-Binet Intelligence Scale–IV* has a mean of 100 and a standard deviation of 16. Many test manuals provide tables that allow conversion of raw scores to deviation IQ scores.

*Normal Curve Equivalents.* **Normal curve equivalents (NCEs)** are a type of standard score with a mean of 50 and a standard deviation of 21.06. When the baseline of the normal curve

is divided into 99 equal units, the percentile ranks of 1, 50, and 99 are the same as NCE units (Lyman, 1986). One test that does report NCEs is the *Battelle Developmental Inventory.* However, NCEs are not reported for some tests.

*Stanines.* **Stanines** are bands of standard scores that have a mean of 5 and a standard deviation of 2. As illustrated in Figure 3.5, stanines range from 1 to 9. Despite their relative ease of interpretation, stanines have several disadvantages. A change in just a few raw score points can move a student from one stanine to another. Also, because stanines are a general way of interpreting test performance, caution is necessary when making classification and placement decisions. As an aid in interpreting stanines, evaluators can assign descriptors to each of the 9 values:

9—very superior
8—superior
7—very good
6—good
5—average
4—below average

3—considerably below average
2—poor
1—very poor

## Basal and Ceiling Levels

Many tests, because test authors construct them for students of differing abilities, contain more items than are necessary. To determine the starting and stopping points for administering a test, test authors designate basal and ceiling levels. (Although these are really not types of scores, basal and ceiling levels are sometimes called rules or scores.) The **basal level** is the point below which the examiner assumes that the student could obtain all correct responses and, therefore, it is the point at which the examiner begins testing.

The test manual will designate the point at which testing should begin. For example, a test manual states, "Students who are 13 years old should begin with item 12. Continue testing when three items in a row have been answered correctly. If three items in a row are not answered correctly, the examiner should drop back a level." This is the basal level.

Let's look at the example of the student who is 9 years old. Although the examiner begins testing at the 9-year-old level, the student fails to answer correctly three in a row. Thus, the examiner is unable to establish a basal level at the suggested beginning point. Many manuals instruct the examiner to continue testing backward, dropping back one item at a time, until the student correctly answers three items. Some test manuals instruct examiners to drop back an entire level, for instance, to age 8, and begin testing (Overton, 1992).

When computing the student's raw score, the examiner includes items below the basal point as items answered correctly. Thus, the raw score includes all the items the student answered correctly plus the test items below the basal point.

The **ceiling level** is the point above which the examiner assumes that the student would obtain all incorrect responses if the testing were to continue; it is, therefore, the point at which the examiner stops testing. "To determine a ceiling," a manual may read, "discontinue testing when three items in a row have been missed."

A false ceiling can be reached if the examiner does not carefully follow directions for determining the ceiling level. Some tests require students to complete a page of test items to establish the ceiling level.

## Standard Error of Measurement and Confidence Intervals

### Standard Error of Measurement

The administration of a test is subject to many errors: errors can occur in the testing environment, the examiner may make errors, the examinee may not be exhibiting the best performance, and the test itself may not able to evoke the best performance from the examinee. All these errors contribute to lowering the reliability of a test.

The **standard error of measurement (SEM)** is related to reliability and is very useful in the interpretation of test performance. The standard error of measurement is the amount of error associated with individual test scores, test items, item samples, and test times. A **true score** is the score an individual would obtain on a test if there were no measurement errors. (The obtained score is the score that a student gets on a test.) Figure 3.6 shows the distribution of the SEM around the estimated true score.

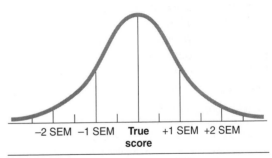

**FIGURE 3.6** *Standard Error of Measurement*

If examiners expect that the reliability or the standard error of measurement will differ for different populations, SEMs should be reported for each population taking the test.

When the SEM is small, we can be more confident of a score; when the SEM is large, there is less confidence in the score. Thus, it follows that the more reliable a test is, the smaller the SEM and the more confidence we can have. The less reliable a test, the larger the SEM, and the more uncertainty we have in a score.

### Confidence Intervals

Although educators can never know a student's true score, we can use the concept of confidence intervals to give us a range within which the true score can be found. Because it is inadvisable to present a student's score as an exact point, the concept of **confidence intervals** is an important one to use when reporting a student's test score.

We can determine the probability that a student's score will fall within a particular range. Three equivalent terms can describe this range:

band of error, confidence interval, and confidence band (Table 3.4). The higher the probability level, the more confidence we can have that a student's score falls within a specific range. The lower the probability, the less confidence we have that a score falls within a particular range. For instance, we can be 50, 68, 90, 95, 98, or 99 percent confident that a student's true score can be found within a range of scores. The percent of confidence that is chosen depends on the preference of the test examiner. However, we prefer to use 90 percent level or higher. In the Snapshot, teacher Gayle Aker explains a student's test performance using confidence intervals.

### Scoring Guidelines

After you have administered the test, you must carefully score it. If you have used a standardized test, you must use the specific procedures for scoring described in the test manual. Score the test as soon as possible after you have administered it. Be sure to allot sufficient time so that you do not feel rushed. Scoring must be accurate. Check all calculations carefully. Many tests have computer programs that will calculate the

**TABLE 3.4**    *Average Bands of Error for Comprehensive Form Subtests and Composites at the 90 Percent Level of Confidence, by Grade and by Age*

| | Average Band of Error at 90% Confidence Level | |
|---|---|---|
| **Subtest of Composite** | **Grades 1 to 12 (Grade Norms)** | **Ages 6 to 18 (Age Norms)** |
| Reading decoding | ± 6 | ± 5 |
| Reading comprehension | ± 7 | ± 6 |
| Reading composite | ± 5 | ± 4 |
| Mathematics applications | ± 8 | ± 7 |
| Mathematics computation | ± 8 | ± 7 |
| Mathematics composite | ± 6 | ± 5 |
| Spelling | ± 7 | ± 6 |
| Battery composite | ± 4 | ± 3 |

*Source: Kaufman Test of Educational Achievement Normative Update (K-TEA/NU)* Table 3.1 from p 57 of the Comprehensive Form Manual by Alan S. Kaufman and Nadeen L. Kaufman © 1985 American Guidance Servivce, Inc., 4201 Woodland Road, Circle Pines, Minnesota 55014-1796. Reproduced with permission of publisher. All rights reserved. www.agsnet.com

*Several students read in the classroom library corner.*

test scores for you. These can be very helpful in avoiding errors in computation.

### Completing the Test Record Form

***Biographical Information.*** The test record form contains a section for the examiner to complete biographical information about the student (Figure 3.7). Usually, this section is on the front of the test record form. The form, in general, asks for the following information: student's name, gender, name(s) of parent(s), home address, home telephone, grade in school, age when tested, date of birth, student's home-

### SNAPSHOT ■ *Confidence Intervals*

Gayle Aker, the special education consultant, had just finished administering the Comprehensive Form of the *Kaufman Test of Educational Achievement (K-TEA/NU)* to Cindy, a 7-year-old who was suspected of having a learning disability. After Gayle had marked the raw scores and the standard scores on the front of the Comprehensive Form (Figure 3.7) she was ready to write down the confidence interval. Gayle decided to use the 90 percent level of confidence. Like many tests, the developers of the K-TEA/NU have calculated the confidence bands so that test administrators do not need to make the calculations themselves. Gayle, using the K-TEA/NU manual, found the tables that listed the bands of confidence for Cindy's standard scores.

When Gayle met with Cindy's family she was able to report her scores in this way: "I am very confident when I say that Cindy's performance on the Battery Composite on the K-TEA/NU showed that her score was 86 ± 3. This means that her true score is between 83 and 89. It is more accurate to report her performance within a range of scores because test scores tend to fluctuate or change. There may be small changes in her scores if I were to retest her within a short time interval."

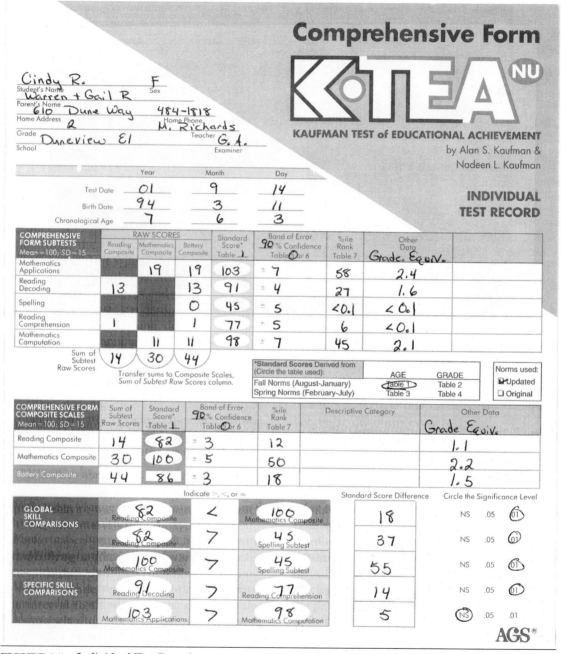

**FIGURE 3.7    *Individual Test Record***

*Source: Kaufman Test of Educational Achievement Normative Update (K-TEA/NU).* Individual Test Record summary page by Alan S. Kaufman and Nadeen L. Kaufmann © 1985 American Guidance Service, Inc., 4201 Woodland Road, Circle Pines, Minnesota 55014-1796. Reproduced with permission of publisher. All rights reserved. www.agsnet.com

room teacher, name of school, and examiner's name. If the student needs to use corrective lenses or a hearing aid, the examiner should note this also.

***Chronological Age.*** Often it is necessary to calculate the student's chronological age, the precise age of the student in years and months. If testing took place over several days, use the first test date to calculate the chronological age. Figure 3.8 shows the steps in calculating chronological age.

***Calculating Raw Scores.*** The raw scores are the number of items that the student answered correctly. Directions for computing the raw score may vary from one test to another. Within each subtest you will need to add the total number of items the student answered correctly. Each test will have its own system for indicating the student's correct and incorrect answers. Following the directions given in the test manual or on the test record form, the examiner will designate the correct answers by marking either a plus sign (+) or by designating points (e.g., 1, 2, or 3 points) for each correct answer. When calculating the raw score, the examiner will need to follow the test manual directions for calculating basal and ceiling scores.

After calculating the raw scores, the examiner writes these scores on the test form and transfers them to the section that summarizes the student's scores. For many test forms, this section is on the front of the test form.

***Transforming Raw Scores to Derived Scores.*** Calculating derived scores allow educators to make comparisons between test scores. Developmental scores and scores of relative standing are two types of derived scores. We prefer to use scores of relative standing: percentiles, standard scores, and stanines.

Test manuals have norm tables that allow the examiner to convert raw scores to one or more types of derived scores. Some test manuals contain tables for age and grade norms for tests

**FIGURE 3.8** *Three Examples of Calculating Chronological Age*

---

*Example 1*

Begin with the right column and subtract days, then months, and finally years. In this example no borrowing is required.

|  | Year | Month | Day |
|---|---|---|---|
| Test Date | 2002 | 6 | 15 |
| Birth Date | 1987 | 3 | 13 |
| Chronological Age | 15 | 3 | 2 |

---

*Example 2*

If the day for the test date is smaller than the day for the birth date, it is necessary to borrow one month (30 days) from the month column and add the 30 days to the day column. When borrowing one month always borrow 30 days.

|  | Year | Month | Day |
|---|---|---|---|
| Test Dates | 2002 | 5 | 33 |
|  |  | ~~6~~ | ~~3~~ |
| Birth Date | 1987 | 3 | 13 |
| Chronological Age | 15 | 2 | 20 |

---

*Example 3*

If the month for the test date is smaller than the month for the birth date, it is necessary to borrow one year (12 months) from the year column and add the 12 months to the month column.

|  | Year | Month | Day |
|---|---|---|---|
| Test Dates | 2001 | 14 | 15 |
|  | ~~2002~~ | ~~2~~ |  |
| Birth Date | 1987 | 3 | 13 |
| Chronological Age | 14 | 11 | 2 |

In general, chronological age is reported in days and months. If the number of days exceeds 15, add 1 month. If the number of days is equal to or is smaller than 15, do not change the months.

conducted during the fall, winter, or spring; other test manuals will have norm tables for tests administered at any time during the year. You may need to use more than one of the norm tables in the test manual. The section of the test form that summarizes the student's scores will indicate which type of derived score to use.

***Indicating Confidence Intervals.***    All test performance, you will recall, is prone to errors of measurement. Confidence intervals indicate the probability that a student's true score will fall within a particular range. Many test manuals provide tables of the bands of error for standard scores. In fact, because the standard score is not an exact score, the examiner should always use a confidence interval when reporting standard scores. The test record form often requires the examiner to record the band of error, indicated by a plus sign (+) and minus sign (–) on the test record form. It is up to the examiner to determine the specific level of confidence, 50, 68, 90, 95, 98, or 99 percent, that should be used. For most assessment decisions, we recommend a confidence level of 90 percent or higher because examiners can have greater confidence when interpreting test performance.

***Graphing Scores.***    Many test record forms allow the examiner to plot a graph or profile of the student's test scores. A graph allows the examiner to depict test scores visually and assists in the interpretation of test performance. To develop a graph, the examiner transfers the student's scores to the designated section of the test record form and creates a graph. Some record forms also allow bands of error to be plotted.

## Interpreting Test Performance

Conclusions and interpretations about a student's performance based on the results of one test, measure, or observation are limited. A student's performance on only one measure indicates a narrow slice of information about the student. Because many sources of variability and error are present in any assessment situation and because

many of the assessment approaches have limitations, we recommend that examiners use several *different* sources of assessment data. Sources of assessment data include: standardized measures; portfolio assessment; performance-based assessment; interviews with family members, teachers, and the student; and observations in classrooms, playground, cafeteria, and the student's home, if appropriate.

When making interpretations about a student's performance, include observations of the behavior of the student and observations of the environment.

## Behavioral Observations

Describe the student's behavior during formal and informal testing. The examiner will want to note whether the student was cooperative, distractible, attentive, tired, shy, or exhibited other behaviors. What was the student's behavior at the beginning of the testing? during the testing? at the end? To a certain extent the testing situation is artificial, and examiners must consider this when drawing conclusions about a child's behavior (Sattler, 2001). A child's behavior can vary in different settings and with different examiners. Systematic observations, as discussed in Chapter 5, can be important sources of information.

The following list of behaviors is a starting point for discussion (Sattler, 2001):

- physical appearance
- reactions to test session and to the examiner
- general behavior
- typical mode of relating to the examiner
- language style
- general response style
- response to failures
- response to successes
- response to encouragement
- activity level
- attitude toward self
- attitude toward the examiner and the testing process
- visual-motor ability

- unusual habits, mannerisms, or verbalizations
- the examiner's reaction to the child

### Observations of the Environment

Note any factors in the environment such as interruptions, excessive noise, or unusual temperature that may affect the student's test performance and behavior. Approaches to assessing the environment will be discussed in Chapter 5.

### Discussion of Results

When reporting the results of standardized tests, use the same types of scores throughout. Most professionals prefer standard scores, percentiles, or stanines. Report two or more types of scores, such as standard scores and percentiles. If a graph of the student's performance is available, be sure to use it.

## How Should Assessment Approaches Be Evaluated?

We have discussed many concepts in this chapter. It is important for you to understand these concepts when using a test. Table 3.5 can be helpful when determining the adequacy of assessment approaches.

Before using individual tests, professionals would do well to consult independent reviews. There are numerous resources available that provide independent evaluations of tests. The *Mental Measurements Yearbooks* (MMY) and *Tests in Print*, which are published by the Buros Institute of Mental Measurements at the University of Nebraska–Lincoln (University of Nebraska at Lincoln, Lincoln, Nebraska 68588), are probably the best-known sources of test reviews. *Test Critiques*, published by the Test Corporation of America (4050 Pennsylvania, Suite 310, Kansas City, Missouri 64112), is another source.

The Internet provides a wealth of information. The website of the ERIC Clearinghouse on Assessment and Evaluation provides information and access to the ERIC database on tests and measurement, newsletters on tests and mea-

surement, descriptions of tests, information on locating tests and test reviews, research studies and essays, and links to numerous Internet resources on tests and measurement. The Buros Institute of Mental Measurements website has information on locating tests and test reviews. Other Internet resources include the United States Department of Education; the National Center for Research on Evaluation, Standards, and Student Teaching (CRESST); and the National Association of Test Directors.

Many journals contain reviews of tests. Journals that may be of particular interest to special educators include: *Diagnostique, Exceptional Children, Journal of Early Intervention, Journal of Learning Disabilities, Journal of Reading, Journal of School Psychology, Journal of Special Education, Mental Retardation, Remedial and Special Education*, and *Topics in Early Childhood Special Education*.

Finally, test publishers provide catalogues that describe their products. Catalogues provide overviews of tests as well as information about how to purchase tests, record forms, and technical materials. Remember that the primary goal of test publishers is to sell tests. It is essential that professionals examine independent reviews of tests, such as those contained in MMY, *Tests in Print, Test Critiques*, and various journals.

### Preferred Practices

When using standardized, norm-referenced tests, educators must determine whether they are measuring consistent student performance and whether tests measure what the authors describe as the purpose of the tests. Test manuals provide information about technical aspects of tests, including the development of norms and test scores. Teachers, test examiners, and administrators need to carefully review tests before using them to satisfy themselves that each test has acceptable levels of reliability and validity. Professionals should apply the technical concepts we have discussed in this and previous chapters to the assessment approaches, procedures, and techniques.

**TABLE 3.5** *Evaluation of a Test or Other Assessment Approach*

**Name of Assessment Test or Approach** _____

**Author(s)** _____

**Publisher** _____  **Date of Publication** _____

*About the Assessment Test or Approach*

1. Purpose(s) (according to the manual)
2. Extent to which individual items or tasks match the purpose(s)
3. Length of time for test administration
4. Group or individual

*About Administration Requirements*

1. Education and experience of examiner requirements
2. Additional training requirements

*About the Student*

1. Considerations/adaptations for disability
2. Considerations/adaptations for language
3. Considerations/adaptations for culture/race/ethnicity

*About the Technical Aspects*

1. Norms, goals, standards, outcomes. If relevant, indicate:
   a. Type
   b. Age, grade, language, culture, gender
   c. Representativeness
   d. Relevance of sample to student(s) tested
   e. Method of selection of sample
   f. Date of development of norms, goals, standards, outcomes
2. Reliability. What are the coefficients and how were they determined?
   a. Test-retest
   b. Alternate form
   c. Split-half
   d. Internal consistency
   e. Interscorer/interrater/interobserver

3. Validity. What is the justification for each type of validity?
   a. Content
   b. Concurrent
   c. Predictive
   d. Construct
   e. Consequential validity

*About the Results and Aids to Interpretation*

1. Types of scores
2. Interpretation aids

*About Fairness*

1. Is the norm or comparison group appropriate?
2. Are considerations made for race, culture, gender, language, socioeconomic status, or disability?

*About the Usefulness of This Test or Approach*

1. Is it appropriate for the student(s)?
2. Is it fair?
3. Is it technically adequate?
4. Report from an independent source (*The Mental Measurements Yearbooks, Tests in Print, Test Critiques*, journal article, or Internet)

*Conclusions*

1. Overall strengths
2. Overall weaknesses
3. Summary and recommendations

*About References*

1. List of references consulted
2. List of other sources consulted

## Extending Learning

1. What are the advantages of using norm-referenced tests?
2. Imagine that you are the director of testing for a large metropolitan school district and that you will be giving a one-day workshop to your staff. What topics should you discuss relating to the technical adequacy of tests? Why did you choose each of these topics?
3. Clara received a score of 64 on an achievement test. How can the special education teacher use the concept of confidence intervals to explain Clara's performance to her family?
4. Several different types of test scores are discussed in this chapter. Which ones do you prefer to use? Why?
5. Obtain two or more test manuals and read the sections pertaining to the standardiza-

tion samples. Compare and contrast the development of two tests, based on these descriptions. How closely does the norm sample of each test represent students in the community in which you live? What conclusions can you make?

(On p. 63 we asked: Which measure of central tendency—the mean, median, or mode—should Brendan use in his discussion with Ken? Answer: Brendan should use the median score of 79 because most of the scores in the class cluster around this score. The score represents the division between the top 50 percent of students and the bottom 50 percent of students. The mean score of 73 should not be used. Notice how this score was strongly influenced by the bottom score of 20.)

## References

American Educational Research Association, American Psychological Association, and National Council on Measurement in Education (1999). *Standards for educational and psychological testing.* Washington, DC: American Educational Research Association.

Berk, R. A. (1988). Criterion-referenced tests. In *Educational research, methodology, and measurement: An international handbook*, ed. J. P. Keeves, 365–370. Oxford: Pergamon Press.

Cronbach, L. J. (1971). Test validation. In *Educational measurement*, ed. R. Thorndike, 443–507. Washington, DC: American Council on Education.

DeVellis, R. F. (1991). *Scale development.* Newbury Park, CA: Sage.

Gronlund, N. E., and R. L. Linn (1990). *Measurement and evaluation in teaching.* New York: Macmillan.

Kaufman, A., and N. L. Kaufman (1988). *Kaufman test of educational achievement/Normative update (K-TEA/NU).* Circle Pines, MN: American Guidance Service.

Lyman, H. 1986. *Test scores and what they mean.* 4th ed. Englewood Cliffs, NJ: Prentice-Hall.

Mardell-Czudnowski, C., and Goldenberg, D. S.

(1998). *Developmental indicators for the assessment of learning.* 3rd ed. Circle Pines, MN: American Guidance Service.

McLean, M., D. B. Bailey, and M. Wolery (1996). *Assessing infants and preschoolers with handicaps.* Columbus, OH: Merrill.

Mehrens, W. A., and I. J. Lehmann (1991). *Measurement and evaluation in education and psychology.* Fort Worth, TX: Holt, Rinehart & Winston.

Overton, T. (1992). *Assessment in special education.* New York: Merrill.

Rudner, L. M., J. C. Conoley, and B. S. Plake (1989). *Understanding achievement tests: A guide for school administrators.* Washington, DC: ERIC Clearinghouse on Assessment and Evaluation. (ERIC Document Reproduction Service, no. ED 314 426).

Sattler, J. (2001). *Assessment of students.* San Diego, CA: Jerome M. Sattler.

Zeller, R. A. (1988). Validity. In *Educational research, methodology, and measurement: An international handbook*, ed. J. P. Keeves, 322–330. Oxford: Pergamon Press.

# 4

## *Reliability and Validity*

### Overview

Reliability and validity, two closely related concepts, are discussed in this chapter. This chapter also continues the discussion on responding to diversity. Being responsive to diversity means that assessment procedures are fair. Fairness in assessment indicates that assessment methods are equitable, free of bias, adapted for students with disabilities, sensitive to diverse groups of students, and considerate of contemporary views of growth and development, aptitude, cognition, learning, behavior, and personality.

## Chapter Objectives

After completing this chapter, you should be able to:

- Define reliability and describe the different types of reliability.
- Define validity and describe the different types of validity.

- Describe the application of the concepts of reliability and validity as they apply to all forms of assessment.
- Explain why assessment approaches should be responsive to diversity.

## What Shapes Our Views

The measurement concepts we discuss in this chapter are central to an understanding of assessment. Using reliability and validity as the basis of assessment is like constructing a house with a strong foundation. An assessment approach that has a sturdy foundation will be much more useful than one in which reliability and validity are weak.

## Reliability

Reliability is one of the most important considerations when selecting tests and other assessment tools. A test must be constructed so that examiners can administer the test with minimal errors and can interpret the performance of students with confidence.

The assessment process is subject to error from many sources. Errors in measurement can stem from the testing environment, the student, the test, and the examiner. Sources of error in the testing environment include:

- noise distractions;
- poor lighting; and
- uncomfortable room temperature.

Sources of error associated with the student include:

- hunger;
- fatigue;
- illness;

- difficulty in understanding test instructions; and
- difficulty in understanding or interpreting language used.

Sources of error stemming from the test include:

- ambiguously worded questions;
- biased questions; and
- different interpretations of the wording of test questions.

An examiner who is not prepared or who incorrectly interprets administration or scoring guidelines contributes to measurement errors. Sources of error associated with test administration include:

- unclear directions;
- difficulty in achieving rapport;
- insensitivity to student's culture, language, preferences, or other characteristics;
- ambiguous scoring; and
- errors associated with recording information about the student.

Reliability information that is reported in test manuals should be evaluated. While there are some books and journal articles that report evaluations of tests, tests are not given "seals of approval." To be useful, they must meet certain standards. Three professional organizations, the American Educational Research Association, the American Psychological Association, and the National Council on Measurement in Education (1999) have published *Standards for Educational and Psychological Testing*, which provides criteria for evaluating tests, testing practices, and the effects of test use on individuals.

The 1999 edition of *Standards for Educational and Psychological Testing* describes reliability and provides a departure from more traditional thinking about reliability. In this edition, reliability refers to the "scoring procedure that enables the examiner to quantify, evaluate, and interpret behavior or work samples. Reliability refers to the consistency of such measurements when the testing procedure is repeated on a population of individuals or groups" (p. 25).

Test developers convey reliability of assessment instruments in various ways. Traditionally, test developers have been responsible for reporting evidence of reliability. Test users and consumers must use this evidence in deciding the suitability of various assessment instruments. While no one approach is preferred, educators should be familiar with all of the approaches in order to judge the usefulness of instruments. These approaches are: (1) one or more correlation coefficients; (2) variances or standard deviations of measurement errors; and (3) technical information about tests known as IRT (item response theory).

## Approach 1: Using Correlation Coefficients

Traditionally, **reliability** has been described as the stability or consistency of test performance. The teacher needs to know that a student's test performance is stable over time and over different test items that have similar objectives. Of course, it is impractical and unnecessary for a student to take a test every day. If a teacher administers a test to a student on a given day, that teacher wants to have some assurance that the student, if retested on the following day, will score about the same on both tests. Or, if a student takes one form or version of a test, the teacher needs to know that the test scores of the student, if taking a similar form of a test, will be about the same.

This type of reliability also provides an estimate of the consistency of test results when administering a test under similar conditions. This consistency or agreement is described by means of a correlation coefficient. Some test manuals use the term *reliability coefficient* in place of the term *correlation coefficient*. In order to understand this type of reliability, it is useful to know about the concepts of correlation and correlation coefficients.

*Correlation.* A **correlation** indicates the extent to which two or more scores vary together. It measures the degree to which a change in one score has a relationship with a change in another score. For example, in general, the higher a student's intelligence score, the higher will be the student's score on a vocabulary test. Usually, students with higher intelligence quotient (IQ) scores tend to have higher vocabulary scores and students with lower IQ scores will probably have lower vocabulary test scores. IQ and vocabulary level correlate with each other. However, examiners must use caution when interpreting relationships; just because two scores correlate does not mean that one score causes a change in the other score. The correlation between shoe size and reading achievement is an example of a strong correlation but lack of causation. As shoe size increases, reading achievement may also increase, but this is pure coincidence; a person's shoe size has nothing to do with how well that person reads.

*Correlation Coefficient.* A **correlation coefficient** measures the correlation, or relationship, between tests, test items, scoring procedures, observations, or behavior ratings. A correlation coefficient quantifies a relationship and provides information about whether there is a relationship, strength of the relationship, and the direction of the relationship. The symbol for correlation coefficient is a lower case $r$. Test developers conduct research studies to determine correlation coefficients and report these coefficients in test manuals.

*Strength of a Relationship.* The value of a correlation coefficient can vary from +1.00 to –1.00. The closer the correlation coefficient is to 1.00, either +1.00 or –1.00, the stronger the relationship. The closer the correlation coefficient is to 0.00, the weaker the relationship. For example, a coefficient of .89 is stronger than a coefficient of .15 because .89 is closer to 1.00, just as a coefficient of –.54 is stronger than a coefficient of –.45 because –.54 is closer to –1.00.

*Direction of a Relationship.* The presence of a plus (+) or minus (–) sign determines the direction of a correlation. A plus sign indicates that a relationship is positive; and a negative (minus) sign indicates that a relationship is negative. When positive correlation coefficients are written, the plus sign is usually omitted. When one test score increases as another test score increases, the relationship is positive. In a positive relationship, the scores either increase together or decrease together. However, when one test score decreases while the other test score increases, the relationship is negative. The relationship between IQ and vocabulary achievement is a positive relationship, because both of these variables usually increase together.

*Positive relationship:* If there were a perfect relationship between IQ level and vocabulary achievement, the correlation would be expressed as either +1.00 or 1.00. If for every increase in IQ score there is a corresponding increase in vocabulary scores, the relationship between IQ and vocabulary level would be perfect and the resulting correlation coefficient would be 1.00. However, because there are so many other variables that influence both IQ and vocabulary achievement, this relationship will never be a perfect 1.00. Figure 4.1 illustrates this relationship.

*Negative relationship:* A perfect negative relationship is indicated by –1.00. The relationship between level of achievement and the number of errors made is a negative relationship. As the achievement increases, the number of errors that an individual makes decreases. Figure 4.2 illustrates this relationship.

*Zero relationship:* The relationship between an individual's score on an intelligence test and the height of that individual is zero. When arranged on a scatter plot, most of the intelligence test scores and the height

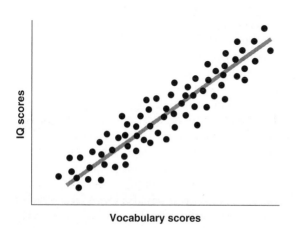

**FIGURE 4.1** *Scatter Plot of a Positive Relationship*

**FIGURE 4.2** *Scatter Plot of a Negative Relationship*

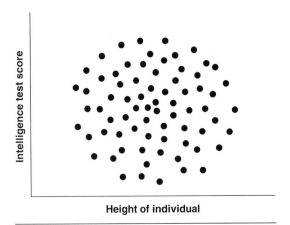

**FIGURE 4.3**   *Scatter Plot of a Zero Relationship*

measurements are not associated with each other; the scores do not vary with each other. Figure 4.3 illustrates this relationship.

### Applying Correlation Coefficients to Reliability.

In test manuals, a lowercase *r* designates a reliability or correlation coefficient. For example, when a test manual reports that r = .92, the reliability for the test is .92. Because .92 is close to a perfect correlation coefficient of 1.00, a teacher can have confidence that the test has adequate reliability. For guidance in evaluating correlation coefficients, Nitko (2001) recommends that when making major educational decisions, a reliability coefficient of at least .90 is the preferred standard.

### Types of Reliability That Involve Correlation Coefficients.

The traditional view of reliability conceptualizes five types of reliability: test-retest, alternate form, split-half, internal consistency, and interscorer/interobserver/interrater reliability. For these types of reliability, it is incumbent upon test publishers to report information fully in test manuals. Test publishers should tell how they obtained the samples of students, individuals, or observations from which they determine their reliability coefficients. Interpretations of total test scores, subscores, or combinations of scores should include stated relevant reliabilities. Similarly, when tests have both long and short versions, test publishers must report reliabilities of each version based on separate independent administrations of each version.

*Test-Retest Reliability.* **Test-retest reliability** can be obtained when administering the same test to the same student twice by correlating the scores on the first and second administrations and obtaining a reliability coefficient. This coefficient is a measure of the stability of the test score. Because the same test is administered twice, test developers need to state the time interval between the two administrations of the test. Too short an interval will inflate the reliability coefficient. When the time interval is too long, a student may experience developmental changes that will affect the reliability coefficient.

There are several drawbacks to this type of reliability. Having seen the test items and the directions for taking the test over two test administrations, the student may obtain a higher test score on the second testing.

*Alternate Form Reliability.* **Alternate form reliability** is also known as equivalent form or parallel form reliability. Frequently, there is a need for two forms of a test that contain different test items but that evaluate the same knowledge and skills. This procedure is especially useful when pretesting and posttesting students. The two forms have different designations. For example, some forms are designated A and B; others may be labeled X and Y or L and M.

Like test-retest reliability, alternate form reliability has several disadvantages. It is difficult to develop two parallel forms of a test. In addition, as with test-retest reliability, a shorter interval between test administrations can inflate the reliability coefficient and the effect of practice on similar test items.

*Split-Half Reliability.*   **Split-half reliability** is measured by administering a test to a group of students, dividing the total number of test items in half to form two tests, and correlating the scores on the two halves of the test. For example, suppose a test has 20 items. We could administer the entire test to a group of students and then divide the test into two halves, each containing 10 items. We can use different methods to break a test into two halves: by separating the first half from the second half or by separating the even numbered items from the odd numbered items. We can then correlate the items on the two halves to determine the relationship between the scores from the first half of the test and the scores from the second half.

Dividing a test into a first half and a second half can cause problems in determining the reliability. Fatigue, practice effect, failure to complete the test, and print quality can all affect the reliability coefficient (DeVellis, 1991). Assuming random order of the test items, we could divide the test by odd-even items or by balancing the halves. Balancing halves could involve item length, response type, or another characteristic that is appropriate for the test. The most appropriate method of splitting the halves of a test will depend on the test and the testing situation (DeVellis, 1991).

With the split-half procedure, we administer the test only once. Therefore, this procedure gives reliability coefficients that are a measure of internal consistency, not of the temporal stability of test performance.

*Internal Consistency Reliability.*   Internal consistency reliability is similar to the split-half method. **Internal consistency reliability** is an estimate of the homogeneity or interrelatedness of responses to test items. Students take this test only once. Usually test developers use one of the Kuder-Richardson formulas to find the average coefficient by calculating all the possible split-half coefficients. The more similar the test items are to each other, the higher will be the reliability coefficient. Like split-half reliability, internal consistency reliability does not provide an estimate of the stability of the test over time.

The advantage of using internal consistency instead of the split-half method is that internal consistency provides the average of all split-half correlations—all possible ways of dividing the test into two halves. The split-half method allows only one division of the test in half. The Snapshot of Prentice Dillon and Erin Gates illustrates how teachers consider this type of reliability.

## SNAPSHOT   ■   *Prentice Dillon and Erin Gates*

After all the students had left school for the day, Prentice Dillon, a special education teacher, decided that he needed to review the test manual for a recently purchased school test. He read the initial chapters in the manual that described the test and the administration procedures. Okay so far. Dillon began the chapter that described the reliability of the test. The section that described internal consistency reliability said, "The reliability coefficient for the composite scores was described as r = .92. This is greater than the reliability coefficients for the subtest scores." Prentice asked himself, "Why were the reliability coefficients of the composite scores higher than the reliability coefficients of the individual subtests?" Prentice decided to see what Erin Gates, the other special educator in his building, knew about this test.

After reading the reliability section of the manual, Erin explained that it was not unusual for composite scores to have higher reliability coefficients than individual subtests because test developers use more test items to calculate the reliability coefficients associated with composite scores than with individual subtests. Composite scores, in general, show higher reliability coefficients than do individual subtests.

*Interscorer/Interobserver/Interrater Reliability.*
**Interscorer/interobserver/interrater reliability** is a measure of the extent to which two or more scorers, observers, or raters agree on how to score a test. Interscorer/interobserver/interrater reliability is important when errors in scoring or differences in judgment can affect the test outcomes. This type of reliability should be reported when:

1. There is a possibility that errors can be made in computing the test score(s).
2. A test item can have more than one answer.
3. A response to a question can have more than one interpretation.
4. Observations are made about the behaviors of one or more students.
5. Interviews are used to collect information.

## Approach 2: Variances or Standard Deviations of Measurement Errors

The true score is the score an individual would obtain on a test if there were no measurement errors. The **obtained score** is the actual score that a student obtains on a test. This is the best estimate we have of a student's performance. If all testing conditions were perfect and there were no errors of measurement, the obtained score and the true score would be the same. But, since error is always present, the true score cannot be known. However, an individual's true score can be measured by using the formula $X = T + E$ where the student's obtained or observed score, $X$, equals the true score, $T$, plus the errors that are associated with measurement, represented by $E$, the error score.

Standard errors of measurement are especially important when evaluators need to make immediate decisions with limited information. Examiners should report the standard error of measurement (SEM) for derived scores including standard scores, grade or age equivalents, and percentile ranks. SEM is of special concern when using cut scores. **Cut scores** are prespecified scores that determine how to select or classify students. Typically, evaluators may select or classify students who score at or below a pre-specified cut score, such as 30, for special education or labeling. When using cut scores, test publishers must specify the measurement error associated with each cut score. Standard errors of measurement are also important to consider when making score comparisons such as between achievement and ability and when interpreting score profiles.

## Approach 3: Item Response Theory (IRT)

Technical information about tests is known as **item response theory (IRT).** IRT involves a statistical calculation that determines how well the instrument differentiates between individuals at various levels of measured abilities or characteristics. If test publishers, authors, and researchers choose to demonstrate reliability using IRT, they should provide sufficient information in test manuals. Test publishers should clearly and comprehensively describe the procedures they used to determine reliability.

## Factors That Influence Reliability

Several factors can affect the reliability of a test (Mehrens and Lehmann, 1991; Sattler, 2001):

1. *Test length.* Generally, the longer a test is, the more reliable it is.
2. *Speed.* When a test is a speed test, reliability can be problematic. It is inappropriate to estimate reliability using internal consistency, test-retest, or alternate form methods. This is because not every student is able to complete all of the items in a speed test. In contrast, a power test is a test in which every student is able to complete all the items.
3. *Group homogeneity.* In general, the more heterogeneous the group of students who take the test, the more reliable the measure will be.
4. *Item difficulty.* When there is little variability among test scores, the reliability will be low.

Thus, reliability will be low if a test is so easy that every student gets most or all of the items correct or so difficult that every student gets most or all of the items wrong.

5. *Objectivity.* Objectively scored tests, rather than subjectively scored tests, show a higher reliability.

6. *Test-retest interval.* The shorter the time interval between two administrations of a test, the less likely that changes will occur and the higher the reliability will be.

7. *Variation with the testing situation.* Errors in the testing situation (e.g., students misunderstanding or misreading test directions; noise level; distractions; and sickness) can cause test scores to vary.

## *Validity*

**Validity** is the most important consideration when developing, evaluating, and interpreting tests. Reliability is a prerequisite of validity. A test must demonstrate reliability before test developers or test users can consider evidence of validity. A test that is reliable is not necessarily valid. According to *Standards for Educational and Psychological Testing* (American Educational Research Association et al., 1999), "Validity refers to the degree to which evidence and theory support the interpretations of test scores entailed by the proposed tests" (p. 9). In order to establish validity of a test and of test interpretations, test developers usually gather evidence in multiple forms over a period of time. The determination of validity is the obligation of both the test developer and test user. Test developers should provide information about validity in test manuals. Ultimately, it is incumbent upon the test user to review the evidence and determine the extent to which a test is valid and the interpretations of the test are valid. The test user should consider: process used to construct the instrument; score reliability; test administration procedures; scoring procedures; the standards-setting process; and the extent to

which the test is fair. We describe fairness in detail later in this chapter.

### *Traditional View of Validity*

Traditionally, validity has several aspects: content, criterion-related (which includes concurrent and predictive validity), and construct. A correlation coefficient (r) commonly represents criterion-related and construct validity. From our discussion of reliability, you will recall that r is also a measure of reliability. Therefore, it is important that users pay attention to whether the r values refer to reliability or validity.

***Content Validity.*** Content validity measures the extent to which the test items reflect the content domain of a test. Content validity is the most important type of validity for achievement tests because achievement tests typically measure content knowledge such as reading, writing, mathematics, science, and social studies.

An estimate of the content validity of a test is obtained by thoroughly and systematically examining the test items to determine the extent to which they reflect and do not reflect the content domain. In general, a panel composed of curriculum experts and specialists in tests and measurements evaluate content validity by determining the extent to which the test items reflect the test objectives. Test developers should provide information about the experts who reviewed the test content.

Most norm-referenced tests represent the curricula that are taught in various geographic regions of the United States. Because these tests are so broad, they may inadequately represent the curricula in many schools. Thus, as a rule, test users must ensure the content validity of norm-referenced tests before a test user can be confident that a particular test is appropriate in this respect.

***Criterion-Related Validity.*** **Criterion-related validity** refers to the extent to which scores from one test, instrument, or measure relate to scores from another test, instrument, or measure. When determining criterion-related validity, test developers compare their test with another outcome or criterion: another test, school grades, or observations. If test developers use this type of validity they should report their findings in the test manuals.

When assessing the criterion-related validity of a test, it is important to verify the criterion measure's validity as well. Concurrent and predictive validity are two types of criterion-related validity.

*Concurrent Validity.*    **Concurrent validity** is the extent to which the results of two different tests administered at about the same time correlate with each other. To obtain concurrent validity, test developers administer two different tests within a brief interval and calculate the correlation between the scores from the tests. This method of estimating validity is especially useful when constructing a new test.

Suppose a test publisher wanted to develop a new way to test the hearing abilities of students. The publisher would administer this new test and also a standard hearing test. Next, the publisher would establish concurrent validity by examining the relationship between the scores from the two tests.

The test publisher wants to know the extent to which a known instrument and a new test measure the same objectives. If the new test correlates highly with the established instrument, the test publisher can conclude that the new test is valid and that it has an acceptable level of concurrent validity.

*Predictive Validity.*    How accurately can current performance predict future performance or behavior? Predictive validity is the standard for forecasting student performance or behavior from a test score.

Be careful not to confuse concurrent validity with predictive validity. There are some important differences. While concurrent validity is a measure of the extent to which two sets of test scores relate to each other, **predictive validity** is an estimate of the extent to which one test

accurately predicts future performance or behavior. When scores on one test accurately predict performance on another test or criterion, we can say that there is high predictive validity.

*Construct Validity.*    **Construct validity** is the extent to which a test measures a particular trait, construct, or psychological characteristic. Examples of constructs include reasoning ability, spatial visualization, reading comprehension, sociability, and introversion.

Construct validity is the most difficult type of validity to establish. Test developers need a long period of time and numerous research studies before verifying construct validity for a particular test. Zeller (1988) compares the establishment of construct validity to a detective's search for clues, accumulating evidence bit by bit. The clues assist the test developer in determining the consistency of the evidence in the interpretation of construct validity. If the evidence falls into a systematic pattern, then test developers and test examiners can have confidence in the validity of the construct. Prentice Dillon and Erin Gates continue their conversation in the Snapshot.

## Validity of Test Interpretations

The interpretation of test results can have profound consequences for students, families, and educators. Thus, test publishers should provide validity information for each proposed interpretation and use of test scores, subtests, subscores, score differences, and test profiles (American Educational Research Association et al., 1999). Test publishers should also provide evidence of validity, including the statistics they used to conduct analyses, composition of samples they used to collect the data, and conditions under which they collected the data, for each proposed interpretation.

Test users should evaluate the evidence in order to determine the extent of support for the proposed interpretations. If evidence is unavailable or inconsistent, test publishers should

**SNAPSHOT** ■ *Prentice Dillon and Erin Gates Continue Their Conversation*

Prentice continued reading the manual of the new test that his school had purchased. After finishing the reliability section, he decided to turn to the validity section. The manual said, "The achievement subtests were correlated with the cognitive subtests and the coefficients ranged from .20 to .65." Prentice knew that coefficients that approach 1.00 indicate that there is a very close relationship. But, when evaluating the validity of a test, what did correlations between .20 and .65 mean?

Erin Gates was still in her classroom when Prentice asked if she could help him understand validity. Erin explained that the authors of the test manual were presenting evidence for the construct validity of their test. Construct validity is the extent to which a test measures a particular trait, construct, or psychological characteristic, such as achievement and cognitive ability. In determining construct validity, the test author describes the construct, indicating how it differs from other constructs.

Erin told Prentice that the correlations between .20 and .65 indicate that there is, in fact, some relationship between achievement and cognitive ability because achievement and cognitive ability are actually two different, but not totally separate, constructs. In fact, if the correlations were close to 1.00, for example, .90, .93, or .95, it would mean that the achievement subtests and the cognitive subtests were too closely related and that they were measuring the same constructs!

disclose this information to test users. Similarly, if a test user would like to use a test in a way for which validity evidence is lacking, the user should refrain from using the test until publishers can provide sufficient evidence.

### Consequential Validity

**Consequential validity** describes the extent to which an assessment instrument promotes the intended consequences (Linn and Baker, 1996). Test publishers use consequential validity to describe performance-based assessments. Performance-based assessment, which we discuss in Chapter 7, provides information about what a student can do with knowledge in real-life, real-world settings rather than with isolated bits of knowledge. Domains such as dance and music have long used performance-based assessments to evaluate students. Performances are far more appropriate for evaluating how students dance or play musical instruments than are multiple-choice questions.

One of the primary reasons for using performance-based assessments is to improve student learning. Consequential validity reflects the extent to which performance-based assessment improves student learning. Factors that can affect student learning positively, and thus impact consequential validity, include school improvement activities, instructional improvements, staff development activities, levels of student achievement, and accountability systems (Linn and Baker, 1996).

### Participation of Students with Disabilities in State- and Districtwide Assessments

IDEA requires that an accountability system be in place to evaluate the progress that students with disabilities make toward the established general education performance goals and indicators that apply to all students. State- and districtwide assessments must include all students with disabilities. Students with disabilities convicted as adults under state law and incarcerated in adult prisons are the only students who are exempted from participation in general state- and districtwide assessments (Heumann and Warlick, 2000).

Since the law requires that all students with disabilities must participate in state- and districtwide assessments, the IEP team does not determine *whether* students with disabilities will participate. However, the IEP team can determine *how* students with disabilities participate. The IEP team determines whether accommodations or modifications should be made to the test or to the procedures used in test administration so that the student can participate. Test accommodations do not mean adaptations or changes to the test but rather to the test's format, response, setting, timing, or scheduling. These changes should not significantly alter the way examiners make test interpretations or comparisons (Heumann and Warlick, 2000).

### Alternate Assessment

Some students with severe or significant disabilities are unable to participate in large-scale assessments even when accommodations and modifications are made. Alternate assessments enable students with severe or significant disabilities to participate in general large-scale assessments. Alternate assessments must align with the same curriculum standards that all students use. States and local education agencies and districts must, by law, develop guidelines for alternate assessments.

### Out-of-Level Testing

**Out-of-level testing** occurs when examiners assess students in one grade level using tests that were designed for students in other, usually lower, grade levels. IDEA does not specifically prohibit out-of-level testing; however, out-of-level testing should be discouraged for the following reasons (Heumann and Warlick, 2000):

1. Out-of-level testing may not assess the same grade-level content areas as the large-scale assessment that the majority of students in the state or district take.
2. Out-of-level testing may lower expectations for students with disabilities.
3. Scores from out-of-level testing are difficult to aggregate or group together with scores from students taking the general, large-scale assessment.

4. Scores from out-of-level testing are difficult to compare with scores from students taking the general, large-scale assessment.
5. Out-of-level testing may provide inadequate or insufficient information about how students with disabilities perform on the established goals and standards that apply to all students in the state or district.

## Responding to Diversity: Fairness in Assessment

Assessment has a great influence on curriculum, instruction, classroom, and school organization, and on educational and career opportunities for students. Fairness in assessment means that all assessment approaches, including standardized tests, performance assessment, portfolio assessment, and informal measures, are free from bias and that methods of student assessment are equitable and sensitive to diverse student populations. Assessment should be fair to all students so as not to limit students' present education and their future opportunities (National Forum on Assessment, 1995). Fairness in assessment means that assessment methods reflect the following:

- equity;
- nonbiased assessment;
- linguistic diversity;
- accommodations and modifications for students with disabilities;
- sensitivity to diverse student populations;
- consideration of contemporary views of growth and development, aptitude, cognition, learning, behavior, and personality; and
- consideration of possible adverse consequences to students of any applicable assessment devices.

### Equity

Differences in test results may be due to differences in educational opportunities, resources, or cultural expectations. This is especially true when considerations about culture, ethnicity, race, language, geographic region of origin, gender, disability, or economic status are a concern. **Equity** in assessment means that assessment is approached in a fair, impartial, and just manner. Assessment tools must be more than reliable and valid. Valid assessments arise only when the assessment is fair. Fair assessments mean that all students have access to and can participate in a variety of assessment approaches.

## Nonbiased Assessment

Assessment tools must be nonbiased. When groups know approximately the same amount of material but one group scores consistently higher than other groups on a test it may indicate test bias. For example, a test may portray individuals in stereotypic ways in test problems that contain references applying to only males, to only middle-class individuals, to only a particular culture, or to topics that carry status with only those groups. When evaluating student behavior in such tests, some behaviors considered aberrant for one group may be proper for another group.

## Linguistic Diversity

There are important considerations when testing students who are nonnative speakers of English or who speak languages other than English. Translation of an assessment tool or use of an interpreter is not always appropriate (American Educational Research Association et al., 1999). Translation alone does not ensure that an assessment procedure is comparable in content, difficulty level, reliability, or validity to the original version.

Both the language dominance and language proficiency of test takers should be considered (American Educational Research Association et al., 1999). **Language dominance** refers to the individual's preferred language. **Language proficiency** refers to level of expertise in a language. A student who may be bilingual, or even trilingual, may have different levels of proficiency in speaking, reading, and writing. Test administrators should determine the language proficiency of the students and administer tests in the language in which the student is most proficient.

When recommending a test for use with linguistically diverse test takers, test developers and publishers should provide the information for appropriate test use and interpretation. When translating a test from one language or dialect to another, test administrators need to establish the test's reliability and validity for the uses intended in the linguistic groups they will test.

## Accommodations and Modifications for Students with Disabilities

Assessment activities must be accessible to students with disabilities, and they must be able to provide evidence about what the student knows and can do. Test accommodations indicate changes in format, response, setting, timing, or scheduling but no adaptations or changes in the test. Accommodations do not alter in a significant way in which evaluators make test interpretations or comparisons. Modifications mean changes or adaptations in a test. These modifications involve a nonstandard administration of the test.

The purpose of making accommodations and modifications is to reduce the impact of student characteristics and the testing environment on testing performance. Accommodations and modifications should respond to the needs of the student, and test administrators should document and describe them in the testing report. Although two students may have the same disability, such as a learning disability, the accommodations and modifications each student may need can differ.

Test manuals should describe appropriate accommodations and modifications and provide evidence of the validity of the test when examiners implement them. When evidence about the

**TABLE 4.1**    *Frequently Used Accommodations and Modifications*

| Type of Accommodation or Modification | Examples of Accommodations (*No changes to the test but changes in format, response, setting, timing, or scheduling have been made*) | Examples of Modifications (*Changes made to the test*) |
|---|---|---|
| Location of the test administration | • Test is administered in an area that has reduced distractions.<br>• Test is administered in a separate area of the classroom.<br>• Test is administered while student is using special furniture.<br>• Test is administered in space that has special lighting. | |
| Presentation mode | • Test is administered individually rather than administered in a group.<br>• Examiner reads items out loud (except when student is tested in reading).<br>• Large print forms are used.<br>• Magnifying devices are used for students with visual difficulties.<br>• Markers are used to keep the place.<br>• A specific examiner may be chosen who is able to develop (or who already has) rapport with the student. | • Instructions are placed next to the test items to which they are associated.<br>• Key words in the test directions are highlighted or color coded.<br>• Student is allowed to restate test directions.<br>• Examiner paraphrases the directions.<br>• Examiner uses prompts.<br>• Student takes a computer presentation of test that is not typically available on a computer.<br>• Braille form of the test is used.<br>• Test directions and items are signed.<br>• Test alternates quiet and active tasks or items.<br>• Examiner states student's name before asking test questions.<br>• Examiner uses physical proximity and touch to cue the student.<br>• Examiner makes frequent checks on student's progress toward completion.<br>• Examiner breaks test into short segments.<br>• Examiner allows for frequent breaks. |
| Response mode | • Teacher or helper marks the responses as indicated by the student.<br>• Student uses pencil or pen that is adapted in size or that has a finger grip.<br>• Student gives the responses verbally rather than in writing.<br>• Student uses a speech-to-text or text-to-speech reader.<br>• Student uses assistive technology such as a switch, alternate keyboard, or visual magnification.<br>• Time limits for responding are extended or modified. | • Student is allowed to use a computer or calculator.<br>• Examiner accepts key word responses instead of complete sentences.<br>• A teacher or peer records responses for the student. |

| **...commodations**
...test but
...response,
...scheduling | **Examples of Modifications**
*(Changes made to test)* |
|---|---|
| | • Nonvisual items are substituted for students with visual impairments.
• Items that are not dependent on the hearing of specific sounds are substituted for students who are hard of hearing or deaf.
• For a writing test, student is allowed to use a spell checker or dictionary. |
| ...s per page is ...
...agnified. Student ...ses on paper ...a grid. | • Prior to the test, examiner provides the student the opportunity to do a practice test.
• Student learns test-taking skills. |

effects of accommodations and modifications on test performance is lacking, examiners should interpret tests cautiously. Table 4.1 describes frequently used accommodations and modifications.

Despite the practice of modifying tests for students with disabilities, there are several major problems to consider. Many experts believe that unless test developers norm a test using specific modifications, the test is invalid. Very few research studies demonstrate the effects of accommodations and modifications on test performance. Because of technical considerations relating to test development, it is difficult to equate the performance of students who have various accommodations or modifications with the performance of students who do not have accommodations or modifications. A test accommodation or modification may change the underlying construct of the test (American Educational Research Association, 1999). For example, a test of written language may become a test of spoken language if the student is permitted to dictate the response rather than writing it.

A concern of the reporting of test scores or test performance is whether or not to report the accommodation or modification. Some experts believe that not identifying modifications is misleading. Persons with disabilities have countered that modifying test procedures provides opportunities to demonstrate their abilities and that not modifying test procedures is unfair. Further, flagging or identifying accommodations or modifications can lead to discrimination and stigmatization (American Educational Research Association et al., 1999).

## Sensitivity to Diversity

Good practice requires that examiners use a variety of assessment tasks. Students should have opportunities to answer in other languages, to demonstrate their abilities and skills in various forms, to use materials from various cultures, and to accommodate alternative ways of responding.

## Consideration of Adverse Consequences

Some students do not perform well on assessments simply because they lack the background

*A teacher talks to students about current events.*

or experiences with certain methods of assessment. Teachers can try to ameliorate this by providing all students with instruction and practice in the assessment approaches that are used in evaluations.

Assessment developers and users must actively avoid assessment approaches, instruments, and techniques that may have adverse consequences on groups that currently are targets of discrimination or have previously been the targets of discrimination. Proper assessment assists in providing learning opportunities for students rather than in placing students in tracks or limiting educational opportunities (National Forum on Assessment, 1995).

## Preferred Practices

Test manuals provide information about reliability and validity. However, teachers, test examiners, and administrators should review tests and test manuals and satisfy themselves that each test has acceptable levels of reliability and validity. Test users must be skilled examiners as well as informed consumers of tests. Fairness in assessment means that teachers use only those assessment approaches judged to be reliable and valid. Fairness also means that bias has been minimized, that the assessment is equitable, and that the measures are sensitive to diverse populations.

## Extending Learning

1. The director of testing has asked you to evaluate the reliability and validity of a test that he is considering for purchase. What standards of reliability and validity will you use when evaluating this measure?

2. Working with a small group of other students, review a test manual. Identify the types of reliability and validity the manual reports. Explain the meaning of these two terms, using your own words.

3. Imagine that you found the following excerpt in a test manual: "The authors of the test determined that the achievement test lacks evidence of validity but has high reliability. The reliability coefficient is 1.15." What are two problems with this excerpt?

4. Yizhong, who recently moved to this country from Asia, may have a learning disability. What must the examiner consider when deciding which tests to use when assessing Yizhong?

5. A test publisher is in the process of developing a new measure of cognitive ability. What advice can you give the publisher about making sure that the instrument is fair?

6. A student who has a learning disability in mathematics is using a calculator while completing a test. How would you explain this in the test report? Would this modification affect the outcomes of the test?

## References

American Educational Research Association, American Psychological Association, and National Council on Measurement in Education (1999). *Standards for educational and psychological testing.* Washington, DC: American Educational Research Association.

DeVellis, R. F. (1991). *Scale development.* Newbury Park, CA: Sage.

Heumann, J., and K. R. Warlick (2000). Memorandum: Questions and answers about provisions in the Individuals with Disabilities Education Act amendments of 1997 related to students with disabilities and state and district-wide assessments. Office of Special Education and Rehabilitative Services, Office of Special Education Programs, August 24.

Linn, R. L., and E. L. Baker (1996). Can performance-based student assessments be psychometrically sound? In *Performance-based student assessment:* *Challenges and possibilities,* ed. J. B. Baron and D. P. Wolf, 84–103. Chicago, IL: University of Chicago Press.

Mehrens, W. A., and I. J. Lehmann (1991). *Measurement and evaluation in education and psychology.* Fort Worth, TX: Holt, Rinehart & Winston.

National Forum on Assessment (1995). *Principles and indicators for student assessment systems.* Cambridge, MA: National Center for Fair and Open Testing.

Nitko, A. J. (2001). *Educational assessment of students.* 3d ed. Upper Saddle River, NJ: Prentice-Hall.

Sattler, J. M. (2001). *Assessment of children: Cognitive applications.* Jerome M. Sattler, Publisher.

Zeller, R. A. (1988). Validity. In *Educational research, methodology, and measurement: An international handbook,* ed. J. P. Keeves, 322–330. Oxford: Pergamon Press.

# 5

## *Observation, Interview, and Conferencing Skills*

## Overview

Conducting observations, interviews, and conferences with others are valuable techniques that enhance other assessment approaches. Observations focus on the student, teacher, and environment; they often provide information not easily obtained by other means. Interviews gather information about the individual perspectives of students, parents, colleagues, and professionals. Observing and interviewing usually involve conferences and collaboration with other professionals to gather information and share results. This chapter provides information on how to plan and design observations and interviews and how to build skills in working with others.

## *Chapter Objectives*

After completing this chapter, you should be able to:

- Provide a rationale for planning and conducting observations.
- Compare and contrast the use of anecdotal records, running records, event recordings, duration recordings, intensity recordings, latency recordings, interval recordings, category recordings, rating scales, checklists, and questionnaires.

- Conduct observations.
- Describe concerns relating to reliability and validity.
- Describe the process for planning and conducting interviews.
- Apply skills in conferencing and collaborating with others.

## *What Shapes Our Views*

**Direct observation** is the systematic process of gathering information by looking at students and their environments. How independently is the student functioning? Does the student use age-appropriate skills? Does the student socialize with students without disabilities in a nonstructured setting? What factors in the classroom environment provide guidelines for appropriate behavior? Does the learning environment support the student's special needs? How does the classroom environment encourage collaboration and a feeling of well-being among students?

For students with or at risk for disability, IDEA requires observations as part of an initial assessment and as part of any reevaluation of the student. In fact, observations of the student and the environment provide valuable information during each of the steps in the assessment process: screening, prereferral, referral, determining eligibility, program planning, monitoring progress, and conducting evaluations. Observations may be conducted by special educators and general educators, as well as parents, therapists, and other related services providers.

Observations of a student provide information about achievement levels, growth, development, characteristics, social skills, and behaviors. Student observations involve looking at students and recording their behaviors, responses, characteristics, and products of their play and work. Using observations, professionals can collect information about the physical arrangement of the classroom, student groupings, teacher expectations, classroom procedures, and many other aspects of the learning and social environments.

## *General Guidelines for Planning Observations*

Planning observations involves identifying the assessment question(s), defining the event or behavior to be observed, specifying the location(s) for the observations, and deciding the method to use in recording observation data. Planning should address the accuracy of the observations as well as how to integrate the information with other assessment information. In the following section we will examine each of these areas in more detail.

### *Observation Questions*

Observations can help answer assessment questions during each of the steps of the assessment process. The observation may focus on the environment, or on one or more students. Since there are many events going on in a classroom at one time, the observer needs to focus on specific areas that will help respond to the assessment question. It is important to state the question clearly. For example, "How independently is the student functioning in the regular classroom?"

## Event or Behavior

Defining an event or behavior in observable terms helps the observer know when to record an observation. A detailed definition helps ensure that the recordings are reliable. For example, "We will define the student's independent functioning as behaviors that require only a verbal prompt."

Teachers need to collect observation information over a period of time; that is, observations should take place on several different occasions. Frequency increases reliability and, as the information is synthesized, trends become apparent.

## Location

Observations take place in the classroom, cafeteria, playground, other school settings, or in the home. Teachers and parents can usually observe students without disrupting routines. However, when an observer is not a usual part of the setting, the presence of the outsider can change aspects of the environment or of the students' behavior. Additional equipment, such as a video camera, can also adversely affect the results of the observations.

## Recording

There are many different ways of recording information: anecdotal records, running records, event recording, duration recording, intensity recording, latency of behavior, interval recording, category recording, rating scales, checklists, and questionnaires. Teachers carefully select the recording method that will be the most effective one in answering the assessment question(s), during the planning stage.

## Accuracy

Recording information takes skill and practice. Some of the important considerations include: Are your observations accurate? Are your findings consistent with what you might observe

tomorrow? Do your findings agree with others who conduct the same observation? Later in this chapter we discuss in detail methods of ensuring accuracy and consistency when using observation assessments.

## Integration

Observation data will need to be integrated with other assessment information that has been gathered. We describe a process for integrating assessment information in Chapter 18.

## Recording Methods

There are a number of different methods from which to choose in planning observations. These methods allow for collecting and recording data in various formats. The type of student behavior you will observe will influence the method you choose (Table 5.1). Let's examine the different types of recording methods and some of the advantages as well as disadvantages of these methods.

## Anecdotal Record

An **anecdotal record** is a brief narrative description of an event or events that the observer felt was important to record. Anecdotal records are recorded after the events have occurred, usually in the form of notes. The writer records the date, time, and place of the event and, as accurately as possible, describes the event as it took place, including verbal and nonverbal cues and direct quotations. The observation should be as objective as possible, describing only what the observer saw and heard. Interpretive comments should not be part of the description of the episode.

Let's consider a question that came before a student assistance team. Leo's parent had contacted the school to inquire whether the classroom teacher would observe any changes in behavior over the next two weeks. The physician planned to change Leo's level of medication and

**TABLE 5.1**   *Selecting a Method for Observation*

| Recording Format | When the Behavior Is | | | | | | |
|---|---|---|---|---|---|---|---|
| | Clear Begin/End | Frequent | Infrequent | Brief | Lengthy | Unanticipated | Sequential |
| Anecdotal recording | | | | | | × | |
| Duration recording | | | | × | × | | |
| Event recording | × | × | × | × | | | |
| Interval recording | × | × | | × | | | |
| Running record | | | | | | | × |

Adapted from Sulzer-Azaroff, B., and R. G. Mayer (1991). *Behavior analysis for lasting change.* Fort Worth, TX: Holt, Rinehart & Winston.

wanted to monitor any effects, both at home and at school. The student assistance team met to plan aspects of the observation. The team decided that the classroom teacher should complete a daily anecdotal record. Figure 5.1 is an example of the anecdotal record that Leo's classroom teacher logged.

There are several advantages to maintaining anecdotal records:

1. The method requires little special training.
2. Observers can record unanticipated events.
3. Observations record actual behavior in a natural setting.

4. The method provides a check on other types of assessment.

However, there are several disadvantages to this technique:

1. The recording of anecdotal records is dependent on the memory of the observer.
2. Bias may occur if the observer selects only certain aspects or incidents to record.
3. The technique may not completely describe specific behaviors.
4. There are difficulties associated with validating narrative recordings.

**FIGURE 5.1**   *An Anecdotal Record*

| Date: October 15 | Time Period: 1:00–1:50 |
|---|---|
| Student: Leo B. | Class activity: Science |

Leo worked in a small group with two other students for the first part of the period. The group used the classroom computer in locating information about bats for their presentation next week. Leo typed in much of the search information on the computer and worked well with the other two students. However, when they returned to their desks, he had trouble settling down. He asked to go to the bathroom twice, broke his pencil three times, and then spent the remainder of the class period with his head on the desk.

*Comment:*
L. seems to be very interested in this topic. Today was the first time he has worked for a steady 20 minutes. Is it the topic or use of computer? Or medication change?

Tomorrow I'll try having his group use other materials for searching for information.

5. The recording of the behavior can be time-consuming.
6. Records of several anecdotal observations may be difficult to summarize (Beaty, 1998; Gronlund and Linn, 1990; Sattler, 2001).

Gronlund and Linn (1990) provide the following suggestions for recording anecdotal records:

1. Before observing, decide what behaviors to observe.
2. When observing, watch out for any unusual behaviors that need recording.
3. Observe and record the complete incident. This includes any precipitating behaviors as well as behaviors that occur as a consequence of the incident.
4. As soon as possible after the observation, record the incident.
5. Record individual incidents in separate anecdotal records.
6. The anecdote should just be a record of what you observed; keep any interpretations separate from the description of the behavior.
7. Be sure to record both positive and negative behaviors.
8. Before making inferences about a student's behavior, record a number of anecdotes. It is difficult to generalize from one or two observations.
9. Training and practice in writing anecdotes are important.

## Running Record

A **running record,** sometimes called a continuous record, is a description of events written as they occur. Unlike an anecdotal record in which the observer records events sometime after they occur, a running record describes events while they are taking place. A running record provides a rich description of events and is helpful in analyzing the behavior of students. Unlike the anecdotal record, which is a selective record of events, the running record includes everything that is observed; it is a comprehensive, detailed account of events.

Let's examine an example: A special education teacher was gathering information about Sami's progress in preparation for the annual IEP meeting. One of the questions that the team was likely to raise was how Sami functioned in homeroom. The special education teacher decided to use a running record to gather information about Sami's interactions with other students during this time (Figure 5.2).

When recording information, the observer must carefully describe the events. It is much better to provide a factual, detailed account than to be judgmental. Factual accounts are less likely to be influenced by observer bias. The observer strives to write not only accurate but detailed descriptions of the observed events. Instead of simply recording, "the student moved toward the doorway," the observer can write "ran toward the doorway"; "skipped to greet the teacher"; or "moved slowly to avoid the boxes on the floor."

Beaty (1998) describes several disadvantages of running records:

1. Writing a running record can be time-consuming.
2. Recording all observable events is difficult; some details may be overlooked.
3. This technique is useful when observing individual students but is difficult when observing a group or groups of students.

One of the major disadvantages of anecdotal records and running records is that they are subject to observer bias and judgment. In addition, while they can provide rich descriptions of events, it is difficult to quantify behaviors. For these reasons, other types of recording systems have been developed.

## Event Recording

**Event recording,** or frequency recording, is a procedure in which the observer records a

**FIGURE 5.2**   *A Running Record*

| Date: **May 10** | Student: **Sami G.** |
|---|---|
| Period: **Homeroom** | Focus: **Sami's interactions with other students during free time** |

| | |
|---|---|
| 7:45  Sami enters the room with two other students. One student grabs Sami's hat and turns it around backward. Sami grins and says "haaay." | *Observer comments:* Students entering the classroom. Several students seated; about 15 students standing around. |
| 7:47  Sami wanders toward the back of the classroom and stops at JR's desk. | |
| 7:48  JR asks "How's the man?" | |
| 7:49  Sami gives him a high five. | |
| 7:50  The homeroom teacher enters and asks everyone to take their seats. | |
| 7:52  Sami heads for his desk but stops to watch Joe and Mark arm wrestle. | |
| 7:55  The teacher again asks everyone to take their seats. | About 7 of the 25 students are milling around. |
| 7:56  Sami makes his way to his desk and sits down. He looks at Jen (sitting to his left) and asks her if she watched HBO last night. | Sami is the only student not in his seat. |
| 7:59  The teacher takes attendance and asks students to indicate if they are taking hot lunch. Sami raises his hand. | |
| 8:05  Bell for first period rings. | |

behavior each time it occurs during a given period. For example, if an observation lasts for 20 minutes, the observer records each occurrence of the behavior during the 20-minute period. The observer must pay close attention to the student and precisely tally the number of times that the behavior occurs. Before beginning event recording, the observer must carefully define the behavior to be observed, including a description of the beginning of the behavior and the end of the behavior so that there is no ambiguity about whether the behavior occurred or not. Event recording is useful for behaviors that occur very frequently or very infrequently. Event recording is sometimes referred to as event sampling.

Several different procedures are effective for recording events. The simplest one is a tally. Each time the behavior occurs a line is drawn on the page and then the number of lines are totaled:

     ЦН̄     ЦН̄     ǀǀ       12

Observers use event recording frequently to answer questions about students with disabilities. For example, an IEP team wondered if accommodations to the classroom environment had helped Pedrico feel more comfortable in volunteering in class. An event recording was used to gather this information (Figure 5.3).

In monitoring another student's individualized education program, the IEP team wondered to what degree the regular classroom environment was providing opportunities for Tia to communicate with her peers. The teacher aide completed an event recording form

**FIGURE 5.3**   *An Event Recording*

| | | |
|---|---|---|
| **Date:** December 1 | | **Student:** Pedrico G. |

**Observation questions:** Does Pedrico participate in class discussions?

**Class activity:** Reading          **Behavior observed:** volunteers by raising his hand or by responding to teacher-directed questions

**Observer:** Jake Orone

| Time | Frequency | Comments |
|---|---|---|
| :00 | | Beginning of class discussion. |
| :05 | I | P. immediately raises hand and teacher calls on P. After P's comment, teacher says, "That's an interesting idea about why the author chose to open the story with a flashback. What do other people think?" |
| :10 | | P. stares out the window. Is he distracted by the noise of the dump truck outside? |
| :15 | IIII | P. raises his hand to each of the next four questions but teacher does not call on him. |
| :20 | | P. plays with pencil, doodling on paper. |

**FIGURE 5.4**   *Observations of Tia's Communication with Peers (Event Recording)*

**Student:** Tia Blackwell

**Date:** Week of September 5 to September 16

**Assessment question:** Is the general education classroom providing opportunities for Tia to communicate with her peers?

**Behavior:** Communication (verbal communication)

**Observer:** T. Morrill, personal aide

| Schedule | Time | 9/5 | 9/6 | 9/7 | 9/8 | 9/9 | 9/12 | 9/13 | 9/14 | 9/15 | 9/16 |
|---|---|---|---|---|---|---|---|---|---|---|---|
| *Homeroom | 7:30–7:45 | 0 | 0 | 0 | 1 | 1 | 0 | 2 | 0 | 1 | 0 |
| *Art/music rotation | 7:50–9:00 | 1 | 0 | 0 | 0 | 1 | 1 | 0 | 0 | 1 | 2 |
| Functional life skills | 9:10–10:20 | 3 | 0 | 1 | 2 | 1 | 0 | 1 | 3 | 2 | 0 |
| *Physical education | 10:30–11:40 | 2 | 1 | 3 | 1 | 2 | 3 | 3 | 0 | 2 | 3 |
| *Cafeteria/lunch | 11:50–12:20 | 0 | 0 | 1 | 2 | 1 | 0 | 2 | 2 | 1 | 1 |
| Vocational training | 12:30–1:50 | 2 | 0 | 1 | 2 | 3 | 1 | 1 | 3 | 2 | 2 |
| Leisure | 2:00–2:20 | 1 | 0 | 0 | 1 | 1 | 1 | 2 | 1 | 2 | 2 |
| Prepare for departure/Bus | 2:30–2:45 | 1 | 1 | 2 | 3 | 2 | 0 | 3 | 2 | 3 | 3 |

*General education settings

to document Tia's communication with peers during her daily schedule (Figure 5.4).

Sometimes teachers wish to know the rate of behavior over time. With event recording, they can calculate rate of occurrences of the behavior. This is helpful when observation times vary, when evaluating behaviors before and after an intervention, or when comparing the behaviors of various students. For example, suppose the teacher is using a teaching strategy to decrease Stacy's disruptiveness in class and wants to judge its effectiveness. Two months ago, an observer counted that Stacy engaged in shouting 30 times during a 15-minute period. To obtain a rate of occurrence we divide the number of occurrences of the behavior by the length of time observed. The calculation follows:

$$\frac{N}{T} = \text{Rate of occurrence}$$

where $\quad N$ = the number of occurrences of the behavior

$\quad\quad T$ = the length of time of the observation

$$\frac{30 \text{ occurrences}}{15 \text{ minutes}} = 2 \frac{\text{occurrences of shouting per}}{\text{minute}}$$

In a recent observation, Stacy engaged in shouting 15 times during a 10-minute observation. What is the rate of occurrence? Would you say that there has been an improvement in Stacy's behavior? See the Extending Learning section at the end of this chapter to find the answer.

Event recording has several advantages (Beaty, 1998; Sattler, 2001):

1. The behavior or event remains intact, thus facilitating analysis.
2. It is possible to monitor behaviors that occur infrequently.
3. It is possible to record changes in behavior over a period of time.

Despite the advantages, event recording also has several disadvantages (Beaty, 1998; Sattler, 2001):

1. Because the event is taken out of context, it may be difficult to analyze events that preceded the behavior.
2. Patterns of behavior may remain undetected.
3. The method cannot record behaviors that are difficult to define.
4. Reliability between observers is difficult to establish.
5. Unless the length of the observation periods across the sessions is constant, it is difficult to make generalizations.

## Duration Recording

**Duration recording** is a measure of the length of time a specific event or behavior persists. For example, in developing instructional goals, the teacher wants to know how long a tantrum lasts or how long a student works independently. Duration recording is an effective method to use when it is important to know the length of time the behavior or event lasted rather than whether it occurred.

The duration of a behavior or event can be hard to measure; because of the difficulties involved with this method, we recommend its use only when information about duration is essential. Before the observer begins duration recording, precise definitions for the beginning and ending of the behaviors must be set. For example, the definition of when independent play begins could be when the child begins to look at the object, when the child approaches the object, or when the child actually picks up the object. Once the observer has determined how to define the beginning and ending of a behavior or event, a stopwatch can time the length of the behavior.

Besides simply recording the duration of a behavior or event, teachers may wish to further analyze the data. The observer can determine the percentage of time a behavior or event occurs or calculate the average length of the behavior or event (Sattler, 2001).

An observer may want to know the percent of time that the behavior or event occurs. This is known as the **percentage duration rate**. To calculate the percentage duration rate, the observer divides the total duration of the behavior or event by the total time of the observation and multiplies this answer by 100 to obtain a percentage.

$$\frac{d}{t} \times 100$$

where    d = the total duration of the behavior or event

t = the total length of the observation period

For example, in planning Ian's program, the IEP team is interested in determining his ability to work independently. The observer, using a stopwatch, watches Ian for a 30-minute interval, and records the information (Figure 5.5). The duration recording shows that Ian worked independently during two time periods, of 8 minutes and 4 minutes for a total duration of 12 minutes.

To calculate the percent of time Ian worked independently during this time period, the numbers are inserted into the formula:

$$\frac{12}{30} \times 100 = 40\% \text{ of the observation period}$$

## Intensity Recording

**Intensity recording** is a measure of the degree of a behavior. Since the degrees are usually defined as high, medium, or low, the observer's judgment can be very subjective and unreliable. Before using an intensity recording, the teacher must specify the ways in which the various levels differentiate.

For example, Carlos' IEP team wanted to know if the teaching strategies for including students with and without disabilities were enabling him to generalize the skills to other settings. The team asked the special education teacher to observe Carlos' behavior on the playground during informal play and games. The teacher decided not to use event recording because the information needed (level of involvement) went beyond whether or not Carlos simply participated in outdoor games with students without disabilities. The teacher defined the degrees of involvement in the following ways:

**FIGURE 5.5**  *A Duration Recording*

| Date: October 12 | Class: |
|---|---|
| Student: Ian B. | Observer: |
| **Purpose:  to observe Ian working independently** | |

| Time: | Comments: |
|---|---|
| 10:00–10:08 | works independently |
| 10:08 | asks for help in reading paragraph |
| 10:15 | returns to seat |
| 10:16 | drops pencil, gets up to sharpen pencil |
| 10:20 | returns to seat |
| 10:22 | starts working |
| 10:23–10:27 | works independently |
| 10:28–10:30 | glances around room |

*High involvement:* The target student participated fully in the activity and showed great interest through interactions with other students, body language, and general overall affect.

*Medium involvement:* The target student joined the other students in the activity but showed little interest in the progression of the activity, either by lack of interactions or affect.

*Low involvement:* The target student primarily watched the other students, occasionally shouting words of encouragement or adding comments to the activity.

*No involvement:* The target student ignored the activity.

Using these descriptors, the teacher was able to complete an accurate, reliable recording.

## Latency Recording

**Latency recording** is a measure of the amount of time between a behavior or event (or request to begin the behavior) and the beginning of the prespecified or target behavior. For example, suppose we wanted to know the length of time that elapsed between the moment Darcy was encouraged to use a switch to select an activity and when she depressed the switch. Using a stopwatch, the observer can determine the amount of time that elapses between the initiation of the request and when Darcy begins the requested behavior. In a variation of latency recording, instead of recording the time it takes to begin the requested behavior, the observer records the time between the initial request and the completion of the behavior (Alessi and Kaye, 1983).

Latency recording can be difficult to measure. The observer must carefully define the stimulus behavior (the behavior that actually signals the request to initiate behavior), the beginning of the target behavior, and the end of the target behavior.

## Interval Recording

**Interval recording** is an observational method that involves the recording of specific events or behaviors during a prespecified time interval. Interval recording is effective for behaviors that are visible and occur frequently.

The period of observation is divided into equal time segments, and in each time slot the observer records the presence or absence of the behavior. Generally, the length of the time interval ranges from 5 seconds to 30 seconds. During each interval the observer records whether the behavior has occurred. The observer proceeds from one interval to the next until the end of the observation period.

An easy way to set up interval recording is to indicate time intervals on graph paper. For example, intervals of 30 seconds each can be drawn on graph paper using a ruler. If the observer will be watching for 10 minutes, there will be twenty 30-second intervals; for a 20-minute observation period, there will be forty 30-second intervals.

Generally, educators should use a combination of interval and event recording for behaviors that occur frequently. Let's examine why a teacher might select this method. The top section of Figure 5.6 illustrates an interval-event recording during fifteen one-minute time intervals to collect information about a student's disruptive behavior, defined as "poking others with a pencil, name-calling, and whistling." Here the educator recorded the number of disruptive behaviors (events) that the target student, D, and a typical student, T, displayed during each minute (interval) of the fifteen-minute observation period. The bottom section of Figure 5.6 shows the same information scored as an interval-only recording. By looking at both of these recordings one can see that interval-only scoring does not provide information about the increase in disruptive behaviors during the latter part of the observation period—only the presence of the behavior. By examining the interval-event recording, one can see a sudden increase in the behaviors after minute 9. Likewise, the interval-only rcording is not as sensitive to the difference between the two students. In minutes 7, 11, 13, and 15 both students participated in disruptive behavior but by examining the interval-event

---

**FIGURE 5.6**    *A Comparison of the Sensitivity of Event-Interval and Interval-Only Recordings*

Disruptive Behavior: Student pokes others with pencil, name calls, and whistles during instructional time.

*One-minute interval-event recording*

**One-Minute Intervals**

| Student | 1 | 2 | 3 | 4 | 5 | 6 | 7 | 8 | 9 | 10 | 11 | 12 | 13 | 14 | 15 | Total number during observation period |
|---|---|---|---|---|---|---|---|---|---|---|---|---|---|---|---|---|
| D | 0 | 0 | // | / | /// | / | / | / | // | //// | //// | /// | //// | //// | /// | 33 |
| T | 0 | 0 | 0 | 0 | 0 | 0 | / | 0 | 0 | 0 | / | 0 | / | 0 | / | 4 |

*One-minute interval-event recording*

**One-Minute Intervals**

| Student | 1 | 2 | 3 | 4 | 5 | 6 | 7 | 8 | 9 | 10 | 11 | 12 | 13 | 14 | 15 | Percent of intervals |
|---|---|---|---|---|---|---|---|---|---|---|---|---|---|---|---|---|
| D | 0 | 0 | × | × | × | × | × | × | × | × | × | × | × | × | × | 87% |
| T | 0 | 0 | 0 | 0 | 0 | 0 | × | 0 | 0 | 0 | × | 0 | × | 0 | × | 27% |

*Source:* From Cohen, Libby G., and Loraine J. Spenciner, *Assessment of Young Children.* Copyright © 1994. White Plains, NY: Longman Publishers. Reprinted/adapted by permission by Allyn & Bacon.

scoring, one can see that the target student's disruptive behavior was more frequent during each of these time intervals than the typical student.

***Establishing a Recording Interval.*** Sometimes it is difficult for the observer to continue to observe while recording. Proceeding from one interval to the next can be especially demanding when the observation interval is very brief, the behavior to be observed is complex, or the observer is recording the behaviors of a number of students. To help alleviate this problem, the observer can establish a recording interval. With this technique, the student is observed for a time interval, such as 30 seconds, and then the observer records the data during the next 30-second time interval. The observer then proceeds from one interval to the next, observing, recording, observing, and so on. This type of recording can be helpful in comparing the behavior of students like Maria, who displays hyperactive behavior, with two of her fellow students (see Figure 5.7; Snapshot).

## Category Recording

**Category recording** is a system of recording behavior in discrete groupings. Figure 5.8 shows two different observation instruments that use category recording. Category recording can be as simple as two categories (e.g., on-task and off-task) or complex enough to contain many

**FIGURE 5.7**   *Comparison of On-Task Behavior (First Five Minutes of a Twenty-Minute Recording Interval Form)*

| | :00 | :30 | 1:00 | 1:30 | 2:00 | 2:30 | 3:00 | 3:30 | 4:00 | 4:30 |
|---|---|---|---|---|---|---|---|---|---|---|
| | | | | | **One-Minute Intervals** | | | | | |
| Student | O | R | O | R | O | R | O | R | O | R |
| Anna | | × | | × | | × | | × | | |
| Maria | | | | × | | × | | | | |
| Nan | | × | | | | × | | | | × |
| | | | | | | | | | | |

O = observe
R = record

**FIGURE 5.8**   *Category Reporting*

**Student's name:  Tara**

| | | | | | | | | | | |
|---|---|---|---|---|---|---|---|---|---|---|
| | | | | | **Two-Minute Intervals** | | | | | |
| On-task | × | | | | × | × | × | × | | |
| Off-task | | × | × | × | | | | | × | × |

*Two-Category Instrument*

**Student's name:  Tara**

| | | | | | | | | | | |
|---|---|---|---|---|---|---|---|---|---|---|
| | | | | | **Thirty-Second Intervals** | | | | | |
| Uses words to express needs | × | | × | | | | × | × | | |
| Raises hand to signal teacher for help | × | | | | | | | × | | |
| Regards speaker | | × | × | × | | × | | × | | |
| Complies with requests | | | × | | | | × | | | |

*Four-Category Instrument*

## SNAPSHOT ■ *Maria*

Maria's teacher, Mr. Ramsdell, feels that she is hyperactive and is unable to attend in the classroom. He discusses his concerns with the special education teacher, who team teaches with him several mornings a week. They decide to plan and conduct several observations of Maria and two other students who were selected because Mr. Ramsdell identified them as typical students. The purpose of the observation is to provide a brief picture of Maria's behavior compared to other students in her classroom and to answer questions regarding her hyperactivity. The teachers decided that because the observation would focus on several students, a recording interval form (Figure 5.7) should be used to allow the observer time to record multiple data.

---

categories (e.g., uses words to express needs, raises hand to signal teacher for help, regards speaker, complies with requests). As with other types of observations, the behaviors must be discrete, be carefully defined, and have an observable beginning and end.

### Rating Scales

**Rating scales** can help answer questions about the learning environment or about one or more students. Environmental rating scales measure the degree to which the setting meets a certain criterion. These rating scales assist team members in problem solving around issues of a particular learning environment or of the teaching strategies currently in place. Environmental rating scales can be helpful when conducting program planning and when identifying the environment that will meet the student's needs.

Student rating scales measure the degree to which a student exhibits a prespecified behavior. These scales are useful when they are combined with other types of assessment, such as with data obtained from interval recording, event recording, and the results of other assessment approaches. Rating scales can help to evaluate the quality of the behavior of one student or many students.

While rating scales can be useful, they have been criticized as being impressionistic, lacking interrater reliability, and being affected by the subjectivity of the observer (Sattler, 2001).

Teachers can increase reliability by using rating scales with **descriptors** (Figure 5.9). Descriptors provide detailed information regarding each of the levels of the rating scale.

### Checklists

**Checklists** are similar to rating scales and are used in observing the environment or in observing one or more students. A checklist is a list of characteristics or behaviors arranged in a consistent manner that allows the evaluator to check the presence or absence of the characteristic or behavior. While rating scales help to evaluate the degree or frequency of an item or a behavior, checklists usually require a simple yes or no response.

Checklists can be used to assess behaviors as well as products of one or more students. Some checklists provide space for comments or descriptions. Checklists are fairly easy to develop. The following guidelines are helpful when developing checklists (Beaty, 1998; Gronlund and Linn, 1990):

1. Checklist items should be brief, yet detailed and easily understood.
2. Word construction must be parallel. That is, the word order, subject, and verb tense should be the same for all items.
3. The items are nonjudgmental.
4. The checklist should stress positive behavior. Emphasis is placed on what the student can do as opposed to what the student cannot do.

**FIGURE 5.9**  *An Example of Descriptors in a Rating Scale*

| Behavior | 1 | 2 | 3 | 4 |
|---|---|---|---|---|
| Student participates in small group activity. | Student regards others who are talking. | Student regards others who are talking and participates in group discussion. | Student uses materials to assist in group activity and all of #2. | Student evaluates own role in group activity and all of #3. |
| Student shows respect for personal boundaries. | At school, student keeps hands to self. | At school, student maintains personal space when speaking with others and keeps hands to self. | Student identifies behavior appropriate to the environmental setting (school, home, community) and all of #2. | Student displays behavior appropriate to the setting (school, home, community). |

5. The items should not repeat in different parts of the checklist.
6. The items should be representative of students' behavior.
7. Arrange the items in the order in which they are expected to appear.
8. Provide a procedure for indicating each behavior as it occurs (e.g., check mark, yes-no, plus or minus sign).

Checklists, like rating scales, have greater utility when they are combined with other assessment approaches. Checklists can supplement the information obtained from observations, can help to evaluate a student's behavior, and can apply to one or more students. Criticisms include a lack of interrater reliability, and a tendency to reflect the subjectivity of the rater. In addition, they miss behaviors that are not on the list and they do not provide information about the quality of the behavior (Beaty, 1998).

## Observing the Student within the Classroom Environment

Teachers assess the needs of individual students within the context of the classroom environment. How should I deal with Katya's behavioral outbursts? What can I do to help Timmy, a student with disabilities, feel a part of our classroom? How can we assist Boyanna in becoming more independent? The interaction of student learning and behavior is complex. The classroom environment can affect learning and behavior adversely, or the environment can be structured to promote positive behaviors, enhance positive conduct, and build self-esteem.

Three aspects of the classroom environment affect the student's learning and behavior: the physical environment, the learning or instructional environment, and the social environment. Rating scales and checklists are the most common ways of gathering information about the classroom environment. In the following sections, we examine both teacher-constructed tools and commercial instruments for observing these three aspects of the classroom environment.

### Physical Environment

The physical environment consists of seating arrangements, lighting, noise level, distractions, temperature, overall atmosphere, and general layout of the classroom. Some of the areas to consider in planning an observation of the physical environment include:

1. *Seating*
   - positioning

     Do the height and size of the chair give the student proper support?

     Are the student's feet supported (either resting flat on the floor or supported by a footrest)?

     Is the student seated in close proximity to other students?

     Does the student's position allow full view of the board, teacher, and other students?

     Does the student's position readily allow communication with the teacher and other students?

2. *Lighting*
   - lighting intensity

     Is the degree of lighting appropriate?

     Is the board or screen free from glare that might make reading difficult?
   - type of lighting

     Is fluorescent lighting used?

     Is natural light available?

3. *Noise*
   - minimum noise level

     Is the noise level of student work groups appropriate?

4. *Distractions*
   - sight

     Does the room have displays that are visually distracting?
   - sound

     Is there noise distraction (such as a clock ticking or a radiator pinging)?
   - events and activities

     Are there activities in the room that are distracting to the student?

5. *Climate*
   - temperature

     Is the temperature level of the classroom comfortable?

6. *Classroom*
   - atmosphere

     Is the classroom atmosphere warm and accepting?

     Does the student appear to be comfortable?

7. *General layout*
   - layout of the room and type and placement of furniture, equipment, and materials

     Are all areas of the classroom accessible to the student?

     Are classroom materials accessible to the student?
   - amount and type of space

     Is there enough space to meet the student's needs?

     Is there an accessible place to store adapted materials and equipment?

     Can the student easily move between areas of the room?

The amount and arrangement of physical space affects student functioning. For example, grouping desks in sets of three or four encourages students to discuss and share ideas. The placement of furniture, equipment, and materials is critical for students with disabilities. Furniture and adaptive equipment need to maximize the student's potential for independent participation. The availability of accessible space allows a student with a physical disability full classroom access. Differences in texture or color of carpet between centers enable a student who is blind or has multiple disabilities to increase orientation and independent travel (mobility) skills. An organized environment helps all students learn appropriate storage of materials. Accessible storage of materials assists students with disabilities in locating and using materials independently.

Figure 5.10 illustrates a teacher-made checklist for observing the physical environment. Information about the physical layout of this kindergarten classroom proved very helpful. The drawing helped the teaching team to think about the classroom layout and how they might improve learning opportunities. The teachers decided to try moving the science and mathematics center closer to the block area to allow children to use the blocks in various mathematics and science activities. The teachers also discussed how the location of adjacent areas contributed to difficulties that they had experienced during circle

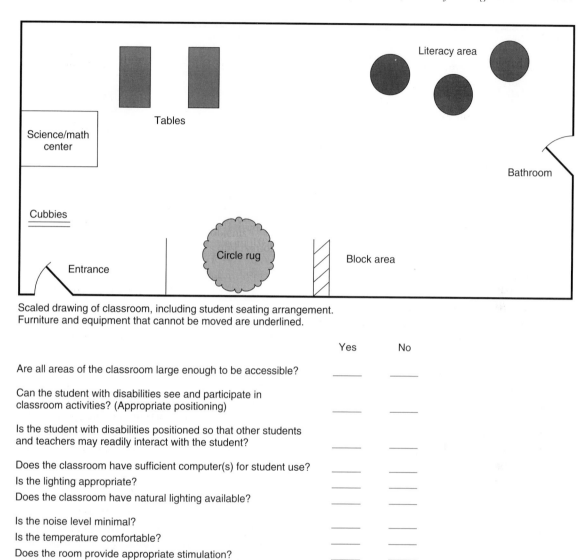

Scaled drawing of classroom, including student seating arrangement.
Furniture and equipment that cannot be moved are underlined.

|  | Yes | No |
|---|---|---|
| Are all areas of the classroom large enough to be accessible? | ____ | ____ |
| Can the student with disabilities see and participate in classroom activities? (Appropriate positioning) | ____ | ____ |
| Is the student with disabilities positioned so that other students and teachers may readily interact with the student? | ____ | ____ |
| Does the classroom have sufficient computer(s) for student use? | ____ | ____ |
| Is the lighting appropriate? | ____ | ____ |
| Does the classroom have natural lighting available? | ____ | ____ |
| Is the noise level minimal? | ____ | ____ |
| Is the temperature comfortable? | ____ | ____ |
| Does the room provide appropriate stimulation? (Neither over- nor understimulation) | ____ | ____ |
| Does the classroom have a minimum of interruptions? | ____ | ____ |

**FIGURE 5.10   *Kindergarten Teacher–Made Drawing and Checklist for Observing the Physical Environment***

time. They decided to move the circle area away from the block center, which was distracting to two students. They changed the center of the room to accommodate space for circle activities and added individual carpet squares to the area to help children understand individual space and reduce the likelihood of disruptive behavior. Figure 5.11 represents the rearranged environment.

An environmental rating scale is helpful to teachers in that it identifies the important components in a quality program. The rating scale provides a structured way of recording obser-

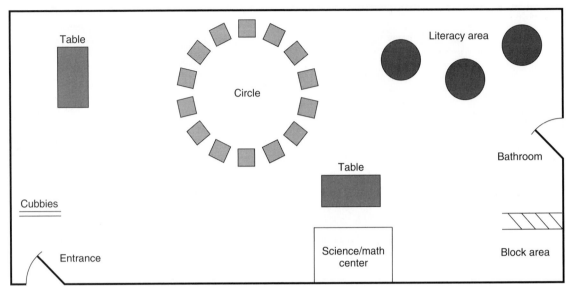

Scaled drawing of classroom, including student seating arrangement.
Furniture and equipment that cannot be moved are underlined.

**FIGURE 5.11**    *Rearranged Physical Environment*

vations by organizing items in specific categories. While a checklist can indicate whether or not an item is present, a rating scale provides a judgment on the degree of an item. Teachers may use rating scales to identify the areas of strength in the classroom as well as the areas that need improvement.

***Commercial Rating Scales.***    Commercial rating scales provide teachers with an identified list of items by which to measure the environment. Usually these scales are standardized, and include a manual that describes information concerning their reliability and validity. The following section looks at one example of a commercial environmental rating scale for preschool and developmental early education programs in public school.

***Early Childhood Environment Rating Scale–Revised Edition (ECERS–R).***    The *Early Childhood Environment Rating Scale–Revised Edition (ECERS–R)* (Harms, Clifford, and Cryer,

1998) is effective for use in a variety of settings, including Head Start programs, parent cooperative preschools, private preschools, playgroups, and pre-K and kindergarten programs. The *ECERS–R* consists of seven subscales: Space and Furnishings, Personal Care Routines, Language-Reasoning, Activities, Interaction, Program Structure, and Parents and Staff. The purpose of the scale is to examine the current environmental quality a center or school provides and to offer a background for planning improvements. Box 5.1 lists indications for use of this scale.

*Administration.*    Administering this scale calls for a trained observer. Each of the 43 items is rated according to a 7-point **Likert scale.** On Likert scales, the lowest rating (generally 1) indicates, for example, that the item never occurs, and the highest rating (in this case, 5) indicates that the item always occurs. A small amount of space after each item allows the observer to record additional information.

**BOX 5.1** *Early Childhood Environment Rating Scale– Revised Edition*

*Publication Date:* 1998

*Purposes:* Useful in assessing early childhood program environments

*Age/Grade Levels:* Most appropriate for preschool programs; some aspects may be helpful to primary grades.

*Time to Administer:* Need to observe greeting and departure activities; 10 to 15 minutes for other information.

*Technical Adequacy:* Adequate for first edition. The revised edition needs additional studies to determine technical adequacy.

*Suggested Use:* Valuable tool to assist teachers in designing a classroom environment that supports children's development.

*Scores.* Each item includes descriptors associated with each of the numeric ratings. Examiners then tally item ratings for a subtotal of each category. This instrument includes a profile sheet on which to record each category subtotal. The profile allows the user to quickly identify areas, or subcategories, of strength and weakness, as seen in Figure 5.12.

*Standardization.* Teachers field-tested the first edition of the *ECERS* in 25 classrooms in 17 child care centers in St. Louis. The *ECERS–R* manual does not include any information about further standardization nor does it include any details concerning the classrooms that participated in the original standardization.

*Reliability and Validity.* The manual reports three measures of reliability: interrater reliability by item, interrater reliability by classroom, and internal consistency. Internal consistency data provide support for the subscales as separate

constructs. Additional reliability and validity studies are necessary before determining the technical adequacy of the revised edition.

*Summary.* The *Early Childhood Environment Rating Scale–Revised Edition* is applicable to a variety of programs that serve young children through age 6. The information provided in describing each of the items is very helpful for several steps of the assessment process, including planning and evaluating the program. This scale is also useful in understanding the quality of the physical environment. Given the philosophical differences among early childhood programs, the potential user should examine this scale to ensure that it will be valid for a given program.

## Learning Environment

What are the expectations of the classroom? How can the classroom be adapted to accommodate the student's learning needs? The learning or instructional environment consists of the teaching strategies that the teacher uses and the materials that are available for student use. Observing the learning environment involves examining the instructional materials as well as the methods of instruction. Some of the areas to consider in planning an observation of the learning environment include:

1. *Materials*
   - variety
     Do students have access to a variety of materials?
   - format
     Is the format of the materials appropriate?
2. *Manipulatives*
   - availability and appropriateness
     Are manipulatives available?
     Are manipulatives appropriate?
3. *Learning Activities*
   - instructional methods
     Does the teacher use a variety of instructional methods?

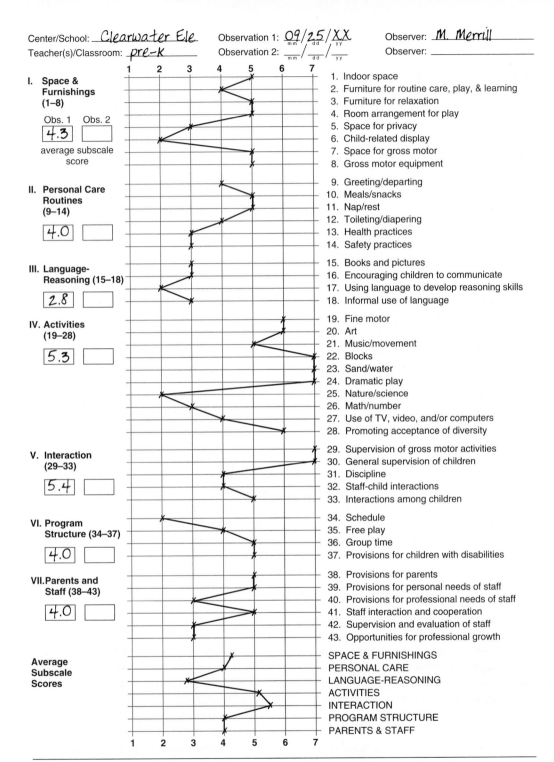

Center/School: _Clearwater Ele_    Observation 1: _09_/_25_/_XX_    Observer: _M. Merrill_
                                              mm   dd   yy
Teacher(s)/Classroom: _pre-k_    Observation 2: ___/___/___    Observer: _____
                                               mm   dd   yy

I. Space & Furnishings (1–8)

Obs. 1    Obs. 2
[4.3]     [   ]

average subscale score

1. Indoor space
2. Furniture for routine care, play, & learning
3. Furniture for relaxation
4. Room arrangement for play
5. Space for privacy
6. Child-related display
7. Space for gross motor
8. Gross motor equipment

II. Personal Care Routines (9–14)

[4.0]     [   ]

9. Greeting/departing
10. Meals/snacks
11. Nap/rest
12. Toileting/diapering
13. Health practices
14. Safety practices

III. Language-Reasoning (15–18)

[2.8]     [   ]

15. Books and pictures
16. Encouraging children to communicate
17. Using language to develop reasoning skills
18. Informal use of language

IV. Activities (19–28)

[5.3]     [   ]

19. Fine motor
20. Art
21. Music/movement
22. Blocks
23. Sand/water
24. Dramatic play
25. Nature/science
26. Math/number
27. Use of TV, video, and/or computers
28. Promoting acceptance of diversity

V. Interaction (29–33)

[5.4]     [   ]

29. Supervision of gross motor activities
30. General supervision of children
31. Discipline
32. Staff-child interactions
33. Interactions among children

VI. Program Structure (34–37)

[4.0]     [   ]

34. Schedule
35. Free play
36. Group time
37. Provisions for children with disabilities

VII. Parents and Staff (38–43)

[4.0]     [   ]

38. Provisions for parents
39. Provisions for personal needs of staff
40. Provisions for professional needs of staff
41. Staff interaction and cooperation
42. Supervision and evaluation of staff
43. Opportunities for professional growth

Average Subscale Scores

SPACE & FURNISHINGS
PERSONAL CARE
LANGUAGE-REASONING
ACTIVITIES
INTERACTION
PROGRAM STRUCTURE
PARENTS & STAFF

**FIGURE 5.12**  *Early Childhood Environmental Rating Scale–Revised Summary Profile*

*Source: Early Childhood Environment Rating Scale, Revised Edition* by Thelma Harms, Richard M. Clifford, and Debby Cryer. Reprinted by permission of the publisher. (New York: Teachers College Press © 1998 by Thelma Harms, Richard M. Clifford, and Debby Cryer. All rights reserved.), p. 59.

- opportunities to make choices
  Does the classroom teacher provide students opportunities to make choices during learning activities?
- opportunities to share ideas
  Are student comments and questions respected and encouraged?

4. *Instructional Demands*
   - clear instructions for completing the assignments
     Does the teacher provide clear instructions and check for student understanding before students begin learning activities and assignments?
   - assignments that are appropriate in difficulty and in length
     Are students assigned work that is appropriate in difficulty and length?
   - learning activities and assignments that are relevant to the students
     Do students perceive that the work is useful?
     Can students use a variety of materials?

5. *Modifications*
   - changes in furniture, equipment, or materials
     Is there easy and convenient access to furniture and equipment?
     Can students use the materials or is there a need for accommodations or modifications?

6. *Grouping*
   - grouping of students
     Do students complete some work independently?
     Can students work with a peer?
     Do students have opportunities to work cooperatively with others?

7. *Instruction*
   - adjustments
     Are the instructional strategies appropriate or is there a need for revision?
     Is there a variety of instructional methods in use?
   - pace of instruction
     Is the pace of instructional delivery appropriate?

- adequate levels of assistance
  Does the teacher (or teaching assistant) provide prompts and other types of assistance on an as-needed basis to students?
  Is assistance faded as soon as possible?

8. *Expectations*
   - demands placed on students
     Are the teacher's expectations appropriate?

9. *Student Involvement*
   - teacher support
     Does the teacher encourage student involvement?
     Is the student actively involved in learning activities?
     Does the student participate in classroom discussions?
   - peer support
     Do other students interact with the student?
     Does the student interact with other students?

10. *Assessment*
    - tools
      Does the teacher use a variety of assessment approaches in assessing student instructional needs and progress?
    - format
      If appropriate, does the teacher implement alternative formats?
    - feedback
      Does the teacher give students feedback and suggestions for improvement?

11. *Curriculum*
    - curriculum reform and standards
      Does the curriculum reflect recent reform, standards, and contemporary views?

12. *Schedule*
    - predictability of the daily schedule
      Does the classroom teacher follow a regular schedule?
      Is the schedule posted for students to see?
      Is there a minimum of interruptions?

13. *Transitions*
   - preparation and follow-through
     Does the teacher prepare students for the transition from one activity to another?
     Does the teacher provide time for students to transition?

Teacher expectations, teaching methods, and student requirements may be very different from one classroom to the next. These differences vary from the materials and equipment that are available to assist students in their work, to teaching methods that may require different skills from the students.

The classroom examples in the Snapshots of Stoney Brook Elementary and Lincoln High illustrate the variety of teaching methods, materials, and demands that students may encounter in the same grade. Students with disabilities at Stoney Brook or Lincoln High may experience difficulties in one or more of these classrooms.

### The Instructional Environment System–II (TIES–II).

*The Instructional Environment System–II (TIES–II)* (Ysseldyke and Christenson, 1993) is a comprehensive tool for assessing the environment and provides information that assists teachers in designing classroom interventions to promote positive behavior and achievement, whether or not a student is receiving special education services. Box 5.2 describes the parameters of this assessment tool.

*TIES–II* consists of 12 components that involve not only the physical environment but the learning and social environments as well. These components are:

- instructional match
- teacher expectations
- classroom environment
- instructional presentation
- cognitive emphasis
- motivational strategies
- relevant practice
- informed feedback
- academic engaged time
- adaptive instruction
- progress evaluation
- student understanding

*Administration.* TIES–II involves the gathering of information from five sources: a structured classroom observation, a student interview, a classroom teacher interview, a parent interview in order to understand the student's support for instructional needs in the home, and an instructional needs checklist. *TIES–II* includes an inter-

---

**SNAPSHOT ■ *Stoney Brook Elementary Learning Environments***

Stoney Brook Elementary School has three fourth-grade classrooms. The school district has adopted the state curriculum framework for English language arts and, among other areas, all fourth graders must demonstrate competency in researching and writing a paper about a topic of their interest. The fourth-grade teachers approach the teaching of skills in researching information in different ways. In one classroom, the teacher invites an author to come in and talk with students. The author shares resource materials and shows how his or her information was researched. The author's enthusiasm for writing sparks the children's interest. In a second classroom, the teacher makes arrangements to take the students to the library, where the school librarian gives them a tour of the library's resources and discusses ways to find information in the on-line catalogue. Later, the children will be divided into small work groups and return to the library to use the materials. In the third classroom, the children already use the computer daily to search and download information from the Internet. Their teacher will encourage them to use their skills independently in locating information for their individual papers.

## SNAPSHOT ▪ *Lincoln High Learning Environments*

The English teachers at Lincoln High use the state curriculum framework for secondary English language arts and approach student learning in different ways, use a variety of teaching strategies in the classroom, and hold different expectations for student achievement. Let's visit two classrooms to see what students experience.

In the first classroom, the teacher plans learning activities around projects that last from a few weeks to several months. There are computers available for student writing and editing, including word processing programs with word prediction features. The teacher encourages students to work together in small groups and plans conference meetings with individual students several times a week to monitor student progress.

Next door, the teacher relies primarily on the textbook to provide the curriculum content. Students complete daily assignments from textbook readings. Each class begins with a lecture that reviews the previous reading and provides some supplemental information. The teacher requires students to take notes. The teacher assesses student learning by short-answer tests that cover the textbook and classroom lectures.

vention planning form to assist team members in developing intervention strategies that include both classroom and home support.

*Scores.* After completing a classroom observation and student and teacher interviews, the examiner synthesizes the information and rates the extent to which each of the 12 components is present in the student's instructional environment. The results influence decisions regarding intervention recommendations. The manual offers suggestions for improving instructional environments that have received low scores. Figure 5.13 illustrates a section of the classroom observation form.

*Standardization.* TIES–II is a structured system that gathers qualitative information. It is not a norm-referenced instrument.

*Reliability and Validity.* The manual reports limited information regarding reliability and validity studies. Both interrater reliability and content validity are adequate.

*Summary.* TIES–II consists of 12 instructional environment components and this information can be very useful to teachers in planning classroom interventions and in improving classroom teaching strategies. Sharing and discussing the home support for learning components with parents could assist in supporting student learning at home. Because this tool requires several sources of information for use, the examiner must be skilled in synthesizing information.

---

| **BOX 5.2** | *Instructional Environment System–II (TIES–II)* |

*Publication Date:* 1993

*Purposes:* Used to assess various aspects of the classroom environment and to identify interventions that may help individual students.

*Age/Grade Levels:* K–12. Some areas may not be appropriate in preschool or primary settings.

*Time to Administer:* Not stated.

*Technical Adequacy:* Interrater reliability and content validity are adequate.

*Suggested Use:* A valuable instrument for collecting information about the physical, learning, and social environments in order to plan interventions for students who are having difficulties in being successful.

**FIGURE 5.13    TIES–II** *Observation Record*

| Observation Record | Page 2 |
|---|---|

**Instructional Planning**
- Instructional Match
- Teacher Expectations

How are the student's performance and behavior affected by instructional planning?

_____
_____
_____
_____
_____

**Instructional Management**
- Classroom Environment

How are the student's performance and behavior affected by instructional management?

_____
_____
_____
_____
_____

**Instructional Delivery**
- Instructional Presentation
- Cognitive Emphasis
- Motivational Strategies
- Relevant Practice
- Informed Feedback

How are the student's performance and behavior affected by instructional delivery?

_____
_____
_____
_____
_____

**Instructional Monitoring and Evaluation**
- Academic Engaged Time
- Adaptive Instruction
- Progress Evaluation
- Student Understanding

How are the student's performance and behavior affected by instructional monitoring and evaluation?

_____
_____
_____
_____
_____

*Source:* Reprinted with permission, Sopris West Educational Services, *TIES–II* Ysseldyke. Copyright 1993–1996.

## Questionnaires

**Questionnaires** consist of a set of questions designed to gather information. Educators and other professionals design questionnaires to collect various types of information and to assist in answering questions. For example, school personnel may develop and distribute a ques-tionnaire to parents to determine the level of support and interest in a new swimming pool, or a group of concerned educators may develop a questionnaire to determine the need for after-school care in the community.

In this section, we focus on questionnaires developed for the purpose of gathering infor-mation about the student. For example, a special education teacher who is working with a student with problem behaviors might ask the general education teacher, parents, and others who know the student well to complete a questionnaire about the student's behavior at school, at home, and in the community.

Another special educator, who is working with a student with learning disabilities, wants to improve the learning environment. The teacher wonders, "How does this student learn best? What are the most effective ways we can structure the learning environment?" The teacher designs the set of questions in Figure 5.14, to be completed by the student. Do you think the questionnaire would provide helpful information to you, if you were the teacher?

## Social Environment

The social environment consists of the general classroom atmosphere as well as the relationships among students and between students and teachers. The overall atmosphere or classroom climate is important for student success. Some of the areas to consider when planning an observation of the social environment include:

1. *Teacher-student interactions*
   - respect for oneself and others
     Are all students valued for themselves? Does the teacher expect students to respect others?
   - supportive social environment
     Are interactions warm and friendly?

---

**FIGURE 5.14**   *Student Questionnaire*

### Student Questionnaire

Name _____    Date _____

Teacher _____    Grade _____

Your teacher is planning a learning activity for _____ (teacher or student can fill in the subject).

1. What kind of task would you like it to be? What should the teacher give you to do?

2. Would you like to work on this task alone or would you like help? If you would like help, whom would you like to help you?

3. If it were up to you, how would you show the teacher what you had learned?

4. If your parent or other relative were coming to school to see your work, what work would you show them?

5. What work would you probably not show them?

*Source:* Adapted from S. L. McNeely (1997). *Observing Students and Teachers through Objective Strategies.* Boston: Allyn & Bacon.

- interactions
  Does the teacher know how to communicate with students with disabilities?
  Does the teacher encourage students to interact appropriately with the teacher?
2. *Behavioral interventions*
  - positive behavioral supports
    Does the teacher use positive teaching strategies in helping students learn appropriate behavioral expectations?
- behavior management
  Are behavior management strategies effective?
  Are expectations of behavior posted?
3. *Peer interactions*
  - student-to-student interactions
    Do students know how to communicate with students with disabilities?
    Do students interact appropriately with each other?

**FIGURE 5.15** *Teacher-Designed Checklist for Observing Classroom Learning and Social Environments*

| Classroom | Check | Suggestions |
|---|---|---|
| Are interactions between students free from bullying? | | |
| Does the teacher communicate positively with each student on a regular basis? | | |
| Does the teacher encourage student attempts? | | |
| Does the teacher provide opportunities for making choices? | | |
| Does the teacher require students to take notes? | | |
| Does the teacher expect students to work independently? | | |
| Is the student required to respond to information orally? | | |
| Is the student required to respond to information in writing? | | |
| Is the student required to memorize material? | | |

Are students courteous, respectful, and supportive of learning?
4. *General atmosphere*
   • positive classroom climate
   Does the teacher have high expectations for all students?
   Is there an atmosphere of enthusiasm and support for students?
   Does the student appear to be comfortable in the social environment?
   • distractions
   Are distractions kept to a minimum?

Figure 5.15 illustrates a teacher-developed checklist to assist in observing the learning and social environments of the regular classroom.

## *Observing the Student: Responding to Diversity*

Does Jesse communicate with peers? Does Andre socialize with others? How prevalent is Ennio's behavior? Conducting observations of a student is one of the best methods for obtaining specific information regarding that student's behavior. Observers use a variety of recording methods in collecting information about assessment questions (Table 5.2).

For the observer who is sensitive and responsive to diversity, these observations create a picture of the uniqueness of the student. Some of the areas to consider in planning an observation include:

1. *Work habits*
   • time
   How long does it take the student to get started?
   How long is the student able to stay on task?
   • levels of assistance needed
   What can the student do independently?
   How frequently does the student need prompting?
   What types of prompts are helpful (physical, verbal, gestural)?

**TABLE 5.2** *Questions and Methods of Observation*

| Assessment Question | Recording Methods |
| --- | --- |
| How independently is the student functioning? | Anecdotal record<br>Latency recording<br>Category recording<br>Rating scale<br>Checklist |
| How does the student communicate with peers? | Anecdotal record<br>Running record<br>Duration recording<br>Rating scale<br>Checklist |
| Does the student socialize with students without disabilities in a nonstructured setting? | Running record<br>Event recording<br>Interval recording<br>Category recording |

   • reinforcements used
   What types of reinforcement are effective?
   How does the student react to the reinforcement?
2. *Interactions with others*
   • other students
   Does the student have a variety of ways to communicate?
   Do other students communicate with the student?
   Does the student socialize with other students?
   • teacher
   Does the student have a variety of ways to communicate?
   Can the teacher communicate with the student?
   Is the student given opportunities to demonstrate competence?
3. *Facial expression and affect*
   • eye contact
   Does the student make eye contact with others?

- affect
  Does the student have appropriate affect?
4. *Body movements*
   - independent skills
     Does the student have independent mobility skills?
   - quality of movement
     Is the quality of gross and fine motor responses adequate (not jerky)?
5. *Adaptive skills*
   - independent skills
     Can the student eat independently?
   - appropriate skills
     Does the student use appropriate grooming skills?
     Does the student dress in an age-appropriate manner?
6. *Participation in play and games*
   - level of participation
     Does the student participate in unorganized play (free time, recess)?
     Does the student understand the rules of the game?
     Does the student play cooperatively?

## Steps in Planning and Conducting Student Observations

Conducting observations is more than just watching the student and writing down impressions of what you have seen. An observation is a systematic procedure that involves informed attention and focused recording of what you witness. The observer must complete several steps in planning and conducting observations.

1. Identify the purpose of the observations. What information is needed?

   Rebecca is a 17-year-old student who attends the Life Skills Program at Central High School. Two of her IEP goals focus on increasing independent functioning and increasing prosocial behavior skills. The purpose of the observation is to collect information regarding the IEP goals in preparation for the annual review.

2. Define the behavior in terms that are observable and measurable. The observer wrote:

   Independent functioning is defined as an ability to complete a task without prompting.

   The second goal of increasing prosocial skills was discussed in more detail by the IEP Team. One of the impediments to prosocial skills has been Rebecca's angry outbursts. A special education teacher was asked to note Rebecca's angry outbursts during the lunch period and in homeroom. What is meant by "angry outbursts"? In planning the observation, the behavior must be defined. Angry behavior could be defined by physical and/or verbal aggression. Sometimes anger is not expressed. An individual may suppress angry feelings or show them in unexpected ways. The special educator asked the general education teacher to give some examples of Rebecca's angry outbursts, and subsequently, they developed this definition: "screeching and screaming and hitting others." They decided that the observation should include both the verbal outbursts (screeching and screaming) as well as the physical contacts (hitting others). They wrote:

   Rebecca's behavior to be observed includes verbal outbursts (screeching and screaming) as well as the physical contacts (hitting others).

3. Identify where the observations will occur. Observations of the student may take place in any number of settings, depending on the assessment question:

   - in the classroom
   - in the resource room
   - in the cafeteria
   - on the playground
   - in the community
   - at home

   The teachers decided that the observations of Rebecca will be conducted in the classroom and in the cafeteria.

The details of the observations can include:

- the physical setup of the cafeteria line
- the arrangement of tables
- the types of assistance from other students
- the types of assistance from teachers or cafeteria monitors
- the methods Rebecca uses to approach other students
- the initiations of other students talking to Rebecca

A direct observation such as this example may focus on the target student or on the target student interacting with other students. Several observations are necessary to ensure consistency or reliability of results.

4. Plan how the behavior will be recorded. Different methods of recording behavior are used, depending on the assessment question (Table 5.2).

5. Integrate the results with other information about the student. After completing an observation, obtain feedback from the classroom teacher. You will need to know if the class time that you observed was typical or not. If there is no opportunity to talk, you may leave a brief form with the teacher that requests the following information: How typical was today's class? In what ways was it different?

## Sources of Error in Recording Observations

Three types of errors affect the accuracy of observations: (1) errors of omission, (2) errors of commission, and (3) errors of transmission. Familiarity with these sources of error will help reduce the possibility of their occurrence.

### Errors of Omission

To leave out information that is helpful or important to understanding a student's behavior is an error of omission. Adding comments that provide a more complete picture of the observation is helpful in preventing errors of omission. Consider the Snapshot of Jon.

The teacher could record this observation in terms of the number of minutes that Jon was in the cafeteria before he began the self-abusive behavior (that is, latency recording), or the teacher could record the magnitude or degree of the behavior (intensity recording). However, these recordings would be incomplete. One important event has been omitted; namely, what happened when the student joined Jon. The question remains, "Did he affect Jon's behavior?"

Missing part of the sequence of events, even by a temporary distraction, jeopardizes the accuracy of an observation. In this case, the student who joined Jon may have sat too close or acted in a way that disturbed Jon. Perhaps Jon's abusive behavior was a communication

**SNAPSHOT** ■ *Observations of Jon*

Jon is a 10-year-old student with autism. He has a number of self-abusive behaviors, including biting his wrists and banging his head. His teacher, concerned that the incidence of these behaviors is increasing, decided to conduct a series of classroom observations. The first observation was conducted during lunch in the cafeteria. Jon was observed as he entered the cafeteria and chose a seat at one of the tables. Another student sat down beside him at the table. Jon quickly opened his lunch box and began eating while the observer was momentarily distracted when two students briefly obstructed the view. Jon began to slap his head with his hand, and the behavior escalated until the teacher assistant noticed the self-abuse and went over to speak to Jon.

attempt in response to the other student. Errors of omission can result from simply missing behaviors that occur.

### Errors of Commission

Including information that did not actually occur is an error of commission. Errors of commission frequently occur when the observer is not able to take complete notes during the observation but must rely on memory to record the information at a later time.

### Errors of Transmission

An error of transmission occurs when observers record behaviors in an improper sequence. Since many behaviors relate to each other and the order in which they occur is important, make precautions to guard against this type of error. Recording the time at which you observe a particular behavior or recording the number of times that a particular behavior begins or ends can reduce errors of transmission.

## Reliability of Direct Observations

Reliability is an important concern when discussing direct observations. Reliability is the consistency or stability of the observations. When conducting direct observations, determining interobserver reliability is very important. Repp, Neiminen, Olinger, and Brusca (1988) discuss several factors that affect the accuracy of observers. These include reactivity, observer drift, reliability checks, observer expectancy, the characteristics of the student, and the setting.

### Reactivity

Reactivity refers to the changes that individuals make in behaviors during an observation. Teachers may alter their instructions, give additional prompts, or increase the amount of feedback when someone is observing them. Students

may improve behavior because of the "visitor," or they put on a good "show." These changes in behavior are threats to the accuracy of an observation. The use of videotapes and audiotapes also increases reactivity.

### Observer Drift

Observer drift occurs when the observer shifts away from the original objectives of the observation. Usually, the observer is not aware of this alteration. To prevent this phenomenon from occurring, the observer needs to periodically check the established purposes and criteria for conducting the observation.

### Reliability Checks

The conduct of reliability checks can also affect the accuracy of observations. If an observer is aware that the accuracy of an observation is being monitored, the observer may change the usual methods of conducting the observation. Reliability of observations tends to increase when an observer is aware that someone is checking the observations.

### Predetermined Expectations

Bias can occur if the observer has a predetermined expectation about the observation. For example, if an observer knows that the target student has been referred for aggressive behavior, expectations of this behavior may influence the observation.

### Student and Setting Characteristics

Certain characteristics of the student and the setting can influence the accuracy of an observation. The gender of the student, the complexity of the behaviors under observation, the predictability of the student's behaviors, and the observer's familiarity with the setting can all affect accuracy.

Thus, reactivity, observer drift, reliability checks, observer expectancy, and the characteristics of the student and the setting can all affect the accuracy of observations. To minimize these threats, Repp et al. (1988) recommend that:

1. Observers be well trained.
2. Observers use uncomplicated codes to record observations.
3. Both male and female observers conduct observations.
4. Observers avoid interaction with one another during the observation.
5. Observers check the accuracy of observations against a criterion.
6. Both observers and students have a period of time in which they can adapt to each other.
7. Observers conduct observations as unobtrusively as possible.
8. Teachers and other professionals conduct observations frequently and systematically.

## Calculating Interobserver Reliability

There are several ways of determining reliability of observations (Alessi and Kaye, 1983; Frick and Semmel, 1978). To calculate reliability it is important that (1) observers collect all data independently, (2) at least two observers conduct observations, and (3) the observers look at the same phenomenon. If it is not possible for two observers to be present at the same time, a videotape or audiotape can be used for the second observer (Alessi and Kaye, 1983).

### Event Recording

One way of determining interobserver reliability for event recording is to determine the percentage of agreements between the observers (Alessi and Kaye, 1983). The following formula can be used:

$$r = \frac{a}{a+d} \times 100$$

The number of times that the observers agreed with each other (a) is divided by the total number of times that the observers agreed (a) and disagreed (d) with each other. This number is then multiplied by 100 to give the percentage of agreements between the observers. For example, suppose two observers were using event recording to observe the number of times a student interrupted other students. The observers agreed 10 times and disagreed 4 times. Using the formula:

$$r = \frac{10}{10+4} \times 100$$

$$r = \frac{10}{14} \times 100$$

$$r = 71\%$$

Thus, the percentage of agreement between the observers in this example is 71 percent.

### Duration Recording

Computing interobserver reliability for duration recording is similar to calculating interobserver reliability for event recording. The formula for duration recording is:

$$\% A_{dr} = \frac{t_1}{t_2} \times 100$$

where $\% A_{dr}$ = percentage agreement for duration recording

$t_1$ = time recorded by the observer with the smaller time duration

$t_2$ = time recorded by the observer with the larger time duration

For example, suppose two observers are recording the length of time a child plays independently. One observer records 180 seconds; the other observer records 190 seconds. Using the formula:

$$\% A_{dr} = \frac{180}{190} \times 100$$

$$\% A_{dr} = 95\%$$

In this example, there is 95 percent agreement between the observers.

## Rating Recording

When computing agreement between two raters or observers, the following formula can be used (Sattler, 2001):

$$\% A_r = \frac{A_r}{A_r + D} \times 100$$

where   $\% A_r$ = percentage agreement for rating recording

   $A_r$ = number of items for which observers agreed on the rating

   $D$ = number of items for which observers disagreed on the rating

For example, suppose two observers, using a 15-item rating scale, agree on the ratings for 12 of the 15 items. Using the formula, we have:

$$\% A_r = \frac{12}{12 + 3} \times 100$$

$$\% A_r = 80\%$$

In this example, there is 80 percent agreement between the two observers.

## Validity of Direct Observations

The validity of observational measures is a very important concern. Validity is the extent to which an instrument measures what it is intended to measure. Validity standards depend on the observability of behaviors, the objectivity of the instrument, observer variability, and the representativeness by instrument items of the behaviors that are observed (Herbert and Attridge, 1975). While there is some evidence of validity for some observational instruments, the validity of many instruments is either unsubstantiated or questionable.

Hoge (1985), who makes several recommendations for assuring validity, advises that observers use existing instruments when possible. Using existing instruments has several advantages: (1) time and effort are saved; (2) reliability and validity information are often available; and (3) information about the use of these instruments can lead to the development of sounder measures. Hoge cautions observers to take care that the instruments are reliable. Finally, he believes that instruments that broadly define behavior (e.g., on-task, off-task) are more likely to be valid than instruments that categorize behaviors into numerous subskills and categories. Remember that although it may be more difficult to determine the validity of observational measures, validity is a very important area of concern.

## Developing Informal Norms

Developing informal norms will help observers to evaluate the behavior they observe. The behavior of one or more students in the group can serve as the norm or comparison group for the student who is to be observed. In this instance, the other students in the group are known as the norm group, and the student who is to be observed is referred to as the target student. Without informal norms, it is difficult to determine if the target student's behavior is atypical or abnormal.

There are three ways to develop informal norms. The first is to take several students or a group of students as the norm sample and to use the scan-check method. The observer scans the sample group of students for several seconds over the observation period and counts the number of students who are exhibiting the behavior under observation. For example, every minute an observer scans a group of students for 5 seconds and counts the number of students who are working independently. After this scan-check, the observer can watch the target student to see whether the student is working independently. Figure 5.16 is an example of the scan-check method.

The second method of establishing an informal norm sample is to ask the teacher to identify a student whose behavior is typical or representative of the behavior of the students in the group. By watching the behavior of the typical student, the observer can use the scan-check method to compare the typical student's behavior with that of the target student.

A third way to develop an informal norm is to compare several observations of the behavior of the target student that were conducted

---

Child s name: _Ben_      Observer: _D. Southard_

Age: _4–8_      Date: _November 12_

School: _North_      Teacher: _Blesson_

Reason for Observation: _to determine the extent that Ben's behaviors differ from his peers_

Activity Observed: _Circle time_

Observation Technique Used (e.g., interval recording, duration recording): _1 min. intervals_

| Behavior Codes | Grouping Codes | Teacher and Peer Reaction Codes |
|---|---|---|
| **T** On-task | **L** Large group | **AA** Attention to all |
| **O** Off-task | **S** Small group | **A+** Positive attention |
| **P** Passive activity | **O** One-to-one | **A−** Negative attention |
| **M** Motor activity | **C** Cooperative play | **NA** No attention |
| **W** Watching | **P** Parallel play | **NT** Neutral attention |
| | **I** Individual | |

| Time | Child behavior | Compare Child beh. | Class Scan | Anecdotal Notes | Group | Teacher | Peer |
|---|---|---|---|---|---|---|---|
| 9:16 | O | T | 80% | making faces | L | A− | A+ |
| 17 | M | T | | walks away | L | A− | A+ |
| 18 | M | T | 70% | | L | NA | NA |
| 19 | O | O | | plays with blocks | L | NA | NA |
| 20 | M | T | 80% | | L | NA | NA |
| 21 | M | T | | returns circle | L | A+ | NT |
| 22 | T | O | 90% | attends to group | L | AA | NT |
| 23 | T | T | | | L | AA | NT |
| 24 | T | T | 80% | | L | AA | NT |
| 25 | P | T | | | L | AA | NT |
| Total | 3/10 30% | 8/10 80% | 80% | | L | | |

**FIGURE 5.16** *Scan-Check Recording Sheet*

*Source:* Adapted from G. J. Alessi and J. H. Kaye (1983). *Behavior Assessment for School Psychologists.* Kent, OH: National Association of School Psychologists.

during separate observation periods. In this way, the behavior of the target student is compared with previous observations of that same behavior (Alessi, 1980; Sattler, 2001).

## Interviewing

The interview allows a face-to-face meeting in which participants discuss and share their individual perspectives. Interviews may be conducted with students, parents, colleagues, and other professionals. In Chapter 2 special considerations in interviewing parents and other family members were discussed.

Interviewing consists of asking the right questions and listening carefully to what the other person is saying. This skill demands that you know yourself and not let your own biases overshadow what is being told to you. If you use this technique, you must want to hear what the other person is saying. Being a good listener is a complex skill that calls for sensitivity and respect for others. Skillful interviewing requires training and practice.

The interview makes certain assumptions about the give and take of the communication process between individuals. Professionals need to be sensitive to assumptions that members of the dominant group hold about this communication process; these assumptions may not be the same for members of less dominant groups.

### Planning and Conducting Interviews with Teachers and Other Professionals

In Chapter 2 we discuss planning and conducting interviews with family members. The steps are similar when working with other teachers and professionals. We will briefly review these steps applied to fellow professionals.

***Planning the Interview.***  In preparing to conduct an interview, contact the individual and state the purpose of the meeting. Plan a convenient time and place to meet.

State the purpose of the interview. The purpose may be to follow up on a student referral: "I'd like to sit down and talk further about your concerns about Sharda."

Arrange a convenient time and meeting place: "Do you have some time in the next few days that we could meet?" Since information shared during the interview may be confidential in nature, take care to arrange a meeting place that can ensure confidentiality. Locations that are public gathering spots, such as the cafeteria or teachers' lounge, may not be appropriate.

***Beginning the Interview.***  Establish rapport with the individual. Some interviewers spend a few minutes talking about a shared activity of mutual interest before sitting down to work. Acknowledge the fact that the individual has set aside time for the meeting. Begin the interview with broad questions and gradually ask more specific and focused questions (Nitko, 2001).

***Conducting the Interview.***  Show a genuine interest in what the individual has to say. Create a positive tone by your respect, support, and warmth.

Ask questions and rephrase statements to help clarify important points. Many professionals find it helpful to prepare a few questions in advance. As you think about the types of questions that would be helpful, consider the wording of the questions and the type of answers that may result. Open-ended questions are usually more helpful. For example, ask "What have you tried?" or "What are you thinking about doing?" Too often the teacher or other professional requesting assistance receives questions in the form "Have you tried x?" This line of questioning may produce single-word responses and a sense of frustration.

Listen not only to hear but to understand what the individual is saying.

***Completing the Interview.***  Generally, interviews should not exceed an hour in length. Conclude the interview by summarizing the discussion.

## Conducting Interviews with Students

Interviews with students are helpful both when students are having academic difficulties and when students are doing well. The interview provides information about a student's perspective in a wide variety of areas, and is especially productive in giving insight into the student's overall patterns of behavior (Salvia and Ysseldyke, 2001) and self-concept. Student interviews are helpful in making adjustments to the classroom environment.

Interviews should be used with caution, however, as they can present difficulties for students with disabilities and for students from some cultural and ethnic groups. The interview technique requires skills in understanding and speaking the language of the interviewee. For example, an interviewer can inadvertently cut off students with processing difficulties, who may take longer to compose a response. Students who are not proficient in English can experience difficulty, even when a translator is present. The translator may or may not be proficient in the student's dialect, or the student may misinterpret the translation because the nuances in the language do not transfer.

### Steps in Conducting Student Interviews.
Merrell (1994) describes the steps in conducting a student interview:

1. Begin by asking generally for the student's reasons for having the interview. Allow time for discussion of the student's interests and attitudes.
2. Lead the discussion toward a specific probing of the problem. For example, the interviewer might ask the student to describe what happens just before the student gets involved in a fight.
3. Ask the student to describe any behavioral assets the student has.
4. Obtain the student's perspective on what positive and appropriate behaviors the student can marshal as well as a description of likes and dislikes.

5. Use this information along with other assessment information to develop a plan for addressing the problem behavior.

## Conferencing and Collaborating

### Conferencing

**Conferencing** involves meeting with parents, teachers, therapists, or professionals in other agencies to share information, concerns, and ideas regarding common issues.

The conference involves a planned meeting with two people or meeting with a small or large group of individuals. The key aspects of conducting conferences are:

### Planning the Conference
1. Setting a meeting time and location
   - Find a time and location that is convenient for each person.

### During the Conference
1. Identifying and clarifying the situation
   - Describe the areas of concern: "I understand that Roberto has been having a difficult time. Could you describe what has been happening?"
   - Ask questions or restate what has been said, if you are unsure of the issues.
   - Determine the history and the frequency of the problem.
2. Generating ideas
   - Work together to brainstorm a list of interventions.
   - Write down each idea.
3. Making decisions
   - Identify possible solutions.
   - Build consensus.
4. Keeping focused
   - Maintain the purpose of the meeting. Participants should feel that they are making progress. Don't waste time by letting the meeting become sidetracked with other conversations or interruptions.

*Collaboration with colleagues encourages good interpersonal skills and a commitment to teamwork.*

**5.** Developing a time line
- Write down a time line for activities and interventions that will be tried.
- Clarify the responsibilities of each member.
- Schedule a follow-up meeting.

### Following the Conference
**1.** Keeping track of improvements
- Share ideas of good experiences and solutions that have worked. (Adapted from Ferguson, 1994; Heward, 2001)

## Collaborating

**Collaborating** is a more active process than simply meeting with others to discuss common issues. Collaboration involves a commitment on an individual's part to work cooperatively with others toward a common goal.

Building expertise in conferencing and collaborating begins with good interpersonal skills.

Some individuals seem to have strong interpersonal skills; others need to develop and practice these faculties. Professionals improve interpersonal competence by working with others who demonstrate a strong commitment to teamwork and collaboration. Let's examine some of the characteristics of effective interpersonal skills:

- Individuals with strong interpersonal skills communicate in a positive, genuine manner. They are interested in what others are saying and in the ideas that others have.
- Interpersonal skills involve both verbal and nonverbal communication. Verbal communication refers not only to the spoken words but to the tone and pitch the speaker uses. Nonverbal communication consists of facial expression, body language, and gestures. Nonverbal customs can send strong messages to the speaker. For example, one of the expected norms in communication among some groups is that the speaker makes eye contact

with the listener and that a good listener indicates interest by returning the eye contact. Professionals must be aware that expected norms typical for members of the dominant group may not be held by professionals who are members of less dominant groups. In some cultural groups, the "lack" of eye contact is a scruple, a behavior that signifies respect for the speaker rather than lack of interest.

- Listen and hear the speaker out. Don't interrupt when a colleague is talking. Knowing all the answers is not important—or possible. Working together to create solutions is critical.
- Use everyday language and eliminate the use of jargon. The field of special education is filled with initials, numbers, and acronyms. Professionals from other disciplines may not be familiar with many of the terms that special educators use frequently.

## Preferred Practices

In conducting observations, the examiner needs to be aware of the sources of error that affect the accuracy of observations. Examiners must take care to ensure that observations are both reliable and valid and to take precautions against bias.

Examiners gather information in observations and synthesize and integrate it with other assessment data to assist the team in answering the assessment questions during one or more steps of the assessment process. This data includes observations of the student and of the environment.

Observing and interviewing involve working closely with other professionals. Conferencing and collaborating entail strong interpersonal organizational skills. Being sensitive to these skills and having opportunities to practice them in working with others are the first steps in becoming a skillful practitioner.

## Extending Learning

1. Darcy is a new student in your classroom who is frequently aggressive to others. The aggression is sometimes physical and sometimes verbal. You plan to observe Darcy's behavior for instances of aggression to find out what kinds of situations make her upset. Describe how you would proceed in planning and conducting the observation. Design or adapt an observation form to assist you in collecting information.

2. The assessment team has asked you to gather information regarding the degree to which a student is independent of others. You need to know examples of situations in which the student works independently and does not seek direction or assistance from others. Select three different time periods during the day to observe the student. Adapt one of the observation forms to assist you in collecting the information. Use your form to conduct the observation. What would you report back to the team?

3. Help the teachers who are planning to conduct student observations! Complete the missing information in Figure 5.17.

4. Select two students to observe using the event sampling technique. Record their responses to others in terms of affect and expression. Complete an interpretation of your observations, including a summary of the responses of each student and a comparison of the range of responses and intensity of expression.

5. Sometimes teachers assess out-of-seat behavior. Explain why duration recording is preferable to event recording for collecting this data. (Hint: Are all out-of-seat behaviors equivalent as time away from the student's desk?)

6. Interview a teacher to collect information about one or two learning or behavior problems in the classroom. Identify questions or additional information that would be helpful in addressing the problem. Based on these

**FIGURE 5.17**    *Teacher's Questions about Students and Methods of Recording Observations*

| Assessment Questions | Behavior | Method of Recording Observation Information |
|---|---|---|
| 1. How often does Tia interact with her classmates? | Interact is defined as making eye contact | Event or latency |
| 2. How long does it take Ben to finish cleaning up? | | |
| 3. Is MJ late to class today? | | |
| 4. In math class, is Carla more disruptive than other students? | | |
| 5. Can Harold complete the job application form in a reasonable amount of time? | | |

question(s), construct a checklist to help you gather this information.

7. Plan to conduct a student interview regarding the student's interests and school work. Use the steps in conducting an interview to plan your meeting. After you have conducted the interview, write an evaluation of the interview process. What aspects went well? What would you do differently next time?

8. Choose one of the schools described in the Snapshots of Stoney Brook Elementary and Lincoln High. How might the methods, materials, and demands affect a student who is experiencing academic problems?

9. College professors often use group assignments to foster skills in collaboration. Consider a situation in which you have worked together with a group of classmates on a problem or assignment. Was the group project successful overall? Did members encounter difficulties in working together? Define what the problems were and discuss possible solutions.

(On p. 99 we asked if Stacy's behavior had improved after a two-month interval. The answer is:

$$\frac{15\ occurrences}{10\ minutes} = 1.5\ occurrences\ per\ minute$$

This represents an improvement.)

## References

Alessi, G. J. (1980). Behavioral observation for the school psychologist: Responsive-discrepancy model. *School Psychology Review* 9: 31–45.

Alessi, G. J., and J. H. Kaye (1983). *Behavior assessment for school psychologists.* Kent, OH: National Association of School Psychologists.

Beaty, J. (1998). *Observing development of the young child.* 3rd ed. Upper Saddle River, NJ: Merrill.

Cohen, Libby G., and Loraine J. Spenciner (1994).

*Assessment of young children.* White Plains, NY: Longman.

Ferguson, D. L. (1994). Magic for teacher work groups. *Teaching Exceptional Children* 27(1): 42–47.

Frick, T., and M. I. Semmel (1978). Observer agreement and reliabilities of classroom observational measures. *Review of Educational Research* 48: 157–184.

Gronlund, N. E., and R. L. Linn (1990). *Measurement and evaluation in teaching.* New York: Macmillan.

Harms, T., R. M. Clifford, and D. Cryer (1998). *Early childhood environment rating scale—revised.* New York: Teachers College Press.

Herbert, J., and C. Attridge (1975). A guide for developers and users of observation systems and manuals. *American Educational Research Journal* 12: 1–20.

Heward, W. L. (2001). *Exceptional children: An introduction to special education.* 6th ed. Upper Saddle River, NJ: Prentice-Hall, Pearson Education.

Hoge, R. D. (1985). The validity of direct observation. *Review of Educational Research* 55: 469–483.

McNeely, S. L. (1997). *Observing students and teachers through objective strategies.* Boston: Allyn & Bacon.

Merrell, K. W. (1994). *Assessment of behavioral, social, and emotional problems: Direct and objective methods for use with children and adolescents.* White Plains, NY: Longman.

Nitko, A. J. (2001). *Educational assessment of students.* 3rd ed. Upper Saddle River, NJ: Prentice-Hall, Pearson Education.

Repp, A. C., G. S. Nieminen, E. Olinger, and R. Brusca (1988). Direct observation: Factors affecting the accuracy of observers. *Exceptional Children* 55: 29–36.

Salvia, J., and J. E. Ysseldyke (2001). *Assessment.* 8th ed. Boston: Houghton Mifflin.

Sattler, J. (2001). *Assessment of children.* 4th ed. La Mesa, CA: Jerome M. Sattler.

Sulzer-Azaroff, B., and R. G. Mayer (1991). *Behavior analysis for lasting change.* Fort Worth, TX: Holt, Rinehart & Winston.

Ysseldyke, J. E., and S. L. Christenson (1993). *The instructional environment system–II.* Longmont, CO: Sopris West Educational Services.

# 6

# *Achievement:*
# *Overall Performance*

## Overview

**Achievement testing** is the assessment of past learning that is usually the result of formal and informal educational experiences. This chapter is concerned with approaches that assess the achievement of students. Several other chapters in this book also address aspects of the assess-ment of achievement. Chapter 7 discusses performance-based, authentic, and portfolio assessments, Chapters 8 and 9 examine the assessment of reading and written language, and Chapter 11 examines the assessment of mathematics.

## Chapter Objectives

After completing this chapter you should be able to:

- Describe assessment questions, purposes, and approaches relating to the assessment of achievement.
- Explain the integral link between instruction and assessment.
- Compare approaches to the assessment of achievement, including norm-referenced

standardized tests, curriculum-based assessment, criterion-referenced assessment, and alternative assessments such as performance-based assessment, self-assessment, and peer assessment.
- Describe how the assessment of the physical, learning, and social environments influences achievement.

## What Shapes Our Views

The assessment of achievement occurs regularly throughout students' school careers. Achievement tests are designed for groups of students or for individual students in order to assess their formal and informal learning experiences. The questions, purposes, and approaches that apply to the assessment of achievement are described in Table 6.1.

## Responding to Diversity

The assessment of achievement must be sensitive to an individual's culture, ethnicity, race, language, geographic region of origin, gender, disability, and economic status. Assessment approaches, including standardized tests, performance-based assessment, and the other approaches this chapter describes must be free from bias. There are several ways in which achievement tests can show bias (Howell and Rueda, 1996):

- in the format of the test
- if the test directions are too technical or do not translate easily into another language
- if the content of achievement tests differs in importance across cultures
- if the examinee test-taking behaviors vary from one culture to another
- if the examiner personality characteristics influence the examinee's responses

- if the underlying psychological construct of the test is not universal
- if the individual examinee does not represent the norm group

Using a variety of approaches when assessing achievement reflects sensitivity to the student as well as a thorough attempt to understand what the student has learned. The assessment of achievement includes standardized testing in addition to a variety of these other approaches:

- curriculum-based assessment
- criterion-referenced assessment
- alternative forms of assessment, such as systematic observations, anecdotal records, interviews with family members and the students themselves, samples of students' work, videotapes, audiotapes, performances, portfolios, and exhibitions.

## Standardized Instruments

Standardized tests of achievement are tests that follow strict procedures for administration, scoring, and interpretation. A standardized test is usually norm-referenced. A **norm-referenced test** (NRT) is a measure that compares a student's test performance with that of similar students who have taken the same test. The construction of a standardized test is often a lengthy and costly project that involves considerable research and development.

**TABLE 6.1** *Assessment Questions, Purposes, and Approaches*

| Assessment Questions | Steps and Purposes | Approaches |
|---|---|---|
| | **Screening** | |
| Is there a possibility of a disability in achievement? | To determine whether students *may* have a disability and should be referred for further assessment | Norm-referenced instruments<br>Curriculum-based assessments<br>Criterion-referenced assessments<br>Observations<br>Checklists |
| | **Eligibility** | |
| Does the student have a disability?<br>What disability does the student have?<br>Does the student meet the criteria for services?<br>What are the strengths and weaknesses?<br>In what areas is the student having difficulty?<br>What does the student understand? | To determine if there is a disability<br>To compare the student's performance with the performance of the peer group<br>To determine specific strengths and weaknesses<br>To understand why the student is having difficulty | Norm-referenced instruments<br>Curriculum-based assessments<br>Criterion-referenced assessments<br>Observations<br>Probes<br>Error analysis<br>Interviews<br>Checklists<br>Student, parent, and/or teacher conferences<br>Performance assessments |

*Connecting Instruction with Assessment*

| | **Program Planning** | |
|---|---|---|
| What does the student not understand?<br>Where should instruction begin? | To understand what the student knows and does not know<br>To plan the student's program<br>To determine instructional approaches | Norm-referenced instruments<br>Curriculum-based assessments<br>Criterion-referenced assessments<br>Observations<br>Probes<br>Error analysis<br>Interviews<br>Checklists<br>Student, parent, and/or teacher conferences<br>Performance assessments |

## Steps in the Development of a Standardized Achievement Test

1. Test developers create specifications for the test.

2. Test items are written.

3. Test developers conduct an item tryout of initial draft items on a large group of individuals.

4. Test developers analyze the results of the item tryout; discard, or modify some items;

**TABLE 6.1**   *Continued*

| Assessment Questions | Steps and Purposes | Approaches |
|---|---|---|
| | **Program Monitoring** | |
| Once instruction begins, is the student making progress? Should the instruction be modified? | To understand the pace of instruction<br>To understand what the student knows prior to and after instruction<br>To understand the strategies and concepts the student uses<br>To monitor the student's program | Curriculum-based assessments<br>Criterion-referenced assessments<br>Observations<br>Probes<br>Error analysis<br>Interviews<br>Checklists<br>Student, parent, and/or teacher conferences<br>Portfolios<br>Exhibitions<br>Journals<br>Written descriptions<br>Oral descriptions |
| | **Program Evaluation** | |
| Has the student met the goals of the IEP?<br>Has the instructional program been successful for the student?<br>Has the student made progress?<br>Has the instructional program achieved its goals? | To determine whether the IEP goals have been met<br>To determine whether the goals of the program have been met<br>To evaluate program effectiveness | Curriculum-based assessments<br>Criterion-referenced assessments<br>Observations<br>Probes<br>Error analysis<br>Interviews<br>Checklists<br>Student, parent, and/or teacher conferences<br>Portfolios<br>Exhibitions<br>Journals<br>Written descriptions<br>Oral descriptions<br>Surveys |

create new items; and develop methods of scoring and interpretation.

5. Test developers conduct a national standardization of the test. They select a national standardization sample representative of the United States, based on the results of the most recent census data. The sample participants represent balanced criteria for age, socioeconomic status, geographic region, urban/rural/suburban residence, race, ethnicity, and gender. The sample may include additional variables, depending on the purposes of the test.

6. Test developers analyze the data from the national tryout and develop norm tables. Norm tables help examiners compare the performance of individual students with the performance of the students' peers.

7. Final test materials, including test manuals, answer sheets, and scoring guides result from these steps.

## *Benefits*

The benefits of using standardized tests are that the test materials describe the development of the tests in detail, including the test content, administration, norms, reliability, validity, scoring, and interpretation. Because standardized tests are usually norm-referenced, testers can make comparisons between the performance of an individual student, the student's peers, and the students in the standardized sample group. In addition, the tests allow for comparisons between a student's performance on several subtests or on several separate tests in order to identify relative strengths and weaknesses. Depending on the test, standardized achievement tests are helpful in screening, determining eligibility, program planning, monitoring progress, and program evaluation.

## *Disadvantages*

Although standardized achievement tests have a number of advantages, they also have many disadvantages for students with special needs:

- The tests assume that all students have been exposed to the content tested.
- Many tests assume that students come from a homogeneous culture.
- Many tests show bias against students with disabilities, females, and certain cultures, ethnic groups, and economic groups.
- Many tests do not test what the curriculum has taught in schools.
- Many tests do not measure or consider creativity, interest, initiative, motivation, and values.
- Many tests result in labeling or mislabeling of students.
- The tests encourage teachers to teach toward the test.
- The tests result in competition among students, teachers, and schools.

- The tests generate fear (Nitko, 1996).
- Test standards usually require that students be able to read and write independently.

## *Steps and Purposes of Standardized Achievement Testing*

***Screening.*** One frequent use of standardized achievement tests is to identify students who perform below, at the same level, or above their peers. That is, the utility of achievement test results in the screening process is in identifying students who need further assessment. Examples of achievement tests to use for screening are the *Iowa Tests of Basic Skills* and the *Peabody Individual Achievement Test–Revised/Normative Update*.

***Determining Eligibility.*** Using standardized achievement tests in conjunction with other types of tests can help determine eligibility for services. For example, using the *Wechsler Individual Achievement Test, Second Edition (WIAT®–II)*, with a measure of cognitive ability can help determine eligibility for services.

***Program Planning.*** Program planning and monitoring student progress connect instruction with assessment. Achievement tests can aid in instructional planning and can be helpful in identifying what the student knows and can do. Two useful tests for program planning are the *Peabody Individual Achievement Test–Revised/NU* and the *KeyMath–Revised/NU*. The teacher can also utilize other assessment approaches discussed in this chapter to assist with program planning.

***Monitoring Progress.*** Regularly monitoring students' progress in literacy, mathematics, and other academic content areas is important. Norm-referenced tests may not be as useful in monitoring progress as are other assessment approaches because they are not sensitive to small changes in performance. Frequent monitoring assists the teacher in modifying instruction to meet the needs of the student. As with program planning, the teacher may also use other assessment approaches discussed in this chapter.

***Program Evaluation.*** Teachers and other professionals employ achievement tests to conduct two types of program evaluation: Individual student programs as specified in an IEP, and, more broadly, the progress that a class, grade, school, or the school district itself has made over a period of time. See Chapter 19 for further discussion of program evaluation.

## Group Tests

Group tests of achievement are usually administered to groups of students in classrooms. Students with special needs who are in regular classrooms frequently participate in group achievement testing. The purposes of group achievement tests are to: (1) assist in screening students, (2) evaluate the relative performance of students when compared with their peers, (3) describe the relative effectiveness of methods of instruction, and (4) evaluate curricula. IDEA requires that general state- and districtwide assessments include students with disabilities, using appropriate accommodations where necessary.

Most group tests require using scripted directions that the test publisher provides. The tests usually have booklets that contain test items and separate answer sheets. Hand scoring is common, although some publishers either request or require that schools return the answer sheets for machine scoring. Group tests report a variety of types of scores, including standard scores, percentiles, stanines, and age and grade equivalents. These scores can generate profiles, thus facilitating the comparison of students, classrooms, individual schools, and school districts.

***Benefits.*** Group testing with standardized tests permits the testing of large groups of students using the same administration, scoring, and interpretation procedures. While it is appropriate to administer group tests to individual students, it is not appropriate to administer individual tests to groups.

***Disadvantages.*** Group testing has several disadvantages for students with special needs. The tests routinely require that students read and write independently. Further, many group achievement tests have separate test booklets that contain the test items and separate answer sheets. Some students may be able to correctly answer the questions but have difficulty transferring their answers to the answer sheet. Finally, many group achievement tests have multiple-choice answers. Students with disabilities as well as students from various culture or ethnic groups may have difficulty using this format.

There are a number of published group achievement tests available. Table 6.2 presents a comparison of commonly used tests.

## Individual Achievement Tests

When testing individual students, achievement tests provide the examiner with the opportunity to get to know students. The student and the test examiner can establish a rapport, and the examiner can help the student feel at ease. Individual testing allows the examiner to observe the student's appearance, adjustment to the testing, cooperation, effort, motivation, attitudes, speech patterns, anxiety level, activity level, flexibility, impulse control, fine and gross motor abilities, distractibility, and mood (Sattler, 1988). The examiner can individualize the test administration according to the needs of the student. For example, if a student is tired or hungry, the examiner can stop the test so that the student can take a break. A list of published individual achievement tests can be found in Table 6.3.

## Published Achievement Tests

### Basic Achievement Skills Individual Screener

The *Basic Achievement Skills Individual Screener (BASIS)* (Sonnenschein, 1983) measures skills in reading, mathematics, spelling, and writing for

**TABLE 6.2**    *Group Tests of Achievement*

| Test | Grade |
| --- | --- |
| *\*Aprenda: La Prueba de Logros en Español* (1997) Coordinated with Stanford Achievement Test Series | K through 13 |
| *California Achievement Tests/Terra Nova* (CTB/Macmillan/McGraw-Hill, 2000) | K through 12 |
| *Iowa Tests of Basic Skills: Form M* (Hoover, Hieronymous, Frisbie, and Dunbar, 1996) | K through 9 |
| *Iowa Tests of Educational Development: Form M* (Feldt, Forsyth, Ansley, and Alnot, 1996) | 9 through 12 |
| *Metropolitan Achievement Tests* (8th ed.) (Balow, Farr, and Hogan, 2000) | K through 12 |
| *SRA Achievement Series* (Naslund, Thorpe, and Lefever, 1985) | K through 12 |
| *Stanford Achievement Test: New Norms* (Harcourt Brace Educational Measurement, 2001) | K through 13 |
| *Supera®* (CTB, McGraw-Hill, 1997) | 1 through 9 |
| *TerraNova® Assessment Series* (CTB, McGraw-Hill, 2000) | K through 12 |
| *Tests of Achievement and Proficiency* (Scannell, Hough, Lloyd, and Risinger, 1993) | 9 through 12 |

*Spanish form

students in grades 1 through 12 and post–high school students. The test is both criterion-referenced and norm-referenced and produces scores that range from grades 1 through 12. Box 6.1 on page 138 gives a brief summary of the test.

The test arranges each of the following content-areas items in grade-level clusters:

*Reading.* The items in this cluster range from readiness through grade 8. The purpose of this subtest measures reading comprehension by asking upper-grade students to read graded passages and supply the missing words. This is known as the *cloze technique.*

*Mathematics.* The items in this cluster range from readiness through grade 8. The student must solve computational problems using a pencil. The examiner dictates word problems.

*Spelling.* The items in this cluster range from grades 1 through 8. The student writes words that the teacher dictates.

*Writing.* The writing subtest is optional. After being assigned a topic by the examiner, the student writes for 10 minutes. The examiner scores the sample holistically and compares it with average writing samples for students in grades 3 through 8.

***Administration.*** The examiner administers the subtests individually. The test has no set time limit and takes less than one hour. There is one form.

**TABLE 6.3**    *Individual Tests of Achievement*

| Name | Ages/Grades |
| --- | --- |
| *Basic Achievement Skills Individual Screener (BASIS)* (Sonnenschein, 1983) | grades 1 through 12 and post–high school |
| *\*Bateria Woodcock Munzo–Revisada* (2000) Co-normed test of cognitive ability and achievement; normed on 800+ Spanish-speaking subjects from five countries | ages 4 years through 20 years |
| *Diagnostic Achievement Battery–3 (DAB–3)* (Newcomer, 2001) | ages 6 years through 14 years |
| *Diagnostic Achievement Test for Adolescents–2 (DATA–2)* (Newcomer and Bryant, 1993) | grades 7 through 12 |
| *Kaufman Test of Educational Achievement/Normative Update (K-TEA/NU)* (Kaufman and Kaufman, 1998) | grades 1 through 12 ages 6 years to 18 years, 11 months |
| *Peabody Individual Achievement Test–R/Normative Update (PIAT–R/NU)* (Markwardt, 1998) | grades K through 12 ages 5 years to 18 years, 11 months |
| *Wide Range Achievement Test–3 (WRAT–3)* (Wilkinson, 1993) | ages 5 years through 75 years |
| *Wechsler Individual Achievement Test–II (WIAT®–II)* (Harcourt Brace Educational Measurement, 2001) | grades K through 12, ages 5 years through adulthood |
| *Woodcock-Johnson Tests of Achievement–III (WJ®–III)* (Woodcock, McGrew, and Mather, 2001) | grades K through 12 ages 2 years through adulthood |

*Spanish form

**Scoring.**    The subtests are hand scored. Both normative and criterion-referenced scores are available. The following normative scores are available: percentile ranks, stanines, standard scores, age equivalents, and grade equivalents. Criterion-referenced scoring involves evaluating the student's performance on clusters of items.

**Standardization.**    The *BASIS* was standardized in the fall of 1982. The test sample was representative of students in grades 1 to 12, based on the 1970 U.S. Census.

**Reliability.**    The reliability appears to be adequate. Test-retest reliabilities are greater than .80. Internal consistency reliability is acceptable.

**Validity.**    The selection of items in the construction of the test determine content validity. Sample populations of special students, such as students who were learning disabled, gifted, mentally retarded, emotionally disturbed, and hearing impaired, participated in a number of validity studies. However, the samples were small and additional research is necessary to determine the usefulness of this instrument with special populations.

**Summary.**    The *BASIS* is an individually administered test of reading, mathematics, spelling,

| **BOX 6.1** | *Basic Achievement Skills Individual Screener (BASIS)* |

*Publication Date:* 1983

*Purpose:* A criterion-referenced and norm-referenced individual test that measures skills in reading, mathematics, spelling, and writing.

*Age/Grade Levels:* Students in grades 1 through 12 and post–high school students.

*Time to Administer:* 20 minutes to less than 1 hour.

*Technical Adequacy:* Reliability is adequate. The teacher should examine the test items to determine the extent to which they measure the curriculum that the student has been taught.

*Suggested Use:* Screening.

and writing. The examiner should determine the appropriateness of the test items by comparing them with the student's curriculum. The test is probably best used as a screening instrument rather than as a test of achievement in content areas.

## Kaufman Test of Educational Achievement/Normative Update

The *Kaufman Test of Educational Achievement/ Normative Update (K–TEA/NU)* (Kaufman and Kaufman, 1998) is an individually administered test of achievement for students in grades 1 through 12. Collected data from 1995 to 1996 resulted in a complete renorming of the test. The age-based norms range from 6 years, 0 months to 18 years, 11 months. The *K–TEA/NU* has two forms, the Comprehensive Form and the Brief Form. Although the forms are not interchangeable, they do have overlapping uses. The applications listed for the Brief Form are: contributing to a battery, screening, program planning,

research, pretesting and posttesting, making placement decisions, student self-appraisal, use by government agencies, personnel selection, and measuring adaptive functioning. The Comprehensive Form has all of these uses except screening. In addition, the Comprehensive Form is recommended for analyzing strengths and weaknesses and for analyzing errors. There is some overlap of items between the *K–TEA/NU* and the *Kaufman Assessment Battery for Children (K–ABC)*.

***Description of the Subtests in the Comprehensive Form.*** The Comprehensive Form consists of five subtests: Mathematics Applications, Reading Decoding, Spelling, Reading Comprehension, and Mathematics Computation.

*Mathematics Applications.* The examiner presents the items orally while using pictures and graphs as visual stimuli. The items assess the application of mathematical principles and reasoning.

*Reading Decoding.* The items assess the ability to identify letters and to pronounce words that are phonetic and nonphonetic.

*Spelling.* The examiner pronounces a word and uses it in a sentence, then asks the student to write the word. If students cannot write, they may spell the word orally.

*Reading Comprehension.* The child reads a passage and responds either gesturally or orally to the items in the reading.

*Mathematics Computation.* The student uses a paper and pencil to solve written mathematical problems.

***Description of the Subtests in the Brief Form.*** The Brief Form consists of three subtests: Mathematics, Reading, and Spelling.

*Mathematics.* This subtest measures basic computational skills and the application of mathematical principles and reasoning.

*Reading.* The items assess both decoding, by asking the child to read words, and reading comprehension, by requiring the child to read statements.

*Spelling.* The items consist of words that the examiner reads and uses in a sentence. The student then writes the word or spells it orally, if the student is unable to write.

**Administration.** Persons who have had training in educational and psychological testing as well as persons who have had limited training in these areas can administer the *K–TEA/NU*. For children in grades 1 through 3, the Comprehensive Form takes from 20 minutes to 1 hour to administer; the Brief Form requires from 10 to 35 minutes to administer.

**Scoring.** Raw scores convert to standard scores, with a mean of 100 and a standard deviation of 15. These are available for both fall and spring testing by grade level or by age. In addition, percentile ranks, stanines, normal curve equivalents, age equivalents, and grade equivalents are available. The manual describes the following methods of interpreting *K–TEA/NU* scores: the size of the difference and the significance of the difference between subtests and between composite scores, analyzing strengths and weaknesses, and identifying errors.

**Standardization.** Test publishers renormed both the Comprehensive and the Brief Forms of the *K–TEA/NU* between October 1995 and November 1996. Stratification of the standardization sample followed age, gender, region, race, ethnicity, and economic status as estimated by parental education. The standardization sample of the *K–TEA/NU* was linked to the standardization samples for the *Peabody Individual Achievement Test–Revised (PIAT–R)*, *KeyMath–R*, and the *Woodcock Reading Mastery Tests–Revised (WRMT–R)*. For the *K–TEA/NU*, the renorming sample consisted of students from grade 1 through age 22. To obtain a linking sample, test examinees in the norm sample take one of the complete test batteries and one or more subtests from another battery. This linking approach

permits the making of comparisons of test performance across batteries.

**Reliability.** The reliabilities of the Comprehensive Form's five subtests are in the mid to high .90s.

Test-retest reliability coefficients for the Comprehensive Form are high. Reliabilities of the three subtests of the Brief Form are also high. The reliability of the Battery Composite is high.

**Validity.** The validity of the Comprehensive Form and the Brief Form were estimated using similar procedures. Content validity comes through consultation with curriculum experts in each subject area. Test developers conducted three national tryouts during the fall of 1981 and the spring of 1982. The final selection of the items emerged from these tryouts.

An estimate of construct validity resulted from showing that subtest and composite scores increased across age and grade levels. Correlating the results of the *K–TEA/NU* with the results of other tests given to the same students demonstrated criterion-related validity. These tests included the *Kaufman Assessment Battery for Children (K–ABC)*, *Wide Range Achievement Test– 3 (WRAT–3)*, *Peabody Individual Achievement Test–R (PIAT–R)*, and other tests.

**Summary.** The *Kaufman Test of Educational Achievement/Normative Update* is an individually administered test of achievement for students in grades 1 through 12 whose ages range from 6 years, 0 months to 18 years, 11 months. The *K–TEA/NU* has two forms, the Comprehensive Form and the Brief Form. Although the forms overlap in content, they are not interchangeable. Evidence for the technical adequacy of the test is sufficient. The reliability is excellent and validity of both forms is adequate. As with all achievement tests, educators must evaluate the content validity to determine how well it measures what has been taught. See Box 6.2 for a summary of the test parameters.

### BOX 6.2    *Kaufman Test of Educational Achievement/ Normative Update (K–TEA/NU)*

*Publication Date:* 1998

*Purposes:* The Comprehensive Form measures: Reading Decoding, Spelling, Reading Comprehension, Mathematics Applications, and Mathematics Computation. The Brief Form consists of three subtests: Reading, Mathematics, and Spelling.

*Age/Grade Levels:* Grades 1 through 12; ages range from 6 years, 0 months to 18 years, 11 months.

*Time to Administer:* 20 minutes to approximately 1 hour.

*Technical Adequacy:* Renorming was based on data collected in 1995 to 1996. The reliability and validity of both forms is adequate. As with all achievement tests, educators must evaluate the content validity to determine how well it measures what has been taught.

*Suggested Uses:* The Comprehensive Form can be used to measure overall achievement. The Brief Form should be used for screening.

## Peabody Individual Achievement Test–Revised/Normative Update

The *Peabody Individual Achievement Test–Revised/Normative Update (PIAT–R/NU)* (Markwardt Jr., 1998) is an individually administered, norm-referenced test for students in grades kindergarten through 12 (5 years, 0 months to 18 years, 11 months). The manual states that the *PIAT–R/NU* has the following uses: individual evaluation, program planning, guidance and counseling, admissions and transfers, grouping students, follow-up evaluation, personnel selection, and research. The manual also describes the following limitations: (1) the *PIAT–R/NU* is not a diagnostic test; (2) it does not provide

highly precise measurement of achievement; (3) it cannot sample the curriculum of individual schools—rather, it represents a representative curriculum of schools in the United States; and (4) the background and qualifications of the test administrator can have a varying influence on the interpretation of the test.

The test assesses achievement in six areas:

*General Information.* This subtest measures general knowledge. The examiner reads the open-ended questions aloud and the child answers orally.

*Reading Recognition.* The initial test items consist of ability to recognize the sounds associated with letters. Later test items consist of isolated words. The student reproduces the sounds and reads the words orally.

*Reading Comprehension.* The student reads a sentence silently and then is asked to identify the one picture out of four that best depicts the sentence.

*Mathematics.* Using a multiple-choice format, the test assesses knowledge of basic facts and applications. The examiner reads all of the test items to the student. For the first 50 items, the child sees only the responses and not the test items. For items 50 to 100, the student sees the printed questions and the response choices.

*Spelling.* The format for the responses is multiple choice. The items at the beginning of this subtest measure the student's ability to distinguish a printed letter from an object and to recognize letters after hearing their names or sounds. Later items assess the child's ability to identify the one correctly spelled word out of four that the examiner pronounces.

*Written Expression.* This subtest has two levels. Level I is effective for children in kindergarten or first grade and assesses copying and writing letters, words, and sentences that the examiner dictates. Children in grades 2 through 12 can test in Level II. The student writes a story in response to one of two picture prompts. Children have 20 minutes to complete Level II.

***Administration.*** The manual distinguishes between the qualifications of individuals who administer the *PIAT–R/NU* and those who interpret the results. According to the manual, almost anyone can learn to administer the test. Persons who provide an interpretation should have an understanding of psychometrics and curricula. Depending on the number of items, it takes approximately 30 minutes to an hour to administer the total test.

***Scoring.*** For all of the subtests except Written Expression, the test items are either correct or incorrect. Raw scores can convert to standard scores, percentile ranks, grade and age equivalents, stanines, and normal curve equivalents. A separate scoring guide is in the manual for the Written Expression subtest.

Three composite scores are possible with this test. The Total Reading composite derives from the performance on the Reading Recognition and the Reading Comprehension subtests. The Total Test composite is a composite score from the performance on the first five subtests. There is an optional Written Language composite, which derives from the Written Expression and the Spelling subtests.

***Standardization.*** Renorming of the *PIAT–R/ NU* took place between October 1995 and November 1996. The standardization sample comprised groups according to age, gender, region, race, ethnicity, and economic status as estimated by parental education. The standardization sample of the *PIAT–R/NU* was linked to the standardization samples for the *K–TEA*, *KeyMath–R*, and the *Woodcock Reading Mastery Tests–Revised*. For the *PIAT–R/NU*, the renorming sample consisted of students who were in kindergarten through students age 22. For the linking sample, the test examinees in the norm sample took one of the complete test batteries and one or more subtests from another battery. This linking

approach permits the making of comparisons of test performance across batteries.

***Reliability.*** Split-half reliability coefficients are available by age and grade for all of the subtests, excluding Written Expression. The coefficients range from .84 (Mathematics) to .98 (Reading Recognition). The split-half reliability coefficients for the total test are in the high .90s.

The test provides computed internal consistency reliability coefficients by grade and age for all of the subtests, except Written Expression. With few exceptions, the coefficients were in the mid to high .90s. Internal consistency reliability estimates for Written Expression resulted in reliability coefficients for Level I in the low .60s and .69 (grade 1). Calculations of internal consistency reliability coefficients for Level II of the Written Expression subtest were in the low .70s and high .80s.

In order to estimate test-retest reliability, test developers randomly selected approximately 50 children from grades K, 2, 4, 6, 8, and 10 and retested them within a two- to four-week interval. Median test-retest reliability coefficients for the subtests, excluding Written Expression, ranged from .84 (Mathematics) to .96 (Reading Recognition).

***Validity.*** The manual reports using the development process to establish content validity, and consulting content area experts, tests reviewers, and others. As with any achievement test, however, the teacher should review the test to determine the extent to which the test has content validity.

Subtest and composite scores increased across age and grade levels, demonstrating construct validity. Correlating the results of the *PIAT–R/NU* with the *PIAT* and the *Peabody Picture Vocabulary Test–Revised (PPVT–R)* demonstrated concurrent validity. Additional evidence is necessary to prove construct validity.

***Summary.*** The *Peabody Individual Achievement Test–Revised/Normative Update* is an individually administered, norm-referenced test

*Peabody Individual Achievement Test–Revised/ Normative Update (PIAT–R/NU)*

*Publication Date:* 1998

*Purposes:* Measures overall achievement in the areas of General Information, Reading Recognition, Reading Comprehension, Mathematics, Spelling, and Written Expression.

*Age/Grade Levels:* Grades K through 12; 5 years, 0 months to 18 years, 11 months.

*Time to Administer:* Approximately 30 minutes to 1 hour.

*Technical Adequacy:* The standardization sample and the reliability are acceptable. As with all standardized achievement tests, the teacher should evaluate the content validity of this test.

*Suggested Uses:* Screening; measure of overall achievement in reading, mathematics, spelling, and written expression.

that is useful for children in grades kindergarten through 12. The test assesses achievement in six areas: General Information, Reading Recognition, Reading Comprehension, Mathematics, Spelling, and Written Expression. The standardization and the reliability are acceptable. As with all standardized achievement tests, the teacher should evaluate the content validity of this test. Box 6.3 summarizes the test's parameters.

## Wechsler Individual Achievement Test

The *Wechsler Individual Achievement Test–Second Edition (WIAT®–II)* (The Psychological Corporation, 2001) is an individually administered achievement test for students ages 4 years

through adulthood. The *WIAT®–II* contains nine subtests in four areas:

1. *Oral Expression and Listening Comprehension*
   - Oral Language
   - Listening Comprehension
2. *Written Expression*
   - Written Expression
   - Spelling
3. *Basic Reading Skill and Reading Comprehension*
   - Pseudoword Decoding
   - Word Reading
   - Reading Comprehension
4. *Mathematics Calculation and Mathematics Reasoning*
   - Numerical Operations
   - Mathematics Reasoning

***Administration.*** The *WIAT®–II* is administered individually. The *WIAT®–II* takes approximately 30 minutes to 2 hours to administer.

***Scoring.*** Raw scores convert to grade-based standard scores. Percentiles, age and grade equivalents, normal curve equivalents, and stanines are also available (Figure 6.1). It is possible to determine the discrepancy between *WIAT®–II* standard scores and *Wechsler Preschool and Primary Scale of Intelligence–Revised (WIPPSI–R)* standard scores or *Wechsler Intelligence Scale for Children–III (WISC–III)* standard scores.

***Standardization.*** Sample stratification occurred according to age, grade, gender, race/ethnicity (White, Black, Hispanic, Native American, Eskimo, Aleut, Asian, Pacific Islander, Other), geographic region, and the education of the parent(s) or guardian(s) based on 1998 data from the U.S. Census Bureau.

The *WIAT®–II* links with the *Wechsler Intelligence Scale for Children®–Third Edition (WISC–III)*, the *Wechsler Preschool and Primary Scale of Intelligence™–Revised (WPPSI–R)*, and the *Wechsler Adult Intelligence Scale®–Third Edition (WAIS–III)*. It was co-normed with the

**Record Form**

Wechsler Individual Achievement Test®
Second Edition

|  | Year | Month | Day |
|---|---|---|---|
| | | 6 | 36 |
| Date Tested | 01 | 7 | 6 |
| Date of Birth | 90 | 2 | 7 |
| Age | 11 | 4 | 29 |

Name __Ruth Firestone__     Sex: ☐ Male ☐ Female

School __Carmel School__     Grade _____

Teacher _____     Examiner __H. Gordon__

Referral Source _____

Reason for Referral _____

Behavior Observations _____

## Summary Report

☐ Grade-Based Scores     ☐ Age-Based Scores

| Subtests | Subtest Standard Score | Composite Standard Score | 95% Confidence Interval | Percentile | Other: ☐ NCE ☐ Stanine | Age Equivalent (Use Raw Scores) | Grade Equivalent |
|---|---|---|---|---|---|---|---|
| **Reading** | | | | | | | |
| Word Reading | 100 | | ± 5 | 50 | | 11.4 | |
| Reading Comprehension | 114 | | ± 7 | 82 | | 12.0 | |
| Pseudoword Decoding | 98 | | ± 5 | 45 | | 10.8 | |
| Composite (Sum of Subtest Standard Scores) | 312 | 101 | ± 4 | 53 | | | |
| *Use Table C.2/F.2* | | | | | | | |
| **Mathematics** | | | | | | | |
| Numerical Operations | 83 | | ± 9 | 13 | | 9.8 | |
| Math Reasoning | 105 | | ± 8 | 63 | | 12.0 | |
| Composite (Sum of Subtest Standard Scores) | 188 | 92 | ± 7 | 30 | | | |
| *Use Table C.2/F.2* | | | | | | | |
| **Written Language** | | | | | | | |
| Spelling | 91 | | ± 6 | 27 | | 9.8 | |
| Written Expression | 104 | | ± 13 | 61 | | 12.0 | |
| Composite (Sum of Subtest Standard Scores) | 195 | 96 | ± 8 | 39 | | | |
| *Use Table C.2/F.2* | | | | | | | |
| **Oral Language** | | | | | | | |
| Listening Comprehension | 120 | | ± 14 | 91 | | 16.0 | |
| Oral Expression | N/A | | | | | | |
| Composite (Sum of Subtest Standard Scores) | | N/A | | | | | |
| *Use Table C.2/F.2* | | | | | | | |
| **Total Composite** (Sum of All Subtest Standard Scores) | | N/A | | | | | |
| *Use Table C.2/F.2* | | | | | | | |

## Supplemental Scores

| Reading | Quartile |
|---|---|
| Reading Comprehension | 4 |
| Target Words | 2 |
| Reading Speed | 3 |

| Written Expression | Quartile | Decile |
|---|---|---|
| Alphabet Writing | | N/A |
| Word Fluency | | |
| Word Count | | |

| Oral Expression | Quartile |
|---|---|
| Word Fluency | |

1 2 3 4 5 6 7 8 9 10 11 12 A B C D E

Ψ THE PSYCHOLOGICAL CORPORATION®

A Harcourt Assessment Company

**FIGURE 6.1** *WIAT–III Record Form*

*Wechsler Individual Achievement Test, Second Edition.* Copyright © 2001 by The Psychological Corporation, a Harcourt Assessment Company. Reproduced by permission. All rights reserved. "Wechsler Individual Achievement Test," and "WIAT" are trademarks of The Psychological Corporation registered in the United States of America and/or other jurisdictions.

BOX 6.4   *Wechsler Individual Achievement Test, Second Edition (WIAT–II)*

*Publication Date:* 2001

*Purposes:* Measures strengths and weaknesses in oral expression, listening comprehension, written expression, word reading skill, reading comprehension, spelling, mathematics calculation or mathematics reasoning.

*Age/Grade Levels:* Ages 4 years through adulthood.

*Time to Administer:* Approximately 30 minutes to 2 hours.

*Technical Adequacy:* The standardization sample, reliability, and validity are very good.

*Suggested Uses:* Measure of overall achievement; identifies academic strengths and weaknesses.

*Process Assessment of the Learner (PAL™): Test Battery for Reading and Writing.*

**Validity.**   There is good evidence of construct validity. However, as with all tests, we recommend conducting independent validity studies in order to obtain additional information about the construct validity of the *WIAT®–II.*

**Summary.**   The *WIAT®–II* is an individually administered test that assesses achievement in students ages 4 through adulthood. We encourage additional studies investigating the validity of the *WIAT®–II* and the use of this test with students with disabilities. As with all achievement tests, use caution and carefully examine the test items to determine the degree to which they correspond with the curriculum that the student has been taught. Box 6.4 summarizes the parameters of the *WIAT®–II.* In the Snapshot, a special education teacher talks about the administration of the *WIAT®–II* to Patricia, a student with reading difficulties.

## Wide Range Achievement Test–3

The *Wide Range Achievement Test–3 (WRAT–3)* (Wilkinson, 1993) measures the "codes which are needed to learn the basic skills of reading, writing, spelling, and arithmetic" (p. 10). This purpose is the same as the purposes in the previous editions of this test. The meaning of the word "codes" is unclear, although professionals generally assume that it refers to basic academic skills that are essential in reading, spelling, and arithmetic. The *WRAT–3* has three subtests:

*Reading.* The examiner asks the students to recognize individual letters and words in isolation.

*Spelling.* The examiner asks the students to copy marks, write the student's name, and write single words that the examiner dictates.

*Arithmetic.* The student is asked to read numerals, solve problems that the examiner presents verbally, and to compute arithmetic problems using pencil and paper.

**Administration.**   The *WRAT–3* is individually administered and can be administered to individuals ages 5 to 75. There are two forms.

**Scoring.**   The *WRAT–3* is hand scored and six types of scores are available: raw, absolute, and standard scores, percentiles, normal curve equivalents, and grade equivalents.

**Standardization.**   The standardization sample of the *WRAT–3* was based on the 1990 U.S. Census and consisted of 4,443 individuals. The sample stratifications include age, region of the country, gender, and ethnic group.

**Reliability.**   Reliability appears to be adequate. Twenty-three age groups for each form of the test report internal consistency coefficients ranging from .85 to .91. Alternate form reliability is acceptable and median coefficients are: Reading, .92; Spelling, .93; and Mathematics, .89.

## SNAPSHOT ■ *A Special Education Teacher's Comments*

Patricia is in fourth grade. She has received special education services since kindergarten because of speech and language difficulties. When she was in third grade Patricia's teacher raised concerns about Patricia's behavior in the classroom, and asked Patricia's parent to seek a medical opinion about the possibility that Patricia had an attention-deficit hyperactivity disorder. The parent did not follow this advice, and the school did not follow up. Her current fourth-grade teacher has raised these concerns again and referred Patricia for further evaluation.

As part of the evaluation, I administered the *Wechsler Individual Achievement Test®, Second Edition (WIAT®–II)*. Patricia came willingly to the testing room. She seemed to listen carefully while I explained that some of the questions would be easy but would get harder since this was a test for older children as well. We proceeded through the subtests.

When we came to the Spelling subtest I noticed an immediate change in her behavior and attitude. As soon as I gave her the spelling sheet and a pencil and asked her to write the words given to her, she became restless and silly. Her pencil grip seemed unsteady and she wiggled in her seat. She repeated every word slowly and talked to herself throughout this subtest.

After the Spelling subtest we took a short break, and then I proceeded to administer the remaining subtests in the *WIAT®–II*. The restlessness was still present. When we were finished, I thanked Patricia and walked her back to her classroom.

I returned to my room and scored the test. An analysis of Patricia's performance showed that she had specific strengths and a number of weaknesses. I was very concerned about Patricia's behavioral changes when faced with tasks that involved writing.

Patricia's literacy instruction uses a balanced approach as a base. I wondered if Patricia's behavior was an attempt to hide her perceived discomfort. In preparation for the IEP meeting, I summarized Patricia's performance and asked her teacher to bring samples of Patricia's classroom work and homework to the meeting. I also asked the teacher to bring samples of students who were performing "typically" so that the team would be able to compare Patricia's performance with the performance of students who were performing at this standard. Finally, I arranged for the consultant to conduct systematic observations of Patricia's behavior in her classroom.

*Validity.* We strongly urge examiners to examine the content of the test items. Content validity is highly questionable because it is unclear how well the test items assess the content areas of reading, mathematics, and spelling. Additional research studies are necessary to substantiate the construct validity of this instrument.

*Summary.* The *Wide Range Achievement Test–3* is an individually administered test of reading, spelling, and mathematics achievement. The format of the test has not significantly changed since it was first published. Although the standardization and reliability are acceptable, validity is questionable. We recommend using this instrument as a screening instrument, if at all. Box 6.5 summarizes the tool's parameters.

**BOX 6.5** *Wide Range Achievement Test–3 (WRAT–3)*

*Publication Date:* 1993

*Purposes:* Measures reading recognition, spelling dictated words, and basic arithmetic skills.

*Age/Grade Levels:* Ages 5 years through 75 years.

*Time to Administer:* 15 minutes to 30 minutes.

*Technical Adequacy:* Standardization and reliability are acceptable, validity is questionable.

*Suggested Use:* This instrument is best used as a screening instrument, if at all.

## Woodcock-Johnson Tests of Achievement

The *Woodcock-Johnson® III (WJ® III)* (Woodcock, McGrew, and Mather, 2001) is an individually administered battery that assesses cognitive and academic abilities in individuals ages 2 years through adulthood. The battery consists of two tests: *Woodcock-Johnson® III Tests of Cognitive Ability (WJ® III COG)* and the *Woodcock-Johnson® III Tests of Achievement (WJ® III ACH)*. Each part comprises a Standard Battery and a Supplemental Battery. Standard batteries can be administered alone or with the supplemental batteries. Chapter 13 describes the *WJ® III COG*. Box 6.6 summarizes the battery's parameters.

The *WJ® III* has the following purposes: (1) diagnosis, (2) determination of intra-ability and ability/achievement discrepancies, (3) program placement, (4) individual program planning, (5) guidance, (6) growth assessment, (7) program evaluation, and (8) research. The subtests combine to form five clusters in reading, mathematics, written language, and knowledge (science, social studies, and humanities). A description of the subtests can be found in Table 6.4. There are two parallel forms of the *WJ® III ACH* Standard Battery.

*Administration.* The time to administer the *WJ® III ACH* varies from approximately 20 minutes to over an hour, depending on whether examiners use both the Standard Battery and the Supplemental Battery. Raw scores can convert to age and grade equivalents, percentile ranks, and standard scores. The scoring can be cumbersome and it is advisable to use a computer scoring program.

*Norms.* The *WJ® III* was standardized on 8,818 individuals in over 100 communities. The preschool sample consisted of 1,143 children who were 2 years to 5 years of age and not enrolled in kindergarten. There were 4,783 individuals in the kindergarten through grade 12 sample. The rest of the standardization sample consisted of individuals who were in college or not in school. The sample was stratified according to region, community size, sex, race—Caucasian, African American, Native American, Asian Pacific, Hispanic (non-Hispanic, Hispanic), and other—funding of college/university, type of college/university, and occupation of adults. The norms are continuous-year norms, that is, the norms were collected throughout the year.

*Reliability.* The test manual provides extensive information on reliability for the *WJ® III ACH* including: split-half reliabilities for all achievement subtests except the subtests that rely on speed of response (Reading Fluency, Math Fluency, and Writing Fluency); test-retest reliabilities for the speeded subtests; interrater reliabilities for the achievement subtests (Writing Samples, Writing Fluency, Handwriting) that require subjective judgment of responses; and alternative form reliabilities, for equivalence of Forms A and B. The manual also provides information about standard errors of measurement for

---

**BOX 6.6**  *Woodcock-Johnson® III, Tests of Achievement (WJ® III ACH)*

*Publication Date:* 2001

*Purposes:* Measures overall achievement in reading, mathematics, written language, and general knowledge in science, social studies, and humanities.

*Age/Grade Levels:* Ages 2 years through adulthood.

*Time to Administer:* 20 minutes to over 1 hour.

*Technical Adequacy:* Reliability information is acceptable. Validity is adequate; however, the teacher should determine content validity by comparing the test items with the curriculum that the student has been taught.

*Suggested Uses:* Measure overall achievement; may be used to indicate general areas of strength and weakness.

**TABLE 6.4** *Woodcock-Johnson® III, Tests of Achievement*

There are two parallel forms of the *WJ® III ACH:* Standard Battery and Extended Battery.

The subtests can be combined to form four clusters in reading, mathematics, oral language, written language, and skills.

The *WJ® III Standard Battery* consists of twelve subtests.

1. *Letter-Word Identification.* Assesses the ability to identify letters and words in isolation.
2. *Reading Fluency.* Measures the ability to read statements rapidly and answer "yes" or "no."
3. *Story Recall.* Assesses the ability to listen to and recall details of stories.
4. *Understanding Directions.* Measures the ability to comprehend and follow directions.
5. *Calculation.* Assesses the ability to solve mathematical calculations using a booklet in which the student can respond in writing.
6. *Math Fluency.* Assesses the ability to add, subtract, and multiply rapidly.
7. *Spelling.* Measures the ability to spell orally presented words.
8. *Writing Fluency.* Measures the ability to write fluently.
9. *Passage Comprehension.* Measures the ability to read a short passage and to identify the missing word.
10. *Applied Problems.* Measures the ability to solve practical mathematical problems.
11. *Writing Samples.* Measures the ability to respond in writing to various response demands.
12. *Story Recall–Delayed.* Measures the ability to recall previously presented story.

The *WJ® III ACH Extended Battery* consists of ten subtests.

1. *Word Attack.* Assesses the ability to apply the rules of phonic and structural analysis to read unfamiliar and nonsense words.
2. *Picture Vocabulary.* Measures the ability to identify objects.
3. *Oral Comprehension.* Assesses the ability to identify missing words in a passage that is presented orally.
4. *Editing.* Measures the ability to correct errors in written passages.
5. *Reading Vocabulary.* Assesses the ability to supply one-word synonyms and antonyms after reading words.
6. *Quantitative Concepts.* Assesses the ability to identify mathematics terms, formulas, and number patterns.
7. *Academic Knowledge.* Measures the ability to answer questions about science, social studies, and humanities.
8. *Spelling of Sounds.* Assesses knowledge of letter combinations that form regular patterns in written English.
9. *Sound Awareness.* Measures the ability to rhyme words and to remove, substitute, and reverse parts of words in order to make new words.
10. *Punctuation and Capitalization.* Assesses knowledge of punctuation and capitalization rules.

the subtests. Overall, the reliabilities of the subtests and the clusters are acceptable.

***Validity.*** The manual reports a number of validity studies for the achievement battery. In general, there is evidence to support content, concurrent, and construct validity. The extent to which various subtests reflect students' abilities depends on the instructional orientation of the teacher and the school curriculum.

***Summary.*** The *Tests of Achievements of the Woodcock-Johnson® III* assess academic abilities in individuals ages 24 months through adulthood. The battery is norm-referenced and individually administered. Reliability information is acceptable. A student's performance on the achievement subtests may be a reflection, in part, of the curriculum that has been taught.

## Curriculum-Based Assessment

**Curriculum-based assessment (CBA)** is an approach to linking instruction with assessment. CBA has three purposes: (1) to determine eligibility, (2) to develop the goals for instruction, and (3) to evaluate the student's progress in the curriculum. Based on the performance on a CBA instrument, teachers and other professionals can specify instructional goals. Because there is such a close link between assessment and instruction, it is possible to conduct CBA frequently in order to determine whether to make any changes in instruction or the curriculum. Data collection, interpretation, and intervention are all integral parts of CBA. Other terms for CBA are: curriculum-referenced measurement, curriculum-embedded measurement, frequent measurement, continuous curriculum measurement, and therapeutic measurement. CBA has the following capabilities:

- links curriculum and instruction
- helps the teacher determine what to teach
- can be used frequently
- assists in the evaluation of student progress and program evaluation
- can be reliable and valid
- assists in improving student achievement (Choate, Enright, Miller, Poteet, and Rakes, 1995

### Developing a Curriculum-Based Assessment Instrument

While commercially published CBA instruments exist, there are advantages for teachers to develop their own. One important reason for this is that the curriculum may not correspond to the content of existing instruments. By constructing a CBA instrument using the steps listed below, teachers can specify goals, build into the instrument any special adaptations for test administration, and help to ensure that the CBA instrument is valid.

***Step 1: Identify the Purpose(s).*** Use the instrument to determine eligibility or entry into a curriculum, to develop the goals for intervention, or to evaluate the student's progress in the curriculum. Sometimes, one instrument can serve multiple purposes. For example, teachers can use the CBA instrument to develop goals and to evaluate the student's progress.

***Step 2: Analyze the Curriculum.*** Determine what the curriculum teaches. Determine the specific tasks that the student should be learning.

***Step 3: Develop Performance Objectives.*** Determine if a student has demonstrated progress in the curriculum. Specify behaviors that the student must demonstrate in order to indicate progress in the curriculum.

***Step 4: Develop the Assessment Procedures.*** In this step, develop specific test items that correspond with the performance objectives. The teacher can develop different types of items; for example, observing the student or requesting that the student perform specific actions or specific academic tasks, demonstrate particular behaviors, or answer particular questions.

Make sure to delineate the scoring procedures. You will have to specify how you will determine how well the student performs.

Considerations about reliability and validity are important. The CBA instrument must be valid. It must have a close correspondence with the curriculum.

***Step 5: Implement the Assessment Procedures.*** Once the assessment procedures have been developed, you can collect information. How you decide to record and keep track of the information will be important.

The way in which teachers assess students must be consistent each time. Recording sheets will be helpful in keeping track of the information you collect.

Piloting, or trying out, the CBA items before actual implementation is a good idea. Although a great deal of thought has gone into the development and construction of the items, it is always good practice to try out the items before using them to assess students. You should administer CBA items according to the procedures that have been developed.

### Step 6: Organize the Information.
Summarize the information that you have collected. Tables, graphs, or charts can be useful.

### Step 7: Interpret and Integrate the Results.
Integrate the CBA information with information from standardized tests, observations, anecdotal records, and other forms of assessment. This is the point in the assessment process where instruction and assessment link. The decision-making process continues as educators, along with the team, decide where, when, and how instruction should proceed.

## Criterion-Referenced Tests

A **criterion-referenced test (CRT)** measures a student's performance with respect to a well-defined domain (Anastasi, 1988; Berk, 1988). While norm-referenced tests discriminate between the performance of individual students on specific test items, criterion-referenced tests provide a description of a student's knowledge, skills, or behavior in a specific range of well-defined instructional objectives. This specific range is referred to as a domain. Criterion-referenced tests, instead of using norms, provide information on the performance of a student with respect to specific test items. The results of criterion-referenced testing are not dependent on the performance of other students, as with a norm-referenced test.

There are several characteristics that distinguish CRTs from norm-referenced tests. One of these is mastery. Performance on CRTs provides information on whether students have attained a predetermined level of competence or performance, called mastery. Performance can be interpreted as mastery, nonmastery, or intermediate mastery (Anastasi, 1988). While it is possible to construct a test that is both norm-referenced and criterion-referenced, teachers and other professionals must use caution when interpreting the results of these tests because it is difficult to combine both types of tests in one instrument.

Another distinction between criterion-referenced and norm-referenced tests is the breadth of the content domain that the test covers (Mehrens and Lehmann, 1991). Typical norm-referenced tests survey a broad domain, while CRTs usually have fewer domains but more items in each domain. CRTs typically sample the domain more thoroughly than norm-referenced tests (Mehrens and Lehmann, 1991).

CRTs can also be very useful in helping to make instructional planning decisions. Since they frequently cover a more restricted range of content than norm-referenced tests, they can provide more information about a student's levels of performance.

### Teacher-Developed Criterion-Referenced Tests

Teachers can develop CRTs. The advantage to developing your own CRT is that you can directly link the test items to the curriculum. Use the following steps when developing a CRT (Rivera, Taylor, and Bryant, 1994–1995; Taylor, 1993):

### Step 1: Identify the Knowledge, Processes, or Skills to Be Measured.
Pinpoint the knowledge, processes, skills, and subskills that the student has been taught from the curriculum and from the student's individual educational program (IEP).

### Step 2: Develop Instructional Objectives or Subobjectives for the Skills.
Break down each of the skills and subskills into smaller steps;

*High school students use calculators while collaborating on a mathematics assignment.*

these become the instructional objectives and subobjectives.

***Step 3: Develop Test Items for Each Objective or Subobjective.***   In order to measure each skill, develop test items for each one.

***Step 4: Determine the Performance Standards or Criteria for Performance.***   Give each of the objectives and subobjectives at least one criterion that indicates acceptable levels of performance.

***Step 5: Administer the Test Items.***   Once you have developed the CRT, you can administer the items. An advantage to using criterion-referenced tests is that, unlike norm-referenced tests, you can administer the items on a CRT frequently in order to document the student's progress.

***Step 6: Score the Test Items and Present the Results in a Graph or Chart.***   Record the

student's performance on the CRT. Graphing or charting the results can help both students and teachers in monitoring progress.

***Step 7: Analyze and Interpret the Results.***   Knowledge about the student's level of performance facilitates the development of new instructional objectives and modifications.

### Published Criterion-Referenced Tests

The *BRIGANCE® Diagnostic Inventories* are criterion-referenced tests that are similar in purpose, scoring, administration, and interpretation. They are useful in program planning and in monitoring programs. Table 6.5 summarizes the achievement sections of each of the inventories.

The administration and scoring for the *BRIGANCE®* inventories is similar for all of the inventories. It is not necessary to administer all items or all subtests to a student. The examiner uses professional judgment to determine which items and subtests to administer. Each student has a record booklet which follows the student through several years of school.

Because these inventories are criterion-referenced, teachers can administer them frequently to monitor progress. Color-coding the student's responses to each item enables the teacher to see which skills the student has mastered. There are no summary scores. Instructional objectives accompany the items, facilitating program planning.

## Connecting Instruction with Assessment: Alternative Assessment

The term *informal tests* is an older term that describes approaches to assessment other than standardized tests. The terms *alternative assessment* and *informal assessment* are sometimes used interchangeably to refer to these approaches.

A fundamental principle of alternative approaches is that assessment of achievement

**TABLE 6.5** *BRIGANCE® Inventories*

| Name | Ages/Grades | Achievement Domains |
|---|---|---|
| *BRIGANCE® Inventory of Essential Skills* (Brigance, 1981) | grades 4 through 12 | 1. Mathematics<br>2. Reading<br>3. Writing<br>4. Spelling<br>5. Reference Skills<br>6. Schedules and Graphs<br>7. Measurement<br>8. Money and Finance |
| *BRIGANCE® Comprehensive Inventory of Basic Skills–Revised* (Brigance, 1999) | pre-K through 9 | 1. Mathematics<br>2. Reading<br>3. Writing<br>4. Spelling<br>5. Reference Skills<br>6. Graphs and Maps<br>7. Measurement |
| *BRIGANCE® Assessment of Basic Skills–Spanish Edition* (Brigance, 1984) | grades K through 8 | 1. Reading<br>2. Mathematics<br>3. Writing<br>4. Measurement |
| *BRIGANCE® Diagnostic Inventory of Early Development–Revised* (Brigance, 1991) | ages birth to 7 years | 1. Reading<br>2. Writing<br>3. Mathematics |
| *BRIGANCE® Diagnostic Employability Skills Inventory* (Brigance, 1995) | vocational secondary adult education job training | 1. Reading<br>2. Writing<br>3. Mathematics |

should link to the curriculum. Linking instruction to the assessment of achievement means that:

• Assessment occurs as a normal part of the student's work. Assessment activities should emerge from the curriculum and the teaching situation. The student does not stop work to do an assessment; the work and the assessment are linked. Examples of this type of assessment include the use of journals, notebooks, essays, oral reports, homework, classroom discussions, group work, and interviews. These assessment activities can occur individually or in small groups and can take place during one session or over multiple sessions (Marolda and Davidson, 1994).

• The conditions for assessment need to be similar to the conditions for doing meaningful tasks. Students should have sufficient time, have access to peers, be able to use appropriate tools (books, calculators, manipulatives, etc.), and have the chance to revise their work.

• Assessment tasks should be meaningful and multidimensional. For example, they should provide students with the opportunity to demonstrate solving problems, drawing conclusions, understanding relationships, making inferences, and generating new questions.

• Feedback to students should be specific, meaningful, and prompt, and should inform the students' thinking.

• Students participate in the assessment process. They help to generate and apply standards or rubrics. A rubric is an assessment scale that defines criterion for use in evaluating students. Self-assessment and peer assessment are part of the assessment process.

### Assessment Approaches

Assessment activities and feedback from peers and teachers help promote student achievement. Ways in which the teacher can gather information and provide feedback to parents and students include:

• probes
• error analysis
• oral descriptions
• written descriptions
• checklists
• questionnaires
• interviews
• conferences
• student journals and notebooks
• performance-based assessment
• portfolios
• exhibitions

(National Council of Teachers of Mathematics, 1991)

***Probes.*** A **probe** is a diagnostic technique that modifies instruction in order to determine whether an instructional strategy is effective. Probes can help diagnose student problems and assist in planning instruction. For example, suppose a teacher wants to determine whether a fourth-grade student who is engaged in science investigations is ready to proceed to the next investigation. The teacher can present a science problem to the student and observe the strategies that the student uses to solve it. The teacher probes with questions such as, "What will happen if the temperature is increased?" The student in this case is able to successfully solve the problem, but has difficulty understanding that an experiment may work under certain conditions but not under other conditions. The teacher then helps the student by further probing and guiding the student through the steps of the experiment.

The teacher can implement instructional probes during the process of instruction, using the following steps to design the probe:

1. The teacher identifies the targeted area of achievement and measures whether the student can perform the task. For example, in science the student is studying how pushing or pulling affects moving objects.

**2.** The teacher probes by modifying the task. For example, the teacher adds weight to one of the objects. (See the next section for examples of other instructional modifications.)

**3.** The teacher measures whether the student can perform the task.

When conducting a diagnostic probe the teacher should document the student's performance during step 1 (baseline), step 2 (instruction), and step 3 (baseline).

*Types of Modifications for Use with Probes.* Types of modifications that can apply to instruction include:

### Instructional modifications
- change from written presentation to oral presentation
- combine verbal instruction with written explanation
- require fewer problems to be completed
- provide additional practice
- slow the pace of instruction
- provide additional time to complete problems

### Materials modifications
- use manipulatives
- place fewer questions, problems, or items on a page
- use color, word, or symbolic cues
- simplify the problem or the wording
- combine tactile mode with visual, oral, or kinesthetic modes

### Environmental modifications
- change location of instruction or probe
- change time of day for instruction or probe
- provide a work area that is quiet and free of distractions
- change lighting of work area
- change seating arrangements

***Error Analysis.*** The purposes of **error analysis** are to: (1) identify the patterns of errors or mistakes that students make in their work, (2) understand why students make the errors, and (3) provide targeted instruction to correct the errors. When conducting an error analysis, the teacher checks the student's work and categorizes the errors.

After conducting an error analysis, the teacher summarizes the error patterns. However, many errors that students make may not fall into a pattern. Alternatively, if a pattern emerges it does not mean that the problem is serious. Teachers should view error analysis as a preliminary form of assessment, and should always conduct further evaluation of the student's work.

Teachers frequently use this approach to analyzing student work when assessing students' reading abilities. Error analysis, when it is applied to reading, is commonly referred to as *miscue analysis*. When conducting a miscue analysis, teachers look for patterns of errors. According to Goodman (1984; 1989) these are "natural" errors rather than mistakes. Chapter 8 and Chapter 11 describe the application of error analysis to the assessment of reading and mathematics, respectively.

***Oral Descriptions.*** Verbal descriptions of a student's work provide immediate feedback to a student by a teacher or peer. Oral descriptions are especially useful because they are quick, efficient, direct, and integrate easily into instruction. They are effective for program planning and program evaluation.

Oral descriptions do have several drawbacks, however. They can be subjective and, since the descriptions are verbal, there is no permanent record. In addition, specific disabilities may limit the ability of the student to understand, remember, or reply to what has been said.

***Written Descriptions.*** A written description is a brief narrative that records feedback about the student's work. The teacher can share the narrative with students, teachers, or parents. A written description, like an oral description, conveys an impression of important aspects of the student's work. Teachers can use written descriptions for program planning and program evaluation.

Before writing the narrative, the teacher should carefully review the student's work. The teacher writes the description, noting areas of strength as well as problem areas. A written description provides feedback to the student about the quality of the work. Because it is recorded, it becomes a reference as the student continues to work. For example, a student who is engaged in environmental science has the following project: Investigate the migration patterns of killer bees. After developing graphs that depict migration patterns and studying the habitats of killer bees, the student develops conclusions and makes predictions about future migrations to new geographic areas.

After examining the student's work, a teacher can comment on: labeling, graphing, spelling, and use of language. In addition, the teacher can discuss the use of graphing and knowledge of geography to solve real-world problems, completeness of the results, the student's disposition toward science, the ability to plan ahead, work habits, and attention to detail (Kulm, 1994). Two

disadvantages of using written descriptions are that the parents may have difficulty reading or they may not have knowledge of written English.

***Checklists and Questionnaires.***  Checklists and questionnaires are convenient ways to provide feedback about a student's work or attitudes. A checklist can be a quick and easy assessment approach. Figure 6.2 is an example of a checklist that provides feedback about student confidence, willingness, perseverance, and interest. Checklists are helpful for screening, diagnosis, program planning, and program evaluation.

Questionnaires provide an opportunity for teachers and students to collect information in more detail than checklists. Questionnaires can be open-ended, allowing respondents to express their attitudes, opinions, and knowledge in depth or they can have a more structured format so that the respondents just need to fill in one or two words, circle responses, or indicate the appropriate picture or icon.

***Interviews.***  In Chapter 5 we discuss the topic of conducting interviews. Interviews help guide

---

**FIGURE 6.2**  *Assessing Attitudes, Interests, and Habits*

**My Beliefs about School**

| | | | |
|---|---|---|---|
| 1. I like to go to school | most of the time | sometimes | never |
| 2. My favorite subjects are | language arts<br>social studies | mathematics<br>health | science<br>physical education |
| 3. When I am at school I like to | read<br>use the computer | write<br>use the library | do projects<br>use the playground |
| 4. I like to work | by myself | with one other<br>person | with several peers |
| 5. I do homework | most of the time | sometimes | never |
| 6. If I need help doing homework,<br>I usually ask | my parent<br>no one | my brother or sister | a friend |
| 7. Some things I like about my<br>teacher are: | | | |

discussions, encourage students, determine motivation and enthusiasm, and identify work and study habits. One basic approach is to interview students individually about their likes and dislikes. Asking questions such as the following can be informative: "What do you like about social studies?" "What are your interests?" "What don't you like?" Interviews are useful for screening, diagnosis, program planning, and program evaluation.

Structured interviews provide a more systematic way to assess achievement. A structured interview offers the opportunity to observe, question, and discuss areas of achievement.

An example of using a structured interview in science is to ask students to observe the sky several times during one evening and the next day to answer the following questions:

1. What is the pattern of the stars as they move across the sky?
2. What is the pattern of the planets?
3. Do the planets follow the same pattern as the stars?
4. After showing students several pictures of the planets and stars, ask students to develop several hypotheses about their size, appearance, and motion.

*Conferences.*   A conference is a conversation about the student's work that can include the student, educators, and parents. In a conference, participants share their views of the student's work with the goal of providing feedback and recommendations. Teacher-student conferences are helpful when assessing one piece of work or when summarizing the student's work over a period of time. The discussion in a conference can be strictly verbal or it can be on audiotape, videotape, or written in summary form. Conferences can be useful for diagnosis, program planning, and program evaluation.

*Student Journals.*   Students can keep a notebook or journal that allows them to record their work as well as their attitudes and feelings. A journal provides students the opportunity to record the steps to plan for an assignment, reflect on their own work, communicate about their learning, and document their progress (Kulm, 1994). In a journal, students can indicate what they like and don't like and areas in which they have difficulty. Journals are effective for program planning and program evaluation. The following is a sample mathematics journal outline (Kulm, 1994, p. 48):

Today's topic:

Two important ideas:

What I understood best:

What I need more work on:

How this topic can be used in real life:

*Performance-Based Assessment.*   When used to assess achievement, **performance-based assessment** is the demonstration of knowledge, skills, or behavior. Performance assessment requires students to develop a product or to demonstrate an ability or skill based on an understanding of concepts and relationships. Chapter 7 describes performance-based assessment in detail.

*Portfolios.*   A **portfolio** is a systematic collection of a student's work, assembled over a period of time. When documenting and assessing achievement, portfolios can provide information about conceptual understanding, problem solving, reasoning, communication abilities, habits, motivation, enthusiasm, creativity, work habits, and attitudes. Portfolios help students see that knowledge is interconnected. They are useful for program planning and program evaluation. A more extensive discussion of the use of portfolios can be found in Chapter 7.

*Exhibitions.*   An exhibition is a display of a student's work that demonstrates knowledge, abilities, skills, and attitudes. Exhibitions are discussed in Chapter 7.

## Self-Assessment

Self-assessment provides students with an opportunity to review concepts and identify processes. It is an occasion for students to reflect on their learning. Figure 6.3 is an example of a checklist that students use when assessing their own learning.

## Peer Assessment

Peer assessment allows students insight into the thinking and reasoning abilities of their peers. When conducting peer assessments, students have an opportunity to reflect on the learning processes of their peers as well as their own. Figure 6.4 is an example of a checklist that students use when conducting a peer assessment.

## Report Card Grades as Measures of Achievement

Report card grades can be helpful in understanding a student's achievement levels, strengths, and weaknesses. Report cards from the current and previous years can provide information about whether the student's problems are new or long-standing. They can indicate trends in student achievement. Is the problem recent? Has the student had difficulty during previous years? Is the problem in one area or in several areas? In what areas does the student do well?

## Report Card Grading

There are two major viewpoints regarding the assignment of report card grades to students with disabilities (Gersten, Vaughn, and Brengelman, 1996). The first position considers grading standards to be absolute. Report card grades for all students should be based on the same standards; that is, an A, B, C, or failing grade means the same for a student with a disability or a student without a disability. The second perspective is that grading should be based on individual effort. However, this second option has several drawbacks: (1) it is difficult to measure effort; (2) basing grades on effort can prevent students from making progress because the grade creates the illusion that the student *is* making progress; (3) it is difficult to use just one grade to communicate multiple meanings such

**FIGURE 6.3**   *Self-Assessment Checklist—Social Studies*

| Student's Name | | | | Date | |
|---|---|---|---|---|---|
| **After completing my social studies assignment, I can** | *1* *Great!* | *2* | *3* | *4* | *5* *Need more work* |
| 1. make comparisons among different points of view. | | | | | |
| 2. distinguish between fact and opinion. | | | | | |
| 3. apply new skills in using information. | | | | | |
| 4. understand new vocabulary. | | | | | |
| 5. make inferences about events. | | | | | |
| 6. integrate new information. | | | | | |
| 7. discuss new concepts and theories. | | | | | |

**FIGURE 6.4** *Peer Assessment—Science*

| Student's Name | Date | | |
|---|---|---|---|
| Peer's Name | | | |
| | Yes | No | Somewhat |
| 1. My peer used new information to solve a problem. | | | |
| 2. My peer used new vocabulary. | | | |
| 3. My peer demonstrated the ability to think analytically. | | | |
| 4. My peer integrated and synthesized information. | | | |
| 5. My peer made several generalizations. | | | |

as progress, effort, and peer comparisons (Bursuck, et al., 1996).

### Grading Students with Disabilities

Alternatives to traditional report cards for students with disabilities are:

*Supplementary progress reports.* This is a written narrative that accompanies the traditional report card and that describes the student's academic and behavioral performance during a specific ranking period (Mehring, 1995).

*Contracts.* This is a written agreement between the student and the teacher that specifies the level of performance that the student must sustain to obtain a particular grade (Mehring, 1995).

*Progress checklist.* This is a list of skills or competencies that are taught. Evaluation of the skills or competencies is made by checking a box under the column "mastered" or "needs improvement" (Mehring, 1995).

*Modifications list.* A list of options for the teacher when grading a student with a disability can be used. These modifications can be jointly developed by the teacher, student, and parents. Figure 6.5 presents suggested modifications.

### Observing the Student within the Environment

Chapter 5 discusses the importance of considering the student within the physical, learning, and social environments. The interactions between the student and the environment are important assessment considerations.

### Physical Environment

The physical environment can influence the student's performance. The temperature, lighting, and seating arrangements of teaching and learning spaces can affect how well the student performs. Figure 6.6 on page 159 is a checklist for studying the physical environment.

### Learning Environment

A comfortable learning environment facilitates the acquisition of a positive disposition and contributes to achievement. The curriculum, instructional methods, materials, and the assessment approaches are all areas of concern. A positive learning environment contributes to developing a positive disposition. Figure 6.7 on page 160 is a checklist that can help to determine the appropriateness of the learning environment.

**FIGURE 6.5**    *Sample of Criteria for Grading a Student Who Receives Special Education Services*

The following procedures could be jointly developed by the school, student, and parent when specifying grading options.

**Tests**

- Administer test orally, with questions and answers.
- Teacher, other student, or resource teacher reads regular test to student. (Please give resource teacher at least one day's notice.)
- Administer regular test using open book, class notes, or both.
- Modify modality of tests, written or oral, such as multiple choice instead of essay questions.
- Redo test if not passed.
- Lower criterion for passing.

**In-Class Assignments**

- Give regular assignments with lower criteria for passing.
- Shorten the regular assignment (e.g., half the questions).
- Grade assignments as "complete" rather than with a letter grade.
- Modify the set of questions students will answer.

- Pair the student with another student for help.
- Require the student to give oral answers to teacher.
- Redo assignments if incorrect.
- Give credit for appropriate behaviors not normally graded, such as taking notes.

**Homework**

- Same options as "In-Class Assignments."

**Class Participation, Behavior, and Effort**

- Same expectations as for other class members, but student may need extra encouragement and frequent feedback from teacher.
- Focus on a specific study skill or behavior deficit by giving a Pass/No Pass each day for that behavior. (Examples: coming prepared to class to class with correct materials, or volunteering anwers during class discussions.)

**Other Considerations**

- Give extra credit for projects that student or teacher suggests.
- Have student aide tape reading assignments or read aloud to student.
- Set expectations for attendance.

*Source:* "ASCD Yearbook 1996 Communicating Student Learning." Edited by Thomas R. Guskey, 1996, Alexandria, VA: Association for Supervision and Curriculum Development, Figure 5.1, pp. 52, and Figure 9.2, pp. 94.

## Social Environment

Relationships with students and teachers can affect achievement. The social environment is important to the development of self-concept and self-esteem. These, in turn, contribute to a positive disposition toward achievement. By observing the social environment, teachers can study the relationships students have with peers and adults. Figure 6.8 on page 161 is a checklist that can help to determine the appropriateness of the social environment.

## Preferred Practices

Achievement tests, when carefully chosen, can be important sources of information. The achieve-

ment approaches discussed in this chapter include multiple sources of information that are useful when assessing achievement. School records and past and current classroom performance are important sources of information. Other sources include criterion-referenced assessment, curriculum-based assessment, journals, notebooks, essays, oral reports, homework, discussions, group work, interviews, alternative assessment, performance testing, self-assessment, peer assessment, systematic observations, anecdotal records, interviews with teachers and students, and samples of student's work.

Assessment and instruction are closely linked and intertwined. When assessing achievement, the teacher must be knowledgeable about the *taught* curriculum in contrast to

◀ **POINT STREET SCHOOL** ▶
**Physical Environment**

Student's Name ___Karen S.___

Observer ___T.S.___

Date ___3/13___  Time ___10:35___

Location ___English___

| Characteristic | Always | Sometimes | Never |
|---|---|---|---|
| **1. Seating** Is the student seated properly? | | | X |

▶ Suggestions for improvement: Karen's feet do not reach the floor when she is sitting at her desk. She needs to have a foot rest.

| | | | |
|---|---|---|---|
| **2. Lighting** Is the lighting appropriate? | X | | |

▶ Suggestions for improvement:

| | | | |
|---|---|---|---|
| **3. Noise** Is the noise level appropriate? | | X | |

▶ Suggestions for improvement: There are times when the noise level seems high. This may make it difficult for Karen and other students to concentrate. Suggest that the teacher and students monitor the noise level.

| | | | |
|---|---|---|---|
| **4. Distractions** Is the student distracted by activities in the room? | | X | |

▶ Suggestions for improvement: While Karen is distracted at times, she is able to refocus on the tasks at hand.

| | | | |
|---|---|---|---|
| **5. Temperature** Is the temperature of the room appropriate? | | X | |

▶ Suggestions for improvement: There are times when the room is too hot. This does not seem to affect Karen's performance. However, this should be monitored.

| | | | |
|---|---|---|---|
| **6. General Atmosphere** Does the student appear to be comfortable in the environment? | X | | |

▶ Suggestions for improvement:

**FIGURE 6.6**   *Observing the Physical Environment*

**◄ POINT STREET SCHOOL ►**
**Learning Environment**

Student's Name ___Karen S.___          Date __3/13__  Time __10:35__

Observer ___T.S.___                    Location ___English___

| Characteristic | Always | Sometimes | Never |
|---|---|---|---|
| **1. Materials**<br>Are a variety of materials available? | X | | |
| ▶ Suggestions for improvement: | | | |
| **2. Manipulatives**<br>Are appropriate manipulatives available? | | | |
| ▶ Suggestions for improvement: *N/A* | | | |
| **3. Curriculum**<br>Does the curriculum reflect recent reform standards? | X | | |
| ▶ Suggestions for improvement: | | | |
| **4. Activities**<br>Is instruction oriented toward the use of various materials rather than paper and pencil tasks? | | X | |
| ▶ Suggestions for improvement: *Karen performs best when actively involved in projects. Suggest that options for assignments be developed for Karen and other students.* | | | |
| **5. Instructional Demands**<br>Are the instructional demands appropriate for the student? | | X | |
| ▶ Suggestions for improvement: *Karen needs to have directions for assignments clarified. She should be asked to repeat the directions to make sure that she understands what is expected.* | | | |
| **6. Modifications**<br>Have modifications been made to instruction to accommodate the learning needs of the student? | X | | |
| ▶ Suggestions for improvement: | | | |

**FIGURE 6.7**   *Observing the Learning Environment*

◄ **POINT STREET SCHOOL** ►
**Social Environment**

Student's Name ___Karen S.___          Date __3/13__ Time __10:35__

Observer ___T.S.___          Location ___English___

| Characteristic | Always | Sometimes | Never |
|---|---|---|---|
| **1. Teacher-Student Interactions**<br>Are interactions warm and friendly? | X | | |
| ▶ Suggestions for improvement: | | | |
| **2. Disruptions**<br>Are disruptions kept to a minimum? | | X | |
| ▶ Suggestions for improvement: *Announcements and the public address system interruptions can distract Karen and other students in the class. An effort should be made to reduce these interruptions.* | | | |
| **3. Behavioral interventions**<br>Are behavioral interventions effective and appropriate? | X | | |
| ▶ Suggestions for improvement: | | | |
| **4. Peer interactions**<br>Are peer interactions appropriate? | X | | |
| ▶ Suggestions for improvement: | | | |
| **5. General Atmosphere**<br>Does the student appear to be comfortable in the social environment? | X | | |
| ▶ Suggestions for improvement: | | | |

**FIGURE 6.8** *Observing the Social Environment*

the *written* curriculum. Achievement tests should measure what has been *taught*. Teachers should carefully examine the test content in order to determine that there is a very close match between the test items and the taught curriculum. The information that teachers gather through the assessment process should inform and support learning and instruction.

## Extending Learning

1. Identify one topic for instruction. Develop two assessment tasks that link the instruction directly to assessment.

2. Obtain a copy of a standardized achievement test. Review the test items in one curriculum area. What items represent the curriculum that is being taught in the local schools? What items differ? What conclusions and recommendations can you offer?

3. Mr. Lincoln, a new teacher, suspected that Simon, an 8-year-old in second grade, was having difficulty keeping up with his classroom peers. Ms. Sloan, who taught high school students, was puzzled when Katy, a 15-year-old, was falling behind her classmates. Choose one of these teachers. What suggestions could you give the teacher for assessing the achievement of these students?

4. Compare the test items of a group achievement test with an individual achievement test. What are the similarities? Differences? When would it be appropriate to use each of these tests?

5. Choose a curriculum area with which you are familiar. Working with a partner, identify a unit of instruction. Using the steps suggested in this chapter, develop a criterion-referenced test. Share your CRT with other groups and provide feedback.

## References

American Educational Research Association, American Psychological Association, and National Council on Measurement in Education (1985). *Standards for educational and psychological testing.* Washington, DC: American Educational Research Association.

Anastasi, A. (1988). *Psychological testing.* New York: Macmillan.

Balow, I. H., R. C. Farr, and T. P. Hogan (2000). *Metropolitan achievement test 8.* San Antonio, TX: The Psychological Corporation.

Berk, R. A. (1988). Criterion-referenced tests. In *Educational research, methodology, and measurement: An international handbook,* ed. J. P. Keeves, 365–370. Oxford: Pergamon Press.

Brigance, A. H. (1981). *BRIGANCE® inventory of essential skills.* No. Billerica, MA: Curriculum Associates.

Brigance, A. H. (1999). *BRIGANCE® comprehensive inventory of basic skills–revised.* No. Billerica, MA: Curriculum Associates.

Brigance, A. H. (1984). *BRIGANCE® assessment of basic skills–Spanish edition.* No. Billerica, MA: Curriculum Associates.

Brigance, A. H. (1991). *BRIGANCE® inventory of early development–revised.* No. Billerica, MA: Curriculum Associates.

Brigance, A. H. (1995). *BRIGANCE® employability skills inventory.* No. Billerica, MA: Curriculum Associates.

Bursuck, W., E. A. Polloway, L. Plante, M. J. Epstein, J. Jayanthi, and J. McConeghy (1996). Report card grading and adaptations: A national survey of classroom practices. *Exceptional Children* 62: 301–318.

Choate, J. S., B. E. Enright, L. J. Miller, J. A. Poteet, and T. A. Rakes (1995). *Curriculum-based assessment and programming.* Boston: Allyn & Bacon.

CTB/Macmillan/McGraw-Hill (2000). *Terra Nova®.* Monterey, CA: McGraw-Hill.

CTB/McGraw-Hill (1997). *Supeva®.* Monterey, CA: CTB/McGraw-Hill.

Engel, B. (1990). An approach to assessement in early literacy. In *Achievement testing in the early grades,* ed. C. Kamii, 119–134. Washington, DC: National Association for the Education of Young Children.

Feldt, L. S., R. A. Forsyth, T. N. Ansley, and S. D. Alnot (1996). *Iowa tests of educational development.* Chicago: Riverside.

Gersten, R., S. Vaughn, and S. U. Brengelman (1996). Grading and academic feedback for special education students and students with learning difficulties. In *ASCD yearbook,* ed. T. R. Guskey, 47–57.

Alexandria, VA: Association for Supervision and Curriculum Development.

Goodman, K. (1984). Unity in reading. In *Becoming readers in a complex society: The 83rd yearbook of the national society of the study of education, Part I*, eds. A. Purves and O. Niles, 79–114. Chicago, IL: University of Chicago Press.

Goodman, K. (1989). Roots of the whole-language movement. *Elementary School Journal* 90: 207–222.

Guskey, T. R. (1996). *Communicating student learning: 1996 ASCO yearbook*. Alexandria, VA: Association for Supervision and Curriculum Development.

Harcourt Brace Educational Measurement (2001). *Stanford achievement test: New norms*. San Antonio, TX: Harcourt Brace Educational Measurement.

Hoover, H. D., A. N. Hieronymous, D. A. Frisbie, and S. B. Dunbar (1996). *Iowa tests of basic skills*. Itasca, IL: Riverside.

Howell, K. W., and R. Rueda (1996). Achievement testing with culturally and linguistically diverse students. In *Handbook of multicultural assessment*, ed. L. S. Suzuki, P. J. Meller, and J. G. Ponterotto. San Francisco: Jossey-Bass.

Kaufman, A. S., and N. L. Kaufman (1998). *Kaufman test of educational achievement/Normative update (KTEA/NU)*. Circle Pines, MN: American Guidance Service.

Kulm, G. (1994). *Mathematics assessment*. San Francisco: Jossey-Bass.

Markwardt, Jr., F. C. (1998). *Peabody individual achievement test–revised/normative update*. Circle Pines, MN: American Guidance Service.

Marolda, M. R., and P. S. Davidson (1994). Assessing mathematical abilities and learning approaches. *Windows of opportunity*, ed. C. A. Thornton and N. S. Bley, 83–113. Reston, VA: National Council of the Teachers of Mathematics.

Mehrens, W. A., and I. J. Lehmann (1991). *Measurement and evaluation in education and psychology*. Fort Worth, TX: Holt, Rinehart & Winston.

Mehring, T. A. (1995). Report card options for students with disabilities in general education. In *Report card on report cards*, ed. T. Azwell and E. Schmar. Portsmouth, NH: Heinemann.

Naslund, R. A., L. P. Thorpe, and D. W. Lefever (1985). *SRA achievement series*. Chicago: Science Research Associates.

National Council of the Teachers of Mathematics. (1991). *Mathematics assessment*. Reston, VA: National Council of the Teachers of Mathematics.

Newcomer, P. L. and B. R. Bryant (1993). *Diagnostic achievement tests for adolescents*. Austin, TX: PRO-ED.

Nitko, A. J. (1996). *Educational assessment of students*. Upper Saddle River, NJ: Prentice-Hall.

Prescott, G. A., I. H. Balow, T. R. Hogan, and R. C. Farr. (1984). *Metropolitan achievement tests 6: Survey battery*. San Antonio, TX: Harcourt Brace Educational Measurement.

The Psychological Corporation (2001). *Wechsler individual achievement test, second edition (WIAT®–II)*. San Antonio, TX: The Psychological Corporation.

Rivera, D. P., R. L. Taylor, and B. R. Bryant (1994–1995). Review of current trends in mathematics assessment for students with mild disabilities. *Diagnostique* 20: 143–174.

Salvia J., and J. E. Ysseldyke (1995). *Assessment*. Boston: Houghton Mifflin.

Sattler, J. (2001). *Assessment of children*. San Diego: Jerome M. Sattler.

Scannell, D. P., O. M. Hough, B. H. Lloyd, and C. F. Risinger (1993). *Tests of achievement and proficiency*. Itasca, IL: Riverside.

Sonnenschein, J. L. (1983). *Basic achievement skills individual screener*. San Antonio, TX: Harcourt Brace Educational Measurement.

Taylor, R. L. (1993). *Assessment of exceptional students*. 3d ed. Boston, MA: Allyn & Bacon.

Wilkinson, G. (1993). *Wide range achievement test–3*. Wilmington, DE: Wide Range.

Woodcock, R. W., K. S. McGrew, and N. Mather (2001). *Woodcock-Johnson® III*. Itasca, IL: Riverside.

# 7

# *Performance-Based, Authentic, and Portfolio Assessments*

## *Overview*

This chapter examines alternatives to traditional assessment approaches. Each of the alternative methods, performance-based assessment, authentic assessment, and portfolio assessment, is evolving as we search for improved practices and tools for linking instruction with assessment. Portfolios, performance tasks, exhibitions, or other documentation of students' achievement are a measure of student accomplishments. While norm-referenced tests have their place in the assessment process, alternatives to norm-referenced tests provide a rich variety of methods to collect information about student progress, skills, and achievement.

## Chapter Objectives

After completing this chapter, you should be able to:

- Provide a rationale for the use of alternative assessment methods.
- Describe performance-based assessment, authentic assessment, and portfolio assessment.
- Develop and implement performance-based assessment methods.
- Develop scoring rubrics.

## What Shapes Our Views

Contemporary views of learning have influenced the development of alternative assessment approaches. From cognitive learning theory we know the following (Byrnes, 1996; Dixon-Krauss, 1996; Herman, Aschbacher, Winters, 1992; Mayer, 1998):

1. *Students can construct knowledge by connecting new information and prior learning.* Implications for assessment:

   - Students learn divergent thinking, rather than searching for one right answer and multiple solutions.
   - Students develop multiple forms of expression.
   - Students develop critical thinking skills.
   - Students relate new information to prior knowledge.

2. *Students of all ages and abilities can solve problems.* Implications for assessment:

   - All students participate in problem solving activities.
   - Problem solving and critical thinking do not have to be contingent on mastery of basic skills.

3. *Students approach learning with a multiplicity of learning styles, attention spans, and developmental and cognitive differences.* Implications for assessment:

   - Multiple choices in how to demonstrate what has been learned are available.
   - Teachers allot enough time to complete assessment tasks generously.

4. *Students do better when they know the goals and understand how their performance will be evaluated.* Implications for assessment:

   - Students participate in establishing goals.
   - Students can discuss and describe criteria for performance.
   - Students routinely receive examples of acceptable levels of performance.

5. *Students should know when to use knowledge and how to direct their own learning.* Implications for assessment:

   - Students have opportunities to monitor and evaluate their own learning.
   - Teachers utilize authentic (real-world) opportunities for assessment.

6. *Students' learning is affected by motivation, effort, and self-esteem.* Implications for assessment:

   - Teachers consider motivation, self-esteem, and the promotion of best efforts in designing assessments.

## Performance-Based Assessment

Performance-based assessment describes one or more approaches for measuring student progress, skills, and achievements. Performance-based assessment consists of portfolios, performance tasks, exhibitions, or other documentation of student accomplishments. One way of looking at performance assessment is to think of it as the ultimate form of linking instruction with assessment. Wiggins (1993) has been a strong proponent of performance assessment. He has urged educators to use "clear, apt, published, and consistently applied teacher criteria in grading work and published models of excellent work that exemplifies standards" and create "ample opportunities [for students] to produce work that they can be proud of (thus, ample opportunity in the curriculum and instruction to monitor, self-assess, and self-correct their work)" (p. 28).

Gardner (1991) has described performance-based assessments according to developmental levels. Gardner views students as learners who are at various points in their learning. For example, some students might exhibit the performance of beginning learners while others would demonstrate the performance of experts. Evaluations do not just have to focus on what students demonstrate about their academic or cognitive abilities but can determine the extent to which students work cooperatively, are sensitive to others, or contribute to the group.

Performance-based assessment is particularly useful when students are working on long-term projects. In this way, they are able to bring into play a variety of resources and to demonstrate mastery of various concepts and principles. Performance-based assessments relate most closely to the types of assessments that students will most likely engage in after they leave school.

For teachers of standards-based education, performance-based assessment serves several important functions (Arter and McTighe, 2001):

- Performance criteria help define the standards by specifying what one would look for as evidence of standards achievement.
- When made public, the performance criteria and scoring guides provide clear and consistent targets for students, parents, teachers, and others.
- Using performance-based assessment consistently across classrooms, school, and districts makes the evaluation of student performance more reliable.
- Teaching criteria to students helps improve the very skills under assessment, thus integrating assessment and instruction. (pp. 15–16)

## Developing Performance-Based Assessments

There are four questions that can guide us as we think about performance assessment (Diez and Moon, 1992):

1. *What is important for students to know and to be able to do?* This question requires us to re-think curricula, standards, and approaches to teaching.

2. *What is acceptable performance?* In establishing criteria for performance, we must think about mastery. What does mastery of a specific skill or behavior look like? The criteria must be general enough so that students can practice those skills on which they will be evaluated.

3. *How can expert judgments be made?* In developing the criteria for acceptable performance, we must be able to specify them in advance. For example, suppose we want to know how well a student can retell a story or demonstrate knowledge about the community in which the student lives. Criteria that could be specified in advance include the use of details, accuracy, vocabulary, and expression.

4. *How can feedback be provided?* Performance assessment always requires more than one solution or one type of performance. Is the student using the skills under consideration in school and at home? How can the family, educators, and peers provide feedback to the student? The criteria for making judgments become the goals for instruction and progress.

Figure 7.1 is a checklist for use in developing performance-based assessments.

## Authentic Assessment

**Authentic assessment** is similar to performance assessment except that the student completes or demonstrates knowledge, skills, or behavior in a real-life context (Meyer, 1992) and real-world standards measure the student's knowledge, skills,

**FIGURE 7.1**   *Checklist for Developing Performance-Based Assessments*

**Performance Tasks "Worth Doing"**

| Criteria | Never | Sometimes | Definitely |
|---|---|---|---|
| 1. *Essential*—The task is a "big idea" that fits the core of the curriculum. | | | |
| 2. *Authentic*—The task relates to real-world problems. | | | |
| 3. *Rich*—The task leads to new problems and raises questions. | | | |
| 4. *Engaging*—The task is absorbing and thought-provoking. | | | |
| 5. *Active*—The student is involved in developing solutions and creating new problems. | | | |
| 6. *Feasible*—The task can be done within a reasonable time frame, is appropriate, and is safe. | | | |
| 7. *Equitable*—The completion of the task requires a variety of learning styles. | | | |
| 8. *Open*—The task has more than one solution. | | | |

*Source:* Adapted from National Council of the Teachers of Mathematics (1991). *Mathematics Assessments.* Alexandria, VA: National Council of the Teachers of Mathematics.

or behavior. Authentic assessment is not a new concept for teachers working with students with moderate to severe disabilities (Alper, Ryndak, and Schloss, 2001). Learning and performing daily living and job-related skills has been a part of the functional life skills curriculum for some time.

The conditions for the authentic assessment are quite different from those of the performance assessment. In performance assessment, the circumstances are often contrived or artificial, while in authentic assessment the tasks are part of a real-world setting. For example, learning activities could focus on a student-run snack shop where students plan and order materials, and make and sell items. Just as with performance-based assessment, evaluators must develop the criteria for authentic assessment.

Cushman (1990) discusses four characteristics of authentic performance:

### Structure
- The activities are public.
- The activities involve an audience or panel.
- The activities require some collaboration.
- The activities are worth practicing.
- The activities involve the modification of school policies and schedules to support them.

### Design
- The activities are essential.
- The activities are enabling.
- The activities are contextualized.
- The activities involve complex processes, not isolated tasks or outcomes.
- The activities assess habits, attitudes, behaviors, motivation, and creativity.
- The activities are representative.
- The activities are engaging.
- The activities are open-ended.

### Scoring
- The activities involve criteria that are essential.
- The activities are graded according to performance standards.
- The activities involve self-assessment.

*Fourth-grade students design a playground for the new primary school.*

- The activities use multifaceted scoring, not one grade.

### Equity
- The activities are fair.
- The activities involve multiple areas of learning.
- The activities are responsive to culture, gender, learning style, and language.

Table 7.1 presents a list of examples of authentic assessments.

## Portfolio Assessment

A **portfolio** is a systematic collection of a student's work covering an extended period of time. Portfolios can include works in progress, a student's best work, or work of which the student is most proud. Materials in the portfolio are a direct link to a student's individualized education program and show growth toward the

program's objectives (Swicegood, 1994; Wesson and King, 1996).

### Purposes of Portfolios

Special educators find portfolios helpful in answering questions regarding what a student knows and can do. First, portfolios demonstrate a student's growth and progress over time. Students can develop portfolios over the course of a school year and share them during parent-teacher conferences and during annual reviews of the student's individualized educational program. Portfolios may become part of the student's records, which move with the student from one grade or level to the next.

Second, portfolios present examples of the student's best work(s). Portfolios can reflect development over one or more years and be part of graduation requirements, be part of evaluations of individualized programs, or be part of the student's resume for potential employers to see the student's achievements.

**TABLE 7.1**  *Examples of Authentic Assessment*

| Literacy | Science | Mathematics |
|---|---|---|
| audiotape of reading | experiment | solving real-life problems |
| videotape of peer conferencing | original investigation | using a checking account |
| book review | journal of observations | designing and building a structure |
| book poster | investigation of local pollution | development of a budget |
| article for school newspaper | problems | teaching a lesson |
| job application | designing and building a bridge | **Social studies** |
| resumé | developing a solar car | |
| **The Arts** | **Oral Expression** | map of a nature trail |
| | | development of a museum exhibit |
| scenery design for a play | debate | development of a political |
| play performance | book talk | campaign |
| musical performance | play reading | design of a children's playground |
| design for a public space | phone call to obtain information | |
| sculpture | speech | |
| dance performance | | |

Adapted from Poteet, J. A., J. S. Choate, and S. C. Stewart (1993). Performance Assessment and Special Education: Practices and Prospects. *Focus on Exceptional Children* 26: 1–20.

## Benefits

Portfolio assessment provides benefits to students, teachers, and family members (Airasian, 2001; Rogers and Graham, 2000; Stiggins, 1997; Wiggins and McTigue, 1998). These benefits include:

- *For students:*
    selecting items to include in the portfolios
    engaging in a noncompetitive activity
    experiencing a collaborative climate among students through peer collaboration activities
    having ownership and tangible evidence of learning
    building self-esteem
    clarifying expectations
    reflecting and judging their own works
    having ongoing feedback regarding their works
- *For teachers:*
    connecting assessment and instruction
    providing diagnostic information about a student's strengths and instructional needs

generating meaningful examples of student growth
constructing knowledge of what constitutes high-quality work
having concrete examples of student performance to discuss with family members

- *For family members:*
    viewing student progress over time
    having easy-to-understand examples

In one study (Shepard and Bliem, 1995) parents reported that talking about their child's progress and seeing samples of their child's work were very useful (77 percent and 60 percent, respectively), whereas, only 43 percent of parents reported report cards useful and 14 percent reported standardized tests useful.

## Contents of a Portfolio

The contents of a portfolio consist of product as well as process items. Product items are works, such as papers, drawings, photographs, models, language samples, creative art, and other artifacts. Process items include successive drafts of a paper, works in progress, works in which students have cooperated with others, and self-reflections about a particular unit of study. Students' reflective statements are critical components of a portfolio (Cole, Ryan, and Kick, 1995). Finally, a portfolio may include teacher and parent comments, scores of standardized tests, school attendance records, and school activities.

## Organizing the Portfolio

Materials in the portfolio can be organized according to curriculum areas, skill areas, or chronological order. In this section, we will examine ways to organize portfolios at various grade levels.

1. *Early Education:* The two models in Figure 7.2 apply to young children and illustrate ways that a teacher can conceptualize portfolios. Model A reflects curriculum areas, and Model B focuses on skill and knowledge areas. Model A shows some content modifications for a student with disabilities in the classroom, which relate to the student's IEP. Daryl, a fourth grade student with a learning

disability, is working on a portfolio linked to his IEP goals. You can read more about his work in the Snapshot.
2. *Middle School.* Portfolios can focus on documenting academic progress and on assisting students in understanding themselves. Figure 7.3 on page 172 illustrates the portfolio components from one middle school.
3. *Secondary School.* Portfolios can help students synthesize information about career plans (Figure 7.4 on page 172) or may be a graduation requirement.

Portfolios, because of their breadth and integrative format, are useful as part of graduation requirements. Central Park East Secondary School requires students to complete a portfolio across fourteen categories and to display their portfolios to a graduation committee (Darling-Hammond, Ancess, and Falk, 1995). The portfolio derives from the individual student's work; however, some portfolios have the group work requirements. Students present seven of the fourteen categories orally to a graduation committee comprising the student's faculty advisor, another faculty member, an adult chosen by the

**SNAPSHOT ■** *Linking Daryl's IEP with Portfolio Assessment*

Last year, when Daryl was in third grade, he was identified as having a learning disability. He had difficulties in reading, written language, and getting along with other students, and he was often argumentative. One of Daryl's IEP goals is that he will improve in reading.

His fourth-grade teacher is using portfolios to document student progress. His teacher believes that Daryl can demonstrate progress in language and literacy by documenting activities in the portfolio. Daryl will keep a reading log that lists the books that he has read and a brief summary of each. Periodically, Daryl will complete a more extensive book report. Daryl will use a word processing program with a word prediction feature that will allow him to record his thoughts more efficiently. Daryl will add copies of his writing drafts to the portfolio

periodically. Daryl's teacher will share these materials with the IEP team during the annual review of Daryl's individualized education program.

Daryl's portfolio will also include a section on Working with Others. This area relates directly to another IEP goal for building social skills. Daryl and his teacher discussed ways in which Daryl can make and keep friends and decided how they should document his progress. One of the ideas that they discussed was for Daryl to complete a daily self-assessment checklist. The teacher talked about her observations of Daryl on the playground this week and some examples of cooperating with others. They agreed that she will continue to share her observations with Daryl at the end of the day and together they will record positive examples on a graph.

**FIGURE 7.2** *Portfolio Models in Early Education*

## Model A: Curriculum Areas

### Language and Literacy

*1. Audiotapes of child retelling a story
2. Drawing of favorite part of the story
*3. Writing samples using word prediction software
4. List of favorite books written or dictated by child

### Science and Mathematics

1. Paper and pencil drawings and written descriptions of mathematics problems
2. Written log/drawings of child's observations of science experiments
3. Chart with a series of predictions
4. Photographs of child engaged in measuring, sorting, classifying, or seriation activities
5. Child's graph of group data from the class

### Art and Music

1. Paintings and drawings
2. Audiotape of song/music created by child
3. Photographs of art projects
4. Copies of projects drawn using software

### Community and Culture

1. Student maps of the classroom, school, or community
2. Copies of student e-mail sent to pen pal in another city or state
3. Photographs and teacher-transcribed descriptions of field trips
4. Copies of student thank-you letters to community speakers

### Physical Education

1. Photographs of child on climbing structure

*2. Checklist of child's skills completed by the teacher
*3. Videotapes of child participating in an activity
4. List of favorite activities written or dictated by child

### Social Skills

*1. Child's evaluation of cooperative learning activities
2. Copies of peer evaluations of cooperative learning activities
*3. Videotapes of student working with others
*4. Checklists of skills or observations completed by the teacher

## Model B: Knowledge and Skills

### Academic

1. Writing log and videotape of integrated unit activity
2. Student notes from learning a search process on the Internet

### Self-esteem

1. A series of drawings about feelings
2. Comments from teachers and peers on accomplishments

### Cooperative group

1. Teacher feedback notes regarding a cooperative learning activity
2. Student products, reflections on group activities

### Citizenship

1. Summary of a community project and self-reflection
2. List of activities regarding "How I Helped My School"

*Some of the contents in this portfolio have been modified for a student with disabilities. The items that are asterisked (*) show how the teacher modified the contents for this portfolio.

student, and another student. The student candidates may have to answer questions about the other seven categories during the Graduation Committee Hearing. Students also complete a final project that is in an area of particular interest to the student, such as one of the portfolio items explored in greater depth. Students can

create and present the portfolio in any number of ways—there is no one "right" way.

## Helping Students Construct Portfolios

Students learn a great deal from making selections, assembling and reviewing their materials,

**FIGURE 7.3** *Portfolio Model for Middle School Students*

I. Who I am
  A. Interests
  B. Friends
  C. Family
  D. Other
II. Skills that I am developing
  A. Working independently
  B. Working cooperatively with others
  C. Problem solving
  D. Conflict resolution
  E. Other
III. My academic progress
  A. Language Arts (reading, writing, listening, speaking)
  B. Mathematics
  C. Science
  D. Social Studies
  E. Music
  F. Art
  G. Other
IV. Service to my community
  A. Volunteer work
  B. Special projects
  C. Other

*Source:* Adapted from portfolio models developed by Milton Union School faculty, June 1993, and Joan Schindler (Incarnation); Alvine Wilson, Mary Galdeen, Deborah Carey, Rae Ann Herman (West Carrollton Junior High School); and Cindy Hill (Weisenborn Institute), June 1993, as cited in Cole, D. J., C. W. Ryan, and F. Kick, 1995. *Portfolios Across the Curriculum and Beyond.* Thousand Oaks, CA: Corwin Press, pp. 40–42.

**FIGURE 7.4** *Portfolio Model for Students in an Alternative High School*

I. Introduction
  A. Title page
  B. Table of contents
  C. Preface (student's reflection on the portfolio)
II. Student Profile
  A. Autobiography
  B. School service projects
  C. Community service
III. Educational Achievement
  A. My beliefs about my education (a personal philosophy)
  B. My education goals
  C. Copies of exceptional work
  D. Evaluations of education progress
  E. Other
IV. Preparing for the Future
  A. Interest surveys
  B. Career exploration
  C. Home and family
  D. Recreation
  E. Other

*Source:* Adapted from portfolio models developed by LIMA OWE faculty, November 1991, as cited in Cole, D. J., C. W. Ryan, and F. Kick, 1995. *Portfolios Across the Curriculum and Beyond.* Thousand Oaks, CA: Corwin Press, p. 44.

and refining their portfolios. Teachers help students during each step in the construction process:

**1.** *Deciding what they want to demonstrate in their portfolios.* For portfolios to be valid, students must understand the performance they demonstrate. Teachers should discuss with students at the beginning of the year what to include in the portfolio and explain the evaluation process.

**2.** *Incorporating self-reflections, which are important components of a portfolio.* A self-reflection is a writing activity in which the student analyzes learning and accomplishments. In the written reflection students describe their views of the learning process and the importance of the task. To help students become more familiar with the process of reflection, a teacher can use class discussions to encourage students to think about an activity or event. The teacher can model self-reflection or provide examples of student reflections. Students also should have opportunities to practice reflection with each other.

Cole, Ryan, and Kick (1995) suggest that the teacher develop several questions to assist students in reflecting on their works in progress or their completed works:

a. Why is this your best work?

b. How did you go about accomplishing this task?

c. What would you do differently if you did a task like this again?

d. Where do you go from here? (p. 16)

**3.** *Understanding portfolio evaluation.* It is important that students understand how teachers will evaluate their portfolios. Teachers need to spend time discussing with the class the many ways of evaluating a work. Consider the following example of two elementary students who responded to an interviewer's question:

*First Classroom:*

INTERVIEWER: "What kind of reader are you?"

TARA: "Pretty good."

INTERVIEWER: "What makes you say that?"

TARA: "I'm in the Red Group."

*Second Classroom:*

INTERVIEWER: "What kind of reader are you?"

SHEILA: "I like funny stories and books about animals, but often I just kind of get stuck on the same author for months at a time." (Adapted from Johnston, as cited in Hewitt, 1995, p. 188)

**4.** *Choosing the pieces to include.* Students learn a great deal in choosing and selecting the materials to include in the portfolio. Teachers help students by choosing assignments that require a diversity of skills and with individual student ability and areas of interest in mind.

**5.** *Determining how to present the pieces.* Some content areas more readily lend themselves to one format than another. For example, a photograph may better represent the complexity or creativity of a model of a city or construction of a sailboat than a written text could.

A videotape captures areas in which movements or interactions are important.

## Using Technology

Teachers can organize and preserve student information, including text, sound (talking, singing, music, reading), scanned images (pictures, drawings, and photographs), and video (individual and group performances), on digital file and class home pages on the World Wide Web. Student- or teacher-developed Websites can display the students' portfolios.

Incorporating the use of technology offers the capabilities of computer searching and combining information in meaningful ways. Preserving the contents of a portfolio on disk means the disk can follow students from one grade to the next. After graduation, students can provide a disk to prospective employers or to college or university admissions officers to illustrate what they know and are able to do.

## Exhibitions

An **exhibition** is a display of a student's work that demonstrates knowledge, abilities, skills, and attitudes concerning one project or a unit of work. An exhibition provides students with the opportunity to summarize and to synthesize what they have accomplished. Exhibitions are useful in a variety of academic content areas and in interdisciplinary studies because students can realize by their own efforts that learning is more than just a series of worksheets or exercises and that it involves conceptual understanding, problem solving, and reasoning. Exhibitions are useful for program planning and program evaluation.

Teachers and scientists sometimes create partnerships to develop performance tasks and opportunities for students to display their work. The Maine Mathematics and Science Alliance and six Maine high school teachers partnered with the Harvard Smithsonian Center for Astrophysics and Tufts University Wright

Center for Science Education to create a set of embedded performance tasks and classroom activities that utilize the rich X-ray data being generated by the Chandra X-Ray Observatory (Keeley, 2001). One of the many learning tasks that the teachers and scientists developed was "Electromagnetic Pasta" (Figure 7.5).

## Responding to Diversity

Using performance-based, authentic, or portfolio assessment with students with disabilities requires teachers to be sensitive to the unique needs of these students. Gordon and Bonilla-Bowman (1996) report that portfolio assessment serves as a concrete reminder to students of their work and progress. Fuchs (1994) discusses challenges in using portfolio assessment with students with disabilities. Students who are experiencing difficulties in writing are at a disadvantage when constructing a writing portfolio,

for example, because it may be difficult to determine whether an inadequate response results from poor writing skills, poor mastery of the content, poor problem-solving skills, lack of creativity, or a combination of these factors.

Portfolios may not be useful for students with chaotic lives or who have chronic health problems. Portfolios are not effective for students who come infrequently to school (Wolf, 1996). Understanding portfolio expectations requires regular school attendance and ongoing discussions with the teacher regarding one's work.

Gordon and Bonilla-Bowman (1996) discuss teachers' and parents' concerns regarding the use of portfolios with students from diverse cultural, ethnic, and linguistic groups. There are two potential difficulties with portfolio assessment for these students. First, students rely on their own use of language, more so than on standardized tests; and, second, the teacher may introduce bias in assessing the portfolio. Portfolios have the

---

**FIGURE 7.5** *Electromagnetic pasta*

The light that our eyes can see is called visible light. Different wavelengths of visible light are seen as different colors by our eyes. But the sun and stars send us more than just visible light; they send invisible light as well. Both visible and invisible light are referred to as electromagnetic radiation (EMR). Invisible light has either longer wavelengths or shorter wavelengths than the visible light we see with our eyes. When these different forms of light are placed side by side in order of increasing or decreasing wavelength, they make up the **electromagnetic spectrum.**

**Your task:** Using different types of pasta (spaghetti, linguini, cappellini, fettucini, lasagne, orzo, macaroni, rigatoni, manicotti, ziti, etc.), create a combined model/display. You will use these pasta analogies to *explain* the principal classification of the electromagnetic spectrum.

Your model/display must:

1. Clearly characterize each type of EMR.
2. Describe the human uses of each type of EMR.
3. Include an explanation for choosing each type of pasta to represent a portion of the electromagnetic spectrum by making an analogy between the pasta and the EMR it represents.
4. Include a critique of how the pasta analogy/model, providing at least one good explanation of how it does and does not represent the real thing.

You may choose to display your model using any medium you choose. Your display should be neat, well-organized, explanatory, and visually appealing!

*Source:* Developed by Gary Glick (Falmouth [ME] High School) and Page Keeley (Maine Mathematics and Science Alliance) for the Chandra X-Ray Center with funding from NASA under Contract NAS 8-39073.

potential of providing students with ways of demonstrating conceptual understandings beyond the ability to understand English. Yet, in a review of portfolios, Gordon and Bonilla-Bowman (1996) found little evidence or representation of students' home cultures and few portfolios that included students' home languages.

Limited research is available on bias in portfolio assessment. Some research raises questions about bias in alternative assessment in general. For example, Nuttall and Goldstein (as cited in Madaus, Haney, and Kreitzer, 1992) found that the achievement gap between various groups of students was greater on alternative assessment instruments than on traditional tests. Identifying activities that are authentic, especially for students whose lives will be very different from the teacher's, is difficult (Fuchs, 1994).

Much research is needed on the use of portfolios and the effects of this method on student learning. Questions to keep in mind include: Does the use of portfolios in the classroom increase student achievement? Are portfolios effective measures for meeting the goals of the individualized education program for students with disabilities? What types of evidence show learning?

## Developing Scoring Systems

Developing or selecting a scoring system is an important part of classroom-based assessment because effective systems provide valuable feedback to students, teachers, and parents regarding level of performance and progress in the curriculum. Teachers may use anecdotal notes, performance task checklists, or rubrics. Educators frequently use notes and checklists because they provide convenient ways of recording informal information. Yet, anecdotal notes do not provide the student (or teacher and parents) with information as to the evaluation process. Furthermore, teachers who use anecdotal notes may find it difficult to be consistent (and reliable) from one student to the next without more objective criteria.

Checklists on the other hand can list the components of what is under evaluation during the performance. They are also easy to use but they do not provide any detailed information as to the quality of the achievement; they simply record whether or not one of the items in the performance was present or not. In the following section, we will discuss rubrics and how educators are using this scoring system in the classroom.

### Rubric

Rubrics are considered the most useful scoring system for performance-based, authentic, and portfolio assessments because they provide the greatest amount of detail regarding the performance. A **rubric** is an assessment scale that identifies the area(s) of performance and defines various levels of achievement. Within each level, the rubric should include descriptors, or detailed descriptions of each level of achievement. Descriptors provide specific information to students, teachers, and parents regarding what to expect at each achievement level. Descriptors also help teachers in scoring student performances consistently. Scoring systems generally fall into two main types: analytic and holistic.

*Analytic Scoring.* An **analytic scoring** system reports an independent score for each of the criteria of the assessment scale. For a rubric developed for a writing portfolio there might be four criteria: organization, details, voice, and grammar. An analytic scoring system reports separate scores for each of these criteria. Within each of these criteria, the various levels of achievement can be described either numerically or categorically. In an example of a writing portfolio, we might identify the following achievement levels of organization:

### Criterion: Organization
4 = Extensive
3 = Moderate
2 = Slight
1 = Lacking

Notice that we have used both numerical and corresponding categorical descriptions of achievement in this rubric.

In our example, the rubric does not include descriptors of the levels of achievement. Thus, without further descriptions of the terms "moderate" and "slight," one teacher might rank the organization of a student's paper a "3" while another teacher would rank organization a "2." Detailed descriptors are helpful to teachers and others during evaluation procedures and serve to increase interrater reliability.

One example of a rubric that provides detailed descriptors is the Vermont New Standards Rubric. Compare the detailed descriptors given in the fifth-grade analytic scoring rubric for writing reports (Figure 7.6) with the numeric and category listing in the example above. We see that to receive an "accomplished writing" score, the rubric provides detailed information on organizing and conveying information and ideas accurately and effectively.

Descriptors are helpful to students and parents. Detailed information regarding levels of achievement assist students in understanding not only how teachers will evaluate their work but how they can evaluate the work themselves. Descriptors are helpful to parents in understanding what their child can do.

Depending on the richness and detail of the descriptors, analytic scoring can provide diagnostic information about the student's achievement. Teachers can examine scores on the individual criteria to identify areas of strengths and areas of improvement. Because this type of scoring system is an effective diagnostic tool, teachers should report student scores as categorical rather than numerical. By reporting analytic scores numerically, even if they show totals and averages, the result is a loss of rich analytic information (Hewitt, 1995).

Let's return to the Electromagnetic Pasta activity (Figure 7.5). The activity asked students to describe the different types of wavelengths, to explain how the pasta types represented the information, and to critique their pasta model. The analytic scoring rubric that the teachers and sci-entists developed (Figure 7.7 on page 179) provides detailed information for each level of achievement in content level, use of model or display, and critique of how their pasta model does and does not represent the real thing.

***Holistic Scoring.*** **Holistic scoring** is a type of scoring in which the teacher assigns a single score to the student's work (Figure 7.8 on page 180). For example, the writing portfolio receives a single overall score. The teacher does not analyze the writing by separate criteria such as organization, details, voice, and grammar. Like analytic scoring, holistic scoring should include descriptors of each of the achievement levels.

This type of scoring lacks the depth of information contained in analytic scoring; however, it tends to be easier to design and score than analytic scoring.

## Benchmarks

**Benchmarks** are examples of student work that illustrate each scoring level on the rubric, either analytic or holistic. Teachers evaluate student work by using scoring standards and benchmarks. Benchmarks can be in the form of papers, such as example essays, or a small sample of student work, such as possible answers to a question. Student papers that represent writing at different levels of performance are sometimes called **anchor papers.** Figure 7.9 on page 181 illustrates an example from a set of anchor papers developed by teachers in Vermont (2000–2001 5th Grade Writing Benchmarks).

Hewitt (1995) cautions teachers to select benchmark examples that demonstrate the mid-range of each of the achievement levels. When a teacher scores a student's portfolio, benchmarks provide the teacher with a framework and serve to increase reliability.

Benchmarks can be helpful to students in understanding how teachers will assess their performance or portfolio. However, benchmarks should be shared carefully with students so that they will not think they must replicate the example, thus losing the individual nature of

**FIGURE 7.6** *Fifth Grade Analytic Scoring Rubric for Reports: Writing to Inform*

| | Vermont New Standards Rubric for Reports: Writing to Inform | | | | |
|---|---|---|---|---|---|
| *Standard 1.8* In written reports, students organize and convey information and ideas accurately and effectively. | | | | | |
| Criteria | Score Point 5 Exceeds the Standards | Score Point 4 Accomplished Writing | Score Point 3 Intermediate Writing | Score Point 2 Basic Writing | Score Point 1 Limited Writing |
| **Purpose, Stance, Voice/ Tone (Controlling Idea)**<br><br>• Evidence of gathered information<br>• Analysis of a situation followed by a sug-gested course of action<br>• Prediction of possible outcomes of a situation<br>• Appropriate stance<br>• Anticipation of reader needs | Meets all the criteria listed in score point 4 and uses strategies not always thought of for reporting information— e.g., personal anecdotes or dramatization impart informa-tion in an entertaining way.<br><br>Precise use of language conveys intent clearly and concisely.<br><br>The writer may reflect on the significance of the information.<br><br>Shows an exceptional awareness of readers' concerns and needs. | A sense of purpose stated strongly or implied, unifies and focuses the report.<br><br>Shows a clear sense of direction appropriate to its purpose.<br><br><br><br><br>Stance is that of a knowledgeable person presenting relevant information (voice and tone).<br><br><br><br>Context is clear throughout. | States control-ling idea/focus but may not use it effectively to unify report.<br><br>Shows evidence of having a general rather than a focused purpose in presenting information.<br><br>Stance is that of a person who has a desire to convey gathered information but sense of audience is vague (voice and tone).<br><br>Establishes sufficient context. | Defines subject with a simple statement rather than controlling idea/focus.<br><br><br>Conveys a lack of evident purpose.<br><br><br><br><br><br>May be a monotone (voice and tone).<br><br><br><br><br><br>May offer little context. | May only state topic.<br><br><br><br><br>Rarely conveys writer's intent.<br><br><br><br><br>Monotone (voice and tone).<br><br>Stance is undeveloped.<br><br><br>Seems unaware of reader concerns or needs; no context. |
| **Organization and Coherence**<br><br>• Appropriate patterns: chronologi-cal; histori-cal; specific to general; general to specific; causal; sequential; other, appropriate | May demon-strate an unusual pattern or framework in which to embed information. | Organized in a pattern or framework suited to purpose, audience, and context.<br><br>Strong overall coherence and balance; uses transitions. Tight construction without extrane-ous material. | Generally uses a predictable pattern.<br><br><br><br>Has overall coherence; uses some transitions. | Usually shows an organized plan but may have digressions.<br><br>Has general coherence, stays on topic but may show weak transitions between paragraphs or sentences. | Shows little or no evidence of purposeful organization.<br><br>May lack coherence; no transitions. |

*Score Point 0   Unscorable   There is no evidence of an attempt to write a report.*

*(continued)*

**FIGURE 7.6**  *Continued*

| Criteria | Score Point 5 Exceeds the Standards | Score Point 4 Accomplished Writing | Score Point 3 Intermediate Writing | Score Point 2 Basic Writing | Score Point 1 Limited Writing | Score Point 0 Unscorable |
|---|---|---|---|---|---|---|
| **Vermont New Standards Rubric for Reports: Writing to Inform** *Standard 1.8* In written reports, students organize and convey information and ideas accurately and effectively. | | | | | | |
| for specific report • Overall coherence | The writer is extremely selective in presenting information, including relevant material and excluding that which would clutter the report. | Compelling opening, strong informative body, and satisfying conclusion (organization). | Clear beginning, middle, and end; may provide considerable information. | May have a lengthy opening and abrupt closure; may present random bits of information. | | There is no evidence of an attempt to write a report. |
| **Elaboration Strategies, Details** • Using specific, concrete strategies • Comparing, contrasting • Naming, describing • Reporting conversation • Reviewing the history • Explaining the possibilities • Creating a scenario | | Uses a variety of elaboration strategies effectively and appropriately; cites references as needed. Details are relevant to the topic, purpose, and audience. Provides depth of information. | General information, not well supported by concrete examples. Some information may be irrelevant. | Relies on general rather than specific details. May use irrelevant details, often presented in a list. May rely on opinion rather than facts. | Random, disconnected, and/or unfocused opinions with some scattered facts. Presents very little information. | |

*Source:* Reprinted with permission of the Vermont Department of Education.

**FIGURE 7.7**  *Analytic Scoring Rubric for Electromagnetic Pasta*

| Scoring Critera | Scoring Rubric: The Universe Rated R! | | | |
| --- | --- | --- | --- | --- |
| | **1** <br> **Attempted** <br> **Demonstration** | **2** <br> **Partial** <br> **Demonstration** | **3** <br> **Proficient** <br> **Demonstration** | **4** <br> **Distinguished** <br> **Demonstration** |
| **Content Knowledge** <br><br> Students' ability to describe the different types of electromagnetic radiation (EMR), including their uses by humans. | Student attempts to describe at least 3 types of EMR. Student attempts to arrange them by some criteria, and/or describes at least 3 human applications. There may be major errors. | Student describes at least 5 types of EMR, arranges them by increasing or decreasing wavelength, and describes at least 5 human applications. There may be slight omissions or minor errors. | Student correctly describes 7 types of EMR, arranges them by increasing or decreasing wavelength, and describes a human application of each. | Student correctly describes, in supporting detail, 7 types of EMR, arranges them by increasing or decreasing wavelength, and describes a human application of each. Student may offer sophistcated and/or insightful details. |
| **Communicate with a Model/ Display** <br><br> Students' ability to represent the electromagnetic spectrum with a physical model/ display that draws analogies between the model and the material used. | Student creates a physical model/ display of at least 3 components of the electromagnetic spectrum, using pasta, and draws at least 1 analogy between the characteristics of the pasta and the EMR it represents. The model/display may contain major errors. | Student creates a physical model/ display of at least 5 components of the electromagnetic spectrum, using pasta, and draws at least 3 effective analogies between the characteristics of the pasta and the EMR it represents. The model/display may contain minor errors. | Student creates an effective, neat and organized physical model/display of the 7 components of the electromagnetic spectrum, using pasta, and draws effective analogies between the characteristics of the pasta and the EMR it represents. | Student creates a highly effective, visually appealing, well-organized, self-explanatory physical model/display of the 7 components of the electromagnetic spectrum, using pasta, and draws effective and logical analogies between the characteristics of the pasta and the EMR it represents. Student may offer sophisticated and/or insightful details. |
| **Critique of a Model** <br><br> Students' ability to critique a model. | Student critiques the model providing at least 1 reason why it is either like or unlike the real electromagnetic spectrum. Reason(s) may be irrelevant, overly obvious, or illogical. | Student critiques the model providing at least 1 reason why it is either like or unlike the real electromagnetic spectrum. | Student critiques the model providing at least 1 significant reason why it is both like and unlike the real electromagnetic spectrum. | Student effectively critiques the model providing at least 2 significant reasons why it is both like and unlike the real electromagnetic spectrum. Reasons given may indicate higher level reasoning beyond the obvious features of the model. |

*Source:*  Developed by Gary Glick (Falmouth [ME] High School) and Page Keeley (Maine Mathematics and Science Alliance) for the Chandra X-Ray Center with funding from NASA under Contract NAS 8-39073.

**FIGURE 7.8**  *Holistic Rubric for Scoring Student Writing*

| Description | Numerical Score |
|---|---|
| The paper is well organized, provides a sufficient number of explicit details in supporting statements, and contains no major grammatical errors. | 4 |
| The paper shows organization but may lack coherence, details are appropriate, and/or it contains some grammatical errors. | 3 |
| The paper lacks consistency in organization, details are not elaborate, and/or it contains many grammatical errors. | 2 |
| The paper has serious problems in organization, lack of details, and/or it contains frequent grammatical errors. | 1 |

their work. Providing students with several different examples of benchmarks at various achievement levels can reduce this potential problem.

## Ensuring Technical Adequacy

### Reliability

The purpose of the assessment affects how crucial the issue of reliability is. Some assessments are low-stakes assessments; that is, the consequences of the assessment do not have a major impact on the student's future. For example, an assessment designed to answer questions regarding student progress is a low-stakes assessment.

Assessments that are part of graduation requirements have much higher stakes. High-stakes assessments refer to situations in which the collected information will have a direct and potentially adverse impact on the student. In high-stakes assessment, issues of reliability are critical.

***Consistency and Stability.***    Reliability of performance-based assessments focuses on the consistency and the stability of the assessment. When using performance-based assessment, students frequently have multiple opportunities to perform individually. For example, a teacher is able to create a number of opportunities that require students to work together cooperatively; however, individual oral presentations on a unit of study occur infrequently because of the amount of class time these presentations require. In this case, consistency of student response is unknown due to low frequency of performance.

Multiple categories or points on the assessment scale affect the degree of interrater agreement. The more categories or points, the more difficult it may be to obtain interrater agreement, especially if the categories are vague. We have discussed one method of increasing consistency by including detailed descriptors in each of the achievement levels. We have examined how descriptors assist evaluators in making determinations regarding students' scores and help students evaluate their own work.

Another approach to addressing consistency actually adjusts for differences between evaluators by accepting adjacent scores (Hewitt, 1995).

**FIGURE 7.9    *Example of a Fifth-Grade Writing Benchmark***

<u>**Trying to Convince Someone Not to Smoke**</u>
*Topic is clearly stated in the title*

I am trying to convince a friend not to smoke. My first reason is it's bad for you. My second reason is it's expensive. My third reason is it's social pressure. *Introduction is weak. States appropriate arguments.*

<u>It's bad for you.</u> You could get cancer. Smoking takes away your appetite and you don't eat as much. Smoking will make you have bad breath and teeth. Smoking is addicting. *Arranges ideas in a simple way, listing without relating to each other.*

*Lacks transitions*
<u>It's expensive.</u> Medical care for your health will cost alot because it's addicting. Dental care will cost alot of money for your teeth because the tar in cigarettes make your teeth black. The cost of the habit is over one thousand dollars a year. *Provides some supporting evidence for argument.*

*Coherence is weak between and within paragraphs.*
<u>Social pressure.</u> Cigarette advertisements make smoking look harmless and fun. Some advertisements help you stop. There are warning labels saying that if you're pregnant your baby could probably have birth weight. The labels are called Surgeon General Warnings. Just because someone you know or like smokes don't mean you have to smoke.

I never want to smoke and I hope you feel the same way. I hope you make the right chose and save money. *Conclusion is weak.*

*The writer assumes the reader will find these ideas credible.*

*Source:* Reprinted from "2000–2001 5th Grade Writing Benchmarks" with permission of the Vermont Department of Education.

For example, two teachers reviewed a student's writing using the holistic scoring system in Figure 7.8. The first reader rated the paper a 1; the second reader rated the paper a 2. Since the evaluators have adjacent scores, they adjust the difference by averaging the two scores, and the student receives a score of 1.5.

Teachers also want assurance that the performance will be stable. Stability is a function of the scoring system and environmental factors. Errors in the scoring systems affect stability; for example, when the teacher assigns an incorrect score or makes a calculation error. Environmental factors also affect stability. The learning and social environments of the classroom impact the student's motivation, attitude, self-esteem, confidence, and anxiety, which in turn can alter the student's performance.

## Consequential Validity

Consequential validity is the extent to which an assessment instrument promotes the intended consequences (Linn and Baker, 1996). This type of validity can describe performance-based assessments. One of the primary reasons for using this type of assessment is to improve student learning, and the extent to which performance-based assessment improves student learning defines consequential validity. Factors that can affect student learning, and thus impact consequential validity, include school reform activities, instructional improvements, staff development activities, levels of student achievement, and accountability systems (Linn and Baker, 1996).

Both student and teacher perspectives can affect consequential validity.

*From the student's perspective:* For the assessment to be valid, students must know what to expect. Students must know what skills and knowledge are in the assessment, what types of performance demonstrate these skills and knowledge, and what type of evaluation their performance will receive.

*From the teacher's perspective:* For the assessment to be valid, teachers must take care in designing tasks that accurately reflect achievement for students from nondominant cultures. For example, oral presentations may be difficult for students whose first language is not English. An oral presentation in science, for example, might be supplemented by information presented in another format, such as a detailed drawing to illustrate the concepts presented.

***Fairness.*** Fairness of the assessment instrument is an important aspect of consequential validity. One of the driving forces behind the evolution of performance-based assessment has been the impetus to develop assessment instruments that are fair to students. Tests are opportunities for students to demonstrate learning regardless of culture, gender, race, socioeconomic status, or disability. Fairness means minimal bias, equitable assessment, and measures that are sensitive to diverse populations.

## Improving Reliability and Validity

Airasian (2001) suggests several guidelines to improve reliability and validity of performance-based and portfolio assessments:

1. Know the purpose of the assessment.
2. Teach and give students practice on the assessment criteria.
3. State the criteria in observable behaviors.
4. Select criteria that are at an appropriate level of difficulty for the students.
5. Limit the number of criteria to a manageable number.
6. Maintain a written record.
7. Be sure the performance assessment is fair to all students. (pp. 254–255)

## Cautions When Using Performance-Based, Authentic, and Portfolio Assessment

Careful design of performance, authentic, and portfolio assessments is important to ensure that educators, parents, and students draw appropriate conclusions. If we are unclear about our expectations, then we diminish the usefulness of the assessment. There are several questions that can guide us in using these assessment techniques.

Is the assessment representative of the student's work? For example, a performance task could demonstrate how a student develops a first draft of a book review, but not a finished one. Videotapes might contain images of play rehearsals, but not the opening-night production.

Are the criteria for assessment clear to all evaluators and students? Ambiguity, inconsistency in judging performance and authentic assessments, and subjectivity can be major problems. Both students and the educators must know what the assessment tasks are, what the performance conditions are, and what the criteria for evaluation are.

Have the criteria for evaluation changed over time? When designing an assessment the educator may have specified the evaluation of all of the student's creative writings. Later, it may be unclear whether this meant all the finished writing or all the writing whether finished or not.

Who evaluates the contents? Depending on who evaluates the performance or authentic assessment tasks, interpretations can vary; and depending on the training of the educator, different conclusions can be reached (Arter and Spandel, 1991).

Are performance and authentic assessments fair? The use of performance and authentic assessments does not automatically mean that they show no bias toward students with disabilities, certain cultural groups, minorities, economic groups, and those to whom English is a second language.

## Preferred Practices

The development and implementation of performance-based assessments present challenges to educators. Although they are not without problems, these assessment procedures have the potential of helping us develop valid and fair approaches to assessing students. However, as this area continues to develop, we must proceed carefully. Table 7.2 summarizes the advantages and limitations of alternative assessment procedures.

Educators in professional organizations and state departments of education have developed sets of standards that specify what students should know and achieve. Assessment procedures should assist educators and policymakers in improving instruction and learning. If assessment is to be beneficial, the procedures must provide useful information about the capabilities of students. We believe that performance-based, authentic, and portfolio assessment will continue to be a valuable assessment approach. If the purposes of assessment are not beneficial, then neither the assessment nor the assessment procedures are valid.

All assessment procedures have to be fair to all students. Assessment procedures should contain no bias; and they should be attentive to differences in development and disabilities and to differences in culture, race, socioeconomic standing, and gender. Students must be given multiple opportunities to demonstrate what they know. A single test score cannot determine educational decisions.

The assessment tasks must be reliable and valid and represent the standards that children are to achieve. Multiple-choice tests give children inadequate opportunities to demonstrate what they know. Alternatives to traditional assessment, such as performance-based assessment, portfolios, and exhibitions are rich sources of information (Hymes, Chafin, and Gonder, 1991).

Educators involve themselves in the development and implementation of assessment procedures. Because assessment forms a close link with instruction, educators must participate in the development, administration, scoring, and interpretation of assessment procedures. We need to continue to develop and revise effective authentic and performance tasks.

Teachers and other evaluators should use caution when applying portfolios to high-stakes testing. High-stakes testing is the use of assessments to make classification, retention, or promotion decisions about students. The pressure of such a situation can compromise student work. The lack of a research base in this relatively new type of assessment and concerns regarding validity and reliability are additional reasons why practitioners should not use portfolios in high-stakes testing.

In constructing a portfolio, students take responsibility for planning and illustrating their learning. Portfolios provide a vehicle for students to slip into the driver's seat and acquire ownership of their learning. However, this road remains untested; until there is a stronger research base, teachers and other evaluators should use portfolios with caution. Perhaps there will always be a place for different types of assessment practices. Consider the following parable:

> There is a big difference between naming hammers and pounding nails in a wall. However, lest anyone believe that naming hammers is not important, just ask someone to get a particular type of hammer and see what happens if the person fetching it doesn't know the types of hammers. On the other hand, and more importantly, standing with a hammer in one's hand and knowing its name doesn't make one a builder or tell one how to use it. Could there be a place for both knowledge and application? (Farr and Tone, cited in Gillespie et al., 1996, p. 490)

**TABLE 7.2** *Advantages, Limitations, and Pitfalls of Alternative Types of Classroom Assessment Techniques*

| Assessment Alternatives | Advantages for Teachers | Disadvantages for Teachers | Suggestions for Improved Use |
|---|---|---|---|
| | *Formative Assessment Techniques* | | |
| 1. Conversations and comments from other teachers | (a) Fast way to obtain certain types of background information about a student. <br> (b) Permit colleagues to share experiences with specific students in other learning contexts, thereby broadening the perspective about the learners. <br> (c) Permit attainment of information about a student's family, siblings, or peer problems that may be affecting the student's learning. | (a) Tend to reinforce stereotype and biases toward a family or a social class. <br> (b) Students' learning under another teacher or in another context may be quite unlike their learning in the current context. <br> (c) Others' opinions are not objective, often based on incomplete information, personal life view, or personal theory of personality. | (a) Do not believe hearsay, rumors, biases of others. <br> (b) Do not gossip or reveal private and confidential information about students. <br> (c) Keep the conversation on a professional level, focused on facts rather than speculation and confidential so it is not overheard by others. |
| 2. Casual conversations with students | (a) Provide relaxed, informal setting for obtaining information. <br> (b) Students may reveal their attitudes and motivations toward learning that are not exhibited in class. | (a) A student's mind may not be focused on the learning target being assessed. <br> (b) Inadequate sampling of students' knowledge; too few students assessed. <br> (c) Inefficient: students' conversation may be irrelevant to assessing their achievement. | (a) Do not appear as an inquisitor, always probing students. <br> (b) Be careful so as not to misperceive a student's attitude or a student's degree of understanding. |
| 3. Questioning students during instruction | (a) Permits judgments about students' thinking and learning progress during the course of teaching; gives teachers immediate feedback. <br> (b) Permits teachers to ask questions requiring higher-order thinking and elaborated responses. <br> (c) Permits student-to-student interaction to be assessed. | (a) Some students cannot express themselves well in front of other students. <br> (b) Requires education in how to ask proper questions and to plan for asking specific types of questions during the lesson. <br> (c) Information obtained tends to be only a small sample of the learning outcomes and of the students in the class. | (a) Be sure to ask questions of students who are reticent or slow to respond. Avoid focusing on verbally aggressive and pleasant "stars." <br> (b) Wait 5 to 10 seconds for a student to respond before moving on to another. <br> (c) Avoid limiting questions to those requiring facts or a definite correct answer, thereby narrowing the focus of |

the assessment inappropriately.

(d) Do not punish students for failing to participate in class question sessions or inappropriately reward those verbally aggressive students who participate fully.

(e) Remember the students' verbal and nonverbal behavior in class may not indicate their true attitudes/values.

(a) Remember that this method assesses learning that is only in the formative stages. It may be inappropriate to assign summative letter grades from the results.

(b) Failure to complete homework or completing it late is no reason to punish students by embarrassing them in front of others or by lowering their overall grade. Learning may be subsequently demonstrated through other assessments.

(c) Do not inappropriately attribute poor test performance to the student not doing the homework.

(d) Do not overemphasize the homework grade and overuse homework as a teaching strategy (e.g., using it as a primary teaching method).

---

(d) Some learning targets cannot be assessed by spontaneous and short oral responses; they require longer time frames in which students are free to think, create, and respond.

(e) Records of students' responses are kept only in the teacher's mind, which may be unreliable.

(a) Tend to focus on narrow segments of learning rather than integrating large complexes of skills and knowledge.

(b) Sample only a small variety of content and skills on any one assignment.

(c) Assignment may not be complete or may be copied from others.

---

(d) Permits assessment of students' ability to discuss issues with others orally and in some depth.

**4.** Daily homework and seatwork

(a) Provide formative information about how learning is progressing.

(b) Allow errors to be diagnosed and corrected.

(c) Combine practice, reinforcements, and assessment.

**TABLE 7.2** *Continued*

| Assessment Alternatives | Advantages for Teachers | Disadvantages for Teachers | Suggestions for Improved Use |
|---|---|---|---|
| | *Formative Assessment Techniques* | | |
| 5. Teacher-made quizzes and tests | (a) Although primarily useful for summative evaluation, they may permit diagnosis or errors and faulty thinking. (b) Provide for students' written expression of knowledge. | (a) Require time to craft good tasks useful for diagnosis. (b) Focus exclusively on cognitive learning targets. | (a) Do not overemphasize lower-level thinking skills. (b) Use open-ended or constructed response tasks to gain insight into a student's thinking processes and errors. (c) For better diagnosis of a student's thinking, use tasks that require students to apply and use their knowledge to "real-life" situations. |
| 6. In-depth interviews of individual students | (a) Permit in-depth probing of students' understandings, thinking patterns, and problem-solving strategies. (b) Permit follow-up questions tailored to a student's responses and allow a student to elaborate answers. (c) Permit diagnosis of faulty thinking and errors in performances. | (a) Require a lot of time to complete. (b) Require keeping the rest of the class occupied while one student is being interviewed. (c) Require learning skills in effective educational achievement interviewing and diagnosis. | (a) If assessing students' thinking patterns, problem-solving strategies, etc., avoid prompting student toward a prescribed way of problem solving. (b) Some students need their self-confidence bolstered before they feel comfortable revealing their mistakes. |
| 7. Growth and learning progress portfolios | (a) Allow large segments of a student's learning experiences to be reviewed. (b) Allow monitoring a student's growth and progress. (c) Communicate to students that growth and progress are more important than test results. | (a) Require a long time to accumulate evidence of growth and progress. (b) Require special effort to teach students how to use appropriate and realistic self-assessment techniques. (c) Require high-level knowledge of the subject matter to diagnose and guide students. | (a) Be very clear about the learning targets toward which you are monitoring progress. (b) Use a conceptual framework or learning progress model to guide your diagnosis and monitoring. (c) Coordinate portfolio development and assessment with other teachers. |

| | Characteristics | Cautions | Guidelines |
|---|---|---|---|
| | **(d)** Allow student to participate in selecting and evaluating material to include in the portfolio.<br>**(e)** Can become a focus of teaching and learning. | **(d)** Require the ability to recognize complex and subtle patterns of growth and progress in the subject.<br>**(e)** Results tend to be inconsistent from teacher to teacher. | **(d)** Develop scoring rubrics to define standards and maintain consistency. |
| **8.** Attitude and values questionnaires | **(a)** Assess effective characteristics of students.<br>**(b)** Knowing student's attitudes and values in relation to a specific topic or subject matter may be useful in planning teaching.<br>**(c)** May provide insights into students' motivations. | **(a)** The results are sensitive to the way questions are worded. Students may misinterpret, not understand, or react differently than the assessor intended.<br>**(b)** Can be easily "faked" by older and testwise students. | **(a)** Remember that the way questions are worded significantly affects how students respond.<br>**(b)** Remember that attitude questionnaire responses may change drastically from one occasion or context to another.<br>**(c)** Remember that your personal theory of personality or personal value system may lead to incorrect interpretations of students' responses. |

*Summative Assessment Techniques*

| | Characteristics | Cautions | Guidelines |
|---|---|---|---|
| **1.** Teacher-made tests and quizzes | **(a)** Can assess a wide range of content and cognitive skills.<br>**(b)** Can be aligned with what was actually taught.<br>**(c)** Use a variety of task formats.<br>**(d)** Allow for assessment or written expression. | **(a)** Difficult to assess complex skills or ability to use combinations of skills.<br>**(b)** Require time to create, edit, and produce good items.<br>**(c)** Craft task requiring students to apply knowledge to "real life." Class period is often too short for a complete assessment.<br>**(d)** Focus exclusively on cognitive outcomes. | **(a)** Do not overemphasize lower-level thinking skills.<br>**(b)** Do not overuse short-answer and response-choice items.<br>**(c)** Craft task requiring students to apply knowledge to "real life." |
| **2.** Tasks focusing on procedures and processes | **(a)** Allow assessments of nonverbal as well as verbal responses. | **(a)** Focus on a narrow range of content knowledge and cognitive skills. | **(a)** Investigate carefully the reason for student's failure to complete the task successfully. |

**TABLE 7.2** *Continued*

| Assessment Alternatives | Advantages for Teachers | Disadvantages for Teachers | Suggestions for Improved Use |
|---|---|---|---|
| | | *Summative Assessment Techniques* | |
| | (b) Allow students to integrate several simple skills and knowledge to perform a complex, realistic task.<br>(c) Allow for group and cooperative performance and assessment.<br>(d) Allow assessment of steps used to complete an assignment. | (b) Require great deal of time to properly formulate, administer, and rate.<br>(c) May have low interrater reliability unless scoring rubrics are used.<br>(d) Results are often specific to the combination of student and task. Students' performance quality is not easily generalized across different content and tasks.<br>(e) Tasks that students perceive as uninteresting, boring, or irrelevant do not elicit the students' best efforts. | (b) Use a scoring rubric to increase the reliability and validity of results.<br>(c) Do not confuse the evaluation of the process a student uses with the need to evaluate the correctness of the answers.<br>(d) Allow sufficient time for students to adequately demonstrate the performance. |
| 3. Tasks focusing on products and projects | (a) Same as 2(a), (b), and (c).<br>(b) Permit several equally valid processes to be used to produce the product or complete the project.<br>(c) Allow assessment of the quality of the product.<br>(d) Allow longer time than class period to complete the tasks. | (a) Same as 2(a), (b), (c), (d), and (e).<br>(b) Students may have unauthorized help outside of class to complete the product or project.<br>(c) All students in the class must have the same opportunity to use all appropriate materials and tools in order for the assessment to be fair. | (a) Same as 2(a), (b), (c), and (d).<br>(b) Give adequate instruction to students on the criteria that will be used to evaluate their work, the standards that will be applied, and how students can use these criteria and standards to monitor their own progress in completing the work.<br>(c) Do not mistake the aesthetic appearance of the product for substance and thoughtfulness.<br>(d) Do not punish tardiness in completing the project or product by lowering the student's grade. |

| | | | |
|---|---|---|---|
| **4. Best work portfolios** | **(a)** Allow large segments of a student's learning experience to be assessed.<br>**(b)** May allow students to participate in the selection of the material to be included in the portfolio.<br>**(c)** Allow either quantitative or qualitative assessment of the works in the portfolio.<br>**(d)** Permit a much broader assessment of learning targets than tests. | **(a)** Require waiting a long time before reporting assessment results.<br>**(b)** Students must be taught how to select work to include as well as how to present it effectively.<br>**(c)** Teachers must learn to use a scoring rubric that assesses a wide variety of pieces of work.<br>**(d)** Interrater reliability is low from teacher to teacher.<br>**(e)** Require high levels of subject matter knowledge to evaluate students' work properly. | **(a)** Be very clear about the learning targets to be assessed to avoid confusion and invalid portfolio assessment results.<br>**(b)** Teach a student to use appropriate criteria to choose the work to include.<br>**(c)** Do not collect too much material to evaluate.<br>**(d)** Coordinate portfolio development with other teachers.<br>**(e)** Develop and use scoring rubrics to define standards and maintain consistency. |
| **5. Textbook-supplied tests and quizzes** | **(a)** Allow for assessment of written expression.<br>**(b)** Already prepared, save teachers time.<br>**(c)** Match the content and sequence of the textbook or curricular materials. | **(a)** Often do not assess complex skills or ability to use combinations of skills.<br>**(b)** Often do not match the emphases and presentations in class.<br>**(c)** Focus on cognitive skills.<br>**(d)** Class period is often too short for a complete assessment. | **(a)** Be skeptical that the items were made by professionals and are of high quality.<br>**(b)** Carefully edit or rewrite the item to match what you have taught.<br>**(c)** Remember that you are personally responsible for using a poor quality test. You must not appeal to the authority of the textbook. |
| **6. Standardized achievement tests** | **(a)** Assess a wide range of cognitive abilities and skills that cover a year's learning.<br>**(b)** Assess content and skills common to many schools across the country.<br>**(c)** Items developed and screened by professionals, resulting in only the best items being included. | **(a)** Focus exclusively on cognitive outcomes.<br>**(b)** Often the emphasis on a particular test is different from the emphasis of a particular teacher.<br>**(c)** Do not provide diagnostic information. | **(a)** Avoid narrowing your instruction to prepare students for these tests when administrators put pressure on teachers.<br>**(b)** Do not use these tests to evaluate teachers.<br>**(c)** Do not confuse the quality of the learning that did occur in the classroom with the results on standardized tests when interpreting them. |

**TABLE 7.2** *Continued*

| Assessment Alternatives | Advantages for Teachers | Disadvantages for Teachers | Suggestions for Improved Use |
|---|---|---|---|
| | *Summative Assessment Techniques* | | |
| | (d) Corroborate what teachers know about pupils; sometimes indicate unexpected results for specific students.<br><br>(e) Provide norm-referenced information that permits evaluation of students' progress in relation to students nationwide.<br><br>(f) Provide legitimate comparisons of a student's achievement in two and more curricular areas.<br><br>(g) Provide growth scales so students' long-term educational development can be monitored.<br><br>(h) Useful for curriculum evaluation. | (d) Results usually take too long to get back to teachers, so are not directly useful for instructional planning. | (d) Educate parents about the tests' limited validity for assessing a student's learning potentials. |

*Source: Educational Assessment of Students,* 3d ed., by Nitko, Anthony J. © 2001. Reprinted by permission of Pearson Education, Inc., Upper Saddle River, NJ.

## *Extending Learning*

1. Working with a small group of students, develop a set of questions for two or more chapters in this textbook. Your question sets should include multiple-choice, short-answer, and essay questions. Next, review the same chapters and identify how knowledge of the information could be demonstrated by either performance or portfolio assessment. What method of assessment do you prefer? Why?

2. Compare the various methods of scoring performance-based assessments. What are the advantages and disadvantages of each?

3. How are educators in your local school districts using performance-based assessments with students with disabilities? Make arrangements to interview a local special educator or administrator.

4. Why are concerns relating to reliability and validity so important when using performance-based assessments?

5. Develop a resource of websites that illustrate well-designed rubrics. Select a curriculum area and use a search engine to narrow your search to locate five to eight sites that you would recommend in English Language Arts, Science, Mathematics, Social Studies, or other curriculum areas. Share your findings with the class.

## *References*

Airasian, P. W. (2001). *Assessment in the classroom*. 4th ed. New York: McGraw-Hill.

Alper, S., D. L. Ryndak, and C. N. Schloss (2001). *Alternate assessment of students with disabilities in inclusive settings*. Boston: Allyn & Bacon.

Arter, J., and J. McTighe (2001). Scoring rubrics in the classroom. In *Experts in assessment*, ed. T. R. Guskey and R. J. Marzano. Thousand Oaks, CA: Corwin Press.

Arter, J. A., and V. Spandel (1991). *Using portfolios of student work in instruction and assessment*. Portland, OR: Northwest Regional Education Laboratory.

Byrnes, J. P. (1996). *Cognitive development and learning in instructional contexts*. Boston: Allyn & Bacon.

Chandra X-Ray Observatory. *Electromagnetic pasta*. Retrieved June 26, 2001, from the World Wide Web: http://chandra.harvard.edu/edu/formal/pasta/task1.html.

Cohen, P. (1995). Designing performance assessment tasks. *Education update* 37(1): 4–5, 8.

Cole, D. J., C. W. Ryan, and F. Kick (1995). *Portfolios across the curriculum and beyond*. Thousand Oaks, CA: Corwin Press.

Cushman, P. (1990). Performances and exhibitions: The demonstration of mastery. *Horace* 6: 17–24.

Darling-Hammond, L., J. Ancess, and B. Falk (1995). *Authentic assessment in action*. New York: Teachers College Press.

Diez, M. E., and C. J. Moon (1992). What do we want students to know? . . . and other important questions. *Educational Leadership* 49: 38–41.

Dixon-Krauss, L. (1996). *Vygotsky in the classroom*. White Plains, NY: Longman.

Fuchs, L. (1994). *Connecting performance assessment to instruction*. Reston, VA: Council for Exceptional Children.

Gardner, H. (1991). *The unschooled mind*. New York: Basic Books.

Gillespie, C. S., K. L. Ford, R. D. Gillespie, and A. G. Leavell (1996). Portfolio assessment: Some questions, some answers, some recommendation. *Journal of Adolescent and Adult Literacy* 39(6): 480–491.

Gordon, E.W., and C. Bonilla-Bowman (1996). Can performance-based assessments contribute to the achievement of educational equity? In *Performance-based student assessment: Challenges and possibilities*, ed. J. B. Baron and D. P. Wolf, 32–51. Chicago, IL: University of Chicago Press.

Herman, J. L., P. R. Aschbacher, and L. Winters (1992). *A practical guide to alternative assessment*. Alexandria, VA: Association for Supervision and Curriculum Development.

Hewitt, G. (1995). *A portfolio primer: Teaching, collecting, and assessing student writing*. Portsmouth, NH: Heinemann.

Hymes, D. L., A. E. Chafin, and P. Gonder (1991). The changing face of testing and assessment, problems and solutions. Arlington, VA: American Association of School Adminstrators.

Keeley, P. (2001). High school: Chandra performance tasks. Maine Science Teachers Network Listserv [Online]. Available: maine_science@list.terc.edu.

Linn, R. L., and E. L. Baker (1996). Can performance-based student assessments be psychometrically sound? In *Performance-based student assessment: Challenges and possibilities*, ed. J. B. Baron and D. P.

Wolf, 84–103. Chicago, IL: University of Chicago Press.

Madaus, G., W. Haney, and A. Kreitzer (1992). *Testing and evaluation.* New York: Council for Aid to Education.

Maine Learning Results. Retrieved June 26, 2001, from the World Wide Web: http://www.state.me.us/education/lres/lres.htm.

Mayer, R. E. (1998). *The promise of educational psychology.* Upper Saddle River, NJ: Merrill/Prentice-Hall.

Meyer, C. A. (1992). What's the difference between *authentic* and *performance* assessment? *Educational Leadership* 49: 39–40.

National Council of the Teachers of Mathematics (1991). *Mathematics assessment.* Alexandria, VA: National Council of the Teachers of Mathematics.

Nitko, A. J. (2001). *Educational assessment of students.* Upper Saddle River, NJ: Prentice-Hall.

Poteet, J. A., J. S. Choate, and S. C. Stewart (1993). Performance assessment and special education: Practices and prospects. *Focus on Exceptional Children* 26: 1–20.

Rogers, S., and S. Graham (2000). *The high performance toolbox: Succeeding with performance tasks, projects, and assessments* (3rd ed.). Evergreen, CO: Peak Learning Systems.

Shepard, L., and C. L. Bliem (1995). Parents' thinking about standardized tests and performance assessment. *Educational Researcher* 24(8): 25–32.

Stiggins, R. J. (1997). *Student-centered classroom assessment* (2nd ed.). Upper Saddle River, NJ: Merrill.

Swicegood, P. (1994). Portfolio-based assessment practices. *Intervention in School and Clinic* 30(1): 6–15.

Thompson, S. J., R. F. Quenemoen, M. L. Thurlow, and J. E. Ysseldyke (2001). *Alternative assessments for students with disabilities.* Thousand Oaks, CA: Corwin Press.

Vermont Department of Education (2001). *2000–2001 5th grade writing benchmarks.* Montpelier, VT: Author.

Wesson, C. L., and R. P. King (1996). Portfolio assessment and special education students. *Teaching Exceptional Children* 28(2): 44–48.

Wiggins, G. P. (1993). *Assessing student performance.* San Francisco: Jossey-Bass.

Wiggins, G., & J. McTigue (1998). *Understanding by design.* Alexandria, VA: Association for Supervision and Curriculum Development.

Wolf, D. (1996). Performance-based student assessment: Challenges and possibilities. Paper presented at the annual meeting of the American Educational Research Association, April. New York, New York.

# 8

# *Reading*

## Overview

Literacy involves being able to read, write, think, and communicate. Probably no other subject receives as much emphasis in the early grades. As students progress through the grades, we expect them to be literate. In school, achievement implies literacy. Once students leave school, being able to read and write is a prerequisite of everyday life, career success, socioeconomic status, and personal satisfaction. Yet, students continue to experience difficulties in learning to be literate.

Attempts to improve literacy have received renewed attention. Efforts have focused on improving classroom practices and generating attitudes and skills that foster the development of lifelong readers. One of the priorities of school reform efforts is an emphasis on connecting and integrating assessment with improvements in classroom practices (Langer et al., 1995).

Current instructional practices stress the integral link between reading and writing. This chapter focuses on the assessment of reading. Chapter 9 discusses the assessment of written language.

## *Chapter Objectives*

After completing this chapter you should be able to:

- Contrast several theoretical perspectives regarding the development of literacy.
- Explain the appropriate use of standardized achievement tests in the assessment of literacy.
- Describe specific tests of literacy.

- Describe the use of alternative assessment instruments that form a direct linked to instruction, program planning, and program evaluation.
- Describe how the physical, learning, and social environments influence literacy performance.

## *What Shapes Our Views*

The assessment of reading abilities and skills should involve a variety of approaches in order to reflect an understanding of what students know and are able to do. Assessment of reading and writing should reflect integrated activities that evaluate students' ability to think, rethink, construct, and interpret knowledge. This means that as students read they should know when to read, how to read, how to think about what they have read, and how to communicate their knowledge and understanding (Langer et al., 1995). Table 8.1 on page 196 describes reading assessment purposes and approaches.

## *Reading Theories*

Many theorists have studied the development of reading and have influenced current thinking about the link between reading and writing instruction and assessment (Rhodes and Shanklin, 1993).

### *Psycholinguistic Theory*

Goodman (Goodman, 1984, 1989; Rhodes and Shanklin, 1993) considers reading and its development to be a psychological process in which the reader constructs meaning. The construction of meaning involves using background knowledge to make predictions, confirm predictions, integrate information, and interpret information.

Goodman terms errors that occur in reading **miscues,** or "natural" errors rather than mistakes. As we assess reading, these miscues help us to view the cognitive processes that the student uses while reading. These errors may be omissions, substitutions, additions, repetitions, self-corrections, and pauses.

### *Schema Theory*

Cognitive psychologists have theorized that individuals use **schemas** to help make sense of new information. A schema is an "interlocking knowledge network" (Rhodes and Shanklin, 1993, p. 151). Schemas assist in the organization, remembering, and integration of knowledge. As we learn, we develop and refine schemas. Some readers may lack schemas, may not use schemas, or may be unable to maintain the schemas they have. Schemas relate to the individual's knowledge of graphophonics, semantics, syntax, and pragmatics.

**Graphophonics** refers to the knowledge of letters and their associated sounds. **Semantics** reflects an understanding of the meaning of language; for example, the ability to understand the meaning of the word *time* in distinguishing "What time is it?" from "He came on time." **Syntax** is the system of rules that dictate how words combine into meaningful phrases and sentences. Knowledge of syntax governs the arrangement of word sequences. For example, in the English language the most frequently used word order is subject, verb, direct object. In

**TABLE 8.1**   *Assessment Questions, Purposes, and Approaches*

| Assessment Questions | Steps and Purposes | Approaches |
|---|---|---|
| | **Screening** | |
| Is there a possibility of a disability in reading? | To determine whether students *may* have a disability in reading and should be referred for further assessment | Norm-referenced instruments<br>Curriculum-based assessments<br>Criterion-referenced assessments<br>Observations<br>Checklists<br>Norm-referenced instruments |
| | **Eligibility** | |
| Does the student have a disability?<br>What disability does the student have?<br>Does the student meet the criteria for services?<br>What are the strengths and weaknesses?<br>Why is the student having difficulty reading? | To determine if there is a disability<br>To compare the student's performance in reading with the performance of the peer group<br>To determine specific strengths and weaknesses in reading<br>To understand why the student is having difficulty | Curriculum-based assessments<br>Criterion-referenced assessments<br>Observations<br>Probes<br>Error analysis<br>Interviews<br>Checklists<br>Student, parent, and/or teacher conferences<br>Performance assessments |

*Connecting Instruction with Assessment*

| | | |
|---|---|---|
| | **Program Planning** | |
| What does the student not understand about reading?<br>Where should instruction in reading begin? | To understand what the student knows and does not know<br>To plan the student's program<br>To determine instructional approaches | Norm-referenced instruments<br>Curriculum-based assessments<br>Criterion-referenced assessments<br>Observations<br>Probes<br>Error analysis<br>Interviews<br>Checklists<br>Student, parent, and/or teacher conferences<br>Performance assessments |

*(continued)*

other languages, the verb may come first in the sentence, and the subject last. Finally, **pragmatics** refers to how individuals use language in a specific context. For example, knowledge of what to say upon first being introduced to someone reflects pragmatic ability.

## Transactional Theory

Rosenblatt (1995), a leading proponent of transactional theory, believes that readers use different strategies depending on the purpose of reading. Reading is a unique event that engages

**TABLE 8.1** *Continued*

| Assessment Questions | Steps and Purposes | Approaches |
|---|---|---|
| | **Program Monitoring** | |
| Once instruction begins, is the student making progress in reading?<br>Should reading instruction be modified? | To understand the strategies and concepts the student uses<br>To monitor the student's program | Curriculum-based assessments<br>Criterion-referenced assessments<br>Observations<br>Probes<br>Error analysis<br>Interviews<br>Checklists<br>Student, parent, and/or teacher conferences<br>Portfolios<br>Exhibitions<br>Journals<br>Written descriptions<br>Oral descriptions |
| | **Program Evaluation** | |
| Has the student met the goals of the IEP in reading?<br>Has the instructional program been successful for the student?<br>Has the student made progress?<br>Has the instructional program achieved its goals? | To determine whether the IEP goals have been met<br>To determine whether the goals of the program have been met<br>To evaluate program effectiveness | Curriculum-based assessments<br>Criterion-referenced assessments<br>Observations<br>Probes<br>Error analysis<br>Interviews<br>Checklists<br>Student, parent, and/or teacher conferences<br>Portfolios<br>Exhibitions<br>Journals<br>Written descriptions<br>Oral descriptions<br>Surveys |

the reader and the text at a particular time and under particular circumstances. During the transaction, the reader responds to the text in a variety of ways that are specific to the text and the individual's personal and cultural experiences. Gender, ethnicity, culture, and socioeconomic context are important factors that influence reading.

## Socio-Psycholinguistic Theory

Smith's theory of reading is complex and includes several aspects of the theories previously discussed (Rhodes and Shanklin, 1993; Smith, 1988). Smith emphasizes the importance of short-term and long-term memory in the reading process. Long-term memory guides the reading process while short-term memory assists in the recognition of information. Smith is credited with recognizing that the nonvisual information individuals bring to reading helps to facilitate the reading process.

## Synthesis of the Theories

These theories emphasize the contributions of cognitive psychology to our understanding of the reading process and reading development. Together, they construct contemporary beliefs about reading:

- Background knowledge influences reading performance.
- Schemas relate to the creation of meaning.
- Social and cultural factors affect reading.
- Knowledge of graphophonics, semantics, syntax, and pragmatics influence the reading process.
- Skilled readers are fluent.
- Reading involves the restructuring, application, and flexible use of knowledge in new situations.

## Instructional Approaches

Teachers apply theories of reading in various ways in the teaching and learning process (Stahl and Kuhn, 1995). Depending on background and orientation, the teacher may use one or more of the approaches in Table 8.2 on page 198.

## Assessment Principles

In 1991 the International Reading Association (IRA) (Rhodes and Shanklin, 1993) issued "Resolutions on Literacy Assessment." These resolutions are comprehensive and state that the two major purposes of literacy assessment are: (1) to inform learning and instruction and (2) to demonstrate that literacy programs are effective. Among the resolutions are several that are pertinent to the assessment of students with special needs:

- Assessments should include a variety of observations that consider the complexity of the processes involved in reading, writing, and in using language. The assessment tasks must include high-quality texts, various genres, and authentic tasks.
- Assessment tasks should be age-appropriate.
- Assessment tools should not reflect bias.
- Assessment of reading, writing, and language must include a variety of approaches.
- Assessment approaches should consider the purposes of each assessment tool and the settings in which the assessment is conducted.
- Assessment activities should reflect instruction.

## Twelve Principles of Literacy Assessment

According to Rhodes and Shanklin (1993), there are twelve principles of literacy assessment:

**1.** *Assess authentic reading and writing.* When students read and write they must know the letters and their associated sounds (graphophonics), understand the meaning of language (semantics), and grasp the flow of the language (syntax).

**2.** *Assess reading and writing in various contexts.* An understanding of students' reading and writing abilities must consider the contexts in which reading and writing occur. Contexts relate to the types of reading materials, the purpose of the reading, and strategies in use.

**3.** *Assess the literacy environment, instruction, and students.* Reading and writing assessment must consider the environments in which reading occurs, the types of instruction in use, and the characteristics of students.

**4.** *Assess processes and products of reading.* The assessment of reading processes and students' products can provide a comprehensive understanding of students' abilities.

**5.** *Analyze error patterns.* The understanding of patterns of errors in reading and writing can help improve student performance. Errors

**TABLE 8.2**    *Instructional Approaches in Reading*

| Instructor Variables | Direct Instruction | Explicit Instruction | Cognitive Approach | Whole Language |
|---|---|---|---|---|
| Orientation to reading | Emphasis is on the teaching of subskills (e.g., phonics, sight words, etc.) | Strategies are explicitly taught | Meaning is constructed from the text | Immersion in a print environment |
| Instruction | Directed by teacher | Directed by teacher | Teacher and student collaborate | Student, with teacher guidance |
| Instructional materials | Workbooks, worksheets, basal readers | Worksheets, basals, literature-based program | Literature-based program, small discussion groups | Literature-based program, integrated writing, individual and small discussion groups |

*Source:* Adapted from Stahl, S. A., and H. R. Kuhn (1995). Does Whole Language or Instruction Matched to Learning Styles Help Children Learn to Read? *School Psychology Review* 24: 393–404.

in reading include miscues, omissions, substitutions, additions, repetitions, self-corrections, and pauses.

**6.** *Include the assessment of background knowledge.* Experience, prior learning, and background knowledge influence reading and writing performance.

**7.** *Consider developmental patterns in reading and writing.* Knowledge of typical developmental patterns in reading and writing can contribute to our understanding of reading and writing abilities.

**8.** *Use sound principles of assessment.* Use sound principles or standards when assessing students. These standards apply to reliability, validity, observation, and scoring. Chapters 3 and 4 discuss many of these principles.

**9.** *Use triangulation.* **Triangulation** means that conclusions about student performance

derive from multiple (here, at least three) sources of information. Rhodes and Shanklin advise caution when drawing conclusions about students when using only one source of information.

**10.** *Include students, parents, teachers, and other school personnel in the assessment process.* The involvement of students, parents, and other educators in the assessment process provides for the inclusion of multiple perspectives.

**11.** *Assessment activities should be ongoing.* Assessment activities should occur frequently and routinely. In this way, assessment activities integrate into and inform instruction.

**12.** *Record, analyze, and use assessment information.* Assessment information is effective only when it is in use. Record assessment data frequently, analyze it, and use it on a routine basis to guide instruction.

## Standardized Instruments

There are many standardized tests of reading (Table 8.3). In addition, Table 8.4 lists achievement batteries that contain reading subtests.

## Gray Oral Reading Tests–4

The *Gray Oral Reading Tests–4 (GORT–4)* (Wiederholt and Bryant, 2001) is an individually administered norm-referenced test of reading comprehension and oral reading for students ages 6 years through 18 years. Each of the two forms of the *GORT–4* contains 13 reading passages arranged in order of difficulty. Although the title of the test indicates that the *GORT–4* is a revision of the previous edition,

this test is almost identical to its predecessor, *Gray Oral Reading Tests–3 (GORT–3).*

***Administration.*** For each passage, the examiner reads one or two sentences that provide motivation. After reading each passage orally, the student responds to five multiple-choice questions that the examiner reads aloud. The examiner records the student's responses.

***Scoring.*** The test reports scores as age and grade equivalents; percentiles; standard scores for the total scores for rate, accuracy, and comprehension; and Oral Reading Comprehension Score.

***Standardization.*** The *GORT–4* was standardized on more than 1,600 students, ages 6

**TABLE 8.3** *Standardized Tests of Reading*

| Test | Ages/Grades | Abilities |
|---|---|---|
| *Gray Oral Reading Tests–4* (Wiederholt and Bryant, 2001) | Ages 6 years through 18 years | Comprehension, oral reading skills |
| *Nelson-Denny Reading Test* (Brown, Fishco, and Hanna, 2000) | Grade 9 through college | Vocabulary, comprehension, reading rate |
| *Standardized Reading Inventory–2* (Newcomer, 1999) | Preprimer through grade 8 | Oral reading, word recognition, comprehension |
| *Stanford Diagnostic Reading Test 4* (Harcourt Brace Educational Measurement, 1995) | Grades 1.5 through 13 | Phonetic ability, vocabulary, comprehension |
| *Test of Early Reading Ability, Third Edition* (Reid, Hresko, and Hammill, 2001) | Ages 3 years through 9 years, 11 months | Contextual meaning, alphabet, conventions |
| *Test of Phonological Awareness* (Torgeson and Bryant, 1994) | K through grade 2 | Awareness of individual sounds in words |
| *Test of Reading Comprehension–3* (Brown, Hammill, and Wiederholt, 1995) | Ages 7 years through 17 years, 11 months | Vocabulary, syntactic similarities, comprehension, sentence sequencing |
| *Woodcock Reading Mastery Tests–Revised/Normative Update* (Woodcock, McGrew, and Mather, 1998) | K through adulthood | Visual-auditory learning, letter identification, word identification, word attack, word comprehension |

**TABLE 8.4** *Test Batteries That Contain Reading Subtests*

| Test | Ages/Grades |
|------|-------------|
| *BRIGANCE® Inventory of Essential Skills* (Brigance, 1981) | Grades 6 through adulthood |
| *BRIGANCE® Comprehensive Inventory of Basic Skills–Revised* (Brigance, 1999) | Grades 1 through 6 |
| *BRIGANCE® Assessment of Basic Skills–Spanish Edition* (Brigance, 1984) | Grades K through 8 |
| *Basic Achievement Individual Skills Screener (BASIS)* (Sonnenschein, 1983) | Grades 1 through 12 and post–high school |
| *Diagnostic Achievement Battery–2 (DAB–2)* (Newcomer, 1990) | Ages 6 years through 14 years |
| *Diagnostic Achievement Test for Adolescents–2 (DATA–2)* (Newcomer and Bryant, 1993) | Grades 7 through 12 |
| *Kaufman Assessment Battery for Children (K–ABC)* (Kaufman and Kaufman, 1983) | Ages 2 years, 6 months through 12 years, 6 months |
| *Kaufman Test of Educational Achievement/Normative Update (K–TEA/NU)* (Kaufman and Kaufman, 1998) | Grades 1 through 12; ages 6 years to 18 years, 11 months |
| *Peabody Individual Achievement Test–R/Normative Update (PIAT–R/NU)* (Markwardt, 1998) | Grades K through 12; ages 5 years to 18 years, 11 months |
| *Wide Range Achievement Test–3 (WRAT–3)* (Wilkinson, 1993) | Ages 5 years to 75 years |
| *Wechsler Individual Achievement Test–II (WIAT–II)* (Harcourt Brace Educational Measurement, 2001) | Grades K through 12; ages 5 years to 19 years, 11 months |
| *Woodcock-Johnson Psychoeducational Battery–III (WJ–III)* (Woodcock, McGrew, and Mather, 2001) | Grades K through 12; ages 2 years through adulthood |

years through 18 years. The sample selection came from U.S. Census reports and was stratified according to geographic region, race, grade, gender, and ethnicity.

*Reliability.* Average internal consistency reliability coefficients are .90. In general, the reliability coefficients are adequate.

*Validity.* For the most part, the *GORT–4* bases concurrent validity on the *GORT–3*. The major criticism of the validity of this test is that the manual does not report whether the *GORT–4* actually measures the authors' stated purposes.

*Summary.* The *Gray Oral Reading Tests–4* is an individually administered norm-referenced test of reading comprehension and oral reading. The standardization is adequate. However, information is lacking as to the socioeconomic status of the sample, and whether test developers systemically included students with disabilities and students whose first language is not English. While the reliability is acceptable, additional evidence of validity is needed.

## Stanford Diagnostic Reading Test

The *Stanford Diagnostic Reading Test 4 (SDRT4)* (Harcourt Brace Educational Measurement,

1995) is a norm-referenced test for students in grades 1.5 through 13. The test has six overlapping levels:

| Grade | Level |
|---|---|
| 1.5 through 2.5 | red |
| 2.5 through 3.5 | orange |
| 3.5 through 4.5 | green |
| 4.5 through 6.5 | purple |
| 6.5 through 8.9 | brown |
| 9.0 through 13.0 | blue |

The purposes of the *SDRT4* are to assist in making eligibility decisions, diagnose difficulties in reading, evaluate programs, and provide information about program effectiveness. The test assesses phonetic ability, vocabulary, reading comprehension, and the ability to scan for information.

***Administration.*** The *SDRT4* is a group-administered test. Examiners need not administer all subtests. The examiner can decide to administer only one or two of the subtests. The items are a combination of multiple choice and free response. Examiners can administer this test individually following standardized procedures for test administration.

***Scoring.*** Raw scores convert to percentiles, stanines, normal curve equivalents, grade equivalents, and scaled scores. Teachers can score the *SDRT4* by hand (using a stencil provided by the publisher) or send it away for machine scoring.

***Standardization.*** The standardization sample is representative of socioeconomic status, size of school district, and geographic region.

***Reliability.*** The test reports both alternate form and internal consistency reliabilities. The reliability coefficients are adequate.

***Validity.*** The test reports content and criterion-related validity. Teachers should examine the test items to determine the extent to which the *SDRT4* matches reading as they have taught it.

***Summary.*** The *Stanford Diagnostic Reading Test 4* is a norm-referenced test for students in grades 1.5 through 13. The test has six overlapping levels and is applicable to groups of students. However, it can be useful for individual students. The items consist of both multiple-choice and free-response items.

## Test of Reading Comprehension–3

The *Test of Reading Comprehension–3 (TORC–3)* (Brown, Hammill, and Wiederholt, 1995) is an individually administered norm-referenced test of vocabulary and silent reading comprehension for students ages 7 years through 17 years, 11 months. The *TORC–3* contains eight subtests:

*General Vocabulary.* The student reads three words and then selects two other words that relate to the three words.

*Syntactic Similarities.* The student reads five sentences and then chooses the two sentences that are most closely related.

*Paragraph Reading.* After reading brief paragraphs, the student answers multiple-choice questions for each paragraph.

*Sentence Sequencing.* After reading five sentences, the student must arrange them in a logical sequence.

*Mathematics Vocabulary.* This subtest is similar to the General Vocabulary subtest, except that the vocabulary consists of words related to mathematics.

*Social Studies Vocabulary.* This subtest is similar to the General Vocabulary subtest except that the vocabulary consists of words related to social studies.

*Science Vocabulary.* This subtest is similar to the General Vocabulary subtest except that the vocabulary consists of words related to science.

*Reading the Directions of Schoolwork.* The student reads directions and responds on the answer sheet.

**Administration.** The *TORC–3* is individually administered. However, teachers can administer it to small groups of students.

**Scoring.** Raw scores convert to age and grade equivalents, percentiles, and standard scores.

**Standardization.** *TORC–3* is the third edition of the *TORC*, originally published in 1968. It was revised in 1986. This third edition was renormed. The test reports information about the proportion of students by age, geographic region, gender, residence, race, ethnicity, and disabilities in the standardization sample.

**Reliability.** The test reports test-retest and internal consistency reliability coefficients. Reliabilty for the *TORC–3* is adequate.

**Validity.** The test reports content and criterion-related validity. Teachers should examine

the test items to determine the extent to which the *TORC–3* matches reading as they have taught it.

**Summary.** The *Test of Reading Comprehension–3* is a norm-referenced test of vocabulary and reading comprehension. Evidence of reliabilty and validity is adequate. However, the teacher should examine the test items in order to determine congruence with the school curriculum. Box 8.1 describes the test's parameters.

## Woodcock Reading Mastery Test–Revised/Normative Update

The *Woodcock Reading Mastery Test–Revised/ Normative Update (WRMT–R/NU)* (Woodcock, 1998) is an individually administered test of reading skills and reading comprehension for individuals from kindergarten through age 75. The *WRMT–R/NU* consists of six tests arranged in clusters. The Visual-Auditory Learning and Letter Identification tests compose the Readiness Cluster. The Word Identification and Word Attack tests form the Basic Skills Cluster and the Word Comprehension and Passage Comprehension tests consitute the Reading Comprehension Cluster. Form G of the test includes a Supplementary Letter Checklist. The following section describes each of the tests.

*Visual-Auditory Learning.* The student looks at rebuses representing words and must "read" the rebuses.

*Letter Identification.* The student looks at upper- and lowercase letters of the alphabet and must name each of the letters.

*Supplementary Letter Checklist (Form G only).* The student must recognize and name letters in sans serif type.

*Word Identification.* The student must read single words that are in the test.

*Word Attack.* The student must demonstrate a knowledge of phonics and word attack skills by pronouncing nonsense syllables.

---

**BOX 8.1** *Test of Reading Comprehension–3 (TORC–3)*

*Publication Date:* 1995

*Purpose:* Measures vocabulary and reading comprehension.

*Age/Grade Levels:* Ages 7 years through 17 years, 11 months.

*Time to Administer:* One to three hours, depending on the age of the student.

*Technical Adequacy:* Evidence of reliabilty and validity is adequate. Test items should be examined by the evaluator in order to determine congruence with reading instruction.

*Suggested Use:* Measure of vocabulary; indicates strengths and weaknesses in silent reading comprehension.

*Word Comprehension.* This subtest is composed of three parts: Antonyms, Synonyms, and Analogies. The student must connect words according to these categories.

*Passage Comprehension.* The student reads a brief passage and supplies the missing words.

**Administration.** The *WRMT–R/NU* is administered individually.

**Scoring.** Raw scores are converted to standard scores, percentiles, and age and grade equivalents. In addition, there is a relative performance index (RPI) that provides an estimate of expected performance. The *WRMT–R/NU* scoring forms include visual profiles for describing performance.

**Standardization.** For the 1998 edition, test publishers did not collect new norms, but rather, reanalyzed existing standardization data. The school-age sample data are from 1983 to 1985. The college and university sample data are from 1984 through 1985. Adult data are from 1984 through 1985. The standardization sample represents age, gender, region, race, ethnicity, and economic status as estimated by parental education. The standardization sample of the *WRMT–R/NU* forms a link with the standardization samples for the *Kaufman Test of Achievement (K–TEA/NU), Peabody Individual Achievement Test–Revised/NU (PIAT–R/NU)*, and the *KeyMath–R*. The renorming sample for the *WRMT–R/NU* consisted of students in kindergarten through age 22. There is no update for the sample of individuals over the age of 22. For the linking sample, the test examinees in the norm sample took one of the complete test batteries and one or more subtests from another battery. This linking approach permits the making of comparisons of test performance across batteries.

**Reliability.** Test publishers report internal consistency reliability coefficients only for grades 1, 3, 5, 8, and 11, and for adults. The coefficients are in the .80s and .90s. Test-retest reliability coefficients are not available.

**Validity.** The manual provides evidence of content validity. The test reports concurrent validity with the *Woodcock-Johnson Psychoeducational Battery–Revised*. The *WRMT–R/NU* uses a traditional, somewhat outdated approach to reading. Evidence to support the validity of the clusters is lacking. Examiners should carefully review the test in order to determine the correspondence between test items and the literacy curriculum.

**Summary.** The *WRMT–R/NU* is an individually administered test of reading skills and reading comprehension for individuals from kindergarten through adulthood, consisting of

---

**BOX 8.2**    *Woodcock Reading Mastery Test–Revised/NU (WRMT–R/NU)*

---

*Publication Date:* 1998

*Purposes:* Measures reading readiness, reading skills, and reading comprehension.

*Age/Grade Levels:* Kindergarten through adulthood.

*Time to Administer:* 30 minutes to 50 minutes.

*Technical Adequacy:* For the 1998 edition, new norms were not collected. Existing standardization data were reanalyzed. Reliability is adequate. Validity is acceptable; however, teachers should examine the test items to determine the extent to which the items assess the curriculum taught. Many of the test items reflect a skills approach to learning to read.

*Suggested Use:* As a limited measure of overall reading achievement. Examiners should evaluate the test items because the test does not reflect contemporary approaches to the teaching of literacy.

six tests in three clusters. The *NU* edition does not update the norms. There is some question about validity of the test in view of current approaches to teaching literacy. Box 8.2 describes the test's parameters.

## Concerns about Standardized Reading Tests

Norm-referenced tests of reading can be useful in identifying students with reading difficulties, pinpointing strengths and weaknesses, and evaluating programs. However, many experts have voiced concerns about those tests. In 1991 the International Reading Association directly addressed concerns about the use of standardized reading tests when it "resolved that literacy assessments must be based in current research and theory, not limited by traditional psychometric concepts, and must reflect the complex and dynamic interrelationship of reading, writing, and language abilities" (Rhodes and Shanklin, 1993, p. 47). Most experts in reading believe that standardized norm-referenced tests of reading have a number of shortcomings.

| Norm-Referenced Tests of Reading | Contemporary Theories of Reading Assessment |
|---|---|
| Contain brief, incomplete passages | Have longer, complete passages |
| Fail to tap background knowledge | Encourage the reader to use background knowledge while reading |
| Pose literal questions | Encourage the use of higher-order thinking; which involves the restructuring, application, and flexible use of knowledge in new situations |
| Can contain biased questions | Offer equitable assessment strategies |

*Several students discuss the books that they selected for their book group.*

| Norm-Referenced Tests of Reading | Contemporary Theories of Reading Assessment |
|---|---|
| Pose multiple-choice questions | Pose open-ended questions |
| Have only one correct answer to each question | Encourage more than one answer |
| Fail to assess the use of a variety of reading strategies | Assess a variety of reading strategies |
| Do not assess reading attitudes and habits | Assess reading attitudes and habits |
| Offer few or no direct links to instruction | Directly link assessment tools to instruction |

## Connecting Assessment with Instruction

Curriculum-based assessment (CBA), introduced in Chapter 6, is a broad approach to linking assessment with instruction. CBA has three purposes: (1) to determine eligibility, (2) to develop the goals for instruction, and (3) to evaluate the student's progress in the curriculum. There are a number of approaches to developing and using curriculum-based assessment instruments in the assessment of literacy. We will examine two approaches: curriculum-based assessment and curriculum-based measurement.

### Curriculum-Based Assessment: Idol, Nevin, Paolucci-Whitcomb Model

Curriculum-based assessment can measure the rate of reading, reading errors, accuracy, and reading comprehension. Although the developers (Idol, Nevin, and Paolucci-Whitcomb, 1996) presume a basal reading series as part of the curriculum, this model can adapt to a literature-based reading program. Teachers can use instruction materials to construct the CBA and to establish levels of mastery. The following steps describe how to develop and administer the CBA:

**1.** The teacher photocopies three 100-word passages from the first quarter of each of the basal readers for grades 1 through 6. For preprimers and primers, teachers select passages of 25 or 50 words, then label and arrange them in order of difficulty.

**2.** On three successive days, beginning with the easiest passage and proceeding to the more difficult ones, the student reads orally one of the passages. The teacher records the total number of seconds it took for the student to read the passage. From this, the teacher can determine the number of correct words the student reads per minute.

**3.** The teacher records errors made while the student is reading. Types of errors include omissions, substitutions, additions, repetitions, self-corrections, and pauses. To determine the percentage of reading accuracy, the number of words read correctly is divided by the total number of words in the passage. For example, Peter read a 100-word passage and made five errors. To calculate reading accuracy, his teacher followed these steps:

- Subtract total number of errors from number of words in the passage

  $100 - 5 = 95$ words read correctly

- Divide the number of words read correctly by the total number of words in the passage

  $\frac{95}{100} = 95\,\%$ level of accuracy

**4.** After each passage is read, the teacher asks the student six comprehension questions that the teacher has constructed. The acceptable level of performance is answering 5 of the 6 questions correctly. Teachers should construct the questions as follows:

- *Two text-explicit (TE) questions.* These are questions with answers that the student can find precisely in the passage.

Example: What is the name of the main character?

- *Two text-implicit (TI) questions.* These are questions with answers that the passage implies.

Example: What is a solar system?

- *Two script-implicit (SI) questions.* These are questions that require the reader to combine prior knowledge with details from the passage.

Example: What is the moral of the story?

## Curriculum-Based Measurement

Curriculum-based measurement (CBM) (Marston, 1989) is a type of curriculum-based assessment that emphasizes repeated direct measurement of student performance. CBM is based on the belief that reading fluency depends on speed and accuracy of reading. Like the previous model, CBM emphasizes: (1) the direct link between the assessment and the student's curriculum, (2) brief, frequent assessments, (3) multiple forms of the assessment instrument, (4) the low cost of developing assessment materials, and (5) a sensitivity to measuring the improvement of student performance.

To construct a CBM, the teacher selects a brief passage or word list and asks the student to read it orally. When the student finishes reading, the teacher counts the number of correctly and incorrectly read words. The teacher and the student use a graph to plot the number of correctly read words. Teachers can repeat this process many times in order to document the progress that the student makes.

## Criterion-Referenced Assessment

Instead of comparing a student's performance to a norm group, criterion-referenced assessments measure a student's performance with respect to a well-defined content domain (Anastasi, 1988), as Chapter 6 discusses. Criterion-referenced tests are applicable to each of the assessment approaches described in Table

8.1. While norm-referenced tests in reading discriminate between the performance of individual students on specific test items, criterion-referenced tests provide a description of a student's curriculum-referenced knowledge, skills, or processes.

The *BRIGANCE® Inventories* are criterion-referenced tests that are similar in purpose, scoring, administration, and interpretation. Chapter 6 describes the tests in detail, and Table 8.5 summarizes the reading sections of each of the inventories.

## Principles

It is a fundamental principle that instruction in reading links directly with assessment. Connecting instruction to assessment in reading means that:

- Assessment occurs as a normal part of the student's work. Assessment activities emerge from the teaching situation. The student does not stop work to do an assessment; the work connects with the assessment. Examples of this type of assessment include the use of journals, notebooks, essays, oral reports, homework, classroom discussions, group work, and interviews. These assessment activities can occur individually or in small groups and can take place during one session or over multiple sessions.

- The conditions for assessment should be similar to the conditions for doing meaningful tasks. Students must have sufficient time, have access to peers, be able to use appropriate literacy materials, and have the chance to revise their work.

- Assessment tasks need to be meaningful and multidimensional. They should provide students with the opportunity to demonstrate a variety of reading abilities and skills.

- Feedback to students is frequent, specific, meaningful, and prompt, and assists students' acquisition of reading.

- Students participate in the assessment process. They help to generate and apply

**TABLE 8.5   BRIGANCE® *Inventories***

| Name | Ages/Grades | Reading Abilities |
|---|---|---|
| *BRIGANCE® Inventory of Essential Skills* (Brigance, 1981) | Grades 4 through 12 | 1. Word Recognition<br>2. Oral Reading<br>3. Reading Comprehension<br>4. Word Analysis<br>5. Functional Word Recognition |
| *BRIGANCE® Comprehensive Inventory of Basic Skills–Revised* (Brigance, 1999) | Pre-K through grade 9 | 1. Word Recognition<br>2. Oral Reading<br>3. Reading Comprehension<br>4. Word Analysis<br>5. Functional Word Recognition |
| *BRIGANCE® Assessment of Basic Skills–Spanish Edition* (Brigance, 1984) | Grades K through 6 | 1. Functional Word Recognition<br>2. Oral Reading<br>3. Reading Comprehension<br>4. Word Analysis<br>5. Listening |
| *BRIGANCE® Inventory of Early Development–Revised* (Brigance, 1991) | Ages birth to 7 years | 1. Letter Recognition<br>2. Word Recognition<br>3. Oral Reading<br>4. Letter-Sound Recognition |
| *BRIGANCE® Life Skills Inventory* (Brigance, 1994) | Vocational<br>Secondary<br>Adult education | 1. Words on Common Signs<br>2. Words on Common Labels |
| *BRIGANCE® Employability Skills Inventory* (Brigance, 1995) | Vocational<br>Secondary<br>Adult education<br>Job training | 1. Reading Grade-Placement<br>2. Direction Words<br>3. Words Related to Employment<br>4. Abbreviations |

standards or rubrics. Self-assessment and peer assessment are part of the assessment process.

## Assessment Approaches

Formal assessment and feedback from peers and teachers encourage the development of reading abilities. Ways in which the teacher can gather information and provide feedback to parents and students include:

- probes
- miscue, or error, analysis
- cloze procedure
- think-alouds
- retelling
- oral descriptions
- written descriptions
- checklists and questionnaires
- interviews
- conferences
- student journals and notebooks
- performance-based assessments
- sharing portfolios
- exhibitions
- self-assessment
- peer assessment

## Probes

A probe is a diagnostic technique in which instruction is varied in order to examine whether an instructional schema is working. As Chapter 6 indicates, probes are valuable for diagnosing student problems and assisting in planning instruction. For example, suppose a teacher wants to determine whether a student is ready to proceed to a more difficult reading book. The teacher can present the student with a selection from the book and observe the strategies that the student uses when reading. The student may be able to read the words on the page but needs some help learning new vocabulary. The teacher can then help the student by introducing the new vocabulary and providing background knowledge.

Teachers implement instructional probes during the process of instruction. When designing an instructional probe, we suggest the following steps:

1. The teacher identifies the area of reading that is to be the target and determines whether the student is able to do the tasks or use certain reading strategies. Examples include locating the title page, retelling a story, and recognizing common warning signs such as Danger and Keep Out.

2. The teacher modifies the assignment. For example, to facilitate the recognition of warning signs the teacher can have the student say, trace, recognize, and write the words. To assist in retelling, a teacher can ask: What happened after? Tell me more about where the story takes place.

3. The teacher determines whether the student can read the words or can retell the passage.

When conducting a diagnostic probe, the teacher should document the student's performance during step 1 (baseline), step 2 (instruction), and step 3 (baseline).

## Miscue (or Error) Analysis

As defined in Chapter 6, the purposes of error analysis are: (1) to identify the patterns of errors or miscues that students make in their work, (2) to understand why students make the errors, and (3) to provide instruction to help correct the errors. In a miscue or error analysis of reading skills, the student reads aloud and the teacher categorizes the errors. Figure 8.1 shows common symbols and how teachers use them when marking miscues.

After conducting a miscue analysis, the teacher should summarize the error patterns. However, many errors will not have a pattern, and a pattern of errors does not mean that there is a serious problem. Miscue analysis is always a preliminary form of assessment; teachers should always conduct further evaluation of the student's work.

Students will frequently correct their own miscues. Calling attention to the student's miscues can interrupt the student's understanding of the passage. Teachers should allow students to proceed to the end of the sentence or paragraph before providing feedback. Teachers can gather useful assessment information when observing whether the student makes self-corrections when rereading a passage.

The *Classroom Reading Miscue Assessment (CRMA)* (Rhodes and Shanklin, 1993) (Figure 8.2) was developed to assist teachers in using miscue analysis. As the student reads a passage, the teacher uses the CRMA to determine the types of miscues that the student makes. To begin, the teacher selects a complete passage or story, from 300 to 500 words in length, with which the student is unfamiliar. The passage should be at an acceptable level of difficulty, which is estimated at between 1 and 9 semantically unacceptable miscues in the first 100 words that the student reads. As the student reads the passage, the teacher marks the miscues.

Once the teacher identifies the miscues, the teacher asks the student to retell the story. The teacher can use open-ended probes to assist in

| | |
|---|---|
| *brothers*<br>bothers | Longhand superscriptions denote substitution miscues—oral observed responses that differ from expected responses to printed text. |
| ∧ | Insertion miscue (word not printed in text, added by oral reader).<br>Example:   Gwen ∧ poured him a big glass.  *(proudly)* |
| (word) | Circled word or words; circled period or other punctuation indicates omission miscue—word in printed text, omitted in oral reading. |
| *st-* | In substitution miscues, partial word plus hyphen stands for partial word substituted in oral reading for text word. |
| Billy\|cried, | Reversal miscue of words in text by oral reader. |
| ℝ Then he | In passages recording miscues, underlines denote repetitions—portions the reader repeats in oral reading. |
| ℂ | Miscue corrected through regression.<br>Example:   ℂ *the* Then he … |
| ⓤⓒ | Miscue with unsuccessful attempt at correction through regression.<br>Example:   ⓤⓒ *All* Tell me what you see … |
| ⒶⒸ | Reader abandons correct form. Reader replaces an initially correct response with an incorrect one. |
| ⓓ with | Circled letter d preceding a miscue superscription denotes a variation in sound, vocabulary, or grammar resulting from a dialect difference between the author and the reader. |
| $ | Nonword miscue. The reader either produces a nonword orally in place of text word or supplies a phonemic dialect variation.<br>Examples:   $ *larther* I sat in a large leather chair.<br>$ *cawed* What his mother called him depended on what he did last. |
| + | Oral reader sounds out the word in segments.<br>Example:   $ *sooth + thing* I guess they do have a soothing sound. |

**FIGURE 8.1   *Miscue Symbols***

*Source:* Reprinted by permission of Lynn K. Rhodes and Nancy L. Shanklin from *Windows into Literacy: Assessing Learners K–8.* Portsmouth, NH: Heinemann, A division of Reed Elsevier, Inc., 1993, p. 163.

Reader's Name __Richard_____ Date _____

Grade level __Gr 4-Chapter 1_____ Teacher _____

Selection read ____Wolf_____

## CLASSROOM READING MISCUE ASSESSMENT

**I.   What percent of the sentences read make sense?**

| | Sentence by sentence tally | Total |
|---|---|---|
| Number of semantically acceptable sentences | THL THL THL THL THL THL THL THL THL THL I | 51 |
| Number of semantically unacceptable sentences | THL III | 8 |

% Comprehending score:

$$\frac{\text{Number of semantically acceptable sentences}}{\text{Total number of sentences read}} \times 100 = \underline{\quad 86 \quad} \%$$

**II.  In what ways is the reader constructing meaning?**

| | Seldom | Sometimes | Often | Usually | Never |
|---|---|---|---|---|---|
| A. Recognizes when miscues have disrupted meaning | ① | 2 | 3 | 4 | 5 |
| B. Logically substitutes | ① | 2 | 3 | 4 | 5 |
| C. Self-corrects errors that disrupt meaning | ① | 2 | 3 | 4 | 5 |
| D. Uses picture and/or other visual clues | 1 | 2 | 3 | ④ | 5 |

**In what ways is the reader disrupting meaning?**

| | Seldom | Sometimes | Often | Usually | Never |
|---|---|---|---|---|---|
| A. Substitutes words that don't make sense | 1 | ② | 3 | 4 | 5 |
| B. Makes omissions that disrupt meaning | ① | 2 | 3 | 4 | 5 |
| C. Relies too heavily on graphophonic cues | 1 | ② | 3 | 4 | 5 |

**III. If narrative text is used:**

| | No | | Partial | | Yes |
|---|---|---|---|---|---|
| A. Character recall | 1 | 2 | 3 | 4 | ⑤ |
| B. Character development | 1 | 2 | 3 | 4 | ⑤ |
| C. Setting | 1 | 2 | 3 | 4 | ⑤ |
| D. Relationship of events | 1 | 2 | 3 | 4 | ⑤ |
| E. Plot | 1 | 2 | 3 | ④ | ⑤ |
| F. Theme | 1 | 2 | 3 | 4 | 5 |
| G. Overall retelling | 1 | 2 | 3 | 4 | ⑤ |

**If expository text is used:**

| | No | | Partial | | Yes |
|---|---|---|---|---|---|
| A. Major concepts | 1 | 2 | 3 | 4 | 5 |
| B. Generalizations | 1 | 2 | 3 | 4 | 5 |
| C. Specific information | 1 | 2 | 3 | 4 | 5 |
| D. Logical structuring | 1 | 2 | 3 | 4 | 5 |
| E. Overall retelling | 1 | 2 | 3 | 4 | 5 |

**FIGURE 8.2  *Classroom Reading Miscue Assessment***

*Source:* Reprinted by permission of Lynn K. Rhodes and Nancy L. Shanklin from *Windows into Literacy: Assessing Learners K–8.* Portsmouth, NH: Heinemann, A division of Reed Elsevier, Inc., 1993, p. 177.

the retelling. Figure 8.3 provides examples of probes to use in the retelling.

### Cloze Procedure

The cloze procedure is generally used to determine whether reading material is within a student's ability. The teacher selects a passage to be read and reproduces it, leaving out every fifth word. The assumption of the technique is that if the student can fill in the blanks, the reading is within the student's ability. Some alternatives to using the fifth-word rule are:

- The teacher decides which words to omit.
- The teacher can read orally and ask the student to fill in the missing word.

- Blanks can be left so that various parts of speech are omitted. (Rhodes and Shanklin, 1993)

### Think-Alouds

A think-aloud is the verbalization of a student's thoughts about a text before, during, or after reading. Think-alouds provide insight into the student's comprehension abilities and thinking processes. For example, before beginning to read a story about immigrants in the United States, the teacher could ask, "What do you think that this story will be about?" or "What do you already know about immigrants?" During the reading, the student might verbalize, "I don't know that word" or "My mother told me about that."

---

**FIGURE 8.3**   *Probes*

| | |
|---|---|
| Character Recall: | Who else was in the story? |
| Character Development: | What else can you tell me about _____? |
| Setting: | Where did _____ happen? |
| | When did _____ happen? |
| | Tell me more about _____ place. |
| Events: | What else happened in the story? |
| | How did _____ happen? |
| Event Sequence: | What happened before _____? |
| | What happened after _____? |
| Plot: | What was _____'s main problem? |
| Theme: | What did you think (the major character ) learned in the story? |
| | What do you think the author might have been trying to tell us in this story? |
| Good probes to use with expository text are: | |
| Major Concept(s): | What was the main thing the author wanted you to learn? |
| Generalizations: | What other important information about _____ did the author tell you? |
| Specific Information: | Is there any other information you remember the author told about? |
| | What specific facts do you remember? |
| Logical Structuring: | How did the author go about presenting the information? (comparison, examples, steps in a process, etc.) |

*Source:*  Reprinted by permission of Lynn K. Rhodes and Nancy L. Shanklin from *Windows into Literacy: Assessing Learners K–8.* Portsmouth, NH: Heinemann, A division of Reed Elsevier, Inc., 1993, p. 181.

After reading, the student might say "I didn't understand that" or "That was hard."

When eliciting think-alouds, teachers can use the following procedures:

1. Ask students to think aloud while they are reading. Explain that thinking aloud will help students to understand the text.
2. Indicate where the student should stop reading in order to think aloud.
3. Model how a think-aloud is done.
4. While the student is thinking aloud, record the student's comments.
5. Analyze the think-aloud for patterns, such as the use of context clues, substitutions, misunderstandings, inferences, use of information, and the addition of information to the text. (Rhodes and Shanklin, 1993)

## Retelling

Retelling is a comprehension exercise in which the student retells as much of a text as can be remembered after reading it. Retelling provides considerable information about comprehension. The following procedures are useful in retelling:

1. Tell the student that you will request a retelling at the end of the reading.
2. Once the student has finished reading, request the retelling.
3. Audiotape the retelling.
4. Once the student has finished the retelling, ask if there is anything else that the student would like to add.
5. At this point, you can choose to ask questions or use prompts to elicit additional information.
6. Use a checklist or record form to analyze the retelling for patterns and trends in knowledge of story structure, story elements, use of details, and use of language. (Rhodes and Shanklin, 1993)

## Oral Descriptions

Verbal descriptions of a student's work can provide immediate feedback to a student by a teacher or peer. Oral descriptions are useful because they are quick, efficient, direct, and integrate easily into instruction. They are adaptable for program planning and program evaluation. An example of providing oral feedback to a student who has just completed reading a passage is: "You did a nice job recognizing when words didn't make sense. You understood the events that occurred in the passage and retold the story with only two prompts."

Oral descriptions do have several drawbacks, however. They are subjective and, since the descriptions are given verbally, there is no permanent record. In addition, specific disabilities may limit the ability of the student to understand, remember, or reply to what has been said.

## Written Descriptions

A written description is a brief narrative that records feedback about the student's work and that teachers can share with the student, other teachers, or parents. A written description, like an oral description, conveys an impression of important aspects of the student's work. Written descriptions are also useful for program planning and program evaluation.

Before writing the narrative, the teacher should carefully review what the student has accomplished. The teacher then writes the description, noting areas of strength as well as problem areas. Such written description provides feedback to the student about the quality of the student's reading. Because it is recorded, the student can refer to it and can also share it with other teachers or family. The disadvantage of using written descriptions arises when parents have difficulty reading or do not have knowledge of written English.

## Checklists and Questionnaires

Checklists and questionnaires are convenient ways to provide information about a student's work. A checklist is a procedure that a teacher

**FIGURE 8.4**   *Checklist for Assessing Reading Attitudes, Interests, and Habits*

**My Beliefs about Reading**

| | | | |
|---|---|---|---|
| **1.** I like to read at school | most of the time | sometimes | never |
| **2.** I like to read | books | magazines | newspapers |
| **3.** I like to read the following types of stories | fiction<br>history/politics | biography/<br>autobiography<br>science fiction | science<br><br>adventure |
| **4.** I like to read at home | most of the time | sometimes | never |
| **5.** I talk with my friends about what I read | most of the time | sometimes | never |
| **6.** I think I am a good reader | most of the time | sometimes | never |
| **7.** Some books that I like are: | | | |

can complete quickly. Figure 8.4 is an example of a checklist for students that provides feedback to parents and teachers about students' reading habits and attitudes. Figure 8.5 is a checklist for gathering information about students' knowledge of books. Checklists are useful for screening, diagnosis, program planning, and program evaluation.

**FIGURE 8.5**   *Checklist for Assessing Knowledge of Books*

**Student's Name** _____   **Date** _____

**Teacher's Name** _____

**Directions: Show a book that is unfamiliar to the student. Ask the student to tell you about the book.**

| Concept | Demonstrates | Does Not Demonstrate | Observations |
|---|---|---|---|
| **1.** front | | | |
| **2.** back | | | |
| **3.** title | | | |
| **4.** author | | | |
| **5.** letters | | | |
| **6.** words | | | |
| **7.** pictures | | | |
| **8.** page numbers | | | |
| **9.** punctuation | | | |

Questionnaires provide an opportunity for teachers and students to collect information in more detail than checklists permit. Open-ended questionnaires allow respondents to express their attitudes, opinions, and knowledge in depth. Structured questionnaires ask only that the student fill in one or two words or circle a response.

## Interviews

There are special considerations when using interviews in reading assessment. Interviews are helpful when guiding discussions, encouraging students, and determining reading attitudes and habits. One basic approach is to interview students individually about their likes and dislikes. Asking questions such as "What do you like about reading?" "What are your interests?" or "What don't you like?" can be informative. Interviews are also useful for screening, diagnosis, program planning, and program evaluation. Figure 8.6 is an example of a parent interview that is gathering information about how parents view their child's development as a reader.

## Conferences

A conference is a conversation about the student's work that can include the student, educators, and parents. In a conference, participants share their views of the student's work with the goal of providing feedback and recommendations. Teacher-student conferences are helpful when assessing the student's reading ability. The discussion in a conference can be strictly verbal, or it can be audiotaped, videotaped, or summarized in written form. Conferences are useful for diagnosis, program planning, and program evaluation. Figure 8.7 on page 216 is an example of a progress report that a teacher can use as a guide when having a conference with a parent.

## Student Journals and Notebooks

Students can keep a notebook or journal that allows them to record their work as well as their attitudes and feelings about reading and what they have read. In a journal, students can indicate what they like and don't like about reading and list areas in which they have difficulty. A journal provides students the opportunity to reflect on their reading, to communicate about their learning, and to document their progress. Journals can be used for program planning and program evaluation. The following is a sample reading journal outline:

What I read today:

Two important ideas:

What I liked best about the passage or story:

What I didn't like about the passage or story:

What the author was telling us:

## Performance-Based Assessment

When measuring reading ability, performance-based assessment refers to the demonstration of reading and writing abilities, skills, and behavior. Performance-based assessment requires students to demonstrate that they can read a passage or story for a purpose, use one or more cognitive skills as they construct meaning from the text, and write about what they read, usually in response to a prompt or task (Farr and Tone, 1994). This assessment approach is useful in program planning and program evaluation. The following are examples of performance tasks teachers might ask students to undertake after reading a book or story:

- Write a poem.
- Draw pictures with captions.
- Build a model.
- Develop a story map.
- Write a review for the newspaper.
- Interview the author or a character in the story.

**FIGURE 8.6** *Parent Interview*

Name _____ Date _____

Child's Name _____ Grade _____

### PARENT INTERVIEW

1. How do you think your child is doing as a reader/writer? Why? (If a young child: What signs have you seen that your child is ready to learn to read/write?)
_____
_____
_____
_____

2. What would you like your child to do as a reader/writer that he or she isn't doing now?
_____
_____
_____

3. Do you ever notice your child reading/writing at home? Tell me about it.
_____
_____
_____
_____

4. What do you think your child's attitude is toward reading/writing? What do you think has helped to create this attitude?
_____
_____
_____
_____

5. What sorts of questions about your role in helping your child become a better reader/writer might you like to ask me?
_____
_____
_____
_____

6. Since I like to help the children read and write about things they are interested in, it helps me to know each individual child's interests. What kinds of things does your child like to do in his or her free time?
_____
_____
_____
_____

7. Is there anything about the child's medical history that might affect his or her reading/writing? Is there anything else that might affect his or her reading/writing?
_____
_____
_____
_____

8. Is there anything else that you think would be helpful for me to know in teaching your child?
_____
_____
_____
_____

*Source:* "Parent Interview" by Lynn K. Rhodes. Reprinted by permission from *Literary Assessment: A Handbook of Instruments*, edited by Lynn K. Rhodes, Portsmouth, NH: Heinemann, A division of Reed Elsevier Inc., 1993, pp. 152–153.

**FIGURE 8.7**  *Progress Report*

|  | 1st | 2nd | 3rd | 4th |
|---|---|---|---|---|
| **READING** |  |  |  |  |
| Level at which child is working |  |  |  |  |
| Phonics and word attack skills |  |  |  |  |
| Word recognition |  |  |  |  |
| Comprehension |  |  |  |  |
| Reference skills |  |  |  |  |
| Oral reading |  |  |  |  |
| Independent reading |  |  |  |  |
| Completes assignments |  |  |  |  |
| Demonstrates effort |  |  |  |  |
| **SPELLING** |  |  |  |  |
| Mastery of spelling words |  |  |  |  |
| Application of spelling skills in written work |  |  |  |  |
| Completes assignments |  |  |  |  |
| Demonstrates effort |  |  |  |  |
| **LANGUAGE** |  |  |  |  |
| Correctly uses language mechanics |  |  |  |  |
| (punctuation, capitalization, etc.) |  |  |  |  |
| Grammar (word usage/sentence structure) |  |  |  |  |
| Demonstrates creative written expression |  |  |  |  |
| Oral expression |  |  |  |  |
| Completes assignments |  |  |  |  |
| Demonstrates effort |  |  |  |  |
| **HANDWRITING** |  |  |  |  |
| Conforms to letter form, size, spacing, and slant |  |  |  |  |
| Writes legibly and neatly in daily work |  |  |  |  |
| Demonstrates effort |  |  |  |  |

*Source:* Reprinted by permission of Lynn K. Rhodes and Nancy L. Shanklin from *Windows into Literacy: Assessing Learners K–8*. Portsmouth NH: Heinemann, A division of Reed Elsevier, Inc., 1993, p. 385.

- Have a discussion with a peer, teacher, or other adult.
- Write a letter to the author.
- Write a letter to the editor of a newspaper or magazine.
- Write a report about a subject related to the story.
- Adapt a nonfiction article or book to fiction.
- Write lyrics to a song.
- Write a play.

## *Sharing Portfolios*

A portfolio is a deliberate collection of a student's work that demonstrates the student's efforts, progress, and achievement. When documenting and assessing reading ability, portfolios provide information about reading, skills, comprehension, attitudes toward reading, work habits, and written communication abilities. Portfolios in literacy assessment are useful for program planning and program evaluation. Chapter 7 provides a more extensive discussion of the applications of portfolios.

A portfolio is not just a folder of worksheets or of all the work that the student has completed. Selecting the pieces to include in the portfolio requires careful consideration. The following are suggestions for inclusion in student portfolios:

- writing samples collected over time
- photographs of student projects
- student logs
- projects that involve students in portraying characters or plot
- journals in which students record their thoughts about what they have read
- written dialogues between student and teacher
- audiotapes of students reading
- videotapes of students conferencing with each other
- teacher-developed tests

- anecdotal records
- student think-alouds

## *Exhibitions*

An exhibition is a display of a student's work that demonstrates knowledge, abilities, skills, and attitudes concerning one project or a unit of work. An exhibition offers an opportunity to summarize and to synthesize the student's accomplishments. In reading and writing assessment, exhibitions are valuable because students can realize that reading and writing involves integration, understanding, problem solving, and reasoning. This tool is useful for program planning and program evaluation. Examples of exhibitions in reading and writing include:

- storyboards
- series of letters to editors
- diary of one of the characters in the story
- reviews of related books
- dialogues among the characters
- maps depicting the travels of the characters

## *Self-Assessment*

Self-assessment provides students with an opportunity to analyze their own reading and writing. It is an occasion for students to reflect on their learning. Figure 8.8 is an example of a checklist that students use when assessing their own learning.

## *Peer Assessment*

Peer assessment allows students insight into reading and writing abilities of their peers. Students have an opportunity to reflect on the learning processes and strategies of others as well as on their own. Figure 8.9 is an example of a checklist that students use when conducting a peer assessment.

**FIGURE 8.8**  *Self-Assessment Checklist*

| Student's Name | | Date | | | |
|---|---|---|---|---|---|
| **After reading the story I:** | *1*<br>*Great!* | *2* | *3* | *4* | *5*<br>*Darn!* |
| 1. understand the assignment. | | | | | |
| 2. believe that I can restate the assignment. | | | | | |
| 3. feel that I can complete the assignment in a timely manner. | | | | | |
| 4. feel that I am a usually successful reader. | | | | | |

## Observing the Student within the Environment

In Chapter 6 you learned about the importance of considering the student within the physical, learning, and social environments. The interactions between the student and the environment are important assessment considerations.

### Physical Environment

The physical environment influences the student's reading performance. The tempera-ture, lighting, and seating arrangements of the spaces used for teaching and learning can affect how well the student performs. Figure 8.10 is a checklist that serves as an example study of the physical environment.

### Learning Environment

A comfortable learning environment facilitates the development of reading and writing abilities, positive attitudes, and habits. The curriculum, instructional methods, books, materials, and the assessment procedures are all areas of

| | 😦 | 😐 | 😊 |
|---|---|---|---|
| Student's Name _____  Date _____ | | | |
| Peer's Name _____ | | | |
| 1. My peer understood the story. | | | |
| 2. My peer understood the assignment. | | | |
| 3. My peer completed the assignment. | | | |
| 4. My peer conferenced with me. | | | |
| 5. My peer's work is neat. | | | |

**FIGURE 8.9**  *Peer Assessment Checklist*

**◀ POINT STREET SCHOOL ▶**
**Physical Environment ▶ Literacy**

Student's Name ___Chris___     Date __10/19__  Time __9:15__
Observer ___Mr. T.___     Location ___Classroom___

| Characteristic | Always | Sometimes | Never |
|---|---|---|---|
| **1. Seating**<br>Is the student seated properly? | X | | |
| ▶ Suggestions for improvement: | | | |
| **2. Lighting**<br>Is the lighting appropriate? | | X | |
| ▶ Suggestions for improvement: Due to Chris' vision problems, the lighting should be adjusted. The curtains should be adjusted so that the glare is eliminated. | | | |
| **3. Noise**<br>Is the noise level appropriate? | | X | |
| ▶ Suggestions for improvement: When group activities are underway, the noise level of the classroom tends to rise. Both teacher and students should monitor this. | | | |
| **4. Distractions**<br>Is the student distracted by activities in the room? | X | | |
| ▶ Suggestions for improvement: | | | |
| **5. Temperature**<br>Is the temperature of the room appropriate? | X | | |
| ▶ Suggestions for improvement: | | | |
| **6. General Atmosphere**<br>Does the student appear to be comfortable in the environment? | | X | |
| ▶ Suggestions for improvement: The physical layout of the room should be arranged so that Chris does not trip or bump into the tables. An emergency exit should be planned in case of fire. | | | |

**FIGURE 8.10**  *Observing the Physical Environment*

◀ **POINT STREET SCHOOL** ▶
Learning Environment ▶ Literacy

Student's Name ____Chris____                    Date __10/19__  Time __9:15__

Observer _____Mr. T._____                    Location ____Classroom____

| Characteristic | Always | Sometimes | Never |
|---|---|---|---|
| 1. **Materials** <br> Are a variety of reading materials available? | X | | |
| ▶ Suggestions for improvement: | | | |
| 2. **Curriculum** <br> Does the reading/writing curriculum reflect contemporary views of reading and writing? | X | | |
| ▶ Suggestions for improvement: | | | |
| 3. **Activities** <br> Is instruction oriented toward the use of various reading and writing materials? | X | | |
| ▶ Suggestions for improvement: | | | |
| 4. **Instructional Demands** <br> Are the instructional demands appropriate for the student? | | X | |
| ▶ Suggestions for improvement: Although Chris is severely myopic (nearsighted), he is capable of keeping up with his peers. Instructional demands should be appropriate in keeping with his abilities. | | | |
| 5. **Modifications** <br> Have modifications been made to instruction in order to accommodate the learning needs of the student? | | X | |
| ▶ Suggestions for improvement: Chris needs software which enlarges print on the computer screen. | | | |
| 6. **Assessment** <br> Are a variety of assessment tools used to provide feedback to the student? <br> Is information collected on the student's progress and performance? | X | | |

**FIGURE 8.11**    *Observing the Learning Environment*

| | | | |
|---|---|---|---|
| ▶ Suggestions for improvement: | | | |
| **7. Grouping**<br>If grouping is used, is it appropriate? | | X | |
| ▶ Suggestions for improvement: *Chris should be grouped with students who can actively engage Chris in group discussions in projects.* | | | |
| **8. Expectations**<br>Are teacher expectations appropriate? | | X | |
| ▶ Suggestions for improvement: *Teacher expectations should be high. Although it may take Chris longer to complete assignments, he is able to achieve at a high level.* | | | |
| **9. Student Involvement**<br>Is the student actively involved in reading and writing activities? | X | | |
| ▶ Suggestions for improvement: | | | |
| **10. Instruction**<br>Is instruction matched to the assessed needs of the student?<br>Are a variety of instructional methods used? | X | | |
| ▶ Suggestions for improvement: | | | |
| **11. Pace of Instruction**<br>Is the pace of instruction appropriate? | X | | |
| ▶ Suggestions for improvement: | | | |
| **12. Schedule**<br>Is the student's schedule appropriate? | | X | |
| ▶ Suggestions for improvement: *Chris needs a longer time than his peers to change classrooms.* | | | |
| **13. Transitions**<br>Are transitions made smoothly? | | X | |
| ▶ Suggestions for improvement: *Planning for transitions should occur. Chris needs extra time to take out and put away materials.* | | | |

**FIGURE 8.11** *Continued*

## ◀ POINT STREET SCHOOL ▶
### Social Environment ▶ Literacy

Student's Name ____Chris____        Date __10/19__  Time __9:15__

Observer ____Mr. T.____             Location ____Classroom____

| Characteristic | Always | Sometimes | Never |
|---|---|---|---|
| **1. Teacher-Student Interactions** <br> Are interactions warm and friendly? | X | | |
| ▶ Suggestions for improvement: | | | |
| **2. Disruptions** <br> Are disruptions kept to a minimum? | X | | |
| ▶ Suggestions for improvement: | | | |
| **3. Behavioral Interventions** <br> Are behavioral interventions effective and appropriate? | X | | |
| ▶ Suggestions for improvement: | | | |
| **4. Peer Interactions** <br> Are peer interactions appropriate? | | X | |
| ▶ Suggestions for improvement: Due to Chris' vision problems, he is reluctant to initiate peer interactions. A circle of friends should be convened. | | | |
| **5. General Atmosphere** <br> Does the student appear to be comfortable in the social environment? | | X | |
| ▶ Suggestions for improvement: Some students seem to be uncomfortable with Chris' disabilities. With Chris' permission, the special education teacher could be asked to explain Chris' disabilities to the students. Chris can also be asked to share his feelings with the students. | | | |

**FIGURE 8.12**   *Observing the Social Environment*

concern. Students will be willing to engage in reading and writing activities when: (1) the activities are challenging; (2) students realize that the assignments and the assessment activities are worth doing; (3) reading and writing assignments and assessment activities are accessible to a wide range of students; (4) teachers use a variety of instructional approaches, books, and materials; and (5) teachers use multiple assessment procedures. Figure 8.11 on pages 220 and 221 is a checklist that can help to determine the appropriateness of the learning environment.

### Social Environment

Relationships with students and teachers can affect performance in reading and writing. The social environment is important to the development of self-concept and self-esteem. These, in turn, contribute to positive attitudes toward literacy development. By observing the social environment, teachers can study the relationships students have with peers and adults. Figure 8.12 is a checklist designed to determine the appropriateness of the social environment.

## Preferred Practices

The assessment of literacy must reflect the integral link between reading and written language,

occur frequently, and produce results useful in planning instruction.

Evaluators should use individual standardized tests of reading cautiously. Many norm-referenced tests do not reflect contemporary views of reading and writing. Because reading and writing instruction varies considerably throughout the United States, it is important to carefully screen assessment instruments in order to select the instrument that best matches the curriculum.

Most standardized achievement tests show bias toward students from various cultural, linguistic, ethnic, and socioeconomic groups. Test construction may not reflect cultural patterns of teaching and learning. Low socioeconomic status limits access and participation in educational activities.

Teachers should utilize multiple approaches in the assessment of reading, including standardized tests, curriculum-based assessment, criterion-referenced assessment, and alternative forms of assessment. Teachers also need to conduct assessments routinely. The slogan for the assessment of literacy is "multiple, multiple, and frequent"—use multiple approaches, multiple instruments, and assess frequently!

## Extending Learning

1. Develop two assessment tasks that link instruction in reading directly to assessment of reading.
2. Develop a checklist or rating scale that assesses students' attitudes and habits in reading.
3. Examine a norm-referenced standardized reading test. Compare the development of this test with the contemporary views of reading assessment discussed in this chapter.

4. Develop an interview guide for use with parents to assess students' reading attitudes and habits at home.
5. Identify three assessment approaches the chapter discusses. Compare the purposes, advantages, and disadvantages of each approach.

# *References*

Anastasi, A. (1988). *Psychological testing*. New York: Macmillan.

Brigance, A. H. (1981). *BRIGANCE® inventory of essential skills*. No. Billerica, MA: Curriculum Associates.

Brigance, A. H. (1999). *BRIGANCE® comprehensive inventory of basic skills–revised*. No. Billerica, MA: Curriculum Associates.

Brigance, A. H. (1984). *BRIGANCE® assessment of basic skills–Spanish edition*. No. Billerica, MA: Curriculum Associates.

Brigance, A. H. (1991). *BRIGANCE® inventory of early development–revised*. No. Billerica, MA: Curriculum Associates.

Brown, J. I., V. V. Fishco, and G. S. Hanna (2000). *Nelson-Denny reading test*. Itasca, IL: Riverside.

Brown, V. L., D. D. Hammill, and J. L. Wiederholt (1995). *Test of reading comprehension–3*. Austin, TX: PRO-ED.

Farr, R., and B. Tone (1994). *Portfolio and performance assessment*. Fort Worth, TX: Harcourt Brace College .

Goodman, K. (1984). Unity in reading. In *Becoming readers in a complex society: The 83rd yearbook of the national society of the study of education, part I*, eds. A. Purves and O. Niles, 79–114. Chicago, IL: University of Chicago Press.

Goodman, K. (1989). Roots of the whole-language movement. *Elementary School Journal* 90: 207–222.

Harcourt Brace Educational Measurement (1995). *Stanford diagnostic reading test 4*. 4th ed. San Antonio, TX: Harcourt Brace Educational Assessment.

Idol, L., A. Nevin, and P. Paolucci-Whitcomb (1996). *Models of curriculum-based assessment*. Austin, TX: PRO-ED.

Kaufman, A. S., and N. L. Kaufman (1983). *Kaufman assessment battery for children*. Circle Pines, MN: American Guidance Service.

Kaufman, A. S., and N. L. Kaufman (1998). *Kaufman test of educational achievement/Normative update (K-TEA/NU)*. Circle Pines, MN: American Guidance Service.

Langer, J. A., J. R. Campbell, S. B. Neumann, I. V. S. Mullis, H. R. Persky, and P. L. Donahue (1995). *Reading assessment redesigned*. Washington, DC: U.S. Department of Education.

MacGinitie, W. H., and R. K. MacGinitie (1989). *Gates-MacGinitie reading tests*. Itasca, IL: Riverside.

Markwardt Jr., F. C. (1998). *Peabody individual achievement test–revised/Normative update*. Circle Pines, MN: American Guidance Service.

Marston, D. (1989). A curriculum-based measurement approach to assessing academic performance: What it is and why do it. In *Curriculum-based measurement*, ed. M. R. Shinn, 18–78. New York: The Guilford Press.

Newcomer, P. L. (1990). *Diagnostic achievement battery*. 2d ed. Austin, TX: PRO-ED.

Newcomer, P. (1999). *Standardized reading inventory–2*. Austin, TX: PRO-ED.

Newcomer, P. L., and B. R. Bryant (1993). *Diagnostic achievement test for adolescents*. 2d. ed. Austin, TX: PRO-ED.

The Psychological Corporation (2001). *Wechsler individual achievement test,® second edition (WIAT®–II)*. San Antonio, TX: The Psychological Corporation.

Reid, D. K., W. P. Hresko, and D. D. Hammill (2001). *Test of early reading ability*. 3d ed. Austin, TX: PRO-ED.

Rhodes, L. K., and N. Shanklin (1993). *Windows into literacy: Assessing learners K–8*. Portsmouth, NH: Heinemann.

Rosenblatt, L. (1995). *The reader, the text, the poem*. Carbondale, IL: Southern Illinois University Press.

Slosson, R. L. (1990). *Slosson oral reading test*. East Aurora, NY: Slosson Educational Publications.

Smith, F. (1988). *Understanding reading*. 4th ed. New York: Holt, Rinehart & Winston.

Sonnenschein, J. L. (1983). *Basic achievement individual skills screener*. San Antonio, TX: Harcourt Brace Educational Measurement.

Stahl, S. A., and M. R. Kuhn (1995). Does whole language or instruction matched to learning styles help children learn to read? *School Psychology Review* 24: 393–404.

Torgeson, J. K., and B. R. Byrant (1994). *Test of phonological awareness*. Austin, TX: PRO-ED.

Wiederholt, L., and B. Bryant (2001). *Gray oral reading test–4*. Austin, Tex.: PRO-ED.

Wilkinson, G. (1994). *Wide range achievement test–3*. Wilmington, DE: Jastak Associates.

Woodcock, R. (1998). *Woodcock reading mastery tests–revised/normative update*. Circle Pines, MN: American Guidance Service.

Woodcock, R. W., K. S. McGrew, and N. Mather (2001). *Woodcock-Johnson psychoeducational battery–III*. Itasca, IL: Riverside.

# 9

# *Written Language*

## Overview

Contemporary instructional practices stress the integral link between reading and writing for both instruction and assessment. In the previous chapter we discussed approaches to the assessment of literacy, emphasizing the assessment of reading. This chapter continues this discussion and highlights the assessment of written language.

## Chapter Objectives

After completing this chapter you should be able to:

- Understand contemporary views of written language instruction.

- Explain the integral link between reading instruction, written language instruction, and assessment.

225

- Describe approaches to written language assessment, including norm-referenced standardized tests, writing samples, journals, notebooks, essays, homework, discussions, group work, interviews, alternative assessment, performance testing, self-assessment, and peer assessment.
- Describe how physical, learning, and social environments influence written language performance.

## What Shapes Our Views

Contemporary views of the assessing written language have as their basis the essential link between reading and written language. Teachers apply theories of the development of written language in various ways in the teaching and learning process. Some teachers emphasize the link between the development of reading and writing and view the development of written language as a process. Other teachers emphasize the development of specific skills, such as correct spelling, punctuation, capitalization, and grammar. Some teachers use a combination of these approaches. Depending on their background and orientation, teachers may use one or more of the assessment approaches in Table 9.1.

Assessing written language usually means making a direct connection between reading and writing and following these principles:

**1.** *Assess reading and writing in various contexts.* Reading and writing varies with the

**TABLE 9.1**    *Instructional Approaches in the Development of Written Language*

| Instructor Variables | Direct Instruction | Explicit Instruction | Cognitive Approach | Whole Language |
|---|---|---|---|---|
| Orientation to reading and writing | Emphasis is on the teaching of subskills (e.g., punctuation, capitalization, grammar, spelling etc.) | Skills are explicitly taught | Meaning is constructed from the text | Immersion in a print environment; close link between reading and writing activities |
| Instruction | Directed by teacher | Directed by teacher | Teacher and student collaborate | Student, with teacher guidance |
| Instructional materials | Workbooks, worksheets, spelling lists | Worksheets, literature-based program | Literature-based program, small discussion groups, writing projects | Literature-based program, integrated writing, individual and small discussion groups |

Adapted from Stahl, S. A., and M. R. Kuhn (1995). Does Whole Language or Instruction Matched to Learning Styles Help Children Learn to Read? *School Psychology Review* 24: 393–404.

context. Contexts relate to the types of reading materials, the purpose of the writing, and strategies students use. An understanding of students' reading and writing abilities must consider the contexts in which reading and writing occur.

**2.** *Assess the literacy environment, instruction, and students.* Reading and writing assessment must consider environments in which reading and writing occurs, types of instruction, and student factors.

**3.** *Assess processes and products of writing.* The assessment of writing processes as well as the products can provide a comprehensive understanding of students' abilities.

**4.** *Analyze error patterns.* Understanding the patterns of errors in writing improves student performance.

**5.** *Include the assessment of background knowledge.* Experience, prior learning, and background knowledge influence reading and writing performance.

**6.** *Consider developmental patterns in reading and writing.* Knowledge of typical developmental patterns in reading and writing contributes to our understanding of reading and writing abilities.

**7.** *Use sound principles of assessment.* Employ sound principles or standards when assessing students. These standards apply to reliability, validity, observation, and scoring, discussed in previous chapters.

**8.** *Use triangulation.* Triangulation signifies that conclusions about student performance are the result of multiple (here, at least three) sources of information. In turn, teachers should corroborate information about students by using several sources of data. Teachers must proceed with considerable caution when drawing conclusions about students and using only one source of information.

**9.** *Include students, parents, teachers, and other school personnel in the assessment process.* The involvement of students, parents, and other educators in the assessment process ensures the inclusion of multiple perspectives.

**10.** *Assessment activities should be ongoing.* Assessment activities can inform instruction best when they occur frequently and routinely.

**11.** *Record, analyze, and use assessment information.* Assessment information is useful only when it is in use. Record assessment data frequently, analyze it, and use it on a routine basis to guide instruction. Linking instruction with assessment means that:

- Assessments include a variety of observations that consider the complexity of the processes involved in reading, writing, and language.
- Assessment tasks are age-appropriate.
- Assessment tools are unbiased.
- Assessment of reading, writing, and language must incorporate a variety of approaches.
- Assessment approaches should consider the purposes of each assessment tool and the settings in which the assessment is conducted.
- Assessment should reflect classroom instruction. (Rhodes and Shanklin, 1993)

## Assessment Questions, Purposes, and Approaches

The assessment of written language abilities and skills requires a variety of approaches in order to reflect an understanding of students' abilities, developmental levels, maturity, gender, and ethnic and racial background. Assessment techniques must include standardized testing as well as a variety of other approaches. Table 9.2 describes some of the questions, purposes, and approaches that are part of written language assessment.

## Standardized Tests of Written Language

Standardized norm-referenced tests of written language can be useful in identifying students

**TABLE 9.2** *Assessment Questions, Purposes, and Approaches*

| Assessment Questions | Steps and Purposes | Approaches |
|---|---|---|
| | **Screening** | |
| Is there a possibility of a disability in written language? | To determine whether students may have a disability in writing and should be referred for further assessment | Norm-referenced instruments<br>Curriculum-based assessments<br>Criterion-referenced assessments<br>Observations<br>Checklists |
| | **Eligibility** | |
| Does the student have a disability?<br>What disability does the student have?<br>Does the student meet the criteria for services?<br>What are the strengths and weaknesses?<br>Why is the student having difficulty writing? | To determine if there is a disability<br>To compare the student's performance in writing with the performance of the peer group<br>To determine specific strengths and weaknesses in writing<br>To understand why the student is having difficulty | Norm-referenced instruments<br>Curriculum-based assessments<br>Criterion-referenced assessments<br>Observations<br>Probes<br>Error analysis<br>Interviews<br>Checklists<br>Student, parent, and/or teacher conferences<br>Performance assessments |
| *Connecting Instruction with Assessment* | | |
| | **Program Planning** | |
| What does the student not understand about writing?<br>Where should instruction in writing begin? | To understand what the student knows and does not know<br>To plan the student's program<br>To determine instructional approaches | Norm-referenced instruments<br>Curriculum-based assessments<br>Criterion-referenced assessments<br>Observations<br>Probes<br>Error analysis<br>Interviews<br>Checklists<br>Student, parent, and/or teacher conferences<br>Performance assessments |

with writing difficulties, pinpointing strengths and weaknesses, and evaluating programs.

## Content Validity

Content validity is a primary concern of any achievement test, including tests of written language. This type of validity measure relates the extent to which the test items reflect the instructional objectives of a test. An estimate of the content validity of a test results from thoroughly and systematically examining the test items to determine the extent to which they reflect the intended instructional objectives and content.

**TABLE 9.2**    *Continued*

| Assessment Questions | Steps and Purposes | Approaches |
|---|---|---|
| Once instruction begins, is the student making progress in written language? Should writing instruction be modified? | **Program Monitoring** To understand the strategies and concepts the student uses To monitor the student's program | Curriculum-based assessments Criterion-referenced assessments Observations Probes Error analysis Interviews Checklists Student, parent, and/or teacher conferences Portfolios Exhibitions Journals Written descriptions Oral descriptions |
| Has the student met the goals of the IEP in written language? Has the instructional program been successful for the student? Has the student made progress? Has the instructional program achieved its goals? | **Program Evaluation** To determine whether the IEP goals have been met To determine whether the goals of the program have been met To evaluate program effectiveness | Curriculum-based assessments Criterion-referenced assessments Observations Probes Error analysis Interviews Checklists Student, parent, and/or teacher conferences Portfolios Exhibitions Journals Written descriptions Oral descriptions Surveys |

While the test developer must describe the process that established the content validity of a test, the test examiner must make an independent determination. This is especially important when deciding on the content validity of written language tests. The test examiner has to compare the test objectives, format, number of responses or prompts, and types of responses or prompts with the taught curriculum.

## Scoring

Scoring tests of written language can be problematic for the test examiner. Students vary in

*A teacher and student work on a writing assignment together.*

their writing abilities and many test manuals contain general directions, which are sometimes ambiguous, for scoring writing samples. Because the test examiners must use judgment in scoring, there may be variations and inconsistencies between test scores.

There are a number of standardized tests of written language. Table 9.3 lists tests of written language and tests that have subtests in the areas of handwriting, spelling, mechanics, grammar, or written language. This section describes some of the commonly used individual, standardized tests of written language. All of these tests use standardized procedures for norm-referencing, administering, and scoring. The tests yield a variety of scores, including standard scores, percentiles, age equivalents, grade equivalents, and normal curve equivalents.

## Oral and Written Language Scales

The *Oral and Written Language Scales (OWLS)* (Carrow-Woolfolk, 1996) is an individualized test of oral and written language. The *OWLS* has three scales: Listening Comprehension, Oral Expression, and Written Expression. The description of the *OWLS* in this chapter will focus on the Written Expression Scale. The Listening Comprehension and Oral Expression scales are described in Chapter 10. The Written Expression Scale is for individuals ages 5 years through 21 years. The Written Expression Scale consists of four overlapping sets of items in the following areas:

*Use of conventions:* Measures skills including letter formation, correct spelling, punctuation, capitalization, and conventions.

*Use of linguistic forms:* Measures abilities, including the use of language forms such as modifiers, verb forms, and complex sentences.

*Content:* Measures the ability to communicate subject matter in a meaningful way.

***Administration.*** The *OWLS* can be administered individually or to a small group.

**TABLE 9.3** *Instruments That Contain Subtests of Spelling and Written Language*

| Name | Ages/Grades | Group/Individual | Areas |
|---|---|---|---|
| *Basic Achievement Skills Individual Screener (BASIS)* (Sonnenschein, 1983) | Grades 1 through 12 and post–high school | Individual | Spelling<br>Written language |
| *BRIGANCE® Inventory of Essential Skills* (Brigance, 1981) | Grade 6 through adulthood | Individual | Spelling<br>Handwriting<br>Mechanics |
| *BRIGANCE® Comprehensive Inventory of Basic Skills–Revised* (Brigance, 1999) | Grades 1 through 6 | Individual | Spelling<br>Handwriting<br>Mechanics |
| *BRIGANCE® Assessment of Basic Skills–Spanish Edition* (Brigance, 1984) | Grades K through 8 | Individual | Handwriting |
| *Diagnostic Achievement Battery–2 (DAB–2)* (Newcomer, 1990) | Ages 6 years through 14 years | Individual | Spelling<br>Grammar<br>Mechanics<br>Written language |
| *Diagnostic Achievement Test for Adolescents–2 (DATA–2)* (Newcomer and Bryant, 1993) | Grades 7 through 12 | Individual | Spelling<br>Grammar<br>Written language |
| *Kaufman Test of Educational Achievement/Normative Update (K–TEA/NU)* (Kaufman and Kaufman, 1998) | Grades 1 through 12; ages 6 years to 18 years, 11 months | Individual | Spelling |
| *Oral and Written Language Scales/OWLS* (Carrow-Woolfolk, 1996) | Ages 5 years through 21 years | Individual or small group | Use of conventions<br>Use of linguistic forms<br>Content |
| *Peabody Individual Achievement Test–Revised/Normative Update (PIAT–R/NU)* (Markwardt, 1998) | Grades K through 12; ages 5 years to 18 years, 11 months | Individual | Spelling<br>Written language |
| *Test of Adolescent and Adult Language–3 (TOAL–3)* (Hammill, Brown, Larsen, and Wiederholt, 1994) | Ages 12 years through 24 years, 11 months | Individual or group | Grammar<br>Written language |
| *Test of Early Written Language–2 (TEWL–2)* (Hresko, Herron, and Peak, 1996) | Ages 3 years through 10 years, 11 months | Individual | Spelling<br>Mechanics<br>Written language |
| *Test of Written Expression (TOWE)* (McGhee, Bryant, Larsen, and Rivera, 1995) | Ages 6 years, 6 months through 14 years, 11 months | Individual or group | Spelling<br>Mechanics<br>Grammar<br>Written language |

*(continued)*

**TABLE 9.3**    *Continued*

| Name | Ages/Grades | Group/Individual | Areas |
|------|-------------|------------------|-------|
| *Test of Written Language–3 (TOWL–3)* (Hammill and Larsen, 1996) | Ages 7 years, 6 months through 17 years, 11 months | Individual or group | Spelling<br>Mechanics<br>Grammar<br>Written language |
| *Test of Written Spelling–4 (TWS–4)* (Larsen, Hammill, and Moats, 1999) | Grades 1 through 12 | Individual or group | Spelling |
| *Wide Range Achievement Test–3 (WRAT–3)* (Wilkinson, 1993) | Ages 5 years through 75 years | Individual | Spelling |
| *Wechsler Individual Achievement Test–II (WIAT–II)* (The Psychological Corporation, 2001) | Ages 5 years to 19 years, 11 months | Individual | Spelling<br>Written language |
| *Woodcock-Johnson Psychoeducational Battery–III (WJ–III)* (Woodcock, McGrew, and Mather, 2001) | Ages 2 years through adulthood; grades K through 12 | Individual | Spelling<br>Mechanics<br>Written language |

**Scoring.** Depending on the item, the examiner follows from 1 to 11 scoring rules. Raw scores convert to standard scores, percentiles, normal curve equivalents, stanines, and age and grade equivalents.

**Standardization.** Standardization of the *OWLS* occurred between April 1992 and August 1993. Test developers drew the standardization sample of 1,985 individuals, who represented groups by age, gender, race, ethnic group, geographic region, and economic status, based on the mother's level of education, from the 1991 U.S. Census data from the 1991 *Current Population Survey* and co-normed the three scales of the *OWLS*.

**Reliability.** The test presents reliability information for split-half reliability, test-retest reliability, and interrater reliability. For the Written Expression Scale the coefficients range from .77 (ages 19 years through 21 years) to .89 (age 6 years). For test-retest reliability the coefficient for ages 8 years through 10 years, 11 months was .88; for ages 16 years through 18 years, 11 months, the coefficient was .87. Interrater reliability ranged from .91 (ages 12 years through 14 years) to .98 (ages 5 years through 7 years).

**Validity.** Adequate evidence of content, criterion-related, and construct validity is available. The *OWLS* was administered concurrently with the *Kaufman Test of Educational Achievement, Comprehensive Form, Peabody Individual Achievement Test–Revised, Woodcock Reading Mastery Test–Revised, Peabody Picture Vocabulary Test–Revised, Clinical Evaluation of Language Fundamentals–Revised, Wechsler Intelligence Scale for Children–III,* and *Kaufman Brief Intelligence Test.*

Students who were identified as language impaired, mentally disabled, learning disabled, hearing impaired, or as receiving Chapter One assistance in reading participated in small studies. Students from these studies were not in the standardization sample. The results of these studies are inconclusive because each group participated in only one study and because the samples were so small.

**BOX 9.1**    *Oral and Written Language Scales (OWLS), Written Expression Scale*

*Publication Date:* 1996

*Purposes:* Measures use of conventions, use of linguistic forms, and the ability to communicate subject matter in a meaningful way.

*Age/Grade Levels:* 5 through 21.

*Time to Administer:* Approximately 30 to 45 minutes.

*Technical Adequacy:* The standardization sample is appropriate. Reliability and validity are adequate.

*Suggested Use:* The test is based on contemporary views of written language and is effective for assessing overall ability to use written language and areas of strength and weakness.

**Summary.** The *Oral and Written Language Scales* is an individualized test of oral and written language. The test is based on contemporary views of written language. Reliability and validity are adequate. Box 9.1 describes the test's parameters.

## Test of Early Written Language–2

The *Test of Early Written Language–2 (TEWL–2)* (Hresko, Herron, and Peak, 1996) is a revision of the first edition. Designed for use with students ages 4 years through 10 years, 11 months, the *TEWL–2* is a downward extension of the *Test of Written Language (TOWL–3)*, which we describe below. The *TEWL–2* contains two subtests:

*Basic Writing.* This subtest contains 57 items and assesses spelling, capitalization, punctuation, sentence construction, and metacognitive knowledge.

*Contextual Writing.* This subtest contains 14 items and assesses the student's ability to write a story when presented with a picture prompt.

## Test of Written Expression

The *Test of Written Expression (TOWE)* (McGhee, Bryant, Larsen, and Rivera, 1995) is intended for students ages 6 years, 6 months through 14 years, 11 months. This test can be administered to individuals or groups. The *TOWE* assesses written language skills, such as ideation, grammar, vocabulary, capitalization, punctuation, spelling, and general ability to produce written language.

## Test of Written Language–3

The *Test of Written Language–3 (TOWL–3)* (Hammill and Larsen, 1996) is the third edition of this test. The *TOWL–3* is intended for use with students ages 7 years, 6 months through 17 years, 11 months. It contains eight subtests organized into two formats: spontaneous and contrived. The spontaneous format assesses students' written essays, and the contrived format directly assesses specific skills associated with writing.

| Subtest | Abilities/Skills Assessed |
|---|---|
| *Spontaneous Format* | |
| Contextual Conventions | Capitalization, punctuation, spelling |
| Contextual Language | Vocabulary, syntax, grammar |
| Story Construction | Plot, character development, general composition |
| *Contrived Format* | |
| Vocabulary | Word usage |
| Spelling | Correct spelling |
| Style | Capitalization, punctuation |
| Logical Sentences | Rewriting of sentence so that they make sense |
| Sentence Combining | Rewrite one sentence from two sentences |

***Administration.*** The *TOWL–3* is individually administered. However, it can be administered to small groups of students.

***Scoring.*** Raw scores convert to percentiles and standard scores.

***Standardization.*** The *TOWL–3* is the third edition of the *TOWL*, originally published in 1978. It was revised in 1988. This renormed third edition, published in 1994, reports information about the age, geographic region, gender, residence, race, ethnicity, income of parents, education of parents, and disabilities factors that the standardization sample represents.

***Reliability.*** The test reports test-retest and internal consistency reliability coefficients. The reliabilty for the *TOWL–3* is adequate.

***Validity.*** The test reports content, criterion-related, and construct validity. Teachers should examine the test items to determine the extent to which the *TOWL–3* matches writing in the taught curriculum.

---

**BOX 9.2**     *Test of Written*
             *Language–3 (TOWL–3)*

---

*Publication Date:* 1996

*Purposes:* Assesses writing conventions, grammar, syntax, vocabulary, spelling, sentence construction, and story construction.

*Age/Grade Levels:* Ages 7 years, 6 months through 17 years, 11 months.

*Time to Administer:* 1.5 hours.

*Technical Adequacy:* The standardization sample is adequate. Reliability is good; requires further evidence of validity.

*Suggested Use:* Provides evidence of strengths and weaknesses in written language, spelling, and vocabulary. Examiners should evaluate the test items to determine the extent to which they reflect writing as it has been taught to the student.

---

***Summary.*** The *Test of Written Language–3* is a third-edition norm-referenced test of skills and abilities associated with written language and the writing process. Evidence of reliabilty and validity is adequate. However, the teacher should examine the test items in order to determine congruence with the school curriculum. Box 9.2 describes the test's parameters.

## Test of Written Spelling–4

The *Test of Written Spelling–4 (TWS–4)* (Larson, Hammill, and Moats, 1999) is the fourth edition of this test and is for use with students in grades 1 through 12. The *TWS–4* assesses predictable words (words with spellings that are predictable using letter-sound patterns) and unpredictable words (words with spellings that are unpredictable, or are "word demons"). In administering the test, examiner says a word, says a sentence that contains the word, and says the word again. The student writes the word only; words are not written in sentences.

## *Concerns about Standardized Tests of Written Language*

The International Reading Association directly addressed concerns about the use of standardized reading tests in 1991. Most experts in literacy believe that standardarized, norm-referenced tests of writing have a number of shortcomings.

| Norm-referenced Tests of Written Language | Theories of Written Contemporary Language Assessment |
| --- | --- |
| Assess writing abilities separately from reading abilities | Link the assessment of writing with the assessment of reading |
| Fail to tap background knowledge | Encourage the writer to use background knowledge while writing |

| Norm-referenced Tests of Written Language | Theories of Written Contemporary Language Assessment |
|---|---|
| Emphasize skills (spelling, punctuation, capitalization, grammar, etc.) | Assess a variety of writing processes |
| May show bias in the questions | Demonstrate equitable assessment strategies |
| Present multiple-choice questions | Present open-ended questions |
| Do not assess writing attitudes and habits | Assess writing attitudes and habits |
| Show few or no direct links to instruction | Link assessment tools directly to instruction |

## Connecting Assessment with Instruction

It is a fundamental principle that assessment of written language abilities and skills must form a direct link to reading instruction. Linking instruction to assessment in reading and written language means that:

• Assessment occurs as a normal part of the student's work. Assessment activities should emerge from the teaching and learning situation. Examples of this type of assessment include the use of journals, notebooks, essays, oral reports, homework, classroom discussions, group work, and interviews. These assessment activities can occur individually or in small groups and can take place during one session or over multiple sessions.

• The conditions for assessment are similar to the conditions for doing meaningful tasks. Students should have sufficient time, have access to peers, be able to use appropriate literacy materials, and have the chance to revise their work.

• Assessment tasks are meaningful and multidimensional. They should provide students with the opportunity to demonstrate a variety of writing abilities and skills.

• Feedback to students is specific, meaningful, prompt, and informs the students' work.

• Students participate in the assessment process. They help to generate and apply standards or rubrics. Self-assessment and peer assessment are part of the assessment process.

Ways in which the teacher can gather information and provide feedback to parents and students include:

• curriculum-based measurement
• criterion-referenced assessment
• probes
• error analysis
• oral descriptions
• written descriptions
• checklists and questionnaires
• interviews
• conferences
• student work samples and products
• student journals and notebooks
• performance-based assessment
• portfolios
• exhibitions
• self-assessment
• peer assessment

## Curriculum-Based Measurement

Chapter 6 introduced curriculum-based measurement (CBM). To construct a CBM in writing, the teacher selects a brief story starter or topic sentence and asks the student to write it out in three minutes. When the student finishes writing, the teacher has four choices for scoring: (1) count the number of words written correctly; (2) count the number of words spelled correctly; (3) count the number of letters written correctly; or (4) count the number of correct word sequences. Word sequences are two words together that are both correctly spelled and grammatically correct. The teacher and the student can then use a graph to plot the results. By repeating this process many times, the teacher can document the progress that the student makes.

## Criterion-Referenced Assessment

Teachers can create criterion-referenced tests in written language. Such teacher-developed criterion-referenced tests are useful for screening, determining eligibility, diagnosis of strengths and needs, program planning, progress monitoring, and program evaluation. For example, a teacher can enumerate spelling words that the student must spell correctly, can identify punctuation that the student must use accurately, or can list words that require correct capitalization in order to develop a criterion-referenced test.

**BRIGANCE® Inventories.** The *BRIGANCE® Inventories* are criterion-referenced tests that contain subtests in written language. The inventories are similar in purpose, scoring, administration, and interpretation. Chapter 6 describes the tests in detail, but Table 9.3 summarizes those sections of the *BRIGANCE®* inventories that assess aspects of written language.

## Probes

A probe is a diagnostic technique that can be especially useful in diagnosing student problems and in planning instruction in written language. For example, suppose a teacher wants to determine whether a student has considered feedback from peers when revising a writing sample. The teacher can review the student's written draft, inquire about the use of peer feedback, and assist the student in incorporating peer feedback into a revision of the draft.

## Error Analysis

The purposes of error analysis are to: (1) identify the patterns of errors or mistakes that students make in their work; (2) understand why students make the errors; and (3) provide instruction so as to correct the errors. A systematic approach to error analysis helps both the student and the teacher identify errors and correct them.

**FIGURE 9.1**  *Toni's Editing Checklist*

**Checking and Correcting Work**

| Editing | Checked | | Corrected | |
|---|---|---|---|---|
| | yes | no | yes | no |
| 1. Grammar | | | | |
| 2. Periods | | | | |
| 3. Question marks | | | | |
| 4. Exclamation points | | | | |
| 5. Quotation marks | | | | |
| 6. Paragraphing | | | | |
| 7. Spelling | | | | |

A checklist, developed by the teacher, the student, or through collaboration, can be helpful in identifying errors. Figure 9.1 is an example of a checklist that Toni, a sixth grader, developed with her teacher to help Toni with editing.

**Spelling.**  Error analysis is important in the development of spelling. Spelling evaluation should be a part of the process of developing written language rather than a finished product. Teachers should consider four principles in evaluating spelling (Wilde, 1989a):

1. Evaluate spelling on the basis of natural writing rather than by tests of words in isolation.
2. Evaluate spelling analytically rather than as correct or incorrect.
3. Analyze spelling by discovering the strategies the student used in the context of writing.
4. As a matter of good professional practice in this area, learn about language development and about language disabilities and how they can affect the development of written language.

Questions to ask about a student's spelling include:

1. Is the word spelled as it sounds?
2. Is the spelling unusual?
3. Is the word a sight word?
4. Is the word a real word?
5. Is the word a "placeholder"?
6. Is a homophone used?
7. What strategies does a student use when the spelling is unknown?
   a. writes down what it sounds like
   b. writes down what student thinks the word looks like
   c. looks around the classroom to find the word
   d. thinks about parts of the word
   e. uses spelling rules
   f. uses a dictionary or spell checker
   g. asks someone for the correct spelling
   h. uses a personal spelling list (Rhodes and Shanklin, 1993; Wilde, 1989a; Wilde, 1989b)

### Oral Descriptions

Verbal descriptions of a student's work provide immediate feedback to the student by a teacher or peer. Oral descriptions are quick, efficient, and direct, and they integrate easily into instruction. However, they should not be off-the-cuff expressions, but rather as well thought out as written descriptions. Oral descriptions are useful for program planning and program evaluation. An example of providing oral feedback to a student who has just completed writing a first draft is, "You did a nice job getting your ideas down. While developing your ideas you consulted several sources and asked a peer for help with spelling."

Notwithstanding, oral descriptions do have several drawbacks. They can be subjective, and there is no permanent record. In addition, specific disabilities may limit the ability of the student to understand, remember, or reply to them.

### Written Descriptions

A written description is a brief narrative that records feedback about the student's work and that the student, other teachers, or parents can review. A written description, like an oral description, conveys an impression of important aspects of the student's work. Written descriptions are effective for program planning and program evaluation.

Before writing the narrative, the teacher carefully reviews what the student has accomplished. The teacher should write the description noting areas of strength as well as problem areas. A written description provides feedback to the student about the quality of the student's writing, and because it provides a record, the student can refer to it and share it with the student's family.

Two potential problems of written descriptions are that parents who have difficulty reading or who do not have knowledge of written English are at a disadvantage.

### Checklists and Questionnaires

Checklists and questionnaires are convenient ways to provide feedback about a student's work. A checklist is fast and easy to complete.

Questionnaires enable teachers and students to collect information in more detail than checklists. Questionnaires can be open-ended, allowing respondents to express their attitudes, opinions, and knowledge in depth, or they can be structured so that the student just needs to fill in one or two words or to circle a response. Figure 9.2 is an example of an open-ended questionnaire.

### Interviews

In Chapter 5 we discussed the topic of conducting interviews. There are special considerations when using this technique in the assessment of written language. Interviews are useful in developing ideas for writing, encouraging students, learning more about a student's written piece, and determining writing attitudes and habits. Asking questions such as the following can be informative: "What do you like about writing?" "Describe the process you use in developing a new piece of writing." "What are your interests?" "What don't you like?" Interviews are

---

**FIGURE 9.2**  *Open-Ended Writing Questionnaire*

**What Kind of Writer I Am**

---

1. Things I like to write at home (examples: notes, letters, poems, stories, etc.)
2. What other people think of my writing:
3. What I think of myself as a writer:
4. Things I like to write at school:
5. What I like about my writing:
6. What I don't like about my writing:

---

helpful for screening, diagnosis, program planning, and program evaluation.

## Conferences

A conference is a conversation about the student's work that can include the student, educators, and/or parents. In a conference participants share their views of the student's work with the goal of offering feedback and recommendations. Teacher-student conferences can be helpful when assessing the student's written language. The discussion can be strictly verbal or it can be audiotaped, videotaped, or summarized in written form. Conferences are useful for diagnosis, program planning, and program evaluation.

## Student Work Samples and Products

Examining students' written work provides an opportunity to identify the skills, abilities, and processes that the student uses while developing the written piece. The writing process breaks down into overlapping steps (Rhodes and Shanklin, 1993):

**1.** *Writing authentic work.* Students should have opportunities to engage in authentic writing. This means that when students write in school they must write for the same reasons they write outside of school. Students need to

have control over their writing. They should have the necessary materials available, know how to use them, know the purposes for writing, and know how much time is available to them.

**2.** *Rehearsing writing.* Rehearsing means that students know what to expect and are able to choose the type of writing that is appropriate for the purpose. Rehearsing can involve drawing pictures, developing semantic webs, taking notes, and brainstorming.

**3.** *Developing the first draft.* Writing the first draft entails fluency, spelling, and rereading. Fluency is being able to put ideas into writing and having the thoughts flow. Spelling is a consideration in this step as well, because like writing, spelling is a process. Reading and rereading the draft are important because this allows the student to identify and correct errors and to elaborate ideas.

**4.** *Conferencing with peers and/or teachers.* Feedback from peers or teachers can yield important suggestions and ideas as the student develops the written piece.

**5.** *Revising the written piece.* Revising a piece of writing gives the student an opportunity to reflect on his or her own reading of it and on the feedback from peers and teachers. The student can choose to elaborate, clarify, take away information, make corrections, and change the sentence or paragraph structure.

**6.** *Editing.* Editing allows the student to make surface corrections to the written piece. This means making the piece conform to writing conventions and it also involves organization and ideas (Rhodes and Shanklin, 1993).

**7.** *Producing and sharing the finished piece.* The final piece can take various forms, depending on the purpose for writing. For example, the written piece may be a newspaper article, review of a story, poem, play, story, or report. Figure 9.3 is a checklist for use when assessing writing samples to provide feedback to students.

## Student Journals and Notebooks

Keeping a notebook or journal allows students to record their work as well as their attitudes and feelings about reading and writing. A journal can contain sample pieces the student has written as well as spontaneous types of entries. Journals are useful in program planning and program evaluation. The following samples of written language can be part of a journal:

- poems
- short stories
- writing fragments
- student's comments about writing
- log entries on specific topics
- interdisciplinary writing
- quotations from the student's readings
- comments by peers or teachers

## Performance-Based Assessment

Performance-based assessment of reading and writing abilities measures the integration of reading and writing and evaluates demonstrations of reading and writing abilities. Performance-based assessment requires students to read a passage or story for a purpose, use one or more cognitive skills as they construct meaning from the text, and write about what they read, usually in response to a prompt or task (Farr and

Tone, 1994). Performance-based assessment can be used in program planning and program evaluation.

## Portfolios

A portfolio, as we have discussed, is a deliberate collection of a student's work that demonstrates the student's efforts, progress, and achievement. When documenting and assessing written language ability, portfolios provide valuable information about reading, writing, spelling skills, comprehension, attitudes, and work habits. Portfolios in literacy assessment are useful for program planning and program evaluation. See Chapter 7 for a more extensive discussion of portfolio use.

The following are suggestions for materials that students could include in student writing portfolios:

- newsletter articles
- student logs
- plays
- poems
- lyrics to a song
- creative writing
- nonfiction writing
- projects that involve students in portraying characters or plot
- journals in which students record their thoughts about what they have read
- written dialogues between student and teacher
- videotapes of students conferencing with each other
- photographs of student writing projects

## Exhibitions

An exhibition displays a student's work and demonstrates how the student combines knowledge, abilities, skills, and attitudes. This tool gives students the opportunity to summarize and synthesize their accomplishments. In reading and writing assessment, exhibitions are useful because students realize that reading and

FIGURE 9.3  *Assessing the Writing Process*

| Writing Process | | | |
| --- | --- | --- | --- |
| Student's Name _____ | **Date** _____ | | |

| *Authentic Writing* | *Always* | *Sometimes* | *Never* |
| --- | --- | --- | --- |
| 1. Does the writer have an authentic, meaningful reason to write? | | | |
| 2. If the written piece is to be shared, does the writer know the audience? | | | |
| 3. Is the writer able to take risks in order to express ideas? | | | |
| 4. Is the writer able to critique the written text? | | | |
| ❏ Suggestion for improvement: | | | |

| *Rehearsal of Writing* | *Always* | *Sometimes* | *Never* |
| --- | --- | --- | --- |
| 5. To what extent does the writer think or plan before writing? | | | |
| 6. To what extent does the writer consult with others before writing? | | | |
| 7. To what extent does the writer use readings as a source of ideas? | | | |
| 8. To what extent does the writer help others develop ideas? | | | |
| ❏ Suggestion for improvement: | | | |

| *Developing the Draft* | *Always* | *Sometimes* | *Never* |
| --- | --- | --- | --- |
| 9. To what extent is the writer able to put thoughts on paper? | | | |
| 10. Do the ideas flow? | | | |
| 11. Is the writer able to physically write? Is an alternative input device or communication device used? | | | |
| 12. Is the writer hindered due to spelling difficulties? | | | |
| 13. Does the writer's attitude support writing? | | | |
| 14. Does the writer read and reread the written text? | | | |
| 15. Does the writer need to be prompted to read and reread the written text? | | | |
| 16. Does the writer make changes based on the reading and rereading of the written text? | | | |

**FIGURE 9.3    *Continued***

| Revising | Always | Sometimes | Never |
|---|---|---|---|
| **17.** Does the writer elaborate or add information? | | | |
| **18.** To what extent does the writer incorporate feedback? | | | |
| **19.** Does the writer use transition? | | | |
| **20.** Does the writer develop one or more introductions or endings to determine which is suitable? | | | |
| ❑ Suggestion for improvement: | | | |

| Editing | Always | Sometimes | Never |
|---|---|---|---|
| **21.** To what extent is the writer able to edit:<br>    **a.** spelling<br>    **b.** capitalization<br>    **c.** punctuation<br>    **d.** grammar<br>    **e.** paragraphing | | | |
| **22.** Is the writer willing to edit the draft? | | | |
| ❑ Suggestion for improvement: | | | |

*Source:* Adapted from Rhodes, L. K., and N. Shanklin (1993). *Windows into Literacy: Assessing Learners K–8.* Portsmouth, NH: Heinemann.

writing involves integration, understanding, problem solving, and reasoning. In this way, teachers have concrete information for program planning and program evaluation.

The elements of an exhibition that involve writing do not necessarily occur in a sequential order but they are useful when thinking about the development of exhibitions (Willis, 1996):

• *Prompt:* A prompt is what teachers ask students to do. This can be as basic as "write a research report about the city in which you live," "write a description of a new tool that would make a task easier," or as comprehensive as "develop an exhibition of your vision for the city of the future."

• *Vision:* A vision is what the exhibition will be like. For example, the exhibition on cities will include oral, written, and multimedia components that demonstrate students' skills and abilities to reflect on their learning, to analyze, to conduct research, and to synthesize. Teachers may ask students to integrate one or more disciplines, to write reports, create multimedia presentations, and incorporate the arts.

• *Agreement on Standards:* Educators and students must agree on what makes an exhibition good. Various scoring systems or rubrics can assist in the evaluation of exhibitions.

• *Audience:* Students' work is exhibited to other students, educators, parents, or community members.

• *Coaching:* Peers and teachers should coach students toward the development of their exhibitions. Coaching, rather than evaluating, is important in the development phase of the exhibition.

• *Reflection:* All participants should reflect on their exhibitions. This allows all of the participants to develop an appreciation for what they have learned and accomplished. Reflection also provides an opportunity to think about how to do it better the next time.

Examples of exhibitions in reading and writing include:

• storyboards
• series of letters to editors
• diary of one of the characters in the story
• reviews of related books
• dialogues among the characters
• maps depicting the travels of the characters

## Self-Assessment

Self-assessment provides students with an opportunity to analyze their own writing and to reflect on their own learning. Figure 9.4 is an example of a questionnaire that students can use when assessing their own writing.

## Peer Assessment

When conducting peer assessments, students have an opportunity to reflect on the writing processes, skills, and strategies of their peers as well as on their own writing processes, skills, and strategies. Figure 9.5, on page 244, is an example of a checklist that students use when conducting a peer assessment.

## Scoring

Teachers use two types of scoring, holistic and analytic, when evaluating writing samples, written products, portfolios, performance assessments, and exhibitions. After reading this section, use one or more of the types of scoring to assess Seth's story, in the Snapshot, "A Day in the Life of My Cat."

## Holistic Scoring

Holistic scoring (Figure 9.6, page 245) is a quick and efficient type of scoring. Holistic scoring produces one score that provides an impression of writing ability. Holistic scoring rests on the assumption that all of the elements of writing, such as organization, mechanics, and fluency, work together in the whole text. This type of scoring can be useful when the teacher is looking for one or two previously identified characteristics in a student's work. One important disadvantage of holistic scoring is that it does not provide detailed information about the success of the student in specific areas of writing (Spandel and Stiggins, 1990).

## Analytic Scoring

Analytic scoring (Figure 9.7, page 246) is a type of scoring that produces a detailed analysis of the written text. The teacher uses a scale or rubric to assign points to different levels of performance in each of the assessed areas. For example, a teacher wants to describe the writing performance of students to organize, use mechanics, and use paragraphing. The teacher rates the students' writing samples on a scale, from 1 to 5 or 1 to 6, in each of these three areas and the student receives three separate scores. Teachers should take care when scoring each of these areas not to let their impressions in one area—for example, organization—influence the impression in another area—such as mechanics in this example (Spandel and Stiggins, 1990).

Analytic scoring is frequently done by two or more raters, working independently, who rate the same written text. When they have

**FIGURE 9.4**  *Self-Assessment Checklist*

**Name** _____    **Date** _____

*Authentic Writing*                                                *My Comments*

1. I know my audience.
2. I take risks when I write.

**Rehearsal of Writing**

3. I think or plan ahead when I write.
4. I consult with my peers.
5. I use print and nonprint media as sources.
6. I help others to write.

**Developing the Draft**

7. I feel that I can put my thoughts down on paper.
8. I have a good attitude toward writing.
9. I am able to spell most words.
10. I know which words to capitalize.
11. I know how to use punctuation.
12. I make changes to my text based on rereading.

**Revising**

13. I incorporate feedback.
14. I make changes, such as beginnings, transitions, and endings.

**Editing**

15. I am willing to edit my draft.
16. I am able to edit and correct spelling.
17. I am able to edit and correct punctuation.
18. I am able to edit and correct capitalization.
19. I am able to edit and correct grammar.
20. I am able to edit and correct paragraphing.

finished, comparisons are made between their ratings to determine their similarity. If the ratings are dissimilar, the two teachers can discuss why they gave certain ratings or a third teacher can rate the text.

## Anchor Papers

Anchor papers are students' papers that represent writing at different levels of performance. They can be useful in the development of rubrics. For example, after a group of students completes a writing assignment, the teacher reviews all of the papers to determine which three represent, by degrees, high-quality performance, typical or average performance, and low performance. These are the anchor papers. Next, the teacher evaluates all of the student papers, using the anchor papers as a guide to determine high, typical, or low performance.

| | ☹ | 😐 | ☺ |
|---|---|---|---|
| Student's Name _____  Date _____  Peer's Name _____ | | | |
| 1. My peer writes for a purpose. | | | |
| 2. My peer consulted me before writing. | | | |
| 3. My peer made changes based on my feedback. | | | |
| 4. My peer conferenced with me. | | | |
| 5. My peer uses transitions. | | | |
| 6. My peer is able to edit the written text. | | | |

**FIGURE 9.5    *Peer Assessment Checklist***

---

*SNAPSHOT* ■ *Seth*

Seth is a curious and energetic sixth grader. One of his most favorite things to do is spend time with his cat. Seth's teacher recently asked him to write a creative story. After reading Seth's story about his cat, describe how you could assess Seth's written language.

### A Day in the Life of My Cat

### by Seth

For those of you who don't now me, you probably don't now my cat. Since this story is going to be about him, you may find it helpful for me to give you a discription him. His name sounds like a good place start. It is Kelev which in Hebrew means dog. This sounds crazy but since my dad wanted a dog we named the cat Kelev. He is huge 20 pound black and white tabby with large green eyes. By the way, this story will be written from the cat's point of view. Most of the dialog in the story is what the cat thnking.

Buzzzzzzzzzzzzz, meooooooooooooooow. I hate that kid's didgatal alarm. It startles me every morning. How come I'm the only one awake? It is supposed to wake him up, too, but he just sleeps through it like a dead mouse. I think it is about time to bther his parants.

Soon the boy and his mothr and fathr leave the house. O boy! I hve the hous to myself.

Soon, the son comes home and the family eats dinner. I keep them compeny and wander around the boy's chair hoping to get a scrap of food. After suppar, everyone, including me, retreat into the TV room and relax. I crawl up on top of the boy and down. He pats me. I then get up for some more food. When I finish, I journey to the bathroom and open the cabinet to reveal my little house. I go to sleep in it. I wake to find the house silent. Everyone is sleeping. Again, I make a trips to the boy's bed, where he is now sleeping and I sit down. I now wait for that scary buzz I hear every morning.

**FIGURE 9.6** *Holistic Scoring*

| | Holistic Scoring Guide—Writing |
|---|---|
| *Score* | *Criteria* |
| 5 | The paper is superb. The ideas are very well developed. If there are any errors in mechanics, grammar, or spelling, they are very minor. Sentence structure is very clear and varied. There is a clear sense of purpose and audience. Ideas are explained and very well supported. |
| 4 | The paper is very good. The ideas are very well developed. There are few errors in mechanics, grammar, or spelling. Sentence structure is clear and varied. There is a clear sense of purpose and audience. Ideas are explained and supported. |
| 3 | The paper is good. The ideas are well developed. There are some errors in mechanics, grammar, or spelling. Sentences follow a similar pattern. There is some sense of purpose or audience. Ideas are not always explained or supported. |
| 2 | The paper is moderate. Some ideas are developed. There are frequent errors in mechanics, grammar, or spelling. Sentences follow a similar pattern. There may be sentence fragments. There is little sense of purpose or audience. Ideas are infrequently explained or supported. |
| 1 | The paper is poor. Ideas are rarely developed. There are many errors in mechanics, grammar, or spelling. Sentences follow a similar pattern. There are sentence fragments. There is no sense of purpose or audience. Ideas are rarely explained or supported. |

## Observing the Student within the Environment

In previous chapters we have discussed the influence of the physical, learning, and social environments on teaching and learning. Temperature, lighting, and seating arrangements affect how well the student reads and writes. A comfortable learning environment facilitates the development of writing abilities and positive attitudes and habits. Finally, the relationships that students have with peers and teachers affect performance.

## Preferred Practices

The assessment of literacy must reflect the close link between the development of reading and written language. Best practice requires that teachers conduct literacy assessment frequently and use the results to guide instruction.

Reliance on individual standardized tests can be dangerous. Many norm-referenced tests do not reflect contemporary views of reading and writing. Selecting an instrument requires careful consideration to match the curriculum and the test content. Reading and writing instruction varies considerably throughout the United States. Therefore, selection of an instrument that best matches the curriculum is essential.

Most standardized achievement tests show bias toward students from many cultural, ethnic, and socioeconomic groups. Tests may not reflect cultural patterns of teaching and learning. Low socioeconomic status often limits access and participation in educational activities.

Scoring tests can be problematic. Students vary in their abilities and most test manuals

**FIGURE 9.7** *Analytic Scoring*

| Analytic Scoring—Writing | | | | | |
|---|---|---|---|---|---|
| | *1* | *2* | *3* | *4* | *5* |
| Development of Ideas | Little understanding of audience; little elaboration of ideas | Some understanding of audience; some elaboration of ideas | Good understanding of audience; good elaboration of ideas | Very good understanding of audience; very good elaboration of ideas | Excellent understanding of audience; superb elaboration of ideas |
| Organization | No evidence of an organized plan for writing; ideas and paragraphs run together | Some evidence of an organized plan for writing; ideas and paragraphs are loosely organized | Good evidence of an organized plan for writing; ideas and paragraphs are organized | Very good evidence of an organized plan for writing; ideas and paragraphs are well organized | Excellent evidence of organized plan for writing; ideas are original and paragraphs are well organized |
| Fluency | Language is very limited and repetitive; written text is very brief | Language is somewhat limited and repetitive; written text is brief | Language is good and there are few repetitions; written text has adequate elaboration | Language is very good and varied; there are no repetitions; written text has very good elaboration | Language is excellent and varied; there are no repetitions; written text has excellent elaboration |
| Spelling | Few words are spelled correctly | Most words are spelled phonetically; most sight words are spelled correctly | Most words are spelled correctly; some errors with homophones and endings | Words are spelled correctly; there are few errors | Words are spelled correctly; errors are minor |
| Capitalization and Punctuation | No capitalization or punctuation | Some evidence of correct capitalization and punctuation | Good evidence of capitalization and punctuation | Very good evidence of capitalization and punctuation; few errors | Excellent evidence of capitalization and punctuation; errors are rare |

contain general directions for scoring. The test examiner must use judgment in scoring. This can be a problem because the test examiners' judgment differs, which can lead to inconsistencies in scoring and interpretation.

Performance-based assessment, portfolios, and exhibitions can be problematic as well.

Questions remain about the reliability and validity of these approaches.

Assessment of literacy requires the use of multiple approaches, including standardized tests, curriculum-based assessment, criterion-referenced assessment, and alternative forms of assessment.

## Extending Learning

1. Develop two assessment tasks that link the instruction in writing directly to assessment of writing.

2. Develop a checklist or rating scale that assesses students' attitudes and habits in writing.

3. After reading the following writing sample that Yizhong, a fourth grader, wrote, develop a checklist and use it to analyze Yizhong's writing.

### Pangea

Pangea was the supercontenient that was made up of the seven other continents linked together. This explains how I think the continents dissembled themselves and how they got where they are today. South America which was nestled in the curve of Africa rotated 90° to the right and moved westward. North America above South America was connected to Europe with the middle part of Canada. This medium size continent made another 90° right turn and again moved to the west. After these continents unhooked themselves Africa followed by moving south west detaching itself from Saudi Arabia and Europe. Now it was Australia's turn to slide out the Bengal bay and float south east. Aisa and Europe which was the main link for Pangea stayed where they were. This explains how continents moved with the continental drift.

4. Examine a norm-referenced, standardized writing test. Compare the development of this test with the contemporary views of assessment discussed in this chapter.

5. Identify three assessment approaches this chapter discusses. Compare the purposes, advantages, and disadvantages of each approach.

## References

Brigance, A. H. (1981). *BRIGANCE® inventory of essential skills.* No. Billerica, MA: Curriculum Associates.

Brigance, A. H. (1999). *BRIGANCE® comprehensive inventory of basic skills–revised.* No. Billerica, MA: Curriculum Associates.

Brigance, A. H. (1984). *BRIGANCE® assessment of basic skills–Spanish edition.* No. Billerica, MA: Curriculum Associates.

Carrow-Woolfolk, E. (1996). *Oral and written language scales.* Minneapolis, MN: American Guidance Service.

Farr, R., and B. Tone (1994). *Portfolio and performance assessment.* Fort Worth, TX: Harcourt Brace College.

Hammill, D. D., V. L. Brown, S. C. Larsen, and J. L. Wiederholt (1994). *Test of adolescent and adult language.* 3d ed. Austin, TX: PRO-ED.

Hammill, D. D., and S. C. Larsen (1996). *Test of written language.* 3d ed. Austin, TX: PRO-ED.

Hresko, W. P., S. R. Herron, and P. K. Peak (1996). *Test of early written language.* 2d ed. Austin, TX: PRO-ED.

Kaufman, A. S., and N. L. Kaufman (1998). *Kaufman test of educational achievement/normative update (K–TEA/NU).* Circle Pines, MN: American Guidance Service.

Larsen, S. C., D. D. Hammill, and D. Moats (1999). *Test of written spelling.* 4th ed. Austin, TX: PRO-ED.

Markwardt Jr., F. C. (1998). *Peabody individual achievement test–revised/normative update.* Circle Pines, MN: American Guidance Service.

McGhee, R., B. R. Bryant, S. C. Larsen, and D. M. Rivera (1995). *Test of written expression.* Austin, TX: PRO-ED.

Newcomer, P. L. (1990). *Diagnostic achievement battery.* 2d ed. Austin, TX: PRO-ED.

Newcomer, P. L., and B. R. Bryant (1993). *Diagnostic achievement test for adolescents.* 2d ed. Austin, TX: PRO-ED.

Psychological Corporation (2001). *Wechsler individual*

*achievement test–II*. San Antonio, TX: The Psychological Corporation.

Rhodes, L. K., and N. Shanklin (1993). *Windows into literacy: Assessing learners K–8*. Portsmouth, NH: Heinemann.

Sonnenschein, J. L. (1983). *Basic achievement skills individual screener*. San Antonio, TX: Harcourt Brace.

Spandel, V., and R. J. Stiggins (1990). *Creating writers*. New York: Longman.

Stahl, S. A., and M. R. Kuhn (1995). Does whole language or instruction matched to learning styles help children learn to read? *School Psychology Review* 24: 393–404.

Wilde, S. (1989a). Looking at invented spelling: A kidwatcher's guide to spelling, Part I. In *The whole language evaluation book*, ed. K. S. Goodman, Y. M. Goodman, and W. J. Hood, 213–226. Portsmouth, NH: Heinemann.

Wilde, S. (1989b). Understanding spelling strategies: A kidwatcher's guide to spelling, Part II. In *The whole language evaluation book*, ed. K. S. Goodman, Y. M. Goodman, and W. J. Hood, 227–236. Portsmouth, NH: Heinemann.

Wilkinson, G. (1993). *Wide range achievement test*. 3d ed. Wilmington, DE: Jastak Associates.

Willis, S. (1996). *Student exhibitions put higher-order skills to the test*. Education Update 38 (March): 1, 3.

Woodcock, R. W., K. S. McGrew, and N. Mather (2001). *Woodcock-Johnson psychoeducational battery–III*. Itasca, IL: Riverside.

# 10

# *Oral Language*

## Overview

Language involves the use of symbols to communicate thoughts, feelings, ideas, and information. To communicate meaning, humans speak these symbols or produce them through synthesized speech, write them by using the visual symbols of the language, or express them manually through signing or gestures. Each of us uses these symbols of language every day.

Oral language relates closely to other assessment areas described in this book. The assessment of oral language skills is important when assessing achievement, development, ability, and behavior. As you read this chapter, keep in mind how assessment of children and youth in one domain might relate to assessment in another area.

## Chapter Objectives _____

After completing this chapter, you should be able to:

- Contrast several theoretical perspectives regarding the development of oral language.
- Discuss examples of best practice when assessing English language learners.
- Describe the use of standardized tests for assessing oral language.

- Compare assessment approaches that form a link with instruction, program planning, and program evaluation.
- Describe how the physical, learning, and social environments influence oral language.

## *What Shapes Our Views*

Contemporary perspectives on the development of speech and language skills and abilities provide a basis for the various approaches to assessment. We examine three different perspectives: the behavioral approach, the social learning theory approach, and the psycholinguistic approach.

### *Behavioral Approach*

This approach emphasizes the importance of external factors (outside of the individual) in influencing and promoting language development. Verbal ability develops as a result of the contingent relationship among the antecedent, the behavior, and the consequence. Speech and language develop as a result of adult interaction with the child (stimulus, or antecedent), the child's vocalization (verbal response behavior), and the reinforcement (the consequence of vocalization). Language abilities become refined through the process of **shaping,** or reinforcing, the sounds or word as the vocalization more closely approximates the sound or word in the language.

For example, a caregiver talks to an infant, "Here's your juice . . . juice . . . umm . . . good juice!" The child makes responses to the caregiver's voice, "oooo" . . . "ummm." As time goes on, the child's responses approximate the actual word, "umm juuu." The caregiver smiles and responds, "Yes!!! Juice!" Gradually, the child's responses duplicate the actual word.

Shaping is a behavioral term that refers to reinforcing the behavior (each progressive step) as it becomes more and more like the target behavior. Thus, as children become older, gradual reinforcement for making sounds common to the language occurs. Eventually, children shape strings of sounds to approximate words:

**CHILD:** "Ma jus."

**ADULT:** "That's right! More juice!"

***Effect on Assessment Practices.***    Assessment practices that follow this theoretical perspective focus on the stimulus or antecedent (A), the verbal response or behavior (B), and the reinforcements or consequences (C) offered in the environment. This type of assessment is often referred to as the ABC approach. The behavior (B) may be divided into smaller steps, depending on the needs and abilities of the individual. Breaking the behavior into small, discrete, sequential steps is called **task analysis.** Chapter 15 contains a detailed explanation of the ABC approach and of task analysis procedures in assessment practices.

### *Social Learning Theory*

According to this perspective, individuals learn a set of rules about the syntax of language through the modeling of language (Bandura, 1977). As defined earlier, syntax is the system of rules that dictate how people combine words into meaningful phrases and sentences; syntax governs the arrangement of word sequences. This set of rules allows people to produce new and novel combinations of words, such as phrases or sentences, that they have never heard or produced before. When a child develops competence in syntax, the child can speak and understand an infinite number of sentences.

Adults frequently use a technique called **expansion** to increase language development. Expansion involves restating the child's language and adding words and more complex phrases.

CHILD:  "Wan dawg."

ADULT:  "You want to pat the dog?"

CHILD:  "Wan pa dawg."

***Effect on Assessment Practices.***   Assessment practices that follow this theoretical perspective emphasize the importance of adults and peers in the student's environment and their effect on the development of language. The modeling of language, the use of syntax, and the expansion of language are areas of assessment focus.

### Psycholinguistic Approach

The psycholinguistic approach, developed by Noam Chomsky (1967), rests on the belief that children are born ready to develop language skills and that they have an inborn language-developing ability that helps them understand and learn language. This is called the "language acquisition device," and it enables the child to interpret language, construct grammatical rules, and generate an infinite variety of phrases and sentences.

***Effect on Assessment Practices.***   This perspective presents difficulties to educators who work with students with language disabilities. The view that children and youth are innately predisposed and have an inborn ability implies that individuals with language impairments are not born with this ability and will never have this ability. This approach provides little encouragement for intervention and instruction for students who are experiencing delays in language development.

## Understanding Speech and Language Disorders

Students with suspected speech and language disorders are screened first for possible hearing loss. The hearing screening consists of listening to several tones within the speech range. If a student has difficulty hearing one or more of these tones, the examiner refers the student for a complete hearing assessment. Chapter 16 describes a hearing assessment.

### Speech Disorders

A speech disorder refers to a difficulty in articulation, such as the way words are pronounced; the fluency of speech, including rate and rhythm; and the pitch, volume, and quality of the voice. Ricardo, a student in the Snapshot on page 252, has a speech disorder. You can follow his teacher's questions and the steps that she took to help Ricardo.

Assessment questions arise when a parent or teacher has difficulty in understanding a student's speech. A speech and language pathologist (SLP) usually conducts the assessment. In fact, the speech and language pathologist is the primary practitioner to plan assessment in this area.

Students who have difficulty producing the correct sounds of speech generally have problems in one or more of four areas of speech production.

**1.** *Respiration:* To produce sounds, an individual must be able to control the inhaling and exhaling of breath. This must occur while forcing air through the larynx.

**2.** *Phonation:* An individual must contract specific muscles to allow the vocal folds of the larynx to be drawn together. Forcing air through the larynx causes the air to vibrate and produce sound.

## SNAPSHOT ■ *Ricardo*

"Cccan I sh-sh-sharpen my pencil?"

Ms. Wong looked up to see Ricardo waving his hand in the air. She nodded and motioned toward the pencil sharpener. As Ricardo left his work group of three other students, Ms. Wong thought again about Ricardo's stuttering problem.

He was a new student in her class this year. When she had first observed his stuttering problem, she had checked the records that were forwarded by Ricardo's former school. They contained no mention of a stuttering problem. She thought that Ricardo might overcome the stuttering with time; but it did not seem to disappear. In fact, today marked the beginning of the third week of school and he seemed to be having more difficulty getting his ideas across as time went on.

Will the stuttering become worse or will he outgrow it in time? Should she try to correct him? She wrote herself a reminder to fill out a referral form concerning Ricardo's speech problems before the end of the week. The referral form would be sent to the school's coordinator of the assessment team.

By the end of the school year, Ricardo was very grateful to his teacher for recognizing his speech problem and referring him for assessment. Through the IEP process, Ricardo received services from the speech and language pathologist, who taught him specific strategies to counter his stuttering. By learning ways to control his breathing and plan what he wanted to say in class, Ricardo was able to learn life skills in decreasing his stuttering problem.

Questions and concerns about a student's oral language always need to be referred as soon as possible to the assessment team. In Ricardo's case, after filling out the referral form his teacher should consult with members of the team, such as the speech and language pathologist, about ways to work with Ricardo in the classroom. She needs to address her questions regarding how to handle classroom stuttering as soon as she notices the difficulty.

---

**3.** *Resonation:* The vibrating air passes through the throat, mouth, and sometimes the nasal cavities, shaping the quality of the sound.

**4.** *Articulation:* The formation of specific sounds of speech are produced by the position of the tongue, lips, teeth, and mouth.

### Language Disorders

A **language disorder** refers to a difficulty or inability in decoding or encoding the set of symbols used in language or an inability to effectively use inner language. The Snapshot of Bethany describes some of the difficulties experienced by one student with a language disorder. Assessment questions focus on the student's expressive language, receptive language, or inner language. Some standardized instruments such as the *Oral and Written Language Scales* (Carrow-Woolfolk, 1996) assess these language areas.

**Expressive language** refers to the student's ability to use language to communicate information, thoughts, feelings, and ideas with others. Assessing expressive language involves examining the actual production of sound, speech, and language. **Speech** is the production of oral language for the purpose of expression.

**Receptive language** refers to the student's understanding of the language of others. Assessment of receptive language usually involves having the student listen to words or phrases and then demonstrating understanding. For example, a student might be asked to put the book on top of or under the table or to point to the picture that shows the boy putting on a jacket. Many standardized instruments measure expressive and receptive language.

**Inner language** involves the use of language during thinking, planning, and other mental processes. The assessment of inner language skills and abilities is a complex process

## SNAPSHOT ■ *Bethany*

The teacher's words fell on Bethany's ears at an overwhelming rate. Bethany knew that the teacher was explaining the assignment for tomorrow. Although Bethany has average intelligence, she is not able to comprehend all that the teacher says. Before dismissing the class, Bethany's teacher handed her a written copy of the assignment, and Bethany smiled quickly as she gathered her books.

Bethany's teacher returned the smile as she remembered the problems that Bethany had experienced earlier in the year. Through the referral and assessment process, the teacher was able to discover Bethany's difficulty in comprehending oral directions and in following class discussions.

It all began early in the year, after the school nurse had conducted a hearing screening on all the students in her classroom. Bethany passed the screening with no problems. However, as the first month of school passed, Bethany's teacher observed that even though Bethany seemed to be attentive, she had difficulty in following daily class discussions. Bethany frequently submitted incomplete homework assignments and, when questioned, would apologetically add that she didn't ". . . know we had to do that." As the difficulty seemed to persist, the teacher decided to confer with Bethany's former teachers. Both teachers vaguely remembered that Bethany was not consistent in her work. Some of the assignments were done well, they remembered. One teacher felt that she did not seem to be motivated.

The following week, the teacher called Bethany's parents and asked them to come in for a conference. Both parents were surprised to hear about the teacher's concerns. When asked if Bethany needed to have the volume high on the television, her mother replied that Bethany seldom seemed to be interested in watching television or in going to the movies. Bethany's parents were concerned about her missing assignments. They tried to pinpoint some of their concerns: Why doesn't Bethany turn in complete assignments? Why doesn't she participate in class discussions? Is there a reason why Bethany does not like to watch television or go to the movies? They agreed that the teacher should make a referral to the assessment team. Perhaps the team might be able to provide some answers to these puzzling questions.

Through the assessment process, the team identified Bethany's problem. She had difficulty processing oral language. Her teacher used several accommodations, such as written assignment slips and outlines of lecture material, to help Bethany be more successful in the classroom.

---

and continues to evolve as more and more research addresses this area.

## Responding to Diversity

Today, many children are English language learners; that is, English is not their first language. They come from homes in which the family's native language is spoken exclusively or nearly exclusively. School personnel consider the home language to be the students' first language; and regard them as culturally and linguistically diverse students. As the United States continues to become an increasingly diverse society, children from culturally and linguistically diverse backgrounds make up a greater percentage of the school population. In some large-city school districts, these students comprise up to 80 percent of the student body (Improving Results for Culturally and Linguistically Diverse Students, 2000).

In order to benefit from their education program, many children who are culturally and linguistically diverse need second language instruction. Some children need additional tutoring due to limited linguistic experiences, but most children who are culturally and linguistically diverse do not have a special need that requires a referral to special services.

How can teachers distinguish language differences from speech and language disorders in linguistically and culturally diverse students? First, a teacher can observe speech production and refer the student if the student's speech contains mispronunciations, dysfluencies, unusual pitch, rate, hoarseness, omitted words or word endings, words used in unusual ways, or atypical sequences when compared to dialect peers (Moran, 1996).

Second, a teacher should refer a linguistically and culturally diverse student to the assessment team when the teacher observes some of the following behaviors in comparison to similar peers:

1. Nonverbal aspects of language are culturally inappropriate.
2. The student does not express basic needs adequately.
3. The student rarely initiates verbal interaction with peers.
4. When peers initiate interaction, the student responds sporadically/inappropriately.
5. The student replaces speech with gestures, and communicates nonverbally when talking would be appropriate and expected.
6. Peers give indications that they have difficulty understanding the student.
7. The student often gives inappropriate responses.
8. The student has difficulty conveying thoughts in an organized, sequential manner that is understandable to listeners.
9. The student shows poor topic maintenance ("skips around").
10. The student has word-finding difficulties that go beyond normal second-language acquisition patterns.
11. The student fails to provide significant information to the listener, leaving the listener confused.
12. The student has difficulty with conversational turn-taking skills (may be too passive, or may interrupt inappropriately).
13. The student perseverates (remains too long) on a topic even after the topic has changed.
14. The student fails to ask and answer questions appropriately.
15. The student needs to hear things repeated, even when they are stated simply and comprehensibly.
16. The student often echoes what others say. (Roseberry-McKibbin, 1995)

The focus of the assessment question, "How does the student communicate within the first-language setting?" and the standard that teachers can apply is whether the student's language reflects characteristics that are different from the student's first-language community (Moran, 1996). Teachers should not identify students as having a speech and language disability simply by comparing the student's language with the dominant language—such as European American English—of the school community.

There is a shortage of teachers and other professionals qualified to assess culturally and linguistically diverse students and many standardized instruments are woefully inadequate (Burnette, 2000). To help IEP team members who are struggling with insufficient training and materials, a number of solutions and best practice have been identified (Figure 10.1).

## *Speech and Language Assessment*

An assessment of speech and language reflects, to some degree, the perspectives of the examiner who is gathering the information as well as the choice of the assessment approach. Many standardized instruments focus only on expressive and receptive language, whereas authorities in the field (Bloom and Lahey, cited in Kaiser, Alpert, and Warren, 1988; Semel, Wiig, and Secord, 2002) describe oral language as consisting of three main areas or components: form, content, and use.

**FIGURE 10.1**  *Best Practice for IEP Team Members Working with Students Who Are Linguistically and Culturally Diverse*

What should IEP team members do when assessing to determine eligibility for special education services for a student who shows linguistically and culturally diverse traits?

- ❏ Gather information to determine whether the difficulties stem from language or cultural differences, from a lack of opportunity to learn, or from a disability as part of a preferral and intervention process.

- ❏ Include interpreters, bilingual educators, and an individual who is familiar with the student's culture and language as members of the IEP team.

- ❏ Assess the student's language dominance and proficiency to determine which language to use in the assessment process for special education services, if the student's home language is other than English.

- ❏ Select nonbiased, appropriate instruments along with other sources of information (observation, interviews) from a variety of environments (school, home, community) to produce a multidimensional assessment.

*Source:* Adapted from Burnette, J. (2000). Assessment of culturally and linguistically diverse students for special education eligibility. (ERIC EC Digest No. E604). Retrieved April 26, 2001. http://ericec.org/digests/e604.html.

## Form

Form relates to the structural properties of language, including the sounds and written symbols of language and the letters that form a unit of meaning. The term **phonology** refers to the system of speech sounds of a language. The smallest units of sound are **phonemes.** For example, the English language makes use of only about 44 different phonemes. The word *truck* consists of four phonemes (/T/R/U/K/). Students with articulation disorders often have difficulty in producing sounds. Substituting one phoneme for another and omitting phonemes are common mistakes that students make. Speech and language pathologists may describe this as a problem in articulation. For example: substituting letter(s) (wabbit for rabbit) or omitting letter(s): (car for cars).

Some students have difficulty in associating phonemes with their written equivalents, called **graphemes.** One of the reasons that English is such a difficult language is that: (1) a single grapheme can represent more than one phoneme (for example, *c—cake c—circus*) and (2) different graphemes can represent the same phoneme (for example, *c—cake k—kite*) (Polloway and Smith, 2000). In teaching that a single grapheme can represent more than one phoneme, we say that a letter has different sounds. For example, how many sounds does the letter *a* have?

*Morphology.*  **Morphology** is the study of the units of letters that form a single unit of meaning. The basic unit of meaning is a **morpheme.** Morphemes can be a word such as *house*, or *car*, or a meaningful part of a word such as *re* in *renew*. Prefixes and suffixes, such as *re-, in-, -s, -er* are morphemes. Because morphemes are units of meaning, examiners frequently use them to measure expressive language development by obtaining a sample of the student's language and counting the individual morphemes per speech utterance. A speech utterance is the single phrase or sentence that the student expresses. The number of morphemes is totaled and divided by the number of speech utterances to obtain the average **mean length of utterance (MLU).**

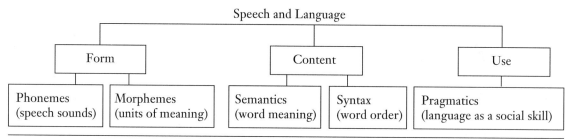

**FIGURE 10.2** *Linguistic Aspects of Speech and Language*

The following conversation was part of a five-minute observation of Andre during free play in the kindergarten classroom.

**DIANE:**    My block . . . [2 morphemes]

**ANDRE:**    No, I want this. [4 morphemes]

**ANDRE:**    You can be the driver. [6 morphemes; -er is a suffix]

Adding up Andre's use of morphemes, the total comes to 10 and is divided by the number of Andre's speech utterances (2). Although the MLU may be an oversimplification of the concept of spoken language, the MLU is useful in comparing levels of linguistic development and increases in individual mastery of expressive language (Polloway and Smith, 2000). Other considerations that will affect the MLU are (1) the length of the recording needed to obtain an adequate language sample of speech utterances; and (2) the environment(s) that will be observed.

### Content

Content relates to the meaning of language. Content includes semantics and syntax.

*Semantics.*    Semantics is the study of word meanings. Development of semantics begins with association of single concrete morphemes, for example, the association of *mama* with a particular person. Development typically progresses to understanding complex utterances; for example, "Please, get me the book" and

more complex language such as, "It's raining cats and dogs."

*Syntax.*    Syntax refers to the rules for arranging words into a sentence or phrase. In English, for example, adjectives are commonly placed before nouns. The combination of syntax and morphology is known as grammar.

### Use

Pragmatics refers to the ability to use language in functional ways: for example, the ability to use language in taking turns, to enter into a conversation or discussion with other children (or adults), to continue the conversation, to interpret the meaning of the speaker, or to "read" the listener's nonverbal cues.

Figure 10.2 illustrates the relationship between the aspects of speech and language we have discussed.

### Assessment Questions, Purposes, and Approaches

Questions regarding a student's oral language abilities and skills require the practitioner to employ a variety of assessment approaches in order to obtain an understanding of the student's ability and developmental level. These approaches should include language probes, language samples, MLUs, oral descriptions, interviews, conferences, videotapes, discussions, and standardized tests (Table 10.1).

**TABLE 10.1**     *Assessment Questions, Purposes, and Approaches*

| Assessment Questions | Steps and Purposes | Approaches |
|---|---|---|
| Is the student's speech and language typical for the student's age? | **Screening**<br>To determine whether students *may* have speech and language delays or disabilities and should be referred for further assessment | Norm-referenced instruments<br>Curriculum-based assessments<br>Criterion-referenced assessments<br>Observations<br>Questionnaires<br>Checklists |
| Does the student have a severe language disability?<br>Does the student meet the criteria for services?<br>What are the strengths and weaknesses?<br>Why does the student have a speech and language disorder?<br>How extensive is the disability? | **Eligibility**<br>To determine if there is a disability and the extent of the speech and language problems<br>To determine the need for special education and related services<br>To compare the student's performance with the performance of the peer group<br>To determine specific strengths and weaknesses<br>To understand why the student is having difficulty | Norm-referenced instruments<br>Curriculum-based assessments<br>Criterion-referenced assessments<br>Observations<br>Probes<br>Error analysis<br>Interviews<br>Checklists<br>Student, parent, and/or teacher conferences<br>Performance assessments |

*Connecting Instruction with Assessment*

| | | |
|---|---|---|
| What types of services should be provided?<br>What classroom modifications and adaptations should be implemented?<br>What skills does the student have?<br>What should be taught?<br>When behavior impedes learning or that of others, what strategies, including positive behavioral interventions and supports, to address that behavior should be included? | **Program Planning**<br>To determine the locations and type of services(s) to be received<br>To assess the physical, learning, and social classroom environments<br>To understand what the student knows and does not know<br>To plan the student's program<br>To determine where instruction should begin<br>To determine instructional approaches | Norm-referenced instruments<br>Curriculum-based assessments<br>Criterion-referenced assessments<br>Observations<br>Probes<br>MLUs<br>Language samples<br>Error analysis<br>Interviews<br>Checklists<br>Questionnaires<br>Student, parent, and/or teacher conferences<br>Performance assessments |
| Once instruction begins, is the student making progress?<br>Should the instruction be modified? | **Program Monitoring**<br>To understand the pace of instruction<br>To understand what the student knows prior to and after instruction | Curriculum-based assessments<br>Criterion-referenced assessments<br>Observations<br>Probes<br>MLUs |

*continued*

**TABLE 10.1** *Continued*

| Assessment Questions | Steps and Purposes | Approaches |
|---|---|---|
| | **Program Monitoring**<br>To understand the strategies and concepts the student uses<br>To monitor the student's program | Language samples<br>Error analysis<br>Interviews<br>Checklists<br>Questionnaires<br>Student, parent, and/or teacher conferences<br>Portfolios<br>Exhibitions<br>Journals<br>Written descriptions<br>Oral descriptions |
| Has the student made progress?<br>Has the student met the goals of the IEP?<br>Has the instructional program been successful for the student?<br>Has the instructional program achieved its goals? | **Program Evaluation**<br>To determine whether the IEP goals have been met<br>To determine whether the goals of the program have been met<br>To evaluate program effectiveness | Curriculum-based assessments<br>Criterion-referenced assessments<br>Observations<br>Probes<br>Error analysis<br>Interviews<br>Checklists<br>Questionnaires<br>Student, parent, and/or teacher conferences<br>Portfolios<br>Exhibitions<br>Journals<br>Written descriptions<br>Oral descriptions<br>Surveys |

## *Standardized Tests of Oral Language*

There are a number of standardized tests of oral language (Table 10.2). This section highlights some of the commonly used individual, standardized tests of oral language. All the tests in this section are norm-referenced and use standardized procedures for administering and scoring. The tests yield a variety of scores, including standard scores, percentiles, stanines, age equivalents, and normal curve equivalents (NCEs).

## Clinical Evaluation of Language Fundamentals–3

As Box 10.1 shows, the *Clinical Evaluation of Language Fundamentals–3 (CELF–3)* (Semel, Wiig, and Secord, 1995a) identifies, diagnoses, and follows up the evaluation of language skills deficits in students ages 6 through 21. The *CELF–3* contains 11 subtests that measure selected receptive and expressive skills in morphology, syntax, semantics, and memory. The Examiner's Manual includes a chapter on

**TABLE 10.2** *Standardized Instruments of Oral Language*

| Instrument | Age Range | Type | Areas Assessed | Comments Regarding Technical Adequacy |
|---|---|---|---|---|
| *Brigance® Inventory of Early Development–Revised* (Brigance, 1991) | Birth through 7 years | Criterion-referenced | Speech and language, including receptive language, gestures, vocalizations, expressive language, sentence length, and auditory memory | Skill sequences and associated age levels were developed by a review of the literature. |
| *Brigance® Comprehensive Inventory of Basic Skills–Revised* (Brigance, 1999) | 5 years through 15 years | Criterion-referenced | Speech, including syntax and fluency, expressive language, articulation, and speech quality; listening skills, including auditory discrimination, auditory memory, and receptive language | Skill sequences and associated grade levels were developed by a review of the literature. |
| *Clinical Evaluation of Language Fundamentals–3 (CELF–3)* (Semel, Wiig, and Secord, 1996) | 6 years through 21 years | Norm-referenced | Receptive and expressive language, morphology, syntax, semantics, and memory | Adequate |
| *Comprehensive Receptive and Expressive Vocabulary Test–Second Edition (CREVT–2)* (Wallace and Hammill, 2002) | 4 years through adulthood | Norm-referenced | Expressive and receptive language | Adequate |
| *Expressive Vocabulary Test (EVT)* (Williams, 1997) | 2 years, 5 months through 90+ years | Norm-referenced | Expressive vocabulary and language retrieval | Pictures contain a good balance of gender and ethnic representations. Adequate reliability and validity. |

*(continued)*

**TABLE 10.2** *Continued*

| Instrument | Age Range | Type | Areas Assessed | Comments Regarding Technical Adequacy |
|---|---|---|---|---|
| *Expressive One–Word Picture Vocabulary–2000 Edition (EOWPVT–2000)* (Brownell, 2000) English and Spanish Forms* | 2 years through 18 years | Norm-referenced | Expressive language | Limited information regarding norming sample |
| *Oral and Written Language Scales (OWLS)* (Carrow-Woolfolk, 1996) | 3 years through 21 years | Norm-referenced | Vocabulary, syntax, pragmatics, and higher-order thinking | Internal and test-retest reliability is weak for some age groups. |
| *Peabody Picture Vocabulary Test–Third Edition (PPVT–III)* (Dunn and Dunn, 1997) | 2 years, 5 months through 90+ years | Norm-referenced | Receptive language | During test development, items were reviewed for bias and cultural sensitivity. Adequate reliability and validity. |
| *Prueba del Desarrollo Inicial del Lenguaje* (Hresko, Reid, and Hammill, 1982)* | 3 years through 7 years | Norm-referenced; norming sample consisted of 549 Spanish-speaking children from Mexico, Puerto Rico, and the U.S. | Receptive and expressive language for Spanish-speaking children | This test is a direct translation of the *Test of Early Language Development*. |
| *Test de Vocabulario en Imágenes Peabody (TVIP)* (Dunn, Lugo, Padilla, and Dunn, 1986)* | 2 years, 5 months through 18 years | Norm-referenced; norms are available for Mexican and Puerto Rican standardization samples | Receptive language for Spanish-speaking children and adolescents | This test is a direct translation of the *Peabody Picture Vocabulary Test–R* (Dunn and Dunn, 1981). |
| *Preschool Language Scale–3 (PLS–3)* (Zimmerman, Steiner, and Pond, 1992)* | Birth through 6 years, 11 months | Norm-referenced | Auditory comprehension, expressive language | Adequate |

**TABLE 10.2** *Continued*

| | | | |
|---|---|---|---|
| Test of Adolescent and Adult Language–Third Edition (TOAL–3) (Hammill, Brown, Larsen, and Wiederholt, 1994) | 12 years through 24 years, 11 months | Norm-referenced | Expressive and receptive language, syntax semantics, and phonology, reading and writing | Adequate for measuring components of oral language |
| Test of Early Language Development–Third Edition (TELD–3) (Hresko, Reid, and Hammill, 1999) | 2 years through 7 years | Norm-referenced | Expressive and receptive language, syntax and semantics | Adequate |
| Test of Language Development: Third Edition (TOLD–P:3) (Newcomer and Hammill, 1997) | 4 years through 8 years | Norm-referenced | Expressive and receptive language, syntax, semantics, and phonology | Adequate |
| Test of Language Development–Intermediate: Third Edition (TOLD–I:3) (Hammill and Newcomer, 1997) | 8 years, 6 months through 12 years | Norm-referenced | Expressive and receptive language, syntax, semantics, and phonology | Adequate |
| Test of Pragmatic Language (Phelps-Terasaki and Phelps-Gunn, 1992) | 5 years through 13 years | Norm-referenced | Pragmatic language | Additional information concerning reliability and validity would be helpful. |
| Woodcock Language Proficiency Battery–Revised English Form (Woodcock, 1991) | 2 years through adulthood | Norm-referenced | Auditory memory, expressive and receptive language, verbal analogies, reading and written language | Adequate |

*(continued)*

TABLE 10.2 *Continued*

| Instrument | Age Range | Type | Areas Assessed | Comments Regarding Technical Adequacy |
|---|---|---|---|---|
| *Woodcock Language Proficiency Battery–Spanish Form* (Woodcock and Muñoz-Sandoval, 1995)* | 2 years through adulthood | Norm-referenced; norming sample of Spanish version included individuals from Argentina, Costa Rica, Mexico, Peru, Puerto Rico, Spain, and several locations within the United States | Auditory memory, expressive and receptive language, verbal analogies, reading and written language | Spanish version is an adaptation, not a direct translation of, the English Form. |
| *Woodcock-Muñoz Language Survey, Normative Update, English and Spanish Forms* (Woodcock and Muñoz-Sandoval, 2001)* | 4 years through adulthood | Norm-referenced; the normative update is based on the norming population of the *Woodcock Johnson III* (over 8,000 individuals); original norming sample of Spanish version included individuals from Argentina, Costa Rica, Mexico, Peru, Puerto Rico, Spain, and several locations within the United States | Oral language including picture vocabulary and verbal analogies, reading (letter-word identification) and writing (spelling, punctuation, capitalization, and word usage) | A screening test. Spanish version is an adaptation, not a direct translation of, the English Form. |

*Spanish form available

## BOX 10.1 *Clinical Evaluation of Language Fundamentals–3 (CELF–3)*

*Publication Date:* 1995

*Purposes:* Measures selected receptive and expressive skills in morphology, syntax, semantics, and memory.

*Age/Grade Levels:* Ages 6 through 21.

*Time to Administer:* 30 minutes to 45 minutes.

*Technical Adequacy:* The standardization sample, reliability, and validity are adequate.

*Suggested Uses:* Identify, diagnose, and follow up the evaluation of language skills deficits. For Spanish-speaking individuals, the CELF–3 Spanish Edition is a parallel, not translated, version of the instrument.

extension testing and instructional objectives with many excellent examples of follow-up probes that are useful in assessing and monitoring students in the classroom.

The Examiner's Manual also presents a timely chapter devoted to dialectal variations and cultural sensitivity. The authors have addressed issues of bias in assessment of oral language by submitting the *CELF–3* test materials to a panel of experts who reviewed the test specifically for gender, racial/ethnic, and regional biases. For Spanish-speaking individuals, the *CELF–3* Spanish Edition is a parallel, not translated, version of the instrument.

**Administration.** The *CELF–3* is administered individually and takes 30 minutes to 45 minutes.

**Scoring.** Raw scores convert to standard scores, percentile ranks, stanines, or normal curve equivalents. Confidence intervals may be 68 percent and 90 percent.

**Standardization.** The *CELF–3* standardization process took place between 1994 and 1995.

The standardization sample consisted of 2,450 individuals who represented age, gender, race/ethnicity, geographic region, and parent education strata. None of the individuals in the standardization sample received language therapy or had a diagnosed or identified language disorder.

Only individuals who could understand and speak English and were English-language dominant participated in the standardization. Approximately 30 percent of the standardization sample included individuals with regional or dialectal differences, including Black English, Southern English, General American, Appalachian English, Western Pennsylvania, Middle Atlantic, among others.

**Reliability.** Reliability information for internal consistency, test-retest reliability, and interrater reliability is as follows: Internal consistency coefficients for composite scores ranged from .83 (receptive language for age 15 and ages 17 through 21) to .95 (total language for ages 7 through 11). Test-retest coefficients for composite scores ranged from .77 (receptive and expressive language for age 13) to .94 (total language for age 10). There is only one small interrater reliability study, which showed adequate results.

**Validity.** The test presents adequate evidence of content, construct, and concurrent validity. The *CELF–3* was administered concurrently with the *Clinical Evaluation of Language Fundamentals–Revised*, the *Clinical Evaluation of Language Fundamentals–Preschool*, and the *Wechsler Intelligence Scale for Children–III*.

**Summary.** The *Clinical Evaluation of Language Fundamentals–3* is designed to identify, diagnose, and follow up the evaluation of language skills deficits in students ages 6 through 21. The *CELF–3* contains 11 subtests that measure selected receptive and expressive skills in morphology, syntax, semantics, and memory. The authors have addressed cultural sensitivity and test bias; and the examiner's manual addresses dialectal variations. Technical characteristics are adequate with the exception that additional studies are necessary regarding concurrent validity with instruments other than the *CELF* series. Additional studies concerning interrater reliability would be helpful.

## Expressive Vocabulary Test

The *Expressive Vocabulary Test (EVT)* (Williams, 1997) measures expressive vocabulary and word retrieval for Standard American English in individuals ages 2 years, 5 months through 90+ years. Box 10.2 describes the test's parameters. The *EVT* is administered using a stimulus book with pictures that contain a good balance of gender and ethnic representations.

The examinee must respond to two types of items, labeling and synonyms. For labeling items, the examiner points to a picture or a part of the body and asks a question. For the synonyms, the examiner presents a picture and a stimulus word.

***Administration.*** The *EVT* is administered individually and takes 10 minutes to 25 minutes.

***Scoring.*** Raw scores convert to standard scores, percentile ranks, stanines, NCEs, or age equivalents, with calculable confidence intervals

---

**BOX 10.2**    *Expressive Vocabulary Test (EVT)*

---

*Publication Date:* 1997

*Purposes:* Measures expressive vocabulary and word retrieval.

*Age/Grade Levels:* Ages 2 years, 5 months through 90+ years.

*Time to Administer:* 10 minutes to 25 minutes.

*Technical Adequacy:* The standardization sample, reliability, and validity studies are adequate.

*Suggested Uses:* Identify, diagnose, and follow up the evaluation of expressive language and word retrieval skill deficits.

---

at the 90 and 95 percent level. The *EVT* standard score has a mean of 100 and a standard deviation of 15.

***Standardization.*** The *EVT* was standardized on 2,725 individuals, the same population used in the *Peabody Picture Vocabulary Test–III* standardization. Based on the 1990 census data, test developers controlled the sample for age, gender, race/ethnicity, region, and SES (based on parent or self education level).

***Reliability.*** Test-retest reliability ranged from .77 to .90; split-half reliability ranged from .83 to .97. Internal reliability was high.

***Validity.*** The test presents evidence for content and construct validity. Criterion-related validity studies for the *EVT* and the *Oral and Written Language Scales (OWLS)* showed correlations in the moderate to high range. The reason for this range is that the *EVT* only measures one area of language, expressive vocabulary, while the *OWLS* measures language in a broad context. Additional criterion-related validity studies would be helpful.

Several small studies examined the performance of different clinical groups matched to control groups. Children in clinical groups represented specific diagnostic or special education categories including: speech impairment, language delay, language impairment, mental retardation, learning disability (reading), and hearing impairment. Clinical groups also included gifted students and adults with mild mental retardation. Individuals from these studies were not in the standardization sample.

***Summary.*** The *Expressive Vocabulary Test* measures expressive vocabulary and word retrieval for Standard American English in individuals representing a wide age range (ages 2 years, 5 months through 90+ years). The test has adequate technical characteristics, although additional criterion-related validity studies would be helpful.

# Oral and Written Language Scales

The *Oral and Written Language Scales (OWLS)* (Carrow-Woolfolk, 1996) is an individualized test of oral and written language. Box 10.3 describes the test's parameters. The *OWLS* has three scales: Listening Comprehension, Oral Expression, and Written Expression. Chapter 9 discusses the Written Expression Scale. In this section we will examine the Listening Comprehension and Oral Expression Scales which are intended for use with children and young adults ages 3 through 21. The *OWLS* measures vocabulary, syntax, pragmatics, and higher-order thinking, including interpretation of figurative language, inference, synthesizing information, and so on.

*Administration.* The Listening Comprehension and Oral Expression Scales are individually administered.

*Scoring.* Raw scores convert to standard scores, including percentile ranks, normal curve equivalents, and stanines with possible confidence intervals of 68 percent, 90 percent, or 95 percent.

---

**BOX 10.3**  *Oral and Written Language Scales (OWLS)*

---

*Publication Date:* 1996

*Purposes:* Measures written and oral language including vocabulary, syntax, pragmatics, and higher-order thinking including interpretations of figurative language, inference, and so on.

*Age/Grade Levels:* Ages 3 through 21.

*Time to Administer:* 15 minutes to 25 minutes.

*Technical Adequacy:* Standardization sample is adequate, reliability is weak for some age groups. Validity is adequate.

*Suggested Uses:* Assesses listening comprehension, oral expression, and written expression.

---

*Standardization.* Standardization of the *OWLS* occurred between April 1992 and August 1993. The standardization sample was based on 1991 U.S. Census Bureau data and included 1,985 individuals who represented strata of age, gender, race, ethnic group, geographic region, and economic status, based on the mother's level of education. The three scales of the OWLS were co-normed.

*Reliability.* The test presents reliability information for split-half reliability, test-retest reliability, and interrater reliability. For the Listening Comprehension Scale, the split-half reliability coefficients range from .75 (age 8) to .89 (age 4); for the Oral Expression Scale, the coefficients range from .76 (ages 19 through 21) to .91 (age 4). For test-retest reliability, the coefficients for the Listening Comprehension Scale range from .73 to .80; for the Oral Expression Scale the coefficients range from .77 to .86. Interrater reliability for the Oral Expression Scale ranged from .90 to .93.

*Validity.* The test presents adequate evidence of content, criterion-related, and construct validity. The *OWLS* was administered concurrently with the *Test for Auditory Comprehension of Language–Revised, Peabody Picture Vocabulary Test–Revised, Clinical Evaluation of Language Fundamentals–Revised, Kaufman Assessment Battery for Children, Wechsler Intelligence Scale for Children–Third Edition, Kaufman Brief Intelligence Test, Kaufman Test of Educational Achievement, Comprehensive Form,* and the *Woodcock Reading Mastery Tests–Revised.*

While test developers conducted small studies with students who were identified as having a speech impairment, language delay, language impairment, mental disability, learning disability, hearing impairment, or as receiving Chapter One assistance in reading, these studies were not part of the standardization sample. These studies produced limited results because each group participated in only one study and because the samples were so small.

*Summary.* The *OWLS* is an individualized test of oral and written language. The instrument provides in-depth information regarding the use of oral language, including vocabulary, syntax, pragmatics, and higher-order thinking, and the use of written language. Internal and test-retest reliability is weak for some age groups. Interrater reliability is good for the Oral Expression Scale. The test presents adequate evidence of validity.

## Peabody Picture Vocabulary Test–Third Edition

The *Peabody Picture Vocabulary Test–Third Edition (PPVT-III)* (Dunn and Dunn, 1997) measures receptive language (vocabulary) for individuals 2 years, 5 months through 90+ years of age. In the development of this revised instrument, a bias review panel reviewed test items, and an analysis for item bias by race/ethnicity, gender, and region was completed. Box 10.4 shows the test's parameters.

The test consists of a series of pictures or test plates that include depictions of individuals from various ethnic backgrounds and individuals with disabilities. Each plate has four pictures

---

**BOX 10.4**    *Peabody Picture Vocabulary Test–Third Edition (PPVT–III)*

*Publication Date:* 1997

*Purposes:* Measures receptive language skills in children, youth, and adults.

*Age/Grade Levels:* Ages 2 years, 5 months through 90+ years.

*Time to Administer:* 5 minutes to 10 minutes.

*Technical Adequacy:* Standardization sample, validity, and reliability adequate.

*Suggested Uses:* Assesses receptive language skills for Standard American English. A Spanish edition, the *Test de Vocabulario en Imágenes Peabody (TVIP)*, is based on items translated from the *PPVT–R*.

---

and the examinee must point to the one that best tells the meaning of the word (Figure 10.3). This instrument has two parallel forms, Form IIIA and Form IIIB. This test is also available in Spanish *(TVIP: Test de Vocabulario en Imágenes Peabody)*. The *TVIP* (Dunn, Lugo, Padilla, and Dunn, 1986) measures the receptive vocabulary of Spanish-speaking students, ages 2 years, 5 months through 18 years.

*Administration.* The *PPVT–III* is an individually administered test.

*Scoring.* Examiners record the individual's response to each test item and mark the item pass/fail. Raw scores are converted to standard scores, percentiles, stanines, NCEs, or age equivalents and evaluators can calculate confidence intervals at the 68, 90, and 95 percent level. The *PPVT–III* standard score has a mean of 100 and a standard deviation of 15.

*Standardization.* The norming sample consisted of 2,725 individuals ages 2 years, 5 months through 90 years. Based on the 1994 population survey, the sample reflects controls for age, gender, race/ethnicity, region, and SES (based on parent or self education level). In the Spanish version, norms are available for both combined and separate Mexican and Puerto Rican standardization samples.

*Reliability.* Internal consistency reliabilities indicated a high degree of item uniformity within each of the forms: correlations ranged from .83 to .97 with a median reliability of .94 for Form IIIA and .91 for Form IIIB. Test-retest and alternate form reliabilities were high.

*Validity.* The test manual reports rationale to support content and construct validity. The results of criterion-related validity studies with instruments of intelligence and oral language and two small studies with the *PPVT–III* and the *OWLS* show correlations in the moderate to high range (.63 to .83). The reason for this range is

Training Plate D

**FIGURE 10.3    Peabody Picture Vocabulary Test–Third Edition**

*Source:* From the *Peabody Picture Vocabulary Test–Third Edition* © 1997 by Lloyd M. Dunn and Leota M. Dunn. America Guidance Service, Inc., 4201 Woodland Road, Circle Pines, MN 55014. Reprinted with permission of the Authors/ Publisher. All rights reserved.

that the *PPVT–III* only measures one area of language, receptive vocabulary, while the *OWLS* measures language in a broad context. Additional criterion-related validity studies would be helpful.

Several small studies examined the performance of different clinical groups matched to control groups. The clinical groups represented specific diagnostic or special education categories including: speech impairment, language delay, language impairment, mental retardation, learning disability (reading), and hearing impairment, and included gifted students as well as adults with mild mental retardation.

***Summary.***    The *Peabody Picture Vocabulary Test–III* is a standardized instrument for assessing receptive language skills in children, youth, and adults from 2 years, 5 months through 90+

years of age. The drawings that illustrate the stimulus words consist of gender and ethnic balance. The instrument is well normed and technically adequate, although additional criterion-related validity studies would be helpful.

This instrument is available in Spanish, *TVIP: Test de Vocabulario en Imágenes Peabody*, and assesses receptive vocabulary of Spanish-speaking students. The *TVIP* is a direct translation of an earlier version of the *PPVT–III*, the *Peabody Picture Vocabulary Test–R* (Dunn and Dunn, 1981).

## Preschool Language Scale–3

The *Preschool Language Scale–3 (PLS–3)* (Zimmerman, Steiner, and Pond, 1992) measures language acquisition and prelanguage skills in children ages birth through 6 years, 11 months. See Box 10.5 for the test's parameters. The test has two subscales: an auditory comprehension and an expressive communication that includes preverbal communication skills. The test also has a Spanish-language version, the *Preschool Language Scale–3, Spanish Edition*, that is designed to test receptive and expressive language in Span-

ish. According to the manual, common dialectal variations are listed for testing children who live in different Spanish-speaking regions, including Cuba, Mexico, Guatemala, and Puerto Rico.

*Administration.* This instrument takes approximately 20 minutes to 30 minutes to administer. Both English and Spanish versions use the same materials.

*Scoring.* The test reports scores as standard scores and percentile ranks by age. Language age equivalents are also available.

*Standardization.* Approximately 1,200 children from ages 2 weeks through 6 years, 11 months participated in the standardization sample. The sample was stratified by race, parent education level, and geographic region. The sample approximated the 1980 U.S. Census. Spanish-speaking children from various regions in the United States participated in the standardization sample for the Spanish version.

*Reliability.* The test reports three types of reliability: internal consistency, test-retest, and interrater reliability. Reliability coefficients for each type were within the acceptable range.

*Validity.* The test reports three types of validity: content, construct, and concurrent. The authors claim to demonstrate content validity in the fact that the literature documents the language skills that the *PLS–3* tests.

Test developers assessed construct validity by examining whether or not the instrument differentiated between children with no language needs and children with language disorders.

Concurrent validity studies compared the *PLS–3* with several standardized instruments (*Denver Developmental Screening Test II, Preschool Language Scale–Revised,* and the *Clinical Evaluation of Language Fundamentals–Revised*).

*Summary.* The *Preschool Language Scale–3* is a standardized instrument for measuring

---

| **BOX 10.5** | *Preschool Language Scale–3 (PLS–3)* |
|---|---|

*Publication Date:* 1992

*Purposes:* Measures auditory comprehension and expressive communication that includes preverbal communication skills.

*Age/Grade Levels:* Ages 2 weeks through 6 years, 11 months.

*Time to Administer:* 20 minutes to 30 minutes.

*Technical Adequacy:* Norming sample is based on 1980 U.S. Census and will need to be renormed and restandardized.

*Suggested Uses:* Assesses language acquisition and prelanguage skills in children. A Spanish edition is designed to test receptive and expressive language in Spanish.

preverbal and language skills in young children ages birth through 6 years, 11 months. The norming sample is representative of the 1980 U.S. Census according to race, parent education level, and geographic region of the country. Reliability studies report good internal consistency and high test-retest and interrater reliability coefficients. Construct validity studies found the instrument to be somewhat successful in identifying children who had previously been identified as having a language disorder. The *Preschool Language Scale–3, Spanish Edition*, assesses Spanish expressive and receptive language skills. The instrument addresses the common Spanish dialects and is useful for children who come from different geographic regions.

## Test of Adolescent and Adult Language–3

The *Test of Adolescent and Adult Language–3 (TOAL–3)* (Hammill, Brown, Larsen, and Wiederholt, 1994) assesses language skills in individuals ages 12 years through 24 years, 11 months. The test consists of ten areas, including listening, speaking, reading, writing, spoken language, written language, vocabulary, grammar, receptive language, and expressive language. Box 10.6 describes the test's parameters.

***Administration.*** The *TOAL–3* can be administered individually or to a small group. Administration time is one to three hours.

***Scoring.*** Raw scores transform to composite quotients, with a mean of 100 and a standard deviation of 15 for each of the ten areas assessed. Additionally, obtaining an Overall Language Ability quotient is possible.

***Standardization.*** The standardization sample derives from the 1990 U.S. Census. The *TOAL–3* was standardized on approximately 3,000 individuals who reflect controls for region, gender, age, race, and residence.

***Reliability.*** The test presents reliability information for internal consistency and test-retest reliability, and all coefficients exceed .80.

***Validity.*** The test gives adequate evidence of content, criterion-related, and construct validity. The *TOAL–3* was administered concurrently with the *Test of Language Development–I:2, Peabody Picture Vocabulary Test, Detroit Test of Learning Abilities–3*, and *Test of Written Language–2*.

***Summary.*** The *TOAL–3* assesses language skills in individuals ages 12 years through 24 years, 11 months. The test consists of ten areas: listening, speaking, reading, writing, spoken language, written language, vocabulary, grammar, receptive language, and expressive language. Evidence of reliability and validity appears to be adequate.

---

**BOX 10.6**    *Test of Adolescent and Adult Language–3 (TOAL–3)*

*Publication Date:* 1994

*Purposes:* Assesses listening, speaking, reading, writing, spoken language, written language, vocabulary, grammar, receptive language, and expressive language.

*Age/Grade Levels:* Ages 12 years through 24 years, 11 months.

*Time to Administer:* One to three hours.

*Technical Adequacy:* The standardization sample, reliability, and validity are adequate.

*Suggested Uses:* Assesses language skills in youth and young adults.

---

## Test of Language Development–Primary: Third Edition

The *Test of Language Development–Primary: Third Edition (TOLD–P:3)* (Newcomer and Hammill, 1997) is for children ages 4 through 8. According to the manual, the purposes of the *TOLD–P:3* are (1) to identify children who are

BOX 10.7 *Test of Language Development–Primary: 3 (TOLD–P:3)*

*Publication Date:* 1997

*Purposes:* Assesses language skills.

*Ages/Grade Levels:* Ages 4 through 8.

*Time to Administer:* 30 minutes to one hour.

*Technical Adequacy:* The standardization sample, reliability, and validity are adequate.

*Suggested Use:* As part of a comprehensive assessment in determining eligibility or in evaluating a child's progress.

significantly below their peers in language proficiency, (2) to determine specific strengths and weaknesses in language skills, (3) to document progress in language as a result of an intervention program, and (4) to measure language in research studies. The test consists of the following nine subtests: Picture Vocabulary, Relational Vocabulary, Oral Vocabulary, Grammatic Understanding, Sentence Imitation, Grammatic Completion, Word Discrimination, Phonemic Analysis, and Word Articulation. Box 10.7 describes the test's parameters.

*Administration.* There are no time limits on the *TOLD–P:3* and the time to administer the test may vary from 30 minutes to one hour.

*Scoring.* Test examiners may transform raw scores into standard scores, percentiles, and age equivalent quotients for the composites. The manual explains the calculation of composite scores well.

*Standardization.* One thousand children from 28 states, selected to represent 1990 U.S. census data, participated in the *TOLD–P:3* standardization.

*Reliability.* The examiner's manual reports three types of reliability: internal consistency, test-retest, and interscorer. The *TOLD–P:3*

meets acceptable criteria (r = .80) for subtests as well as composites.

*Validity.* The examiner's manual provides evidence for content, construct, and criterion validity.

*Summary.* The *Test of Language Development–Primary: Third Edition (TOLD–P:3)* is a norm-referenced instrument. The test is for use with children ages 4 through 8 and is individually administered. Reliability and validity are adequate. The test may be useful in identifying children with speech and language impairments.

## Concerns about Standardized Tests of Oral Language

### Receptive Language

The assessment of receptive language requires determining the student's understanding of language. Many standardized tests use symbols in test items to represent word meanings, then take symbol recognition as a key measure of receptive language; therefore teachers must examine these symbols for appropriateness and clarity. We know that during an individual's cognitive development, understanding of symbols moves from concrete to abstract levels. A test item that measures the student's understanding of common objects in the environment might include the task, "Point to the ball." Test developers vary in how they represent the object "ball," that is, some pictures provide a more abstract representation than others. In the following list of test materials, how could the items be ordered from most concrete to most abstract?

black and white line drawing of a ball

cartoon of a ball

photograph of a ball

The test should represent items in an appropriate way for the student. For example, items presented in abstract terms or items that are culture-bound may not be a true measure of the student's receptive language. The type of symbols used, the inclusion of regional or cultural items familiar to the individual, and the response method that the student receives to indicate a choice are all particularly salient factors in the assessment of receptive language skills.

## Expressive Language

An individual must have a reason for using language as well as one for wanting to respond. Young children may not care to perform, or a student may not want to comply with the examiner's request. The student's need or desire to communicate will directly affect the assessment results from standardized instruments.

## Connecting Assessment with Instruction

Alternative assessment approaches can be more effective in connecting assessment with instruction than the use of standardized instruments. In the following section, we examine some of these assessment approaches.

## Language Probes

A **language probe** is a sampling of words or sounds that elicit specific information on a receptive or expressive skill (Polloway and Smith, 2000). For example, the high school special education teacher in a life skills class selects six objects from a job setting. The teacher presents each object to the student twice and the teacher asks, "What is this? What is this used for?" The teacher sets the criteria of correct responses for each item. Probes are helpful diagnostic techniques and assist in planning instruction because they take advantage of the natural environment.

## Language Samples

**Language samples** are examples of a student's use of language, such as explaining a topic of interest, telling a story, or stating and supporting an opinion. Language samples yield information about the student's vocabulary, use of syntax, understanding of semantics, proficiency in articulation, and the ability to use language in functional ways. Samples should also include examples of conversations with peers.

Samples of the student's language can be tape-recorded or written on a chart. Teachers and parents collect samples of the student's language during various daily routines, activities, and assignments. Commercial instruments for assessing speech and language skills can supplement this information.

## MLUs

Earlier in this chapter we described the term mean length of utterance (MLU) and the way teachers calculate MLUs by using a child's language sample. Sometimes teachers who want a quick sample of a child's language will gather several MLUs over the course of the day. MLUs are useful in monitoring a young child's progress in language development or an older student's progress in the increasing use of language for communication in functional life skills.

## Other Approaches

In previous chapters, we describe and examine other helpful approaches in linking assessment questions to instruction. In assessing oral language, these approaches aid the teacher in gathering information and providing feedback to students and parents regarding skill-level and progress. These approaches include:

- oral descriptions
- written descriptions
- checklists and questionnaires
- interviews
- conferences
- audio- and videotapes
- discussions with students, parents, and teachers

*Physical, learning, and social environments enhance communication skills.*

## Observing the Student within the Environment

In previous chapters we discuss the importance of considering the student within the physical, learning, and social environments. The interactions between the student and the environment are important assessment considerations when assessing oral language.

### Physical Environment

The physical setting can influence the student's development and use of language. Observations outside the regular classroom, such as in the hallways, cafeteria, and playground, provide a better understanding of the student's language than in the more structured classroom (Moran, 1996).

### Learning Environment

The learning environment influences and promotes the development of a student's language. For example, the types of questions a teacher asks directly influence the level of response that a student gives. Which of the following questions would encourage you to continue the conversation? Did you go to the movies this weekend? What was the name of the movie you saw? What was the movie about? Some questions require a yes or no; these are minimal-response questions. Some questions require students to think about the materials that they are using; these are thought-provoking questions and may require a phrase or a few sentences to answer. Other questions require students to think and weigh possible responses; they are open-ended questions.

In addition to questioning techniques, there are other teaching strategies to promote the development of oral language. Expansion and modeling are two such strategies that are effective in the classroom.

*Expansion.*    Expansion is a strategy that helps students learn syntax by supplying omitted structures. Billy, who is in kindergarten, told his teacher, "I want to use that thing." His teacher answered, "You want to use the scale at the science table?" The Snapshot of Nina describes how her teacher is helping Nina develop oral language skills.

*Modeling.*    In addition to expansion, teachers can assist students in learning semantic features by modeling or by combining the two.

*Conversation one:*

**AGATA:**  My brother got shot at the doctor's yesterday.

**TEACHER:**  Don't say "got" say "had a shot."

*Conversation two:*

**AGATA:**  My brother got shot at the doctor's yesterday.

**TEACHER:**  Your brother had a shot at the doctor's yesterday? And did you get a shot at the doctor's too?

If you were Agata, which conversation would encourage you to continue telling about your experience? Teachers are more effective when they use expansion and modeling frequently and use correction sparingly. A checklist of strategies for supporting language can be found in Figure 10.4.

## Social Environment

The social environment is important to the development of self-concept and self-esteem. These, in turn, contribute to skills in communicating effectively with others, in communicating

**SNAPSHOT ■ *Nina***

Nina is in the ninth grade and enjoys all her classes in school. Nina also has mental retardation and receives special education and related services. Her IEP states that the speech and language pathologist will work with Nina and will consult with her special education teacher. Her special education teacher has been working with the speech and language pathologist to provide a rich language environment not only for Nina but for all the students in her classroom. Her teacher encourages Nina to expand her vocabulary and to articulate clearly so that others can understand her. Assessment focuses on planning for instruction and evaluating progress.

Each week the teacher invites the students to share a story or discuss current community and national events. Each student has an individual audiotape and is encouraged to make a recording of his or her individual participation. The following segment reflects Nina's latest recording.

> The School Boar (Board) is going to meet tonight. My father is going. They are going to vo (vote). Many people want low (lower) tax (taxes). I don't want them to cut the swim (swimming program). Everyone should vo (vote).

Nina's teacher will replay the sample for Nina, and they will discuss whether to add it to Nina's portfolio.

**FIGURE 10.4**    *Checklist for Observing a Language-Rich Environment*

**Observation setting:**

*Physical Environment*

1. How does the physical setting encourage conversations among students?

*Learning Environment*

2. Does the teacher provide materials and activities that encourage discussion?
3. Does the teacher create student groups during some learning activities?
4. Does the teacher use appropriate modeling of language?
5. Does the teacher provide opportunities for students to use language for different purposes?

   For example:
   _____ recalling a story or event
   _____ dictating directions
   _____ presenting facts or an opinion
   _____ other

6. Does the teacher provide opportunities for using language with different audiences?

   For example:
   _____ telling a fable to younger children
   _____ making a presentation to the PTA
   _____ describing an exhibit to community members
   _____ taking a position on an issue and defending it to peers
   _____ other

7. Does the teacher employ techniques to enhance language opportunities?

   For example:
   _____ using expansion techniques
   _____ asking questions that are thought-provoking or open-ended
   _____ other

*Social Environment*

8. Does the school day provide for "free time" socialization among students?

   For example:
   _____ informal time before classes begin
   _____ informal time before departure at end of day
   _____ other

9. Is lunchtime scheduled in such a way as to support socialization?

   _____ sufficient time to eat and socialize
   _____ students have choices where they may sit
   _____ students are allowed to talk
   _____ other

with a variety of audiences, and in listening to others. By observing the social environment, teachers can study the relationships students have with peers and adults. Positive and supportive relationships influence language usage.

## Students with Severe Communication Disorders

Some students have severe communication disorders as a result of or in combination with other disabilities, including motor impairments, developmental disabilities, or pervasive developmental disorder (PDD). These disabilities affect the ability to communicate.

### Augmentative or Alternative Communication Systems

Some students with severe physical disabilities are not able to use oral language efficiently. For example, ten-year-old Felix is an honor-roll student who loves basketball games. He has cerebral palsy and uses a motorized wheelchair. The cerebral palsy has affected Felix's ability to use oral language. Although he can produce some sounds, his oral speech is not an effective way to communicate.

Felix, like many other students with severe physical disabilities, uses an **augmentative or alternative communication (AAC)** system for oral language assistance. AAC, which IDEA considers to be assistive technology, is any method or device that assists communication. IDEA provides for the functional evaluation of a child with a disability and assistance in selecting, acquiring, and using an assistive technology (AT) device. An AAC device could be a picture book or a communication board comprising symbols. These materials require the student to point to a picture, symbol, or letter by using a finger, toe, or headstick.

Many AAC systems program synthesized speech (produced electronically) or digitized speech (human speech recorded using a microphone) into the device. This type of AAC enables students with severe communication disabilities to participate more fully among peers without disabilities. Students may access the device in any number of ways: by pointing to pictures, by using a single switch, or by activating the device through eye gaze. These access methods provide a wider range of input options than traditional communication books and boards. The communication device can store frequently used messages, and allows the user to access a prestored message with only one keystroke. Some systems have a word prediction feature for older children who are using written language. However, it is important to remember that AAC is only a part of a student's communication system. AAC users, as well as other people, employ a variety of communication forms, including gestures or eye gaze, eye blinks, and winks.

***Assessment for AAC.*** The assessment and selection of a specific communication device should be a team decision, including the individual (when possible), family members, a speech and language pathologist, an occupational therapist, and an educator, as well as other interested team members. The assessment of an individual for an augmentative/alternative communication device depends on a number of factors, including chronological age, imitative ability, motor control, cognitive ability, and visual needs. As members of the team, educators contribute information on classroom and academic performance. Educators assist other team members by defining the communications skills the student needs to complete academic and vocational courses and to interact with classmates. Some of the key questions for teachers, students, and family members to consider during an assessment are listed in Figure 10.5.

***Concerns about Assessing Students with Severe Speech and Language Disabilities.*** Evaluators must use caution in assessing communication development and in identifying prerequisite skills, as well as in drawing assumptions. Students with some types of disabilities such as autism or pervasive developmental disorder (PDD) conventionally experience great

**FIGURE 10.5** *Questionnaire for Assessment of an Augmentative/Alternative Communication Device for a Student*

1. What are the environments where the student spends a portion of the day?
   _____ home
   _____ school
   _____ after-school care
   _____ other (please specify)

2. What types of communication does the student presently use?     How well do others understand?

   _____ points                                                    poor     good     excellent
   _____ gestures                                                  poor     good     excellent
   _____ eye gazes                                                 poor     good     excellent
   _____ other (please  specify)                                   poor     good     excellent

3. During a typical day:

   **a.** with whom might the student interact?

   _____   _____   _____

   _____   _____   _____

   _____   _____   _____

   **b.** what are some messages that the student might use?

   To state a feeling:

   To make a request:

   To ask a question:

   To greet someone or say good-bye:

4. How could additional opportunities to communicate be provided:

   **a.** by modifying the present system?

   **b.** by using another device?

difficulty with expressive language. Students with severe communication disorders can have poor—or excellent—receptive language skills but show little indication of them.

## Preferred Practices

Teachers must identify young students who are experiencing difficulties as soon as possible or early problems in oral language will develop into difficulties with written language and reading.

Once teachers have identified students, best practice recommends ongoing assessment activities for the purpose of planning instruction. Teachers also need opportunities to conduct observations of language-rich classrooms. Classroom observations should focus on aspects that support language development and build language skills. Teachers need opportunities to plan and discuss helpful strategies with other teachers and the speech and language pathologist. Coordinating classroom activities with speech and language therapy will enhance student skills.

## Extending Learning

1. Create a checklist for observing the physical, learning, or social environment. Visit two different classrooms and use your checklist to identify aspects in the environment that support the students' oral language.

2. Ask a friend to tape a conversation of you working with a student. Conduct an analysis of the tape. How did you support the student's use of language? Did you use expansion or modeling strategies? What types of questions did you pose (minimal response, thought-provoking, or open-ended)? What might you do differently next time?

3. Interview a speech and language pathologist regarding assessment tools. What assessment approaches does this individual use in gathering information about content, form, and use?

4. Reread the Snapshot about Nina. What would you say about Nina's language sample on a simple analysis form?

    Form:

    Content:

    Use:

    How might the teacher use this information in planning instruction? Check your ideas with the suggestions described in the section of this chapter on the learning environment.

5. Obtain two or more standardized tests for assessing oral language. Compare and contrast the content of the two instruments. Would one of these instruments be helpful in answering assessment questions identified in one of the Snapshots in this chapter?

6. Evaluate the technical aspects of one of the commercial instruments. Develop your own format for evaluating or use the format suggested in Chapter 3.

## References

Bandura, A. (1977). *Social learning theory.* Englewood Cliffs, NJ: Prentice-Hall.

Brigance, A. H. (1991). *Brigance® inventory of early development–revised.* No. Billerica, MA: Curriculum Associates.

Brigance, A. H. (1999). *Brigance® comprehensive inventory of basic skills–revised.* No. Billerica, MA: Curriculum Associates.

Brownell, R., (ed.) (2000). *Expressive one-word picture vocabulary test.* Novato, CA: Academic Therapy.

Burnette, J. (2000). Assessment of culturally and linguistically diverse students for special education eligibility (ERIC EC Digest N. E604) [online]. Retrieved April 26, 2001. Available: http://ericec.org/digests/e604.html.

Carrow-Woolfolk, E. (1996). *Oral and written language scales.* Minneapolis, MN: American Guidance Service.

Chomsky, N. (1967). The formal nature of language. In *Biological foundations of language*, ed. E. Lenneberg. New York: John Wiley.

Dunn, L. M., and L. M. Dunn (1981). *Peabody picture vocabulary test–revised.* Circle Pines, MN: American Guidance Service.

Dunn, L. M., and L. M. Dunn (1997). *Peabody picture vocabulary test–third edition.* Circle Pines, MN: American Guidance Service.

Dunn, L. M., D. E. Lugo, E. R. Padilla, and L. M. Dunn (1986). *Test de vocabulario en imágenes Peabody.* Circle Pines, MN: American Guidance Service.

Hammill, D. D., and P. L. Newcomer (1997). *Test of language development–intermediate: third edition.* Austin, TX: PRO-ED.

Hammill, D. D., V. L. Brown, S. C. Larsen, and J. L. Wiederholt (1994). *Test of adolescent and adult language: third edition.* Austin, TX: PRO-ED.

Hresko, W. P., D. K. Reid, and D. D. Hammill (1999). *Test of early language development: third edition.* Austin, TX: PRO-ED.

Hresko, W. P., D. K. Reid, and D. D. Hammill (1982). *Prueba del desarrollo inicial del lenguaje.* Austin, TX: PRO-ED.

Improving results for culturally and linguistically diverse students. (2000). *Research Connections* 7 (Fall): 1.

Kaiser, A. P., C. L. Alpert, and S. F. Warren (1988). *Language and communication disorders.* In *Handbook of developmental and physical disabilities*, ed. V. B. VanHasselt, P. S. Strain, and M. Hersen. New York: Pergamon Press.

Moran, M. R. (1996). Educating children with communication disorders. In *Exceptional children in today's schools*, 3d ed., ed. E. L. Meyen (281–314). Denver, CO: Love.

Newcomer, P. L., and D. D. Hammill (1997). *Test of language development–primary: third edition.* Austin, TX: PRO-ED.

Phelps-Terasaki, D., and T. Phelps-Gunn (1992). *Test of pragmatic language.* Austin, TX: PRO-ED.

Polloway, E. A., and T. E. C. Smith (2000). *Language instruction for students with disabilities.* 2d ed. Denver, CO: Love.

Roseberry-McKibbin, C. (1995). Distinguishing language differences from language disorders in linguistically and culturally diverse students. *Multicultural Education* (Summer): 12–16.

Semel, E., E. H. Wiig, and W. Secord (1996a). *Clinical evaluation of language fundamentals.* 3d ed. San Antonio, TX: The Psychological Corporation, Harcourt Brace Jovanovich.

Semel, E., E. H. Wiig, and W. Secord (1996b). *Technical manual.* San Antonio, TX: The Psychological Corporation, Harcourt Brace Jovanovich.

Tanchak, T. L., and C. Sawyer (1995). Augmentative communication. In *Assistive technology: A resource for school, work, and community,* ed. K. F. Flippo, K. J. Inge, and J. M. Barcus. Baltimore: Paul H. Brookes.

Wallace, G., and D. D. Hammill (2002). *Comprehensive receptive and expressive vocabulary test.* 2d ed. Austin, TX: PRO-ED.

Williams, K. T. (1997). *Expressive vocabulary test.* Circle Pines, MN: American Guidance Service.

Woodcock, R. W. (1991). *Woodcock language proficiency battery–revised English form.* Itasca, IL: Riverside.

Woodcock, R. W., and A. F. Muñoz-Sandoval (1995). *Woodcock language proficiency battery–Spanish form.* Itasca, IL: Riverside.

Woodcock, R. W., and A. F. Muñoz-Sandoval (2001). *Woodcock/Muñoz language survey, normative update.* Itasca, IL: Riverside.

Zimmerman, I. L., V. G. Steiner, and R. E. Pond (1992). *Preschool language scale–3.* San Antonio, TX: The Psychological Corporation.

# 11

# *Mathematics*

## Overview

The National Council of the Teachers of Mathematics (NCTM) introduced a vision of mathematics instruction that has changed the direction of teaching and assessment of mathematics (National Council of the Teachers of Mathematics, 1989, 1991a). This comprehensive approach to mathematics instruction means that students engage in a study of mathematics that

> includes the ability to explore, conjecture, and reason logically; to solve nonroutine problems; to communicate about and through mathemat-

ics; and to connect ideas within mathematics and between mathematics and other intellectual activity. Mathematical power also involves the development of personal self-confidence and a disposition to seek, evaluate, and use quantitative and spatial information in solving problems and in making decisions. Students' flexibility, perseverance, interest, curiosity, and inventiveness also affect the realization of mathematical power. (NCTM, 1991b, p. 1)

The thrust of this initiative is the precept that *all* students regardless of their ability, culture, ethnicity, race, language, geographic region of origin, gender, disability, or economic status will receive high-quality mathematics instruction and assessment. The study of mathematics builds on students' knowledge or prior experiences and actively involves them as doers of mathematics.

## Chapter Objectives

After completing this chapter you should be able to:

- Understand contemporary views of mathematics instruction.
- Explain the integral link between mathematics instruction and assessment.

- Describe approaches to mathematics assessment.
- Describe how the physical, learning, and social environments influence mathematics performance.

## What Shapes Our Views

The contemporary view of mathematics instruction derives from the following beliefs:

- All students need to learn mathematics in order to function successfully in the world today.
- All students must develop skills and confidence that will enable them to be capable problem solvers.
- All students should be able to communicate and reason mathematically.
- All students need to value mathematics as important and useful. (Trafton and Claus, 1994)

Today's mathematics programs should comprise rich mathematics problems that build on students' knowledge or prior experiences and that actively engage students in accomplishing mathematics. According to the National Council of the Teachers of Mathematics (NCTM), knowing mathematics means doing mathematics. The doing of mathematics necessarily involves students in problems and tasks that

- are mathematically meaningful
- require students to think rather than to memorize

- require students to hypothesize and to generalize
- generate further mathematics questions or problems
- require that students learn while solving a task
- allow for more than one acceptable answer (Speer and Brahier, 1994).

## Evaluating Mathematical Power

According to the *Statement of Principles on Assessment in Mathematics and Science Education* (U.S. Department of Education and the National Science Foundation (NSF), n.d.), all assessment programs have as their foundation the equity principle. This means that, "Assessment should support every student's opportunity to learn important mathematics and science" (p. 9). In designing the *Statement of Principles*, the U.S. Department of Education and the NSF emphasize that *all* students are to participate in instruction and assessment activities and that assessment instruments by design and intent are to be equitable. While not specifically mentioning students with disabilities, these major government organizations indicate that all assessment tools must consider or be applicable to *all* students and that they must yield information that will improve student learning. Accordingly, all assessment programs should

- assess knowledge and understanding in complex ways and include the assessment of higher-order thinking and problem solving
- be fair, valid, and reliable
- demonstrate knowledge of how students develop and learn
- demonstrate administration procedures that can be interpreted only for the program's designed purposes
- work to improve instruction and develop curriculum
- promote equity by providing optimal opportunities for students to demonstrate their knowledge

Equitable evaluation of mathematical abilities and skills presupposes a variety of approaches in order to reflect an understanding of students' abilities, culture, ethnicity, race, language, geographic region of origin, gender, disability, and economic status in assessments. Educators must place an emphasis on students solving real-world problems that involve making conclusions, understanding relationships, and generating new questions (Marolda and Davidson, 1994). Assessment methods include standardized testing as well as other kinds of approaches. Table 11.1 describes the assessment purposes and approaches of mathematics assessment.

## *Responding to Diversity*

Multicultural mathematics is the study of the way persons all over the world use mathematics in a variety of activities, including counting, measuring, performing calculations, using calendars, building homes, and playing games. Attention to the ways persons of various cultures use mathematics is important to our understanding of equity in the teaching and the assessment of mathematics (Zaslavsky, 1996). Consider the following:

- The Mende people of Sierra Leone and the Yup'ik (Innuit, or Eskimo) count by twenties. They count fingers, and toes are counted symbolically.
- The Chinese, Islamic, and Hebrew calendars are lunar. For the Islamic calendar time is reckoned from 622 C.E.
- People often base measures of length on body parts. In fact, the "foot" is still part of our system. Other cultures use the palm, hand span, and the cubit. (The cubit is an old measure based on the length of a person's forearm.) The Yup'ik people use the width of the fingers to measure the openings for fish traps.

These few examples point out the importance of using assessments that are sensitive to specific customs and practices. A student's culture, ethnicity, race, language, geographic region of origin, gender, disability, and economic status has to be considered when assessing mathematics performance.

## *Standardized Instruments*

This section describes the use of standardized, norm-referenced tests of mathematical abilities. Referring to the instruments listed in Table 11.2 on page 284, standardized, norm-referenced tests are effective for screening, determining eligibility, and conducting a program evaluation. Evaluators can compare scores from these tests with the performance of students of similar age or grade who are part of a national standardization sample. In addition to the individual tests of mathematical abilities in Table 11.2, Table 11.3 on page 285 contains a list of tests that have mathematics subtests.

## KeyMath–Revised/Normative Update: A Diagnostic Inventory of Essential Mathematics

*KeyMath–Revised/Normative Update: A Diagnostic Inventory of Essential Mathematics (KeyMath–R/NU)* (Connolly, 1998) is an individually

**TABLE 11.1** *Assessment Questions, Purposes, and Approaches*

| Assessment Questions | Steps and Purposes | Approaches |
|---|---|---|
| | **Screening** | |
| Is there a possibility of a disability in mathematics? | To determine whether students may have a disability in mathematics and should be referred for further assessment | Norm-referenced instruments<br>Curriculum-based assessments<br>Criterion-referenced assessments<br>Observations<br>Checklists |
| | **Eligibility** | |
| Does the student have a disability in mathematics?<br>What disability does the student have?<br>Does the student meet the criteria for services?<br>What are the strengths and weaknesses in mathematics?<br>Why is the student having trouble doing mathematics?<br>What does the student understand? | To determine if there is a disability in mathematics<br>To compare the student's performance in mathematics with the performance of the peer group<br>To determine specific strengths and weaknesses<br>To understand why the student is having difficulty | Norm-referenced instruments<br>Curriculum-based assessments<br>Criterion-referenced assessments<br>Observations<br>Probes<br>Error analysis<br>Interviews<br>Checklists<br>Student, parent, and/or teacher conferences<br>Performance assessments |

*Connecting Instruction with Assessment*

| | | |
|---|---|---|
| | **Program Planning** | |
| What does the student not understand?<br>Where should instruction in mathematics begin? | To understand what the student knows and does not know in mathematics<br>To plan the student's program in mathematics<br>To determine instructional approaches | Norm-referenced instruments<br>Curriculum-based assessments<br>Criterion-referenced assessments<br>Observations<br>Probes<br>Error analysis<br>Interviews<br>Checklists<br>Student, parent, and/or teacher conferences<br>Performance assessments |
| | **Program Monitoring** | |
| Once instruction begins, is the student making progress in mathematics?<br>Should the instruction be modified? | To understand the pace of instruction<br>To understand what the student knows prior to and after instruction<br>To understand the strategies and concepts the student uses | Curriculum-based assessments<br>Criterion-referenced assessments<br>Observations<br>Probes<br>Error analysis<br>Interviews<br>Checklists |

**TABLE 11.1**  *Continued*

| Assessment Questions | Steps and Purposes | Approaches |
|---|---|---|
| | To monitor the student's program | Student, parent, and/or teacher conferences<br>Portfolios<br>Exhibitions<br>Journals<br>Written descriptions<br>Oral descriptions |
| Has the student met the goals of the IEP in mathematics?<br>Has the instructional program in mathematics been successful for the student?<br>Has the student made progress in mathematics?<br>Has the instructional program achieved its goals? | **Program Evaluation**<br>To determine whether the IEP goals in mathematics have been met<br>To determine whether the goals of the program have been met<br>To evaluate program effectiveness | Curriculum-based assessments<br>Criterion-referenced assessments<br>Observations<br>Probes<br>Error analysis<br>Interviews<br>Checklists<br>Student, parent, and/or teacher conferences<br>Portfolios<br>Exhibitions<br>Journals<br>Written descriptions<br>Oral descriptions<br>Surveys |

administered test of mathematics skills, concepts, and operations. Box 11.1 describes the test's parameters. The *KeyMath–R/NU* is intended for use with children in kindergarten through grade 9. There are two forms and, according to the author, the *KeyMath–R/NU* has the following five uses:

1. To guide general instructional planning
2. To develop remedial instruction
3. To assist in global assessment by making comparisons with the results of other instruments
4. To use as a pretest and posttest instrument when conducting research and program evaluation
5. To assist in assessing the usefulness of mathematics curriculum

When developing the scope and sequence of the test content, the author surveyed the basal mathematics textbooks of many publishers as well as materials published by the National Council of the Teachers of Mathematics, then organized the resulting scope and sequence into three areas: Basic Concepts, Operations, and Applications. These comprise 13 strands, which in turn comprise four domains (Table 11.4 on page 286).

*Administration.* The *KeyMath–R/NU* can be administered by regular and special education teachers, aides, paraprofessionals, counselors, and school psychologists. Depending on the age of the student, it takes approximately 35 minutes to 50 minutes to administer this test. The Snapshot of Kara on page 288 describes how

**TABLE 11.2** *Standardardized Tests of Mathematics*

| Name | Ages/Grades | Group/Individual |
| --- | --- | --- |
| *Diagnostic Screening Tests Math (DSTM)* (Gnagey, 1980) | Grades 1 through 10 | Individual or group |
| *KeyMath–R/NU* (Connolly, 1998) | Grades K through 9 | Individual |
| *Slosson–Diagnostic Math Screener* (S–DMS) (Erford and Boykin, 1996) | Ages 6 years through 13 years | Individual or group |
| *Stanford Diagnostic Mathematics Test* (4th ed.) (Harcourt Brace Educational Measurement, 1995) | Grades 1 through 8 | Individual or group |
| *Test of Early Mathematics Ability (TEMA–2)* (Ginsburg and Baroody, 1990) | Ages 3 years through 8 years, 11 months | Individual |
| *Test of Mathematical Abilities–2 (TOMA–2)* (Brown, Cronin, and McEntire, 1994) | Grades 3 through 12 | Individual |

her teacher evaluated her performance on this test.

***Scoring.*** Raw scores are converted to standard scores, percentile ranks, grade and age equivalents, stanines, and normal curve equivalents. Using an optional scoring procedure for domain scores, evaluators can rate a student's scores as weak, average, or strong. Figure 11.1 on page 287 shows the front cover of the test record form.

***Standardization.*** The *KeyMath–R/NU* was renormed between October 1995 and November 1996. Stratification of the standardization sample reflects categories of age, gender, region, race, ethnicity, and economic status as estimated by parental education. The standardization sample of the *KeyMath–R/NU* was linked to the standardization samples for the *Kaufman Test of Individual Achievement (K–TEA), Peabody Individiual Achievement Test–Revised (PIAT–R)*, and the *Woodcock Reading Mastery Tests–Revised (WRMT–R)*. For the *KeyMath–R/NU* the renorming sample comprised students who were in kindergarten through age 22. Test examinees in the norm sample took one of the complete test batteries and one or more subtests

from another battery to create the linking sample. This linking approach permits the making of comparisons of test performance across batteries.

---

**BOX 11.1** *KeyMath–Revised/ Normative Update: A Diagnostic Inventory of Essential Mathematics (KeyMath–R/NU)*

*Publication Date:* 1998

*Purposes:* Measures mathematics concepts, skills, operations, and applications.

*Age/Grade Levels:* Kindergarten through grade 9.

*Time to Administer:* 35 minutes to 50 minutes.

*Technical Adequacy:* Standardization sample is acceptable. The reliabilities for the subtests and the areas are too low to make instructional decisions. Examiners should determine content validity by comparing the test items with the curriculum for congruence.

*Suggested Use:* Provides evidence of strengths and weaknesses in mathematics knowledge and skills.

**TABLE 11.3**  *Test Batteries That Contain Mathematics Subtests or Mathematics-Related Subtests*

| Name | Ages/Grades |
|------|-------------|
| *BRIGANCE® Inventory of Essential Skills* (Brigance, 1980) | Grades 6 through adulthood |
| *BRIGANCE® Comprehensive Inventory of Basic Skills–Revised* (Brigance, 1999) | Grades K through 9 |
| *BRIGANCE® Assessment of Basic Skills–Spanish Edition* (Brigance, 1984) | Grades K through 8 |
| *BRIGANCE® Life Skills Inventory* (Brigance, 1994) | Vocational Secondary Adult education |
| *BRIGANCE® Employability Skills Inventory* (Brigance, 1995) | Vocational Secondary Adult education job training |
| *BRIGANCE® Inventory of Early Development–Revised* (Brigance, 1991) | Ages birth to 7 years |
| *Basic Achievement Skills Individual Screener (BASIS)* (Sonnenschein, 1983) | Grades 1 through 12 and post–high school |
| *Diagnostic Achievement Battery 2d ed. (DAB–2)* (Newcomer, 1990) | Ages 6 years through 14 years |
| *Diagnostic Achievement Test for Adolescents–2* (Newcomer and Bryant, 1993) | Grades 7 through 12 |
| *Kaufman Assessment Battery for Children (K–ABC)* (Kaufman and Kaufman, 1983) | Ages 2 years, 6 months through 12 years, 6 months |
| *Kaufman Test of Educational Achievement/NU (K–TEA/NU)* (Kaufman and Kaufman, 1998) | Grades 1 through 12; ages 6 years to 18 years, 11 months |
| *Peabody Individual Achievement Test–Revised/NU* (Markwardt, 1998) | Grades K through 12; ages 5 years to 18 years, 11 months |
| *Wide Range Achievement Test–3 (WRAT–3)* (Wilkinson, 1993) | Ages 5 years to 75 years |
| *Wechsler Individual Achievement Test–II* (Harcourt Brace Educational Measurement, 2001) | Grades K through 12; ages 5 years to 19 years, 11 months |
| *Woodcock-Johnson Psychoeducational Battery–III* (Woodcock, McGrew, and Mather, 2001) | Grades K through 12; ages 2 years to 90 years |

***Reliability.***   The author determined alternate-form reliability by retesting approximately 70 percent of the children in grades kindergarten, 2, 4, 6, and 8 who took part in the fall standardization. The tests took between two and four weeks to administer. The reported reliability coefficients are for the subtests, areas, and the total test score. Alternate-form reliability is not available for each grade. For the subtests, the reliability coefficients ranged from .50s to .70s; for the areas, the correlations were in the low .80s. The average alternate-form correlation for the total test was .90.

The test reports split-half reliabilities by grade and calculates them by correlating the odd and even test items. For the subtests, most of the correlations were in the .70s and .80s; for the areas, the split-half reliability coefficients

**TABLE 11.4** *Content Specification of KeyMath-R/NU: Areas, Strands, and Domains*

| AREAS: | Basic Concepts | Operations | Applications |
|---|---|---|---|
| **Strands and domains:** | **Numeration**<br>1. Numbers 0–9<br>2. Numbers 0–99<br>3. Numbers 0–999<br>4. Multidigit numbers and advanced numeration topics<br><br>**Rational Numbers**<br>1. Fractions<br>2. Decimals<br>3. Percents<br><br>**Geometry**<br>1. Spatial and attribute relations<br>2. Two-dimensional shapes and their relations<br>3. Coordinate and transformational geometry<br>4. Three-dimensional shapes and their relations | **Addition**<br>1. Models and basic facts<br>2. Algorithms to add whole numbers<br>3. Adding rational numbers<br><br>**Subtraction**<br>1. Models and basic facts<br>2. Algorithms to subtract whole numbers<br>3. Subtracting rational numbers<br><br>**Multiplication**<br>1. Models and basic facts<br>2. Algorithms to multiply whole numbers<br>3. Multiplying rational numbers<br><br>**Division**<br>1. Models and basic facts<br>2. Algorithms to divide whole numbers<br>3. Dividing rational numbers<br><br>**Mental Computation**<br>1. Computation chains<br>2. Whole numbers<br>3. Rational numbers | **Measurement**<br>1. Comparisons<br>2. Using nonstandard units<br>3. Using standard units—length, area<br>4. Using standard units—weight, capacity<br><br>**Time and Money**<br>1. Identifying passage of time<br>2. Using clocks and clock units<br>3. Monetary amounts to one dollar<br>4. Monetary amounts to one hundred dollars and business transactions<br><br>**Estimation**<br>1. Whole and rational numbers<br>2. Measurement<br>3. Computation<br><br>**Interpreting Data**<br>1. Charts and tables<br>2. Graphs<br>3. Probability and statistics<br><br>**Problem Solving**<br>1. Solving routine problems<br>2. Understanding nonroutine problems<br>3. Solving nonroutine problems |

*Source:* Connolly, A. J. (1998). *KeyMath–Revised/NU.* Circle Pines, MN: American Guidance Service, p. 6. Reprinted with permission of the publisher.

**FIGURE 11.1** KeyMath–Revised/NU Individual Test Record

*Source: KeyMath: A Diagnostic Inventory of Essential Mathematics Revised Normative Update (KeyMath-R/NU) Individual Test Record Summary by Austin J. Connolly © 1988 American Guidance Service, Inc., 4201 Woodland Road, Circle Pines, Minnesota 55014-1796. Reproduced with permission of publisher. All rights reserved. www.agsnet.com*

## SNAPSHOT ■ *Kara*

Kara is a 12-year-old in sixth grade. Her interests include drawing and soccer. Kara has an exuberant sense of humor and loves to play jokes on her friends and family. She has just finished making a book of her drawings that she intends to give to her grandmother who lives with Kara, her 5-year-old brother, John, and her mother and father. Kara was diagnosed as having a learning disability in mathematics when she was in third grade.

### Observation

Kara was observed in her sixth-grade classroom. The 25 other students in the classroom were working in small groups solving problems that the teacher had assigned. The class was lively and the students were engaging in their work—all except Kara. Kara sat with a small group of three other students. Kara appeared to be unsure of how she could contribute to the problem-solving activity. She was quiet, had a puzzled look on her face, and was listening to the students in the group.

### Teacher's Comments

Kara has lagged considerably behind her peers in mathematics. The rest of the class has been working on graphing, geometry, and probability. An examination of Kara's recent homework showed that she has trouble with basic number facts and that she reverses numbers when writing them.

### Summary of Test Performance

At the end of the last school year, the IEP team met to review Kara's program. The special education consultant reported that Kara's full scale intelligence as measured by the *Wechsler Intelligence Scale–III (WISC–III)* was 118, above average. On the *Kaufman Test of Educational Achievement (K–TEA/NU)*, Kara scored above average on the reading and spelling subtests but considerably below average on the Mathematical Applications and Mathematical Computation subtests. On the *KeyMath–Revised/NU* her scores in the areas of Basic Concepts, Operations, and Applications were all well below average.

were in the .90s. The total test reliability coefficients were in the middle to high .90s.

**Validity.** When developing the *KeyMath–R/NU*, the author developed a test blueprint, which detailed the content of the test for the areas, strands, and domains. Next, the author developed items according to the blueprint that was intended to assess mathematics achievement. When using these achievement tests, educators must determine the content validity themselves. Test examiners should review the taught curriculum and determine the extent to which the test items measure the curriculum.

According to the manual, test developers determined construct validity in several ways. The manual presents evidence demonstrating that knowledge about mathematics increases with age, that the subtests intercorrelate with the areas and the total test score, and that scores

on the *KeyMath–R/NU* correlate with scores on other tests of mathematical achievement.

**Summary.** The *KeyMath–Revised/Normative Update: A Diagnostic Inventory of Essential Mathematics* is an individually administered test of mathematics achievement. The reliabilities for the subtests and the areas are too low to make instructional decisions. The educator should determine content validity by comparing the test items with the curriculum for congruence.

## Stanford Diagnostic Mathematics Test

The *Stanford Diagnostic Mathematics Test (SDMT4)* (Harcourt Brace Educational Measurement, 1995) is a norm-referenced test for students in grades 1.5 through 13. The test follows NCTM standards and has six overlapping levels:

| Grade | Level |
|-------|-------|
| 1.5 through 2.5 | red |
| 2.5 through 3.5 | orange |
| 3.5 through 4.5 | green |
| 4.5 through 6.5 | purple |
| 6.5 through 8.9 | brown |
| 9.0 through 13.0 | blue |

The purposes of the *SDMT4* are to assist in making eligibility decisions, diagnose difficulties in mathematics, and evaluate programs and provide information about program effectiveness. The test assesses basic skills and concepts in mathematics, problem solving, and problem-solving strategies.

***Administration.*** The *SDMT4* is a group-administered test. It is not necessary to administer all subtests; the examiner can decide to administer only one or two of the subtests. The items are a combination of multiple choice and free response. Examiners can administer this test individually following standardized procedures for test administration.

***Scoring.*** Raw scores convert to percentiles, stanines, normal curve equivalents, grade equivalents, and scaled scores. Evaluators can hand score the *SDMT4* using a stencil provided by the publisher, or send the test away for machine scoring by the publisher.

***Standardization.*** The standardization sample shows stratification according to socioeconomic status, size of school district, and geographic region.

***Reliability.*** The test reports both alternate-form and internal consistency reliabilities. The reliability coefficients are adequate.

***Validity.*** The test reports content and criterion-related validity. Teachers should examine the test items to determine the extent to which the *SDMT4* matches reading as they have taught it.

***Summary.*** The *Stanford Diagnostic Mathematics Test 4* is a norm-referenced test for students in grades 1.5 through 13. The test has six overlapping levels. The test is intended for group administration. However, it can be useful when administered to individual students.

## Test of Early Mathematics Ability–2

The *Test of Early Mathematics Ability–2 (TEMA–2)* (Ginsburg and Baroody, 1990) is a norm-referenced test that assesses several aspects of mathematical abilities in children ages 3 years through 8 years, 11 months. The *TEMA–2* has 35 informal problems and 30 formal problems. The informal problems measure concepts of relative magnitude, counting skills, and calculation. The formal problems measure reading and writing numerals, number facts, calculated algorithms, and base-ten concepts. Box 11.2 describes the test's parameters.

---

**BOX 11.2**    *Test of Early Mathematics Ability–2 (TEMA–2)*

---

*Publication Date:* 1990

*Purposes:* Measures concepts of relative magnitude, counting skills, calculation, reading and writing numerals, number facts, calculated algorithms, and base-ten concepts.

*Age/Grade Levels:* 3 years through 8 years, 11 months.

*Time to Administer:* 20 minutes.

*Technical Adequacy:* Lacks adequate reliability and validity. The *TEMA–2* is useful as a screening device and may be helpful in identifying strengths and weaknesses. Caution should be used when administering this test to young children because the *TEMA–2* requires listening, reading, writing, and speaking.

*Suggested Use:* May be used for screening purposes.

---

*Administration.* The *TEMA–2* is administered individually to students in approximately 20 minutes. The test requires children to read calculations, listen, respond verbally and nonverbally, and to write numerals.

*Standardization.* The standardization sample combines the sample from the previous edition with additional students selected to approximate the 1980 U.S. Census.

*Scoring.* Raw scores convert to standard scores, percentiles, and age equivalents.

*Reliability.* Internal consistency reliability coefficients range from .92 to .96. The test reports test-retest reliability only for the previous edition.

*Validity.* While there is some evidence of validity, much of it is based on the previous edition. Examiners should carefully compare the mathematics curriculum with the test items in order to determine content validity.

*Summary.* The *Test of Early Mathematics Ability–2 (TEMA–2)* is a norm-referenced test for use with children ages 3 years through 8 years, 11 months. The *TEMA–2* lacks adequate reliability and validity. It may be useful as a screening device and may be helpful in identifying strengths and weaknesses. Educators should be cautious when administering this test to young children because the *TEMA–2* requires listening, reading, writing, and speaking.

## Test of Mathematical Abilities–2

The *Test of Mathematical Abilities–2 (TOMA–2)* (Brown, Cronin, and McEntire, 1994) is a norm-referenced test of attitudes toward mathematics, mathematics vocabulary, computation, general information relating to mathematics, and mathematical story problems. The *TOMA–2* can be individually administered or group-administered to students in grades 3 through 12, and contains five subtests:

*Attitude Toward Math.* Students respond to questions on a 3-point scale on their opinions about mathematics. This scale is an adaptation of the *Estes Attitude Scales* (Estes, Estes, Richards, and Roettger, 1981).

*Vocabulary.* Students read 20 mathematical terms and define them in writing in English. This subtest is administered to students who are at least 11 years old.

*Computation.* Students solve 25 arithmetic problems in writing in an answer booklet.

*General Information.* Students respond orally to 30 problems relating to general applications about mathematics.

*Story Problems.* After reading a word problem, students respond in writing in an answer booklet. This subtest is not administered to students who are nonreaders.

*Administration.* The *TOMA–2* can be individually administered or group-administered.

*Scoring.* Raw scores convert to standard scores and percentile ranks. Subtest scores have a mean of 10 and a standard deviation of 3. The total test scores are called Math Quotients; they have a mean of 100 and a standard deviation of 15. The test examiner can perform an error analysis on individual responses to items that students have written in the student answer booklet.

*Standardization.* The standardization sample for *TOMA–2* includes approximately 1,500 students residing in five states. The sample approximated U.S. Census information according to gender, residence, geographic region, and race.

*Reliability.* Reliability coefficients are in the .80s and .90s. Reliability is acceptable.

*Validity.* While there is some evidence of validity, much of it is from the previous edition. Examiners should carefully compare the mathematics curriculum with the test items in order to determine content validity.

***Summary.*** The *Test of Mathematical Abilities–2 (TOMA–2)* is an individually administered and a group-administered test of various aspects of mathematical abilities. Information of reliability and validity is sketchy. Test examiners should evaluate the content validity of the test. The *TOMA–2* is most useful as a screening test. Box 11.3 lists the test's parameters.

## Connecting Assessment with Instruction

A fundamental principle is that assessment of mathematical abilities and skills form a link with mathematics instruction. Linking instruction with assessment in mathematics means that

• Assessment occurs as a normal part of the student's work. Assessment activities should

---

**BOX 11.3**    *Test of Mathematical Abilities–2 (TOMA–2)*

*Publication Date:* 1994

*Purposes:* Measures attitudes toward mathematics, mathematics vocabulary, computation, general information relating to mathematics, and mathematical story problems.

*Age/Grade Levels:* Grades 3 through 12.

*Time to Adminster:* 45 minutes to 90 minutes.

*Technical Adequacy:* Information on reliability and validity is sparse. Test examiners are encouraged to evaluate the content validity of the test. The *TOMA–2* is best used as a screening measure.

*Suggested Use:* Provides some evidence of strengths and limitations in mathematics knowledge and skills. Should be used in combination with other instruments.

*A teacher discusses a spreadsheet with a student.*

emerge from the teaching situation. The student does not stop work to do an assessment; the work and the assessment are linked. Examples of this type of assessment include the use of journals, notebooks, essays, oral reports, homework, classroom discussions, group work, and interviews. These assessment activities can occur individually or in small groups and can take place during one session or over multiple sessions (Marolda and Davidson, 1994).

• The conditions for assessment are similar to the conditions for doing meaningful tasks. Students should have sufficient time, have access to peers, be able to use appropriate tools (books, calculators, manipulatives, etc.), and have the chance to revise their work.

• Assessment tasks are meaningful and multidimensional. They should provide students with the opportunity to demonstrate mathematical abilities, including problem solving, drawing conclusions, understanding relationships, and generating new questions.

• Feedback to students is specific, meaningful, prompt, and informs the students' thinking about mathematics.

• Students participate in the assessment process. They help to generate and apply standards or rubrics. Self-assessment and peer assessment become part of the assessment process.

One of the most important aspects of assessment is feedback. Standardized, norm-referenced assessment coupled with feedback from peers and teachers encourages the development of mathematical and scientific thinking. Ways in which the teacher can gather information and provide feedback to parents and students include

• criterion-referenced assessment
• probes
• error analysis
• oral descriptions
• written descriptions
• checklists and questionnaires

• interviews
• conferencess
• student journals and notebooks
• performance-based assessment
• portfolios
• exhibitions (NCTM, 1991a)

## Criterion-Referenced Assessment

Instead of comparing a student's performance to a norm group, criterion-referenced tests measure a student's performance with respect to a well-defined content domain (Anastasi, 1988; Berk, 1988). Teachers can use criterion-referenced tests in each of the assessment steps described in Table 11.2. While norm-referenced tests in mathematics allow for discrimination between the performance of individual students on specific test items, criterion-referenced tests provide a description of knowledge, skills, or behaviors in a specific range, or domain, of test items.

**BRIGANCE® Diagnostic Inventories.** The *BRIGANCE® Diagnostic Inventories* are criterion-referenced tests that are similar in purpose, scoring, administration, and interpretation. These inventories assess mastery of mathematics skills and concepts (Table 11.5), and they are useful in program planning and in monitoring programs. Chapter 6 contains a detailed description of the tests.

## Probes

As we discuss in previous chapters, a probe is a diagnostic technique in which the examiner modifies instruction. Probes are helpful in diagnosing and assisting with student problems and assist in planning instruction. For example, suppose a teacher wants to determine whether a third-grade student is ready to proceed to a two-step word problem after mastering one-step word problems.

**TABLE 11.5  BRIGANCE® Inventories**

| Name | Ages/Grades | Mathematics Skills |
|---|---|---|
| *BRIGANCE® Inventory of Essential Skills* (Brigance, 1980) | Grades 4 through 12 | 1. Numbers<br>2. Number Facts<br>3. Computation of Whole Numbers<br>4. Fractions and Mixed Numbers<br>5. Decimals<br>6. Percents<br>7. Measurement<br>8. Metrics<br>9. Math Vocabulary<br>10. Money and Finance |
| *BRIGANCE® Comprehensive Inventory of Basic Skills–Revised* (Brigance, 1999) | Pre-K through 9 | 1. Numbers<br>2. Number Facts<br>3. Computation of Whole Numbers<br>4. Fractions and Mixed Numbers<br>5. Decimals<br>6. Percents<br>7. Measurement/Geometry<br>8. Metrics<br>9. Time<br>10. Money |
| *BRIGANCE® Assessment of Basic Skills–Spanish Edition* (Brigance, 1984) | Grades K through 6 | 1. Number Sequences<br>2. Operations<br>3. Measurement |
| *BRIGANCE® Diagnostic Inventory of Early Development–Revised* (Brigance, 1991) | Ages birth to 7 years | 1. Number Concepts<br>2. Rote Counting<br>3. Reads Numerals<br>4. Numeral Comprehension<br>5. Ordinal Position<br>6. Numerals in Sequence<br>7. Writes Following and Preceding Numerals<br>8. Writes Numerals Dictated<br>9. Addition Combinations<br>10. Subtraction Combinations<br>11. Recognition of Money<br>12. Time |
| *BRIGANCE® Diagnostic Life Skills Inventory* (Brigance, 1994) | Vocational<br>Secondary<br>Adult education | 1. Money<br>2. Operations<br>3. Finance<br>4. Money Management |
| *BRIGANCE® Diagnostic Employability Skills Inventory* (Brigance, 1995) | Vocational<br>Secondary<br>Adult education<br>Job training | 1. Operations<br>2. Fractions<br>3. Measurement<br>4. Geometry<br>5. Math Vocabulary |

The teacher presents a basic two-step word problem to the student and observes the strategies that the student uses to solve the problem. The student may be able to successfully solve the problem, but has difficulty organizing the work. The teacher then can help by showing the student how to draw a grid on paper and put each step of the problem in a cell of the grid. Eventually, using another probe, the teacher is able to use fading to gradually lighten the lines of the grid until the student does not need the grid to successfully complete the problem.

Teachers can implement instructional probes during the process of instruction. When conducting an instructional probe the teacher should document the student's performance during each of the following steps: step 1 (baseline), step 2 (instruction), and step 3 (baseline):

Step 1 (Baseline). The teacher identifies the area of mathematical performance that needs observation and measures whether the student can perform the task. Examples include number recognition, counting, addition, subtraction, and so on.

Step 2 (Instruction). The teacher probes the task. For example, to facilitate number recognition the teacher asks the student to say, trace, recognize, and write a numeral.

Step 3 (Baseline). The teacher measures whether the student can perform the task.

The following list contains three types of modifications for use in probes in mathematics instruction, including examples.

1. *Instructional modifications for use with probes*
   - change from written presentation to oral presentation
   - combine verbal instruction with written explanation
   - require fewer problems to be completed
   - provide additional practice
   - slow the pace of instruction
   - provide additional time to complete problems
   - take tests orally

2. *Materials modifications*
   - use manipulatives
   - place fewer problems on a page
   - use color cues or other cues for mathematical operations
   - simplify the problems
   - combine tactile mode with visual, oral, or kinesthetic modes

3. *Environmental modifications*
   - change location of instruction or test
   - change time of day for instruction or test
   - provide a work area that is quiet and free of distractions
   - change lighting of work area
   - change seating arrangements

## Error Analysis

The purposes of error analysis are to (1) identify the patterns of errors or mistakes that students make in their work; (2) understand why students make the errors; and (3) provide targeted instruction so as to correct the errors. When conducting an error analysis, the teacher checks the student's mathematics problems and categorize the errors. The following is a list of errors that students commonly make in various mathematical areas (Ashlock, 1986; Berman and Friederwitzer, 1981; Kilian, Cahill, Ryan, Sutherland, and Taccetta, 1980; Tindal and Marston, 1990).

### Addition and Subtraction
- lack of understanding of regrouping
- confusion of 1s and 10s in carrying and writing
- forgetting to carry 10s and 100s
- forgetting to regroup when subtracting 10s and 100s
- regrouping when it is not required
- incorrect operation (the student subtracts instead of adding)
- lack of knowledge of basic number facts

### Multiplication and Division
- forgetting to carry in multiplication
- carrying before multiplying

- ignoring place value in division
- recording the answer from left to right
- lack of alignment of work in columns
- lack of knowledge of basic number facts

### Fractions
- incorrect cancellation
- failure to reduce to lowest common denominator
- ignoring the remainder
- incorrect conversion of mixed numbers to fractions

### Word Problems
- difficulty in reading
- inability to relate to context of problem
- inability to understand the language and vocabulary of the problem
- difficulty in identifying the relevant and the irrelevant information
- difficulty in identifying the number of steps required to solve the problem
- trouble in doing mathematical operations (addition, subtraction, multiplication, division)

After conducting an error analysis, summarize the error patterns. Notice, however, that many errors that students make do not fall into a pattern and some patterns that emerge do not indicate a serious problem. Teachers must view error analysis as a preliminary form of assessment and should conduct further evaluation of the student's work.

## Oral Descriptions

Verbal descriptions of a student's work provide immediate feedback to a student by a teacher or peer. Oral descriptions are quick, efficient, and direct, and blend easily into instruction. They must not be off the cuff; oral descriptions should be as well thought out as written descriptions. Oral descriptions are helpful for program planning and program evaluation.

Oral descriptions do have several drawbacks, however. They can be subjective and, since the descriptions are given verbally, there is no permanent record. In addition, specific disabilities limit the ability of the student to understand, remember, or reply to the description.

## Written Descriptions

A written description is a brief narrative that records feedback about the student's work that the student, teachers, or parents can share. A written description, like an oral description, conveys an impression of important aspects of the student's work. Written descriptions are useful for program planning and program evaluation.

Before writing the narrative, the teacher carefully reviews the student's work. The teacher then writes the description, noting areas of strength as well as any problems. A written description provides information to the student about the quality of the work. Because it is a record, the student can refer to it as the student continues to work.

For example, a student is asked to solve the following problem:

> Luke wants to paint one wall of his room. The wall is 20 feet wide and 8 feet high. It takes one can of paint to cover 80 square feet, and the paint is sold at $4.99 a can. What else does Luke need to think of? Make a plan for Luke's trip to the store for supplies for this painting job. (Kulm, 1994, p. 12)

After examining the student's solution, a teacher can comment on the organization, labeling, problem-solving processes, computations, spelling, and language use. Moreover, the teacher can discuss the use of mathematics to solve real-world problems, completeness of the solution, the student's disposition toward mathematics, the ability to plan ahead, work habits, and attention to detail (Kulm, 1994). Two disadvantages to using written descriptions are that the parents may have difficulty reading or they may not have knowledge of written English.

## Checklists and Questionnaires

Checklists and questionnaires are convenient ways to provide feedback about a student's work.

Teachers can quickly complete a checklist. Figure 11.2 is an example of a checklist for teachers to provide feedback about the mathematical disposition or student confidence, willingness, perseverance, and interest in doing mathematics. Checklists are useful for screening, diagnosis, program planning, and program evaluation.

Questionnaires allow teachers and students to collect information in more detail than checklists. Open-ended questionnaires allow respondents to express their attitudes, opinions, and knowledge in depth; structured questionnaires allow respondents simply to fill in one or two words or circle a response.

## Interviews

Chapter 5 discusses the topic of conducting interviews. There are special considerations when using this technique in mathematics assessment. Interviews can guide discussions, encourage students, and determine disposition toward mathematics. One basic approach is to interview students individually about their likes and dislikes, asking questions such as "What do you like about mathematics?" "What are your interests?" "What don't you like?" Interviews can help in screening, diagnosis, program planning, and program evaluation.

| What students have experienced: | Date and Activity | |
|---|---|---|
| 1. Confidence in using mathematics | 10/29 Correctly solved all problems assigned. | 1/19 Actively worked as part of small group that solved a problem. |
| 2. Flexibility in doing mathematics | 11/2 Generated several ways of solving an addition problem. | 4/8 Students challenged each other on solution methods. |
| 3. Persevering at mathematical tasks | 4/29 Worked all day on collecting and displaying data – favorite ice cream. | 2/5 Kept working on different ways of making change for 50¢ – all ways found. |
| 4. Curiosity in doing mathematics | 11/10 Solved a "what if" question, expressing answer in own words. | 4/7 In small group generated own units for measuring room. |
| 5. Reflecting on their own thinking | Every day students explain working on a problem. | their thinking after |
| 6. Valuing applications of mathematics | 2/23 All students brought in pictures for math applications bulletin board. | 5/24 field trip to science museum to see how mathematics is used. |
| 7. Appreciating role of mathematics | 10/15 Brought in newspaper articles that used mathematical terms. | 1/29 Appreciated place-value system by finding sums using Roman numerals. |

**FIGURE 11.2**   *Inventory of Mathematical Disposition Experiences Checklist*

*Source:* Reprinted with permission from *Curriculum and Evaluation Standards for School Mathematics,* copyright 1989 by the National Council of Teachers of Mathematics. All rights reserved.

Structured interviews are a more systematic way to assess mathematics performance. A structured interview is an opportunity to observe, question, and discuss mathematics, and to elicit unexpected information about the student. Kulm (1994) describes three reasons for using structured interviews in mathematics:

- The teacher can question a student about the performance of a physical activity, such as measuring the length of a table.
- Students who lack reading skills, oral language skills, or whose native language is not English can communicate nonverbally, through pantomime, or can use manipulatives to demonstrate answers and solutions.
- Gifted students may find it easier to communicate about mathematics at high cognitive levels, such as making judgments, justifying, and evaluating.

One example of using a structured interview is to give students a piece of rectangular-shaped paper. The teacher records the students' answers to the following questions (Kulm, 1994):

1. What is a perimeter of a rectangle?
2. What is a perimeter used for?
3. Show me the perimeter of the rectangle.
4. How could you measure the perimeter?
5. How would you estimate the perimeter?
6. What do you estimate the perimeter to be?
7. Here is a ruler. Can you use this to check your estimate by measuring the perimeter?
8. How could we use this information?
9. Are there other ways to find the perimeter without measuring all four sides?

## Conferences

A conference is a conversation about the student's work that can include the student, educators, and/or parents. Participants in a conference share their views of the student's work with the goal of providing feedback and recommendations. Teacher-student conferences can be helpful when assessing one piece of work or when summarizing the student's work over a period of time. The discussion in a conference can be strictly verbal or the teacher or evaluator may choose to audiotape it, videotape it, or summarize it in written form. Conferences are effective for diagnosis, program planning, and program evaluation.

## Student Journals

Journals induce students to reflect on their own work, communicate about their learning, and document their progress (Kulm, 1994). Students can keep a notebook or journal that allows them to record their work, attitudes, and feelings about mathematics. In a journal students can indicate what they like and don't like about doing mathematics and which areas are giving them difficulty. Journals are effective for program planning and program evaluation. The following is a sample mathematics journal outline (Kulm, 1994):

Mathematics topic:

Two examples of problems that I solved:

Two important ideas:

What I understand best:

What I need more work on:

How I can use this topic in real life:

## Performance-Based Assessment

As a measure of mathematics instruction, performance-based assessment requires students to demonstrate mathematical abilities, skills, and dispositions, such as developing a product or demonstrating an understanding of concepts and relationships. This type of assessment is useful in program planning and program evaluation. The following are examples of performance tasks:

- Pretend we own a children's shoe store. We need to know whether to have more cloth shoes or more leather shoes for sale in our store. What could we decide to do? (NCTM, 1989, p. 55).

- Here is a rectangle. About how many centimeters long would you estimate its perimeter to be? Use the ruler to measure the perimeter. How close was your estimate? (Kulm, 1994, p. 44).
- Use a spreadsheet program to make a table of multiples of the first five whole numbers (Kulm, 1994, p. 45).

Figure 11.3 is an example of a rubric for describing mathematics performance.

## Portfolios

As Chapter 7 defines it, a portfolio is a deliberate collection of a student's work over time that demonstrates the student's efforts, progress, and achievement. When documenting and assessing mathematical abilities, portfolios provide information about conceptual understanding, problem solving, reasoning, communication abilities, disposition toward mathematics, creativity, work habits, and attitudes. Mathematics portfolios help students see that the study of mathematics is more than discrete rules and procedures (Kulm, 1994). Portfolios in mathematics assessment aid in program planning and program evaluation. Chapter 7 provides a more extensive discussion of the use of portfolios.

A portfolio is not just a folder of practice worksheets or of all the work that the student has completed. The selection of the contents of

---

**FIGURE 11.3    *Math Descriptors***

| Descriptors for Grades K–2 | Descriptors for Grades 3–5 |
|---|---|
| *Exploration:* Becoming aware of math concepts; interacts with materials. | *Emergent:* Descriptors supplied by the teacher. |
| *Emergent:* Benefits from monitoring and help in problem solving; is beginning to understand math concepts; needs assistance to produce work. | *Beginning:* Can solve problems and complete assignments with support; some understanding of math concepts; requires support to produce accurate work, is learning to use math facts. |
| *Beginning:* Solves problems with assistance; needs assistance learning math concepts; needs support to complete math tasks successfully; beginning to learn and use math facts. | *Developing:* Completes required assignments; solves problems with assistance; needs assistance learning math concepts; needs support to produce accurate assignments; beginning to use math facts. |
| *Developing:* Solves problems with occasional assistance; understands math concepts; usually completes math tasks accurately; can recall and use some math facts. | *Capable:* Completes required assignments; solves problems with occasional assistance; understands math concepts; usually accurate on assignments; recalls and uses math facts. |
| *Capable:* Solves problems independently; applies previously learned math concepts; shows accuracy on math tasks; recalls and uses math facts. | *Strong:* Does some enrichment/extra credit math work; solves problems independently; applies previously learned math concepts; shows accuracy on assignments; confidently recalls and uses math facts. |
| *Experienced:* Uses a variety of strategies to solve problems independently; independently applies previously learned math concepts; demonstrates high accuracy on math tasks; confidently recalls and uses all math facts. | *Exceptional:* Extends self with math enrichment/extra credit work; uses thinking strategies to solve problems independently; independently applies previously learned math concepts; demonstrates high accuracy on assignments; confidently recalls and uses all math facts. |

*Source:* "ASCD Yearbook 1996 Communicating Student Learning." Edited by Thomas R. Guskey, 1996, Alexandria, VA: Association for Supervision and Curriculum Development, Figure 5.1, pp. 52, and Figure 9.2, pp. 94.

a portfolio is always a carefully considered process. The following are suggestions for inclusion in student mathematics portfolios:

- photographs of students' bridge-building projects, using rods of different lengths
- worksheets that involve students in creating new shapes
- projects that involve students in using software to design quilts from squares
- performance tasks that require students to demonstrate knowledge of geometry
- journals in which students record problem solving processes
- experiments with probability
- audiotapes of students collaborating on projects
- videotapes of students constructing designed structures or demonstrating what they have learned after analyzing data on rainfall. (National Research Council, 1993; Kulm, 1994)

## Exhibitions

An exhibition is a display of a student's work that summarizes and synthesizes what the student has accomplished. Customarily, it demonstrates knowledge, abilities, skills, and attitudes concerning one project or a unit of work. In mathematics assessment, exhibitions are useful because students realize that doing mathematics is more than just a series of worksheets or exercises, that it involves conceptual understanding, problem solving, and reasoning, and teachers find them effective in program planning and program evaluation.

## Self-Assessment

Self-assessment provides students with an opportunity to review concepts and identify mathematical processes. It is an occasion for students to reflect on their learning. Figure 11.4 is an example of a checklist that students use when assessing their own learning.

## Peer Assessment

Peer assessment allows students insight into the thinking and reasoning abilities of their peers. By engaging in collaborative learning and problem solving, students have an opportunity to reflect on the learning processes of their peers as

**FIGURE 11.4** *Self-Assessment Checklist*

| Student's Name | | Date | | | |
|---|---|---|---|---|---|
| **After reading the mathematical word problem, I can:** | *1*<br><br>*Great!* | *2* | *3* | *4* | *5*<br><br>*Darn!* |
| 1. draw a picture to help solve the problem. | | | | | |
| 2. identify the operations to solve the problem. | | | | | |
| 3. list the steps to solve the problem and explain why each step is necessary. | | | | | |
| 4. use correct labeling. | | | | | |
| 5. use numbers and symbols to write equation(s) to solve the problem. | | | | | |
| 6. verify the results. | | | | | |
| 7. interpret the results. | | | | | |

well as on their own. Figure 11.5 is an example of a checklist that students use when conducting a peer assessment.

## Observing the Student within the Environment

In Chapter 5 you learned about the importance of considering the student within the physical, learning, and social environments. The interactions between the student and the environment are crucial assessment considerations.

### Physical Environment

The physical environment can influence the student's mathematics performance. The temperature, lighting, and seating arrangements of the teaching and learning spaces affect how well

the student performs. Figure 11.6 is a checklist for studying the physical environment.

### Learning Environment

A comfortable learning environment facilitates the acquisition of a positive disposition toward mathematics and can contribute to mathematics achievement. The curriculum, instructional methods, materials, and the assessment procedures are all areas of concern. The learning environment can promote a positive disposition toward mathematics. Students will be willing to do mathematics when (1) mathematics problems are challenging; (2) students realize that mathematics problems are worth doing; (3) mathematics problems are accessible to a wide range of students; (4) a variety of instructional approaches are available; and (5) multiple assessment procedures check learning. Figure 11.7 on page 302 is a checklist that can help to determine the appropriateness of the learning environment.

| Student's Name _____    Date _____ Peer's Name _____ | ☹ | 😐 | ☺ |
|---|---|---|---|
| 1. My peer used the data in the tables to solve the mathematical story problem. | | | |
| 2. My peer used correct mathematical notation. | | | |
| 3. My peer used pictures to illustrate the story problem. | | | |
| 4. My peer used labeling. | | | |
| 5. My peer's work is neat. | | | |

**FIGURE 11.5**  *Peer Assessment*

◀ **POINT STREET SCHOOL** ▶
**Physical Environment** ▶ **Mathematics**

Student's Name _____S.C._____      Date __5/21__ Time __10:15__

Observer _____Ms. P._____      Location _____classroom_____

| Characteristic | Always | Sometimes | Never |
|---|---|---|---|
| **1. Seating** <br> Is the student seated properly? | X | | |
| ▶ Suggestions for improvement: | | | |
| **2. Lighting** <br> Is the lighting appropriate? | X | | |
| ▶ Suggestions for improvement: | | | |
| **3. Noise** <br> Is the noise level appropriate? | | X | |
| ▶ Suggestions for improvement: *When group activities are underway, the noise level of the classroom tends to rise. Both teacher and students should moniter this.* | | | |
| **4. Distractions** <br> Is the student distracted by activities in the room? | X | | |
| ▶ Suggestions for improvement: | | | |
| **5. Temperature** <br> Is the temperature of the room appropriate? | X | | |
| ▶ Suggestions for improvement: | | | |
| **6. General Atmosphere** <br> Does the student appear to be comfortable in the environment? | | X | |
| ▶ Suggestions for improvement: *Group activities take up much of the class time. At times S.C. has difficulty moving from one group to the next.* | | | |

**FIGURE 11.6** *Observing the Physical Environment*

## ◀ POINT STREET SCHOOL ▶
### Learning Environment ▶ Mathematics

Student's Name ____S.C.____          Date __5/21__  Time __10:15__

Observer _____Ms. P._____          Location ____Classroom____

| Characteristic | Always | Sometimes | Never |
|---|---|---|---|
| **1. Materials** <br> Are a variety of mathematics materials available? | X | | |
| ▶ Suggestions for improvement: | | | |
| **2. Manipulatives** <br> Are appropriate manipulatives available? <br> Are a variety of manipulatives available? | X | | |
| ▶ Suggestions for improvement: | | | |
| **3. Curriculum** <br> Does the curriculum reflect recent reform efforts and standards? | X | | |
| ▶ Suggestions for improvement: | | | |
| **4. Activities** <br> Is instruction oriented toward the use of various materials rather than paper and pencil tasks? | X | | |
| ▶ Suggestions for improvement: | | | |
| **5. Modifications** <br> Have modifications been made to instruction in order to accommodate the learning needs of the student? | | X | |
| ▶ Suggestions for improvement: S.C. needs to use a talking calculator. | | | |
| **6. Instructional Demands** <br> Are the instructional demands appropriate for the student? | X | | |

**FIGURE 11.7** *Observing the Learning Environment*

## Social Environment

Relationships with students and teachers affect mathematics achievement. The social environment is pivotal in the development of self-concept and self-esteem. These, in turn, contribute to a positive disposition toward mathematics. By observing the social environment, teachers can study the relationships students have with peers and adults. Figure 11.8 (on page 304) is a checklist for examining the appropriateness of the social environment.

## Preferred Practices

Recent reform initiatives in mathematics have a major impact on curriculum, instruction, and assessment in mathematics. While reform efforts do not specifically identify students with disabilities, the new initiatives do emphasize that *all* students are to benefit from the initiatives. As special educators, we must monitor and be responsive to these reforms.

The reform efforts in mathematics provide a welcome opportunity for educators to involve students with special needs in mathematics and to link instruction directly to assessment activities. Specifically, educators can orient instruction and assessment approaches:

- toward classrooms as mathematical communities—away from classrooms as simply collections of individuals
- toward logic and mathematical evidence as verification—away from the teacher as the sole authority for right answers
- toward conjecturing, inventing, and problem solving—away from an emphasis on mechanistic answer-finding
- toward connecting the learning of mathematics to its fundamental ideas and its applications—away from treating mathematics as a body of isolated concepts and procedures (National Council of the Teachers of Mathematics, 1991a, p. 3)

## Extending Learning

1. Identify one topic for instruction in mathematics. Develop two assessment tasks that link the instruction directly to assessment.
2. Develop a checklist or rating scale that assesses students' dispositions in mathematics.
3. A teacher suspects that Frances, a 10-year-old in fourth grade, is having difficulty doing mathematics. What suggestions can you give the teacher for determing whether these suspicions are correct?
4. Examine a norm-referenced standardized mathematics test. Compare the development of this test with the vision of mathematics assessment discussed in this chapter.
5. Identify three assessment approaches discussed in the chapter. Develop a table that shows the purposes, advantages, and disadvantages of each approach.
6. Visit a school and observe a mathematics class in session. How does the environment affect student learning? Use the Point Street School form in this chapter or develop your own checklist to collect information about the learning environment.
7. Obtain two or more standardized tests. Compare the test items. Read the instructor's manual of one of the tests and evaluate the technical characteristics.
8. Working with one or two other students, identify a unit of study in mathematics. Develop a criterion-referenced test to assess this unit.

◀ **POINT STREET SCHOOL** ▶
Social Environment ▶ Mathematics

Student's Name ____S.C.____                           Date __5/21__  Time __10:15__

Observer ____Ms. P.____                               Location ____Classroom____

| Characteristic | Always | Sometimes | Never |
|---|---|---|---|
| **1. Teacher-Student Interactions**<br>Are interactions warm and friendly? | X | | |
| ▶ Suggestions for improvement: | | | |
| **2. Disruptions**<br>Are disruptions kept to a minimum? | X | | |
| ▶ Suggestions for improvement: | | | |
| **3. Behavioral Interventions**<br>Are behavioral interventions effective and appropriate? | | X | |
| ▶ Suggestions for improvement: *Consultation with the behavioral specialist should be undertaken in order to revise the behavioral plan for S.C.* | | | |
| **4. Peer Interactions**<br>Are peer interactions appropriate? | | X | |
| ▶ Suggestions for improvement: *Due to S.C.'s behavioral problems, peers are reluctant to interact with S.C. The behavioral plan should be revised.* | | | |
| **5. General Atmosphere**<br>Does the student appear to be comfortable in the social environment? | | X | |
| ▶ Suggestions for improvement: *Some students seem to be uncomfortable with S.C.'s behavior. Strategies for successful interactions should be developed.* | | | |
| **6. Schedule**<br>Is the student's schedule appropriate? | | X | |
| ▶ Suggestions for improvement: *S.C. may need additional one-to-one instruction in mathematics.* | | | |
| **7. Transitions**<br>Are transitions made smoothly? | X | | |
| ▶ Suggestions for improvement: | | | |

**FIGURE 11.8**  *Observing the Social Environment*

# *References*

American Association for the Advancement of Science (AAAS) (1993). *Benchmarks for science literacy.* New York: Oxford University Press.

Anastasi, A. (1988). *Psychological testing.* New York: Macmillan.

Ashlock, R. B. (1986). *Error patterns in computation: A semi-programmed approach.* 5th ed. Columbus, OH: Merrill.

Berk, R. A. (1988). Criterion-referenced tests. In *Educational research, methodology, and measurement: An international handbook*, ed. J. P. Keeves, pp. 365–370. Oxford: Pergamon Press.

Berman, B., and F. J. Friederwitzer (1981). A diagnostic-prescriptive approach to remediation of regrouping errors. *Elementary School Journal* 82: 109–115.

Brigance, A. H. (1981). *BRIGANCE® inventory of essential skills.* No. Billerica, MA: Curriculum Associates.

Brigance, A. H. (1984). *BRIGANCE® assessment of basic skills–Spanish edition.* No. Billerica, MA: Curriculum Associates.

Brigance, A. H. (1991). *BRIGANCE® inventory of early development–revised.* No. Billerica, MA: Curriculum Associates.

Brigance, A. H. (1994). *BRIGANCE® life skills inventory.* No. Billerica, MA: Curriculum Associates.

Brigance, A. H. (1995). *BRIGANCE® employability skills inventory.* No. Billerica, MA: Curriculum Associates.

Brigance, A. H. (1999). *BRIGANCE® comprehensive inventory of basic skills–revised.* No. Billerica, MA: Curriculum Associates.

Brown, V. L., M. E. Cronin, and E. McEntire (1994). *Test of mathematical abilities.* 2d ed. Austin, TX: PRO-ED.

Connolly, A. J. (1998). *KeyMath–revised/normative update: A diagnostic inventory of essential mathematics.* Circle Pines, MN: American Guidance Service.

Enright, B. E. (1989). *ENRIGHT® Diagnostic Inventory of Basic Arithmetic Skills.* No. Billerica, MA: Curriculum Associates.

Erford, B. T., and R. R. Boykin (1996). *Slosson-diagnostic math screener.* East Aurora, NY: Slosson Educational Publications.

Estes, T. H., J. J. Estes, H. C. Richards, and D. Roettger (1981). *Estes attitude scales.* Austin, TX: PRO-ED.

Ginsburg, H. P., and A. J. Baroody (1990). *Test of early mathematics ability.* 2d ed. Austin, TX: PRO-ED.

Gnagey, T. D. (1980). *Diagnostic screening tests math.* East Aurora, NY: Slosson Educational Publications.

Guiskey, T. R. (1996). *Communicating student learning: 1996 ASCD yearbook.* Alexandria, VA: Association for Supervision and Curriculum Development.

Harcourt Brace Educational Measurement (1995). *Stanford diagnostic mathematics test 4.* 4th ed. San Antonio, TX: Harcourt Brace Educational Measurement.

Harcourt Brace Educational Measurement (2001). *Wechsler individual achievement test–II.* San Antonio, TX: Harcourt Brace Educational Measurement.

Kaufman, A. S., and N. L. Kaufman (1983). *Kaufman assessment battery for children.* Circle Pines, MN: American Guidance Service.

Kaufman, A. S., and N. L. Kaufman (1998). *Kaufman test of educational achievement/normative update (K–TEA/NU).* Circle Pines, MN: American Guidance Service.

Kilian, L., E. Cahill, C. Ryan, D. Sutherland, and D. Tacetta (1980). Errors that are common in multiplication. *Arithmetic Teacher* 27: 22–25.

Kulm, G. (1994). *Mathematics assessment.* San Francisco: Jossey-Bass.

Lake, K., and K. Kafka (1996). Reporting methods in grade K–8. In *Communicating student learning*, ed. T. R. Guskey, 90–118. Alexandria, VA: Association for Supervision and Curriculum Development.

Markwardt, Jr., F. C. (1998). *Peabody individual achievement test–revised/normative update.* Circle Pines, MN: American Guidance Service.

Marolda, M. R., and P. S. Davidson (1994). Assessing mathematical abilities and learning approaches. In *Windows of opportunity*, ed. C. A. Thornton and N. S. Bley, 83–113. Reston, VA: National Council of the Teachers of Mathematics.

Mathematics Curriculum Framework and Criteria Committee (1992). *Mathematics framework for California public schools.* Sacramento, CA: California Department of Education.

National Council of the Teachers of Mathematics (1989). *Curriculum and evaluation standards for school mathematics.* Reston, VA: National Council of the Teachers of Mathematics.

National Council of the Teachers of Mathematics (1991a). *Mathematics assessment.* Reston, VA: National Council of the Teachers of Mathematics.

National Council of the Teachers of Mathematics (1991b). *Professional standards for the teaching of mathematics.* Reston, VA: National Council of the Teachers of Mathematics.

National Research Council (1993). *Measuring up.* Washington, DC: National Academy Press.

Newcomer, P. L. (1990). *Diagnostic achievement battery.* 2d ed. Austin, TX: PRO-ED.

Newcomer, P. L., and B. R. Bryant (1993). *Diagnostic achievement test for adolescents.* 2d ed. Austin, TX: PRO-ED.

Sonnenschein, J. L. (1983). *Basic achievement skills individual screener.* San Antonio, TX: Harcourt Brace Educational Measurement.

Speer, W. R., and D. J. Brahier (1994). Rethinking the teaching and learning of mathematics. In *Windows of opportunity*, ed. C. A. Thornton and N. S. Bley, 41–59. Reston, VA: National Council of the Teachers of Mathematics.

Tindal, G. A., and D. B. Marston (1990). *Classroom-based assessment*. Columbus, OH: Merrill.

Trafton, P. R., and A. S. Claus (1994). A changing curriculum for a changing age. In *Windows of opportunity*, ed. C. A. Thornton and N. S. Bley, 19–39. Reston, VA: National Council of the Teachers of Mathematics.

U.S. Department of Education, and National Science Foundation (n.d.). *Statement of principles on assessment in mathematics and science education*. Washington, DC: U.S. Department of Education and National Science Foundation.

Wilkinson, G. (1993). *Wide range achievement test*. 3d ed. Austin, TX: PRO-ED.

Woodcock, R. W., K. S. McGrew, and N. Mather (2001). *Woodcock-Johnson–III*. Itasca, IL: Riverside.

Zaslavsky, C. (1996). *The multicultural math classroom: Bringing in the world*. Portsmouth, NH: Heinemann.

# 12

## *Development of Young Children*

## *Overview*

Gathering information about the development of young children before they are enrolled in school is very different from the assessment of school-age children. Working with young children and their families can involve locating a mother and her preschool child in a homeless shelter, receiving a referral form from a community clinic, or working with a family recently arrived from another country where services for young children and families are not available. Assessment ques-

tions focus on the young child's general development in one or more areas. These areas, or **developmental domains,** concern physical, cognitive, communication, social-emotional, and adaptive development. The focus on development differs in significant ways from the focus on academic and achievement difficulties of school-age children and youth we have been discussing.

307

## Chapter Objectives _____

After completing this chapter, you should be able to:

- Explain the considerations involved in assessing young children.
- Identify and describe how to select appropriate screening and developmental assessment approaches.

- Discuss transition assessment of young children.
- Discuss issues in the assessment of school readiness.

## What Shapes Our Views: The Children

Teachers and administrators in public school programs usually define young children as students in grades kindergarten through 3; early intervention specialists define young children as ages birth through 5 years. Thus, the definition of the term "young children" may imply different age ranges, depending on the professional's frame of reference. Two national organizations of professionals, the Division of Early Childhood (DEC) of the Council for Exceptional Children (CEC) and the National Association for the Education of Young Children (NAEYC), define **young children** as children ages birth through age 8. We will use this latter definition in our discussion of young children.

Professionals feel that development, which is influenced by the child's interests, abilities, and opportunities in the natural environment, proceeds at individual variations during the early years. For example, 4-year-old Arron is interested in dinosaurs and can identify which are carnivores and which are herbivores. Will, who is also 4 years old, spends much of his time playing with his dump trucks. He speaks in two- to three-word phrases. The variations between Arron and Will may be due to genetic or biological factors such as the child's temperament or to prenatal factors such as consumption of alcohol or use of tobacco during pregnancy. Moreover, social expectations and ways of caring for Arron and Will or opportunity or its absence can influence their development. Most

probably, according to many developmental theorists, two or more factors interact.

Today, tests can provide screening early in life for young children with special needs who can benefit from special services. Medical professionals identify many newborns with or at risk for a disability before leaving the hospital; visiting nurses and early intervention specialists screen infants in their homes; and early childhood special educators work with toddlers and preschoolers in their homes, child care centers, or early education programs. Professionals working with young children and their families represent a variety of disciplines, including audiology, family counseling, medicine, occupational therapy, physical therapy, psychology, social work, speech and language pathology, as well as education.

## Screening

Screening is a process that identifies children who may have a disability and who need a comprehensive assessment. Some of the common questions raised by parents, caregivers, and early childhood teachers are illustrated in Table 12.1.

Screening typically involves testing large numbers of young children, usually in a short amount of time. Screening does not identify children for services but rather pinpoints children who need further assessment. Using a comprehensive assessment, evaluators may identify some children as needing early intervention or special education and related services.

**TABLE 12.1** *Assessment Questions, Purposes, and Approaches*

| Assessment Questions | Steps and Purposes | Approaches |
|---|---|---|
| | **Screening** | |
| Is the child developing typically?<br>Is there a *possibility* that the child has a delay in development or a disability? | To determine whether the child *may* have a disability and should be referred for further assessment | Norm-referenced instruments<br>Curriculum-based assessments<br>Criterion-referenced assessments<br>Observations<br>Checklists<br>Questionnaires<br>Interviews<br>Parent reports<br>Review of developmental history |
| | **Eligibility** | |
| Does the child have a delay in development or a disability?<br>What disability does the child have?<br>How extensive is the disability or delay?<br>Does the child meet the criteria for services?<br>What are the child's strengths and weaknesses in development?<br>What is the child having trouble doing?<br>What does the child understand? | To determine if there is a disability or a developmental delay<br>To compare the child's performance with the performance of the peer group<br>To determine the need for early intervention or special education and related services<br>To determine specific strengths and weaknesses<br>To understand why the child is having difficulty | Norm-referenced instruments<br>Curriculum-based assessments<br>Criterion-referenced assessments<br>Observations<br>Probes<br>Error analysis<br>Interviews<br>Checklists<br>Questionnaires<br>Parent-teacher conferences<br>Performance assessments<br>Parent reports<br>Review of developmental history |

### Connecting Instruction with Assessment

| | | |
|---|---|---|
| | **Program Planning** | |
| What types of early intervention or special education and/or related services should be provided?<br>At what location(s) should the child and family receive services?<br>What environmental modifications and adaptations should be implemented?<br>When behavior impedes learning or that of others, what strategies, including positive behavioral interventions and supports, to address that behavior should be included? | To plan the child's program<br>To determine family resources, priorities, and concerns<br>To determine the locations and type of services(s) to be received<br>To assess the physical, learning and social environments | Family-directed assessment<br>Norm-referenced instruments<br>Curriculum-based assessments<br>Criterion-referenced assessments<br>Observations<br>Probes<br>Error analysis<br>Interviews<br>Checklists |

*(continued)*

**TABLE 12.1** *Continued*

| Assessment Questions | Steps and Purposes | Approaches |
|---|---|---|
| | *Connecting Instruction with Assessment* | |
| What is the child's knowledge or level of skill development? Where should intervention begin? | To understand the child's level of skill or development To determine where intervention or instruction should begin | Parent-teacher conferences Performance assessments Parent reports Review of developmental history |
| | **Program Monitoring** | |
| Once intervention or instruction begins, is the child making progress? Should the intervention or instruction be modified? | To monitor the child's program To understand the pace of intervention To understand what the child can do prior to and after intervention or instruction | Curriculum-based assessments Criterion-referenced assessments Observations Probes Error analysis Interviews Checklists Parent-teacher conferences Portfolios Exhibitions Journals Written descriptions Oral descriptions |
| | **Program Evaluation** | |
| Has the child met the goals of the IFSP or IEP? Has the child made progress? Has the program been successful for the child and family? Does the child continue to need services? Has the program achieved its goals? | To determine whether the program was successful in meeting the child and family goals (IFSP) To determine if the program was successful in meeting the child's goals (IEP) To determine if the child continues to need services To evaluate program effectiveness | Curriculum-based assessments Criterion-referenced assessments Observations Probes Error analysis Interviews Checklists Questionnaires Parent-teacher conferences Portfolios Exhibitions Journals Written descriptions Oral descriptions Surveys |

In many cases, families are unaware of early childhood screenings and need to learn about the benefits of early intervention and purposes of screening. These awareness activities are known as Child Find. Through Child Find, parents and caregivers become aware of screening activities, the first step in the process of identifying young children who fit the eligibility criteria for special services.

The community can sponsor screenings through the public school, through the state early intervention agency, or through commu-

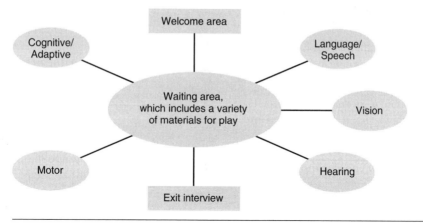

**FIGURE 12.1** *A Community Screening Program with Five Separate Stations*

Source: From Cohen, Libby G., and Loraine J. Spenciner, *Assessment of Young Children.* Copyright © 1994. White Plains, NY: Longman Publishers. Reprinted/adapted by permission by Allyn & Bacon.

nity agencies. Customarily, a screening has several components, such as a physical examination by a doctor or nurse, a developmental history obtained by interviewing the parent, vision and hearing tests, and an assessment of the child's general development, including the physical, cognitive, communication, social-emotional, and adaptive domains. Professionals typically use a screening instrument to assist in making decisions regarding the screening outcome. Figure 12.1 illustrates the setup of a typical community screening program. You can read about one family's experience at a community screening in the Snapshot about Luiz and his mother.

## Choosing Appropriate Screening Instruments

According to Meisels and Wasik (1990) developmental screening tests "should be brief, norm-referenced, inexpensive, standardized in administration, objectively scored, broadly focused across all areas of development, reliable, and valid" (p. 613). Generally, the purpose of screening tests is to evaluate large numbers of children to determine if further assessment is necessary; accordingly, they paint a broad picture and provide general information. Too narrow a focus can result in missing important aspects about the child. Communities can then devote valuable time and money to conducting comprehensive assessments on those children who need further help.

Screening calls for norm-referenced tests, which compare a child's performance with the performance of other children who have taken the test. The norm sample must include children who have similar backgrounds and characteristics to the target child or children. For example, if the children under evaluation come from an inner-city area, then the screening instrument must have included children from urban areas for the norming sample.

Many different professionals and paraprofessionals administer and score screening tests. The administration of screening tests is standardized, as is their scoring. This means that the directions, calculation of scores, and determination of outcomes must contain clear explanations and must be the same for all children who come for screening. The outcomes of screening should not be subject to the judgment and biases of the many individual test examiners who administer and score the tests. Table 12.2 illustrates common screening instruments and their technical characteristics.

**SNAPSHOT ■ *Luiz and His Mother Visit the Community Screening Clinic***

Recently Luiz's mother, Maria Hermetz, heard about a community screening clinic from a friend at the local convenience store. The clinic is held on the first Tuesday of each month at the community center and is free for all children in the community. Health and education professionals are available to answer questions about children's development.

Although Ms. Hermetz does not have any specific questions about 4-year-old Luiz, she decided that she would like to know if he is doing "what he should be doing" at this age. The following month she brought Luiz to the screening.

When Ms. Hermetz arrived at the community center, she observed that the large room had been separated into various areas (Figure 12.1).

The central area had a variety of toys and books for the children and chairs for the parents. "¡Buenos dias!" Ms. Hermetz was greeted by one of the clinic volunteers and asked to complete a brief form with questions regarding her son's development. Ms. Hermetz was relieved to learn that she could choose either an English or Spanish version of the form. Although she speaks English, she prefers to use her native Spanish. An early childhood special education teacher invited Luiz to join two other children who were playing with blocks nearby.

As part of the screening process, the teacher will complete observations of the children as they play alone or together with other children in the waiting area. Earlier, during the planning of the screening program, the screening team identified the questions and the method that the teacher will use for recording the observation data, as Chapter 5 discusses. Observing children, the teacher watched and noted important information in order to answer the following questions: How does the child approach the toys and other children? How does the child interact with the materials? How does the child communicate with adults? With other children?

An early childhood special educator gave Luiz a colorful name tag (Figure 12.2) and invited him to come with her to one of the five screening stations. This teacher, along with other members of the screening team, was using *Developmental Indicators for the Assessment of Learning–Third Edition (DIAL–*

**FIGURE 12.2** *Name Tag*

*3)* (Mardell-Czudnowski and Goldenberg, 1998). They presented Luiz with a number of activities in the areas of motor skills, conceptual abilities, and language skills. See Box 12.1 for a description of *DIAL–3*'s parameters.

Luiz liked pointing to various pictures in the examiner's book. After completing this station, Luiz moved to the next station to work with the speech and language pathologist. Later, he worked with the physical therapist at the motor development station. At the last station, a volunteer checked his hearing and vision. At each station he received another colored sticker on his name tag. This procedure allowed the examiners to quickly determine which stations the child had completed.

After the screening, the nurse met with Ms. Hermetz to talk about the results of the screening and to answer any questions. Depending on the family's needs, the nurse may discuss various community resources. Today, she and Ms. Hermetz chatted about Luiz's development. About a week later, Ms. Hermetz received a letter in the mail that stated that the screening results had been completed and that no further assessment was indicated.

BOX 12.1 *Developmental Indicators for the Assessment of Learning–Third Edition (DIAL–3)*

*Publication Date:* 1998

*Purposes:* Screening test which addresses the following areas: Motor, Language, and Concepts. Parent questionnaire provides information about self-help and social skills.

*Ages/Grade Levels:* Ages 3 years through 6 years, 11 months.

*Time to Administer:* 30 minutes.

*Technical Adequacy:* Reliability and validity are adequate.

*Suggested Use:* For use as part of an overall screening procedure. The Spanish edition was normed on a sample of 605 Spanish-speaking children. The DIAL–3 Spanish edition is not a direct translation but, rather, test developers made efforts to adjust and validate the test for use in a different linguistic or cultural context.

## Planning the Screening Procedure

In planning the screening procedure, the screening team must address several key areas.

**Environment.** The screening should always take place in a setting that is quiet and free from distractions. The child should be in the company of a familiar caregiver during the assessment. It is important never to challenge young children during assessment activities by separating them from their parent or caregiver (Greenspan and Meisels, 1993, p. 14).

**Rapport.** Each examiner must allow time for the child to become familiar with the situation. Many children take time to "warm up" to strangers. If the child does not feel comfortable, the responses the child gives may not reflect the child's ability.

**Physical Status.** As routine practice, an examiner observes the child's current health status. Young children frequently have colds, leading to middle ear infections (a result of which is a temporary decrease in hearing). Can the child hear the directions? Does the child appear to be tired? If so, consider screening at another time. Don't forget that young children have a limited attention span. A child's attention will wander or be lost if the screening test has too many test items.

**Development.** Although educators define separate areas of development (physical, cognitive, communication, social-emotional, and adaptive), these areas are not independent, but interact in complex ways. Screening procedures must be comprehensive in coverage, and not focus on one or two developmental areas.

**Parent Concerns.** Some parents are very anxious about their child's screening test. "When will my child start talking?" or "Will this person find something wrong with my child?" parents may ask—or may not ask, although it is a matter of primary concern. Be sure that parents fully understand the reason for screening their child. An important component of any screening procedure is a period for answering parents' questions, either before or after the testing.

## Limitations of Screening

The screening process has several significant limitations. Members of assessment teams must be knowledgeable about these limits because screening results determine whether the child receives a referral for a comprehensive assessment.

### Snapshots

A screening instrument's results, like some other assessment approaches, show a snapshot of a

**TABLE 12.2** *Selected Screening Instruments for Young Children*

| Instrument | Areas Assessed | Age Range | Reliability | Validity | Norms | Time to Administer |
|---|---|---|---|---|---|---|
| *AGS Early Screening Profiles* (Harrison et al., 1990) | Cognitive/language, self-help/social, articulation survey, behavior survey, motor survey, motor profile, home survey, and health history survey | 2 years to 6 years, 11 months | Internal consistency mean .85; test-retest range .78 to .89; interrater mean .92 | Numerous studies support concurrent, predictive, and construct validity | 1,149 children from 26 states and the District of Columbia stratified by geographic region, race, age, gender, socioeconomic status, and enrollment of school district | 15 minutes to 30 minutes for children; 10 minutes to 15 minutes for teacher and parent questionnaires |
| *Ages & Stages Questionnaires (ASQ)* (Bricker and Squires, 1999) | Communication, gross motor, fine motor, problem solving, and personal-social | 4 months to 60 months | Adequate | Adequate | 2,008 children | 10 minutes to 20 minutes |
| *Brigance® Preschool Screen* (Brigance, 1998) | 11 skill areas | 2 years, 9 months to 5 years | None reported | None reported | Criterion-referenced test | 12 minutes to 15 minutes |
| *Denver Developmental Screening Test II (DDST II)* (Frankenburg, Dodds, Archer, et al., 1990) | Gross motor, language, fine motor-adaptive, and personal-social | Birth through 5 years, 11 months | Limited information reported | Limited information reported | 2,096 children stratified by maternal education, residence, and ethnicity | 5 minutes to 10 minutes |

| Instrument | Areas Assessed | Age Range | Reliability | Validity | Standardization Sample | Administration Time |
|---|---|---|---|---|---|---|
| *Developmental Indicators for the Assessment of Learning–Third Edition (DIAL–3)* (Mardell-Czudnowski, and Goldenberg, 1998)* | Motor skills, conceptual abilities, and language skills | 3 years through 6 years, 11 months | Test-retest reliability .84 to .88; internal consistency adequate | Evidence of validity is adequate | 1,560 English-speaking and 650 Spanish-speaking children, stratified by age, gender, geographic area, race or ethnic group, and parent education level | 30 minutes |
| *Early Screening Inventory–Revised (ESI–R)* (Meisels, Wiske, Marsden, and Henderson, 1997) | Visual-motor/adaptive, language and cognition, and gross motor | *ESI–P* (3 years to 4 years, 6 months) *ESI–K* (4 years, 6 months to 6 years) | Interrater .99 Test-retest .98 / Interrater .98 Test-retest .87 | Limited information / Limited information | 997 children / 5,034 children | 15 minutes to 20 minutes |
| *FirstSTEP* (Miller, 1992) | Cognitive, communication, motor, socio-emotional, and adaptive | 2 years, 9 months to 6 years, 2 months | Test-retest reliability coefficients range from .85 to .92; interrater reliability .77 to .96 | Adequate concurrent validity | 1,433 stratified by gender, geographic regions and race/ethnicity based on 1988 U.S. Census | 15 minutes |

*Available in Spanish

child's development at one point in time. There are many variables that can affect screening results. These include the child's physical, emotional, or motivational states; the examiner's familiarity with the screening tools; the examiner's understanding of child development and ability to establish rapport; the examiner's familiarity with children who are linguistically and culturally diverse; and the screening environment.

Since the results of screening present only a brief picture, best practices in screening suggest that a child receive periodic screening tests. The advantages of giving the child the same standardized instrument for each screening are the ease and usefulness of comparing the child's development on subsequent administrations. However, the cumulative effect of repeating items on periodic screenings and the tendency of some caregivers to "practice" the items with the child reduces the instrument's effectiveness.

## Screening Tasks

Most standardized screening instruments include toys and ask the child to use or to play with the toys in specific ways. For example, a common test item on several screening instruments requires the examiner to tell the child to build a tower with a small pile of 1-inch cubes. Using toys in very specific ways is a new experience for many young children. Most early education programs encourage children to choose a toy, to explore its properties, and to use it in a way that they choose. Thus, when given several small cubes, a child may decide to make a train rather than a tower. To pass this item on a screening test, the child must make a tower; however, a young child may have no motivation or interest to comply with the examiner's request because the child has a more interesting idea (the train or road).

*A teacher collects information about a young child's cognitive, communication, and motor development using observation and classroom materials.*

## SNAPSHOT  ■  *Special Challenges*

Some families face special challenges that impact on Child Find activities and the screening and referral processes. We meet several families in the following snapshots:

- Fourteen-year-old Cheryl and her baby, Samantha, live on the streets of a large urban city. They occasionally sleep at a downtown shelter or in one of the vacant buildings on the waterfront.
- Mindy and her 3-year-old son are illegal immigrants living with her cousin in a small apartment house. Mindy worries that city officials will lo-

cate her and return her and her child to their native country.
- Andreas graduated from college a few years ago and finds himself torn between the responsibilities of his job and his toddler. He often resents the demands that his child makes.
- Rita and Alexander and their three preschoolers live in a trailer at the end of a dirt road several miles from town. They have exhausted their meager savings since the mill closed and both parents lost their jobs. This rural family cannot readily access community resources and services.

### False Negatives

A child who, in fact, does have a disability may pass through the screening without being identified for further assessment. The causes of **false negative** results are a lack of sensitivity of the screening instrument; a lack of training or limited clinical knowledge of the examiner(s); or other factors.

### False Positives

A child who does not have a disability may be identified for further assessment. These **false positive** results increase parental anxiety and place an extra burden on the family until a comprehensive assessment is completed. The causes of false positives are a lack of specificity of the screening instrument; a lack of training or lack of clinical knowledge of the examiner(s); or other factors.

### Special Challenges

Family situations, too, can present special challenges to the screening process. Families who are homeless or who have illegal immigrant sta-

tus may be difficult to locate. You can read more about these special challenges in the Snapshot.

### Comprehensive Developmental Assessment

As a result of screening procedures, a young child may be referred to an assessment team. The team addresses concerns about the child's development and individual team members participate in planning and conducting a comprehensive assessment. Most states require that standardized instruments be part of the developmental assessment to determine eligibility for special eduation services. Team members include the child's parents and professionals representing various disciplines, encompassing education, medicine, occupational therapy or physical therapy, psychology, speech and language pathology, and social work.

Educators play a major role on the assessment team. They often conduct observations of the child in an early education setting or they complete a developmental assessment on the child. Typically, developmental assessments cover a variety of developmental areas, including physical (gross and fine motor), cognitive, communication, social or emotional, and adaptive development.

# What Shapes Our Views: Developmental Assessment

Many of the instruments that assess development derive from various theories of child growth and development.

## Piaget

Jean Piaget developed a theory of cognitive development that emphasizes the interaction of early motor abilities with developing cognitive abilities. During cognitive development, according to Piaget, a child passes through specific developmental stages; however, one child may pass through a stage at a different time than another. Assessment instruments and practices that are built on Piagetian theory include test items that address these cognitive stages: sensorimotor intelligence, preoperational thought, concrete operations, and formal operations. Preoperational thought typically develops between the ages of 2 years and 7 years and is the stage when the child becomes capable of symbolic representations.

***Effect on Assessment Practices.*** An examiner who comes from a Piagetian perspective may choose to gather information about the child's development by observing the child at play. Let's sit in on the observation of two children, both of whom have been referred for a developmental assessment. Jamie, who is 3 years old, picks up the blocks and randomly throws or tosses them away. Occasionally, he puts a block in his mouth. Sarah, who is also 3 years old, lines the blocks up in a double row. She then takes a long rectangular block and starts to push it down the middle of the row. She explains to the observer that she is going shopping at the grocery store for her birthday party.

## Functional Approach

In contrast, the functional (behavioral) approach emphasizes the importance of factors external to the child in skill development. The functional approach emphasizes the skills a child will need to live and play in their natural environment. Many of the instruments are criterion-referenced.

***Effect on Assessment Practices.*** Let's join another examiner who is conducting an assessment of the two 3-year-old children whom we met earlier, Jamie and Sarah. The examiner is using a criterion-referenced instrument, *Hawaii Early Learning Profile (HELP) for Preschoolers* (VORT, 1995). According to this instrument, cognitive skills address reasoning, problem solving, and knowledge. Box 12.2 describes the

**BOX 12.2**    *Hawaii Early Learning Profile (HELP) for Preschoolers*

*Publication Date:* 1995

*Purposes:* A criterion-referenced test that includes the following development areas: cognitive, language, gross motor, fine motor, social-emotional, and adaptive.

*Age/Grade Levels:* 3 to 6 years.

*Time to Administer:* Varies since only areas of interest need to be assessed.

*Technical Adequacy:* Since this is a criterion-referenced instrument, norms were not developed through administering the test but, rather, they were drawn from the literature. The manual does not cite literature references. There is no information concerning reliability and validity.

*Suggested Use:* Assesses a wide area of development in young children. Several strands are particularly helpful to the unique needs of some children, and these areas include sign language, speechreading, and wheelchair skills.

test's parameters. At 3 years of age children should be able to sort objects according to big and little, point to the same item in two different settings, and identify objects based on category. How will this examiner's orientation to gathering information differ in the use of blocks with Jamie and Sarah?

## Biological Approach

A third approach to developmental assessment focuses on the physical state of the child and originates within the fields of neurology and pediatrics. The biological approach emphasizes the importance of the reciprocity between the child's temperament and behavior and the caregiver's response. There appears to be some evidence that assessment within this framework can be used across cultures with infants (Barr, 1989).

## Choosing Appropriate Developmental Assessment Instruments

One of the purposes of a developmental assessment is to answer questions about the child's development using the referral and screening information. The Snapshot of Bennie Laurent

---

**SNAPSHOT ■ *Bennie Laurent***

---

Bennie Laurent is a shy, 36-month-old child who has frequent colds, earaches, and fevers. When he isn't sick, he likes to ride on the family tractor. At the urging of Grandmother, Bennie's father brought him to a well-baby and screening clinic in their rural community. Grandmother was concerned about Bennie's health and his slow development. Just recently he had begun to talk in complete sentences.

As part of the screening process, Bennie took the *Denver Developmental Screening Test II (DDST II)* (Frankenburg, Dodds, and Archer et al., 1990), as did each child who came to the screening clinic. Based on observations conducted during the screening, the parent's report, and the *DDST II*, Bennie was referred to the Developmental Evaluation Clinic for a comprehensive assessment. Box 12.3 describes the test's parameters.

At the Developmental Evaluation Clinic, the assessment team included a physician, a physical therapist, a speech and language pathologist, a psychologist, an educator, and a social worker. Bennie's appointment lasted all morning and part of the afternoon. During this time, each member of the team observed or assessed Bennie and spoke with his dad.

For Bennie and his family, the developmental assessment will be helpful in answering questions about his development: Is there a developmental delay? Does he qualify for special services? What are the child's needs? What skills are developing?

**BOX 12.3** *Denver Developmental Screening Test II (DDST II)*

*Publication Date:* 1990

*Purposes:* A screening tool which assesses the following areas: personal-social, fine motor-adaptive, language, and gross motor.

*Age/Grade Levels:* Birth through 5 years, 11 months.

*Time to Administer:* Approximately 10 minutes.

*Technical Adequacy:* The standardization sample is not representative; additional information is needed concerning reliability and validity.

*Suggested Use:* Screening children for possible problems and monitoring children at risk for developmental problems. The Spanish version consists of a score sheet translated into Spanish. The *DDST II* Spanish version was not normed on Spanish-speaking children.

## SNAPSHOT ■ *The Hodgkin Family*

The Hodgkin family consists of Danny, age 4, Joe, age 7, and their parents. Shortly after birth, Danny was identified as having Trisomy 21 (Down syndrome). Danny and his family have been involved in early intervention services since he was a baby. For the past two years, an early intervention specialist has conducted weekly home visits, helping Danny in his development. Recently, his parents have become increasingly concerned with Danny's lack of progress in talking. An evaluation completed by a speech and language pathologist includes a suggestion that the family begin to explore teaching Danny sign language. Both of Danny's parents hope that he will be able to go to a neighborhood preschool in the fall. Figure 12.3 illustrates a portion of Danny's IFSP, which provides an

---

**Individualized Family Service Plan: Family Considerations**

Child's name: _Danny Hodgkin_ Person providing information _Mrs. Hodgkin_

1. Please describe your child (likes, dislikes, and strengths)

   Danny is a happy, outgoing child. He has not been sick over the last 6 months. He seems to understand a lot that is said to him.

2. What are your concerns or how would you describe your child's needs?

   We are worried about his lack of talking-and his slow progress in speech therapy.

3. What do you believe the strengths of your family are in meeting the child's needs?

   My husband spends time playing with Danny and takes him shopping.

4. What would be helpful for your child and family?

   To understand how to help Danny more. We want to understand what he wants and what he is trying to tell us.

5. Which of the following are concerns or areas about which you would like more information?

   About the child

   ____ feeding
   _X_ communicating
   _X_ learning
   ____ vision or hearing
   ____ problem behaviors
   ____ equipment or supplies

   About the family

   _X_ meeting other families whose child has similar needs
   _X_ finding out more about different services
   ____ child care
   _X_ transportation
   ____ information about my child's disability
   ____ information about SSI or Medicaid

6. Are there other concerns which you would like to discuss at the IFSP meeting?

   We would like to meet families who use sign language with their children.

---

**FIGURE 12.3   *From Danny's IFSP***

## SNAPSHOT ■ *Continued*

opportunity for parents to indicate the areas that are important to them. (From Chapter 2, you may remember that this is called a family-directed assessment.)

Based on family concerns, priorities, and resources as they relate to Danny's development, the team will identify one or more outcome statements that describe what they would like to work on in the next six months. The outcome statements will guide the choice of services Danny will receive. In Danny's IFSP, the outcome statements reflect both child and family outcomes:

**Major Outcomes: Child**

Danny will learn to communicate in order to make his needs known.

**Major Outcomes: Family**

Mr. and Mrs. Hodgkin will receive information about parent groups in the community in order to meet other parents and receive peer parent support regarding issues of mutual interest including learning more about using sign language.

---

describes one family's experience with screening and developmental assessment. For children who have a diagnosed disability, the developmental assessment is helpful in answering questions about program planning. For children who are already receiving services, a developmental assessment provides a method of monitoring progress. Good practice dictates that assessment teams combine developmental assessment instruments with observations of the child and a parent report. The Snapshot about the Hodgkin family describes how all this information helps the team in monitoring Danny's progress.

A number of commonly used instruments, both norm-referenced and criterion-referenced, are for use with a broad age range of young children, ages birth through 2 years and older. For example, the *Bayley Scales of Infant Development II* (Bayley, 1993) assesses children ages 1 month to 42 months; the *Assessment, Evaluation, and Programming System (AEPS)* (Volumes 1–4) (Bricker, 1993; Bricker and Pretti-Frontczak, 1996) is for use with children birth to 6 years.

Box 12.4 describes the *AEPS* parameters. Table 12.3 lists selected instruments and summarizes key areas of information.

---

**BOX 12.4** *Assessment, Evaluation, and Programming System (AEPS)*

*Publication Date:* 1993 (Volumes 1–2); 1996 (Volumes 3–4)

*Purposes:* Criterion-referenced instrument for program planning, monitoring, and evaluating a child's progress. The *AEPS* addresses the following areas: fine motor, gross motor, adaptive, cognitive, social-communication, and social.

*Ages/Grade Levels:* Birth to 3 years (volumes 1–2); ages 3 years through 6 years (volumes 3–4).

*Time to Administer:* Variable, depending on the number of areas assessed.

*Technical Adequacy:* Criterion-referenced instrument; reliability and validity are adequate.

*Suggested Use:* Useful to assist in planning and monitoring child's development across the five developmental domains addressed by IDEA. Volumes 2 and 4 provide excellent curriculum ideas for enhancing the child's development. The *AEPS* comes with a Parent Report, which allows parents to observe and record their child's progress, too.

**TABLE 12.3**  *Selected Developmental Assessment Instruments*

| Instrument | Areas | Age Range | Type | Reliability | Validity |
|---|---|---|---|---|---|
| *Assessment, Evaluation, and Programming System (AEPS) for Infants and Children: Vol. 1, AEPS Measurement for Birth to Three Years* (Bricker, 1993) | Fine motor, gross motor, adaptive, cognitive, social-communication, and social | Birth to 3 years | Criterion-referenced instrument for planning, monitoring, and evaluating a child's progress | Adequate | Teachers and other early intervention providers should examine materials to make decisions for individual programs |
| *Assessment, Evaluation, and Programming System (AEPS) for Infants and Children: Vol. 3. AEPS Measurement for Three to Six Years* (Bricker and Pretti-Frontczak, 1996) | Fine motor, gross motor, adaptive, cognitive, social-communication, and social | 3 years through 6 years | Criterion-referenced instrument for planning, monitoring, and evaluating a child's progress | Adequate | Teachers should examine materials to make decisions for individual programs |
| *Bayley Scales of Infant Development II* (Bayley, 1993) | Mental scale and motor scale | 1 year through 3 years, 6 months | Norm-referenced: 1,700 children participated; stratification based on 1988 U.S. census | Adequate | Adequate |
| *Boehm Test of Basic Concepts, Third Edition–Preschool (Boehm–3 Preschool)* (Boehm, 2001) | Basic relational concepts | 3 years through 5 years, 11 months | Norm-referenced: over 1,600 children, stratified by gender, race/ethnicity, region and parent education level according to the U.S. current population survey, October 1998: school enrollment | Adequate | Adequate |

supplement file, U.S. Bureau of Census

| Test | Construct | Age | Standardization | | |
|---|---|---|---|---|---|
| *Boehm Test of Basic Concepts, Third Edition–Preschool Spanish Edition (Boehm–3 Preschool)* (Boehm, 2001)* | Basic relational concepts | 3 years through 5 years, 11 months | Norm-referenced: over 400 Spanish-speaking children, stratified by gender, race/ethnicity, region, and parent education level. The sample under-represented the northeastern and north central regions and over-represented the southern and western regions. | Adequate | Additional validity studies are needed |
| *Boehm Test of Basic Concepts, Third Edition (Boehm–3)* (Boehm, 2000) | Basic relational concepts | Kindergarten through grade 2 | Norm-referenced: over 10,000 children stratified by race/ethnicity and region according to the U.S. current population survey, October 1998: school enrollment supplement file, U.S. Bureau of Census and socio-economic level of the school district | Adequate | Adequate |

(continued)

TABLE 12.3 *Continued*

| Instrument | Areas | Age Range | Type | Reliability | Validity |
|---|---|---|---|---|---|
| *Boehm Test of Basic Concepts, Third Edition Spanish Edition (Boehm–3)* (Boehm, 2000)* | Basic relational concepts | Kindergarten through grade 2 | Norm-referenced: Over 1,600 children stratified by region and socioeconomic level of the school district; there is a lack of representation from the northeastern region | Internal consistency is adequate; test-retest ranges from .78 to .80 | Additional validity studies are needed |
| *Bracken Basic Concept Scale–Revised* (Bracken, 1998)* | Receptive knowledge of concepts including: color, direction/position, letters, self-social awareness, sizes, texture/materials, comparisons, quantity, shapes, time/sequence, and numbers/counting | 2 years, 6 months to 7 years, 11 months | Norm-referenced | Internal consistency ranges from .78 to .98 for the subtests and .96 to .99 for the total test; test-retest for the total test is .94 | The manual presents evidence for content, concurrent, and predictive validity |
| *BRIGANCE®* *Inventory of Early Development–Revised* (Brigance, 1991) | Preambulatory, gross motor, fine motor, adaptive, speech and language, general knowledge and comprehension, social-emotional, reading readiness, basic reading, writing, and math | Birth to 7 years | Criterion-referenced; norms developed from a literature review | Not reported | Not reported |

| Instrument | Areas assessed | Age range | Type | | |
|---|---|---|---|---|---|
| *Carolina Curriculum for Preschoolers with Special Needs* (Johnson-Martin, Attermeier, and Hacker, 1990) | Cognition, communication, social, adaptive, fine motor, and gross motor | 3 years to 5 years | Criterion-referenced | Not reported | Teachers should review materials to make decisions for individual programs |
| *Developmental Assessment of Young Children* (Voress and Maddox, 1998) | Cognition, communication, social-emotional, physical, and adaptive | Birth through 5 years, 11 months | Norm-referenced: 1,269 children in 27 states participated; comparison of percentages to the *Statistical Abstract of the U.S.* (1996) | Adequate | Adequate |
| *Hawaii Early Learning Profile (HELP) for Preschoolers* (VORT, 1995) | Cognitive, language, gross motor, fine motor, social, and self-help | 3 years to 6 years | Curriculum-based | Descriptions and guidelines in the manual are designed to promote consistency | Teachers should review materials to make decisions for individual programs |
| *Infant-Preschool Play Assessment Scale* (Flagler, 1996) | Cognitive, communication, sensorimotor, fine motor, gross motor, and social-emotional skills | Birth through 5 years | Criterion-referenced | Not reported | Teachers should review materials to make decisions for individual programs |
| *Kaufman Survey of Early Academic and Language Skills (K-SEALS)* (Kaufman and Kaufman, 1993) | Expressive language, receptive language, number, letter, and word skills | 3 years through 6 years | Norm-referenced 1,000 children from 28 states stratified by geographic region, race, age, gender, socioeconomic status, and enrollment of school district | Adequate | Adequate |

*(continued)*

**TABLE 12.3** *Continued*

| Instrument | Areas | Age Range | Type | Reliability | Validity |
|---|---|---|---|---|---|
| *Mullen Scales of Early Learning* (Mullen, 1995) | Gross motor, visual reception, fine motor, receptive language, and expressive language | Birth through 5 years, 9 months | Norm-referenced 1,849 children from 4 geographic regions stratified by age, gender, race/ethnicity, father's occupations, and urban/rural | Adequate for younger age groups | Evidence of construct validity is presented |
| *System to Plan Early Childhood Services (SPECS)* (Bagnato and Neisworth, 1990) | Communication, sensorimotor, physical, self-regulation, cognition, and self/social | 2 years to 6 years | System that links assessment of the child to program planning, development of the individualized plan, and evaluation | Adequate test-retest | Teachers should examine materials and make decisions regarding individual programs |
| *Vineland Social-Emotional Early Childhood Scales (SEEC)* (Sparrow, Balla, and Cicchetti, 1998) | Social-emotional functioning: paying attention, entering into intentional social interactions, understanding expressions of emotion, constructing and observing relationships, and developing self-regulation behaviors | Birth through 5 years, 11 months | Norm-referenced: norms were derived from normative data of the *Vineland Adaptive Behavior Scales (ABS)*, expanded form (items from the *ABS* were used to construct the *SEEC*) | Adequate | Adequate |

*Spanish edition available

## Concerns Regarding the Assessment of Young Children

Practitioners should be aware of a number of issues regarding developmental assessment. First, instruments that focus on assessment of infants, toddlers, and preschoolers typically include the following developmental domains: cognitive, expressive and receptive language, fine and gross motor, and adaptive. Notice that these are not exactly the same as the domains included under the term *developmental delay*. In Chapter 1 we discussed that developmental delay refers to a delay in one or more of the following areas: physical development including fine and gross motor, cognitive, communication, social or emotional, or adaptive development. Many commonly used instruments do not include the social-emotional domain. Yet this area is perhaps one of the most critical in increasing opportunities for young children of differing abilities to play and work together.

Another concern is the fact that criterion-referenced tests group items by the age at which children who are developing typically acquire that skill. However, development may not occur this way, particularly for children with special needs. For example, children who are blind can lag behind their peers in gross-motor development. In addition, acquisition of certain other skills for these children may not follow the same sequence as for children with normal vision. In planning and monitoring children's progress, team members will want to supplement criterion-referenced assessment information with observations, videos and audiotapes, and other assessment approaches.

In discussing appropriate practices for primary grades serving 6- through 8-year-olds, Bredekamp and Copple (1997), writing for the National Association for the Education of Young Children (NAEYC), describe best practices in assessing children's learning, in connecting assessment with instruction, and in avoiding grade retention.

Because they advance through sequential curriculum at different paces, children can progress in all areas as they acquire competence. Children who fall behind receive individualized support, such as tutoring, personal instruction, focused time on areas of difficulty, and other strategies to accelerate learning progress. Efforts are made to avoid grade retention of children who fail to make expected progress, because retention generally does not improve achievement and harmfully alters children's attitude toward school. (p. 176)

## Linking Assessment with Early Childhood Activities

To monitor children's progress, many early childhood educators prefer to use portfolios, exhibits, performances and other performance-based assessments such as those Chapter 7 discusses. Unlike more traditional assessments, these approaches encourage assessment results to be public and visible. Reggio Emilia, originally developed in Italy, is an approach to curriculum planning, implementing, and assessing children's progress that places emphasis on public assessments. Using this approach, teachers set up documentation panels to record children's experiences and progress. Teachers display materials on the documentation panel that include some of the many ways children express their skills and knowledge: photographs, drawings, explanatory notes, and children's comments. Because the panels display documentation prominently in the classroom, children and teachers can refer to it during the day and share the children's work and progress with parents and other classroom visitors. Sometimes teachers use documentation panels in the classroom even though they are not following a Reggio Emilia approach to curriculum. Cooney and Buchanan (2001) describe five guidelines for implementing documentation in the classroom:

1. Decide on the focus/purpose for the documentation panel. Is it to demonstrate one child's progress toward IEP goals? Is it to assess and inform the impact of the curriculum activities on the group of children? If the purpose is to show progress toward IEP goals, decide which IEP goals lend themselves to authentic assessment and how the documentation panel will supplement traditional forms of assessment.

2. When planning curriculum and intervention activities, plan how to record the child's learning process from the beginning to end. Photographing, videotaping, audiotaping, observing and recording, and artifact collecting are useful strategies.

3. During the activities, collect as much information as possible that shows the children's thinking about the concepts related to the lesson. Record children's quotations, collect children's drawings with their explanations, and record children's expression of ideas during other curriculum activities.

4. Carefully choose some of the collected data and neatly organize it on a large panel.

5. Display the panel in the classroom or hallway at the children's eye level. Share it with the children and parents as a way of revisiting the activity to remember it or connect it to future learning activities. (p. 15)

## Working with Families

For some parents, learning that their child has a disability comes as a surprise; but for other parents, the finding comes as a relief. These parents may have had questions and concerns for some time regarding their child's development. Figure 12.4 presents a number of general tips for sharing assessment information with family members.

In sharing knowledge and information, respect the point where the family is at any one period of time. One strategy is to offer choices. For example, in discussing the inconclusive re-

sults of a diagnostic assessment, the practitioner might ask, "Do you want to know the range of options or just the more likely?"

Be honest. Say, "I don't know" when you don't, but also always follow up with "I'll find out" or "The field just doesn't know at this point."

## Transition and Assessment

Children with special needs and their families usually become involved in transitions during three time periods: first, when the child turns 3 years old and moves from infant and toddler early intervention to preschool services; second, when the child turns 5 years old and moves from preschool to school-age services; and, third, when the young adult leaves the education system and moves to the community, to work, or to further education. Transition is

---

**FIGURE 12.4**    *Tips for Sharing Eligibility Information with Families*

- Provide family members with an opportunity to receive the assessment report in a one-to-one setting rather than during a large IFSP or IEP team meeting. This meeting allows the family time to ask questions with an empathetic practitioner and to reflect on the information prior to the larger, full-staff meeting.
- Share information with both parents (or major caregivers) at the same time.
- Be honest and straightforward regarding the disability.
- Be willing to say when you don't know.
- Allow time for families to express their feelings.
- Be sensitive to families if they are not ready to hear details.
- Offer to provide additional information.
- Suggest additional resources.
- Be available to the family for further discussions.
- Arrange to have a native-language interpreter available if families need assistance.

often a difficult time for children and families, perhaps because of a new school program, new teachers and therapists, or new procedures. Rosenkoetter, Hains, and Fowler (1994) describe **transition** as times during which children and families begin working with a new set of professionals, start attending new programs, adjust to new schedules and customs, accept altered expectations, and meet new challenges and opportunities. Figure 12.5 identifies areas of change children and their families experience during the transition process.

**FIGURE 12.5**   *Transition Practices by Component and Age Group*

| Component | Age Group | | |
| --- | --- | --- | --- |
| | **(0–3 years)** | **(4–15 years)** | **(16–21 years)** |
| Curriculum | • Neurobehavioral<br>• Developmentally appropriate<br>• Activity-based<br>• Play-based<br>• Social interaction<br>• Child-directed | • Academics applied to work, community, and daily living<br>• Prevocational skills<br>• Life-based approach<br>• Socialization and independence<br>• Self-determination<br>• Advocacy skills | • Academic<br>• Functional life skills<br>• Vocational evaluation<br>• Employment skills<br>• Inclusive adult world<br>• Independent living<br>• Lifelong learners |
| Location | • Hospital<br>• Home<br>• Day care<br>• Communities | • Preschool<br>• Elementary schools<br>• Middle schools<br>• Communities | • Schools<br>• Communities<br>• Employment settings<br>• Residential settings |
| Futures planning | • IFSP document with transition plans<br>• ICC transition plans<br>• Family-centered | • IEP document with transition plans<br>• Family/student-centered | • Transition IEP document<br>• Family/school-centered<br>• Post-school outcome orientation |
| Multiagency collaboration | • Interagency Collaborative Councils (ICCs)<br>• Public/private day care personnel<br>• Agency personnel (school, work, medical, community) | • ICCs<br>• School advisory councils<br>• Agency personnel (school, work, medical, community) | • ICCs<br>• School advisory councils<br>• Agency personnel (school, work, medical, community)<br>• Adult service provided |
| Family and student focus | • Family-centered<br>• Family as service coordinator<br>• Family needs and outcomes<br>• Family service centers<br>• Family empowerment | • Family/student-centered<br>• Family as service coordinator<br>• Support groups<br>• Family service centers<br>• Family and student advocacy | • Family/student centered<br>• Family/student as service coordinator<br>• Family service centers<br>• Self-advocacy |

*Source:* From Repetto, J. B., and V. I. Correa (1996). Expanding views on transition. *Exceptional Children* 62(6): 551–563. Reprinted with the permission of the publisher.

Transitions involve careful planning by the early childhood team so that the movement between programs can be successful. Assessment questions that the team addresses involve aspects of the new program and needs of the child. Let's examine some of the transition questions regarding the new program.

- What is the physical layout of the room, and what types of adaptations to the environment will the child need?
- What materials are available, and are they accessible to children?
- What are the classroom routines and expectations of children?
    For example: Do children have a designated place for their clothing and materials?
    Are the children permitted to carry materials from one center to other centers?
- What are the classroom procedures?
    For example: Do children clean up after themselves?
    Do children obtain and return materials independently?
    Do some centers have a limit in the number of children who can be at them at any one time?

A teacher can collect information about the new program by means of a checklist or rating scale. By identifying this information early, teachers can complete adaptations to the environment and teach the child some of the routines or expose the child to new procedures before the child enters the new program.

Transition assessment also includes identifying the skills that will be helpful to the child in the new program. Transition activities provide opportunities for parents and teachers to work together, to exchange information, and to build common understandings before a child enters a new program. Sometimes parents and teachers have different expectations. For example, kindergarten teachers identify social skills such as communicating and approaching activities with enthusiasm and curiosity as being important to beginning kindergarten; whereas over 50 percent of the parents identify more academic skills such as counting and knowing the alphabet as important (Table 12.4).

During transition activities, parents and early childhood teachers and caregivers have increased opportunities to facilitate skills before the child enters kindergarten. A checklist (Figure 12.6) for teachers and parents is helpful in collecting this information.

Transition assessment should never aim at excluding children from programs. Transition assessment does not mean assessing school readiness. Rather, it means identifying the

**TABLE 12.4**  *Characteristics Identified as Important for Entering Kindergarten*

| Child Characteristics | Kindergarten Teachers | Parents |
| --- | --- | --- |
| Communicates wants and needs verbally | 84% | 92% |
| Shares and takes turns | 56% | 92% |
| Approaches new activities with enthusiasm and curiosity | 76% | 84% |
| Sits still and pays attention | 42% | 80% |
| Uses pencil or paintbrushes | 21% | 65% |
| Counts to 20 or more | 7% | 59% |
| Knows the letters of the alphabet | 10% | 58% |

Adapted from National Center for Education Statistics (1993). *Readiness for Kindergarten: Parent and Teacher Beliefs.* NCES Publication No. NCES 93-257. Washington, DC: U.S. Department of Education, Office of Educational Research and Improvement; and Welch, M. C., and B. White (1999). *Teacher and Parent Expectations for Kindergarten Readiness* (ERIC Document Reproduction Service No. ED 437 225).

**FIGURE 12.6** *Checklist for Transitioning into Kindergarten*

| Communication | Yes | No |
| --- | --- | --- |
| 1. Communicates wants and needs | | |
| 2. Follows adult requests | | |
| 3. Follows two-step directions | | |
| 4. Initiates and maintains peer interaction | | |

Accommodations, modifications, or supports for
school personnel needed:

| Social-emotional | | |
| --- | --- | --- |
| 1. Shares toys and materials with others | | |
| 2. Respects others' property | | |
| 3. Expresses emotions appropriately | | |
| 4. Takes turns | | |

Accommodations, modifications, or supports for
school personnel needed:

| Adaptive | | |
| --- | --- | --- |
| 1. Puts on and takes off outer clothing | | |
| 2. Cleans up after oneself | | |
| 3. Cares for toileting needs | | |
| 4. Eats independently | | |

Accommodations, modifications, or supports for
school personnel needed:

Adapted from Chandler, L. (1993). Steps in Preparing for Transition: Preschool to Kindergarten. *Teaching Exceptional Children* 25(4): 52–55.

needs and supports that will make entry into the new program as successful as possible.

## Assessing School Readiness

Teachers and other educators working with young children often hear questions about a child's "readiness" for school. The concept that children must obtain certain skills before entering school is troublesome for many educators. In spite of what we know about child development, some schools persist in using school readiness tests to exclude children from regular class placement, testing children before they enter school. Typically, readiness tests derive from the behaviorist tradition, which separates learning into constituent parts or subskills (Shepard, 1990).

Readiness tests are a form of high-stakes testing because they affect decisions about children's entrance into school. High-stakes testing, as we have discussed before, is the use of readiness or achievement tests to make classification, retention, or promotion decisions about children (Meisels, 1989). A child's performance on a school readiness test can determine whether the child will (1) have to wait to enter school; (2) enter school with the child's age-mates; (3) receive a coding of "at-risk" and participate in additional testing; or (4) participate in a special class before entering kindergarten. Many experts regard the latter decision as a form of retention. Thus, a child can be retained before actually entering school.

Shepard (1990) believes that the research on readiness, especially on reading readiness, is "outmoded and seriously flawed" (p. 169) and inadequate. The tests rely on outdated theories in which learning becomes fragmented into skills and subskills. The child is supposed to somehow integrate these skills at a later time. Another criticism of school readiness tests is that they lack predictive validity. That is, for the most part, there are limited data on how accurately school readiness tests predict performance in school. In addition, these tests are inadequate as technical bases for such decisions about school placements as those involving special education placements, two-year kindergarten placements, and delays in school entry (Shepard, 1990).

In contrast to the notion that "children must be ready for school" is the idea that "schools must be ready for children." The Division for Early Childhood of the Council for Exceptional Children (1992) published a position paper stating that schools should be ready to accept and effectively educate all children. Schools must not screen children into or out of early education programs; rather, all children must have an opportunity to learn. Teachers must receive training in a wide variety of devel-

opmentally appropriate curricula, materials, and procedures to maximize each child's growth and development. Schooling will succeed or fail, not children.

## Preferred Practices

Teachers and other professionals need to become familiar with the characteristics of good screening and developmental assessments. The use of observations and the careful recording of data must be integral aspects of assessing young children. Sensitivity to parent concerns and involvement of parents and caregivers throughout the assessment process are key components in working with young children.

Teachers and therapists have to guard against planning the child's program by looking solely at test performance. It is inappropriate for a planning team to identify items that the child fails as discrete items that the child needs to learn. For example, from the test item "Child stacks 3 blocks," an inappropriate objective would be, "Randy will stack 3 blocks." A more appropriate programming activity would provide the child opportunities to manipulate a variety of materials in different ways, one of which might involve stacking.

Finally, assessment should not determine if children are "ready" for school or whether to delay children's entrance into school until they reach a certain level. Rather, children who are entering school for the first time benefit from a transition assessment that identifies needs and supports to make entry into the new program successful.

## Extending Learning

1. Research the position statements of two or more professional organizations such as Division of Early Childhood (DEC), a subdivision of the Council for Exceptional Children (CEC); the National Association for the Education of Young Children (NAEYC); or The Association of Persons

with Severe Handicaps (TASH). What are their positions regarding the assessment of young children? How do these positions compare? Develop your own position statement.

2. Contact your state department of education regarding its eligibility system for young

children. How does the system determine eligibility? What criteria does it use? Does your state use *developmental delay* or other terms in determining eligibility for special services for young children? If so, how is a developmental delay determined?

3. Conduct a comprehensive review of several screening instruments. Compare their administration, standardization, and scoring procedures. What do the manuals state about reliability and validity?

4. A young child received a referral for a comprehensive assessment as a result of the screening test. After examining the results of the comprehensive assessment, team members decided that the child was developing typically and there was no indication of delay. Explain several possible reasons why the child was referred as a result of the screening test.

5. Review two or three developmental assessment instruments. Compare the test items for a particular age group. What are the similarities? How are the items different? If you are assessing for the purpose of planning the child's program, which test items would provide the most helpful information?

6. Refer to the Snapshot that describes "special challenges." Choose one family and discuss how their situation will affect the assessment process.

7. Make arrangements to visit a kindergarten or community screening program. What are the components of the screening program? Compare your visit and observations with the Snapshot of Luiz. Present your observations to the class.

8. For young children, kindergarten screening tests may be a form of high-stakes testing. For older students, what tests are a form of high-stakes testing?

## References

Bagnato, S. J., and J. T. Neisworth (1990). *System to plan early childhood services (SPECS)*. Circle Pines, MN: American Guidance Service.

Barr, R. G. (1989). Recasting a clinical enigma: The case of infant crying. In *Challenges to developmental paradigms: Implications for theory, assessment, and treatment*, ed. P. R. Zelazo and R. G. Barr, 43–64. Hillsdale, NJ: Lawrence Erlbaum Associates.

Bayley, N. (1993). *Bayley scales of infant development.* 2d ed. San Antonio, TX: The Psychological Corporation.

Boehm, A. (2000). *Boehm test of basic concepts, third edition (Boehm–3)*. San Antonio, TX: The Psychological Corporation.

Boehm, A. (2001). *Boehm test of basic concepts, third edition–preschool (Boehm–3 Preschool)*. San Antonio, TX: The Psychological Corporation.

Bracken, B. A. (1998). *Bracken Basic Concept Scale–Revised*. San Antonio, TX: The Psychological Corporation.

Bredekamp, S., and C. Copple (eds.) (1997). *Developmentally appropriate practice in early childhood programs*. Washington, DC: National Association for the Education of Young Children.

Bricker, D. (ed.) (1993). *Assessment, evaluation, and programming system (AEPS) for infants and children: Vol. 1. AEPS measurement for birth to three years*. Baltimore: Paul H. Brookes.

Bricker, D., and K. Pretti-Frontczak (eds.) (1996). *Assessment, evaluation, and programming system (AEPS) for infants and chidren: Vol. 3 AEPS measurement for three to six years*. Baltimore: Paul H. Brookes.

Bricker, D., and J. Squires (1999). *Ages and stages questionnaire (ASQ)*. Baltimore: Paul H. Brookes.

Brigance, A. H. (1991). *BRIGANCE® inventory of early development–revised*. No. Billerica, MA: Curriculum Associates.

Brigance, A. H. (1998). *BRIGANCE® preschool screen for three- and four-year-old children*. No. Billerica, MA: Curriculum Associates.

Chandler, L. (1993). Steps in preparing for transition: Preschool to kindergarten. *Teaching Exceptional Children* 25(4): 52–55.

Cohen, Libby G., and Loraine J. Spenciner (1994). *Assessment of young children*. White Plains, NY: Longman.

Cooney, M. H., and M. Buchanan (2001). Documentation: Making assessment visible. *Young Exceptional Children* 4(3): 10–16.

Division for Early Childhood of the Council for Exceptional Children (1992). DEC position statement on goal one of America 2000: All children should begin school ready to learn. *DEC Communicator* 19(3): 4.

Flagler, S. (1996). *Infant-preschool play assessment scale*. Lewisville, NC: Kaplan.

Frankenburg, W. K., and J. B. Dodds (1990). *Denver II screening manual.* Denver, CO: Denver Developmental Materials.

Frankenburg, W. K., J. Dodds, P. Archer, B. Bresnick, P. Maschka, N. Edelman, and M. Shapiro (1990). *Denver–II.* Denver, CO: Denver Developmental Materials.

Greenspan, S. I., and S. Meisels (1993). Toward a new vision for the developmental assessment of infants and young children. Paper presented at the Zero to Three/National Center for Clinical Infant Programs' Eighth Biennial National Training Institute, December, Washington, DC.

Harrison, P. L., A. S. Kaufman, N. L. Kaufman, R. H. Bruininks, J. Rynders, S. Ilmer, S. S. Sparrow, and D. V. Cicchetti (1990). *AGS early screening profiles.* Circle Pines, MN: American Guidance Service.

Johnson-Martin, N. M., S. M. Attermeier, and B. J. Hacker (1990). *The Carolina curriculum for preschoolers with special needs.* Baltimore: Paul H. Brookes.

Kaufman, A. S., and N. L. Kaufman (1993). *Kaufman survey of early academic and language skills.* Circle Pines, MN: American Guidance Service.

Mardell-Czudnowski, C., and D. S. Goldenberg (1998). *Developmental indicators for the assessment of learning–3, third edition (DIAL–3).* Circle Pines, MN: American Guidance Service.

Meisels, S. J. (1989). High-stakes testing in kindergarten. *Educational Leadership* 46(7): 16–22.

Meisels, S. J., D. B. Marsden, M. S. Wiske, and L. W. Henderson (1997). *Early screening inventory–revised (ESI–R).* Ann Arbor, MI: Rebus.

Meisels, S. J., and B. A. Wasik (1990). Who should be served? Identifying children in need of early intervention. In *Handbook of early childhood intervention,* ed. S. J. Meisels and J. P. Shonkoff, 605–632. Cambridge: Cambridge University Press.

Miller, L. J. (1992). *FirstSTEP: Screening test for evaluating preschoolers.* San Antonio, TX: The Psychological Corporation, Harcourt Brace.

Mullen, E. M. (1995). *Mullen scales of early learning.* Circle Pines, MN: American Guidance Service.

National Center for Education Statistics (1993). *Readiness for kindergarten: Parent and teacher beliefs.* NCES Publication No. NCES 93-257. Washington, DC: U.S. Department of Education, Office of Educational Research and Improvement.

Repetto, J. B., and V. I. Correa (1996). Expanding views on transition. *Exceptional Children* 62(6): 551–563.

Rosenkoetter, S. E., A. H. Hains, and S. A. Fowler (1994). *Bridging early services for children with special needs and their families.* Baltimore: Paul H. Brookes.

Shepard, L. (1990). Readiness testing in local school districts: An analysis of backdoor policies. *Journal of Education Policy* 5(5): 159–179.

Sparrow, S. S., D. A. Balla, and D. V. Cicchetti (1998). *Vineland social-emotional early childhood scales (SEEC).* Circle Pines, MN: American Guidance Services.

Voress, J. K., and T. Maddox (1998). *Developmental assessment of young children.* Austin, TX: PRO-ED.

VORT Corporation (1995). *Hawaii Early Learning Profile (HELP) for preschoolers.* Palo Alto, CA: VORT Corporation.

Welch, M. C., and B. White (1999). *Teacher and parent expectations for kindergarten readiness.* (ERIC Document Reproduction Service No. ED 437 225).

# 13

# *Cognitive Development*

## Overview

What is intelligence? What makes us intelligent? The nature of intelligence has received a great deal of attention over the years. One view of intelligence is that it is an arbitrary concept, impossible to define or quantify. Other views are that intelligence consists of multifaceted, complex, highly organized abilities that are identifiable and measurable. One common conception is that intelligence is the ability to apply prior knowledge to new situations. The specific intelligence tests we describe in this chapter reflect the many views of the construct of intelligence.

## Chapter Objectives

After completing this chapter, you should be able to:

- Explain the concept of intelligence tests as samples of behavior.
- Discuss the stability of test performance.
- Describe specific tests of intelligence.

## What Shapes Our Views

Although there is still a great deal that we do not know about intelligence, Sternberg (1996) has described nine "truths" about intelligence:

1. Intelligence is multidimensional. There is still a great deal that we have to learn about the dimensions of intelligence.
2. The social order of our society is in part the creation of tests, which sort and categorize people according to the abilities they measure.
3. Intelligence is teachable to some extent, but extreme changes are unlikely at this time.
4. Intelligence tests measure skills that are of considerable importance in school and of moderate importance in success on the job.
5. Intelligence tests can be helpful when measuring abilities, but only under proper use and with proper interpretation.
6. Intelligence test scores have been rising since the 1930s in the United States and in other countries.
7. Intelligence is the result of the influences of heredity and environment.
8. We still have much to learn about the relationships between race, intelligence, and environment.
9. While tests of intelligence provide an indication of cognitive skills, they are not measures of the worth of individuals.

## Intelligence Tests as Samples of Behavior

If we were to measure intelligence directly, we would have to monitor the electrical activities, neurochemical changes, and neurobiological changes that occur during cognition. As educators, we rely instead on indirect measures or tests to estimate intelligence. Intelligence tests don't sample intelligence, but rather the behaviors that we associate with intelligence. We use intelligence tests like we would use a knife to cut a piece of cake. The knife reveals a sample of the cake; we assume that the texture and flavor of the cake is the same in the uncut or unsampled portion. This same analogy can be applied to intelligence tests. While the tests sample behaviors, our assumption is that the sample provides information about the intellectual abilities of the individual.

Although there are many intelligence tests, an analysis of them shows that they sample similar behaviors. Salvia and Ysseldyke (2001) have described these behaviors:

1. *Discrimination.* Intelligence tests sample skills that relate to figural, symbolic, or semantic discrimination usually by asking the student to find the item that is different from the other items.

2. *Generalization.* Intelligence tests sample skills relating to figural, symbolic, or semantic understanding by asking students to recognize the response that goes with the stimulus item.

3. *Motor Behavior.* Intelligence tests ask young children to demonstrate a motor response, such as throwing objects, constructing block towers, or placing objects in certain places on a board. The tests ask older students to draw geometric forms, solve mazes, or reproduce designs from memory. In addition to these items, many other test items evaluate motor abilities

by asking students to point out, imitate, or perform other motor activities in order to complete certain test items.

**4.** *General Information.* These items evaluate what the individual has learned. Examples of these items include, "What is the opposite of uncle?" and "How many eggs are in a dozen?"

**5.** *Vocabulary.* Intelligence tests assess knowledge of vocabulary in different ways—by asking individuals to point to a picture the test has named, to define words the examiner presents orally, or to identify a word that matches a definition.

**6.** *Induction.* Intelligence tests present students with several stimuli and ask them to induce or to infer a general principle. For example, after seeing a rock, block of wood, metal object, and a toothpick, the individual must describe the general rule about why certain objects float.

**7.** *Comprehension.* Intelligence tests ask students to demonstrate understanding of or the nature of meaning of certain stimuli. Students have to show that they understand directions, certain materials, or societal customs. Some tests ask the student to respond to certain situations such as, "What should you do if you see a young child playing with an electrical cord?"

**8.** *Sequencing.* Intelligence tests require students to identify the correct sequences for a series of items. The items can, for example, consist of numbers, geometric figures, or abstract geometric designs.

**9.** *Detail Recognition.* A few tests evaluate detail recognition by asking individuals to identify details that are missing from a picture or to draw a picture and evaluate the drawing on the basis of how many details individuals include.

**10.** *Analogies.* Intelligence tests present items consisting of a statement to which the student must give the appropriate response. The stimuli may consist of a series of words, geometric designs, or numbers. An example of an item is: parent : child :: goose :     .

**11.** *Abstract Reasoning.* Intelligence tests present various types of items that assess abstract reasoning by asking students to identify the absurdity in a statement or picture, to state the meaning of a proverb, or to solve problems of arithmetical reasoning.

**12.** *Memory.* Intelligence tests present a variety of test items that evaluate both long-term and short-term memory by asking students to repeat sentences or a series of digits, to retell what they have read, or to reproduce a design from memory.

**13.** *Pattern Completion.* Intelligence tests ask students to complete a pattern or matrix that has a missing piece.

There are many behaviors that intelligence tests do not sample. These behaviors include mechanical, musical, artistic, motivational, emotional, and attitudinal behaviors (Anastasi, 1988). Recent research on the nature of intelligence has begun to explore the contribution of these behaviors to our understanding of intelligence.

## Responding to Diversity

There has been much debate over the years about the value of intelligence testing. Arguments against the use of intelligence testing claim that testing limits opportunities, can be harmful to individuals from various cultural and ethnic groups, and facilitates the placement of students into categories. Advocates of intelligence testing have argued that intelligence testing assists in diagnosis, helps to identify individuals who need specialized instruction or therapy, and promotes educational opportunities (Sattler, 1988).

Membership in a cultural or ethnic group, socioeconomic status, educational attainment, language, and acculturation can affect intelligence test scores. Educators can reduce or prevent bias in the assessment of intelligence by being: (1) aware of individual characteristics; (2) knowledgeable in test use and test selection;

*A teacher discusses a student's test scores with the parents.*

and (3) sensitive when adminstering, scoring, and interpreting performance (Suzuki, Vraniak, and Kugler, 1996).

Intelligence tests provide us with only a part of what we want to know about an individual. The assessment of individuals should never depend on the results of one test; rather, good practice requires that we use the results of additional standardized tests, as well as observations, interviews, checklists, rating scales, samples of work, and other types of assessment, in appropriate combination, to gather information.

In summary, it is important to remember that

- intelligence tests do not measure innate ability
- intelligence test scores change as individuals become older
- intelligence test scores are estimates, or approximations, of abilities
- intelligence is one of many abilities that individuals have

- intelligence scores from various intelligence tests may not have the same meaning
- multiple methods and types of assessment need to be used when assessing an individual (NAEYC Position Statement, cited in Sattler, 1988)

## Standardized Instruments

As stated previously, there are a multitude of standardized tests of intelligence on the market. Table 13.1 lists many of the more commonly available tests of intelligence and some of their application characteristics.

### Batería–R Tests of Cognitive Ability and Achievement

The *Batería–R COG* and the *Batería–R ACH* (Woodcock and Muñoz-Sandoval, 1996) form a parallel Spanish version of the *Woodcock-Johnson Psychoeducational Battery–Revised*. The *Batería–R*

**TABLE 13.1**   *Tests of Intelligence*

| Test | Abilities Measured |
| --- | --- |
| *Batería–R Tests of Cognitive Ability* (Woodcock and Muñoz-Sandoval, 1996)* | Spanish version of the *Woodcock-Johnson Psychoeducational Battery–Revised;* measures cognitive ability, scholastic aptitude, and Spanish oral language |
| *Blind Learning Aptitude Test* (Newland, 1971) | Uses a bas-relief format; assesses discrimination, generalization, sequencing, analogies, and matrix completion; ages 6 years through 12 years |
| *Cognitive Abilities Test, Form 5 (CogAT)* (Thorndike and Hagan, 1993) | Group intelligence test; grades kindergarten through 12 |
| *Columbia Mental Maturity Scale* (Burgenmeister, Blum, and Lorge, 1972) | Nonverbal tests; ages 3 years, 6 months through 9 years, 11 months |
| *Comprehensive Test of Nonverbal Intelligence (CTONI)* (Hammill, Pearson, and Wiederholt, 1996) | Measures nonverbal problem solving and reasoning; ages 6 years through 18 years, 11 months |
| *Detroit Tests of Learning Aptitude–Primary: Second Edition* (Hammill and Bryant, 1991) | Assesses abilities in three domains: linguistic, attentional, motoric; ages 3 years through 9 years, 11 months |
| *Detroit Tests of Learning Aptitude: Fourth Edition* (Hammill, 1998) | Measures intelligence, aptitude, and achievement; ages 6 years through 17 years |
| *Differential Ability Scales–Administration and Scoring Manual* (Elliott, 1990a) | Measures cognitive ability and achievement; ages 2 years, 6 months through 17 years, 11 months |
| *Escala de inteligencia Wechsler para Niños®–Revisada de Puerto Rico (EIWN–R PR)* (Wechsler, 1993)* | Spanish adaptation of the *WISC–R.* Normed on 2,200 Puerto Rican children, ages 6 years through 16 years, 11 months |
| *Escala de Inteligencia Wechsler para Niños®–Revisada (EIWN–R)* (Wechsler, 1983)* | Spanish adaptation of the *WISC–R.* Published without norms, it is intended for use with Chicano, Puerto Rican, and Cuban children |
| *Griffiths Mental Development Scales* (Griffiths, 1979) | Useful with nonverbal children; ages birth through 8 years |
| *Kaufman Adolescent and Adult Intelligence Test* (Kaufman and Kaufman, 1993) | Measures general intelligence; ages 11 years through 85+ years |
| *Kaufman Assessment Battery for Children* (Kaufman and Kaufman, 1983) | Measures mental ability and achievement; ages 2 years, 6 months through 12 years, 6 months |
| *Kaufman Brief Intelligence Test* (Kaufman and Kaufman, 1990) | Measures verbal and nonverbal intelligence; ages 4 years through 90 years |
| *Leiter International Performance Scale* (Roid and Miller, 1997) | Measures nonverbal intelligences; ages 2 years through 12 years |
| *McCarthy Scales of Children's Abilities* (McCarthy, 1972) | Assesses general intellectual ability; ages 2 years, 6 months through 8 years, 6 months |

*(continued)*

**TABLE 13.1**    *Continued*

| Test | Abilities Measured |
|---|---|
| *Slosson Full-Range Intelligence Test–Revised (SFRIT–R)* (Algozzine, 1991) | Assesses verbal intelligence; ages 4 years through 65 years |
| *Slosson Intelligence Test–Revised (SIT–R)* (Algozzine, Eaves, Mann, and Vance, 1998) | Assesses verbal skills, quantitative abilities, memory, abstract reasoning; ages 5 years through adulthood |
| *Stanford-Binet Intelligence Scale: Fourth Edition* (Thorndike, Hagan, and Sattler, 1986c) | Assesses cognitive abilities; ages 2 years through 23 years |
| *Test of Nonverbal Intelligence–Third Edition* (Brown, Sherbenou, and Johnsen, 1997) | Measures abstract figural problem solving; ages 6 years through 85 years, 11 months |
| *Wechsler Intelligence Scale for Children–Third Edition (WISC–III)* (Wechsler, 1991) | Assesses global intellectual ability; ages 6 years through 16 years, 11 months |
| *Wechsler Preschool and Primary Scale of Intelligence–Revised* (Wechsler, 1989) | Measures general intellectual ability; ages 3 years through 7 years |
| *Woodcock-Johnson Tests of Cognitive Ability* (Woodcock, McGrew, and Mather, 2001) | Assesses cognitive and academic abilities; ages 2 years through adulthood |

˚Spanish form

*COG* and *ACH* is an individually administered battery that assesses cognitive, academic, and language abilities in Spanish-speaking individuals ages 2 years through adulthood. The battery consists of two parts, *Tests of Cognitive Ability (Batería–R COG)* and the *Tests of Achievement (Batería–R ACH)*. Box 13.1 describes the test's parameters.

Like the *Woodcock-Johnson Psychoeducational Battery–Revised*, the *Batería–R COG* derives from the Horn-Cattell theory of cognitive processing, which we discuss later in this chapter in the description of the *Woodcock-Johnson Psychoeducational Battery–Revised*.

***Administration.*** The *Batería–R* takes from 20 minutes to more than two hours to administer, depending on whether you are using both parts. Raw scores convert to age and grade equivalents, percentile ranks, and standard scores. The scoring can be cumbersome and it is advisable to use a computer scoring program.

***Technical Adequacy.*** Technical adequacy of the *Batería–R* derives from the *Woodcock-Johnson Psychoeducational Battery–Revised (WJ–R)*. The authors used the standardization sample of the *WJ–R* to develop the scoring procedures and other technical information for the *Batería–R*, and calibrated it on 3,911 native Spanish-speaking individuals from Costa Rica, Mexico, Peru, Puerto Rico, Spain, Arizona, California, Florida, New York, and Texas. The purpose of this calibration was to develop a parallel form of the *WJ–R*.

The authors argue that because of this calibration with the *WJ–R*, reliability and validity information from the *Woodcock-Johnson Psychoeducational Battery–R* is applicable to this test.

***Summary.*** The *Batería–R COG* and the *Batería–R ACH* form a parallel Spanish version of the *Woodcock-Johnson Psychoeducational Battery–Revised*. This norm-referenced, individually

*Batería–R Tests of Cognitive Ability*

*Publication Date:* 1996

*Purposes:* The *Batería–R* is a parallel Spanish version of the *Woodcock-Johnson Psychoeducational Battery–Revised*. The *Batería–R* assesses cognitive, academic, and language abilities in Spanish-speaking individuals.

*Age/Grade Levels:* 2 years through adulthood; grades kindergarten through college.

*Time to Administer:* 20 minutes to more than two hours, depending on whether both the Tests of Cognitive Ability and the Tests of Achievement are administered.

*Technical Adequacy:* Reliability information is lacking. Additional investigation of validity is warranted.

*Suggested Use:* Measures general cognitive abilities, aptitude, and achievement in Spanish-speaking students. Results should be cautiously used.

administered battery assesses cognitive, academic, and language abilities in Spanish-speaking individuals ages 2 years through adulthood. Reliability information is lacking. The tests warrant additional investigation of validity.

# Cognitive Abilities Test

The *Cognitive Abilities Test, Form 5 (CogAT)* (Thorndike and Hagen, 1993) developed out of the *Lorge-Thorndike Intelligence Tests* and consists of a series of group-administered intelligence tests for students in grades kindergarten through 12. The *CogAT* assesses: (1) the ability to follow directions; (2) the ability to hold material in short-term memory; (3) strategies for scanning pictorial and figural stimuli to obtain either specific or general information; (4) general information and verbal concepts; (5) the ability to compare stimuli and detect similarities and differences in relative size, position, quantity, shape, and time; (6) the ability to classify, categorize, or order familiar objects; and (7) the ability to use quantitative and spatial relationships and concepts. Table 13.2 shows the batteries and subtests of the *CogAT*.

*Administration.* The teacher reads aloud all of the directions for Levels 1 and 2. Students do not have to read but must be able to follow the directions of the teacher. The student responds by identifying the one correct response and filling in an oval. Levels A–H are administered to groups of students, rather than to individual students.

*Scoring.* Each battery has a separate score, and there is a Composite score. Individual subtests

**TABLE 13.2** *CogAT Subtests*

| Level | Verbal Battery | Quantitative Battery | Nonverbal Battery |
|---|---|---|---|
| Levels 1 and 2 are for students in grades kindergarten through grade 3. | Verbal Reasoning Oral Vocabulary | Relational Concepts Quantitative Concepts | Figure Classification Matrices |
| Levels A–H are for students in grades 3 through 12. | Verbal Classification Sentence Completion Verbal Analogies | Quantitative Relations Number Series Equation Building | Figure Classification Figure Analogies Figure Analysis |

do not report scores. Reported scores include percentiles, stanines, and standard scores.

***Standardization.*** The *CogAT* was normed at the same time as the *Iowa Tests of Basic Skills* and the *Tests of Achievement and Proficiency* in public schools across the United States according to geographic region, enrollment, and socio-economic status. In addition, there is a sample for private non-Catholic schools and Catholic schools.

***Reliability.*** Internal consistency reliability is acceptable. Other types of reliability are lacking.

***Validity.*** Evidence of validity is absent from the manual.

***Summary.*** The *Cognitive Abilities Test, Form 5* is a group intelligence test for students in kindergarten through grade 12. While the standardization of this test is commendable, evidence of reliability and validity is lacking.

## Comprehensive Test of Nonverbal Intelligence

The *Comprehensive Test of Nonverbal Intelligence (CTONI)* (Hammill, Pearson, and Wiederholt, 1996) is a nonverbal measure of abstract/figural problem solving and reasoning for use with individuals ages 6 years through 18 years, 11 months. It is useful for assessing the performance of individuals who have language or motor problems that in some cases make it difficult for them to respond to more traditional tests. The test is made up of six subtests: Pictorial Analogies, Geometric Analogies, Pictorial Categories, Geometric Categories, Pictorial Sequences, and Geometric Sequences. For each of these subtests, the examinee must solve a visual problem that consists of either pictures (e.g., shoe, ball, cube) or geometric shapes (e.g., triangle, circle, diamond). Box 13.2 describes the test's parameters.

***Administration.*** The test items are contained in a stiff book that is set up like an easel. The examiner can pantomime the instructions or give them orally. If the examiner chooses to pantomime the instructions, the examiner uses facial gestures, hand movements, and head movements. The student shows the correct response by pointing or by some other motor response. This nonverbal method of test administration does have several advantages. The examinee does not have to listen to directions, speak, read, or write. There is no time limit for the test.

***Scoring.*** Examiners score items as either correct or incorrect. Raw scores convert to standard scores, percentile ranks, and age equivalents.

***Standardization.*** The *CTONI* standardization sample consisted of 2,129 individuals, ranging in age from 6 years to 18 years, 11 months. It is unclear whether the sample was stratified accord-

---

**BOX 13.2**    *Comprehensive Test of Nonverbal Intelligence (CTONI)*

*Publication Date:* 1996

*Purposes:* Measures nonverbal abstract/figural problem solving and reasoning in individuals who have language or motor problems that may make it difficult for them to respond to more traditional tests.

*Age/Grade Levels:* Ages 6 years through 18 years, 11 months.

*Time to Administer:* 20 to 45 minutes.

*Technical Adequacy:* Information about the standardization sample is sparse. Reliability is adequate but additional information concerning validity is needed.

*Suggested Use:* The *CTONI* may be useful as a screening instrument. It should be used cautiously until additional information relating to validity can be gathered.

ing to major demographic variables. Characteristics of the sample include age, gender, race (white, black, other), ethnic group (Native American, Hispanic, Asian, African American, other) geographic region, residence (rural, urban), family income, disability status, and educational background of the parents.

***Reliability.*** The test reports internal consistency reliability and test-retest reliability. The average coefficient for internal consistency was .97. The test reports test-retest reliability coefficients only for students enrolled in third grade, eleventh grade, and the total sample. These coefficients ranged from .79 to .94.

***Validity.*** Validity determines whether a test measures what it purports to measure. While the manual reports the results of several validity studies, more extensive research is necessary in order to determine whether this instrument measures the construct of intelligence and to determine its usefulness in measuring intellectual abilities of persons with disabilities.

***Summary.*** The *CTONI* is a nonverbal measure that assesses visual problem solving and reasoning. Reliability is adequate. Teachers should use it cautiously until additional information relating to validity is available.

## Detroit Tests of Learning Aptitude– Primary: Second Edition

The *Detroit Tests of Learning Aptitude–Primary: Second Edition (DTLA–P:2)* (Hammill and Bryant, 1991) measures the intellectual aptitudes or abilities of individuals ages 3 years to 9 years, 11 months. This is the second edition of the *DTLA–P*. According to the authors, the *DTLA–P:2* has four uses: (1) to discover strengths and weaknesses among mental abilities, (2) to identify children who perform significantly below their peers, (3) to predict future performance, and (4) to aid as a research tool when investigating children's aptitude, intelligence, and cognitive ability. De-

pending on the child's age and abilities, the *DTLA–P* takes between 15 and 45 minutes to administer.

The *DTLA–P:2* consists of 100 items arranged in order from the easiest to the most difficult. The items yield six subtest scores and a general, overall mental ability score. The six subtests and the domains in which they are grouped are as follows:

### Linguistic Domain
1. *Verbal Quotient:* Assesses the understanding, integration, and use of spoken language.
2. *Nonverbal Quotient:* Assesses spatial relationship and nonverbal symbolic reasoning abilities.

### Attentional Domain
3. *Attention-Enhanced Quotient:* Evaluates immediate recall, memory, and ability to concentrate.
4. *Attention-Reduced Quotient:* Measures long-term memory, understanding, reasoning ability, and comprehension of abstract relationships.

### Motoric Domain
5. *Motor-Enhanced Quotient:* Assesses complex motor abilities, especially fine-motor abilities.
6. *Motor-Reduced Quotient:* Evaluates aptitude with reduced demands for motor activities. The child indicates the correct response by either pointing or speaking.

***Administration.*** Examiners must have some background in assessment. Directions for administration are on the test protocol. For some items, directions for administration are in the examiner's manual. The test is administered individually. Since the items are in order from least to most difficult, the examiner begins testing at certain entry points. The student's chronological age determines these entry points. When testing reaches a predetermined ceiling, it stops.

*Scoring.* The examiner scores the responses as either correct or incorrect and uses the scores for each item to compute the total score and the subtest scores. Raw scores can convert to age equivalents, percentiles, and quotients, which are standard scores that have a mean of 100 and a standard deviation of 15.

*Standardization.* The standardization sample of the *DTLA–P:2* consisted of 2,095 children in 36 states. In developing this instrument, the authors used data from the standardization sample (March–June 1985) of the *DTLA–P* and tested an additional 619 children between September 1989 and June 1990. These two samples then combined to form the standardization sample for the *DTLA–P:2*. The test reports information on the percentage of children for each of the following variables: gender, residence (urban, rural), race, geographic area (Northeast, North Central, South, West), ethnicity (American Indian, Hispanic, Asian, other), and age.

---

**BOX 13.3**   *Detroit Tests of Learning Aptitude–Primary: Second Edition (DTLA–P:2)*

*Publication Date:* 1991

*Purposes:* Measures general intellectual aptitudes or abilities.

*Age/Grade Levels:* Ages 3 years to 9 years, 11 months.

*Time to Administer:* 15 to 45 minutes.

*Technical Adequacy:* Questions remain as to the appropriateness of the standardization sample, reliability, and validity.

*Suggested Use:* The *DTLA–P:2* can be used as a screening instrument. Caution should be exercised when using test scores to make decisions regarding the identification of students and eligibility for special services.

---

*Reliability.* Test authors used a random sample of 350 protocols from the standardization sample to estimate internal consistency. The average reliabilities for the total score and the six subtests ranged from .88 to .94. The test also reports test-retest reliability, but provides little information about the characteristics of the sample, qualifications of the examiners, or the test-retest interval.

*Validity.* The authors maintain that the *DTLA–P:2* has content validity because it measures behaviors that Salvia and Ysseldyke (1995) have developed. To demonstrate concurrent validity, the authors used evidence from four concurrent validity studies that were conducted with the *DTLA–P*. The size of the samples in each of these correlations ranged from 28 to 68 children. The reported reliability coefficients ranged from .31 to .87.

The *DTLA–P:2* manual contains no evidence of predictive validity. While the authors present evidence of construct validity, additional validity studies are necessary.

*Summary.* The *Detroit Tests of Learning Aptitude–Primary: Second Edition* is an individually administered test for children ages 3 years to 9 years, 11 months. It measures intellectual ability using six subtests and a general, overall score. Questions remain as to the appropriateness of the standardization sample, reliability, and validity. Until the authors present additional evidence, teachers should use the test cautiously. Box 13.3 outlines the test's parameters.

## Detroit Tests of Learning Aptitude: Fourth Edition

The *Detroit Tests of Learning Aptitude–Fourth Edition (DTLA–4)* (Hammill, 1998) measures the intellectual aptitudes or abilities of students ages 6 through 17. According to the author the *DTLA–4* measures intelligence, aptitude, and achievement. Box 13.4 outlines the test's parameters. The *DTLA–4* consists of 10 subtests:

**1.** *Word Opposites:* The student must verbalize the opposite of a word that the examiner says.

**2.** *Design Sequences:* The student must arrange cubes in a pattern from memory after being shown a picture of the pattern for five seconds.

**3.** *Sentence Imitation:* The student repeats a sentence after listening to the examiner say the sentence.

**4.** *Reversed Letters:* The examiner recites a series of letters. The student must record the letters, reversing their order of presentation.

**5.** *Story Construction:* After viewing three pictures, the student makes up three stories.

**6.** *Design Reproduction:* The student must draw a design from memory after being shown a design for five seconds.

**7.** *Basic Information:* The student responds to factual questions.

**8.** *Symbolic Relations:* The student views a design and must choose from among six designs the one that completes the pattern.

**9.** *Word Sequences:* The student repeats a series of unrelated words after listening to the examiner recite the words.

**10.** *Story Sequences:* The student arranges a series of cartoonlike pictures to make a story.

**Administration.** Examiners should have some background in assessment.

Directions for administration are on the test protocol. For some items, directions for administration are in the examiner's manual. Administration takes between 50 minutes and 2 hours.

**Scoring.** Examiners score the responses as either correct or incorrect. The scores for each item make up the computation of the total score and the subtest scores. Raw scores can convert to age equivalents, percentiles, and quotients, which are standard scores that have a mean of 100 and a standard deviation of 15.

**Standardization.** The standardization sample of the *DTLA–4* consisted of 1,350 students in 37 states. In developing this instrument, the author used data from the standardization sample of the *DTLA–3* and selected additional samples. The standardization of the *DTLA–4* is confusing and ambiguous.

**Reliability.** Estimations of internal consistency reliability came from the standardization sample. The average reliabilities for the total score and the six subtests ranged from .82 to .93. Test-retest reliability derived from a sample of 98 students living in Austin, Texas. The coefficients ranged from .71 to .96.

**Validity.** The authors maintain that the *DTLA–4* has content validity because it measures behaviors that Salvia and Ysseldyke (1998) have developed and because it relates the subtests to

---

**BOX 13.4** *Detroit Tests of Learning Aptitude–4 (Fourth Edition) (DTLA–4)*

*Publication Date:* 1998

*Purposes:* Measures general intellectual aptitudes or abilities and achievement.

*Age/Grade Levels:* Ages 6 years through 17 years.

*Time to Administer:* 50 minutes to 2 hours.

*Technical Adequacy:* Questions remain as to the appropriateness of the standardization sample, reliability, and validity.

*Suggested Use:* May be helpful in determining areas of strength and weakness. Exercise caution when using test scores to make decisions regarding the identification of students and eligibility for special services.

the theories of intelligence. While the authors present evidence of construct validity, additional validity studies are necessary.

***Summary.*** The *Detroit Tests of Learning Aptitude–4* is an individually administered test for students ages 6 through 17. Questions remain as to the appropriateness of the standardization sample, reliability, and validity.

## Differential Ability Scales

The *Differential Ability Scales (DAS)* (Elliott, 1990a) is a revision of the *British Ability Scales.* The DAS measures cognitive ability and achievement in individuals ages 2 years, 6 months to 17 years, 11 months. The test does not base itself on any one theory of mental ability. According to the manual, the test

> is built on a collection of subtests that sample a range of human abilities thought to be useful in assessing individuals, particularly students with learning difficulties. The selection of the abilities sampled was influenced by a variety of theoretical approaches. (1990b, p. 14)

The structure of the *DAS* is hierarchical. The first level consists of the subtest scores, at the next level are the cluster scores, and at the general level the *DAS* yields a general cognitive ability score (GCA). The test contains 17 cognitive subtests and 3 school achievement subtests. Not all of the subtests are given to every individual. Teachers administer selected subtests depending on the age of the student. Table 13.3 describes the subtests and clusters.

***Administration.*** The administration of the *DAS* calls for an examiner who has a background in the principles of assessment. The total time to administer the *DAS* is approximately 35 minutes for children ages 2 years, 6 months to 3 years, 5 months; administration to children ages 3 years, 6 months to 5 years, 11 months takes approximately 65 minutes; and it takes

between 65 and 85 minutes for students older than 6 years of age. The manual provides separate directions for administering each of the subtests.

The administration of the *DAS* does have several unique features. These include decision points, alternative stopping points, teaching a failed item, extended selection of subtests, and out-of-level testing. While the starting points for each subtest depend on the individual's age, the administration of items continues until the individual reaches a *decision point*. At that decision point, the examiner decides whether to stop, to continue to administer the difficult items, or to drop back and administer easier items. Alternative stopping points are available so that the examiner can halt the test administration if the items are too difficult or if the examiner and the student have not developed a rapport. In addition to these features, some subtests allow the examiner to teach the individual the failed item. *Extended selection* of subtests refers to the option of allowing the examiner to administer additional subtests that measure similar abilities. This may occur with young children when further assessment is considered necessary. *Out-of-level testing* refers to the administration of additional subtests to individuals who have unusually low or high abilities. These subtests may not be appropriate for individuals who have average ability.

For individuals with hearing impairments or speech or language problems, nonverbal subtests are available. These include Block Building and Picture Similarities. The scores from these subtests form a Special Nonverbal Composite, which, according to the manual, can replace the GCA. However, the test does not include separate norms for special populations.

***Scoring.*** Raw scores compare to Ability Scores. These are scores that are unique to the *DAS* and provide an estimate of the individual's performance on specific subtests. However, ability scores of different subtests have an important limitation: They are not comparable. Converting Ability Scores to T-scores (T-scores have a

**TABLE 13.3   *Differential Ability Scales: Subtests and Clusters***

| Tests | Age Range | Applications |
|---|---|---|
| *Preschool Core Subtests* | | |
| Block Building | 2 years, 6 months to 4 years, 11 months | Measures motor and perceptual abilities. The individual copies wooden block designs. |
| Verbal Comprehension | 2 years, 6 months to 6 years, 11 months | Measures receptive language ability. The child points to named pictures or places objects and chips according to the examiner's instructions (e.g., under the bridge). |
| Picture Similarities | 2 years, 6 months to 7 years, 11 months | Measures nonverbal reasoning ability. After observing a row of four pictures or designs, the child must choose the best picture or design that goes with the ones that are shown. |
| Naming Vocabulary | 2 years, 6 months to 8 years, 11 months | Measures expressive vocabulary. The child names several objects and pictures that are shown. |
| Pattern Construction | 3 years to 17 years, 11 months | Measures visual-spatial problem solving. The individual constructs patterns using foam squares and plastic blocks. |
| Early Number Concepts | 2 years, 6 months to 7 years, 11 months | Measures prenumerical and number concepts and skills. The child counts chips and answers questions about pictures. Many, but not all of the subtests, are nonverbal. |
| Copying | 3 years, 6 months to 7 years, 11 months | Measures ability to copy, motor ability, and the ability to perceive similarities. After observing a line drawing, the child reproduces it. |
| *School-Age Core Subtests* | | |
| Recall of Designs | 5 years through 17 years, 11 months | Assesses short-term recall, motor ability, and visual-spatial ability. After observing a nonpictorial line drawing for five seconds, the individual must draw it from memory. |
| Word Definitions | 5 years through 17 years, 11 months | Measures verbal knowledge. The examiner says a word and the individual must provide the meaning. |

*(continued)*

**TABLE 13.3** *Continued*

| Tests | Age Range | Applications |
|---|---|---|
| *School-Age Core Subtests* | | |
| Pattern Construction | 3 years through 17 years, 11 months | This subtest description is in the *Preschool Core Subtests* section. |
| Matrices | 5 years through 17 years, 11 months | Measures nonverbal reasoning ability. The student observes a series of matrices. For each one, the student chooses the design that best completes the matrix. |
| Similarities | 5 years through 17 years, 11 months | Measures verbal reasoning. The individual must respond orally to a series of questions. |
| Sequential and Quantitative Reasoning | 5 years through 17 years, 11 months | Assesses the ability to perceive sequential patterns or rules in numerical relationships. The items consist of abstract figures or numbers to which the student must respond. |
| *Diagnostic Subtests* | | |
| Matching Letterlike Forms | 4 years through 7 years, 11 months | Measures the ability to visually discriminate among similar letterlike figures. The student matches similar figures that look like letters and are rotated on a page. |
| Recall of Digits | 2 years, 6 months through 17 years, 11 months | Assesses short-term auditory-sequential recall of digits. The individual must repeat a series of 2 to 9 digits. |
| Recall of Objects–Immediate and Delayed | 4 years through 17 years, 11 months | Assesses short-term and delayed verbal memory. The individual recalls as many objects as possible after being shown a card with a number of objects on it. |
| Recognition of Pictures | 2 years, 6 months through 17 years, 11 months | Assesses short-term visual memory. After observing a card with one or more pictures for a few seconds, the individal observes another set of pictures and must point to the pictures that were in the first set. |
| Speed of Information Processing | 5 years through 17 years, 11 months | Assesses speed of simple mental operations. After observing a page consisting of figures or numbers, the individual must mark, as quickly as possible, the circle containing the largest number of boxes or the highest number. |

**TABLE 13.3** *Continued*

| Tests | Age Range | Applications |
|---|---|---|
| *School Achievement Tests* | | |
| Basic Number Skills | 6 years through 17 years, 11 months | Assesses basic computational skills. The individual solves problems on a worksheet. |
| Spelling | 6 years through 17 years, 11 months | Assesses ability to spell based on phonetically regular and irregular words. Children ages 6 years, 0 months to 8 years, 11 months are also asked to write their names. The examiner says the word, uses the word in a sentence, and repeats the word, and the individual writes the words. |
| Word Reading | 5 years through 17 years, 11 months | Assesses ability to decode words in isolation. The student reads a series of words that are shown on a card. |
| *Clusters of the Preschool Level of the Cognitive Battery* | 3 years, 6 months through 5 years, 11 months | Verbal Ability. Assesses learned verbal concepts and knowledge. The subtests that form this cluster are Verbal Comprehension and Naming Vocabulary. |
| Nonverbal Ability | | Assesses complex, nonverbal mental processing. The subtests that form this cluster include Picture Similarities, Pattern Construction, and Copying. |
| *Clusters of the School-Age Level of the Cognitive Battery* | 6 years through 17 years, 11 months | Verbal Ability. Assesses verbal mental processing and acquired knowledge. The subtests that form this cluster are Word Definitions and Similarities. |
| Nonverbal Reasoning Ability | | Assesses nonverbal inductive reasoning and mental processing. The subtests that form this cluster include Matrices, Sequential, and Quantitative Reasoning. |
| Spatial Ability | | Assesses complex visual-spatial processing. The subtests that form this cluster are Recall of Designs and Pattern Construction. |

mean of 50 and a standard deviation of 10), percentiles, and standard scores (mean of 100,
standard deviation of 15) requires another trans-
formation. The test provide age and grade
equivalents for the achievement tests and separate guidelines for scoring each of the subtests.

**Standardization.** The standardization sample
consisted of 3,475 individuals evenly divided by
gender, with 175 individuals for each six-month
interval for ages 2 years, 6 months to 4 years,
11 months and 200 individuals at one-year
intervals for ages 5 years, 0 months to 17 years,
11 months. Other stratification variables were
race/ethnicity (black, Hispanic, white, other
including Asian, Pacific Islander, American
Indian, Eskimo, Aleut), parent education, geographic region, and educational preschool
enrollment.

The standardization sample included individuals with learning disabilities, speech impairments, emotional disturbances, physical
impairments, and mental retardation, as well as
gifted individuals in approximate proportion to
U.S. population data, excluding individuals with
severe disabilities. The test does not provide
separate norms. According to the manual,

> The mere inclusion of individuals with excep-
> tional needs in a norm sample does not make
> the instrument appropriate for use with such
> children, nor does their exclusion make the
> test inappropriate. During item and subtest de-
> velopment, the DAS team sought to create
> tasks that would be suitable in content, format,
> and difficulty for many exceptional children.
> Research that focuses on how the test works
> with such children will determine the success
> of these efforts, like those of any other test de-
> velopment project. (Elliot, 1990b, p. 116)

**Reliability.** The test reports internal reliabilities for each of the subtests and for out-of-
level testing. For the most part, the reliabilities
were within the moderate range.

To estimate test-retest reliability, studies
selected 100 individuals from the standardization sample for each of the following age

ranges: 3 years, 6 months to 4 years, 5 months; 5
years, 0 months to 6 years, 11 months; and 12
years, 0 months to 13 years, 11 months. The
testing interval ranged from two to seven weeks.
While the reliabilities were in the moderate
range for the subtests, the reliabilities of the
clusters and the general cognitive ability score
were higher than the reliabilities for the
subtests.

**Validity.** The manual does provide evidence
of the separate factor structure for the subtests
and the clusters, and reports concurrent validity
with other ability tests and achievement tests. In
addition, studies describe small samples of students labeled educably mentally disabled, learning disabled, reading disabled, and gifted.
However, since this is a relatively new test, independent researchers will need to conduct additional studies in order to confirm and extend
our understanding of the validity of this instrument. Evaluators should use caution when interpreting the performance of individuals with
special needs.

---

**BOX 13.5** **Differential Ability Scales (DAS)**

*Publication Date:* 1990

*Purposes:* Measures cognitive ability and achievement.

*Age/Grade Levels:* 2 years, 6 months through 17 years, 11 months.

*Time to Administer:* 35 to 85 minutes.

*Technical Adequacy:* The standardization sample is acceptable. Reliability is adequate. Additional evidence of validity is needed.

*Suggested Use:* Can be helpful in determining areas of strength and weakness. Exercise caution when using test scores in making decisions regarding identification of students with special needs and determining eligibility for special services.

***Summary.*** The *DAS* is an individually administered ability test for use with individuals ages 2 years, 6 months to 17 years, 11 months. The subtests are designed to measure cognitive ability and selected areas of achievement. Reliability is adequate. However, additional evidence of validity is necessary before educators can use it with confidence for individuals with exceptional needs. Box 13.5 outlines the test's parameters.

## Kaufman Adolescent and Adult Intelligence Test

The *Kaufman Adolescent and Adult Intelligence Test (KAIT)* (Kaufman and Kaufman, 1993) is a test of general intelligence for individuals ages 11 to over 85 years. Three theories of intellectual functioning—Golden's modification of the Luria-Nebraska system of neuropsychological assessment, Piaget's formal operations stage, and the Horn-Cattell theories of fluid and crystallized intelligence—form the basis of the test.

The *KAIT* comprises two scales: crystallized intelligence and fluid intelligence. Crystallized intelligence "measures acquired concepts and depends on schooling and acculturation for success" (p. 1) while fluid intelligence measures "the ability to solve new problems" (p. 1). The test has a Core Battery and an Expanded Battery. In addition, a supplementary subtest assesses the respondent's attention and orientation. Table 13.4 shows a description of the subtests and the abilities they measure.

***Administration.*** The *KAIT* is an individually administered test that requires supervision by persons who have had graduate training in individual assessment of intelligence. The average time to administer the Core Battery is 65 minutes; the Expanded Battery takes approximately 90 minutes.

***Scoring.*** Each of the three intelligence scales, Crystallized, Fluid, and Composite, yields an IQ score with a mean of 100 and a standard deviation of 15. In addition, percentile ranks are obtainable. Each of the ten subtests yields standard scores with a mean of 10 and a standard deviation of 3. Figure 13.1 on page 353 shows the front page from the *KAIT* Individual Test Record Form.

***Standardization.*** The *KAIT* was standardized between 1988 and 1991. Over 2,600 individuals, ages 11 to 94 years, at 60 sites participated in the sample, using census information from 1988. The final standardization sample from the initial group comprised 2,000 individuals composed of 14 age groups.

The proportion of males and females closely approximated census data. The northeastern geographic region was somewhat underrepresented, and the western region was slightly overrepresented. The north central and central regions approximated census data. Socioeconomic status and racial and ethnic groups closely match census information as do data for persons designated as white, black, Hispanic, and other (other includes Native Americans, Asian, Alaskan Natives, Pacific Islanders, and other groups not categorized as white, black, or Hispanic).

***Reliability.*** For split-half reliability of the subtests, average coefficients ranged from .79 (Memory for Block Designs) to .93 (Rebus Learning); for the scales, the average split-half reliability coefficients were .95 (Crystallized, Fluid) and .97 (Composite Intelligence).

Test-retest reliability calculations applied to two test administrations of the *KAIT* to 153 individuals. The interval between the administrations ranged from 6 to 99 days with an average interval of 31 days. Average test-retest coefficients for the scales are .94 (Crystallized), .87 (Fluid), and .94 (Composite). One study reports a sample of 60 individuals who took the test again after an interval of one year. Average test-retest coefficients for the scales are .85 (Crystallized), .79 (Fluid), and .92 (Composite).

***Validity.*** Construct validity is based on studies of age changes on the subtests and the IQ scales, correlations between the subtests and the

**TABLE 13.4    Kaufman Adolescent and Adult Intelligence Test**

*Core Battery Subtests*

| | |
|---|---|
| Definitions | Respondents identify a word after observing the word with several letters missing and after receiving a definition of the word. *(crystallized intelligence)* |
| Rebus Learning | Respondents associate a word or concept with a rebus and then "read" phrases and sentences that comprise several rebuses. *(fluid intelligence)* |
| Logical Steps | Respondents are presented with logical premises in both visual and aural form. They answer a question that relates to these premises. *(fluid intelligence)* |
| Auditory Comprehension | After listening to a recording of a news story, respondents answer literal and inferential questions. *(crystallized intelligence)* |
| Mystery Codes | After looking at the codes associated with several pictures, the respondents solve the code for a pictorial stimulus. *(fluid intelligence)* |
| Double Meanings | After examining two groups of words, respondents recall a word that is associated with the two groups of words. *(crystallized intelligence)* |

*Expanded Battery*

| | |
|---|---|
| Rebus Delayed Recall | Respondents "read" phrases and concepts that are formed from rebuses that they learned earlier in the test. *(delayed recall)* |
| Auditory Delayed Recall | Respondents answer questions about news stories that they listened to earlier in the test. *(delayed recall)* |
| Memory for Block Designs | Respondents construct a block design from memory after briefly looking at a printed copy. *(fluid intelligence)* |
| Famous Faces | After looking at a picture of a famous person and hearing a clue about the person, respondents name the person. *(crystallized intelligence)* |

*Supplementary Subtest*

| | |
|---|---|
| Mental Status | Respondents answer ten questions relating to their attention and orientation to the world. |

IQ scales, factor analyses of the *KAIT*, and correlations between the *KAIT* and other tests.

The studies of age changes on the *KAIT* demonstrate that as individuals grow older, *KAIT* scores change. According to the test manual, this pattern of age changes is consistent with the Horn-Cattell theory of fluid and crystallized intelligence.

The test shows correlations between the *KAIT* subtests and the Composite IQ score. For the six Core subtests, coefficients ranged from

.64 (Mystery Codes) to .75 (Definition), with an average coefficient of .70. These coefficients indicate some support that the *KAIT* subtests measure a unifying ability.

Factor analyses computations support the authors' assertion that the *KAIT* measures theory-based intelligence. Results of the factor analyses demonstrated that the *KAIT*'s two factors are consistent with the crystallized and fluid scales. The authors conducted additional factor analyses between the *KAIT* and the *Wechsler*

**Individual
Test Record**

by Alan S. Kaufman and Nadeen L. Kaufman

| Name | ☐ Male   ☐ Female |
|------|-------------------|

Home address _____   Phone _____

|  | Year | Month | Day |
|--|------|-------|-----|
| Test date | ___ | ___ | ___ |
| Birth date | ___ | ___ | ___ |
| Chronological age | ___ | ___ | ___ |

Parent or Guardian _____
(if applicable)

School _____   Grade _____
(if applicable)

Current or previous occupation _____
(if applicable)

Highest school grade completed _____

Examiner _____

**Mental Status**

| Raw Score | Descriptive Category |
|-----------|---------------------|
|           |                     |

| SUBTESTS | Raw Score | Subtest Scaled Score (Table D.1) M = 10, SD= 3 | | | Per-centile Rank | Other Data Specify: |
|----------|-----------|------------------|------|------------|--------|-----------|
|  |  | Crystallized Scale | Fluid Scale | Delayed Recall | | |
| **CORE BATTERY** 1. Definitions | | | | | | |
| 2. Rebus Learning | | | | | | |
| 3. Logical Steps | | | | | | |
| 4. Auditory Comprehension | | | | | | |
| 5. Mystery Codes | | | | | | |
| 6. Double Meanings | | | | | | |
| **EXPANDED BATTERY** 7. Rebus Delayed Recall | | | **Add only if substituting for Subtest 2, 3, or 5. | | | |
| 8. Auditory Delayed Recall | | *Add only if substituting for Subtest 1, 4, or 6. | | | | |
| 9. Memory for Block Designs | | | ** ( ) | DO NOT ADD | | |
| 10. Famous Faces | | * ( ) | | | | |

| | Crystallized Scale | Fluid Scale | Composite Intelligence Scale | Crystallized and Fluid IQ Comparison |
|--|-------------------|-------------|------------------------------|--------------------------------------|
| **Sum of Three Core Subtest Scaled Scores** | + | = | | Crystallized IQ ⬭ |
| **IQ** | (Table D.2) | (Table D.3) | (Table D.4) | Fluid IQ ⬭ |
| **Confidence Interval** ☐ 90%  ☐ 95% | — | — | — | IQ Difference ⬭ |
| **Percentile Rank** | | | | |
| **Mean Scaled Score** | | | | |
| **Descriptive Category** | | | | |

Statistical Significance (check one)   ☐ NS   ☐ .05   ☐ .01

| Difference Required for Significance at .05 and .01 Levels | | |
|--|--|--|
| Age | Significance Level .05 | .01 |
| 14 or younger | 11 | 14 |
| 15 - 34 | 9 | 12 |
| 35 or older | 8 | 11 |

**FIGURE 13.1**   *Kaufman Adolescent and Adult Intelligence Test*

*Source: Kaufman Adolescent & Adult Intelligence Test (KAIT)* Individual Test Record summary page by Alan S. Kaufman and Nadeen L. Kaufman © 1993 American Guidance Service, Inc., 4201 Woodland Road, Circle Pines, Minnesota 55014-1796. Reproduced with permission of publisher. All rights reserved. www.agsnet.com

*Intelligence Scale for Children–Revised (WISC–R)* and the *Wechsler Adult Intelligence Scale–Revised (WAIS–R)*. These studies indicate that the *KAIT* Fluid Scale and the Wechsler Performance Scales measure different constructs. However, the *KAIT* Crystallized Scale and the Wechsler Verbal Scales are almost the same.

The test reports concurrent validity calculations by computing correlations between the *KAIT* and the *Kaufman Brief Intelligence Test (K–BIT)* and the *Peabody Picture Vocabulary Test–Revised (PPVT–R)*. The correlations between the *KAIT* Composite IQ and the *K–BIT* Composite IQ were .81 at ages 11 to 19 years and .87

at ages 20 to 88 years. The correlations between the *KAIT* Composite IQ and the *PPVT–R* standard scores were .83 for ages 15 to 40 years and .66 for ages 41 to 92 years. Note that the norm tables for the *PPVT–R* only reach 40 years, so concurrent validity calculations used the norm tables for ages 35 to 40. Additional concurrent validity studies are necessary using additional instruments.

The manual reports several studies regarding the diagnostic validity of the *KAIT* using various samples such as Alzheimer's patients and persons with neurological impairments, clinical depression, or reading disabilities. The studies support the diagnostic utility of the *KAIT* in these areas. We commend the authors for their initial investigations of the diagnostic validity of this test and recommend further studies in this area.

***Summary.*** The *Kaufman Adolescent and Adult Intelligence Test* is an individually administered test of general intelligence for persons ages 11 to over 85 years that combines three theoretical models of intelligence. The test is well standardized. There is good evidence for reliability and validity. Box 13.6 describes the test's parameters.

---

**BOX 13.6** *Kaufman Adolescent and Adult Intelligence Test (KAIT)*

---

*Publication Date:* 1993

*Purposes:* Measures general intelligence, crystallized and fluid intellectual abilities.

*Age/Grade Levels:* 11 years to over 85 years.

*Time to Administer:* 65 to 90 minutes.

*Technical Adequacy:* The test is well standardized. There is good evidence for reliability and validity.

*Suggested Use:* Can determine general intellectual ability, areas of strength and weakness.

---

## Kaufman Assessment Battery for Children

The *Kaufman Assessment Battery for Children (K–ABC)* (Kaufman and Kaufman, 1983) assesses the intelligence and achievement of individuals ages 2 years, 6 months through 12 years, 6 months. The test consists of 16 subtests that take from 35 minutes for young children to 75 minutes for elementary school-age children. Examiners administer a maximum of 13 subtests to each individual. The subtests fall into three categories: the Sequential Processing Scale, the Simultaneous Processing Scale, and the Achievement Scale.

Intelligence is "defined in terms of an individual's style of solving problems and processing information" (Kaufman and Kaufman, 1983, p. 2). The intelligence scales base their construction on a theoretical model of mental processing developed by J. P. Das, A. R. Luria, and others that holds that children process information primarily sequentially or simultaneously. The Sequential Processing Scale requires that childrn solve problems in a sequential, or serial, order. The Simultaneous Processing Scale requires children to integrate or synthesize information to obtain a solution.

The Mental Processing Scale is a combination of the Sequential and the Simultaneous Processing scales. It is a measure of total intelligence. The Mental Processing Composite score has a mean of 100 and a standard deviation of 15.

The Achievement Scale assesses knowledge and skills gained through formal and informal experiences. The manual states that the Achievement Scale does not yield a diagnostic assessment of achievement skills; it does provide a global estimate of achievement in the areas of reading, arithmetic, general information, early language development, and language concepts. Table 13.5 gives a description of the subtests.

Depending on the age of the individual, examiners can combine various subtests to form the Nonverbal Scale. The Nonverbal Scale provides an estimate of intelligence for individuals who demonstrate communication problems,

**TABLE 13.5  Kaufman Assessment Battery for Children**

| Scale | Age Range | Applications |
|-------|-----------|--------------|
| *Sequential Processing Scale* | | |
| Hand Movements | 2 years, 6 months to 12 years, 5 months | Perform a series of hand movements in the same sequence as the examiner. |
| Number Recall | 2 years, 6 months to 12 years, 5 months | Repeat a series of digits in the same order as the examiner says them. |
| Word Order | 4 years to 12 years, 5 months | Touch a series of silhouettes of common objects in the same order as the examiner identifies them. |
| *Simultaneous Processing Scale* | | |
| Magic Window | 2 years, 6 months to 4 years, 11 months | The examiner rotates a picture, slowly revealing it behind a narrow window. |
| Face Recognition | 2 years, 6 months to 12 years, 5 months | Identify faces in a group photograph that were exposed on the preceding page. |
| Gestalt Closure | 2 years, 6 months to 12 years, 5 months | Name an object or scene that is depicted in an "inkblot" drawing. |
| Triangles | 4 years to 12 years, 5 months | Form triangles into a pattern that matches a design. |
| Matrix Analogies | 5 years to 12 years, 5 months | Identify a picture or abstract design that best completes a visual analogy. |
| Spatial Memory | 5 years to 12 years, 5 months | Recall the position of pictures on a page that is briefly exposed. |
| Photo Series | 6 years to 12 years, 5 months | Place photographs of an event in chronological order. |
| *Achievement Scale* | | |
| Expressive Vocabulary | 2 years, 6 months to 4 years, 11 months | Identify an object that is pictured in a photograph. |
| Faces & Places | 2 years, 6 months to 12 years, 5 months | Identify a famous person, fictional character, or geographic location. |
| Arithmetic | 3 years to 12 years, 5 months | Demonstrate knowledge of mathematical concepts. |
| Riddles | 3 years to 12 years, 5 months | Name the concept when presented with a list of characteristics. |
| Reading/Decoding | 5 years to 12 years, 5 months | Read letters and words. |
| Reading/Understanding | 7 years to 12 years, 5 months | Demonstrate reading comprehension by following written commands. |

and is useful with children who are deaf, hearing-impaired, speech or language disabled, autistic, or who do not speak English.

*Administration.* The manual provides comprehensive directions for administering the *K–ABC*. A supplement provides instructions for administering the battery in Spanish. The student's chronological age determines the starting point for each subtest and each subtest has a designated stopping point in order to avoid administering too many items to any child. In addition, the test contains a discontinue rule if a student misses a number of items in a row. The first item of each subtest is the sample item and the next two items are teaching items. For the sample and teaching items, it is permissible for the examiner to teach the child how to respond to the items in the subtest. Examiners score each item on the *K–ABC* as correct or incorrect.

The *K–ABC* provides for out-of-level testing for students who are 4 or 5 years old. This helps to provide flexibility in testing young children. At age 5, the number and difficulty of the subtests the child will receive changes. The subtests of Matrix Analogies, Spatial Memory, and Reading/Decoding are introduced. Magic Window, Face Recognition, and Expressive vocabulary are for children younger than 5 years. For children who are between the ages of 5 years, 0 months to 5 years, 11 months and who may be suspected of having mental disabilities or developmental delays, examiners can administer portions of the *K–ABC* that would normally be for 4-year-olds. Similarly, if children ages 4 years, 6 months to 4 years, 11 months show evidence of advanced or gifted skills, examiners may administer subtests for children age 5 and older.

The manual provides separate norms for students who test out-of-level. Out-of-level testing scores, while helpful, demand cautious use. Estimations of student performance extended the norms upward and downward. These extended norms do not represent a nationally tested sample.

For the Nonverbal Scale, the examiner can pantomime the instructions (although this is not a requirement) and the child responds by gesturing, pointing, or demonstrating. The subtests for the Nonverbal Scale are

### Age 4
Face Recognition
Hand Movements
Triangles

### Age 5
Hand Movements
Triangles
Matrix Analogies
Spatial Memory

### Ages 6 to 12
Hand Movements
Triangles
Matrix Analogies
Spatial Memory
Photo Series

*Standardization.* The standardization sample of the *K–ABC* consisted of 2,000 children between the ages of 2 years, 6 months and 12 years, 5 months. Using the 1980 U.S. Census, authors stratified the children within each age group according to gender, geographic region, socioeconomic status, race or ethnicity (African American, Caucasian, Hispanic, other), community size, and educational placement of the child (regular or special classes).

In order to make the *K–ABC* sensitive to the needs of the diverse population in the United States, an additional 469 African American and 119 Caucasian children took the test with the goal of developing sociocultural norms. However, African Americans were overrepresented in the higher education group and underrepresented in the lower education group.

The manual reports subtest scores for the mental processing scales as scaled scores (mean of 10, standard deviation of 3) and percentiles. These subtest scores can combine to yield standard scores (mean of 100, standard deviation of

15) for the Sequential Processing, Simultaneous Processing, Mental Processing Composite, and Nonverbal scales. The manual reports achievement subtests as percentiles and standard scores, provides age equivalents for the Mental Processing Scales, and reports grade equivalents for the Achievement Scale.

*Reliability.* The manual reports split-half, internal consistency, and test-retest reliabilities. For the most part, the reliability coefficients are acceptable. Many coefficients exceed .90 and, in general, the composite scores are more reliable than the individual subtest scores. Mean split-half reliability coefficients ranged from .71 (Gestalt Closure) to .91 (Reading/Understanding). Mean internal consistency coefficients for the global scales ranged from .89 (Sequential Processing) to .97 (Achievement). Test-retest reliability coefficients extended from .77 (Sequential Processing) to .97 (Achievement).

Standard errors of measurement (SEM) vary by age. For school-age students on the subtests, the SEM for the Mental Processing Subtests ranged from 1.1 (Matrix Analogies) to 1.6 (Gestalt Closure); on the Achievement Scale SEM varied from 4.0 (Reading/Decoding) to 5.9 (Faces and Places). For the global scales, the SEM ranged from 2.7 (Achievement) to 5.0 (Sequential Processing).

*Validity.* The manual reports the results of many studies relating to the validity of the K–ABC. The test authors as well as numerous independent researchers have conducted studies investigating its validity. Reviewers of the K–ABC have mixed evaluations of the validity of this instrument (Anastasi, 1985; Coffman, 1985; Merz, 1984; Page, 1985).

In an independent study of 100 Mexican American and 100 Caucasian fifth- and sixth-grade girls and boys (Valencia, Rankin, and Livingston, 1995) concluded that the Mental Processing Scales showed little evidence of bias. However, numerous items on the Achievement Scale displayed bias against Mexican American children.

*Summary.* The *Kaufman Assessment Battery for Children (K–ABC)* assesses the intelligence and achievement of individuals ages 2 years, 6 months through 12 years, 6 months. According to the manual, the test measures sequential processing, simultaneous processing, mental processing composite, and achievement. The K–ABC is sensitive to the preschool population and to the U.S. society, which is becoming increasingly pluralistic. The manual presents extensive evidence for the reliability and validity of the test. Additional research is advisable to confirm that the test does measure sequential and simultaneous processing. There is some concern that the African-American sample shows bias toward the upper education levels. The Achievement Scale shows bias toward Mexican Americans. Box 13.7 outlines the test's parameters.

**BOX 13.7**   *Kaufman Assessment Battery for Children (K–ABC)*

*Publication Date:* 1983

*Purposes:* Assesses intelligence (sequential and simultaneous processing) and achievement in vocabulary, arithmetic, and reading.

*Age/Grade Levels:* 2 years, 6 months through 12 years, 6 months.

*Time to Administer:* 35 to 75 minutes.

*Technical Adequacy:* The standardization sample is dated. Reliability is very good; validity is acceptable. However, additional evidence of validity is needed to support the theoretical basis of this test.

*Suggested Use:* The K–ABC should be used cautiously with students who have diverse backgrounds because some test items may be biased. The K–ABC can be helpful in determining general intellectual ability and overall achievement in vocabulary, arithmetic, and reading.

## Kaufman Brief Intelligence Test

The *Kaufman Brief Intelligence Test (K–BIT)* (Kaufman and Kaufman, 1990) measures verbal and nonverbal intelligence in individuals ages 4 through 90 years old. Because it is a brief test, the authors explain that it is not useful as a substitute for a more comprehensive measure. The test is for screening only, not for diagnostic, placement, or neurological assessment purposes. In addition to its use as a screening instrument, the *K–BIT* provides an estimate of intelligence for persons who may have psychiatric disorders, for job applicants, for people awaiting court hearings, and for individuals whose intellectual status needs periodic monitoring.

The *K–BIT* consists of two subtests, Vocabulary and Matrices. The Vocabulary subtest contains 82 items to which individuals respond verbally. The Vocabulary subtest contains two parts, A and B. Part A, Expressive Vocabulary, contains 45 items that all persons who take this test receive. The individual names a pictured object (e.g., lamp, calendar). Part B, Definitions, contains 37 items that only persons who are older than 8 years of age receive.

The second subtest, Matrices, consists of 48 items to which each individual responds by pointing to the correct response or by saying the corresponding letter. The items on this subtest contain people, objects, abstract designs, and symbols, and the individual must understand the relationship among these items. This subtest measures nonverbal reasoning ability.

*Administration.* A wide variety of professionals can administer the test, including psychologists, special education teachers, educational diagnosticians, remedial reading teachers, counselors, social workers, nurses, and speech and language therapists. In addition, under certain circumstances, technicians and paraprofessionals can administer the *K–BIT*. According to the manual, test administrators require little training to administer the test but a trained professional should interpret the results.

The administration of the *K–BIT* takes from 15 to 20 minutes for children who are between 4 and 7 years of age; for persons older than 7 years, test administration can take up to 30 minutes.

*Scoring.* Examiners score items as either correct or incorrect. Raw scores are converted to standard scores and percentile ranks. Each of the subtests, Vocabulary and Matrices, receives a score, and these can combine to create a composite intellectual ability score. The standard score is similar to intellectual ability scores for other tests. It has a mean of 100 and a standard deviation of 15.

The manual provides some guidance for interpreting test scores. There is evidence that discrepancies between specific subtests can provide helpful diagnostic information. The results of the *K–BIT* are useful in determining discrepancies between the standard scores on the Vocabulary and Matrices subtests. Since this instrument contains only two subtests, the interpretation of discrepancies requires caution and is advisable only after further extensive testing.

The authors reported that the mean *K–BIT* scores were 6 points lower than full scale scores from the *Wechsler Intelligence Scale for Children–Revised (WISC–R)*. This may be of little concern since the *WISC–R* has also undergone revision; however, information is not available on how the *K–BIT* scores compare with scores from the *Wechsler Intelligence Scale for Children–III (WISC–III)*.

*Standardization.* The *K–BIT* used 2,022 individuals between the ages of 4 and 90 years at 60 locations for its standardization sample. Most of the standardization sample was between the ages of 4 and 19. The authors stratified the sample according to gender, geographic region, socioeconomic status, and race or ethnic group. The minority groups included black, Hispanic, and other (Native Americans, Alaskan natives, Asians, Pacific Islanders).

The test examiners were teachers, counselors, psychologists, and graduate students who had received training by watching a videotape and practice in administering the test.

*Reliability.* The test shows split-half reliabilities for the two subtests and for the composite score. For Vocabulary, the split-half reliability coefficients ranged from .89 to .97; for Matrices the split-half reliability coefficients ranged from .74 to .95. The composite split-half reliability varied from .88 to .98. Lower reliabilities occurred at young ages.

To obtain test-retest reliability, the authors administered the *K–BIT* twice to 232 individuals between the ages of 5 and 89. The interval between the two tests ranged from 12 to 145 days, with an average of 21 days. There were 53 children in the age range between 5 and 12 years. For this group, test-retest reliabilities ranged from .83 to .92.

*Validity.* The manual reports concurrent validity studies of the *K–BIT* with the *Test of Nonverbal Intelligence (TONI)* and with the *Slosson Intelligence Test (SIT)*. For the *TONI*, the validity coefficients ranged from –0.04 (Vocabulary subtest) to .36 (Matrices subtest). Correlation coefficients between the *K–BIT* composite score and the *SIT* scores of typical children ranged from .50 to .76; the composite score from the *K–BIT* and *SIT* scores from a gifted sample revealed a validity coefficient of .44.

The manual also reports concurrent validity for the *Kaufman Test of Educational Achievement (K–TEA)* (Comprehensive Form) for normal samples. Using *K–BIT* composite scores, validity coefficients ranged from .33 to .78; and correlation coefficients for the *K–BIT* scores and the *K–TEA* Comprehensive Form scores for two samples of students with learning disabilities ranged from .32 to .65.

Evidence of construct validity stems from five normal samples. As a result of correlating *K–BIT* composite scores with scores from the *Kaufman Assessment Battery for Children (K–ABC)*, *Wechsler Intelligence Scale for Children–Revised (WISC–R)* (1974), and the *Wechsler Adult Intelligence Scale–Revised (WAIS–R)*, validity coefficients ranged from .41 to .80. Thus, while there is some evidence that the *K–BIT* is assessing similar abilities to the *K–ABC*, *WISC–R*, and the *WAIS–R*, it is apparent that it is also assessing some abilities that the other instruments are not. From these conclusions, it would be difficult to justify the use of the *K–BIT* as a substitute for the administration of these other instruments. With regard to testing young children, there is limited evidence as to the usefulness of the *K–BIT* with this population.

*Summary.* The *K–BIT* is a brief intelligence test. It can be useful for a quick screening, but is not a substitute for a more comprehensive intelligence test. Reliability appears to be adequate, and there is some evidence of validity. However, evidence of validity with samples of young children is limited. Utilize the *K–BIT* cautiously when testing young children.

## Stanford-Binet Intelligence Scale: Fourth Edition

The *Stanford-Binet Intelligence Scale: Fourth Edition* (Thorndike, Hagen, and Sattler, 1986) is a revised edition of the *Stanford-Binet Intelligence Scale: Form L-M*. The test was originally developed by Alfred Binet and Theodore Simon in France in 1905. Lewis M. Terman, a professor at Stanford University, revised the Binet-Simon test and introduced it to the United States in 1916. In 1937, Terman, along with Maud A. Merrill, standardized it again and created two revised forms, *Form L* and *Form M*. In 1960, the authors created *Form L-M* from the two forms but did not restandardize the test until 1972. The *Fourth Edition* has some similarities to previous editions: (1) it spans the same age range; (2) many of the item types are the same; and (3) it establishes basal and ceiling levels.

The *Fourth Edition* of the Stanford-Binet assesses cognitive abilities in individuals ages 2 through 23 years. The test contains 15 subtests that evaluate four broad areas titled Verbal Reasoning, Quantitative Reasoning, Abstract/Visual Reasoning, and Short-Term Memory. In addition, there is a composite score which estimates g, general intellectual ability. Administration of specific subtests depends on the age of the individual under assessment; however, examinees do not take all subtests.

The test uses a three-level hierarchical model of intelligence. At the first, or top, level, there is g, general reasoning ability. General ability consists "of the cognitive assembly and control processes that an individual uses to organize adaptive strategies for solving novel problems. In other words, g is what an individual uses when faced with a problem that he or she has not been taught to solve" (Thorndike, Hagen, and Sattler, 1986b, p. 3).

The second level consists of three broad factors: crystallized abilities, fluid-analytic abilities, and short-term memory. Crystallized abilities are defined as "the cognitive skills necessary for acquiring and using information about verbal and quantitative concepts to solve problems" (Thorndike, Hagen, and Sattler, 1986b, p. 4). It is thought that crystallized abilities are affected by experiences in school and outside of school. Fluid-analytic abilities are "the cognitive skills necessary for solving new problems that involve figural or other nonverbal stimuli" (Thorndike, Hagen, and Sattler, 1986c, p. 4). General experiences influence this factor, which relates to flexibility and the ability to deal with novel situations.

The third level includes three factors: verbal reasoning, quantitative reasoning, and abstract/visual reasoning. The rationale for including these factors is that "they have special meaning to clinicians and educators" (1986b, p. 5). Performance on the subtests bears on these three factors; and these factors contribute to the abilities in the second level.

Researchers hypothesize that the *Fourth Edition* measures inferred abilities and influences. Table 13.6 lists the 15 subtests and the abilities that they measure (Delaney and Hopkins, 1987; Sattler, 1988).

***Administration.***    As stated above, the test contains 15 subtests, but no one individual

receives all of the subtests. All of the examinees receive the Vocabulary Test, or the routing test, first. The performance on this subtest, along with the individual's chronological age, determines the remaining subtests the examinee will take. Depending on the age of the individual, these can number between 8 and 13. This can take between one and two hours. The test provides specific instructions for each subtest.

The routing test is sometimes inappropriate for individuals with mental retardation or who have other disabilities because the entry items are too difficult. Because of this, the examiners may have to adjust the entry level in order to make it appropriate for these individuals (Sattler, 1988).

There are several short or abbreviated forms of the test that are useful for screening purposes. A quick screening battery consists of four subtests: Vocabulary, Bead Memory, Quantitative, and Pattern Analysis. Another abbreviated form consists of six subtests: Vocabulary, Bead Memory, Quantitative, Memory for Sentences, Pattern Analysis, and Comprehension. In addition, there is a recommended brief battery for gifted individuals.

The *Examiner's Handbook: An Expanded Guide for Fourth Edition Users* (Delaney and Hopkins, 1987) provides guidelines for modifying the test administration for persons with disabilities, hearing loss, visual impairments, sight loss, or who have limited English proficiency or who are non–language proficient. When making modifications in the test administration, examiners should keep in mind that all individuals possess unique abilities.

***Scoring.***    The manual provides clearly written directions for scoring. The scoring of the subtests varies from one subtest to another. *Fourth Edition* raw scores convert to a Standard Age Score (SAS), which is a normalized standard score with a mean of 50 and a standard deviation of 8. The Standard Age Scores convert to Area Scores and to a Composite SAS. These scores have a mean of 100 and a standard deviation of 16.

There is some evidence that scores on the *Fourth Edition* will be somewhat lower than

**TABLE 13.6   Stanford-Binet Intelligence Scale: Fourth Edition**

*Verbal Reasoning*

| | |
|---|---|
| Vocabulary | Measures recall of expressive word knowledge and verbal comprehension. |
| Comprehension | Reflects verbal comprehension, vocabulary development, verbal expression, social knowledge, and factual information. |
| Absurdities | Assesses visual perception, factual knowledge, discrimination, verbal expression, attention, and social knowledge. |
| Verbal Relations | Assesses vocabulary development, concept formation, discrimination, inductive reasoning, verbal expression, and discrimination of essential details. |

*Quantitative Reasoning*

| | |
|---|---|
| Quantitative | Reflects knowledge of number facts, computation skills, and knowledge of mathematics concepts and procedures. |
| Number Series | Assesses logical reasoning, concentration, mathematics concepts and computation, and inductive reasoning. |
| Equation Building | Reflects knowledge of mathematics concepts and procedures, inductive reasoning, logic, flexibility, and trial and error. |

*Abstract/Visual Reasoning*

| | |
|---|---|
| Pattern Analysis | Measures visual-motor ability, spatial visualization, pattern analysis, and visual-motor coordination. |
| Copying | Measures visual imagery, visual perception, visual-motor ability, and eye-hand coordination. |
| Matrices | Evaluates attention, concentration, visual perception, visual analysis, spatial visualization, and inductive reasoning. |
| Paper Folding and Cutting | Reflects spatial ability, visual perception, visual analysis, and inductive reasoning. |

*Short-Term Memory*

| | |
|---|---|
| Bead Memory | Assesses short-term memory of visual stimuli. Also measures form perception, visual imagery, visual memory, discrimination, and alertness to detail. |
| Memory for Sentences | Measures short-term auditory memory, verbal comprehension, concentration, and attention. |
| Memory for Digits | Evaluates short-term auditory memory and attention. |
| Memory for Objects | Reflects visual comprehension, attention, concentration, and visual memory. |

scores on the *Form L-M*. In one study, 139 children, with an average age of 6 years, 11 months, took the *Fourth Edition* with the *Form L-M* edition. The average Composite score on the *Fourth Edition* was 105.8 with a standard deviation of 13.8; the mean Total score on the *Form L-M* was 108.1 with a standard deviation of 16.7.

*Standardization.* Five variables—geographic region, community size, ethnic group (white, African American, Hispanic, Asian/Pacific Islander), age, and gender—and data from the 1980 census formed the basis for the standardization sample. A total of 5,013 individuals participated in the standardization. Because the sample consisted of too many persons in the upper socioeconomic categories, the authors used weighting procedures to adjust the final sample to the 1980 data on the U.S. population.

*Reliability.* Internal consistency coefficients for the individual subtests ranged from .73 (Memory for Objects) to .94 (Paper Folding and Cutting). In general, the subtest reliabilities for older individuals were higher than the subtest reliabilities for younger children.

For all age groups, the internal consistency of the Composite Score ranged from .95 to .99. The internal consistency reliability of the Area Scores ranged from .82 (Quantitative Reasoning Area for 2-year-olds) to .97 (Abstract/Visual Reasoning for 18- to 23-year-olds), with many of the reliability coefficients in the .90s.

In order to examine test-retest reliability, the authors tested and retested two groups of persons. One group consisted of 57 children who were 5 years old; the second group was composed of 55 persons who were 8 years old. Both groups were retested two to eight months apart. For the 5-year-old group, the subtest reliabilities ranged from .56 (Bead Memory) to .77 (Memory for Sentences). Area Score reliabilities ranged from .71 (Quantitative Reasoning) to .88 (Verbal Reasoning). The Composite Score reliability was .91. For the 8-year-old group, subtest reliabilities varied

from .28 (Quantitative) to .86 (Comprehension). Area Scores extended from .51 (Quantitative Reasoning) to .87 (Verbal Reasoning); and Composite Score reliability was .90.

*Validity.* The authors conducted a factor analysis of the subtest scores across all ages in the standardization sample to measure construct validity. The *Stanford-Binet: Fourth Edition* operates on the theory that the test measures *g*, general ability. Evidence of *g* was found across all ages, although the factor loadings on *g* were greater in the 18- to 23-year-olds than in the younger ages.

Several studies examined concurrent validity. In the study of 139 children with an average age of 6 years, 11 months who took the *Fourth* and the *Form L-M* editions, the correlation between the Composite score *(Fourth Edition)* and the Total score *(Form L-M)* was .81. Another study, with a sample of 205 children with an average age of 9 years, 5 months, investigated the

---

**BOX 13.8**   *Stanford-Binet Intelligence Scale: Fourth Edition*

*Publication Date:* 1986

*Purposes:* Assesses general intellectual abilities (g) and cognitive abilities in four broad areas: Verbal Reasoning, Abstract/Visual Reasoning, Quantitative Reasoning, and Short-Term Memory.

*Age/Grade Levels:* 2 through 23 years.

*Time to Administer:* one to two hours.

*Technical Adequacy:* Well-normed, reliable instrument. Evidence of validity is adequate.

*Suggested Use:* Assesses intellectual ability, strengths and weaknesses. Can be used, in combination with other tests and forms of assessment, to identify students with special needs and determine eligibility for services; can be used when conducting a psycho-educational assessment and for clinical and neuropsychological assessment.

correlations between Area scores and Composite Scores on the *Fourth Edition* and Verbal IQs, Performance IQs, and Full Scale IQs on the *Wechsler Intelligence Scale for Children–Revised (WISC–R)* (1974). Correlations of the four Area Scores with Verbal IQ and Performance IQ ranged from .60 to .72 and the correlation between the Composite Score on the *Fourth Edition* with Full Scale IQ on the *WISC–R* was .83. While the authors present evidence of validity, we recommend additional research over time with varied populations.

***Summary.*** The *Stanford-Binet Intelligence Scale: Fourth Edition* is a well-normed, reliable instrument. Evidence of validity is adequate. However, additional studies must be undertaken that investigate construct validity. While one important strength of the instrument is that a broad age range of individuals can take the test, all examinees do not take all subtests. Thus, comparisons between the performance of examinees over time is difficult. Another disadvantage is that the administering of the *Fourth Edition* can be more time-consuming compared with other intelligence tests. Box 13.8 outlines the test's parameters.

## Test of Nonverbal Intelligence– Third Edition

The *Test of Nonverbal Intelligence–Third Edition (TONI–3)* (Brown, Sherbenou, and Johnsen, 1997) is a nonverbal measure of abstract/figural problem solving for use with individuals ages 6 years to 89 years, 11 months. It can assess the performance of individuals who have language or motor problems that make it difficult for them to respond to more traditional tests. The authors state that it can be useful when assessing persons who have aphasia, hearing impairments, lack of proficiency with spoken or written English, cerebral palsy, stroke, or head trauma. The test has two forms, each containing 45 items. The items consist of a series of abstract figures that require individuals to select the correct response by problem solving.

***Administration.*** The test items sit on an easel and the examiner pantomimes the instructions. The examiner begins the testing by pointing to a blank square in a pattern of figures, making a broad gesture to indicate the possible responses, pointing to the blank square again, and then looking questioningly at the individual. The student shows the correct response by pointing, using an eyeblink, head stick, light beam, or by some other meaningful response. Throughout the administration of this instrument, neither the examiner nor the examinee speaks. This test is untimed, and encourages the examiner to allow examinees sufficient time to respond to each test item. The total time to administer the *TONI–3* is approximately 15 minutes. The advantages of this nonverbal method of test administration are that the examinee does not have to listen to directions, speak, read, or write.

According to the authors, teachers, psychologists, psychological associates, educational diagnosticians, and speech and language therapists can administer the *TONI–3*. Examiners should have sufficient training and knowledge in the area of assessment.

***Scoring.*** Examiners score items as either correct or incorrect. Raw scores convert to deviation quotients (standard scores with a mean of 100 and a standard deviation of 15) and percentile ranks. Since there are no subtests, the *TONI–3* reports only the total score.

***Standardization.*** The *TONI–3* standardization sample consisted of 3,451 individuals, ranging in age from 6 years to 89 years, 11 months stratified by age. The sample groups characteristics according to gender, race, ethnic group, geographic region, residence (rural, urban, suburban), disability status, and income. These demographic characteristics approximated the U.S. population.

***Reliability.*** Test authors calculated reliability for the *TONI–3* in several ways. Internal consistency reliability has a mean reliability coefficient of .93 for both Form A and Form B.

The authors calculated alternate-form reliability for the various age groups in the sample by correlating the scores from Forms A and B after administering them to the same individuals back-to-back. The mean reliability coefficient was .84. Reliability coefficients were: age 6 (.85), age 7 (.79), and age 8 (.79).

The authors also administered the alternate forms in a delayed retest design. Examiners administered both forms of the *TONI–3* seven days apart to individuals ranging in age from 13 years to 40 years. The estimated reliability coefficient was .91.

The manual also reports reliability coefficients for special populations, such as individuals who were learning disabled, deaf, gifted, and Spanish-speaking. The reported coefficients were in the moderate range. However, for the most part, the number of persons included in the special population samples is small and additional research is advisable in this area.

---

**BOX 13.9** *Test of Nonverbal Intelligence–Third Edition (TONI–3)*

*Publication Date:* 1997

*Purposes:* Nonverbal measure of abstract/figural problem solving that can be used when assessing the performance of individuals who have language or motor problems that may make it difficult for them to respond to more traditional tests.

*Age/Grade Levels:* 6 years to 89 years, 11 months.

*Time to Administer:* 15 to 20 minutes.

*Technical Adequacy:* The standardization sample is just acceptable. Reliability and validity coefficients are low to moderate.

*Suggested Use:* The *TONI–3* assesses one aspect of intelligence—problem solving. It is to be used with caution.

*Validity.* Validity is concerned with determining whether a test measures what it purports to measure. The manual reports the results of studies conducted by the authors of the *TONI–3* and by independent researchers. Validity coefficients from a number of validity studies range from low to moderate for correlations of the *TONI–3* and measures of achievement and measures of intelligence.

*Summary.* The *TONI–3* is a nonverbal measure that assesses one aspect of intelligence, namely, problem solving. Reliability and validity coefficients are low to moderate. Caution is advisable when assessing young children. Box 13.9 outlines the test's parameters.

## Wechsler Intelligence Scale for Children–Third Edition

The *Wechsler Intelligence Scale for Children–Third Edition (WISC–III)* (Wechsler, 1991) is a revision of the *Wechsler Intelligence Scale for Children–Revised* and is the third edition of the *Wechsler Intelligence Scale for Children*, which was originally published in 1949. It is an individually administered test that assesses the intellectual ability of children ages 6 years through 16 years, 11 months. Wechsler conceptualizes intelligence as a global ability, which is defined as the "capacity of the individual to act purposefully, to think rationally, and to deal effectively with his or her environment" (Wechsler, 1944, p. 3, cited in Wechsler, 1991). According to the manual, the *WISC–III* is useful for a number of purposes, including psychoeducational assessment, diagnosis of exceptional needs, and clinical and neuropsychological assessment.

The *WISC–III* consists of ten subtests and three optional subtests grouped into two scales, the Verbal Scale and the Performance Scale. The sum of the scores on the Verbal subtests results in a Verbal IQ score; the total of the scores on the Performance subtests results in a Performance IQ score. The scores on both the Verbal and Performance subtests result in a Full Scale IQ score. Figure 13.2 shows a completed *WISC–*

# WISC-III™
## Wechsler Intelligence Scale for Children–Third Edition

Name Loretta M. Flanagan    Sex f

School Cicero Elementary    Grade 6

Examiner Sarah Draper    Handedness R

| Subtests | Raw Scores | Scaled Scores | | | | | |
|---|---|---|---|---|---|---|---|
| Picture Completion | 22 | | 11 | | 11 | | |
| Information | 20 | 13 | | 13 | | | |
| Coding | 53 | | 12 | | | | 12 |
| Similarities | 19 | 11 | | 11 | | | |
| Picture Arrangement | 30 | | 9 | | 9 | | |
| Arithmetic | 22 | 15 | | | 15 | | |
| Block Design | 46 | | 12 | | 12 | | |
| Vocabulary | 42 | 14 | | 14 | | | |
| Object Assembly | 33 | | 12 | | 12 | | |
| Comprehension | 25 | 12 | | 12 | | | |
| (Symbol Search) | 29 | | ((13)) | | | | 13 |
| (Digit Span) | 18 | ((14)) | | | 14 | | |
| (Mazes) | 19 | | ((19)) | | | | |
| Sum of Scaled Scores | | 65 | 56 | 50 | 44 | 29 | 25 |
| | | Verbal | Perfor. | VC | PO | FD | PS |
| | | Full Scale Score **121** | | OPTIONAL | | | |

| | | Year | Month | Day |
|---|---|---|---|---|
| Date Tested | | 91 | 8 | 20 |
| Date of Birth | | 80 | 3 | 10 |
| Age | | 11 | 5 | 10 |

| | Score | IQ/Index | %ile | 90% Confidence Interval |
|---|---|---|---|---|
| Verbal | 65 | 118 | 88 | 112 – 122 |
| Performance | 56 | 108 | 70 | 101 – 114 |
| Full Scale | 121 | 114 | 82 | 109 – 118 |
| VC | 50 | 114 | 82 | 107 – 119 |
| PO | 44 | 107 | 68 | 99 – 113 |
| FD | 29 | 126 | 96 | 115 – 130 |
| PS | 25 | 114 | 82 | 104 – 120 |

Copyright © 1991, 1986, 1974, 1971 by The Psychological Corporation
Standardization edition copyright © 1989 by The Psychological Corporation
Copyright 1949 by The Psychological Corporation
Copyright renewed 1976 by The Psychological Corporation
All rights reserved. Printed in the United States of America.

### Subtest Scores

**Verbal:** Inf 13, Sim 11, Ari 15, Voc 14, Com 12, DS 14

**Performance:** PC 11, Cd 12, PA 9, BD 12, OA 12, SS 13, Mz 9

### IQ Scores

| VIQ | PIQ | FSIQ |
|---|---|---|
| 118 | 108 | 114 |

### Index Scores (Optional)

| VCI | POI | FDI | PSI |
|---|---|---|---|
| 114 | 107 | 126 | 114 |

THE PSYCHOLOGICAL CORPORATION®
HARCOURT BRACE JOVANOVICH, INC.

09–980004

**FIGURE 13.2 Wechsler Intelligence Scale for Children–III, *Record Form***

Source: *Wechsler Individual Achievement Test, Second Edition.* Copyright © 2001 by The Psychological Corporation, a Harcourt Assessment Company. Reproduced by permission. All rights reserved. "Wechsler Individual Achievement Test," and "WIAT" are trademarks of The Psychological Corporation registered in the United States of America and/or other jurisdictions.

**TABLE 13.7    Wechsler Intelligence Scale for Children–III**

*Verbal Scale*

| | |
|---|---|
| Information | The examiner asks common knowledge questions about events, objects, places, and people. |
| Similarities | The examinee explains the correspondence between pairs of words. |
| Arithmetic | The student solves mathematical problems mentally and responds to them verbally. |
| Vocabulary | The examiner presents words orally and the examinee defines them orally. |
| Comprehension | The examiner presents oral questions that assess understanding of familiar problems and social concepts. |
| Digit Span | The individual repeats a series of numbers forward in the Digits Forward section and a series of numbers in reverse order in the Digits Backward section. |

*Performance Scale*

| | |
|---|---|
| Picture Completion | The examinee observes a picture with a missing part and identifies the missing piece. |
| Picture Arrangement | The individual must correctly sequence a series of pictures. |
| Block Design | The examinee reproduces a pattern using blocks. |
| Object Assembly | The individual assembles five jigsaw puzzles. |
| Coding | The examinee copies geometric symbols that are paired with either numbers or shapes. |
| Mazes | The individual completes a series of mazes using a pencil. |
| Symbol Search | The individual searches two groups of paired shapes to locate the target shape. |

*III* Record Form. A description of each of the subtests can be found in Table 13.7.

The *WISC–III* also contains four factor-based index scores: Verbal Comprehension, Perceptual Organization, Freedom from Distractibility, and Processing Speed. Twelve of the 13 subtests yield the four factors. The arrangement of the four factors and their subtests is as follows:

| Factor | Subtests |
|---|---|
| **I.** Verbal Comprehension | Information Similarities Vocabulary Comprehension |
| **II.** Perceptual Organization | Picture Completion, Picture Arrangement, Block Designs, Object Assembly |
| **III.** Freedom from Distractibility | Arithmetic, Digit Span |
| **IV.** Processing Speed | Coding, Symbol Search |

***Administration.*** The *WISC–III* is administered individually. The Snapshot of Andres describes his performance on this test. The manual clearly explains the directions for administration and scoring for each of the 13 subtests. Each subtest has separate starting points, and the rules for stopping vary among the subtests. Administration time is approximately 60 to 90 minutes.

## SNAPSHOT ■ *Andres*

Andres is 11 years old and is in the fifth grade. He grew up in his neighborhood, and he has many friends there. Routinely, when Andres arrives home after school, he has a snack and then races outdoors. Andres has disliked school ever since he can remember. He always had a hard time with reading, writing, and spelling but he achieved somewhat better grades in mathematics.

Last week, there was a meeting at the school to discuss Andres' continuing academic difficulties. Andres attended the meeting along with his parents. His teachers, while praising him for working hard, reported that Andres lags considerably behind his peers in academic areas. His teachers agreed that Andres is a delight to have in class. The participants in the meeting agreed that an assessment of Andres' cognitive abilities should be conducted in order to gain a better understanding of his learning needs.

After permission was obtained from Andres's family, the psychologist administered the *WISC–III* to Andres. Keeping in mind that a standard score of 10 ± 3 falls within the average range, the following is a summary of the results:

| | **Standard Score** |
|---|---|
| *Verbal Scale* | |
| Information | 6 |
| Similarities | 11 |
| Arithmetic | 8 |
| Vocabulary | 9 |
| Comprehension | 7 |
| Digit Span | 7 |
| Verbal Scale IQ | 90 |

Average range is 85 to 115

| *Performance Scale* | |
|---|---|
| Picture Completion | 10 |
| Coding | 8 |
| Picture Arrangement | 15 |
| Block Design | 15 |
| Object Assembly | 8 |
| Symbol Search | 14 |
| Performance IQ | 108 |

Average range is 85 to 115

| | |
|---|---|
| Full Scale IQ | 98 |
| Verbal Comprehension Index | 91 |
| Perceptual Organization Index | 113 |
| Freedom from Distractibility Index | 87 |
| Processing Speed Index | 106 |

Average range is 85 to 115

The psychologist summarized Andres' performance on the *WISC–III*. She wrote that Andres had significant strengths in both verbal and nonverbal concept formation, abstract reasoning, and visual sequencing; and relative weaknesses, although still within the average range, in using short-term memory and in visualizing the whole from the sum of its parts.

The psychologist recommended presenting new concepts globally first and then broken down into their components, taking into consideration the weaknesses in short-term memory when instructing in academic areas. Andres will need repetition in content areas when learning new concepts and help in organizing his thoughts to make connections with prior knowledge in order to retrieve information at a later time.

The *WISC–III* overlaps with the *Wechsler Preschool and Primary Scale of Intelligence–Revised (WPPSI–R)* for children who are 6 years to 7 years, 3 months. The manual recommends using the *WPPSI–R* for children who fall within this age range and who are of low ability; and the *WISC–III* for children who have high ability or are gifted.

*Scoring.*   The manual provides clearly written directions for scoring. The scoring of the subtests varies from one subtest to another. Raw scores convert to scaled scores, which are a form of standard score with a mean of 100 and a standard deviation of 15. The scaled scores determine the Verbal, Performance, and Full Scale IQ scores. The factor-based scores are optional and are calculations from the scaled scores.

When children retest using a revised instrument, there is usually some fluctuation in scores. Comparisons between the *WISC–III* Verbal, Performance, and Full Scale scores with the scores from the *WISC–R* revealed that the *WISC–III* scores were lower than *WISC–R* scores. In general, *WISC–III* Full Scale scores were from 5 to 9 points lower than *WISC–R* scores. Verbal and Performance Scale scores on the *WISC–III* ranged from 2 to 7 points lower than *WISC–R* scores. The average difference between *WISC–III* scores and *WPPSI–R* scores was about 4 points, with *WPPSI–R* scores generally being lower than *WISC–III* scores. However, this difference can be larger with children who fall at the upper or lower ends of the IQ range.

*Standardization.*   The *WISC–III* based its standardization sample on 1988 data from the U.S. Bureau of the Census. The standardization sample consisted of 2,200 children in each of 11 age groups extending from 6 to 16 years and according to age, gender, race, ethnicity, geographic region, and parental education.

The *WISC–III* standardization sample does not include students with exceptional needs nor does it provide separate norms for these children. However, the manual provides summaries of several studies conducted by independent researchers with special populations, including gifted children and those with mental retardation, learning disabilities, and those with attention-deficit hyperactivity disorder, behavior disorder, epilepsy, speech and language delays, and hearing impairment. For the most part, these studies are few in number and contain small samples. However, they are encouraging. Additional research is needed in this area.

*Reliability.*   Reliability refers to the consistency or stability of test performance. The manual reports split-half reliability coefficients for each of the subtests, for the three IQ scales, and for the four factor-based scales. Because the length of a test affects reliability, the highest reliability coefficient was for Full Scale IQ (.96). For the subtests, reliability coefficients ranged from .69 (Object Assembly) to .87 (Vocabulary and Block Design). Reliability coefficients for the factor-based scales ranged from .85 (Processing Speed) to .94 (Verbal Comprehension).

Test-retest reliability is an estimate of the stability of test scores over time. To assess test-retest reliability a separate group of 353 children tested with the instrument twice. The median interval between testings was 23 days. Separate reliability coefficients were calculated for various age groups; for ages 6 and 7, reliability coefficients for the subtests ranged from .60 (Mazes) to .82 (Vocabulary, Picture Completion). Because the reliabilities for the subtests are low, caution is advisable when interpreting the results of individual subtests. For the IQ scores, test-retest reliabilities ranged from .86 (Performance IQ) to .92 (Full Scale IQ); for the factor-based scores test-retest reliabilities ranged from .74 (Freedom from Distractibility) to .89 (Verbal Comprehension).

Like many tests, *WISC–III* scores show a slight increase when the testing interval is short. For example, for children ages 6 and 7, when the median test-retest interval was 23 days, Verbal IQ scores increased 1.7 points, Performance IQ scores increased 11.5 points, and Full Scale IQ scores increased 7 points.

Interscorer reliabilities are available for those subtests that require more judgment in scoring. For the subtests Similarities, Vocabulary, Comprehension, and Mazes, the interscorer reliability coefficients exceeded .90. The manual concludes that scoring for these subtests is reliable.

*Validity.*     According to the manual, because the *WISC–R* is valid, the *WISC–III* is also valid. While it is true that there is considerable evidence for the validity of the *WISC–R*, the *WISC–III* is a substantial revision of the earlier version. Therefore, the evidence for the validity of the *WISC–III* based on the *WISC–R* is reliable with this caveat in mind.

The manual does provide evidence for the separate factor structure of the subtests. In general, Verbal subtests correlate more strongly with each other than with Performance subtests;

Performance subtests correlate more strongly with each other than with Verbal subtests. Factor analyses of the *WISC–III* scores confirm the likelihood of the four factors, Verbal Comprehension, Perceptual Organization, Freedom from Distractibility, and Processing Speed. However, Sattler (1992) has indicated that the Freedom from Distractibility factor may be weak and that evaluators should make interpretations based on this factor cautiously.

The manual reports correlations between *WISC–III* scores and scores from several other tests. This evidence supports the validity of the *WISC–III*. However, additional research studies are necessary in order to add to our knowledge about the validity of the *WISC–III*.

*Summary.*     The *WISC–III* is an individually administered test of intelligence. Reliabilities of the individual subtests, for 6- and 7-year-old children, is lower than for the Full Scale IQ score. Validity appears to be adequate. While additional research is necessary to contribute to our understanding of it, this instrument is useful in the assessment of students. Box 13.10 outlines the test's parameters.

---

**BOX 13.10**  *Wechsler Intelligence Scale for Children–Third Edition (WISC–III)*

---

*Publication Date:* 1991

*Purposes:* Assesses intellectual ability, areas of strength and weakness.

*Age/Grade Levels:* 6 years through 16 years, 11 months.

*Time to Administer:* 60 to 90 minutes.

Technical Adequacy: The standardization sample is excellent. Reliability is very good. Validity is adequate. Rely on evidence for the validity of the *WISC–III* based on the *WISC–R* with caution.

*Suggested Use:* Can be used when conducting a psychoeducational assessment, diagnosis of exceptional needs, determining eligibility for services, and clinical and neuropsychological assessment.

---

## Wechsler Preschool and Primary Scale of Intelligence–Revised

The *Wechsler Preschool and Primary Scale of Intelligence–Revised (WPPSI–R)* (Wechsler, 1989) is a revision of the *Wechsler Preschool and Primary Scale (WPPSI)* (Wechsler, 1967). It is an individually administered test of intelligence for children ages 3 to 7 years. The *WPPSI–R* is similar in format and content to the *WISC–III*. The *WPPSI–R* contains two scales, Verbal and Performance, comprising 12 subtests, two of which are optional. Individual scores are available for each of the subtests. Verbal, Performance, and Full Scale IQ scores derive from the subtest scores. Table 13.8 describes each of the subtests.

**TABLE 13.8    Wechsler Preschool and Primary Scale of Intelligence–Revised**

| | |
|---|---|
| Object Assembly | Pieces of a puzzle are arranged in front of the examinee in a standardized configuration. The individual must put the pieces together within a certain time limit. |
| Information | The examinee must respond to items that demonstrate knowledge about events or objects in the environment. Depending on the level of difficulty of the item, responses can be either verbally or by pointing to a picture of an item. |
| Geometric Design | This subtest includes two types of items. The first asks the examinee to match a visual stimulus with one of the four choices that are presented. For the second type of item, the individual must copy a geometric figure. |
| Comprehension | The individual expresses an understanding of the reasons for certain actions and consequences. |
| Block Design | The examinee must reproduce patterns of two-colored flat blocks that the examiner constructs. |
| Arithmetic | This subtest assesses the individual's understanding of basic quantitative concepts with pictures, counting tasks, and word problems. |
| Mazes | Using paper and pencil the examinee must solve, within specified time limits, printed mazes that increase in difficulty. |
| Vocabulary | Depending on the age of the examinee, the individual must name pictured objects or give oral definitions of words that the examiner presents verbally. |
| Picture Completion | The examinee must identify what is missing from pictured objects or events. |
| Similarities | The individual's understanding of the concept of similarities is assessed in three ways: <br> 1. the examinee points to one of several pictured objects that have a common attribute; <br> 2. the examinee completes a sentence that the examiner presents verbally and that contains an analogy or similarity; and <br> 3. the individual explains orally how two objects or events are similar. |
| Animal Pegs | The examinee must associate a colored peg with each animal according to a key that is at the top of the board. This optional subtest assesses speed and accuracy. |
| Sentences | The examinee repeats a sentence that the examiner says. Like the Animal Pegs subtest, this subtest is optional. |

***Administration.*** Like the *WISC–III*, the *WPPSI–R* is administered individually. The manual presents clear directions for administering and scoring the 12 subtests. The subtests require administering in a specified order, and each subtest has separate starting and stopping points.

The *WPPSI–R* overlaps with the *WISC–III* for children who are 6 years to 7 years, 3 months. The *WPPSI–R* manual recommends using the *WPPSI–R* if a teacher suspects a child of having either average or below average ability, and the *WISC–III* for children who may be gifted.

*Scoring.* The manual clearly explains directions for scoring. Raw scores convert to scaled scores, which have a mean of 100 and a standard deviation of 15. Using these scaled scores evaluators can calculate the Verbal, Performance, and Full Scale IQ scores.

The manual reports comparisons of *WPPSI–R* scores with other tests. *WPPSI* Full Scale IQ scores are approximately 8 points higher than Full Scale IQ scores of the *WPPSI–R*. *WPPSI* Performance Scale IQ scores are approximately 9 points higher and Verbal Scale IQ scores were 5 points higher than *WPPSI–R* scores. The *Stanford-Binet Composite scores and McCarthy Scales of Children's Abilities General Cognitive Index* scores are approximately 2 points higher than *WPPSI–R* Full Scale IQ scores. Similarly, the Mental Processing Composite of the *Kaufman Assessment Battery for Children (K–ABC)* was 6 points higher than the *WPPSI–R* Full Scale IQ score.

*Standardization.* The standardization sample used data from the 1986 Census. The sample consisted of 1,700 children, ages 3 years to 7 years, 3 months. The sample was stratified according to age, gender, geographic region, ethnicity, parental education, and parental occupation. The author oversampled four hundred minority group children in order to investigate item bias.

The standardization sample does not systematically include children with exceptional needs. However, several small studies did include groups of children with exceptional needs. A sample of 16 gifted children who had tested with the *Stanford-Binet* showed that some of these children would not have received the same classification from taking the *WPPSI–R*. Studies of children with mental retardation, learning disabilities, and with speech/language impairments showed that the *WPPSI–R* could be useful with these groups. However, the studies were not wide in scope and additional research is necessary in this area.

*Reliability.* The manual reports interscorer and test-retest reliabilities. Calculations from a sample of 151 scorers determined interscorer reliability of the Comprehension, Vocabulary, Similarities, and Mazes subtests; and for the Geometric Design subtest, the sample comprised 188 scorers. The interscorer reliabilities were: Comprehension .96, Vocabulary .94, Similarities .96, Mazes .94, and Geometric Design .88.

Test-retest reliability came from a randomly selected sample of 175 children from the standardization sample. The test-retest interval ranged from three to seven weeks. Corrected coefficients for the subtests ranged from .52 (Mazes) to .82 (Picture Completion). The correlation coefficients for the three scales were: Verbal Scale .90, Performance Scale .88, and Full Scale IQ .91. Because the coefficients on the subtests are relatively weak, their interpretation is less valuable.

*Validity.* Part of the discussion in the manual on the validity of the *WPPSI–R* refers to previous research conducted on the earlier *WPPSI*. However, the *WPPSI–R* is a comprehensive revision and much of the evidence presented for validity of the *WPPSI* is not applicable to the *WPPSI–R*.

The manual does present descriptions of concurrent validity studies with the *WPPSI–R* and other instruments. In general, the *WPPSI–R* correlated higher with the *WPPSI* and the *Wechsler Intelligence Scale for Children–Revised (WISC–R)*. Moderate correlations arose with the *Stanford-Binet* and the *McCarthy Scales*. Relatively low coefficients resulted when correlating *WPPSI–R* scores with *K–ABC* scores.

*Summary.* The *WPPSI–R* is an individually administered test of intelligence for children ages 3 to 7 years. The standardization is adequate. Information about reliability and validity is limited.

# Woodcock-Johnson® III Tests of Cognitive Ability

The *Woodcock-Johnson® III (WJ III®)* (Woodcock and Johnson, 1989) is an individually administered battery that assesses cognitive and academic abilities in individuals ages 2 years through adulthood. The battery consists of two tests, *Woodcock-Johnson® III Tests of Cognitive Ability (WJ III® COG)* and the *Woodcock-Johnson® III Tests of Achievement (WJ III® ACH)*. The *WJ III®* measures general intellectual ability, specific cognitive abilities, scholastic aptitude, oral language, and academic achievement.

The *WJ III® COG* is an application of the Cattell-Horn-Carroll (CHC) theory of cognitive processing. According to the authors, the *WJ III® COG* measures: General Intellectual Ability, Predicted Achievement, Intra-cognitive Discrepancies, Cognitive Categories (Verbal Ability, Thinking Ability, and Cognitive Efficiency), CHC Factors (Comprehension-Knowledge, Long-Term Retrieval, Visual-Spatial Thinking, Auditory Processing, Fluid Reasoning, Processing Speed, Short-Term Memory), and Clinical Clusters (Phonemic Awareness, Working Memory, Broad Attention, Cognitive Fluency, and Executive Processes).

The *WJ III® COG* comprises two batteries, a Standard Battery and an Extended Battery. Teachers and other professionals can administer the Standard Battery alone or with the Extended Battery. Subtests 1 through 10 make up the Standard Battery and subtests 11 through 20 make up the Extended Battery. Subtests combine to form clusters. Table 13.9 lists the subtests and the Broad Cognitive Abilities that they measure.

***Administration.*** The time to administer the *WJ III®* varies from 20 minutes to several hours depending on whether administering both the *WJ III® COG* and the *WJ III® ACH* and whether including the Standard Battery and the Extended Battery. The test provides age (ages 2 years through adulthood) and grade norms (kindergarten through first year graduate school). A computing scoring program is necessary. Raw scores are converted to age and grade equivalents, percentile ranks, and standard scores. The manual reports confidence bands for standard scores for

the 68 percent, 90 percent, and 95 percent confidence bands. It is possible to make interpretation of intra-individual, intra-cognitive, and intra-achievement discrepancies, and predicted achievement.

***Norms.*** The standardization sample for the *WJ III®* comprised 8,818 individuals in over 100 communities. The preschool sample consisted of over 1,000 children who were 2 to 5 years of age and not enrolled in kindergarten. There were 4,784 individuals in the kindergarten through grade 12 sample. More than 1,000 individuals made up the college/university sample. The rest of the standardization sample consisted of adults. The stratification sample occurred according to Census region, community size, sex, race (Caucasian, African American, Native American, Asian Pacific, Hispanic), type of school (elementary, secondary, public, private, home), type of college/university (two-year college, four-year college or university, public, private), education of adults (less than ninth grade, less than high school diploma, high school diploma, one to three years of college, bachelor's degree, master's degree or higher), occupational status of adults (employed, unemployed, not in labor force), and occupation of adults in labor force (professional/managerial, technical/sales/administrative, Armed Forces/police, farming/forestry/fishing, precision product/craft/repair, operative/fabricator/laborer).

***Reliability.*** The reliability of the *WJ III®* has greatly improved from the previous version of this test. The authors provide extensive information on reliability of the subtest scores, clusters, and the discrepancy scores. Reliabilities for the broad cognitive and achievement clusters are in the .90s.

***Validity.*** The manual reports a number of validity studies for both the cognitive and achievement batteries. In general, there is evidence to support content, concurrent, and construct validity. Evaluators should remember that the

**TABLE 13.9**  *Broad Abilities, Narrow Abilities, and Broad Cognitive Factors Measured by the* Woodcock-Johnson® III, Tests of Cognitive Ability

The Standard Battery of the *WJ® III COG* consists of subtests 1 through 10. The Extended Battery comprises subtests 11 through 20.

| Subtest | Narrow Ability | Broad Cognitive Factor |
|---|---|---|
| 1  Verbal Comprehension | Lexical Knowledge<br>Language Development | Comprehension<br>Knowledge |
| 11  General Information | General Information | |
| 2  Visual-Auditory Learning | Associate Memory | Visual Spatial Thinking |
| 12  Retrieval Fluency | Ideational Fluency | |
| 10  Visual-Auditory Learning—Delayed | Associate Memory | |
| 3  Spatial Relations | Visualization<br>Spatial Relations | Auditory Processing |
| 13  Picture Recognition | Visual Memory | |
| 19  Planning | Spatial Scanning | |
| 4  Sound Blending | Phonetic Coding Synthesis | Auditory Processing |
| 14  Auditory Attention | Speech Sound Discrimination | |
| 8  Incomplete Words | Phonetic Coding Analysis | |
| 5  Concept Formation | Induction | Fluid Reasoning |
| 15  Analysis-Synthesis | Sequential Reasoning | |
| 6  Visual Matching | Perceptual Speed | Processing Speed |
| 16  Decision Speed | Semantic Processing | |
| 18  Rapid Picture Naming | Naming Facility | |
| 20  Pair Cancellation | Attention<br>Concentration | |
| 7  Numbers Reversed | Working Memory<br>Memory Span | Short-Term Memory |
| 17  Memory for Words | Memory Span | |
| 9  Auditory Working Memory | Working Memory<br>Memory Span | |

| BOX 13.11 | *Woodcock-Johnson® III, Tests of Cognitive Ability (WJ III® COG)* |

*Publication Date:* 2001

*Purposes:* Assesses cognitive abilities, general intellectual ability.

*Age/Grade Levels:* 2 years through adulthood.

*Time to Administer:* Approximately one hour.

*Technical Adequacy:* The standardization sample is appropriate. Reliability and validity are strong.

*Suggested Use:* Diagnosis, determining intra-individual, intra-cognitive, and intra-achievement discrepancies, determining predicted achievement, determining eligibility for services, program placement, individual program planning, program evaluation.

cognitive portion represents a single perspective, the Cattell-Horn-Carroll (CHC) theory. The extent to which various subtests and interpretations reflect students' abilities depends on the orientation of the team to assessment.

**Summary.** The *WJ III® COG* is a substantially improved version of its predecessor, the *Woodcock-Johnson Psychoeducational Battery–Revised (WJ–R)* (Woodcock and Johnson, 1989). It is a norm-referenced, individually administered battery that assesses cognitive and academic abilities in individuals ages two years through adulthood. The cognitive battery consists of two parts, Standard Battery and the Extended Battery. Documentation of reliability and validity are extensive. Box 13.11 outlines this test's parameters.

## Preferred Practices

Our understanding of intelligence has developed and changed over the years. Theorists have written about the nature of intelligence and how we should measure it. Although there are differing perspectives, we do know that intelligence is not a unitary construct. Various theorists have conceptualized intelligence as comprising various abilities. However, they have disagreed about the exact nature of these constituent abilities.

New conceptualizations of the construct of intelligence are emerging. Howard Gardner (1991) has developed the theory of multiple intelligences (MI). According to Gardner, individuals

> are capable of at least seven different ways of knowing the world—ways that I have elsewhere labeled the *seven human intelligences.* According to this analysis, we are able to know the world through language, logical-mathematical analysis, spatial representation, musical thinking, the use of the body to solve problems or to make things, an understanding of other individuals, and an understanding of ourselves. (Gardner, 1991, p. 12)

According to MI theory, individuals have different profiles of strengths of the seven intelligences, and individuals differ in the ways they invoke and combine the various intelligences to carry out tasks and to solve problems. Gardner believes that school environments need to develop around these seven ways of knowing. According to Gardner, a curriculum arising from these ways of knowing is worth assessing; if the curriculum does not have an appropriate structure, then the assessment is useless.

MI theory may function as an approach to assessment. Although there are no formal assessment tools stemming from MI theory, Gardner advocates the use of this approach to develop alternative and authentic forms of assessment.

Robert Sternberg (1985) has described a theory of intelligence, called the Triarchic Theory, which has three components: meta-components, performance components, and knowledge-acquisition components. Metacomponents are similar to metacognitive processes in that they help to plan, monitor, and evaluate an individual's performance of a task.

Sternberg (1985) listed ten metacomponents as important to intelligent functioning:

1. recognition that a problem of some kind exists
2. recognition of exactly what the nature of the problem is
3. selection of a set of lower-order, nonexecutive components for the performance on a task
4. selection of a strategy for task performance, combining the lower-order components
5. selection of one or more mental representations for information
6. decision on how to allocate attentional resources
7. monitoring or keeping track of one's place in task performance and of what has been done and needs to be done
8. understanding of internal and external feedback concerning the quality of task performance
9. knowing how to act on the feedback that is received, and
10. implementation of action as a result of the feedback. (p. 62)

Educators can employ performance components to execute a variety of strategies for task performance. These are lower-order processes, and they include:

1. encoding the nature of a stimulus
2. inferring the relations between two stimulus terms that are similar in some ways and different in others
3. applying a previously inferred relation to a new situation. (Sternberg, 1985, p. 62)

Knowledge-acquisition components are processes for learning new information and storing this new information in memory. There are three knowledge-acquisition components:

1. selective encoding, which involves selecting between relevant and irrelevant information
2. selective combination, which involves combining what has been selectively encoded in order to maximize its coherence and connectedness
3. selective comparison, which consists of relating the information that has been selectively encoded and combining it with information already stored in memory in order to optimize the connectedness of the new knowledge. (Sternberg, 1985, p. 62)

When interpreting an individual's performance on an intelligence test, the following cautions should be kept in mind:

1. The examinee's background, environment, motivation, health, and emotional state can affect performance. Other factors include examiner bias, cultural and linguistic differences between the examinee and the examiner, rapport, the skill of the examiner, the test environment, and the demands of the test. (Taylor, 1990)
2. Intelligence tests sample behaviors. Performance on a test helps us in our understanding of the examinee's approach to the demands of the tasks that are presented. There are many behaviors that intelligence tests do not sample and our understanding of these is emerging.
3. Performance on an intelligence test should be regarded as helping to describe rather than to explain behavior. Scores on an IQ test represent the examinee's performance at a given moment in time. We know that, especially with young children, tested intelligence can change over time. (Anastasi, 1988; Sattler, 1988)

## Extending Learning

1. Explain how our conceptualization of intelligence has evolved over time.
2. When measuring intelligence, what special considerations do we need to make when testing a student from another culture?
3. What does the following statement mean:

The results of intelligence tests should describe rather than explain behavior?
4. Examine several different intelligence tests. How do they differ in form and content?
5. What do you think intelligence tests will be like 20 years from now?

## References

Algozzine, B., R. C. Eaves, L. Mann, and H. R. Vance (1993). *Slosson full-range intelligence test*. East Aurora, NY: Slosson Educational Publications.

Anastasi, A. (1985). Review of the Kaufman assessment battery for children. In *Mental measurements yearbook: Vol. 1*, ed. G. Mitchell, 769–771. Lincoln, NE: University of Nebraska.

Anastasi, A. (1988). *Psychological testing*. New York: Macmillan.

Brown, L., R. J. Sherbenou, and S. K. Johnsen (1997). *Test of nonverbal intelligence–3*. Itasca, IL: Riverside.

Burgenmeister, B., L. Blum, and I. Lorge (1972). *Columbia mental maturity scale*. San Antonio, TX: The Psychological Corporation.

Coffman, W. E. (1985). Review of the Kaufman assessment battery for children. In *Mental health measurements yearbook: Vol. 1*, ed. G. Mitchell, 771–773. Lincoln, NE: University of Nebraska.

Das, J. P., J. R. Kirby, and R. F. Jarman (1979). *Simultaneous and successive cognitive processes*. New York: Academic Press.

Das, J. P., and G. N. Molloy (1975). Varieties of simultaneous and successive processing in children. *Journal of Educational Psychology* 67: 213–220.

Delaney, E. A., and T. F. Hopkins (1987). *The Stanford-Binet intelligence scale: Fourth Edition*, Examiner's Handbook. Itasca, IL: Riverside.

Elliot, C. D. (1990a). *Differential ability scales—Administration and scoring manual*. San Antonio, TX: The Psychological Corporation.

Elliot, C. D. (1990b). *Differential ability scales—Introduction and technical handbook*. San Antonio, TX: Psychological Corporation.

Gardner, H. (1991). *The unschooled mind*. New York: Basic Books.

Griffiths, R. (1979). *The abilities of young children*. London: Child Development Research Center.

Hammill, D. D. (1998). *Detroit tests of learning aptitude–4*. Itasca, IL: Riverside.

Hammill, D. D., and B. R. Bryant (1991). *Detroit tests of learning aptitude–primary: second edition*. Itasca, IL: Riverside.

Hammill, D. D., N. A. Pearson, and J. L. Wiederholt (1996). *Comprehensive test of nonverbal intelligence*. Austin, TX: PRO-ED.

Kaufman, A. S., and N. L. Kaufman (1983). *Kaufman assessment battery for children*. Circle Pines, MN: American Guidance Service.

Kaufman, A. S., and N. L. Kaufman (1990). *Kaufman brief intelligence test*. Circle Pines, MN: American Guidance Service.

Kaufman, A. S., and N. L. Kaufman (1993). *Kaufman adolescent and adult intelligence test*. Circle Pines, MN: American Guidance Service.

Leiter, R. G. (1979). *Leiter international performance scale* (rev. ed.). Wood Dale, IL: Stoetling.

McCarthy, D. (1972). *McCarthy scales of children's abilities*. New York: The Psychological Corporation.

Merz, W. R. (1984). Review of the Kaufman assessment battery for children. In *Test Critiques: Vol. 1*, ed. K. Sweetland, 393–404. Kansas City, MO: Test Corporation of America.

Newland, E. T. (1971). *Blind learning aptitude test*. Champaign, IL: University of Illinois Press.

Page, E. B. (1985). Review of the Kaufman assessment battery for children. In *Mental health measurements yearbook: Vol. 1*, ed. G. Mitchell, 773–777. Lincoln, NE: University of Nebraska.

Reid, G., and Miller, M. (1997). *Leiter international performance scale–revised*. Chicago: Stoelting.

Salvia, J., and J. Ysseldyke (1988). *Assessment in special and remedial education*. Boston, MA: Houghton-Mifflin.

Salvia, J., and J. Ysseldyke (2001). *Assessment*. Boston, MA: Houghton-Mifflin.

Sattler, J. (1988). *Assessment of children*. San Diego, CA: Jerome M. Sattler.

Sattler, J. (1992). *WISC–III and WPPSI–R supplement to assessment of children*. San Diego, CA: Jerome M. Sattler.

Slosson, R. (1998). *Slosson intelligence test–revised*. East Aurora, NY: Slosson Educational Publications.

Sternberg, R. (1985). Cognitive approaches to intelligence. In *Handbook of intelligence*, ed. B. B. Wolman, 59–118. New York: John Wiley & Sons.

Sternberg, R. (1996). *Myths, countermyths, and truths*

*about intelligence.* Educational Researcher, 25: 11–16.

Suzuki, L. A., D. A. Vraniak, and J. F. Kugler (1996). Intellectual assessment across cultures. In *Handbook of multicultural assessment*, ed. L. A. Suzuki, P. J. Meller, and J. G. Ponterotto, 141–177. San Francisco: Jossey-Bass.

Taylor, R. (1990). Intellectual assessment tips. *Diagnostique* 16: 52–54.

Thorndike, R. L., and E. Hagen (1993). *Cognitive abilities test, Form 5*. Itasca, IL: Riverside.

Thorndike, R. L., E. P. Hagen, and J. M. Sattler (1986a). *Technical manual Stanford-Binet intelligence scale: Fourth edition*. Itasca, IL: Riverside.

Thorndike, R. L., E. P. Hagen, and J. M. Sattler (1986b). *Guide for administering and scoring the fourth edition*. Itasca, IL: Riverside.

Thorndike, R. L., E. P. Hagen, and J. M. Sattler (1986c). *Stanford-Binet intelligence scale: Fourth edition*. Itasca, IL: Riverside.

Thorndike, R. M., and D. F. Lohman (1990). *A century of ability testing*. Itasca, IL: Riverside.

Valencia, R. R., R. J. Rankin, and R. Livingston (1995). K–ABC content bias: Comparisons between Mexican-American and White children. *Psychology in the Schools* 32: 153–169.

Wechsler, D. (1944). *The measurement of adult intelligence*. 3rd ed. Baltimore: Williams & Wilkins.

Wechsler, D. (1967). *Manual of the Wechsler preschool and primary scale of intelligence*. San Antonio, TX: The Psychological Corporation.

Wechsler, D. (1974). *Wechsler intelligence scale for children–revised*. Itasca, IL: Riverside.

Wechsler, D. (1983). *Escala de inteligencia Wechsler para niños® revisada*. San Antonio, TX: The Psychological Corporaiton.

Wechsler, D. (1989). *WPPSI–R manual*. San Antonio, TX: The Psychological Corporation.

Wechsler, D. (1991). *Wechsler intelligence scale for children–III*. San Antonio, TX: The Psychological Corporation.

Wechsler, D. (1993). *Escala de inteligencia Wechsler para niños® revisada de Puerto Rico*. San Antonio, TX: The Psychological Corporation.

Woodcock, R. W., K. S. McGrew, and N. Mather (2001). *Woodcock-Johnson® III Tests of cognitive ability*. Itasca, IL: Riverside.

Woodcock, R. W., and A. F. Muñoz-Sandoval (1996). *Batería–R tests of cognitive ability*. Itasca, IL: Riverside.

# 14

# *Adaptive Skills*

## *Overview*

Adaptive skills are competencies that an individual has in the following areas: communication, self-care, home living, social skills, community use, self-direction, health and safety, functional academics, leisure, and work (American Association on Mental Retardation, 1992). The concept of adaptive skills is an outgrowth of the term **adaptive behavior,** which is defined as "the quality of everyday performance in coping with environmental demands" (Grossman, 1983, p. 42). The concept of adaptive behavior reflects the in-

fluence of theory, professional practice, politics, and litigation. However, because the concept of adaptive skills reflects a more contemporary approach to this area, we will use the term *adaptive skills* in this book rather than adaptive behavior.

According to the American Association on Mental Retardation, the designation *adaptive skills*

implies an array of competencies and, thus, provides a firmer foundation in several of the definition's key statements; that is, adaptive skill limitations often coexist with strengths in other adaptive skills or other areas of personal competence, and the existence of these limitations and strengths in adaptive skills must be both documented within the context of community environments typical of the individual's age peers and tied to the person's individualized needs for support. (American Association on Mental Retardation, 1992, p. 4)

## Chapter Objectives

After completing this chapter, you should be able to:

- Define and describe the concept of adaptive skills.
- Explain the changing nature of the concepts of adaptive behavior and adaptive skills.
- Describe maladaptive behavior and problem behavior.
- Describe specific tests of adaptive skills, adaptive behavior, and maladaptive behavior.

## What Shapes Our Views

For students who are in school, the measurement of adaptive skills plays a large part in determining whether a student is labeled as having mental retardation. According to the American Association on Mental Retardation

mental retardation refers to substantial limitations in present functioning. It is characterized by significantly subaverage intellectual functioning, existing concurrently with related limitations in two or more of the following adaptive skill areas: communication, self-care, home living, social skills, community use, self-direction, health and safety, functional academics, leisure, and work. Mental retardation manifests before age 18. (American Association on Mental Retardation, 1992, p. 5)

The identification of a student as mentally retarded relates to the identification of at least two limitations in **adaptive skills.** An individual's adaptive skills reflect the competencies that the person has for functioning at home, work, and in the community. Table 14.1 describes the ten adaptive skill areas.

Identification of strengths and weaknesses in adaptive skill areas document the need for supports. **Supports** are

resources and strategies that promote the interests and causes of individuals with or without disabilities; that enable them to access resources, information, and relationships inherent within integrated work and living environments; and that result in their enhanced interdependence/interdependence, productivity, community integration, and satisfaction. (American Association on Mental Retardation, 1992, p. 101)

The assessment of adaptive skills should result in the identification of supports that an individual needs. The desired outcomes of using supports include contributing to personal, social, and emotional development; strengthening the individual's self-esteem and self-worth; and providing opportunities to make contributions. Supports have a number of functions, can come from many resources, and can vary in intensity (American Association on Mental Retardation, 1992). Figure 14.1 on page 382 illustrates the interrelationships between desired outcomes, support resources, support functions, and intensities of support.

### Cautions

Because our views of adaptive skills and adaptive behavior have changed and will continue to

**TABLE 14.1**   *Adaptive Behavior Skills*

| | |
|---|---|
| *Communication* | Skills include the ability to comprehend and express information through symbolic behaviors (e.g., spoken word, written word/orthography, graphic symbols, sign language, manually coded English) or nonsymbolic behaviors (e.g., facial expression, body movement, touch, gesture). Specific examples include the ability to comprehend and/or receive a request, an emotion, a greeting, a comment, a protest, or rejection. Higher level skills of communication (e.g., writing a letter) would also relate to functional academics. |
| *Self-Care* | Skills involved in toileting, eating, dressing, hygiene, and grooming. |
| *Home-Living* | Skills related to functioning within a home, which include clothing care, housekeeping, property maintenance, food preparation and cooking, planning and budgeting for shopping, home safety, and daily scheduling. Related skills include orientation and behavior in the home and nearby neighborhood, communication of choices and needs, social interaction, and application of functional academics in the home. |
| *Social* | Skills related to social exchanges with other individuals, including initiating, interacting, and terminating interaction with others; receiving and responding to pertinent situational cues; recognizing feelings; providing positive and negative feedback; regulating one's own behavior; being aware of peers and peer acceptance; gauging the amount and type of interaction with others; assisting others; forming and fostering of friendships and love; coping with demands from others; making choices; sharing; understanding honesty and fairness; controlling impulses; conforming conduct to laws; violating rules and laws; and displaying appropriate socio-sexual behavior. |
| *Community Use* | Skills related to the appropriate use of community resources, including traveling in the community; grocery and general shopping at stores and markets; purchasing or obtaining services from other community businesses (e.g., gas stations, repair shops, doctor and dentist's offices); attending church or synagogue; using public transportation and public facilities, such as schools, libraries, parks and recreational areas, and streets and sidewalks; attending theaters; and visiting other cultural places and events. Related skills include behavior in the community, communication of choices and needs, social interaction, and the application of functional academics. |
| *Self-Direction* | Skills related to making choices; learning and following a schedule; initiating activities appropriate to the setting, conditions, schedule, and personal interests; completing necessary or required tasks; seeking assistance when needed; resolving problems confronted in familiar and novel situations; and demonstrating appropriate assertiveness and self-advocacy skills. |
| *Health and Safety* | Skills related to maintenance of one's health in terms of eating; illness identification, treatment, and prevention; basic first aid; sexuality; physical fitness; basic safety considerations (e.g., following rules and laws, using seat belts, crossing streets, interacting with strangers, seeking assistance); regular physical and dental check-ups; and personal habits. Related skills include protecting oneself from criminal behavior, using appropriate behavior in the community, communicating choices and needs, participating in social interactions, and applying functional academics. |

**TABLE 14.1**   *Continued*

| | |
|---|---|
| *Functional Academics* | Cognitive abilities and skills related to learning at school that also have direct application in one's life (e.g., writing; reading; using basic practical math concepts, basic science as it relates to awareness of the physical environment and one's health and sexuality; geography; and social studies). It is important to note that the focus of this skill area is not on grade-level academic achievement but, rather, on the acquisition of academic skills that are functional in terms of independent living. |
| *Leisure* | The development of a variety of leisure and recreational interests (i.e., self-entertainment and interactional) that reflect personal preferences and choices and, if the activity will be conducted in public, age and cultural norms. Skills include choosing and self-initiating interests, using and enjoying home and community leisure and recreational activities alone and with others, playing socially with others, taking turns, terminating or refusing leisure or recreational activities, extending one's duration of participation, and expanding one's repertoire of interests, awareness, and skills. Related skills include behaving appropriately in the leisure and recreation setting, communicating choices and needs, participating in social interaction, applying functional academics, and exhibiting mobility skills. |
| *Work* | Skills related to holding a part or full-time job or jobs in the community in terms of specific job skills, appropriate social behavior, and related work skills (e.g., completion of tasks; awareness of schedules; ability to seek assistance, take criticism, and improve skills; money management, financial resources allocation, and the application of other functional academic skills; and skills related to going to and from work, preparation for work, management of oneself while at work, and interaction with coworkers). |

*Source:* American Association on Mental Retardation (1992). Washington, DC: American Association on Mental Retardation, pp. 40–41. Reprinted with permission of the publisher.

change over time, there is considerable disagreement over how current assessment instruments measure these skills. In general, instruments that assess adaptive skills are useful when determining eligibility, engaging in program planning, and monitoring progress. There is also considerable overlap between instruments that assess adaptive skills, adaptive behavior, problem behavior, functional skills, and development. In addition, almost all of the commerically published instruments refer to adaptive behavior rather than to adaptive skills. Finally, adaptive behavior instruments reflect different views of adaptive behavior, and the assessment of adaptive behavior and adaptive skills depends on the orientations of the developers of the instruments.

## Responding to Diversity

Gender, racial, ethnic, or cultural groups, community expectations, and the life cycle all influence adaptive skills. What may be an adaptive skill in one environment may not be so in another environment. The quality of adaptive skills that an individual demonstrates changes at various ages. In addition, the presence of a dis-

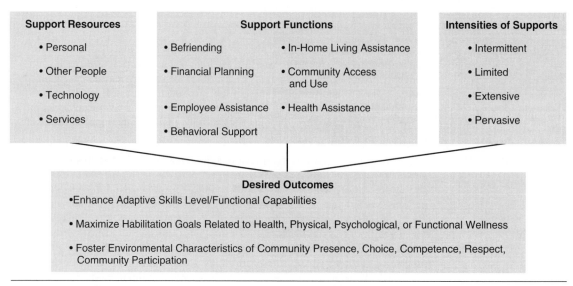

**FIGURE 14.1** *Support Resources, Functions, Intensities, and Desired Outcomes*

*Source:* American Association on Mental Retardation (1992). Washington, DC: American Association on Mental Retardation, p. 102. Reprinted with permission of the publisher.

ability can compound the identification of adaptive skills. Limitations in motor ability, in expressive and receptive abilities, or in other areas can make assessing adaptive skills a difficult or impossible task.

## Informants

Instruments that assess adaptive skills, adaptive behavior, and maladaptive behavior usually rely on an informant. An **informant** is an individual who knows the student well and provides information about the student. The informant responds to questions about the individual either through an interview with the examiner or by completing a checklist or scale. Because the assessment of adaptive skills and adaptive behavior relies on ratings that informants provide, it is possible and advantageous to administer them frequently.

The informant can be a parent, teacher, counselor, aide, nurse, or social worker. Informants provide different information about

students, although there may be considerable overlap. For instance, the teacher, social worker, or counselor provides information about peer relationships while the parent offers information about sibling relationships and activities around the home.

The information that the informants provide is necessarily judgmental, and can vary from one informant to the next. Informants bring their own perspectives, experiences, attitudes, response styles, and biases; and the student is likely to behave differently, depending on the environment or the situation. Because of these variables, it is important to evaluate the reliability and validity of the information that the informant supplies, and to ask more than one informant to complete an instrument or scale (Sattler, 1990)

## Maladaptive Behavior

**Maladaptive behaviors** are those behaviors that are considered to be problem behaviors.

Examples of maladaptive behaviors include bed wetting, unusual physical aggressiveness, poor attention, impulsivity, self-injurious behaviors, rocking back and forth repetitively, and poor eye contact. In general, we consider a student's actions a problem when they adversely affect the student, another student, or the environment (Bruininks, Thurlow, and Gilman, 1987). Problem behaviors affect the extent to which individuals will integrate into social and community settings. With older students, the presence of problem behaviors can have a negative impact on vocational and community placements (Bruininks, Thurlow, and Gilman, 1987).

The concept of maladaptive behavior, like the concept of adaptive behavior, is not without controversy. The assessment of maladaptive behavior relates to expectations tied to the student's age, family, culture, gender, and community. For example, thumb sucking is not a maladaptive behavior for a 2-year-old, but may be so for an 8-year-old.

## Standardized Instruments

The instruments in this chapter have the specific purpose of evaluating adaptive behavior. Many assess adaptive skills and some assess maladaptive behavior. There are many other tests besides these that assess adaptive skills. Tables 14.2, 14.3, and 14.4 give a comprehensive listing of the variety of tests available.

### Adaptive Behavior Inventory

The *Adaptive Behavior Inventory (ABI)* (Brown and Leigh, 1986) is a norm-referenced measure of adaptive development for use with students ages 6 years through 18 years who have disabilities and for students ages 5 through 18 years, 11 months who do not have disabilities. The *ABI* has five subscales: Self-Care Skills, Communication Skills, Social Skills, Academic Skills, and Occupational Skills. Each subscale contains 30

items. A short form of the *ABI*, *ABI–Short*, has 50 items.

***Administration.*** A teacher or other professional can complete the *ABI* and the *ABI–Short* in about 25 minutes.

***Scoring.*** Standard scores and percentile ranks are available for each of the subscales and the full scale.

***Standardization.*** The *ABI* standardized sample comprised 1,296 children with normal intelligence and 1,076 children with mental retardation. Although the characteristics of the sample are present, information about the selection of the sample is lacking.

***Reliability.*** The test provides information about internal consistency and test-retest reliability. For the most part, the reliability coefficients are in the .80s and .90s.

***Validity.*** The manual describes limited information about validity. It does, however, provide information about concurrent validity. Additional information about the validity of the *ABI* is necessary.

***Summary.*** The *ABI* and the *ABI–Short* are norm-referenced instruments that evaluate the adaptive development of students in five areas: Self-Care Skills, Communication Skills, Social Skills, Academic Skills, and Occupational Skills. Additional information about the technical adequacy of this test is necessary.

## Adaptive Behavior Scales

Originally developed by the American Association on Mental Retardation, the *Adaptive Behavior Scales (ABS)* consists of two scales. One, the *Adaptive Behavior Scales–Residential and Community: 2 (ABS–RC:2)* (Lambert, Leland,

and Nihira, 1993a), is for individuals who may be living either in institutional or community settings. It has two parts: Part One assesses personal independence, coping skills, and daily living skills. Part Two, the *Adaptive Behavior Scales–School Edition: 2 (ABS–S:2)* (Lambert, Leland, and Nihira, 1993b), is intended for use with individuals who are from 3 through 18 years, 11 months and who will be attending school or are in school. Here we describe only the *ABS–S:2*.

The *ABS–S:2* is in two parts; Part One comprises the nine domains listed below.

*Independent Functioning.* Assesses eating, toileting, maintaining a clean and neat appearance, dressing, and using transportation and other public facilities.

*Physical Development.* Evaluates physical and motor abilities.

*Economic Activity.* Assesses ability to manage money and to be a consumer.

*Language Development.* Evaluates receptive and expressive language and behavior in social situations.

*Numbers and Time.* Examines basic mathematical skills.

*Prevocational/Vocational Activity.* Assesses skills related to school and job performance.

*Responsibility.* Assesses the extent that an individual can be held accountable for his or her actions, belongings, and duties.

*Self-Direction.* Examines whether individuals choose to maintain an active or passive lifestyle.

*Socialization.* Assesses the ability to interact with others.

Part Two of the *ABS–S:2* focuses on social maladaptation. These behaviors are divided into the seven domains listed below.

*Violent and Antisocial Behavior.* Examines behaviors that are physically or emotionally abusive.

*Rebellious Behavior.* Assesses aspects of rebelliousness.

*Untrustworthy Behaviors.* Examines behaviors that are related to stealing, lying, cheating, and showing disrespect for public and private property.

*Stereotyped and Hyperactive Behavior.* Assesses behaviors such as making inappropriate physical contact, behaving in stereotypical ways, and being overactive.

*Eccentric Behavior.* Examines behaviors considered to be very unusual.

*Withdrawal.* Assesses the degree to which an individual withdraws or fails to respond to others.

*Disturbed Behavior.* Examines bothersome types of behaviors.

***Administration.***     An interviewer administers the *ABS–S:2*.

***Scoring.***     Raw scores convert to standard scores and percentiles. Scores also convert to

**TABLE 14.3**   *Tests of Adaptive Behavior*

| Test | Ages | Behaviors Measured |
|---|---|---|
| *AAMR Adaptive Behavior Scale–School Edition: 2 (ABS–S:2)* (Lambert, Nihira, and Leland, 1993b) | 3 years through 18 years, 11 months | Independent functioning, physical development, economic activity, language development, numbers and time, prevocational/vocational activity, self-direction, responsibility, socialization, social behavior, conformity, trustworthiness, stereotypes and hyperactive behavior, self-abusive behavior, social engagement, disturbing interpersonal behavior |
| *Adaptive Behavior Inventory (ABI)* (Brown and Leigh, 1986) | 5 years through 18 years, 11 months | Self-care, communication, social skills, academic skills, occupational skills |
| *Adaptive Behavior Inventory for Children (ABIC)* (Mercer and Lewis, 1982)<br><br>The manual has been translated into Spanish. The same record form is used for administration in English or Spanish. | 5 years through 11 years | Student role performance in the family, community, peer group, nonacademic settings; earner/consumer activities; self-maintenance |
| *Responsibility and Independence Scale for Adolescents* (Salvia, Neisworth, and Schmidt, 1990) | 12 years through 19 years, 11 months | Responsibility and independence |
| *Checklist of Adaptive Living Skills (CALS)* (Moreau and Bruininks, 1991) | Infant through adult | Personal-living skills, home-living skills, community-living skills, employment skills |
| *Adaptive Behavior Scales–Residential and Community: 2* (Lambert, Leland, and Nihira, 1993a) | 18 years through 80 years | Personal-living skills, community skills |
| *Adaptive Behavior Scales–School Edition: 2* (Lambert, Leland, and Nihira, 1993b) | 3 years through 18 years, 11 months | Self-care, communication, social skills, academic skills |
| *Scales of Independent Behavior–Revised (SIB–R)* (Bruininks, Woodcock, Weatherman, and Hill, 1996) | Infant through adult | Home, social, and community skills |
| *Vineland Adaptive Behavior Scales* (Sparrow, Balla, and Cicchetti, 1984) | Birth through 18 years, 11 months | Communication, daily living skills, socialization, and motor skills |

**TABLE 14.4** *Tests That Include Measures of Adaptive Behavior*

| Test | Ages | Behaviors Measured |
|---|---|---|
| *Early Screening Profiles* (Harrison et al., 1990) | 2 years through 6 years, 11 months | Cognitive language, motor, and self-help abilities; home survey, health survey, and behavior survey |
| *Assessment, Evaluation, and Programming System (AEPS), Vols. 1 and 2* (Bricker, 1993a; Bricker, 1993b) | Birth through 3 years | Feeding, personal hygiene, undressing |
| *Battelle Developmental Inventory (BDI)* (Newborg, Stock, and Wnek, 1988) | Birth through 8 years | Attention, eating, dressing, personal responsibility, toileting |
| *BRIGANCE® Diagnostic Inventory of Early Development–Revised* (Brigance, 1991) | Birth through 7 years | Self-help |
| *The Carolina Curriculum for Infants and Toddlers with Special Needs (CCITSN)* (Johnson-Martin, Jens, Attermeier, and Hacker, 1991) | Birth through 24 months | Eating, dressing, grooming |
| *Carolina Curriculum for Preschoolers with Special Needs (CCPSN)* (Johnson-Martin, Attermeier, and Hacker, 1990) | 2 years through 5 years | Eating, dressing, grooming, toileting, responsibility |
| *Developmental Profile II (DP–II)* (Alpern, Boll, and Shearer, 1986) | Birth through 12 years | Self-help |
| *FirstSTEP Screening Test for Evaluating Preschoolers* (Miller, 1993) | 2 years, 9 months through 6 years, 2 months | Daily living, self management, social interaction, functioning within the community |
| *Hawaii Early Learning Profile (HELP)* (Furano et al., 1988) | Birth through 36 months | Self-help |
| *HELP for Preschoolers* (VORT Corporation, 1995) | 3 years through 6 years | Self-help |

quotients that have a mean of 100 and a standard deviation of 15.

**Standardization.** Standardization of the *ABS–S:2* was covered in 31 states. The sample included both persons with disabilities and those who were not disabled.

**Reliability and Validity.** According to the authors, the *ABS–S:2* is a reliable and valid instrument, and there is considerable research that documents the usefulness of this instrument.

**Summary.** The *Adaptive Behavior Scales–School Edition: 2* is an instrument that assesses

**BOX 14.1**    *Adaptive Behavior Scales–*
*School Edition: 2*
*(ABS–S: 2)*

*Publication Date:* 1993

*Purposes:* To assess personal independence, coping skills, daily living skills, and maladaptive or problem behaviors.

*Age/Grade Levels:* Ages 3 through 21.

*Time to Administer:* Approximately 30 minutes in an interview format.

*Technical Adequacy:* The standardization sample is representative. Reliabilty and validity are very good.

*Suggested Use:* Can be used to determine adaptive and maladaptive (problem) behaviors in individuals who have mental retardation, who are developmentally delayed, or who exhibit problem behaviors. Useful in identification, program planning, and program monitoring.

the adaptive and maladaptive behavior of school-age children. This should be a useful tool. Box 14.1 describes the test's parameters.

## Checklist of Adaptive Living Skills

The *Checklist of Adaptive Living Skills (CALS)* (Moreau and Bruininks, 1991) is a criterion-referenced checklist of approximately 800 items in the areas of self-care, personal independence, and adaptive functioning. It measures the adaptive behaviors of infants through adults and is individually administered, using an interview format, to a respondent who knows the individual well.

The *CALS* relates, conceptually and statistically, to the *Scales of Independent Behavior (SIB)* (Bruininks, Woodcock, Weatherman, and Hill, 1984). The reason for this, according to the manual, was to allow users to predict scores on the *SIB*. The *Adaptive Living Skills Curriculum (ALSC)* (Bruininks, Moreau, Gilman, and Anderson, 1991), which is linked to the *CALS*, contains training objectives, strategies, and activities to facilitate program planning and intervention.

The *CALS* comprises four domains: Personal Living Skills, Home Living Skills, Community Living Skills, and Employment Skills. Each of these domains breaks down into 24 specific skills modules. Each item covers a range of behaviors and proceed in order of difficulty.

*Administration.* The respondent must know the student well. Persons with varied backgrounds, including parents, rehabilitation counselors, teachers, aides, and others can serve as respondents. The student need not test on all items. Because the *CALS* is a criterion-referenced checklist, teachers or other professionals can readminister the items periodically. It takes approximately 60 minutes to complete.

*Scoring.* The examiner checks items if the student performs the skill independently.

*Standardization.* This measure is criterion-referenced and was not standardized. The manual states that 627 individuals who ranged in age from infancy to over 40 years old took the *CALS*. The respondents were from 8 states. Approximately one-half of the sample were individuals with disabilities, and the sample had an approximately equal number of females and males. The manual provides little demographic information about the sample.

*Reliability.* Calculations of internal consistency and split-half reliabilities are available. The information on reliability is limited.

*Validity.* Evidence of criterion-related validity is based on two studies and is very limited.

*Summary.* The *CALS* is a criterion-referenced instrument that shows limited evidence of reliability and content and construct validity. Additional information about the sample is necessary. We recommend using this instrument with caution. It may be most appropriate for program planning.

## Responsibility and Independence Scale for Adolescents

The *Responsibility and Independence Scale for Adolescents (RISA)* (Salvia, Neisworth, and Schmidt, 1990) is a measure of adaptive behavior of individuals who are between the ages of 12 years and 19 years, 11 months. The scale measures responsibility and independence in adolescents. Responsibility is defined as "a broad class of adaptive behaviors that meet social expectations and standards of reciprocity, accountability, and fairness and that enable personal development through self- and social management, age appropriate behavior and social communication" (p. 2). Individuals who are responsible are "dependable, trustworthy, and able to shape, as well as comply with, social rules" (p. 2). Independence is defined as "a broad class of adaptive behaviors that allow individuals to live separately and free from the control or determination of others and to conduct themselves effectively in matters such as domestic and financial management, citizenship, personal organization, transportation, and career development" (p. 2). Independence means that an individual can make good decisions, makes plans, and deals effectively with situations that might affect self-reliance.

The 136 items are arranged in two subtests: Responsibility and Independence. The Responsibility subtest has 52 items that cluster in three areas: Self-Management, Social Maturity, and Social Communication.

*Administration.*    An interviewer administers the *RISA* to an individual who is familiar with the student. Informants can be a parent, guardian, surrogate parent, or spouse. The 136 questions take between 30 to 45 minutes to administer.

*Scores.*    The scoring is dichotomous with a score of 1 given when the informant responds yes, or a variation such as the phrase "I'm pretty sure" (p. 3). A score of 0 given when the informant answers no, or a variation such as the phrase "I don't think so" (p. 3). Scores can convert to percentiles and standard scores. Standard score differences can be available but the manual urges caution when using these differences. Figure 14.2 shows the front of the test form.

*Standardization.*    The sample consisted of ratings of 1,900 adolescents who were from nine age groups. Gender, community size, educational level of the parents or guardians, and geographical region were weighted so that the sample approximated the 1980 census. Race and ethnic group were not weighted because the sample closely represented the proportions in the United States population.

*Reliability.*    The manual reports split-half and test-retest reliability. The coefficients are at least .90 or higher.

*Validity.*    The manual reports three types of validity: content, criterion-related (concurrent), and construct. Content validity appears to be adequate. To demonstrate concurrent validity, the authors correlated the *RISA* with the *Vineland Adaptive Behavior Scales* and the *Scales of Independent Behavior.* The sample consisted of only 93 individuals, thus evidence of concurrent validity is weak. The coefficient for the *Vineland Adaptive Behavior Scales* total scale is .55, and the coefficient for the *Scales of Independent Behavior* total .55. Several studies that the manual reports discuss construct validity. Additional research is necessary to confirm construct validity.

*Summary.*    The *Responsibility and Independence Scale for Adolescents (RISA)* is an individually administered measure of adaptive behavior of adolescents. The scale should measure responsibility and independence. Evidence of

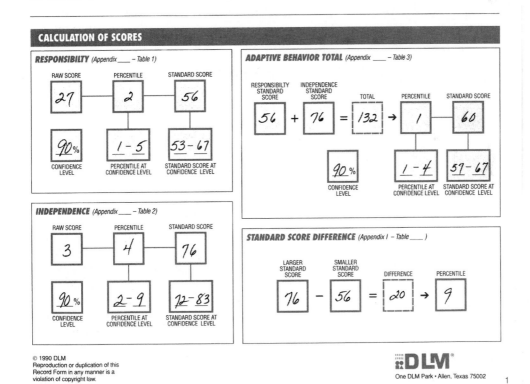

**FIGURE 14.2   RISA *Record Form***

*Source:* Copyright © 1990. From the *Responsibility and Independence Scale for Adolescents*, by John Salvia, John T. Neisworth, and Mary Schmidt, p. 47. Reprinted with permission of The Riverside Publishing Company. All rights reserved.

reliability is adequate. Additional studies are necessary to confirm construct validity.

## Scales of Independent Behavior–Revised

The *Scales of Independent Behavior–Revised (SIB–R)* (Bruininks, Woodcock, Weatherman, and Hill, 1996) is an individually administered, norm-referenced measure of adaptive behavior that measures the adaptive and problem behavior of individuals ages infant through adult. According to the authors, the *SIB–R* is useful for identification, placement, program planning, and monitoring progress. The instrument consists of 14 subscales that form four adaptive behavior clusters: Motor Skills, Social Interaction and Communication Skills, Personal Living Skills, and Community Living Skills. There are four clusters of maladaptive or problem behavior also: General Maladaptive Behavior, Internalized Maladaptive Behavior, Asocial Maladaptive Behavior, and Externalized Maladaptive Behavior. In addition, there are two short forms: *SIB–R Short Form* and the *Early Development Form*.

**Administration.** The Full Scale takes from 30 to 45 minutes to administer, and it takes 15 to 20 minutes for the *Short Form* or the *Early Development Form*.

**Standardization.** The *SIB–R* standardization sample consisted of 2,182 individuals representing the 1990 U.S. Census. It is linked to the *Woodcock-Johnson Psychoeducational Battery–Revised*. (See Chapter 13 for a description of this test.) The sample included persons with and without disabilities.

**Scoring.** The test shows various types of scores, including age scores, percentile ranks, standard scores, stanines, normal curve equivalents, and expected scores.

**Reliability.** Median reliability coefficients for the clusters are in the .80s and .90s.

---

**BOX 14.2** *Scales of Independent Behavior–Revised (SIB–R)*

*Publication Date:* 1996

*Purposes:* Measures adaptive and problem behaviors.

*Age/Grade Levels:* Ages infant through adult.

*Time to Administer:* Approximately 30 to 45 minutes in an interview format.

*Technical Adequacy:* The standardization sample is representative. Reliability and validity are acceptable.

*Suggested Use:* Can be used for identification, placement, program planning, and monitoring progress of individuals who have mental retardation, who are developmentally delayed, or who exhibit problem behaviors.

---

**Validity.** Content validity for the *SIB–R* is adequate. Criterion-related validity was established by correlating the *SIB–R* with other adaptive behavior scales and with the *Woodcock-Johnson Psychoeducational Battery–Revised*. Information relating to content validity and criterion-related validity also support the claims of construct validity.

**Summary.** The *Scales of Independent Behavior–Revised* is an individually administered, norm-referenced measure of adaptive behavior intended to measure the adaptive and problem behavior of individuals ages infant through adult. Evidence of reliability and validity is acceptable. Box 14.2 outlines the test's parameters.

## Vineland Adaptive Behavior Scales

The *Vineland Adaptive Behavior Scales (VABS)* has three forms.

*Expanded Form.* The *Expanded Form* (Sparrow, Balla, and Cicchetti, 1984a) contains 577 items, 297 of which are on the *Survey Form*.

It provides a comprehensive assessment of adaptive behavior and, according to the manual, is useful for developing educational, habilitative, or treatment programs.

*Survey Form.* The *Survey Form* (Sparrow, Balla, and Cicchetti, 1984b) consists of 297 items for use in identifying strengths and weaknesses.

*Classroom Edition.* The *Classroom Edition* (Harrison, 1985) contains 244 items and yields an evaluation of adaptive behavior in the classroom. In addition to items from the *Survey Form* and the *Expanded Form*, the *Classroom Edition* contains items relating to school performance.

All three forms measure communication, daily living skills, socialization, and motor skills. The *Expanded Form* and the *Survey Form* also assess maladaptive behavior. The domains are divided into subdomains: receptive, expressive, written communication, personal, domestic, community daily living skills, interpersonal relationships, play and leisure time, coping skills for socialization, gross and fine motor skills. Mr. Chen, a teacher, describes Jean, one of his homeroom students, in the Snapshot.

*Administration.* Both the *Expanded Form* and the *Survey Form* can be administered in a semistructured interview with a parent, caregiver, or an adult who is disabled. The *Expanded Form*

---

**SNAPSHOT ■ *Jean***

"I'm concerned about Jean," remarked Mr. Chen, referring to Jean, a 14-year-old student who is in Mr. Chen's homeroom. She is currently identified as having a language disability, mental retardation, and a behavior disorder. According to her school records, Jean was administered the *Wechsler Individual Intelligence Scale–III (WISC–III)* last year and obtained a Verbal IQ score of 63 (1st percentile) and a Performance IQ score of 74 (4th percentile), giving her a Full Scale IQ of 66 (1st percentile). The *Vineland Adaptive Behavior Scales (VABS)* were administered in order to evaluate Jean's functional life skills and to review areas of behavioral concern. Jean's mother was the respondent. Jean's scores on the *VABS* revealed her to be functioning well below the average range when compared to other 14-year-old students. The *Adaptive Behavior Composite* was 23 (±6) which constitutes functioning at less than the first percentile. Skill domain scores are:

| | | |
|---|---|---|
| Communications Domain | 23 SS | < 0.1 percentile |
| Daily Living Skills Domain | < 20 SS | < 0.1 percentile |
| Socialization Domain | 34 SS | < 0.1 percentile |

Jean's score in the Maladaptive Behavior Domain was judged to be significant with a score of 19. Areas of noted concern were the student's tendency to be withdrawn and having poor concentration and attention.

In a conference with Jean's teachers, Jean's mother expressed great concern regarding Jean's future. She noted that Jean has "no friends in the neighborhood" and prefers to play with her 6-year-old sister. In thinking about Jean's future, her mother believes that Jean would be able to get a job at a local motel as a chambermaid. She does admit, however, that Jean has generally low levels of skill in this area.

In her conversation with Jean's mother, Jean's special education teacher described Jean as generally withdrawn. She noted that Jean had no friends in the school and that she tended to gravitate toward the youngest and smallest students during recess. The special education teacher commented that Jean had not expressed any interest in a particular vocational activity.

---

*Source:* Brandt, J. E. (1994). *Assessment and transition planning: A curriculum for school psychologists and special educators.* Biddeford, ME: University of New England. Adapted with permission.

takes approximately 60 to 90 minutes to administer; it takes approximately 20 to 60 minutes to administer the *Survey Form*. The *Classroom Edition* is in the form of a questionnaire that a teacher of a child who is between the ages of 3 years through 12 years, 11 months completes. It takes approximately 20 minutes to complete the questionnaire.

**Scores.**    Standard scores are obtainable for the domains and the Adaptive Behavior Composite, as are percentile ranks, stanines, age equivalents, and adaptive levels. Adaptive levels are based on ranges of standard scores and provide a qualitative label for performance, for example, high, moderately high, adequate, moderately low, and low. Tables are available for determining significant and unusual differences. Figure 14.3 shows the scoring on the front of the *Vineland* test form.

**Standardization.**    Test developers did not administer the *Expanded Form* during the standardization, which was done by equating the *Expanded Form* to the *Survey Form* using the common items of each. The *Survey Form* was standardized on 3,000 individuals, with about 100 individuals in each of 30 age groups between birth and 18 years, 11 months. The standardization sample used the 1980 U.S. Census and was stratified according to sex, race/ethnic group, community size, region, and parents' level of education. Supplementary norms for both the *Survey Form* and the *Expanded Form* are also available. These included approximately 1,800 ambulatory and nonambulatory adults who either had mental retardation, were 18 years of age or older, and were clients in residential and nonresidential facilities; or emotionally disturbed, hearing impaired, and visually impaired individuals, 6 through 15 years old, who were clients of residential facilities.

The standardization sample for the *Classroom Edition* consisted of 2,984 children ages 3 years to 12 years, 11 months. Teachers randomly selected the children for the sample, and this resulted in a sample that is largely unrepresentative of the U.S. population as of 1980.

**Reliability.**    The manual reports split-half, test-retest, and interrater reliability for the *Survey Form*. Median split-half reliabilities, based on odd-even correlations, ranged from .83 (Motor Skills) to .90 (Daily Living Skills). The coefficient for the Adaptive Behavior Composite was .94; Maladaptive Behavior, Part 1, coefficients ranged from .77 to .88.

The authors determined test-retest reliability for the *Survey Form* by administering the *Survey Form* twice to parents and caregivers of 484 children and youth from the age of 6 months to 18 years, 11 months. The time interval between the two administrations was from two to four weeks. Most of the coefficients were in the .80s and .90s. The average difference between the first administration and the second was very small.

The authors estimated interrater reliability for the *Survey Form* by interviewing the parents or caregivers of 160 persons in the standardization sample who were from 6 months to 18 years, 11 months of age. The average time between the two interviews was eight days. Coefficients were in the .90s.

The authors estimated reliability information for the *Expanded Form* on data obtained during the standardization of the *Survey Form*. For the *Expanded Form*, estimated median split-half reliability coefficients ranged from .91 (Motor Skills) to .95 (Daily Living Skills). The coefficient for the Adaptive Behavior Composite was .97; Maladaptive Behavior, Part 1, coefficients ranged from .77 to .88.

Test-retest reliability and interrater reliability estimates were not available for the *Expanded Form*.

The *Classroom Edition* showed only internal consistency reliability. Median reliability coefficients ranged from .80 (Motor Skills) to .95 (Daily Living Skills). The median coefficient for the Adaptive Behavior Composite was .98.

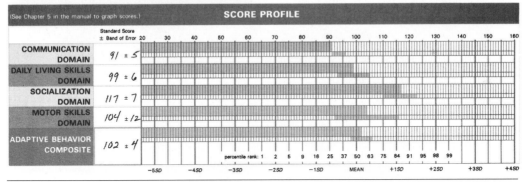

**FIGURE 14.3   Vineland Adaptive Behavior Scales: Classroom Edition**

*Source: Vineland Adaptive Behavior Scales*, Classroom Edition Questionnaire Booklet Score Summary by Sara S. Sparrow, David A. Balla, and Domenic V. Cicchetti © 1985 American Guidance Service, Inc., 4201 Woodland Road, Circle Pines, Minnesota 55014-1796. Reprinted with permission of publisher. All rights reserved. www.agsnet.com

***Validity.***   According to the authors, content validity for the *Survey Form* and *Classroom Edition* is the result of a review of the literature, an analysis of the test items, item tryout, and stan-

dardization. They provide no independent evaluation of content validity.

Criterion-related validity for the *Survey Form* and the *Classroom Edition* was established by correlating the *VABS* with other adaptive be-havior scales and intelligence scales.

Evidence of construct validity for the *Survey Form* and the *Classroom Edition* is demon-strated by a developmental progression of scores over the age span, by factor analysis, and by profiles of scores for supplementary norm groups. Information relating to content validity and criterion-related validity also support the claims of construct validity.

The authors did not conduct independent validity studies for the *Expanded Form*. Accord-ing to the authors, the validity of the *Expanded Form* derives from the *Survey Form*.

***Summary.*** The *Vineland Adaptive Behavior Scales* consist of three forms: the *Expanded Form*, the *Survey Form*, and the *Classroom Edition*. The *VABS* is a norm-referenced, individually admin-istered measure of adaptive and maladaptive

*A teacher provides support for a student in a welding class.*

**BOX 14.3** *Vineland Adaptive Behavior Scales (VABS), Classroom Edition*

*Publication Date:* 1984

*Purposes:* Identifies adaptive and maladaptive behaviors.

*Age/Grade Levels:* Ages 3 years through 12 years, 11 months.

*Time to Administer:* 20 minutes.

*Technical Adequacy:* The standardization sample is appropriate but should be updated. Reliability and validity are good.

*Suggested Use:* Can be used to identify adaptive and problem behaviors in students. Useful for determining eligibility, program planning, and program monitoring.

behavior. Reliability and validity are adequate. However, the reliability and validity of the *Expanded Form* is based on the reliability and validity of the *Survey Form*. Box 14.3 describes parameters for the *Classroom Edition*.

## Preferred Practices

The identification of limitations in adaptive skills along with significantly below-average intellectual functioning plays a large part in determining whether a student will be identified as having mental retardation. Frequently, the term *adaptive behavior* is used instead of the newer term *adaptive skills*.

The assessment of adaptive skills and adaptive behavior is not without controversy. The assessment of adaptive skills and adaptive behavior relates to age, gender, race, cultural and ethnic norms, and disability. As individuals develop, cultural expectations change.

The concepts of adaptive skills and adaptive behavior are dynamic and our views of these constructs change over time. However, the assessment of adaptive skills and adaptive behavior will continue to be important for identification, determining eligibility, program planning, and program evaluation.

## Extending Learning

1. Keeping in mind that the concept of adaptive skills is related to cultural norms, give an example of a behavior that might be considered adaptive in one context and not adaptive in another.
2. In what ways are instruments that assess development similar to ones that assess adaptive skills?
3. In what ways are instruments that assess functional skills similar to adaptive behavior scales?
4. How do the concepts of adaptive skills, adaptive behavior, and intelligence overlap?
5. Examine two or more of the instruments described in this chapter. Compare the test items. Which instrument would you recommend? Why?

## References

Alpern, G., T. Boll, and M. Shearer (1986). *Developmental profile II.* Los Angeles: Western Psychological Services.

American Association on Mental Retardation (1992). *Mental retardation.* 9th ed. Washington, DC: American Association on Mental Retardation.

Brandt, J. E. (1994). *Assessment and transition planning: A curriculum for school psychologists and special educators.* Biddeford, ME: University of New England.

Bricker, D. (1993a). *Assessment, evaluation, and programming system for infants and children: Vol. 1. AEPS measurement for birth to three years.* Baltimore, MD: Paul H. Brookes.

Bricker, D. (1993b). *Assessment, evaluation, and program-*

*ming system for infants and children: Vol. 2.* Baltimore, MD: Paul H. Brookes.

Brigance, A. H. (1991). *BRIGANCE® diagnostic inventory of early development–revised.* No. Billerica, MA: Curriculum Associates.

Brown, L., and J. E. Leigh (1986). *Adaptive behavior inventory.* Austin, TX: PRO-ED.

Bruininks, R. H., M. Thurlow, and C. J. Gilman (1987). Adaptive behavior and mental retardation. *Journal of Special Education* 21(1): 69–88.

Bruininks, R. H., L. E. Moreau, C. J. Gilman, and J. L. Anderson (1991). *Manual for the adaptive living skills curriculum.* Allen, TX: DLM.

Bruininks, R. H., R. W. Woodcock, R. F. Weatherman, and B. K. Hill (1984). *Scales of independent living.* Itasca, IL: Riverside.

Bruininks, R. H., R. W. Woodcock, R. F. Weatherman, and B. K. Hill (1996). *Scales of independent behavior–revised.* Itasca, IL: Riverside.

Furano, S., K. A. O'Reilly, C. M. Hosaka, T. T. Inatsuka, B. Zeisloft-Falbey, and T. Allman (1988). *Hawaii early learning profile.* Palo Alto, CA: VORT Corporation.

Grossman, H. (1983). *Classification in mental retardation.* Washington, DC: American Association on Mental Retardation.

Harrison, P. L. (1985). *Classroom edition manual, Vineland adaptive behavior scales.* Circle Pines, MN: American Guidance Service.

Harrison, P. L., A. S. Kaufman, N. L. Kaufman, R. H. Bruininks, J. Rynders, S. Ilmer, S. S. Sparrow, and D. V. Cicchetti (1990). *AGS early screening profiles.* Circle Pines, MN: American Guidance Service.

Johnson-Martin, N. M., S. M. Attermeier, and B. J. Hacker (1990). *The Carolina curriculum for preschoolers with special needs.* Baltimore, MD: Paul H. Brookes.

Johnson-Martin, N. M., K. G. Jens, S. M. Attermeier, and B. J. Hacker (1991). *The Carolina curriculum for infants and toddlers with special needs.* 2d ed. Baltimore, MD: Paul H. Brookes.

Lambert, N., H. Leland, and K. Nihira (1993a). *Adaptive behavior scales–residential and community edition: 2.* Austin, TX: PRO-ED.

Lambert, N., H. Leland, and K. Nihira (1993b). *Adaptive behavior scales–school edition: 2.* Austin, TX: PRO-ED.

Mercer, J. R., and J. F. Lewis (1982). *Adaptive behavior inventory for children.* San Antonio, TX: The Psychological Corporation.

Miller, L. J. (1993). *FirstSTEP Screening Test for Evaluating Preschoolers.* San Antonio, TX: The Psychological Corporation.

Moreau, L. E., and R. H. Bruininks (1991). *Checklist of adaptive living skills.* Itasca, IL: Riverside.

Newborg, J., J. R. Stock, and L. Wnek (1988). *Battelle developmental inventory.* Itasca, IL: Riverside.

Salvia, J., J. Neisworth, and M. W. Schmidt (1990). *Responsibility and independence scale for adolescents.* Itasca, IL: Riverside.

Sattler, J. (1990). *Assessment of children.* 3d ed. San Diego: Jerome M. Sattler.

Sparrow, S. S., D. A. Balla, and D. V. Cicchetti (1984a). *Interview edition, expanded form manual, Vineland adaptive behavior scales.* Circle Pines, MN: American Guidance Service.

Sparrow, S. S., D. A. Balla, and D. V. Cicchetti (1984b). *Interview edition, survey form manual, Vineland adaptive behavior scales.* Circle Pines, MN: American Guidance Service.

VORT Corporation (1995). *HELP for preschoolers.* Palo Alto, CA: VORT Corporation.

# 15

# *Behavior in the Classroom*

## Overview

In this chapter, we view student behaviors as occurring within the context of various environments. This conceptual framework influences the way we gather assessment information. Assessing behavior in the classroom involves examining classroom management strategies and other aspects of the learning environment as well as observing strategies that classroom teachers employ to help students build skills in working with others. The assessment process also examines the behavior to determine the function that it serves for the student. By organizing and interpreting this information, teachers and other team members are able to develop one or more recommendations.

## Chapter Objectives _____

After completing this chapter, you should be able to:

- Differentiate among various perspectives on emotional and problem behaviors and their effects on assessment practices.

- Describe considerations in assessing the physical, learning, and social environments.

- Discuss the process for conducting a functional behavioral assessment.

- Compare standardized instruments.

## Types of Problem Behaviors Observed in the Classroom

Problem behaviors in the classroom include antisocial behavior, aggression, withdrawal behavior, delayed social skills, and difficulties with interpersonal relationships. The term **externalizing behaviors** refers to a broad array of disruptive and antisocial behavior; whereas the term **internalizing behaviors** includes social withdrawal, anxious or inhibited behaviors, or somatic problems. Educators, school counselors, and school psychologists can measure and change behaviors in the classroom on a number of dimensions (White and Haring, as cited in Alberto and Troutman, 1995). A behavior can occur many times or only occasionally (frequency); a behavior can last a long or a short time (duration); upon the request of the adult or another student, a behavior can occur immediately or after a period of time (latency); a behavior can be described (topography); a behavior can be performed strongly or weakly (intensity); and a behavior can occur in one or more locations (locus).

Along each of these dimensions, cultural expectations dictate a range of behavior. "Typical" behaviors differ, depending on the expectations of the group members. Observers can identify atypical behavior by comparing the individual's behavior with that of members of the comparison group.

In the classroom, students exhibit a range of behavioral dimensions. Students with problem behaviors of high frequency or behaviors that have a strong intensity are easily identifiable.

Students who exhibit low frequency or low levels of intensity of behavior are often equally needy; however, observers may not identify these students as easily because problem behaviors in students who are quiet, withdrawn, or depressed may go unnoticed. You can read more about one teacher's observation of his students in the Snapshot about Mr. Norford's seventh grade class.

## What Shapes Our Views

Examiners may use different perspectives when assessing problem behaviors, depending on their backgrounds and theoretical approaches. Table 15.1 describes some of these. In the following section, we examine some of these perspectives in more detail.

### Behavioral Perspective

The **behavioral perspective** emphasizes the importance of factors external to or outside of the student as catalysts for the development of problem behaviors. Events in the environment provide stimuli for the behaviors to occur and reinforcement for the behaviors to occur more frequently.

*Learning Theory.* A basic principle of the behavioral perspective holds that behaviors are learned as a result of the individual's interactions with the environment. Behaviors may be manipulated by a *stimulus*, such as environmental conditions, or by events, teachers, or other

## SNAPSHOT ■ *Mr. Norford's Seventh-Grade Class*

Andy has difficulty sitting still; he plays with his pencil, shuffles his feet, and jingles the coins in his pocket. Mr. Norford describes his activity level, or frequency of behavior, as high. When Andy becomes upset, he reacts strongly. He becomes angry, shouts, and quickly resorts to pushing and shoving. The intensity of his behavior is also high.

Shelly is an average student. When she becomes upset, she becomes sullen and uncooperative. She refuses to talk with the teacher or to other students. Mr. Norford describes Shelly's level of activity as low; but her intensity is high. Her behavior may be overlooked more readily than Andy's behavior. Shelly's problem behavior may not be as disruptive to the classroom as Andy's problem behavior, but it is disruptive to her learning.

Kenichi enrolled in the middle school last spring, soon after his family moved to this country from Japan. Kenichi had no difficulty understanding English, as he had studied the language for several years. Over the past few months, Mr. Norford has observed that he has become very quiet and rarely speaks in class. Walking between classes and in the cafeteria, Kenichi is usually seen alone. His teacher believes that he is experiencing periods of sadness and depression for many days at a time. The frequency of Kenichi's behavior often is low and the intensity of his behavior is weak. Mr. Norford has observed these behaviors in several locations (locus).

individuals. A stimulus which is presented, contingent upon a response, and which increases the future probability of the response, is called a *positive reinforcer*. A positive reinforcer may or may not be pleasant; howsoever, it has the effect of increasing the probability of the behavior if it is satisfying to the individual. For example, a teacher's angry look can operate as a positive reinforcer if behavior increases in the future after the teacher's look is delivered, contingent upon behavior. To whatever degree, the teacher's attention itself is satisfying to the student.

A *negative reinforcer* involves the removal of a stimulus, contingent upon a response, which increases the future probability of the response. The stimulus could be, for example, a loud noise, a bright light, or extreme cold or heat. Behaviors that are followed by consequences that are satisfying to the individual tend to be repeated, whereas behaviors that result in consequences that are not satisfying tend not to be repeated. Repeated behaviors are learned behaviors.

The events that occur before the behavior occurs are called *antecedents*. The antecedents are the stimuli for the behavior and act as cues for the behavior to reoccur. When the anteced-

ent changes or is no longer there, the behavior may decrease or stop.

Thus, the two basic principles in this approach are (1) Behaviors can be learned, taught, and modified; and (2) Behaviors (B) can be controlled by antecedents (A) and consequences (C).

***Effect on Assessment Practices.*** An examiner using a behavioral perspective conducts observations within a specified time period, defines the behavior in observable terms, and carefully records the consequence(s) that follow the behavior and the antecedent event(s). The assessment focus is on the events that cause and sustain specific problem behaviors. When problem behaviors are serious and reoccurring, teachers work with other team members to conduct a functional behavioral assessment. Later in this chapter, we study this type of assessment in more detail.

***Task Analysis.*** Task analysis is a procedure for identifying the subskills that comprise a specific skill or behavior in order to assist a student in acquiring that skill or behavior. The behavior that will be acquired or eliminated is referred to

**TABLE 15.1**   *Current Perspectives on Assessing Behavior*

| Perspective | Associated Keywords | Focus |
|---|---|---|
| Behavioral | Applied behavior analysis<br>    Antecedents (A)<br>    Behavior (B)<br>    Consequences (C)<br>Learning theory<br>    Task analysis<br>    Chaining | Behavior is learned and can be modified.<br>Learning a complex behavior can be accomplished by identifying the components of the behavior. |
| Biological | Neuroanatomical and/or neurochemical components<br>Biochemical inhibitors | Behaviors are the result of neuroanatomical features or chemical imbalances in the brain.<br>Biologically based brain disorders affect individuals' behavior. |
| Developmental | Critical periods<br>Bonding | A student's early experiences and nurturing are critical in social-emotional development. |
| Ecological | Environment | Behaviors can be improved by altering the environment. |
| Emotional | Emotional intelligence | The individual's emotional intelligence is important for success. |
| Humanistic | Self-direction<br>Self-motivation | The social environment is critical in supporting student behavior. |
| Psychoanalytical | Id<br>Ego<br>Superego<br>Life crises | Assessment is conducted by a licensed psychologist or psychiatrist for the purpose of uncovering the illness or pathology. |
| Psychoeducational | Motivation | The interaction of pathology and the individual's motivation or underlying conflicts result in problem behaviors. |
| Temperament | Rhythmicity<br>Mood<br>Activity<br>Adaptability<br>Distractibility<br>Persistence<br>Threshold<br>Intensity<br>Approach | The relationship between an individual's disposition, behavior, and the environment is critical. |

as the **target behavior.** Target behaviors are acquired (or eliminated) by manipulating the antecedents and consequences. During a task analysis, the examiner follows a series of steps in assessing the target behavior and in planning for instruction (Figure 15.1).

*Effect on Assessment Practices.* Assessment includes a task analysis, data collection, and monitoring procedures. Using task analysis, the observer identifies the target behavior's subskills, assesses the student attempting the skills, and records data on a checklist or rating scale. Assessment occurs while the student actively engages in or carries out an activity.

## Biological Perspective

The biological perspective focuses on the effects of the biological, chemical, neurological, and physical status of the individual and the individual's behavior. A biological approach often is helpful in assessing students with severe emotional behaviors.

*Neurobiological Disorders.* The neurobiological perspective centers on the neuroanatomical and/or neurochemical components of the individual. This kind of analysis is helpful in assessing students who have emotional issues related to an organic disorder. Research focuses on regional neural activity, brain structure, and neuropathological characteristics (Mesulam, 1990), as well as on how excesses or deficiencies of various chemicals in the body impact on the individual's functioning and behavior. Assessment involves the use of medical biochemical tests and diagnosis.

*Temperament.* An individual's disposition or tendencies affect the individual's behavior. Temperament includes a number of general features such as the student's overall demeanor, the ability to adapt to new situations, and the ability to attend to or persist in an activity. A visit to a school classroom reveals individual differences in students. Some students work quietly by themselves; others talk with others or signal frequently for the teacher's attention. There is a reciprocal nature between an individual's temperament and the physical, learning, and social environments. Figure 15.2 illustrates the general features of temperament.

*Effect on Assessment Practices.* Standardized instruments, including behavior rating scales,

---

**FIGURE 15.1** *Steps in Conducting a Task Analysis*

The examiner
1. describes the target behavior in observable terms so that the behaviors can be measured and the student's progress can be evaluated
2. examines the behavior and divides it into small, discrete, sequential steps
3. assesses the student's skill levels in one or more of these sequential steps
4. plans instruction that focuses on the sequential steps of the target behavior
5. links the sequential steps, or subskills, from the task analysis to achieve the more complex target behavior
6. carefully determines the reinforcement by observing the student's behavior
7. carefully arranges antecedent events to elicit behaviors and plan consequences to reinforce behavior. This step serves to increase the frequency and/or intensity of behavior
8. examines the student's everyday routines to determine the behaviors that need to be taught

---

**FIGURE 15.2** *General Features of Temperament*

The general features of temperament (Thomas, Chess, and Birch, 1970; Thomas and Chess, 1977) include:

- *rhythmicity:* the regularity of the student's activity patterns, such as eating, playing, studying, bladder, and bowel functions
- *mood:* the student's overall demeanor, such as happy or sad, friendly or unfriendly
- *activity:* the frequency of movement
- *adaptability:* the ability of the student to adapt to new situations
- *distractibility:* the ease with which the student is interrupted from an activity
- *persistence:* the student's ability to attend to or persist in an activity
- *threshold:* the student's sensitivity to stimuli and changes in the environment, such as noise or temperature
- *intensity:* the student's magnitude of response to a specific stimulus, such as the tendency to smile or laugh when amused or to scream or whimper when hurt
- *approach:* the student's attraction or withdrawal to novel stimuli and situations

---

interviews, and checklists, assess various aspects of temperament. For example, the *Child Behavior Checklist/6–18* (Achenbach, 2001), the *Conners' Rating Scales–Revised* (Connors, 1997), and the *Temperament and Atypical Behavior Scale (TABS)* (Neisworth, Bagnato, Salvia, and Hunt, 1999) contain items that assess aspects of temperament.

## Developmental Approach

The developmental perspective focuses on the social-emotional development of the student. In Chapter 12 you learned that social-emotional development is one of the five areas or domains of development that we assess when working with young children (the others are physical, cognitive, communication, and adaptive).

Theories that focus on a developmental approach to understanding social-emotional development (Brazelton, 1992; Erikson, 1950; Greenspan, 1992; Kopp, 1994; White, 1975; Zero to Three National Center for Clinical Infant Programs, 1995) emphasize that all children progress through regular stages or periods. Individual variations affect the amount of time a given individual remains at a certain stage. Thus, qualitative differences within stages are common, depending on individual differences.

The foundation for social and emotional skills begins during a child's early years. These early years are critical in providing the basis for social-emotional development in later childhood, adolescence, and adulthood. These times are often referred to as **critical periods.** Critical periods refer to "having a certain kind of experience at one point of development that has a profoundly different impact on future behavior than having the same experience at any other point in development" (Bailey, Bruer, Symons, and Lichtman, 2001, p. 4).

*Critical Periods of Development.* The theory of critical periods states that there is an interval of time in which the child is most responsive. If the individual has little or no opportunity to develop the skill or behavior during this period, the individual may have difficulty in doing so later on. Skills and behaviors that are fundamental to success in school begin to develop in the first three years of life (Zero to Three, 1992, p. 3). Children who do not have opportunities to develop these skills (Figure 15.3) can exhibit problem behaviors in the classroom. These behaviors continue to escalate as they become older, unless observers identify the problem behaviors and implement intervention.

---

**FIGURE 15.3**  *Skills and Behaviors Important to School Success*

1. *Confidence:* the child has a sense of being successful and that adults will be helpful.
2. *Curiosity:* the child has a sense that learning is positive and pleasurable.
3. *Intentionality:* the child has a desire to and the capacity to have an impact and to act upon that with persistence.
4. *Self-control:* the child can control personal actions in age-appropriate ways.
5. *Relatedness:* the child can engage with others, can understand, and can be understood.
6. *Capacity to communicate:* the child wants to and has the ability to communicate.
7. *Cooperativeness:* the child has the ability to balance own needs with those of others in a group activity.

Adapted from Zero to Three (1992). *Heart Start: The Emotional Foundations of School Readiness.* Arlington, VA: Zero to Three.

**Effect on Assessment Practices.** Interviews with parents, caregivers, and teachers provide information about the student during critical periods of development.

## Humanistic Perspective

The humanistic perspective is built on the belief that teaching and learning should be meaningful to the student (Rogers, 1983). Humanists believe that students learn best and most efficiently when the learning is personally significant and that choosing the direction of one's learning is highly motivating. Equally important in this view is designing the learning environment so that students may have responsibility for their learning, thereby decreasing problem behaviors. A social environment that is thus responsive to the student's feelings, and an environment that is free from threat enhances learning.

**Effect on Assessment Practices.** Assessment practices focus on understanding problem behavior from the perspective of the student. During assessment activities, student interviews provide information about the problem behaviors from the student's perspective. Observers examine aspects of the learning and social environments and record ways in which the learning environment is responsive to the student.

## What Contributes to Problem Classroom Behaviors?

Expectations of society, the school, and the teacher contribute to or compound problem behaviors in the classroom. Some behaviors may be tolerable or acceptable as the norm in the community; yet these behaviors may not be tolerable to the school or acceptable to the classroom teacher. School and teacher expectations differ widely. The teacher's tolerance for activity level and intensity level affects whether the teacher refers the student for special education services or whether the teacher handles behavior concerns in the classroom.

## Responding to Diversity

Characteristics and expectations of some cultural and ethnic groups influence student behaviors. For example, some Asian and Muslim groups have strict rules about interactions between the sexes. Certain activities that involve body contact between males and females are taboo. Students who must participate in these activities may exhibit problem behaviors (Dresser, 1996).

A student's disability can hasten the development of problem behaviors. For example, a student with Tourette's syndrome develops multiple motor and one or more vocal tics during the illness. These symptoms occur many times throughout the day, although not necessarily simultaneously. Sometimes the student develops patterns of verbal outbursts, such as words and phrases that are inappropriate. The student is not able to repress these outbursts, and medication may not control the problem satisfactorily. The problem behaviors contribute to decreases in the student's self-concept and self-esteem and affect the development of social skills and interpersonal relationships.

Disabilities in communication can foster problem behaviors. Students with disabilities who have difficulty communicating quickly learn to use behaviors that attract another's attention. Some attention behaviors are appropriate while others are antisocial, aggressive, or inappropriate.

Precribed medication for students who have inattention or hyperactivity can affect student behavior. Methylphenidate, sold under the trade name Ritalin, is one of the most frequently prescribed medications. Methylphenidate temporarily controls overactivity, inattention, and impulsivity; however, its side effects (insomnia, irritability, and reduced emotional affect) can influence problem behaviors.

## Observing the Student within the Environment

### Physical Environment

A teacher can positively affect the physical environment by creating a structure and a set of expectations for student behavior. The structure consists of predictable classroom routines, schedules, and behavioral expectations that the teacher clearly displays on a list for all to see.

### Learning Environment

Frequent interruptions, unclear directions, activities that are too difficult, and a variety of other circumstances are apt to foster problem behaviors. Teacher movement throughout the classroom and the position of the teacher in relation to the student can help in preventing behavior problems. One study (Gunter, Shores, Jack, Rasmussen, and Flowers, 1995) found that paraprofessionals responsible for monitoring the student area remained seated 91.7 percent of the time. When the time that they were seated decreased, the time that students remained on-task increased.

### Social Environment

Classroom teachers employ strategies that affect students' behavior and help them build skills in working with others. These strategies allow students to build relationships with their peers by creating an environment that promotes skills in communication, conflict resolution, and respect for others. During a visit to the classroom, the observer may note one or more of these strategies that teachers employ. Classroom strategies that are effective in promoting social relations among students with and without disabilities include the following:

1. Teachers actively facilitate social interactions. Teachers plan and work to facilitate social exchanges between students. They place students in cooperative groupings and encourage collaborative problem solving. Teachers create opportunities for peer tutoring and assign students to various classroom roles of assisting and helping others. Teachers structure the classroom schedule so that students have opportunities to develop social relationships.
2. Teachers involve students in the responsibility for social inclusion of all students.
3. Teachers build a feeling of community in the classroom. Teachers work to create a climate of concern for others among students.
4. Teachers model acceptance.

*Frequently, students who have behavior problems have limited social skills.*

## Classroom Behaviors within an Intervention Context

### Classroom Management Strategies

Assessing behavior problems in the classroom occurs within the context of an intervention sequence. When a behavior problem first occurs, the classroom teacher assesses the use of classroom management strategies. The teacher customarily confers with the school assistance team, behavioral specialist, or special education consultant in order to develop and implement successful management strategies to address problem behaviors. This process can involve implementing one or more different strategies over a period of weeks.

In the Snapshot about Mr. Wing's classroom, you can read about some of the classroom management difficulties that a first year teacher is experiencing. As you reflect on this Snapshot,

consider the following key principles in managing student behaviors. What might you suggest to Mr. Wing?

1. Establish clear guidelines for the expected classroom behavior for students. Ideally, these guidelines are clearly visible in the classroom as a reminder to students.

2. State rules, or guidelines, in terms of what the student should do so that the behavioral expectations are clear. ("We listen when another student is talking.")

3. Provide positive reinforcement to students engaged in appropriate classroom behavior.

4. Use directive statements to tell students how to act correctly and responsibly. ("Holly, if you don't want Sheri to do that, you need to use words to tell her to stop.")

5. Teach pro-social skills such as:

## SNAPSHOT ■ *Mr. Wing's Classroom*

Mr. Wing is beginning his first year of teaching. His class consists of 23 students; three students have been identified as having disabilities. Mr. Wing is concerned about one of these students, Mark D., and how to help him. Mr. Wing worries if he is meeting Mark's needs, and decides to ask the special education consultant, Mr. Sanford, for help.

Mr. Wing describes his concerns: "During class time, Mark never seems to pay attention. When I call on him, he is usually on the wrong page of our book. He rarely knows the answer to my questions. I don't think he has ever participated in class discussions, and he is very disruptive when others are talking. Academically, his grades are very low this first quarter."

Mr. Sanford listened carefully as Mr. Wing talked about Mark. He thought about how he could lead the conversation away from focusing on the student to a more general discussion of classroom management strategies. When there was a pause in the conversation, he asked, "When Mark or some other student disrupts class, what strategies have you found that work well in dealing with this behavior?" The two teachers spent some time talking about strategies and Mr. Wing's apparent frustrations. As the discussion proceeded, Mr. Wing expressed an interest in reviewing his classroom management plan and translating his expectations into procedures and rules.

---

a.  how to ask for help,
b.  how to join a group of students engaged in an activity,
c.  how to join a group discussion,
d.  how to make friends.

6.  Provide consequences for students who disregard behavior guidelines.

7.  Be consistent with all students in their management of classroom behavior.

Figure 15.4 illustrates a behavior management observation form that a special education teacher developed for conferring with classroom teachers.

## Assessment Questions, Purposes, and Approaches

If the problem behavior in the classroom continues after a series of teaching and classroom interventions, the teacher notifies the student's parents and completes a referral to the IEP team. Table 15.2 discusses the questions, purposes, and approaches in assessing behavior problems. Frequently a functional behavioral assessment can address serious and recurring behavior problems.

## Functional Behavioral Assessment (FBA)

When a student's behavior continues to significantly interfere with participation, performance, or achievement, teachers, school psychologists, counselors, and other team members work together to complete a functional behavioral assessment. A **functional behavioral assessment** is a systematic process of gathering information that identifies the causes of and interventions for addressing problem behaviors.

To comply with IDEA requirements, teachers need to know how to conduct functional behavioral assessments. If a student with behavior problems receives disciplinary action, such as carrying a weapon to school or possessing illegal drugs, IDEA requires the IEP team to meet within 10 days to begin a functional behavioral assessment plan. If a behavior plan is already in place, the team must review the plan and revise it, if necessary, to address the behavior.

Typically, a functional behavioral assessment examines the physical environment, the learning environment, and the social environment in which the student's problem behaviors occur. The assessment includes both indirect

---

**◀ POINT STREET SCHOOL ▶**
**Behavior Management**

Student's Name _____     Date _____ Time _____

Observer _____

Teacher _____

Location _____

---

Characteristic

---

1. **Classroom Guidelines**
   Are behavior guidelines posted in the classroom?
   Are guidelines written in positive terms describing the behavior expected of students?
   √ Suggestions for improvement:

2. **Student Understanding**
   Does the student understand the classroom guidelines for behavior?
   √ Suggestions for improvement:

3. **Teacher Reinforcement**
   How does the teacher react when the student behaves appropriately?

   Does the teacher use:
   _____ social reinforcers
   _____ activity reinforcers
   _____ tangible reinforcers
   _____ edible reinforcers
   √ Suggestions for improvement:

4. **Teacher Interventions**
   How does the teacher react when the student behaves inappropriately?

   Does the teacher:

   _____ ignore some behaviors
   Explain:

   _____ use directives
   Explain:

   _____ use contingency contracts

   _____ teach pro-social skills
   Explain:

   ✔ Suggestions for improvement:

5. **Classroom Consequences**
   What consequences does the teacher use when the student behaves inappropriately?

   ✔ Suggestions for improvement:

6. **Classroom Consistency**
   Is the teacher consistent in managing the student's behavior?
   Is the management of the student's behavior consistent with that of all students in the classroom?
   ✔ Suggestions for improvement:

**FIGURE 15.4    *Point Street School Classroom Observation Form***

and direct assessment approaches such as a review of the student's record, interviews with the teachers (and other significant adults), a student interview, and direct observations of the student on several different occasions. These multiple approaches allow teachers and other professionals to gather information from a variety of perspectives concerning the problem behaviors.

Problem behaviors usually serve a function for the student, such as gaining attention from adults or peers. The function, itself, is usually appropriate (most of us like attention) but the behavior itself is not appropriate (such as acting out in class). A functional behavioral assessment involves identifying (1) the behavior and the function that it serves; (2) specific triggers, or

**TABLE 15.2**  *Assessment Questions, Purposes, and Approaches*

| Assessment Questions | Steps and Purposes | Approaches |
|---|---|---|
| | **Screening** | |
| Is the student's behavior typical for the student's age? | To determine whether the student may have emotional or problem behaviors and should be referred for further assessment | Norm-referenced instruments<br>Curriculum-based assessments<br>Criterion-referenced assessments<br>Observations<br>Checklists<br>Questionnaires<br>Rating scales |
| | **Eligibility** | |
| Does the student have a severe emotional or behavior problem?<br>What problem does the student have?<br>Is the problem associated with a disability (ADHD, autism, severe emotional disturbance, traumatic brain injury)?<br>Does the student meet the criteria for special education services? | To determine the extent of emotional or problem behaviors<br>To determine if the behaviors are associated with a specific disability<br>To determine the need for special education and related services<br>To understand why the student is having difficulty | Norm-referenced instruments<br>Curriculum-based assessments<br>Criterion-referenced assessments<br>Observations<br>Probes<br>Error analysis<br>Interviews<br>Checklists<br>Questionnaires<br>Rating scales<br>Student, parent, and/or teacher conferences<br>Performance assessments |

*Connecting Instruction with Assessment*

| | **Program Planning** | |
|---|---|---|
| What types of special education and/or related services should be provided?<br>What classroom modifications and adaptations should be implemented?<br>What skills does the student have?<br>What should be taught?<br>When behavior impedes learning or that of others, what strategies, including positive behavioral interventions and supports, to address that behavior should be included? | To determine the locations and type of services(s) to be received<br>To assess the physical, learning, and social classroom environments<br>To determine where instruction should begin and how the behavior may be managed | Functional behavioral assessment<br>Norm-referenced instruments<br>Curriculum-based assessments<br>Criterion-referenced assessments<br>Observations<br>Probes<br>Error analysis<br>Interviews<br>Checklists<br>Student, parent, and/or teacher conferences<br>Performance assessments |

**TABLE 15.2  *Continued***

| Assessment Questions | Steps and Purposes | Approaches |
|---|---|---|
| Once instruction begins, is the student making progress? Should the instruction be modified? | **Program Monitoring** To understand the pace of instruction To understand what the student knows prior to and after instruction To understand the strategies and concepts the student uses To monitor the student's program | Functional behavioral assessment Curriculum-based assessments Criterion-referenced assessments Observations Probes Error analysis Interviews Checklists Questionnaires Rating scales Student, parent, and/or teacher conferences Portfolios Exhibitions Journals Written descriptions Oral descriptions |
| Has the student made progress? Has the student met the goals of the IEP? Has the instructional program been successful for the student? Has the instructional program achieved its goals? | **Program Evaluation** To determine whether the IEP goals have been met To determine whether the student continues to need special education services To determine whether the goals of the program have been met To evaluate program effectiveness | Functional behavioral assessment Curriculum-based assessments Criterion-referenced assessments Observations Probes Error analysis Interviews Checklists Questionnaires Rating scales Student, parent, and/or teacher conferences Portfolios Exhibitions Journals Written descriptions Oral descriptions Surveys |

antecedents, such as events or actions that preceded the behavior (for example, a teacher-directed lesson); (3) the events or actions that occur after the behavior, or consequences (such as other students laughing), that help maintain the behavior; and (4) developing an intervention plan.

## Conducting a Functional Behavioral Assessment

Team members work together by following a sequence of steps for conducting a functional behavioral assessment (Figure 15.5). In the following sections, we describe these individual steps.

### Verifying the Seriousness of the Problem Behavior.
Because a functional behavioral assessment is time-consuming, the IEP team begins by verifying the seriousness of the problem. Team members address questions such as:

- Does the student's behavior significantly differ from that of other classmates?
- Does the student's behavior lessen the possibility of successful learning for the student and others?
- Have past efforts to address the student's behavior using classroom management strategies been unsuccessful?
- Does the student's behavior represent a behavioral problem, rather than a cultural difference?

- Is the student's behavior serious, persistent, chronic, or a threat to the safety of the student or others?
- If the behavior persists, is some disciplinary action likely to result? (Center for Effective Collaboration and Practice, 1998b)

If the answer to these questions is yes, then the team proceeds with a functional behavioral assessment.

### Defining the Problem Behavior in Observable Terms.
Defining the problem behavior allows teachers and other members to pinpoint the concerns and to plan assessment approaches. Team members will develop a definition of the problem behavior in terms that are observable. Describing the behavior in this way helps to ensure accurate, reliable observations. For example, if the teacher has concerns about a student's "aggressive" behavior, the team needs to agree on how they will know if a student is "aggressive." By developing a definition of aggression that is observable, such as "physically hitting or verbally abusing another person" observers will be able to see and record the behavior whenever it occurs.

Many times a teacher refers a student because of vague concerns. In these cases, the teacher or other team member will need to observe the student's behavior across several different settings to help in defining the behavior. These initial observations often involve watch-

---

**FIGURE 15.5**  *Steps in Performing a Functional Behavioral Assessment*

1. Verify the seriousness of the problem behavior.
2. Define the problem behavior in observable terms.
3. Collect assessment information using multiple approaches, including review of student's records; teacher, parent, and student interviews; and direct observations.
4. Analyze assessment information and examine possible functions of the problem behavior.
5. Develop and implement behavior intervention plan.
6. Monitor and evaluate the behavior intervention plan.

ing and recording two or three students at the same time, including typical peers as well as the student who has been referred to the IEP team. As we discuss in Chapter 5, conducting observations on several students simultaneously allows the observer to determine how different the behavior of the student in question is from the behavior of others. Sometimes initial observations indicate that several students have similar problems and the greater difficulty is one of classroom management, rather than individual student behavior.

When the referred student is linguistically and culturally diverse, team members will need to take into account possible differences in behavioral expectations that are an integral part of cultural beliefs. In these instances, parents can be a valuable source of information to assist team members in their understandings of cultural expectations. Moreover, team members may identify a school or community member who is knowledgeable about the student's cultural background to serve on the IEP team as an additional resource person.

## Collecting Assessment Information Using Multiple Approaches

*Reviewing the Student's Records.* The student's cumulative records provide a starting place to gather information about medical history, school attendance, achievement, assessments, IEPs and behavior management plans, and past disciplinary actions. By reviewing the student's records, a team gleans additional information about medications, patterns of truancy, prolonged difficulties with achievement, positive behavioral intervention, strategies, and supports described in previous behavior management plans, or trends in disciplinary referrals. One or more of these areas can contribute to the current behavior problem.

*Interviewing.* Structured interviews provide information about the student from others who know the student well and the contextual

variable that surrounds problem behaviors (Repp and Horner, 1999). Sometimes the IEP team will select a commercial interview tool or they may decide to construct a structured interview with questions that they have identified. A team member experienced in interviewing techniques, such as the school social worker or school psychologist, usually conducts the structured interviews.

*Teachers.* Teachers and teacher assistants can provide information about how the student interacts with materials and with other students and adults in the classroom. The structured interview might include:

- In what settings and under what conditions do you observe the behavior?
- Are there any settings/situations in which the behavior does not occur?
- Who is present when the behavior occurs?
- What activities or interactions take place just prior to the behavior?
- Are there other events that may trigger the behavior?
- What activities or interactions take place immediately following the behavior?
- Are there other behaviors that occur along with the problem behavior?
- Can you think of any reasons why the student might behave this way?
- What would be a more acceptable way for the student to achieve the same outcome? (Center for Effective Collaboration and Practice, 1998b)

*Parents.* Parents provide yet a different perspective. Parents can share their own expectations regarding their child's behavior. They can provide information about their child's behavior difficulties in the past and the types of interventions that were attempted and successful. They can describe complications or changes in the family structure that the child is currently experiencing at home, including parents' unemployment, death, birth, and divorce, all of which create additional stressors on family members. The structured interview might include:

- Have there been any changes at home or new events in your child's life recently?
- Does your child experience any problems that you are aware of?
- Do you think your child is interested in school this year? Why or why not?
- Do you think that the academic work is too easy or too hard? Could you explain?

*The Student.* The student can provide valuable information in identifying the motivational factors supporting inappropriate behavior (Figure 15.6).

Although functional interviews often yield valuable information, team members are aware, too, that the information may be biased. The teacher may have preconceived ideas about the student and the reasons for the problem behaviors. Although these ideas are recorded as part of the teacher interview, they may not be representative of the actual situation. Or, the parent may deny that a problem exists by not responding in full to the interview questions. Or, the student may misrepresent thoughts and feelings during the structured interview because of embarrassment or shame.

*Conducting Observations.* Chapter 5 discusses the various methods of recording observation data. These same methods—event recording, duration recording, intensity record-

---

**FIGURE 15.6    *Functional Interview with a Student***

**SCHOOL SOCIAL WORKER:** Is there anything that is happening at home that is bothering you?

**STUDENT:** No.

**SCHOOL SOCIAL WORKER:** Is there something new at school that is bothering you?

**STUDENT:** Not really . . . Well, we're getting a lot of homework this year.

**SCHOOL SOCIAL WORKER:** Does it bother you?

**STUDENT:** No, I mean, well . . . it takes a lot of time and I have a part-time job now.

**SCHOOL SOCIAL WORKER:** Let's talk a little about what happened in class today. What was the teacher doing right before you made the comments that made the other students laugh?

**STUDENT:** I don't know, I think he was giving some directions.

**SCHOOL SOCIAL WORKER:** Do you remember what he was asking everyone to do?

**STUDENT:** Well, when he talks so much it's very hard to follow everything. Like he tells us five things and I'm still back on the first.

**SCHOOL SOCIAL WORKER:** Do you remember what were you thinking right before you made the comments?

**STUDENT:** I was just so mad and frustrated!

**SCHOOL SOCIAL WORKER:** When you make noises and comments in class, what usually happens afterward?

**STUDENT:** Everyone laughs and gives me high fives.

**SCHOOL SOCIAL WORKER:** How does that make you feel?

**STUDENT:** Pretty cool, I guess. . . .

ing, latency recording, interval recording and category recording—are useful when conducting direct observations, as part of a functional behavioral analysis. You'll recall that each method has particular strengths, depending on the assessment question. For example, event recording is useful when our question involves "how often" or "how frequently" (Figure 15.7). In conducting observations, team members will gather information not only about occasions when the student displays problem behaviors but also occasions when the student maintains appropriate behavior. Since one observation represents only a snapshot of the student, the team will collect multiple observations to produce more accurate and reliable information.

*Scatter Plots.* A **scatter plot** is a type of interval recording form that the observer uses to record single behaviors or a series of behaviors during the observation period. Scatter plots are useful for initial and follow-up observations to identify patterns of behavior that relate to specific contextual conditions (Center for Effective Collaboration and Practice, 1998b, p. 9). Figure 15.8

is a scatter plot conducted on one student, Trish, during recess. The observer collected information about her appropriate and inappropriate behavior on the playground and the consequences of each during 20-second time intervals. Figure 15.9 illustrates how the observer synthesized data from the four observations to provide a visual representation of Trish's problem behaviors.

*Antecedent-Behavior-Consequence (ABC).* Antecedent-Behavior-Consequence (ABC) recording forms provide a way to record the problem behavior within a contextual condition. These forms are used when an observer wants to organize descriptive information in such a way that classroom conditions that trigger and maintain behavior can be identified. Three columns on the form allow the observer to record the antecedent events, the behavior, and the consequences that followed the behavior. ABC recording sheets can come in various formats and can record various aspects of the behavior, such as the frequency, duration, intensity, or latency of the behavior. Figure

**FIGURE 15.7** *How to Select an Appropriate Observation Recording Method*

**Event recording helps answer questions such as:**
- How many times does (student) . . . ?
- How frequently does (student) . . . ?
- How often does (student) . . . ?
- At what rate does (student) . . . ?

**Duration recording helps answer questions such as:**
- How long does (student) . . . ?

**Intensity recording helps answer questions such as:**
- To what degree does (student) . . . ?
- To what level does (student) . . . ?

**Latency recording helps answer questions such as:**
- Given a request, how long does it take (student) to begin . . . ?

**Interval recording helps answer questions such as:**
- What amount of time does (student) . . . ?
- What percent of time does (student) . . . ?

Student __Trish__   Setting __playground__   Observer(s) _____

Activity __free play__   Date __9/26__

No. of Students __50__   Start Time __9:00__   End Time __9:15__   Total _____

Observation Interval   Time Sampling Procedure

10 sec ___ 15 sec ___ 20 sec _X_   1. Continuous Recording _____   2. Non-Continuous _X_  3. Other _____

(every 3 min.)

APPENDIX A SCATTERPLOTS

ACTIVITY

| Phase | Appropriate Responses | | | | | | Total | Consequences of Appropriate Responses | Inappropriate Responses | | | | | | Total | Consequences of Inappropriate Responses |
|---|---|---|---|---|---|---|---|---|---|---|---|---|---|---|---|---|
| | Peer interaction | Alone | Adult interaction | Organized games | Parallel play | | | | Peer interaction | Alone | Adult interaction | Organized games | Parallel play | | | |
| | | X | | | | | | | | | | | | | | |
| | | X | | | | | | | | | | | | | | |
| | | | | | X | | | | | | | | | | | |
| | | | | | X | | | | | | | | | | | |
| | | | | | | | | | X | | | | | | | Gets football from Marsha |
| | X | | | | | | | Plays catch with Rae | | | | | | | | |
| | X | | | | | | | | | | | | | | | |
| | X | | | | | | | ↓ | X | | X | | | | | |
| | | | | | | | | | X | | X | | | | | |
| | | | | | | | | | X | X | X | | | | | |
| Other | | | | | | | | | | X | X | | | | | |
| Total | | | | | | | | | | | | | | | | |
| Comments: | | | | | | | | | | | | | | | | |

**FIGURE 15.8   *Functional Assessment Scatter Plot***

*Source:* Center for Effective Collaboration and Practice (1998b). Addressing Student Problem Behavior–Part II: Conducting a Functional Behavioral Assessment. Retrieved June 4, 2001, from http://cecp.air.org/fba/problembehavior2/main2.htm. © 2002, Sopris West, Inc., Longmont, CO.

15.10 illustrates an example of an ABC recording form.

*Rubrics.* In Chapter 7, we examine rubrics as types of assessment scales used to measure performance. We discussed how a rubric consists of descriptors that provide detail about each level of achievement. Rubrics are useful tools in functional behavioral assessment, too, when the assessment question concerns the degree of intensity or severity of a behavior, such as disruptive outbursts. To identify the severity of a behavior, the team develops descriptions of the different levels of intensity, assigning a numeric score or categorical label to each level. Figure 15.11 illustrates a rubric that measures the severity of disruptive behavior. When the team uses detailed descriptions and examples for each of the different levels, they increase the reliability of the rubric.

| Student | Trish | | | | Setting | Morning recess | | Observer(s) | Mr. Church | |
| ------- | ----- | - | - | - | ------- | -------------- | - | ----------- | ---------- | - |
| Time 9:00–9:15 | | | | | Intervals 30 Seconds | | | | | |

Code:
- **A** = Appropriate Behavior
- **V** = Verbal Aggression
- **P** = Physical Aggression

| Interval | 10/1 | 10/2 | 10/3 | 10/4 | Total | | | Percentage | | |
| -------- | ---- | ---- | ---- | ---- | ----- | ----- | ----- | ---------- | ----- | ----- |
| | | | | | **A** | **V** | **P** | **A** | **V** | **P** |
| 1 | A | A | A | A | 4 | | | 100 | | |
| 2 | A | A | A | A | 4 | | | 100 | | |
| 3 | A | A | A | A | 4 | | | 100 | | |
| 4 | A | A | A | V | 3 | 1 | | 75 | 25 | |
| 5 | A | V | A | P | 2 | 1 | 1 | 50 | 25 | 25 |
| 6 | A | P | A | P | 2 | | 2 | 50 | | 50 |
| 7 | A | P | A | V | 2 | 1 | 1 | 50 | | 25 |
| 8 | A | V | A | V | 2 | 2 | | 50 | 50 | |
| 9 | A | A | A | A | 4 | | | 100 | | |
| 10 | V | A | A | A | 3 | 1 | | 75 | 25 | |
| 11 | V | A | A | A | 3 | 1 | | 75 | 25 | |
| 12 | P | A | V | A | 2 | 1 | 1 | 50 | 25 | 25 |
| 13 | V | A | P | A | 2 | 1 | 1 | 50 | 25 | 25 |
| 14 | A | A | P | V | 2 | 1 | 1 | 50 | 25 | 25 |
| 15 | A | A | V | A | 3 | 1 | | 75 | 25 | |
| 16 | A | A | A | A | 4 | | | 100 | | |
| 17 | A | A | A | A | 4 | | | 100 | | |
| 18 | V | A | A | V | 2 | 2 | | 50 | 50 | |
| 19 | A | V | A | A | 3 | 1 | | 75 | 25 | |
| 20 | A | P | A | A | 3 | | 1 | 75 | | 25 |
| 21 | A | V | A | A | 3 | 1 | | 75 | 25 | |
| 22 | A | P | A | V | 2 | 1 | 1 | 50 | 25 | 25 |
| 23 | V | V | A | A | 2 | 2 | | 50 | 50 | |
| 24 | V | V | A | A | 2 | 2 | | 50 | 50 | |
| 25 | A | A | A | A | 4 | | | 100 | | |
| 26 | A | A | A | A | 4 | | | 100 | | |
| 27 | A | A | V | A | 3 | 1 | | 75 | 25 | |
| 28 | A | A | P | A | 3 | | 1 | 75 | | 25 |
| 29 | A | A | V | A | 3 | 1 | | 75 | 25 | |
| 30 | A | A | V | A | 3 | 1 | | 75 | 25 | |

**FIGURE 15.9**   *Scatter Plot with Aggregated Data*

*Source:* Center for Effective Collaboration and Practice (1998b). Addressing Student Problem Behavior–Part II: Conducting a Functional Behavioral Assessment. Retrieved June 4, 2001, from http://cecp.air.org.fba.problembehavior2/main2.htm. © 2002, Sopris West, Inc., Longmont, CO.

**FIGURE 15.10**   *Sample ABC Recording Form*

| Student: | | Observer: | | | |
|---|---|---|---|---|---|
| Grade: | | Teacher: | | | |
| Behavior Observed: | | | | | |

| Interval Time (5-minute intervals) | Classroom Activity | Antecedent | Behavior | Consequence | Comments |
|---|---|---|---|---|---|
| 0:00–0:05 | | | | | |
| 0:05–0:10 | | | | | |
| 0:10–0:15 | | | | | |
| 0:15–0:20 | | | | | |
| 0:20–0:25 | | | | | |
| 0:25–0:30 | | | | | |
| 0:30–0:35 | | | | | |
| 0:35–0:40 | | | | | |
| 0:40–0:45 | | | | | |
| 0:45–0:50 | | | | | |
| 0:50–0:55 | | | | | |
| 0:55–1:00 | | | | | |

*Analyzing Assessment Information and Examining Possible Functions of the Problem Behavior.*   Analyzing data involves studying and synthesizing the results of all the information collected, while looking for patterns of behavior. The team considers key questions, such as:

• What student behaviors occurred under different antecedent conditions?
• Did the behavior in question occur under one or more than one antecedent condition?
• What consequences occurred after the behavior in question?

As the team examines the collected information, they look for recurring instances of the problem behaviors and study possible behavioral patterns. They work to synthesize information across the multiple assessment approaches by asking

• How does the information from the interviews corroborate or confirm the ABC observations?
• Based on the review of student records, what other factors may be contributing to the behavior?

**FIGURE 15.11** *Rubric for Measuring Intensity of a Behavior*

**Severity of Disruptive Behavior Rating Rubric**

1. Behavior is confined only to the observed student. May include such behaviors as: refusal to follow directions, scowling, crossing arms, shouting, muttering under student's breath.
2. Behavior disrupts others in the student's immediate area. May include: slamming textbook closed, dropping book on the floor, name-calling, or using inappropriate language.
3. Behavior disrupts everyone in the class. May include: throwing objects, yelling, open defiance of teacher directions, or leaving the classroom.
4. Behavior disrupts other classrooms or common areas of the school. May include: throwing objects, yelling, open defiance of school personnel's directions, or leaving the school campus.
5. Behavior causes or threatens to cause physical injury to student or to others. May include: display of weapons, assault on others.

*Source:* Center for Collective Collaboration and Practice (1998b). Addressing Student Problem Behavior–Part II: Conducting a Functional Behavioral Assessment. Retrieved June 4, 2001, from http://cecp.air.org/fba.problembehavior2/main2.htm. © 2002, Sopris West, Inc., Longmont, CO.

To help in synthesizing all the information, they use a process called triangulation.

*Triangulation.* Triangulation is the process of drawing conclusions based on an analysis of multiple sources of data. A data triangulation chart (Figure 15.12) allows team members to record the multiple sources of data that they have collected and to visually compare the information. Using the data triangulation chart, team members can develop deeper understandings of the behavior and the function that it serves.

*Behavior Pathways.* Another method of analyzing multiple sources of data is the problem behavior pathway (Center for Collective Collaboration and Practice, 1998b). Data is organized by recording information in columns: the setting, antecedents, the behavior, and maintaining consequences (Figure 15.13). A similar form, the competing behavior pathway, can be helpful in testing a hypothesis and in planning intervention. This form organizes the information in similar columns but includes

accommodations and replacement behaviors (Figure 15.14).

***Establishing a Hypothesis: Possible Functions of the Problem Behavior.*** After analyzing the data, team members develop one or more possible explanations for the student's behavior. Let's return to the IEP team that is working with Trish. Using information from the direct observations, including the scatterplot of her playground behavior, discipline referrals, and teacher interviews, the team developed the following hypothesis:

Trish knows how to respond appropriately, based on the four playground observations. If fact, much of the time she engages in appropriate behavior. She is more verbally aggressive than physically aggressive. When she calls other children names, pushes and shoves others, grabs the ball, and hits other children, she usually gets her way. In addition, she receives individual attention from her teachers and the playground supervisors when she engages in inappropriate behavior. In Trish's case, the team feels that Trish's behavior serves as an

**FIGURE 15.12**   *Data Triangulation Chart*

APPENDIX F

## DATA TRIANGULATION CHART

Student _____*Trish*_____                        Date(s) ____*9/26–10/8*____

| Source 1 | Source 2 | Source 3 |
|---|---|---|
| ABC chart: | Interview with playground supervisor: | Scatterplot: |
| Trish yells at students when they don't do what she says. She hits students when she does not get her way. | Trish yells at and hits other girls when she doesn't get her way. This usually happens when there are no adults nearby. | Trish engages in appropriate behavior on the playground about 73 percent of the time; verbally aggressive behavior about 19 percent of the time; and physical aggression 8 percent of the time. |

*Interpretation:*

1. Precipitating events: *Playground, undersupervised games involving girls.*
2. Maintaining consequences: *Trish usually gets her way when she becomes verbally or physically aggressive. She also gets to spend time with the playground supervisor.*
3. Function(s): *Trish's behavior allows her to get her way (albeit for a short time) and play with other girls. She thinks this is an effective way to join groups.*

*Source:* Center for Effective Collaboration and Practice (1998b). Addressing Student Problem Behavior—Part II: Conducting a Functional Behavioral Assessment. Retrieved June 4, 2001, from http://cecp.air.org/fba/problembehavior2/main2.htm. © 2002, Sopris West, Inc., Longmont, CO.

attempt to join her classmates and also to receive attention from adults.

### Developing the Behavior Intervention Plan.

After establishing the hypothesis, team members develop the student's behavior intervention plan. The plan may include manipulating the antecedents and/or consequences, teaching more acceptable behaviors, making accommodations and/or modifications, or acquiring supplementary aids and supports to address the problem behaviors. Let's return once more to Trish's team. As part of her behavior intervention plan, the special education teacher will help Trish learn more appropriate replacement behaviors. The teacher will provide instruction

in social skill training, helping Trish to learn different strategies for joining a group of peers. In addition, the team will ask the playground supervisors and her teachers to begin a conscious effort to recognize Trish for appropriate behavior.

### Monitoring and Evaluating the Behavior Intervention Plan.

A student's behavior intervention plan needs reviewing on a regular basis, at least annually. Problem behaviors can appear and quickly escalate if left unattended. When problem behaviors resurface, team members recognize that the original plan may not be working and reconvene to discuss the student's current needs.

**FIGURE 15.13**   *Problem Behavior Pathway*

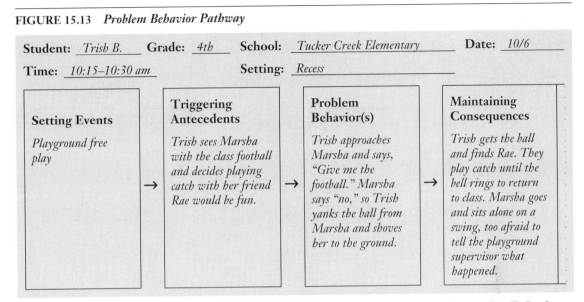

**Student:** *Trish B.*   **Grade:** *4th*   **School:** *Tucker Creek Elementary*   **Date:** *10/6*

**Time:** *10:15–10:30 am*   **Setting:** *Recess*

| **Setting Events** | **Triggering Antecedents** | **Problem Behavior(s)** | **Maintaining Consequences** |
|---|---|---|---|
| *Playground free play* | *Trish sees Marsha with the class football and decides playing catch with her friend Rae would be fun.* → | *Trish approaches Marsha and says, "Give me the football." Marsha says "no," so Trish yanks the ball from Marsha and shoves her to the ground.* → | *Trish gets the ball and finds Rae. They play catch until the bell rings to return to class. Marsha goes and sits alone on a swing, too afraid to tell the playground supervisor what happened.* |

*Source:* Center for Effective Collaboration and Practice (1998b). Addressing Student Problem Behavior—Part II: Conducting a Functional Behavioral Assessment. Retrieved June 4, 2001, from http://cecp.air.org/fba/problembehavior2/main2.htm. © 2002, Sopris West, Inc., Longmont, CO.

## *Standardized Instruments for Assessing Problem Behaviors*

Standardized instruments usually are in the form of rating scales or checklists designed to be completed by school psychologists, teachers, parents, or students themselves. Instruments that assess problem behaviors focus on one or more specific areas. The choice of an instrument depends on the presenting questions and concerns. Table 15.3 illustrates the areas of assessment questions and concerns, standardized instruments that address these areas, and their technical characteristics. The following section describes several of these instruments in more detail.

### Child Behavior Checklist System

The *Child Behavior Checklist System (CBCL)* (Achenbach and Rescorla, 2000b, 2001; McConaughy and Achenbach, 2001b) consists of various behavior checklists and report forms for gathering information about children and youth from 1 year, 6 months to 18 years and about young adults from 18 years through 30 years. The *CBCL System* conceptualizes emotional or behavioral problems as external and internal behavioral clusters. The *System* includes several *Diagnostic and Statistical Manual (DSM)*-oriented scales that are consistent with *DSM* diagnostic categories. Although the *CBCL* is entitled a "checklist," the instruments are really rating scales in that they require the observer to rate items on a numerical scale. These forms have been translated in over sixty languages and are available from the publisher. Published reports describe the use of the *Child Behavior Checklist System* from 50 cultures. The *CBCL* consists of three age levels, each with its own technical manual and scoring system. These include:

*Ages 1½ through 5*

   **1.** *Child Behavior Checklist for Ages 1½–5 (CBCL/1½–5)* (Achenbach and Rescorla, 2001a).

**FIGURE 15.14** *Competing Behavior Pathway*

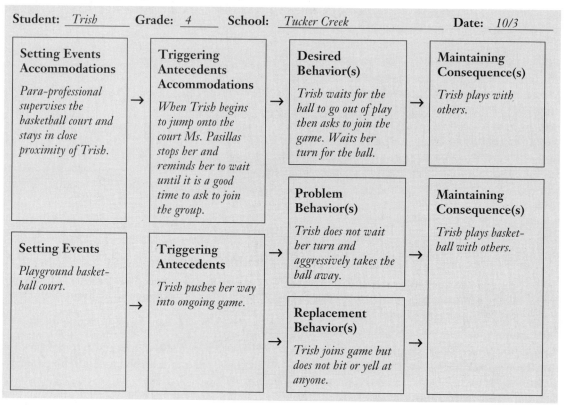

Student: *Trish*    Grade: *4*    School: *Tucker Creek*    Date: *10/3*

| **Setting Events Accommodations** | **Triggering Antecedents Accommodations** | **Desired Behavior(s)** | **Maintaining Consequence(s)** |
|---|---|---|---|
| *Para-professional supervises the basketball court and stays in close proximity of Trish.* | *When Trish begins to jump onto the court Ms. Pasillas stops her and reminds her to wait until it is a good time to ask to join the group.* | *Trish waits for the ball to go out of play then asks to join the game. Waits her turn for the ball.* | *Trish plays with others.* |

| **Problem Behavior(s)** | **Maintaining Consequence(s)** |
|---|---|
| *Trish does not wait her turn and aggressively takes the ball away.* | *Trish plays basketball with others.* |

| **Setting Events** | **Triggering Antecedents** |
|---|---|
| *Playground basketball court.* | *Trish pushes her way into ongoing game.* |

| **Replacement Behavior(s)** |
|---|
| *Trish joins game but does not hit or yell at anyone.* |

*Source:* Center for Effective Collaboration and Practice (1998b). Addressing Student Problem Behavior—Part II: Conducting a Functional Behavioral Assessment. Retrieved June 4, 2001, from http://cecp.air.org/fba/problembehavior2/main2.htm. © 2002, Sopris West, Inc., Longmont, CO.

This checklist consists of 99 items and is designed for the parent or other caregiver to complete. The *CBCL/1½–5* includes the *Language Development Survey (LDS)* for identifying language delays. Similar to the checklist for older children, scores on this instrument can convert to percentile ranks and T-scores. A Spanish version is available.

**2.** *Caregiver-Teacher Report Form/1½–5 (C–TRF)* (Achenbach, 2000). This form obtains ratings by childcare providers and early childhood teachers on 99 items and descriptions of problems or concerns. Similar in layout to the *Child Behavior Checklist for Ages 1½–5*, the forms allow the examiner to compare responses.

*Ages 6 through 18*

**3.** *Child Behavior Checklist for Ages 6–18 (CBCL/6–18)* (Achenbach, 2001a). This scale is designed for the parent to complete and consists of two sections: competence items and problem items. A student's score converts to percentile ranks and T-scores. This checklist has adequate technical characteristics. A Spanish version is available.

**4.** *Teacher's Report Form for Ages 6–18 (TRF)* (Achenbach, 2001b). This scale is similar to the *CBCL/6–18* and is designed for completion by the teacher. The *Teacher's Report Form* consists of three main areas: academic perfor-

**TABLE 15.3**  *Behavior Rating Scales and Checklists*

| Assessment Concerns | Name of Instrument | Grade or Age Range | Technical Characteristics | Comments |
|---|---|---|---|---|
| Autism | *Autism Screening Instrument for Educational Planning Second Edition (ADIEP–2)* (Krug, Arick, and Almond, 1993) | Individuals with language and social skill functioning between 3 months and 49 months | Concerns regarding the norming sample, reliability, and validity | Useful qualitative information, may be used in conjunction with other assessment approaches |
| | *Gilliam Autism Rating Scale* (Gilliam, 1995) | Ages 3 years to 22 years | Norming sample adequate; adequate internal consistency, test-retest reliability, and interscorer reliability (.80–.90) | Uses standard scores and percentiles |
| Attention Hyperactivity Social skills Oppositional behavior | *ADD–H: Comprehensive Teacher's Rating Scale (ACTeRS)–Second Edition* (Ullmann, Sleator, and Sprague, 1991) | Grades K through 8 | Internal consistency adequate; test-retest reliability ranges from .78–.82 | Scores are converted to percentiles and can be plotted on a summary profile sheet. |
| Hyperactivity Impulsivity Inattention | *Attention-Deficit/ Hyperactivity Disorder Test* (Gilliam, 1995) | Ages 3 years to 23 years | High internal consistency and test-retest reliability; evidence for content, construct, and criterion-related validity; concurrent validity established with the *Conners' Rating Scales* and *ADD–H Comprehensive Teacher's Rating Scale* | Based on the diagnostic criteria of *DSM–IV*. Can be completed by teachers and parents |
| Problem behaviors Adaptive skills Externalizing problems Internalizing problems | *BASC: Behavior Assessment System for Children* (Reynolds & Kamphaus, 1992) | Ages 2 years, 6 months through 18 years, 11 months | Adequate reliability and validity | Scores are converted to T-scores and percentiles. *BASC* is available in software that administers and analyzes results. |

*(continued)*

TABLE 15.3 Continued

| Assessment Concerns | Name of Instrument | Grade or Age Range | Technical Characteristics | Comments |
|---|---|---|---|---|
| Problem behaviors Interpersonal relationships | *Behavior Rating Profile–2* (Brown and Hammill, 1990) | Grades 1 through 12 | Internal consistency adequate; concurrent validity established with *Walker Problem Behavior Identification Checklist, Vineland,* and others | Includes six norm-referenced rating scales that are completed by the student, parent, teachers, and student's peers |
| Withdrawal, anxious and depressed Somatic complaints Delinquent behavior Aggressive behavior Social problems Attention and hyperactivity | Child Behavior Checklists* (*CBCL/1½–5*) (Achenbach and Rescorla, 2000a); (*CBCL/6–18*) (Achenbach, 2001a); (*YABCL/18–30*) (Achenbach, 1997); and *Caregiver–Teacher Report Form for Ages 1½–5* (Achenbach, 2000); *Teacher Report Form for Ages 6–18* (Achenbach, 2001b) | Ages 1 year, 6 months through 30 years | Interrater, test-retest, and internal consistency is adequate. Construct validity and criterion-related validity is adequate | Uses direct observation |
| Inattention Impulsivity Hyperactivity Conduct problems/ aggressiveness | *Children's Attention and Adjustment Survey (CAAS)* (Lambert, Hartsough, and Sandoval, 1990) | Ages 5 years through 13 years | Adequate reliability and validity | Consists of two forms: Home Form, which is completed by the parent or primary caregiver, and School Form, which is completed by the teacher. Uses *DSM–IV* criteria |
| Attention Hyperactivity | *Conner's Rating Scales– Revised* (Conners, 1997)* | Ages 3 years to 17 years (Parent) and Grades 4 to 12 (Teacher) | Internal and test-retest reliability adequate; construct validity adequate; continued research on predictive validity needed | *Conners' Rating Scales– Revised* include parent, teacher, and adolescent self-report and *ADHD/ DSM–IV Scales* |

422

| Target behavior | Instrument | Ages/Grades | Technical characteristics | Comments |
|---|---|---|---|---|
| Emotional problems Problem behaviors | *Devereux Behavior Rating Scales* (Naglieri, LeBuffe, and Pfeiffer, 1995) | Ages 5 years through 18 years | Extensive reliability and validity data are provided. | The *Devereux Behavior Rating Scales* consist of the *Devereux Scales of Mental Disorders* and the *Devereux Behavior Rating Scale–School Form.* |
| Internalizing behaviors Externalizing behaviors | *Systematic Screening for Behavior Disorders* (Walker and Severson, 1992) | Grades 1 to 6 | Test-retest adequate for Steps 1 and 2; interrater reliability adequate for Steps 1 and 3. Concurrent and construct validity adequate; predictive validity low to moderate. | Designed to be used as a screening instrument. |
| Problem behavior Social skills | *Social Skills Rating System* (Gresham and Elliott, 1990) | Grades Pre-K through 12 | Good technical characteristics. | Separate questionnaires for preschool, elementary, and secondary level students. Separate forms designed for teachers and parents; self-report form for students. |
| Social-emotional functioning | *Vineland Social-Emotional Early Childhood Scales (SEEC)* (Sparrow, Balla, and Cicchetti, 1998) | Birth through age 5 years, 11 months | Norms were derived from normative data of the *Vineland Adaptive Behavior Scales (ABS),* expanded form. (Items from the ABS were used to construct the *SEEC.*) | Parent report available in English and Spanish. |
| Temperament | *Temperament and Atypical Behavior Scale (TABS)* (Neisworth, Bagnato, Salvia, and Hunt, 1999) | 11 months to 71 months | Normative sample included children both with and without disabilities. Some subtest scores are not sufficiently reliable to make diagnostic decisions for individual children. | This instrument includes both a screener and and assessment tool. |

*Spanish form available

mance, adaptive functioning, and behavioral/emotional problems. Percentiles and T-scores can be calculated.

**5.** *Youth Self-Report for Ages 11–18* (Achenbach, 2001c). This rating scale is for youth ages 11 through 18 years of age. Students must have at least fifth-grade reading ability or the teacher can administer the items orally. Test items are similar to those in the *CBCL/6–18*. Scores can convert to percentile ranks and T-scores. A Spanish version is available.

**6.** *Direct Observation Form for Ages 5–14* (Achenbach, 1986). This form is used to collect observation data on the student during a ten-minute observation period. A list of problem behaviors is provided to assist in organizing observation of the student. Many of the items correspond to the *CBCL/6–18* and the *TRF/6–18*. Percentile and T-scores can be calculated to determine whether the student's behavior falls within clinical or normal range. The *Direct Observation Form* was normed on 287 children (non-referred) who were observed as classroom controls for problem children.

**7.** *Semistructured Clinical Interview for Children and Adolescents (SCICA)* (McConaughy and Achenbach, 2001a). The *SCICA* uses a protocol of questions and probes for interviewing students ages 8 through 18 years. The examiner also completes an observation of the student and the student completes a self-report form. Administration time is 60 to 90 minutes and should be completed by an experienced interviewer.

*Ages 18 through 30*

**8.** *Young Adult Behavior Checklist for Ages 18–30 (YABCL)* (Achenbach, 1997a). The *YABCL* is an upward extension of the *Child Behavior Checklist for Ages 6–18*. Parents and others who know the young adult well complete this form that has 107 items that describe specific behavioral and emotional problems. Like the other checklists, scores can be converted to T-

scores and percentiles. The *YABCL* was normed on 1,074 non-referred young adults.

**9.** *Young Adult Self-Report Form for Ages 18–30 (YASR)* (Achenbach, 1997b). The *YASR* is an upward extension of the *Youth Self-Report*. In addition, there are three other areas concerning adaptive functioning as youth move to adulthood: education, job, and spouse (or partner). These sections are answered only by individuals who have attended secondary or post-secondary institutions, been employed, or

---

**BOX 15.1** *Child Behavior Checklist System (CBCL)*

*Publication Date:* 2000, 2001

*Purposes:* Assesses behavior in terms of internal and external behavior clusters. School-related areas include: academic functioning, adaptive characteristics, and behavioral/emotional problems.

*Age/Grade Levels:* The *Child Behavior Checklist System* consists of two different rating scales, the *CBCL/1½–5* designed for children ages 1 year, 6 months through 5 years and the *CBCL/6–18* designed for students ages 6 years through 18 years. The *System* also includes various teacher and self-report forms, a direct observation form, and a semi-structured clinical interview. For young adults, ages 18 through 30 years, there is the *Young Adult Behavior Checklist (YABCL)*.

*Time to Administer:* 10 to 45 minutes, depending on the amount of information to be recorded.

*Technical Adequacy:* Adequate. The manuals present evidence of adequate reliability and validity.

*Suggested Use:* Measures behaviors from multiple perspectives, including the student, parent, and teacher. Rating scales are available in Spanish. Many of the forms have been translated into other languages and are available from the publisher.

who have lived with a spouse or partner within the past six months. An additional section provides open-ended questions regarding physical problems, disabilities, concerns, and strengths. Scores can be converted to T-scores and percentiles. This instrument was normed on 1,058 young adults aged 18 to 30. One-week test-retest reliability of the total problems scores is r = .89.

***Administration.*** The various forms take 10 to 45 minutes to complete, depending on the amount of information to be recorded.

***Standardization.*** For the *CBCL/6–18*, the norming sample consisted of 1,753 children, ages 6 through 18 years. The sample was stratified by age, gender, geographic region, urban/suburban/rural, socioeconomic status, and ethnicity. For the *CBCL/1½–5*, 700 children participated in the normative sample.

***Scoring.*** Scoring may be completed by hand or by the *Assessment Data Manager (ADM)* software that can be purchased separately.

***Reliability.*** For the *CBCL/6–18*, adequate reliability coefficients are reported for interrater, test-retest, and internal consistency. For the *CBCL/1½–5*, small studies were completed that suggest moderate to adequate reliability. Additional studies are needed.

***Validity.*** Reported evidence supports construct validity for the *CBCL/6–18*. Reported criterion-related validity between the *CBCL* and the *Conners' Rating Scales* and the *Revised Behavior Problem Checklist* is .82 and .81, respectively. Evidence of content validity, criterion-related validity, and construct validity is presented for the *CBCL/1½–5*.

***Summary.*** The *CBCL* is a comprehensive assessment system designed for use with children and youth from 1 year, 6 months through 30 years of age. The system consists of various instruments that are completed by the examiner,

parent, teacher, and student. These multiple sources of information provide a variety of perspectives on the problem behaviors. Box 15.1 describes the test's parameters.

## Conners' Rating Scales–Revised

The *Conners' Rating Scales–Revised (CRS-R)* (Conners, 1997) are designed to assess behaviors in children and youth ages 3 to 17 years. The *CRS-R* consist of a set of main scales and a set of auxiliary scales. Box 15.2 describes the test's parameters.

***Main Scales.*** The three main scales include: two parent, two teacher, and two adolescent self-report scales for assessing problem behaviors, each consisting of two versions, a long form and a shorter form.

---

**BOX 15.2**   *Conners' Rating Scales–Revised (CRS-R)*

---

*Publication Date:* 1997

*Purposes:* Assesses behavior in terms of oppositional-defiant, cognitive problems, hyperactivity-impulsivity, anxious-shy, perfectionism, social problems, psychosomatic (parent scale), a global index (emotional lability and hyperactivity) and ADHD.

*Age/Grade Levels:* The *CRS-R* are designed for children and youth ages 3 to 17 years and are available in English, Spanish (U.S.), and French (Canadian).

*Time to Administer:* Short scales take 5 to 10 minutes to administer; the long scales take between 15 and 20 minutes.

*Technical Adequacy:* Adequate reliability and validity. Additional information regarding the standardization sample would be helpful.

*Suggested Use:* Measures student behavior from the perspectives of the parents, teachers and the individual.

---

**1.** *Long Forms.* The long form is typically used for comprehensive information or for a diagnosis according to the *Diagnostic and Statistical Manual of Mental Disorders–Fourth Edition, Text Revision (DSM–IV–TR)* (American Psychiatric Association, 2000). The *Conners' Parent Rating Scale–Revised: Long Form (CPRS–R:L)* consists of 80 statements to which parents (or guardians) indicate agreement or disagreement regarding their child's behavior over the past month. The statements include a broad range of behaviors, for example, "Does not get invited to friends' houses." and "Clings to parents and other adults." The statements of the *Conners' Parent Rating Scale–Revised: Long Form* are divided among the following 12 subscales:

- Oppositional-Defiant*
- Cognitive Problems*
- Hyperactivity-Impulsivity*
- Anxious-Shy
- Perfectionism
- Social Problems
- Psychosomatic
- Conners' Global Index
- ADHD Index*
- *DSM–IV* Symptom Scale
- *DSM–IV* Inattention
- *DSM–IV* Impulsivity

The "*" indicates the subscales that are also on the short form.

The *Conners' Teacher Rating Scale–Revised: Long Form (CTRS–R:L)* contains the same subscales as the parent long form with the exception of the Psychosomatic subscale. Teachers are asked to consider the student's behavior and actions during the past month. The scales contains 59 items such as "Appears to be unaccepted by group" or "Poor in spelling."

**2.** *Short Forms.* The short version is typically used considering when multiple administrations over time. The parent version, *Conners' Parent Rating Scale–Revised: Short Form (CPRS–R:S)*, contains 27 items divided among the four subscales indicated above by the "*."

For teachers, the Conners' Teacher Rating Scale–Revised: Short Form (CTRS–R:S) contains 29 items and the same subscales as in the short form for parents. The similarities between the forms help facilitate comparisons between parent and teacher responses. Test scores are plotted to create a profile of the problem behaviors.

**3.** *Adolescent Self-Report Scales.* The *Conners-Wells' Adolescent Self-Report Scales: Long Form (CASS:L)* and the *Conners-Wells' Adolescent Self-Report Scales: Short Form (CASS:S)* are useful with adolescents who have at least a fifth-grade reading level. The scales are designed to obtain information that is available from no one else but the individual student. Use the long form when the assessment requires extensive information and *DSM–IV–TR* compliance. Sample items include "My parents' discipline is too harsh" and "My parents do not reward or notice my good behavior."

***Auxiliary Scales.*** The auxiliary scales include a global index (the hyperactivity index in the original *Conners' Rating Scales*) for parents and teachers and a set of *ADHD/DSM–IV* scales for the parent, teacher, and student.

**1.** *Conners' Global Index.* Both the parent and teacher scales, *Conners' Global Index–Parent (CGI–P)* and *Conners' Global Index–Teacher (CGI–T)* consist of 10 items each. The items on this scale, formerly known as the hyperactivity index, are divided between two separate factors: emotional lability and hyperactivity

**2.** *Conners' ADHD/DSM–IV Scales.* These scales include a scale for parents, *Conners' ADHD/DSM–IV Scales–Parent (CADS–P)*, for teachers, *Conners' ADHD/DSM–IV Scales–Teacher (CADS–T)*, and for the student, *Conners' ADHD/DSM–IV Scales–Self Report (CADS–S)*. Each scale contains 30 items that are divided between the following areas:

- ADHD Index
- *DSM–IV* Symptom Scale

- Inattention
- Hyperactivity

For screening purposes, the examiner can choose to administer just the ADHD Index; to confirm *DSM–IV* diagnoses, the examiner can use the *DSM–IV* Symptom Scale.

***Administration.*** All of the short scales take 5 to 10 minutes to administer; the long scales take between 15 and 20 minutes.

***Scoring.*** T-scores may be calculated for each of the scales.

***Standardization.*** The rating scales were originally developed on a clinical population at Johns Hopkins University Hospital in Baltimore. The manual states that 8,000 individuals participated in the norms for the new scales. The manual states that the norm sample included individuals from over 95 percent of the states and provinces in North America and that there were large samples obtained for all of the age groups and for both genders. The manual further states that samples represented minority groups.

***Reliability.*** Internal reliability is adequate for both the short and long forms of the parent and teacher rating scales and the adolescent self-report scales. Test-retest reliability was examined following a 6 to 8 week interval. In general, test-retest reliabilities for the *CRS–R* were adequate across the various forms.

***Validity.*** Reported construct validity for the teacher, parent, and self-report forms is adequate. Small studies report the correlation between the *CRS–R* and the *Children's Depression Inventory* and performance measures. Continued research will be helpful.

***Summary.*** The *Conners' Rating Scales–Revised (CRS–R)* consist of a set of scales for parents, teachers, and students to assist in gathering information about problem behaviors. The revised scales add several important dimensions to the original *Conners' Rating Scales*. The self-report forms provide information from the student's perspective. The auxiliary ADHD forms provide information from parent, teacher, and student perspectives and link the information to *DSM–IV*. Usefulness of the instrument would be enhanced if more information were provided about the sample of individuals who participated in the development of this revised edition. The *CRS–R* is available in English, Spanish (U.S.), and French (Canadian) and can be administered by computer or scored using computer software.

## Preferred Practices

Teachers who have students with emotional or problem behaviors in the classroom must work closely with other professionals. Answering assessment questions and planning, implementing, monitoring, and evaluating an individualized education program for a student with emotional or problem behaviors involves working closely with the school psychologist, social workers, and mental health practitioners. This team of professionals, along with the parents and the student, gather and examine information regarding problem behaviors and the functions that they serve. Together they develop behavioral intervention plans that involve teaching new skills that students lack or replacement behaviors that are more appropriate, while providing positive behavior supports.

## Extending Learning

1. Reread the Snapshot about the students in Mr. Norford's class. If you were the teacher, how would you gather information about these problem behaviors? What additional information would you gather about Kenichi? What resources would be available in your community? Work with a small group of other students to develop your ideas. Present your findings to the class.

2. Make arrangements to visit a classroom and observe student behavior. Create an ABC form and fill in the information that you observe. What classroom behaviors did you witness? What were the consequences that followed each behavior that occurred? Could you identify the antecedent conditions?

3. Visit two or more classrooms and observe one student in each. Compare their classroom behaviors.

4. Wayne is a student in Mrs. Frank's classroom. His teacher reports that he seems to argue constantly with other students. The arguments escalate quickly and often end with the students shoving and pushing each other. Wayne seems to have few friends and often spends his time at recess alone. You have observed that he likes to shoot baskets at the hoop on the playground. Develop a set of questions that you might use in interviewing Wayne.

5. Develop a scale that collects information about student attitudes and interests. What are some of the technical considerations to consider before using your scale?

6. What websites focus on issues in assessing behaviors in the classroom? Share your findings with the class.

## References

Achenbach, T. M. (1986). *Direct observation form for ages 5–14.* Burlington, VT: ASEBA™.

Achenbach, T. M. (1997a). *Young adult behavior checklist for ages 18–30 (YABCL).* Burlington, VT: ASEBA™.

Achenbach, T. M. (1997b). *Young adult self-report for ages 18–30 (YASR).* Burlington, VT: ASEBA™.

Achenbach, T. M. (2000). *Caregiver-teacher report form for ages 1½–5 (C–TRF/1½–5).* Burlington, VT: ASEBA™.

Achenbach, T. M. (2001a). *Child behavior checklist for ages 6–18 (CBC/6–18).* Burlington, VT: ASEBA™.

Achenbach, T. M. (2001b). *Teacher's report form for ages 6–18 (TRF).* Burlington, VT: ASEBA™.

Achenbach, T. M. (2001c). *Youth self-report for ages 11–18 (YSR).* Burlington, VT: ASEBA™.

Achenbach, T. M., and L. A. Rescorla (2000a). *Child behavior checklist for ages 1½–5 (CBC/1½–5).* Burlington, VT: ASEBA™.

Achenbach, T. M., and L. A. Rescorla (2000b). *Manual for the ASEBA preschool forms and profiles.* Burlington, VT: ASEBA™.

Achenbach, T. M., and L. A. Rescorla (2001). *Manual for the ASEBA school-age forms and profiles.* Burlington, VT: ASEBA™.

Alberto, P. A., and A. C. Troutman (1995). *Applied behavior analysis for teachers.* 4th ed. Englewood Cliffs, NJ: Merrill, Prentice-Hall.

American Psychiatric Association (2000). *Diagnostic and statistical manual of mental disorder,* 4th ed., text revision. Washington, DC: American Psychiatric Association.

Bailey, D. B., J. T. Bruer, F. J. Symons, J. W. Lichtman (Eds.) (2001). *Critical thinking about critical periods.*

Brazelton, T. B. (1992). Touchpoints: *Your child's emotional and behavioral development.* Reading, MA: Addison Wesley.

Brown, L., and D. D. Hammill (1990). *Behavior rating profile–2.* Austin, TX: PRO-ED.

Center for Effective Collaboration and Practice (1998a). Addressing student problem behavior: An IEP team's introduction to functional behavioral assessment and behavior intervention plans. Retrieved June 4, 2001. Available: http://cecp.air.org/fba/problembehavior/main.htm.

Center for Effective Collaboration and Practice (1998b). Addressing student problem behavior—Part II: Conducting a functional behavioral assessment. Retrieved June 4, 2001. Available: http://cecp.air.org/fba/problembehavior2/main2/htm.

Cohen, L., and L. Spenciner (1996). Assessment of social-emotional development in young children. In *Behavioral approach to assessment of youth with emotional/behavioral disorders: A handbook for school-based practitioners,* ed. M. Breen and C. Fiedler, 503–580. Austin, TX: PRO-ED.

Conners, C. K. (1997). *Conners' rating scales–revised.* North Tonawanda, NY: Multi-Health Systems.

Dresser, N. (1996). *Multicultural manners: New rules of etiquette for a changing society.* New York: John Wiley & Sons.

Erikson, E. (1950). *Childhood and society.* New York: Norton.

Gilliam, J. E. (1995a). *Attention-deficit/hyperactivity disorder test.* Austin, TX: PRO-ED.

Gilliam, J. E. (1995b). *Gilliam autism rating scale.* Austin, TX: PRO-ED.

Greenspan, S. I. (1992). *Infancy and early childhood: The practice of clinical assessment and intervention with emotional and developmental challenges.* Madison, CT: International Universities Press.

Gresham, F. M., and S. N. Elliott (1990). *Social skills rating system.* Circle Pines, MN: American Guidance Service.

Gunter, P. L., R. E. Shores, S. L. Jack, S. K. Rasmussen, and J. Flowers (1995). On the move. *Teaching Exceptional Children* 28(1): 12–14.

Krug, D. A., J. R. Arick, and P. J. Almond (1993). *Autism screening instrument for educational planning second edition.* Austin, TX: PRO-ED.

Kopp, C. (1994). *Baby Steps: The "whys" of your child's behavior in the first two years.* New York: W. H. Freeman.

Lambert, N., C. Hartsough, and J. Sandoval (1990). *Children's attention and adjustment survey (CAAS).* Circle Pines, MN: American Guidance Service.

McConaughy, S. H., and T. M. Achenbach (2001a). *Semistructured clinical interview for children and adolescents (SCICA).* Burlington, VT: ASEBA™.

McConaughy, S. H., and T. M. Achenbach (2001b). *Manual for the semistructured clinical interview for children and adolescents, 2nd ed. (SCICA).* Burlington, VT: ASEBA™.

Mesulam, M. (1990). Schizophrenia and the brain. *New England Journal of Medicine* 322(12): 842–844.

Naglieri, J. A., P. A LeBuffe, and S. I. Pfeiffer (1995). *Devereux behavior rating scales.* San Antonio, TX: The Psychological Corporation, Harcourt Brace.

Neisworth, J. T., S. J. Bagnato, J. Salvia, and F. H. Hunt (1999). *Temperament and atypical behavior scale (TABS).* Baltimore: Paul H. Brookes.

Repp, A. C., and R. H. Horner (1999). *Functional analysis of problem behavior.* Belmont, CA: Wadsworth.

Reynolds, C. R., and R. W. Kamphaus (1992). *BASC: Behavior assessment system for children.* Circle Pines, MN: American Guidance Service.

Rogers, C. R. (1983). *Freedom to learn for the 80's.* Columbus, OH: Merrill.

Sparrow, S., S. Balla, and D. V. Cicchetti (1998). *Vineland social-emotional early childhood scales.* Circle Pines, MN: American Guidance Service.

Thomas, A., and S. Chess (1977). *Temperament and development.* New York: Bruner/Mazel.

Thomas, A., S. Chess, and H. G. Birch (1970). The origin of personality. *Scientific American* 223: 102–109.

Ullmann, R. K., E. K. Sleator, and R. L. Sprague (1991). *ADD–H: Comprehensive teacher's rating scale (ACTeRS)–2nd edition.* Champaign, IL: Metritech.

Walker, H. M., and H. H. Severson (1992). *Systematic screening for behavior disorders.* 2d ed. Longmont, CO: Sopris West.

White, B. (1975). *The first three years of life.* Englewood Cliffs, NJ: Prentice-Hall.

Zero to Three (1992). *Heart start: The emotional foundations of school readiness.* Arlington, VA: Zero to Three.

Zero to Three/National Center for Clinical Infant Programs. (1995). *Diagnostic classification: 0–3: Diagnostic classification of mental health and developmental disorders of infancy and early childhood.* Arlington, VA: Zero to Three/National Center for Clinical Infant Programs.

# 16

# *Sensory and Motor Abilities*

## Overview

Sometimes teachers have questions regarding a student's hearing or vision, or teachers observe that a student is clumsy or has difficulty in balancing activities. Learning the signs of possible vision, hearing, or motor difficulties helps teachers know when to refer students for further assessments. Correspondingly, a grasp of the common terminology and assessment procedures that therapists and specialized teachers utilize helps classroom teachers in comprehend-

ing assessment reports completed by professionals in other disciplines.

Educators who teach students with sensory or physical disabilities work closely with other professionals, such as itinerant teachers with expertise in blindness and visual impairments, teachers of the deaf, audiologists, physical and occupational therapists. To plan an appropriate educational program for the student, to monitor it and evaluate its progress, the educator must be able to understand and interpret assessments completed by professionals skilled in areas of sensory and motor functioning. This chapter is an introduction to the specialized assessment of students with disabilities in the areas of vision, hearing, and mobility. Through case studies of specific students, we will meet professionals from other disciplines and examine some of the common assessment procedures and instruments that they use.

## Section One

# Identifying and Assessing Students Who Are Blind or Who Have Visual Impairments

## Section Objectives

After completing this section, you should be able to:

- Describe warning signs that indicate the need for referring a student for an eye examination.
- Discuss key aspects in interpreting a vision report.
- Describe the terms and procedures for assessing distance, near, and functional vision.
- Discuss the components of an orientation and mobility assessment.

## Understanding Blindness and Other Visual Impairments

A **visual impairment** is a loss in one or more of the areas of visual functioning, including near and distance acuity, visual field, or color vision. The amount and usefulness of the vision is affected in three ways:

- age of onset
- type of impairment or condition
- extent or degree of the impairment

### Age of Onset

**Congenital visual impairments** (including congenital blindness) are conditions affecting sight that develop during the prenatal period or result from events during the birth process. Other conditions develop during childhood as the result of heredity, accident, or disease and are referred to as **adventitious visual impairments.** Individuals who are adventitiously blind may have some visual memory. Visual memory of objects is helpful in concept development; similarly, visual memory of environments can aid learning of new travel skills.

### Types of Visual Impairments

Visual impairments can affect the entire eye or only a portion of the eye, or result from the absence of all or part of the structures of the eye. Infectious diseases such as toxoplasmosis and trachoma can cause damage to the eye, either before or during birth. Infants who are born prematurely are at a high risk for visual impairments, including retinopathy of prematurity (ROP) (blindness caused by too high a concentration of oxygen given a newborn), amblyopia, strabismus (a muscle imbalance that causes one eye to be turned inward, outward, up, or down), cortical blindness, or extreme nearsightedness (an inability to see objects at a distance), cataracts, glaucoma, and albinism (an inherited disorder that results in lack of pigmentation and low vision). Table 16.1 lists and describes some of the common types of visual impairments.

Some types of visual impairments cause fluctuations in visual acuity, and these fluctuations may be seen periodically or on a regular basis. Thus, a student may have difficulty with a visual task at times while on other days experience no difficulty.

## Extent of Visual Impairments

Almost all students with visual impairments have some vision, albeit limited. In fact, most students who are blind have some usable vision; few students who are "blind" have no sight at all. Often times, students who are blind have enough vision to see hand or finger movement at a close distance. Students unable to see hand movement may have light perception that will enable them to see the shape of large forms and to identify the direction of a light source.

## Signals of Visual Problems

Some visual impairments have no warning signs; other visual impairments have early warning signals. Table 16.2 enumerates some of the more common signals. If a teacher has any doubt, the student should be referred to the school nurse for screening. The teacher or school nurse can then discuss any concerns they have with the student's parents, and encourage them to take their child to an ophthalmologist, a medical doctor who specializes in treating vision and eye problems, or to an optometrist, an individual who examines the eye and prescribes glasses to correct visual acuity.

## Discovering Amblyopia

One of the most common signals of a visual impairment is that the student's eyes appear to be

TABLE 16.1    *Common Effects of Visual Impairments*

| Condition | Effect | Prognosis |
|---|---|---|
| Amblyopia | The image is seen as a double image. Onset is by age 6 and is sometimes referred to as "lazy eye." | Correctable |
| Astigmatism | The image is seen out of focus. | Correctable |
| Cataracts | The image is clouded. | Correctable |
| Glaucoma | The image is hazy and the field of vision is constricted. | Controllable with medication |
| Myopia | The image is blurred. | Correctable |
| Achromatopsia | Sometimes referred to as "colorblindness," this condition is an inability to identify one or more primary colors. | Noncorrectable |
| Cortex damage | A lesion in the cortex area results in a loss of vision. | Noncorrectable |
| Optic nerve damage | Incomplete development or damage to the optic nerve results in a loss of vision. | Noncorrectable |
| Nystagmus | The image is blurred due to the involuntary movement of the eye. | Noncorrectable |

**TABLE 16.2** *Signals of Visual Problems*

1. Student does not track a moving object with both eyes in proper alignment.
2. Student is extremely light sensitive.
3. Student rubs eyes frequently.
4. Student's eyes are frequently red or watery.
5. Student's eyes do not focus properly.
6. Student examines objects at very close range.
7. Student squints when attempting close work.
8. Student experiences difficulty in judging distances.
9. Student avoids close visual work.

out of alignment. This condition, called amblyopia or "lazy eye," results from a muscle imbalance in one of the eyes that causes the individual to receive a double image. This dissonance prompts the brain to suppress the image from the problem eye. Left untreated, the suppressed eye will gradually lose the ability to function. However, if the condition is identified and treated by age 6, there is no permanent loss of vision. Students suspected of having amblyopia should be referred to a specialist for an eye examination. Treatment for amblyopia includes corrective surgery and/or a temporary patch over the dominant eye.

## Screening Instruments

Screening instruments to assess visual functioning require an individual to identify a symbol of an object or a letter in the alphabet. One common tool, the *Lighthouse House, Apple, Umbrella Series Flash Cards* (Lighthouse International), assesses distance acuity using three symbols: an apple, a house, and an umbrella. The symbols are pictured in varying sizes from 20/20 to 20/200 per card and may be used with young children or students with multiple disabilities who are not able to identify letters.

When conducting the screening, the adult checks to make sure that the individual can identify each of the symbols. The student looks at the cards and must name a card while both eyes are open. If the student answers correctly, then the cards are shown at varying distances of 5, 10, and 20 feet. The student tests at each distance, testing each eye separately, then both eyes together.

Another common screening device is *The Pointing Game* using the letter *E* (Prevent Blindness America). First, the adult shows the *E* in various positions and asks the student to point like *E* points. During the actual screening test, the student is seated 10 feet from the eye chart and the adult begins with the largest *E* on line one (Figure 16.1).

If students do not pass the screening test or students are suspected of having a visual impairment, the nurse or other adult refers them to an ophthalmologist.

## Interpreting a Vision Report

An ophthalmological examination furnishes much information about the individual's eye condition. A vision report summarizing this information is helpful to team members in planning the student's educational program, in adapting materials, and in modifying curriculum. The prognosis of the eye condition is helpful in outlining the skills the student will need to acquire and the services that the student should receive.

The ophthalmological vision report (Figure 16.2) contains information about the history of the eye condition, distance and near visual acuity, visual field, color vision, causes of the present eye condition, and prognosis. Let's examine the types of information that are in the report.

### History

Age of onset of the visual impairment and occurrences of infections, injuries, and operations affect an individual's visual memory of the environment.

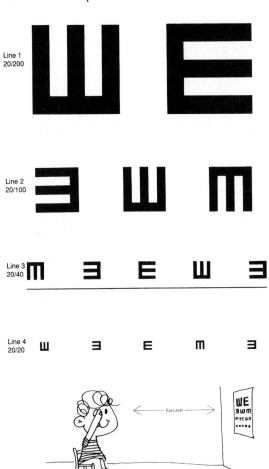

Line 1
20/200

Line 2
20/100

Line 3
20/40

Line 4
20/20

**FIGURE 16.1** *The Pointing Game*

*Source:* Reprinted with permission from Prevent Blindness America.

## Measurements

Measurement of the individual's vision includes both distant and near vision, field of vision, and color perception.

*Distance Acuity.* **Distance visual acuity** is usually measured by twenty feet. Individuals with normal vision are described as having 20/20 vision; a person with a visual impairment may have 20/200. In other words, this person can see at 20 feet what a person with normal vision can see at 200 feet. However, sometimes a

person cannot see the letters or picture symbols at the target distance of 20 feet and needs to have the letters or symbols at a closer range. The eye specialist may then report the distance acuity at 10/200, which means that the individual recognized at 10 feet what a person with normal vision could identify at 200 feet. The following abbreviations are used in reporting acuity in the left, right, and both eyes:

O.D.     Right eye
O.S.     Left eye
O.U.     Both eyes

Persons who have low distance visual acuity may not be able to see figures on the eye chart at any distance; however, they may be able to count fingers, identify hand movement, or recognize a light source. The following abbreviations are typically used to note these acuities:

C.F.      Counts fingers (farthest distance)
H.M.     Hand movement (farthest distance)
L.P.      Light perception (ability to tell whether it is light or dark)
N.L.P.   No light perception

*Near Vision Acuity.* The use of near vision enables the individual to explore their immediate environment and to learn by watching others. Measurements of **near visual acuity** are usually given in inches, meters, or Jaeger chart numbers, a set of numbers that refer to type size.

*Visual Field.* The term "field of vision" refers to central and peripheral vision. Some students may have very good central visual acuity but limited peripheral vision; others may have "islands" of vision in an otherwise restricted field (for example, Reza's right eye in Figure 16.2). For these students, tilting the head or gazing indirectly at the object is the only way to stimulate the usable field. The vision report provides an illustration to indicate field loss. It confirms areas of visual functioning, allowing trained teachers to suggest intervention strategies such

CONFIDENTIAL          **EYE REPORT FOR CHILDREN WITH VISUAL PROBLEMS**

Name of Pupil _____ *Reza* _____ *J.* _____ Sex __*M*__ Race _____
(Type or Print)          (First)          (Middle)          (Last)
Address __ *2 Newberry St.* _____ Date of Birth __*2*__ __*21*__ __*XX*__
          (No. and street)     (City or town)     (Country)     (State)          (Month) (Day) (Year)
Grade _____*6*_____ School _____ Address _____

## I. HISTORY

A. Probable age at onset of vision impairment. Right eye (O.D.) _____ Left eye (O.S.) *early childhood – exact age unknown*

B. Severe ocular infections, injuries, operations, if any, with age at time of occurance _____
_____

C. Has pupil's ocular condition occured in any blood relative(s)? __*yes*__ If so, what relationship(s)? *parent* _____

## II. MEASUREMENTS (see back of form for preferred notation for recording visual acuity and table of approximate equivalents)

A. VISUAL ACUITY

| | DISTANT VISION | | | NEAR VISION | | | PRESCRIPTION | | |
|---|---|---|---|---|---|---|---|---|---|
| | Without correction | With best correction* | With low vision aid | Without correction | With best correction* | With low vision aid | Sph. | Cyl. | Axis |
| Right eye (O.D.) | *5/200* | *5/200* | | | | | | | |
| Left eye (O.S.) | *HM* | *HM* | | | | | | | |
| Both eyes (O.U.) | | | | | | | Date _____ | | |

B. If glasses are to be worn, were safety lenses prescribed in: Plastic _____ Tempered glass _____     *with ordinary lenses

C. If low vision aid is prescribed, specify type and recommendations for use. _____
_____

D. FIELD OF VISION: Is there a limitation? __*yes*__ If so, record results of test on chart on back of form.

What is the widest diameter (in degrees) of remaining visual field?   O.D. _____   O.S. _____

E. Is there impaired color perception? _____ If so, for what color(s) _____

## III. CAUSE OF BLINDNESS OR VISION IMPAIRMENT

A. Present ocular condition(s) responsible for vision impairment. (If more than one, specify all but underline the one which probably first caused severe vision impairment.)

O.D. ╲ *Congenital optic atrophy* _____
O.S. ╱

B. Preceding ocular condition, if any, which led to present condition, or the underlined condition, specified in A.

O.D. _____
O.S. _____

C. Etiology (underlying cause) of ocular condition primarily responsible for vision impairment. (e.g., specific disease, injury, poisoning, heredity or other prenatal influence.)

O.D. ╲ *Hereditary– autosomal dominant* _____
O.S. ╱

D. If etiology is injury or poisoning, indicate circumstances and kind of object or poison involved. _____
_____

## IV. PROGNOSIS AND RECOMMENDATIONS

A. Is pupil's vision impairment considered to be: Stable __X__ Deteriorating _____ Capable of improvement _____ Uncertain _____

B. What treatment is recommended, if any? _____

C. When is reexamination recommended? _____*1 year*_____ *–recommend low vision work-up*

D. Glasses: Not needed _____ To be worn constantly _____ For close work only _____ Other (specify) _____

E. Lighting requirements: Average _____ Better than average __X__ Less than average _____

F. Use of the eyes: Unlimited _____ Limited, as follows: _____

G. Physical activity: Unrestricted _____ Restricted, as follows: _____

**TO BE FORWARDED BY EXAMINER TO:**

Date of examination *August 3, XX* _____
Signature of examiner _____ Degree _____

---

**FIGURE 16.2**   *Reza's Eye Report*

*(continued)*

## PREFERRED VISUAL ACUITY NOTATIONS

DISTANT VISION.  Use Snellen notation with test distance of 20 feet.  (Examples: 20/100, 20/60).  For acuities less than 20/200 record distance at which 200 foot letter can be recognized as numerator of fraction and 200 as denominator.  (Examples: 10/200, 3/200).  If the 200 foot letter is not recognized at 1 foot record abbreviation for best distant vision as follows:

| | |
|---|---|
| HM | HAND MOVEMENTS |
| PLL | PERCEIVES AND LOCALIZES LIGHT IN ONE OR MORE QUADRANTS |
| LP | PERCEIVES BUT DOES NOT LOCALIZE LIGHT |
| No LP | NO LIGHT PERCEPTION |

NEAR VISION.  Use standard A.M.A. notation and specify best distance at which pupil can read.  (Example: 14/70 at 5 in.)

## TABLE OF APPROXIMATE EQUIVALENT VISUAL ACUITY NOTATIONS

These notations serve only as an indication of the approximate relationship between recordings of distant and near vision and point type sizes.  The teacher will find in practice that the pupil's reading performance may vary considerably from the equivalents shown.

| Distant Snellen | Near A.M.A. | Near Jaeger | Near Metric | % Central Visual Efficiency for Near | Point | Usual Type Text Size |
|---|---|---|---|---|---|---|
| 20/20 (ft.) | 14/14 (in.) | 1 | 0.37 (M.) | 100 | 3 | Mail order catalogue |
| 20/30 | 14/21 | 2 | 0.50 | 95 | 5 | Want ads |
| 20/40 | 14/28 | 4 | 0.75 | 90 | 6 | Telephone directory |
| 20/50 | 14/35 | 6 | 0.87 | 50 | 8 | Newspaper text |
| 20/60 | 14/42 | 8 | 1.00 | 40 | 9 | Adult text books |
| 20/80 | 14/56 | 10 | 1.50 | 20 | 12 | Children's books 9-12 yrs |
| 20/100 | 14/70 | 11 | 1.75 | 15 | 14 | Children's books 8-9 yrs. |
| 20/120 | 14/84 | 12 | 2.00 | 10 | 18 ⎫ | Large type text |
| 20/200 | 14/140 | 17 | 3.50 | 2 | 24 ⎭ | |
| 12.5/200 | 14/224 | 19 | 6.00 | 1.5 | | |
| 8/200 | 14/336 | 20 | 8.00 | 1 | | |
| 5/200 | 14/560 | | | | | |
| 3/200 | 14/900 | | | | | |

FIELD OF VISION.  Record results on chart below.

Type of text used: _____    Illumination in ft. candles: _____

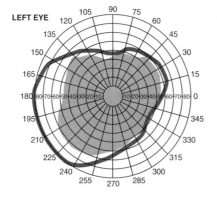

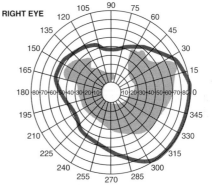

Text object: Color(s) _____ Size(s) _____        Text object: Color(s) _____ Size(s) _____

Distance(s): _____        Distance(s): _____

---

**FIGURE 16.2    *Continued***

*Source:*  Reprinted with permission from Prevent Blindness America.

as positioning and direction of gaze. This information about field loss helps in developing strategies to use in scanning the environment and for using what's called **functional vision.** Functional vision refers to an individual's ability to use vision to complete everyday tasks.

*Color Vision.* Some individuals experience difficulty in distinguishing colors because their retinal cone receptors lack the necessary pigments or are less sensitive in general to certain light waves. These individuals are unable to discriminate some (or all) colors and may exhibit photophobia. Students often compensate for color blindness by detecting brightness or differences in the grayness of colors.

## Causes of Vision Impairment

This section of the vision report describes the type of condition that affects the eye. Sometimes the cause of the visual impairment is unknown.

## Prognosis and Recommendations

Information about the prognosis of the condition is important in program planning. Is the condition stable or will the condition deteriorate? If the condition is not stable, what are some signs that indicate a change in vision? What recommendations should the IEP team include in the individualized education program? In the Snapshot about working with other professionals at Millbrook Middle School, the teaching staff used the vision report to understand and discuss the needs of a new student with low vision.

## Assessments Specific for Students with Visual Impairments

Students with visual impairments have unique needs that require assessments conducted by specialists trained in the field of vision (Table 16.3). Students with visual impairments also require assessment and specific instruction in

curriculum areas beyond that of their sighted peers. Assessing students with visual impairments for the purpose of planning an appropriate education program should involve gathering information about functional vision, braille reading and writing, listening skills, orientation and mobility, and social and recreational skills (Silberman, 1996). A teacher of students with visual impairments, an orientation and mobility specialist, general education and special education teachers, and other team members will address a series of assessment questions regarding the unique needs of the student (Table 16.4). They may select one or more specialized instruments to help in gathering information (Table 16.5).

## Functional Vision

Functional vision is measured in terms of visual efficiency; in other words, how well does the individual use the remaining or residual vision? A **functional vision assessment** is a systematic process of gathering information by a trained teacher of students with visual impairments, or similarly trained professional, to determine the extent of a student's use of residual vision. The examiner begins by carefully reviewing and interpreting the medical information that is available about the student, viewing records specific to vision as well as information about cognitive and other disabilities that the student may have. Following this, the examiner observes the student in the classroom, on the playground, in the cafeteria, and in other school environments to determine therapeutic positioning, lighting, glare, contrast, and color (Utley, Roman, and Nelson, 1998). During these observations the student is performing both near and distance tasks. This information, along with information from medical professionals, parents, related-services providers, and teachers is synthesized and used in developing the IEP.

## Braille Literacy

Assessing skills in reading and writing braille is another area that the teacher, trained to work

SNAPSHOT ■ *Working with Other Professionals at Millbrook Middle School*

Melinda Teraz eased her compact car into the parking lot of Millbrook Middle School. Today, a new student would be joining her class. She thought back to the meeting yesterday afternoon. During their team planning time, Melinda and the other sixth-grade teachers met with the assistant principal, Dr. Wentzel, and two visitors to the school. Dr. Wentzel explained that a new student, Reza J., would be enrolling in the school soon and then introduced the visitors: an itinerant teacher for students with visual impairments, Dan Jenkins, and an orientation and mobility instructor, Sara Walden.

Dan and Sara explained that they would be visiting the school on a regular basis to assist Melinda and the rest of the staff in planning for Reza's needs. Dan discussed the fact that Reza has low vision and shared the vision report from the ophthalmologist (Figure 16.2). He showed the staff the picture of Reza's visual field in his eye report and discussed how students with visual field dysfunction often position their head in an off-mid-line posture in order to bring the object into view. He talked about functional vision and explained that he hoped to complete a functional vision assessment within the next few weeks. Dan continued that this assess-

ment would give the teachers information about the way that Reza uses his remaining vision. Since Reza is a braille reader, Dan will be working with Reza on a regular basis to increase braille literacy skills. Dan explained to the team that he would be a resource to the teachers and that he hoped to participate in their regularly scheduled planning meetings.

Sara gave the staff a brief overview of the areas covered in orientation and mobility instruction. She explained that **orientation** refers to the process that an individual with a visual impairment uses to establish one's position in the environment by using the other senses, and that **mobility** refers to the ability to move safely and efficiently from one place to another. She discussed safety issues after pointing out the door that was partially open. For Reza or any student with low vision, Sara noted, a door that was shut at times and partially opened at other times represents a hazard. Sara said that she would be working with Reza after school for the first few weeks, to orient him to the new surroundings and to help him navigate the building and bus stop. Later, she will be available for consultation on an as-needed basis.

with students with visual impairments, completes. IDEA states that the IEP team must consider (for students who are blind or visually impaired) instruction in braille and the use of braille unless the team determines that instruction or use of braille is not appropriate.

### Orientation and Mobility (O & M) Skills

Orientation refers to the ability to determine one's position in the environment. Different cues such as sounds, light, or pavement surface assist an individual in orientation. Mobility refers to the ability to move from place to place and to travel safely. Learning to use aids such as

a seeing eye dog or a cane increase a person's mobility.

The O & M instructor takes the lead role in assessing formal orientation and mobility skills in conjunction with parents and other team members. Particular skill areas to assess may include:

- the ability to align the body to objects and sounds
- the use of search patterns to explore the environment
- the use of search patterns to recover a dropped object
- the knowledge of how and when to ask for assistance (Hill, 1992)

## *Assessment of Academic and Adaptive Skills*

A comprehensive assessment helps in planning the specialized instruction relating to the individual's visual needs as well as instruction within the general academic program. A comprehensive assessment includes academic achievement; intelligence; motor skills; and, beginning at age 14, transition service needs that focus on

the student's courses of study. A variety of assessment approaches, including performance-based assessment, curriculum-based assessment, interviews, and other approaches that earlier chapters discuss can help in determining the best course of action.

An annotated list of assessment instruments for use with students with visual impairments is available from one of the primary professional and consumer organizations for people with

**TABLE 16.3    *Specialized Assessments: Students with Visual Impairments***

| Type of Assessment | Primary Persons Involved in Assessment | Information Gathered | Purpose |
|---|---|---|---|
| Visual acuity | Ophthalmologist<br><br>Low vision specialist | Near vision<br>Distant vision<br>Visual fields<br>Visual motility<br>Binocularity<br>Etiology<br>Stability of condition<br>Ocular health<br>Color/contrast<br>Photosensitivity<br>Physical restrictions | Understand student's visual status<br><br>Alert others to potential fluctuations in visual performance<br><br>Utilize sun shields for photosensitive students<br><br>Consider the appropriate use of color contrasts |
| Functional vision assessment | O&M specialist<br><br>Teacher of students with visual impairments<br><br>Rehabilitation teacher | Near and distant visual functioning in the classroom, in the school, and in the community<br><br>Effects of lighting<br><br>Color/contrast | Determine student's ability to visually detect information in the classroom, school environment, and in the community<br><br>Determine student's ability to maintain a straight line of travel<br><br>Determine student's ability to avoid obstacles<br><br>Consider the appropriate use of color contrasts for instruction |

*Source:* Adapted from Zimmerman and Roman (1997). Services for children and adults: Standard program design. In B. B. Blasch, W. R. Wiener, and R. L. Welsh (Eds.), *Foundation of orientation and mobility, 2d ed.,* (pp. 383–406). New York: American Foundation for the Blind.

**TABLE 16.4** *Assessment Questions for Planning an Education Program for a Student with a Visual Impairment*

| | |
|---|---|
| *Functional Vision Assessment* | • How does the student use residual vision?<br>• Is the student able to use visual input as a way to gather information about the student's environment?<br>• How does the student use other senses? |
| *Language and Listening* | • Does the student understand important concepts: temporal, quantitative, positional, directional, and sequential? |
| *Braille instruction (unless the IEP team determines that instruction in braille or the use of braille is not appropriate for the student).* | • What are the student's needs for instruction in braille (reading and writing) and the use of braille?<br>• What future needs for instruction in braille or the use of braille does the student have? |
| *Orientation and Mobility Skills* | • How does the student move from place to place?<br>• Does the student move independently?<br>• How does the student travel within the home? school? neighborhood and community? |
| *Academic Skills* | • What is the student's achievement level in braille reading and writing?<br>• Does the student use auditing skills? |

*Source:* Hall, Scholl, and Swallow, 1986; Position Statement from the Council for Exceptional Children, Division on Visual Handicaps, 1991; *Federal Register*, 1999, Sec. 300.346; Utley, Roman, and Nelson, 1998.

visual impairments, Lighthouse International. On their website users may search for instruments by student age or by curriculum area. However, many of the norm-referenced instruments the site describes are not standardized on students with visual impairments.

**Standardized Instruments.** Developing norm-referenced tests for students with visual impairments is problematic. Few reliable and valid instruments exist because of the difficulty in standardizing an instrument (Barraga and Erin, 1992; Silberman, 1996). Since a visual impairment is a low-incidence disability and the variation in types of visual loss and visual functioning among individuals are great, the de-

velopment of a standardized instrument is extremely difficult.

Furthermore, norm-referenced tests that have been developed for sighted students are not always appropriate for students with visual impairments. First, many of the most common instruments do not include students with visual impairments in the norming sample; and second, some of the subtests or individual test items are dependent on vision.

## Preferred Practices

Today, many students have multiple disabilities; vision may be only one area of need. Assessment

**TABLE 16.5**     *Examples of Specialized Assessment Instruments for Students with Visual Impairments*

| Name of Instrument | Areas Assessed |
| --- | --- |
| *Assessment of Braille Literacy Skills* (Koenig and Farrenkopf, 1995) | This instrument includes a braille literacy assessment tool, a summary of skills, and a method of tracking student progress toward attaining literacy skills. |
| *Independent Living: Curriculum with Adaptations for Students with Visual Impairment* (Levack and Lourniet, 1993) | This curriculum resource and guide for assessment, evaluation, and instruction of students with visual impairments includes: social competence, self-care and maintenance of personal environment, play and leisure. |
| *Individualized Systematic Assessment of Visual Efficiency (ISAVE)* (Langley, 1998) | This functional vision assessment tool is for infants, children, and young adults with significant cognitive, neurological, physical, and sensory impairments. Assesses areas including oculomotor skills, acuity skills, visual fields, visual/perceptual skills, ecological factors, and social-attentional gaze. |
| *Learning Media Assessment of Students with Visual Impairments* (Koenig and Holbrook, 1993) | This is a resource guide for assessing a student's skills and deciding on the literacy medium in which the student should begin reading and writing instruction. It includes a process for continuous assessment of literacy media. The appendix contains a specific assessment procedure to compare the effectiveness of various print media for students with low vision. |
| *The Oregon Project for Visually Impaired and Blind Preschool Children, 5th Edition* (Anderson, Davis, and Boigion, 1991) | This criterion-referenced instrument is designed for students up to 7 years of age and assesses cognitive, language, self-help, socialization, and fine and gross motor abilities. |
| *Print, Braille, and Auditory Reading and Writing Assessment* (Ross, 1995) | This assessment includes items relating to print, braille, and auditory access; observations of a student's print and braille reading and writing skills; typing and computing skills. |

teams should ensure that at least one team member has training and expertise in the field of visual impairment so as to avoid misinterpreting assessment tasks and/or assessment information. Lewis and Russo (1998) related how one unskilled examiner required blind students to braille the operations problems presented in the *KeyMath Diagnostic Arithmetic Test*, without recognizing that setting up math problems in

braille requires more skills than the test's publisher intended (p. 55).

Knowledge of the student's visual efficiency will assist team members in assessing areas of achievement, cognitive ability, and transition planning. During the assessment process, the team will need to consider the types of accommodations that the student may need. The educator with specific training in working with students with visual impairments should provide consultation and interpretation.

   Teachers will need to consider the variety of assessment approaches that we describe in earlier chapters. Assessment items and tasks must be carefully examined to ensure that they are fair to the student under assessment. By examining information collected over a period of time, the educator can obtain an accurate account of the student's abilities and needs, especially if the student experiences a fluctuation in vision. Figure 16.3 illustrates some general guidelines for teachers and other team members in assessing the academic skills and achievement of students with visual impairments.

---

**FIGURE 16.3**    *General Guidelines for Assessing the Academic Skills and Achievement of Students with Visual Impairments*

**The Physical Environment**
- Some students may be especially sensitive to echoes and background noise.
- Students need adequate lighting that is free from glare.
- A high intensity light that can be adjusted to individual preferences should be available.
- Table and chair should be at the appropriate height to accommodate braille reading and writing.

**The Examiner**
- Consultation with other specialists is important in understanding the unique assessment needs of the student.
- Allow the student to explore the classroom area, either by walking around it to see the details more clearly or by tactually examining its contents.
- Ask the student's permission to guide the student's hands through a task.
- Encourage the student to use adapted materials or low-vision aids.
- Prior to administering formal instruments, check to see what accommodations and modifications the student presently uses in the classroom. For state- and districtwide assessments, the student will use the same accommodations/modifications as the student uses in the classroom.

**The Materials**
- Identifying unfamiliar pictures without context clues is extremely difficult (Corley and Pring, 1996).
- Computer-generated braille often is unusable because of format errors.
- Tactile representations of three-dimensional objects should not be used, except for students who have had extensive experience with this format.
- Miniature representations may be very similar visually to the real object but very different tactually.
- Whenever possible, pictures should be replaced by real objects. For example, on a curriculum-based mathematics assessment the actual coins, rulers, or calendar should be used.
- Color/contrast affects visual efficiency. Black on white or yellow background provides the greatest contrast for many individuals.
- Use of a san serif font type such as **univers font** is easier to read than a font type with a fancy font, such as **harrington font.**
- If the student does not have an established reading medium, it may be necessary to have braille, largeprint, and standard copies of the material available and allow the student to select the format that is best.

*Source:* Adapted from Lewis, S., and R. Russo, 1998. Educational assessment for students who have visual impairments with other disabilities. In S. Z. Sacks and R. K. Silberman (Eds.), *Educating students who have visual impairments with other disabilities* (pp. 39–72). Baltimore: Paul H. Brookes.

## Section Two

# Identifying and Assessing Students Who Are Deaf or Who Have Hearing Impairments

### Section Objectives

After completing this section, you should be able to:

- Define the terms that describe hearing impairment.
- Identify early signs of hearing impairments.

- Compare methods used in the evaluation of hearing impairments.

## Understanding Hearing Impairments

A **hearing impairment** is an umbrella term that covers all types of hearing losses. As with visual impairments, the amount and usefulness of residual hearing is affected by several factors:

- Age of onset
- Type of impairment or condition
- Extent or degree of the impairment

### Age of Onset

The age of onset directly affects the ability to use speech. A hearing loss that occurs before the child develops language (prelingual) has a greater impact than a loss that occurs after developing language (postlingual). Some conditions that result in deafness or a hearing loss develop during the prenatal period or result from events during the birth process; these situations are referred to as congenital deafness. Other conditions develop during childhood as the result of heredity, an accident, or disease and are referred to as adventitious conditions.

### Types of Hearing Impairments

A hearing loss occurs when one or more of the parts of the ear or auditory nerve do not func-

tion properly. Thus, hearing loss is classified according to the physiological basis for the hearing loss.

***Conductive Hearing Loss.*** A **conductive hearing loss** is due to some barrier to the sound waves that travel from the outer ear to the inner ear. Causes of conductive hearing loss include otitis media (inflammation in the middle ear), severe accumulation of wax, or poorly developed physiological structures in the ear (Bradley-Johnson and Evans, 1991; Ross, Brackett, and Maxon, 1991). Most hearing impairments from conductive losses are correctable through surgery or other medical treatments. A student with a conductive hearing loss may hear speech but certain sounds or discussions can be difficult if they are not loud enough. Amplification of sounds often helps; however, a hearing aid amplifies all sounds. A student wearing a hearing aid will hear all sounds in the environment with equal amplification; this includes extraneous noise in the classroom as well as the teacher talking.

***Sensorineural Hearing Loss.*** Problems with the inner ear or auditory nerve can result in **sensorineural hearing loss.** Sensorineural hearing loss may be due to extended exposure to very loud noise, extended high fevers, tumors in the ear, brain damage, developmental problems, genetic factors, prenatal and/or post-natal infections, anoxia (deficient amounts of oxygen), and trauma (Bradley-Johnson and Evans, 1991; Ross, Brackett, and Maxon, 1991). A student with a sensorineural hearing loss hears distorted sounds even with amplification.

***Mixed Hearing Loss.***   A **mixed hearing loss** is a combination of conductive and sensorineural hearing loss. A student with a mixed hearing loss hears distorted sounds due to the damage to the inner ear and auditory nerve (sensorineural loss) and is unable to hear sounds below a certain decibel level (conductive loss).

### Extent of Hearing Impairments

Hearing impairments range from mild to profound hearing losses, from hearing sound reductions or interruptions to total **deafness.** In general, the term *deaf* is used to describe individuals who are unable to hear and comprehend speech without visual cues, such as speechreading or signing. Students who are deaf have an absence of hearing in both ears. The term *hard of hearing* is generally used to describe persons who can understand speech through listening if other conditions (e.g., lighting, background noise, a properly functioning hearing aid) are adequate. Students who have a hearing impairment have significant hearing loss in one or both ears.

### Signals of Hearing Impairments

Early identification of hearing loss is critical so that intervention can begin as soon as possible. Table 16.6 contains a checklist of symptoms for early detection of hearing loss.

Students suspected of having difficulty hearing must be referred for a hearing test. Referrals can be made to a physician, school nurse, speech-language pathologist, audiologist, or to an **otologist** or **otolaryngologist.** An audiologist is a specialist in testing hearing, an otologist or otolaryngolist is a physician who specializes in disorders of the ear.

**TABLE 16.6**   *Checklist of Symptoms for Early Detection of Hearing Loss*

1. Does the student respond when the student's name is called?
2. Does the student startle when there is a loud noise or bang?
3. Does the student follow directions?
4. Does the student ask to have directions repeated?
5. Does the student speak clearly or demonstrate language difficulties?
6. Does the student have a history of earaches, colds, or allergies?

### Measuring Hearing Loss

Measuring hearing loss and language delays involves professionals from different disciplines (Table 16.7). Early identification of hearing loss maximizes the student's opportunities to benefit from intervention. Early identification has a tremendous impact on a child's speech, social, and academic skills. In this section, we examine four procedures that can determine hearing loss: pure-tone audiometry, bone conduction audiometry, speech audiometry, and immitance audiometry.

### Pure-Tone Audiometry

One of the most common procedures is pure-tone, or air conduction, audiometry. This assessment establishes the type, configuration, laterality, and degree of hearing loss. The type of hearing loss is sensorineural, conductive, or mixed, and the configuration is the pattern of hearing acuity depicted in an **audiogram.** An audiogram is a graph that traces the intensity of sounds detected at five different frequencies. Laterality refers to each ear; that is, the configuration can be different for each ear.

**TABLE 16.7**   *Assessing Students Who Are Deaf or Hard of Hearing*

| Type of Assessment | Primary Persons Involved in Assessment | Information Gathered | Purpose |
|---|---|---|---|
| Hearing | Audiologist | Identification of hearing threshold across frequencies | Determine the need for amplification |
| | Otologist | | Determine treatment |
| | Otolaryngologist | Detection and understanding of speech | |
| | | Evaluation of auditory perceptual disorders | |
| | | Identification of outer ear, middle ear, or sensorineural pathology | |
| Speech and language | Speech and language pathologist | Determination of speech and articulation disorders | Determine instructional plan |
| | Special education teacher | Determination of level of expressive and receptive language skills | |
| | Teacher of the deaf and hearing impaired | Determination of communication needs | |

Audiometers present tones at different levels of loudness (intensity) and pitch. Typically, headphones are placed on the individual's head and the individual is asked to respond to a series of tones by pointing or turning the head. There are many different types of audiometers; some are more specialized than others. An audiometer produces a graph or audiogram that describes the hearing loss (Figure 16.4).

*Loudness.*   The vertical side of the chart measures hearing loss in decibels (dB). Decibels are an indication of loudness or intensity. The range of normal hearing is between 0 dB and 90 dB. For example, a barely audible whisper can be heard at 0 dB; at 50 dB, the sound of an automobile ten feet away can be heard.

*Pitch.*   Frequency of sound waves, hertz (Hz), is measured along the horizontal axis of an audiogram. Frequency is sometimes referred to as pitch. The human ear can detect very low pitch, at about 125 Hz, and very high pitch, at about 8,000 Hz. Speech is in the range of 250 to 4,000 Hz. Each ear is tested separately. On an audiogram an O indicates the right ear and an X indicates the left ear. The audiogram illustrated in Figure 16.4 shows the amount of hearing loss of a child named Chad. You can read more about Chad in the Snapshot.

## Bone Conduction Audiometry

The determination of sensorineural loss is accomplished with bone conduction audiometry.

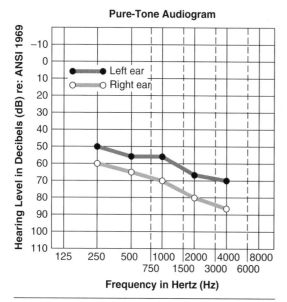

**Pure-Tone Audiogram**

**FIGURE 16.4** *Chad's audiogram*

*Source:* From Cohen, Libby G., and Loraine J. Spenciner, *Assessment of Young Children.* Copyright © 1994. White Plains, NY: Longman Publishers. Reprinted/adapted by permission by Allyn & Bacon.

The bones in the skull can be made to vibrate by a bone-conduction vibrator; this vibration causes electrochemical activity in the inner ear as well as changes in the inner and outer ear.

The examiner tests each ear separately by placing a vibrator on the mastoid bone behind the individual's ear or on the forehead. Testing proceeds as in air conduction, and the results of the bone conduction are reported on the audiogram.

### Speech Audiometry

Pure-tone audiometry and bone conduction audiometry yield limited facts about an individual's ability to hear. Speech audiometry provides information about the ability to *use* audition, or the act or power of hearing. How well an individual is able to understand speech is more important than the ability to hear pure tones. In speech audiometry, the individual wears earphones and the evaluator speaks into a microphone (a tape recording can also be used). Depending on the individual's age and abilities, the student must repeat the words, point to pictures, or write the words the examiner speaks (Madell, 1990; Roeser and Price, 1981).

### Immittance Audiometry

Martin (1991) writes that immittance audiometry, also referred to as impedance audiometry, should be conducted on individuals who are suspected of having a hearing loss. A student can

**SNAPSHOT ■ *Chad***

Chad is an 8-year-old, happy, well-adjusted child who is experiencing moderate to severe developmental delays. He was born after a normal pregnancy and reached the childhood milestones at average ages. He sat alone at 6 months, crawled at 8 months, and walked at 12 months. His speech and language development was typical.

When Chad was 4 years old he had a high temperature and a seizure that lasted for several hours. The blood oxygen supply to his brain was interrupted during the seizure. After the seizure, there was a noticeable regression in Chad's development. He stopped using speech and chose to crawl rather

than walk. This was of great concern to Chad's mother and his pediatrician. He was referred for speech, language, and hearing testing and a severe bilateral hearing loss was discovered. Chad's audiogram can be found in Figure 16.4.

Today, Chad receives special education services in the regular classroom. A sign language interpreter works directly with Chad in his classroom and is also available to consult with Chad's teachers. A therapeutic recreation specialist works with Chad on a biweekly basis and assists in his adaptive physical education program.

have a middle ear disorder, yet pass the audiological evaluation. Immittance audiometry identifies the presence of fluid in the middle ear and other abnormalities in the outer ear and middle ear.

This procedure customarily uses three measures: tympanometry, which evaluates how well the ear transmits energy as air pressure in the ear canal changes; static immittance, which measures the tympanic membrane and the middle ear cavity; and acoustic reflex thresholds, which measure the intensity of the contraction of the stapedius muscle in the middle ear (Ross, Brackett, and Maxon, 1991). The results of immittance screening are plotted on a tympanogram. The graph of the tympanogram in Figure 16.5 shows that the left ear has some otitis media, or inflammation of the middle ear; the right ear appears normal.

## Categories of Hearing Impairments

Although there is some disagreement in the literature, there are established general categories for describing hearing loss (Northern and Downs, 1991, pp. 13–15). Losses 15 to 30 dB are considered mild, 30 to 50 dB are moderate, 50 to 70 dB are severe, and 70 dB or greater are profound. Students with a mild (15 to 30 dB) hearing loss can hear vowel sounds clearly but may miss voiceless consonants. Students with a moderate (30 to 50 dB) hearing loss miss almost all the speech sounds at conversational level. These students may show inattention and difficulty with grammatical rules of language. Prepositions and word endings *(-s, -ed)* are difficult to hear. Hearing aid amplification may help. Students with a severe (50 to 70 dB) hearing loss cannot hear

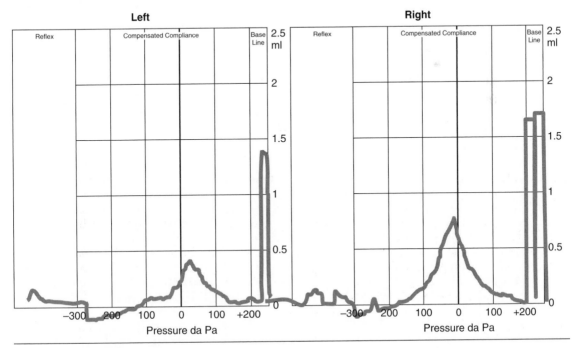

**FIGURE 16.5**  *A Tympanogram*

*Source:* Spenciner, L. J. (1997). [Tympanogram]. Unpublished raw data.

sounds or normal conversation without amplification. With the use of a hearing aid, the student can discern vowel sounds and differences in manner of articulation. The term *deaf* refers to hearing losses that are severe or profound.

Categorizing students on the basis of an audiogram is problematic because so many factors can affect the ability to hear. Describing a student's hearing loss based on an unaided audiogram is misleading and inaccurate. The report, rather, must describe how well a student's hearing functions under normal listening conditions (Moores, 1987).

## Assessments Specific for Students with Hearing Impairments

A complete assessment battery for a student with a hearing impairment consists of evaluations of communications skills, cognitive functioning, academic achievement, and social-emotional skills (Mayer, 1996). If the examiner does not know how to communicate with a student who has a hearing loss, the results of the testing may be of little use. Frequently, examiners will modify administration and response procedures to accommodate the needs of the student. However, examiners must make any accommodations and modifications carefully and render interpretation of performance with due caution. Best practice requires a variety of assessment approaches for planning the program and in monitoring student progress. The IDEA states that the IEP team must consider (for the student who is deaf or hard of hearing) the student's language and communication needs including opportunities for direct communication with peers and professional personnel in the student's language and communication mode, academic level, and opportunities for direct instruction in the student's language and communication mode. Beginning at age 14 the IEP team must consider transition service needs.

*For the student who is deaf, the IEP team must consider opportunities for direct communication with peers in the student's language and communication mode.*

## Standardized Instruments

The use of standardized tests that assess developmental, cognitive, and communication readiness, as well as academic areas to evaluate students who have a hearing loss can be problematic. Many commercially published standardized measures do not systematically include students who are deaf or hard of hearing in the standardization sample. When a student who has a hearing loss is given a test that has not been normed on students with hearing losses, the results of the tests have limited use.

There are some tests that have been normed on students who are deaf or have a hearing impairment.

### Stanford Achievement Test–Ninth Edition Form S.

The *Stanford Achievement Test–Ninth Edition Form S* (Gallaudet Research Institute, 1997–1998), which measures achievement in reading language, spelling, mathematics, science, and social science, was normed on a sample of students who are deaf and hard of hearing. The *Stanford–9* used with deaf students is *not* different from the *Stanford* used with hearing students. Test items and questions are exactly the same for both deaf and hearing students. The *Stanford–9* provides scaled scores, grade equivalent scores, and age-based percentile rankings. Graphs for each of the subtests indicate the student's performance and each graph shows the median score for the 1996 norming sample representing the deaf and hard-of-hearing population, by age.

### Test of Relational Concepts: Norms for Deaf Children.

The *Test of Relational Concepts: Norms for Deaf Children* (Gallaudet Research Institute, 1997–1998) is a quick test of 56 concepts including dimensional adjective (long/short), spatial concepts (front/behind), temporal concepts (before/after), quantitative concepts (more/less), directional concepts (right/left), and qualitative concepts (same/different). The test provides standard scores and percentile ranks for each concept score.

## Preferred Practices

Since sensory impairments are low-incidence disabilities, many classroom teachers have had little exposure to working with students who are deaf or who have a hearing impairment. Figure 16.6 illustrates some general guidelines for teachers and other team members in assessing the academic skills and achievement of students who are deaf or hard of hearing. Team members should schedule meetings and plan carefully to include professionals who work outside of the school community but who can be helpful in answering questions and in planning the student's

---

**FIGURE 16.6**   *General Guidelines for Assessing the Academic Skills and Achievement of Students Who Are Deaf or Hard of Hearing*

**The Physical Environment**

- Background noise may be distracting and interfere with hearing and communication.
- Students using a sign language interpreter will need adequate lighting that is free from glare.

**The Examiner**

- The examiner should be proficient in the student's mode of communication.
- Consultation with other specialists is important in understanding the unique assessment needs of the student.
- Prior to administering formal instruments, check to see what accommodations and modifications the student presently uses in the classroom. For state- and districtwide assessments, the student will use the same accommodations/modifications as the student uses in the classroom.

**The Materials**

- Many students who are deaf and hard of hearing develop reading skills at a slower pace than hearing students of the same age.
- Missing elements, analogies, cloze procedures, and word problems are weighted too heavily on language skills for some students.

individualized education program. For example, the audiologist can help interpret assessment results and alert teachers to any changing conditions.

# Identifying and Assessing Students with Physical Disabilities

## Section Objectives

After completing this section, you should be able to:

- Identify and define specialized terms used in assessing motor development.
- Describe several warning signs of motor problems.

- Discuss key models in the assessment and treatment of students with motor delays.

## Understanding Difficulties and Disabilities in Motor Development

Students with motor difficulties experience problems in one or more of the following areas: muscle development, bones or joints, absence or malformation of a limb or structure, or trauma to the head, neck, or spinal cord. The most common types of difficulty involve muscle deficits. These include:

- *Deficits in **muscle tone**.* Muscle tone refers to the amount of tension that is present in a resting muscle. Muscles that have too little tone appear limp, or **hypotonic**; whereas muscles that are constantly tensed or stretched are referred to as **hypertonic.**

- *Deficits in muscle control.* Problems in muscle control appear as jerky, involuntary movements of the arms and legs, called **tremors.**

- *Deficits in muscle strength.* The student may differ noticeably in muscle strength on the right and left sides of the body or between the limbs. A muscle weakness is referred to as **paresis;** an inability to move is denoted with the combining form *-plegia*. Thus hemiplegia is an inability to move one side of the body.

There are many disorders that cause motor impairments; Table 16.8 lists and briefly describes the most common ones.

## Signals of Motor Difficulties

Good observational skills and knowledge of early signs of motor difficulties are instrumental in the early identification of motor problems. Table 16.9 indicates several early signs that may indicate motor difficulties.

In some progressive disorders such as muscular dystrophy, children experience a decrease

**TABLE 16.8**    *Common Disorders Associated with Motor Disabilities*

| Disorder | Description | Prognosis |
|---|---|---|
| Cerebral palsy | A group of disorders that result from intracranial lesions | Nonprogressive |
| Juvenile rheumatoid arthritis | Inflammation and swelling of the joints | Remission with possible recurrence |
| Muscular dystrophy | Degeneration of the voluntary muscles | Progressive |
| Spina bifida | Congenital malformation of the spinal cord | Nonprogressive, but spinal curvature may develop |
| Spinal cord injuries | Trauma to the spinal cord | Nonprogressive with therapy |
| Traumatic brain injury (TBI) | Severe injuries to the head that may include shearing or tearing of brain tissue | Some individuals will recover some skills, but for others damage is permanent |

in motor coordination. There may also be concerns about equilibrium and posture.

## Common Assumptions Concerning Motor Development

Common assumptions and beliefs about development provide the basis for assessing and working with students with motor delays and deficits. These assumptions are:

**1.** Motor development is one aspect in an integral picture of a student's development and should not be viewed in isolation. Motor, cognitive, and communication skills are interdependent. Delays in motor development can affect cognitive development and language or communication functioning.

**2.** Typical motor development follows a predictable skill sequence, and later skill development is usually dependent upon mastery of earlier skills. Atypical motor development may show a pattern of prolonged stays at an immature stage or acquisition of partial skills that do not fit into any one particular stage. Students who have experienced trauma to the head, neck, or spinal cord have an arrested motor development.

## What Shapes Our Views

There are several different approaches that form the basis of assessment and treatment procedures for students experiencing neuromuscular disorders (Table 16.8). The most common approaches are neurodevelopmental treatment and sensory integration. Each of these perspectives has a fairly narrow focus on the entire assessment and treatment spectrum (Kottke, 1982).

These perspectives arose out of work with particular populations of students; for example, the neurodevelopmental treatment approach was first developed for use with children with cerebral palsy, and sensory integration was developed for use with students with learning disabilities. Conventionally, practitioners will use a combination of approaches in their assessment and treatment procedures.

**TABLE 16.9**  *Early Signs of Motor Difficulties*

1. Abnormal posture or abnormal positioning of arms or legs during play or at rest
2. Tremor in hands or arms when performing an activity
3. Major difference in strength between the left and right sides of the body
4. Poor balance and equilibrium
5. Lack of symmetry between left and right sides of the body
6. Weakness, low muscle tone, and fatigue in gross motor activities
7. Poor coordination during gross and fine motor activities
8. Poor muscle control of lips and tongue
9. Difficulty in accomplishing age-appropriate gross and fine motor tasks
10. Difficulty in maintaining stability while playing or working

Adapted from Cook, R. E., A. Tessier, and M. D. Klein (1999). *Adapting Early Childhood Curricula for Children in Inclusive Settings*, 5th ed. Englewood Cliffs, NJ: Merrill, Prentice-Hall.

## Neurodevelopmental Treatment

The basic principle behind the **neurodevelopmental treatment (NDT)** approach is to facilitate the child's normal, natural movement and to allow the child to experience that feeling through typical activities. NDT utilizes reflex facilitation to reinforce postural activities and works on inhibiting primitive reflexes to facilitate more mature responses. This approach was developed by Karel and Berta Bobath (1972) and emphasizes the need to inhibit hypertonia before beginning therapy. Physical therapists often recommend neurodevelopmental therapy for students with cerebral palsy.

## Sensory Integration

**Sensory integration (SI)** was originally developed by Jean Ayres, who had been working with children with learning and behavior disabilities. The theory of sensory integration focuses on the importance of the organization of sensory input, without which sensory information may either be lost or not fully utilized. During the learning process, the student receives information through the many sensory systems, and the brain takes in, sorts, organizes, and integrates this knowledge with stored information from past experiences. Sensory input comes not only from the five common senses of vision, hearing, taste, smell, and touch but from several other sources as well. Young (n.d.) identified these sources as including:

1. balance or vestibular (from the inner ear) sensation
2. kinesthesia-proprioception—a conscious awareness of one's body position
3. temperature
4. pain
5. chemical receptors in body organs
6. vital receptors to pressure

The theory of sensory integration is based in the importance of the brain being able to accept some and reject other stimuli and then to send the information on to one or more processing centers for integration. This theoretical framework needs empirical research to evaluate its effectiveness.

## Assessments Specific for Students with Physical Disabilities

Team members, including speech and language pathologists, occupational therapists, and physical therapists, need to collect data from a variety of areas, including the student's receptive and expressive language abilities and, for students who do not have intelligible speech, information concerning the augmentative/alternative communication system (see Chapter 10), in planning and monitoring the programs of students with physical disabilities (Table 16.10). Teachers, parents, and other team members provide assistance. Team members will collect information. Assessment will also include details about gross and fine motor skills, the

**TABLE 16.10   *Assessing Students with Physical Disabilities***

| Type of Assessment | Primary Persons Involved in Assessment | Information Gathered | Purpose |
|---|---|---|---|
| Health care needs | IEP team | Health history<br>Physical status<br>Level of adaptive behavior<br>Academic skills and knowledge<br>Social emotional development<br>Need for special health care procedures<br>Activity restrictions | Develop health care plan<br>Develop emergency care plan<br>Develop transportation plan<br>Develop staff training plan |
| Motor functioning | Physical therapist | Evaluation of: movement (including typical and atypical motor patterns), muscle tone, range of motion, muscle strength, and endurance | Determine student's degree of motor ability<br>Determine amount of increased or decreasted tone<br>Determine extent of and interests<br>Determine extent of student's range of motion and interests<br>Determine degree of and interests student's strength and endurance |
| Motor functioning | Occupational therapist<br>Therapeutic recreation specialist | Evaluation of: dexterity; bi-lateral hand movement and coordination; self-help skills including dressing, eating, toileting, and grooming<br>Evaluation of sensory dysfunction<br>Leisure and recreation skills and interests | Determine student's ability and skill level in fine motor activities<br>Determine sensory integration difficulties<br>Determine interests and skills for leisure and recreation |

positioning of the student in order to function in the classroom, and assistive technology needed to complete assignment and classroom activities. IDEA states that the IEP team must consider whether a student with disabilities requires assistive technology devices and services. Beginning at age 14 the IEP team must consider transition service needs.

## Observation

Therapists, teachers, and family members can gather much information about a student's motor skills through observation. This information can include both quantitative measures of movement as well as information about the quality of movement. The Snapshot about Richie describes an occupational therapist's observations of Richie's motor functioning. The IEP team will use this information to assist in planning Richie's program. Neisworth and Bagnato (1987) identify the following questions to consider in observing and appraising patterns of neuromotor development:

1. How does the child's posture and muscle tone change under different conditions and in different positions?

2. Which parts of movement are absent and which contribute to the child's delay in gaining motor milestones?

3. In which positions is the child's postural tone most normal?

4. Which position helps the child to perform the greatest number of voluntary, self-initiated movements?

5. How does the child gather information from the child's surroundings? (p. 336)

## Standardized Instruments

Young children suspected of having motor problems can be assessed by standardized screening instruments such as the *Denver II* or the *Bayley Scales of Infant Development–II)* discussed in Chapter 2. Other instruments to specifically assess motor functioning include the *T.I.M.E™ Toddler and Infant Motor Evaluation* and the *Test of Gross Motor Development–Second Edition (TGMD–2).*

The **T.I.M.E.™ Toddler and Infant Motor Evaluation.**  The *T.I.M.E.™ Toddler and Infant Motor Evaluation* (Miller and Roid, 1994) is a comprehensive norm-referenced instrument,

---

**SNAPSHOT ■ *Richie***

Richie is 10 years old and attends fourth grade. He has an extensive medical history with a suspected partial chromosomal condition. An occupational therapist who consults for the program recently completed the following assessment to help the team in planning Richie's program.

I.  *Sensorimotor Functioning:* During movement activities, Richie stiffens his body and lower trunk area (anterior tilt), which results in difficulties in balance and maintaining his body position in space. He compensates by protective extension (outstretched arms). Richie is also tactile defensive to soft materials. He refuses to handle soft materials, including cheese or fruit. He will not participate in art activities that include working with clay or finger paints.

II.  *Gross Motor:* Richie can hop on two feet but has difficulty in walking along a taped line. He can catch a ball at three feet.

III.  *Fine Motor:* Richie shows a strong preference for using his right hand. He has some difficulty with using a pincer grasp for small objects. Richie uses a palmar grasp when holding a pencil and a "hunt and peck" method in keyboarding.

IV.  *Adaptive:* Mother reports that Richie is learning to dress himself but needs some assistance with pulling his shirt over his head.

**FIGURE 16.7**   *General Guidelines for Assessing the Academic Skills and Achievement of Students with Physical Disabilities*

**The Physical Environment**

- Special positioning and/or seating accommodations may be required.
- Sometimes physical effort can create excessive muscle tone and the student may need to take a break and then try again.
- Sudden, loud noises can increase excessive muscle tone.

**The Examiner**

- Consultation with other specialists is important in understanding the unique assessment needs of the student.
- Prior to administering formal instruments, check to see what accommodations and modifications the student presently uses in the classroom. For state- and districtwide assessments, the student will use the same accommodations/modifications as the student uses in the classroom.

**The Materials**

- Students with physical disabilities may become fatigued easily; allow for rest breaks as necessary.
- Materials should be placed within the student's range of motion.
- Felt tip-pens require less pressure on the paper to write.

---

designed for children from ages 4 months to 3 years, 6 months. The child's raw score can be reported as a standard score or percentile rank. The test includes eight subtests:

*Mobility:* defined as the ability to move one's body in space. Assesses mobility by the maturity and number of variations within a position, the maturity and number of transitions between positions, and the highest developmental pattern obtained from each position.

*Stability:* defined as the dynamic and discrete balance of muscles that results in control over parts of the body. Assesses stability by the highest nonlocomoting position without weight shift, the highest nonlocomoting position with weight shift, the highest locomoting position with weight shift, and the highest reach position.

*Motor organization:* defined as the ability to perform unique motor skills requiring visual and spatial skills, balance, and complex sequential motor abilities.

*Functional performance:* defined as adaptive abilities such as feeding, dressing, and toileting/grooming; self-management and mastery, including independence, play, and personal responsibility; relationships and interactions; and functioning in the community, including functional mobility, functional manipulation, functional communication, social adaptation, and social responsibility.

*Social/emotional abilities:* defined as state, activity level, emotionality, reactivity, temperament, interaction level, and attention span.

*Other:* three additional clinical subtests include atypical positions, quality rating, and component analysis.

### Test of Gross Motor Development–Second Edition (TGMD–2).

The *Test of Gross Motor Development–Second Edition (TGMD–2)* (Ulrich, 2000) is a norm-referenced assessment of gross motor skills for children ages 3 years to 10 years, 11 months. The *TGMD–2* provides standard scores, percentile scores, and age equivalents. The instrument consists of two subtests, locomotor and object control, with six skills assessed in each of the subtests: *locomotor:* run, gallop, hop, leap, jump horizontal, and slide; and *object control:* strike a stationary ball, dribble in place, kick, catch, throw overhand, and roll underhand.

## Assessment of Academic and Social Skills

A variety of assessment approaches are necessary in assessing academic and social skills. To choose an approach, the teacher or examiner will need to consider the accommodations the particular student requires and ensure that these specific modifications to accommodate the student's limited response mode become part of the selected assessment approach (Gleckel and Lee, 1996). Fairness in the assessment approach is critical.

The use of standardized instruments with students with limited motor abilities presents problems. Students may be penalized in two ways: First, students cannot demonstrate motoric responses to questions or to tasks, and second, students with limited ability to speak may be viewed as having mental retardation when they understand but are unable to convey or express that understanding (Gleckel and Lee, 1996).

## Preferred Practices

In assessing students, teachers and therapists must be alert to test items that require motor responses that the student is unable to produce, thus adversely affecting the total test score. Observational information and other assessment approaches we discuss in earlier chapters should assist in this. Home video recordings are an important supplement as well as a means of involving the parent(s) in monitoring their child's progress. Figure 16.7 illustrates some general guidelines for teachers and other team members in assessing the academic skills and achievement of students who have physical disabilities.

## Extending Learning

1. Many states have an educational consultant for students with visual impairments. Contact your state agency to learn about available resources for teachers who have a student with a visual impairment in their classroom.
2. Visit a speech clinic and observe an audiological exam—or have your own hearing tested. What tests were included in the examination? What conclusions would you draw based on the audiogram?
3. Choose one area of low incidence disabilities such as blindness, low vision, deaf, or hearing impairment. Conduct a Web search of assessment resources. Share your findings with the class.
4. Arrange to visit with an occupational or physical therapist in a hospital, clinic, or school setting. What types of assessment procedures do they use?
5. Observe a student with a visual, auditory, or motor disability in school. Interview the classroom teacher and the special education consultant to learn what accommodations or modifications the student uses (if any) during assessment of learning.

## References

Anderson, S., K. Davis, and S. Boigion (1991). *The Oregon project for visually impaired and blind preschool children*. 5th ed. Medford, OR: Jackson Educational Service District.

Barraga, N. C., and J. N. Erin (1992). *Visual handicaps and learning*. Austin, TX: PRO-ED.

Bayley, N. (1993). *Bayley scales of infant development II*. San Antonio, TX: The Psychological Corporation.

Bobath, K., and B. Bobath (1972). Cerebral palsy. In *Physical therapy services in the developmental disabilities*, eds. P. H. Peterson, and C. E. Williams, Springfield, IL: Charles C. Thomas.

Bradley-Johnson, S., and L. D. Evans (1991). *Psychoeducational assessment of hearing-impaired students.* Austin, TX: PRO-ED.

Cohen, L. G., and L. J. Spenciner (1994). *Assessment of young children.* White Plains, NY: Longman.

Cook, R. E., A. Tessier, and M. D. Klein (1999). *Adapting early childhood curricula for children in inclusive settings.* 5th ed. Englewood Cliffs, NJ: Merrill, Prentice-Hall.

Corley, G., and L. Pring (1996). The ability of children with low vision to recall pictures. *Journal of Visual Impairment and Blindness*, 90(1), 58–72.

Division for the Visually Handicapped (1991). *Statements of position.* Reston, VA: Council for Exceptional Children.

*Federal Register* (Vol. 64, No. 48, pp. 12418–12536). Washington, DC: U.S. Government Printing Office, March 12, 1999.

Gallaudet Research Institute (1997–98). *Reviews of four types of assessment instruments used with deaf and hard of hearing students.* Retrieved June 13, 2001. Available: http://gri.gallaudet.edu/~catraxle/ACADEMIC.html.

Gleckel, L. K., and R. L. Lee (1996). Children with physical disabilities. In *Exceptional Children in Today's Schools*, 3d ed., ed. E. L. Meyen, 399–432. Denver: Love.

Hall, A., Scholl, G. T., and R. M. Swallow (1986). Psychoeducational assessment. In *Foundation of education for blind and visually handicapped children and youth*, ed. G. T. Scholl, 187–214. New York: American Foundation for the Blind.

Hill, E. (1992). Instruction in orientation and mobility skills for students with visual handicaps. *DVH Quarterly* 37(2): 25–26.

Koenig, A., and C. Farrenkopt (1995). *Assessment of braille literacy skills.* Abstract retrieved June 13, 2001, from The National Agenda for Blind and Visually Impaired Youths, Including Those with Additional Disabilities. Available: http://www.obs.org/napa/assessme.htm.

Koenig, A., and C. Holbrook (1993). *Learning media assessment of students with visual impairments.* Abstract retrieved June 13, 2001, from The National Agenda for Blind and Visually Impaired Youths, Including Those with Additional Disabilities. Available: http://www.obs.org/napa/assessme.htm.

Kottke, F. J. (1982). Therapeutic exercise to develop neuromuscular coordination. In *Krusen's handbook of physical medicine and rehabilitation*, ed. F. J.

Kottke, G. K. Stillwell, and J. F. Lehmann, 218–252. Philadelphia: W. B. Saunders.

Langley, M. B. (1999). *Individualized systematic assessment of visual efficiency (SAVE).* New York: American Printing House for the Blind.

Levack, N., and R. Lournier (1993). *Independent living: Curriculum with adaptations for students with visual impairment.* Abstract retrieved June 13, 2001, from The National Agenda for Blind and Visually Impaired Youths, Including Those with Additional Disabilities. Available: http://www.obs.org/napa/assessme.htm.

Lewis, S., and R. Russo (1998). Educational assessment for students who have visual impairments with other disabilities. In *Educating students who have visual impairments with other disabilities*, ed. S. Z. Sacks and R. K. Silberman, 39–72. Baltimore: Paul H. Brookes.

Lighthouse International. *Lighthouse, house, apple, umbrella series flash cards.* Available from Lighthouse International, 111 East 59th St., New York, NY 10022.

Madell, J. R. (1990). Audiological evaluation of the mainstreamed hearing-impaired child. In *Hearing-impaired children in the mainstream*, ed., M. Ross, 27–44. Baltimore: York.

Martin, F. N. (1991). *Introduction to audiology.* 4th ed. Englewood Cliffs, NJ: Prentice-Hall.

Mayer, M. H. (1996). Children who are deaf or hard of hearing. In *Exceptional Children in Today's Schools*, 3d ed., ed. E. L. Meyen, 315–350. Denver, CO: Love.

Miller, L. J., and G. H. Roid (1994). *The T.I.M.E.™ toddler and infant motor evaluation.* San Antonio, TX: The Psychological Corporation.

Moores, D. (1987). *Educating the deaf: Psychology, principles, and practices.* 3d ed. Boston: Houghton Mifflin.

Neisworth, J. T., and S. J. Bagnato (1987). *The young exceptional child.* New York: Macmillan.

Northern, J. L., and M. P. Downs (1991). *Hearing in children.* 4th ed. Baltimore: Williams & Wilkins.

Prevent Blindness America. *The pointing game.* Available from Prevent Blindness America, 500 East Remington Road, Schaumburg, IL 60173-5611.

Roeser, R. J., and D. R. Price (1981). Audiometric and impedance measures: Principles and interpretation. In *Auditory disorders in school children*, ed. R. J. Roeser and M. P. Downs, 71–101. New York: Thieme-Stratton.

Ross, D. (1995). *Print, braille, and auditory reading and writing assessment.* Abstract retrieved June 13, 2001, from The National Agenda for Blind and Visually Impaired Youths, Including Those with Additional

Disabilities. Available: http://www.obs.org/napa/assessme.htm.

Ross, M., D. Brackett, and A. B. Maxon (1991). *Assessment and management of mainstreamed hearing-impaired children.* Austin, TX: PRO-ED.

Silberman, R. K. (1996). Children with visual impairments. In *Exceptional Children in Today's Schools*, 3d ed., ed. E. L. Meyen, 351–398. Denver, CO: Love.

Spenciner, L. J. (1997). [Tympanogram]. Unpublished raw data.

Ulrich, D. A. (2000). *Test of gross motor development, second edition.* Austin, TX: PRO-ED.

Utley, B. L., Roman, C., and G. L. Nelson (1998). Functional vision. In *Educating students who have visual impairments with other disabilities*, ed. S. Z. Sacks and R. K. Silberman, 371–412. Baltimore: Paul H. Brookes.

Young, M. H. (n.d.). Sensory integration programming. In *Topics in therapeutic programming for students with severe handicaps (sensory integration programming instructional module)*, ed. P. H. Campbell. Akron, OH: Children's Hospital Medical Center of Akron.

Zimmerman, G. J., and C. A. Roman (1997). Services for children and adults: Standard program design. In *Foundation of orientation and mobility*, 2d ed., ed. B. B. Blasch, W. R. Wiener, and R. L. Welsh, 383–406. New York: American Foundation for the Blind.

# 17

# *Youth in Transition[1]*

## *Overview*

The provision of transition services is critical in helping students with disabilities prepare for adult life. Although students with disabilities continue to fall behind their typical peers in post-school employment, wages, postsecondary education, and residential independence, they are making gains. The federal commitment to supporting transition activities once students leave school has contributed to these improvements (Blackorby and Wagner, 1996). The federal government mandates that students with disabilities

be provided with services that will facilitate their transition from school to post-school activities, including postsecondary education, vocational training, integrated employment (including supported employment), continuing and adult education, adult services, independent living, and community participation.

IDEA requires that schools base individual transition planning on present levels of performance. Transition planning is an outcome-oriented process in which the focus is on the

[1]With Debra Twitchell

attainment of prespecified performance objectives. Assessment of students' transition needs and preferences is an important part of the transition process and should include assessment of vocational, career, academic, personal, social, and living needs. This requires a variety of approaches and because transition planning is a process that occurs over a long period of time, periodic transition assessments and monitoring of transition plans is vital.

## Chapter Objectives

After completing this chapter you should be able to:

- Define the concept of transition.
- Explain the purposes of transition assessment.
- Describe the ways in which students' transition needs and preferences are assessed.
- Compare several approaches to transition assessment.

## What Shapes Our Views

While transitions occur across an individual's life span, the transition from the school setting to adult life is one that requires careful assessment and planning. The effects of this transition have great impact on the individual with a disability. The Division of Career Development and Transition (DCDT) of the Council for Exceptional Children have adopted the following definition when referring to youth who are in transition:

> **Transition** refers to a change in status from behaving primarily as a student to assuming emergent adult roles in the community. These roles include employment, participating in post secondary education, maintaining a home, becoming appropriately involved in the community and experiencing satisfactory personal and social relationships. The process of enhancing transition involves the participation and coordination of school programs, adult agency services, and natural supports within the community. The foundations for transition should be made during the elementary and middle school years, guided by the broad concept of career development. Transition planning should begin no later than age 14, and students should be encouraged to the full extent of their capabilities, to assume a maximum of responsibility for such planning. (Halpern, 1994)

## Legislation

Legislation mandates educational, vocational, and transitional services for individuals with disabilities. Current laws call for an interdisciplinary effort to serve individuals. There are five laws that provide the authorization and the focus for **transition services.** These laws are: the Rehabilitation Act Amendments of 1998 (PL 105–220); The Carl D. Perkins Vocational and Applied Technology Education Act Amendments of 1998 (PL 105–332); Workforce Investment Act of 1998 (PL 105–220); The School-to-Work Opportunities Act of 1994 (PL 103–239); and The Individuals with Disabilities Education Act.

The Rehabilitation Act Amendments of 1998 (PL 105–220) states that a state workforce investment system should coordinate and administer employment and training programs for all individuals. For individuals with disabilities, this means that they will be able to access services and programs that target increased employment, skills, retention, and wages. While the intended outcome is increased employment, the definition of employment is broad enough to include full- or part-time employment, vocational outcomes of supported employment, and other vocational outcomes such as self-employment.

The Carl D. Perkins Vocational and Applied Technology Education Act Amendment of 1998 (PL 105–332) guarantees equal access to vocational education programs and opportunities for all students. Students who are eligible to receive services under the Perkins Act include individuals with disabilities, individuals from economically disadvantaged families, individuals preparing for nontraditional training and employment, single parents, displaced homemakers, and individuals with other barriers to educational achievement, including individuals with limited English proficiency. The Perkins Act links student with disabilities to transition services by mandating that each student who has a disability and who participates in vocational education have

- Equal access to vocational activities,
- Assessment for vocational interests, abilities, and special needs,
- Special services, and
- Guidance, career, and transition counseling.

The purpose of The Workforce Investment Act of 1998 (PL 105–220) is to combine, coordinate, and improve employment, training, literacy, and vocational rehabilitation programs. This act consolidates services through a one-stop delivery system that assists individuals, including those with disabilities. Students with disabilities and their families should, in terms of transition planning, find it easier to access information on employment and vocational training opportunities through this one-stop delivery system.

The School-to-Work Opportunities Act of 1994 (PL 103–239) provides for a national framework (Krieg, Brown, and Ballard, 1995) that supports school-to-work opportunities. Each state determines the implementation of the school-to-work opportunities system, with the ultimate goal of linking youth to productive employment. Because each state determines how it will implement this legislation, the participation of students with disabilities varies from one state to the next.

The Individuals with Disabilities Education Act is the major legislation that mandates transition services. The focus is on assisting the individual with a disability to make a smooth transfer from the school to independent adult life. According to IDEA,

> transition services means a coordinated set of activities for a student designed with an outcome-oriented process, that promotes movement from school to post-school activities, including postsecondary education, vocational training, integrated employment (including supported employment) continuing and adult education. Adult services, independent living, and community participation. (sec. 300.18)

A coordinated set of activities means that all transition activities must meet the student's needs and complement, not duplicate, each other. The transition process involves many individuals and agencies. The coordinated set of activities that IDEA outlines must

1. be based upon the individual student's needs, taking into account the student's preferences and interests; and

2. include
   a. Instruction,
   b. Community experiences,
   c. The development of employment and other post-school adult living objectives, and
   d. If appropriate, acquisition of daily living skills and functional vocational evaluation. (20 U.S.C. 1401 [a] [19])

Although progress has been made there are several challenges that remain. The National Council on Disability has defined these challenges as (1) increasing secondary-aged students' access to relevant and rigorous curricula and information technology, while at the same time increasing the numbers of students who successfully complete high school; (2) expanding the range of options for students who enter employment after graduation from high school; (3) improving access to higher-education opportunities; (4) ensuring that there is wide range of opportunities for vocational and educational opportunities for individuals with disabilities who do not complete a high school program; and (5) increasing the level of accountability in government-funded programs that provide postsecondary education, vocational training, and employment (National Council on Disability and the Social Security Administration, 2000).

## Transition Assessment

Beginning at age 14 (or sooner if determined by the Pupil Evaluation Team) and updated annually, the IEP team must develop a statement of transition services needs of the student that focuses on the student's courses of study. At age 16, the IEP team must discuss and document transition services at every IEP meeting until the student leaves school. Figure 17.1 includes questions that the IEP team should address and methods of collecting data when assessing transition needs. As individuals with disabilities transition from school to adult life, assessment is crucial in career and vocational education and in life-skill development. Transition assessment can be defined as: The ongoing process of collecting data on the individual's strengths, needs, preferences, and interests as they relate to the demands of current and future working, educational, living, and personal and social environments. Assessment data serve as the common thread in the transition process and form the basis for defining goals and services that will make up the Individualized Education Program.

Transition assessment relates to the life roles of individuals with disabilities and the supports they need before, during, and after the transition to adult life. Figure 17.2 illustrates the transition assessment process. The data collected in transition assessment is vital in assisting individuals with disabilities and their families to make choices that take into account the individual's strengths, needs, and preferences about postsecondary education, career development, vocational training, community living and personal and social goals.

## Purposes of Transition Assessment

Transition focuses on facilitating improved postsecondary outcomes for persons with disabilities. Transition assessment assists individuals with disabilities, their families, educators, specialists, employers, and community members to develop, implement, and evaluate the transition process. Transition assessment is integral to instruction and program planning. Because transition planning can begin as early as the elementary years, transition assessment is a process that is on-going. While the purposes of transition change as the student gets older, the major purposes are

1. To identify the person's level of career development
2. To determine the individual's strengths, abilities, interests, and preferences regarding postsecondary education, employment, independent living, community involvement, and personal and social goals
3. To identify the individuals that exhibit interests and skills
4. To identify the accommodations, modifications, supports, and services that the individual will need in order to be a responsible and contributing community member (Sitlington, Neubert, Begun, Lombard, and Leconte, 1996).

## Involving Families

Parental and family involvement and support are integral to the transition process. Beginning in the early elementary years, parental involvement throughout the process is important. Educators should periodically interview parents about their aspirations for their child. As children progress through school, parents' views of their child's abilities will change. Educators should welcome parents as partners throughout the transition process (Wehman, 2001). Questions that can be discussed with parents include

**FIGURE 17.1** *Strengths, Needs, Opportunities, and Worries*

| Assessment Questions to Ask | Methods of Collecting Information |
|---|---|
| *Employment* | |
| 1. What does the student like to do? | Interviews |
| 2. What types of employment options (e.g., supported employment, and competitive employment) are feasible for the student? | • student<br>• family<br>• school personnel<br>• work study teachers<br>• employers |
| 3. What types of accommodations, modifications, and supports will the student need on employment sites? | Situational assessment<br>• in-school jobs |
| 4. What types of skills does the student need to acquire/learn to meet the career goal? | • community-based jobs<br>• vocational courses |
| 5. What types of job benefits does the student need to become an independent member of society? | Work samples<br>Learning style<br>Inventories |
| 6. Does the student have job-seeking skills? | Aptitude testing |
| 7. Does the student need assistance from an adult service provider to find and maintain a job? | Assistive technology assessment |
| *Post-Secondary Education* | |
| 1. Does the student want or need postsecondary education or training programs? | Situational assessment |
| 2. What subject(s)/major is the student interested in studying to prepare for employment? | Interviews<br>• student<br>• family<br>• school personnel |
| 3. Can the student express a desire for support services, accommodations, and modifications if needed? | Background review<br>• medical records<br>• psychological |
| 4. What types of accommodations will the student need in a postsecondary setting? | • financial status |
| 5. Does the student need assistance from an adult agency to attend a postsecondary institution? | Interest inventories<br><br>Functional academics<br><br>Simulated application package |
| *Community Involvement* | |
| 1. What public transportation is the student able to use in the community? | Situational assessment<br>• physical education teacher |
| 2. Does or will the student have a driver's license? | • community recreation services<br>• extracurricular activities |
| 3. Does the student need special travel arrangements made on an ongoing basis? | Interviews<br>• student<br>• family |
| 4. What leisure/community activities does the student enjoy? | • teachers<br>• peers |

*(continued)*

**FIGURE 17.1**    *Continued*

| Assessment Questions to Ask | Methods of Collecting Information |
|---|---|
| 5. Does the student need accommodations, modifications, or supports in order to participate in leisure activities? | Community survey<br><br>Record review |
| 6. Can the student locate/use community services, such as stores, banks, and medical facilities? | |
| 7. Does the student participate in the political process (e.g., voting)? | |
| 8. Is the student knowledgeable about the law? | |

*Personal/Social*

| | |
|---|---|
| 1. Does the student interact with and have support from family members? | Interviews<br>• student<br>• family |
| 2. Does the student have age-appropriate friends? | • teachers<br>• peers |
| 3. Does the student know how to act in social situations? | Background review |
| 4. Is the student able to self-advocate in employment, leisure, and community situations? | Observation<br>• IEP meetings<br>• classrooms<br>• lunchtime |
| 5. Does the student demonstrate an understanding of rights as a person with a disability? | • employment sites<br>• community sites |
| 6. Does the student participate in the IEP process? | Situational assessment<br>• community |
| 7. Is the student able to understand and express strengths, needs, and accommodations? | • employment<br>• role plays |
| 8. Does the student need advocacy support? | |

*Independent Living*

| | |
|---|---|
| 1. What kinds of accommodations/supports will the student need to function in an independent living situation? | Interviews<br>• student<br>• family<br>• teachers |
| 2. Is the student aware of how to find independent living quarters? | • employers |
| 3. Can the student purchase and prepare food? | Functional academics |
| 4. Does the student know how to arrange for utility services? | Background review |
| 5. Can the student follow daily routines (e.g., get up in the morning, do dishes, clean)? | Observations<br>• grocery store<br>• food service class |

**FIGURE 17.1** *Continued*

| Assessment Questions to Ask | Methods of Collecting Information |
|---|---|
| 6. Is the student able to maintain personal and hygiene skills?<br><br>7. Can the student manage money appropriately? | • home<br>• banks<br>• shopping<br><br>Situational assessments<br>• home<br>• community<br>• school<br><br>Simulated class activities |

*Source:* Adapted from Sitlington, P. L., D. A. Neubert, W. Begun, R. C. Lombard, and P. J. Leconte (1996). *Access for Success*. Reston, VA: Council for Exceptional Children.

*Parental Expectations*
• What are your expectations for your child's responsibilities at home?
• What are your child's daily responsibilities at home?
• What are your goals for your child's future employment?

*Experiences*
• What work experiences has your child had?
• To what extent did your child enjoy the work?
• In what types of jobs do you think that your child will be successful?
• In what types of jobs do you think that your child will be unsuccessful?

**FIGURE 17.2** *Transition Assessment*

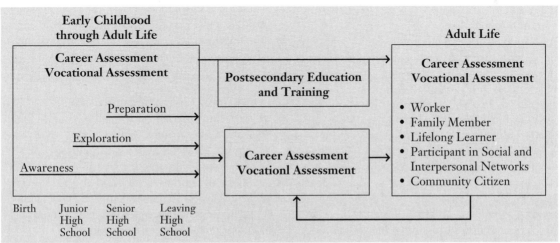

*Source:* Adapted from Transition assessment—where have we been and where should we be going? by P. L. Sitlington, *Career Development for Exceptional Individuals* 19, 1996, page 163. Copyright 1996 by The Council for Exceptional Children. Reprinted with permission.

### *Transportation*
- Does your child drive a car?
- Does your child use public transportation? If so, are there any problems?
- What are your expectations for transportation to take your child to and from work?

### *Education*
- Do you feel that your child will need further education and/or training after completing high school? If so, what types of education or training would be beneficial?
- What steps have you taken to obtain further information on this education and/or training? (Hutchins and Renzaglia, 1998)

## *Person-Centered Planning*

Person-centered planning means that the student with the disability engages in an active meaningful way with parents, educators, community members, and others during the assessment, planning, and service delivery processes. Person-centered planning is focused on self-determination and on the students' hopes, dreams, and desires. Natural supports—the individuals and supports that the general population uses, rather than specialized services—are emphasized. Examples of natural supports include neighbors, employers, clergy, and other community members.

Person-centered planning encourages students with disabilities to take a leadership role during the transition activities. Person-centered planning should result in a comprehensive plan that addresses educational opportunities, employment opportunities, financial and income needs, friendship and socialization needs, transportation needs, health and medical needs, and legal and advocacy needs (Wehman, Everson, and Reid, 2001). Person-centered planning has several characteristics:

1. Person-centered planning focuses on abilities, rather than disabilities.
2. Person-centered planning encourages planning that is oriented toward the future.
3. Involvement of community members and organizations is integral to person-centered planning.
4. Person-centered planning emphasizes supports, connections, and commitment rather than programs and services.
5. Person-centered approaches are individualized according to each student's needs and desires. The student with the disability and family members provide strong direction for transition planning and implementation activities (Wehman, Everson, and Reid, 2001).

When developing IEPs that are person-centered, individuals who are part of the student's personal network should be identified. Along with the student and the family, this personal network develops a vision or dream of the student's future. These individuals can include the student, family members, special educators, general educators, vocational educators, vocational rehabilitation counselors, providers of adult services, and other community members. Each major transition should connect to a part of the student's dream.

The IEP team should identify the experiences, supports, and services that need to be in place in order to achieve the dream. Achieving the IEP goals and objectives should move the student closer to the dream and to inclusion in the community. A variety of instruments can be useful in person-centered planning:

- learning styles inventories
- classroom observation instruments
- curriculum-based assessments
- learning environment assessments
- physical environment assessments
- social environment assessments
- future planning questionnaires
- interviews with students
- interviews with parents and family members
- adaptive behavior instruments
- behavioral and functional assessments
- technology evaluations
- self-determination checklists (Clark, 1996)

## Self-Determination Skills

Student self-determination is at the center of transition planning. All activities in the transition process, including assessment, planning, implementation, and evaluation, must include the individual with the disability as an active participant to the maximum extent possible. Self-determination means that the individual's hopes, dreams, and desires influence the types of assessments that the transition team implements. Figure 17.3 contains an example of a worksheet that may help a student express hopes and dreams. Transition assessment should include and document self-determination skills. Various instruments assist in this process, include one or more interviews with the individual, interviews with parents and family members, checklists, and observations (Sitlington, Neubert, Begun, Lombard, and Leconte, 1996). Suggested questions to ask include

Does the individual understand the transition planning process?

Does the individual understand her rights under the law?

Does the person demonstrate self-advocacy skills?

Can the individual explain his role in the transition planning process?

Can the person identify interests and preferences?

Can the individual describe her transition goals?

## Published Instruments

This chapter contains information on a number of published instruments that provide information on transition assessment. However, many of

## SNAPSHOT ■ *Miguel*

Miguel is 13 years old and in the sixth grade. He has been identified as having mild mental retardation and an emotional disability. Miguel's language abilities are well below the range of an average 14-year-old. Miguel often gets frustrated when he is unable to communicate effectively and sometimes responds inappropriately by striking out at others.

In a conversation with his special education teacher, Shauna Moore, Miguel talked about feeling different from his classmates. He stated that this made him angry and sad. When asked what he likes to do, he responded, "I like to play video games and play with my dog." Shauna asked Miguel what he would like to do for a career when he was older. Miguel indicated that he would like to be a "vet" (veterinarian). When asked why he wanted to be a veterinarian he said, "animals can understand me."

In an interview, Miguel's mother expressed concern about his future. She worries that he will not be able to do the things that other students are going to be doing "like drive a car" or "have a girlfriend." She stated that he prefers to play alone or with his dog, but has "no friends." She does not have many problems understanding her son, but knows that he does get easily frustrated when he is unable to communicate well with others. When asked about Miguel's future after high school, she thought that he might be able to work as a building custodian as long as he was supervised.

Shauna suggested that the team should begin to plan for Miguel's transition by first assessing Miguel's vocational interests and aptitudes. Once these are shared with the team, the team will set goals with Miguel for his life after school and develop a plan of action that will enable him to reach his goals.

**FIGURE 17.3**   *Sample Worksheet for Students*

| S.N.O.W. | |
|---|---|
| *Strengths*<br>What skills have I learned that will help me reach my dreams?<br>Things I can do well are . . . | *Needs*<br>What do I still need to learn to do to reach my dreams?<br>What skills do I have trouble with?<br>What do I need help with? |
| *Opportunities*<br>What is helping me now to reach my dreams?<br>Who can assist me concerning my dreams?<br>How can they help? | *Worries*<br>What worries me when I think about reaching my dreams? |

*Source:* Adapted from the Maine Transition Network/Maine Committee on Transition and So. Me. Advisory Council on Transition, 1997.

these instruments are outdated or have other limitations. As with all assessment instruments, users should carefully review technical aspects and administration procedures and consider how to apply the results of the assessment. Some of these instruments have little relevance in supporting students' preparation for transition; consequently, educators need to think about how to collect more pertinent information.

## Work-Related Behaviors, Skills, and Aptitudes

The *BRIGANCE®* *Inventories* are criterion-referenced tests that are similar in purpose, scoring, administration, and interpretation. The inventories assess skills in literacy, mathematics, speech, listening, and vocational skills; other areas are useful in program planning and program monitoring. Table 17.1 summarizes each of the inventories.

A summary of other instruments that assess work-related behaviors, skills, and aptitudes can be found in Table 17.2. These instruments can help ascertain a student's ability to learn or to succeed in a number of different areas.

## Vocational Interests

The team that is helping to plan for a student's transition may need to gather information about the student's vocational interests. These interest inventories can assist individuals in investigating educational and occupational alternatives, learning about careers, and setting goals for the future. A summary of interest inventories is available in Table 17.3.

**TABLE 17.1**   *Brigance® Inventories*

| Name | Ages/Grades | Transition Related Skills |
|---|---|---|
| *BRIGANCE® Inventory of Essential Skills* (Brigance, 1981) | Grades 4 through 12 | 1. Word Recognition<br>2. Oral Reading<br>3. Reading Comprehension<br>4. Functional Word Recognition<br>5. Word Analysis<br>6. Reference Skills<br>7. Schedules and Graphs<br>8. Writing<br>9. Forms<br>10. Spelling<br>11. Numbers<br>12. Number Facts<br>13. Computation of Whole Numbers<br>14. Fractions and Mixed Numbers<br>15. Decimals<br>16. Percents<br>17. Measurement<br>18. Metrics<br>19. Math Vocabulary<br>20. Money and Finance |
| *BRIGANCE® Comprehensive Inventory of Basic Skills–Revised* (Brigance, 1999) | Grades Pre-K through 9 | 1. Readiness<br>2. Speech<br>3. Word Recognition<br>4. Oral Reading<br>5. Reading Comprehension<br>6. Word Analysis<br>7. Functional Word Recognition<br>8. Listening<br>9. Spelling<br>10. Writing<br>11. Reference Skills<br>12. Graphs and Maps<br>13. Numbers<br>14. Number Facts<br>15. Computation of Whole Numbers<br>16. Fractions and Mixed Numbers<br>17. Decimals<br>18. Percents<br>19. Measurement/Geometry<br>20. Metrics<br>21. Math Vocabulary<br>22. Time<br>23. Money |

*(continued)*

**TABLE 17.1**   *Continued*

| Name | Ages/Grades | Transition Related Skills |
|---|---|---|
| *BRIGANCE® Assessment of Basic Skills–Spanish Edition* (Brigance, 1984) | Grades K through 6 | 1. Readiness<br>2. Word Recognition<br>3. Word Analysis<br>4. Vocabulary<br>5. Handwriting<br>6. Grammar and Mechanics<br>7. Spelling<br>8. Reference Skills<br>9. Math Placement<br>10. Number Sequences<br>11. Operations<br>12. Measurement<br>13. Geometry |
| *BRIGANCE® Life Skills Inventory* (Brigance, 1994) | Vocational<br>Secondary<br>Adult education | 1. Speaking and Listening Skills<br>2. Functional Writing Skills<br>3. Common Signs and Warning Labels<br>4. Telephone Skills<br>5. Money and Finance<br>6. Food<br>7. Clothing<br>8. Health<br>9. Travel and Transportation<br>10. Health Practices and Attitudes<br>11. Self-Concept<br>12. Auto Safety |
| *BRIGANCE® Employability Skills Inventory* (Brigance, 1995) | Vocational<br>Secondary<br>Adult education<br>Job training | 1. Reading<br>2. Career Awareness and Self-Understanding<br>3. Job Seeking Skills<br>4. Self-Concept<br>5. Motor Coordination<br>6. Responsibility<br>7. Speaking and Listening Skills<br>8. Preemployment Writing<br>9. Math Skills and Concepts |

**Reading-Free Vocational Interest Inventory–2.**   The *Reading-Free Vocational Interest Inventory–2 (R–FVII)* (Becker, 2000) is a vocational interest inventory for students who have mental retardation or learning disabilities. The test consists of 55 sets of three pictures. The pic-

tures are black-and-white drawings that depict women and men in work activities.

*Administration.*   The *R–FVII* can be administered to individuals or to groups of students. The examiner reads the directions to the

**TABLE 17.2** *Tests of Work-Related Behaviors, Skills, and Aptitudes*

| Instrument | Individuals | Characteristics |
|---|---|---|
| *A Day in the Life* (Curriculum Associates, 1997) | All disabilities | Evaluates student skills in food service, health, maintenance, retail, clerical, and customer service<br>Computer program |
| *BRIGANCE® Employability Skills Inventory* (Brigance, 1995) | All disabilities | Criterion-referenced |
| *Career Ability Placement Survey (CAPS)* (Knapp and Knapp, 1994) | Mild disabilities<br>Grade 7 through adult | Measures abilities that focus on entry requirements for 14 occupational clusters |
| *Career Planner's Portfolio* (Forest, 1996) | Mild disabilities<br>Grade 5 through adult | Portfolio assessment; self-discovery, educational goals, career choice |
| *Differential Aptitude Tests, Fifth Edition (DAT)* (Bennett, Seashore, and Wesman, 1990) | Mild disabilities<br>Grade 7 through adult | Norm-referenced; verbal reasoning, language usage, numerical reasoning, mechanical reasoning, and space relations<br>Use with Career Interest Inventory |
| *Employability Skills* (Nelson Thomson Learning, 1995) | Mild disabilities | Portfolio assessment; career, educational and personal goals |
| *Kaufman Functional Academic Skills Test (K–FAST)* (Kaufman and Kaufman, 1995) | Mild cognitive disabilities, behavioral disabilities | Norm-referenced, standardized test; assesses performance in reading and mathematics applied to daily life situations |
| *Life-Centered Career Education (LCCE) Knowledge Battery* (Brolin, 1992) | Mild cognitive disabilities, behavioral disabilities | Curriculum-based assessment associated with the LCCE Curriculum |
| *Life-Centered Career Education (LCCE) Performance Battery* (Brolin, 1992) | Mild cognitive disabilities, behavioral disabilities | Criterion-referenced assessment associated with the LCCE Curriculum |
| *Quality of Life Questionnaire* (Schalock and Keith, 1993) | Mild to severe cognitive disabilities<br>Ages 18+ years | Assesses levels of satisfaction, productivity, independence, community integration |
| *Quality of Student Life Questionnaire* (Keith and Schalock, 1995) | All disabilities<br>Ages 14 years through 25 years | Assesses levels of satisfaction, well being, social belonging, and control<br>Interview |

*(continued)*

**TABLE 17.2** *Continued*

| Instrument | Individuals | Characteristics |
|---|---|---|
| *Scales of Independent Behavior–Revised (SIB–R)* (Bruininks, Woodcock, Weatherman, and Hill, 1996) | All disabilities | Norm-referenced; motor skills, social interaction and communications skills, personal living skills, and community living skills |
| *The Ark's Self-Determination Scale* (Wehmeyer and Kelchner, 1995) | All disabilities | Student self-report; global self-determination, autonomy, self-regulation, psychological empowerment, and self-awareness |
| *Transition Behavior Scale* (McCarney and Anderson, 2000) | All disabilities | Assesses work-related behaviors, interpersonal skills, social and community expectations<br>Rated by at least three individuals |
| *Transition Planning Inventory* (Clark and Patton, 1997) | All disabilities | Assesses skills related to employment, education, daily living, leisure, community integration, health communication, interpersonal relationships<br>Rating scale completed by student, parent/guardian, and school personnel |
| *Transition-to-Work Inventory (TWI)* (Friedman, Cameron, and Fletcher, 1996) | Severe disabilities | Job analysis, worker analysis, accommodations and job redesign |
| *Work Adjustment Inventory (WAI)* (Gilliam, 1994) | All disabilities | Norm-referenced<br>Activity, empathy, sociability, assertiveness, adaptability, and emotionality |
| *World of Work Inventory (WOWI)* (Ripley, Hudson, and Neidert, 1992) | Mild disabilities | Norm-referenced vocational training potentials, job satisfaction indicators, career interest activities. Modified version written at fifth-grade level. |

test takers and the test takers circle the drawings that depict the work that they prefer to do. The students require no reading.

*Scoring.* The consumable student booklets are hand scored. Raw scores transform to T-scores, percentiles, and stanines. Scores that fall above the 75th percentile indicate areas of high interest; scores falling below the 25th percentile indicate areas of low interest.

*Standardization.* The *R–FVII* was standardized on over 8,000 students with mild mental retardation or learning disabilities in

**TABLE 17.3** *Interest Inventories*

| Instrument | Grade Level | Reading Level | Administration Time |
|---|---|---|---|
| *APTICOM Occupational Interest Inventory* (Vocational Research Institute, 1991) | Grade 9 through adult | Grade 4 | 90 minutes |
| *Career Interest Inventory* (Impara and Plake, 1998) | Grade 7 through adult | Grades 7 through adult | 30 minutes |
| *Kuder Career Search with Person Match* (Zytowski, 2000) | Grade 7 through adult | Grade 6 | 30 minutes |
| *Career IQ and Interest Test* (PRO-ED, 1997) | Grade 7 through adult | Grade 5 | 25 minutes to 40 minutes |
| *Kuder General Interest Survey–Form E* (Kuder, 1988) | Grades 6 through 12 | Grade 6 | 40 minutes |
| *Kuder Occupational Interest Survey–Form DD* (Kuder, 1985) | Grade 10 through adult | Grade 6 | 60 minutes |
| *Occupational Aptitude Survey and Interest Schedule* (2nd ed.) (OASIS–2) (Parker, 1991) | Grades 8 through 12 | Not reported | 30 minutes |
| *Reading-Free Vocational Interest Inventory–2* (Becker, 2000) | Grade 9 through adult | No reading required | 20 minutes |
| *Strong Interest Inventory* (Campbell and Hansen, 1993) | Grade 8 through adult | Grade 8 | 60 minutes |

grades 7 through 12. In addition, adult norms derived from the test performance of over 3,000 adults with mental retardation and economic or environmental disadvantages. Although the test manual describes a study of students in grades 7 through 12 who showed moderate mental retardation, the norm tables do not incorporate this information. However, the manual suggests that the norms are appropriate for students who show moderate mental retardation.

*Reliability.* Test-retest and internal consistency reliability is adequate, with coefficients generally in the .70s and .80s.

*Validity.* Although the manual states that experts reviewed the items, the description of content validity is sketchy. Concurrent validity was determined by comparing the *R–FVII* with the 1964 revision of the *Geist Picture Interest*

*Inventory* (Geist, 1964). The description of construct validity is limited.

*Summary.* The *Reading-Free Vocational Interest Inventory–2* measures the vocational interests of students with mild mental retardation or learning disabilities who are in grades 7 through 12. The norms need updating to reflect recent census figures. Reliability is adequate; validity is limited. The author should provide evidence of predictive validity so that users can make predictions about vocational interests and actual vocations that are pursued.

### Adaptive Behavior and Life Skills

The *Responsibility and Independence Scale for Adolescents (RISA)* (Salvia, Neisworth, and Schmidt, 1990) is a norm-referenced measure of adolescent adaptive behavior intended for use with students who are between the ages of 12 years and 19 years, 11 months. See Chapter 14 for a detailed description of this instrument.

### Work Samples

Work samples assess students' skills, aptitudes, job preferences, and ability to profit from vocational training. Work sampling evaluates abilities on tasks that simulate actual job tasks. Most commercial work sample systems are based on the *Dictionary of Occupational Titles (DOT)* (U.S. Department of Labor, 1991), a system developed by the U.S. Department of Labor that classifies occupations. Work samples are also helpful in evaluating the progress a student makes in a vocational training program.

In addition to commercial systems, evaluators can construct their own work samples and job simulations. Evaluators must conduct observations of students during vocational training and while working in actual jobs, and also collect information from interviews with job supervisors and written evaluations. Table 17.4 describes commercial work sample systems.

## Connecting Assessment with Instruction

### Curriculum-Based Vocational Assessment

**Curriculum-based vocational assessment (CBVA)** is a type of curriculum-based assessment used in planning and developing vocational education opportunities for students with disabilities (Albright and Cobb, 1988). Conceptually,

**TABLE 17.4   *Work Evaluation Systems***

| Instrument | Reading Level | Group/Individual Administration | Time |
|---|---|---|---|
| *Career Exploration Program* (New Concepts Career Development Corporation, 2000) | No reading | Small group/ individual | 45 minutes |
| *McCarron-Dial Evaluation System* (McCarron and Dial, 1996) | No reading | Individual | 2 to 3 hours |
| *Talent Assessment Program* (Nighswonger, 2001) | No reading | Small group/ individual | 2 to 3 hours |

CBVA is different from traditional vocational assessment, which focuses on occupational areas and consists of formal, standardized measures. Albright and Cobb describe CBVA as an integral aspect of the three different stages of a student's program and list the types of questions on which the assessment should focus at each stage. For example, the first stage of the assessment process occurs prior to and during the first weeks of a student's participation in a vocational program. The sample questions at this stage are: "Which vocational program is most appropriate for the student? What are the special service needs of the student in this particular program? What will be the criteria used to determine student success?" (p. 16).

The second stage of assessment is an ongoing process of evaluation as the student progresses in the vocational education program. The sample questions include: "How is the student performing in the vocational setting? What changes are needed in the student's program?" (p. 16).

The third stage of the assessment process begins when the student exits the program. The sample questions include: "What are the special services needed to help the student transition into employment and/or postsecondary education? Which adult service agencies need to be linked up to the student? How will student adjustment be monitored?" (p. 16).

Lombard, Larsen, and Westphal (1993) developed another approach to CBVA. The Teach Prep Assessment Model consists of five steps named MAGIC. The first step (M) is Making a prediction for the student's future. Informal assessment in this phase involves gathering information about the student's needs, preferences, and interests, and formal assessment consists of the evaluation of occupational interests, vocational aptitude, academic skills, and learning style. The second step (A) is Assess entry-level skills. During this step CBVA is conducted. In the third step (G), Guide skill acquisition to skill mastery, teachers and other personnel conduct a discrepancy analysis between the student's current skills and the entry-level target skills and

develop goals and objectives. The fourth step (I) is Instruct for generalization, and it focuses on using skills in multiple settings. The final step (C) is Conduct maintenance checks. During this last step, there is ongoing assessment to monitor student performance as well as the curriculum and instruction. The final step includes evaluation of both student and program.

Students or employees can assist in monitoring their own demonstration of work-related behaviors and skills. A simple checklist that uses icons is ideal for this purpose (Figure 17.4).

## Performance-Based Assessment

Chapter 7 describes portfolio assessment as the deliberate collection of the products of a student's work in order to demonstrate the student's efforts, progress, and achievement. When applied to transition assessment, portfolios document the transition needs and preferences of students. Documentation of a student's transition needs can include work samples, audiotapes, videotapes, inventories, checklists, observations, and self-reports.

A portfolio that documents transition needs and preferences produces a rich, detailed portrait of the student. It depicts the student in natural work and living environments and provides continuous information, feedback, and growth toward transition needs and goals. Further, portfolio assessment can link interventions directly to the student's activities.

In addition to the assessment tools this chapter describes, the assessment of transition needs can include many of the procedures that previous chapters describe, including:

- oral descriptions
- written descriptions
- checklists and questionnaires
- interviews
- conferences
- student journals and notebooks
- discussions between students, parents, and teachers.

Name: _____

Observer: _____    Date: _____

| I can... | | Yes | No |
|---|---|---|---|
| Tell the time to go to work. | 9:00 AM | | |
| Put on an apron. | | | |
| Find the aisle that needs to be cleaned. | 3 — Coffee — Cereal — Tea — Breakfast food | | |
| Sweep the aisle. • Get the broom • Sweep the aisle and sweep dirt into dustpan • Put dirt in the trash • Put the broom away | | | |
| Mop the aisle. • Get the mop and bucket • Fill the bucket with soapy water • Get the mop wet • Wring out the mop • Mop the aisle • Rinse out the mop • Dump out the water • Put the mop and bucket away | | | |
| Straighten the shelves. | | | |

FIGURE 17.4    *A Picture/Symbol Checklist*

## Preferred Practices

The overall intent of transition assessment is to assist students in making a transition from school to post-school activities, including postsecondary education, vocational training, integrated employment (including supported employment), continuing and adult education, adult services, independent living, and community participation. Transition assessment must include the evaluation of vocational, career, academic, personal, social, and living needs. The assessment of transition needs and preferences

*Friends share a laugh together.*

is an **outcome-oriented process** that begins when the child is young and takes place over a period of time.

Transition assessment involves person-centered planning. This means that the student with the disability engages in an active meaningful way with parents, educators, community members and others during the assessment, planning, and service delivery processes. Person-centered planning focuses on self-determination and on the students' hopes, dreams, and desires.

Cooperation between experts and inter-agency collaboration are essential to the assessment process. Professionals who come from a variety of disciplines and incorporate input from parents, caregivers, and the student should conduct the assessment of transition needs and preferences. Collaboration is important to the success of a student's transition.

A variety of assessment tools is available to conduct transition assessment. These include standardized instruments, curriculum-based assessment, performance-based assessment, direct observation, checklists, and informal approaches. Much more experimentation with various assessment methods, especially in how and when to use them, is necessary in order to continue to develop approaches that educators can apply with confidence.

## Extending Learning

1. After reviewing the purposes of transition assessment, identify specific assessment tools and approaches that fit these purposes.
2. Ideally, at what age should transition assessment begin. Why?
3. How can performance-based assessment contribute to the assessment of transition needs and preferences?
4. Visit a local school and interview a special education teacher who helps provide

transition services. What types of assessment instruments and approaches does this teacher use with students in transition planning? Share your findings with the class.

5. Interview a school guidance counselor or a rehabilitation counselor regarding transition services and assessment approaches that the school offers to students. Share your findings with the class.

## References

Albright, L., and R. B. Cobb (1988). Curriculum-based vocational assessment: A concept whose time has come. *Journal for Vocational Special Needs Education* 10(2): 13–16.

Becker, R. L. (2000). *Reading-free vocational interest inventory–2.* Lutz, FL: Psychological Assessment Resources.

Bennett, G. K., H. G. Seashore, and A. G. Wesman (1990). *Differential aptitude tests, fifth edition.* San Antonio, TX: The Psychological Corporation.

Blackorby, J., and M. Wagner (1996). Longitudinal post-school outcomes of youth with disabilities: Findings from the national longitudinal transition study. *Exceptional Children* 62: 399–413.

Brigance, A. H. (1981). *BRIGANCE® inventory of essential skills.* No. Billerica, MA: Curriculum Associates.

Brigance, A. H. (1984). *BRIGANCE® assessment of basic skills–Spanish edition.* No. Billerica, MA: Curriculum Associates.

Brigance, A. H. (1994). *BRIGANCE® life skills inventory.* No. Billerica, MA: Curriculum Associates.

Brigance, A. H. (1995). *BRIGANCE® employability skills inventory.* No. Billerica, MA: Curriculum Associates.

Brigance, A. H. (1999). *BRIGANCE® comprehensive inventory of basic skills.* No. Billerica, MA: Curriculum Associates.

Brolin, D. E. (1992). *Life-centered career education (LCCE) knowledge and performance batteries.* Reston, VA: The Council for Exceptional Children.

Bruininks, R. H., R. W. Woodcock, R. F. Weatherman, and B. K. Hill (1996). *Scales of independent behavior–revised.* Itasca, IL: Riverside Publishing.

Campbell, D. P., and J. Hansen (1993). *Strong interest inventory.* Stanford, CA: Stanford University Press.

Carl D. Perkins Vocational and Applied Technology Act (PL 99–457). (1990). Washington, DC: U.S. Government Printing Office.

Clark, G.M. (1996). Transition planning assessment for secondary-level students with learning disabilities. *Journal of Learning Disabilities* 29: 79–92.

Clark, G. M., and J. R. Patton (1997). *Transition planning inventory.* Columbia, MO: Hawthorne Educational Services.

Curriculum Associates (1997). *A day in the life: Assessment and instruction.* No. Billerica, MA: Curriculum Associates.

Forest, R. G. (1996). *Career planner's portfolio: A school-to-work assessment tool.* No. Billerica, MA: Curriculum Associates.

Friedman, L., C. Cameron, and J. Fletcher (1996). *Transition-to-work inventory: A job placement system for workers with severe disabilities.* San Antonio, TX: The Psychological Corporation.

Gilliam, J. E. (1994). *Work adjustment inventory.* Austin, TX: The Psychological Corporation.

Halpern, A. S. (1994). The transition of youth with disabilities to adult life: A position statement of the division on career development and transition, the Council for Exceptional Children. *Career Development for Exceptional Individuals* 17: 115–124.

Hutchins, M. P., and A. Renzaglia (1998). Interviewing families for effective transition to employment. *Teaching Exceptional Children* 30, 72–78.

Impara, J.C., and B. S. Plake (eds.) (1998). *Career interest inventory.* San Antonio, TX: The Psychological Corporation.

Individuals with Disabilities Education Act Amendments. PL 101–476. 7 October 1991. Washington, DC: U.S. Government Printing Office.

Kaufman, A. S., and N. L. Kaufman (1995). *Kaufman functional academic skills test (K–FAST).* Circle Pines, MN: American Guidance Service.

Knapp, L. F., and R. R. Knapp (1994). *Career Ability Placement Survey.* San Diego: EdITS/Educational and Industrial Testing Service.

Krieg, F. J., P. Brown, and J. Ballard (1995). *Transition: School to work.* Bethesda, MD: National Association of School Psychologists.

Kuder, G. F. (1985). *Kuder occupational interest survey–Form DD.* Chicago: Science Research Associates.

Kuder, G. F. (1988). *Kuder general interest inventory–Form E.* Chicago: Science Research Associates.

Lombard, R. C., K. A. Larsen, and S. E. Westphal (1993). Validation of vocational assessment services for special populations in tech-prep: A model for translating the Perkins assurances into practice. *Journal for Vocational Special Needs Education* 16(1): 14–22.

McCarney, S. B., and P. D. Anderson (2000). *Transition behavior scale.* Columbia, MO: Hawthorne Educational Service.

McCarron, L., and J. G. Dial (1996). *McCarron-Dial evaluation system.* Dallas, TX: McCarron-Dial Systems.

National Council on Disability and the Social Security Administration. 2000. Transition and post-school outcomes for youth with disabilities: Closing the gaps to post-secondary education and employment [online]. Retrieved November 2000. Available: http://www.ned.gov.

Nelson Thomson Learning (1995). *Employability skills.* Scarborough, ON, Canada: Nelson Thomson Learning.

New Concepts Career Development Corporation (2000). *Career Exploration Program.* Tucson, AZ: New Concepts Career Development Corporaiton.

Nighswonger, J. (2001). *Talent Assessment Program.* Jacksonville, FL: Talent Assessment.

Parker, R. (1991). *Occupational aptitude survey and interest schedule.* 2d ed. Austin, TX: PRO-ED.

PRO-ED (1997). *Career IQ and interest test.* Austin, TX: PRO-ED.

Ripley, R., K. Hudson, and G. P. M. Neidert (1992). *World of Work Inventory.* Tempe, AZ: World of Work.

Salvia, J., J. T. Neisworth, and M. W. Schmidt (1990). *Responsibility and independence scale for adolescents.* Allen, TX: DLM.

Schalock, R. L., and K. D. Keith (1993). *Quality of life questionnaire.* Worthington, OH: IDS.

Schalock, R. L., and K. D. Keith (1995). *Quality of student life questionnaire.* Worthington, OH: IDS.

Sitlington, P. L. (1996). Transition assessment—Where have we been and where should we be going. *Career Development for Exceptional Individuals* 19: 163.

Sitlington, P. L., D. A. Neubert, W. Begun, R. C. Lombard, and P. J. Leconte (1996). *Assess for success.* Reston, VA: Council for Exceptional Children.

U.S. Department of Labor (1991). *Dictionary of occupational titles.* 4th ed. Washington, DC: U.S. Government Printing Office.

Vocational Research Institute (1991). *APTICOM occupational interest inventory.* Philadelphia: Vocational Research Institute.

Wehmeyer, M. L., and K. Kelchner (1995). *The Ark's self-determination scale.* Arlington, TX: The Ark of the United States.

Wehman, P. (2001). *Life beyond the classroom.* 3rd ed. Baltimore, MD: Paul H. Brookes.

Wehman, P., J. M. Everson, and D. H. Reid (2001). Beyond Programs and Placements. In *Life beyond the classroom* ed. P. Wehman, pp. 91–124. Baltimore: Paul H. Brookes.

Zytowski, D. G. (2000). *Kuder career search with person match.* Adel, IA: National Career Assessment Center.

# 18

## *Interpreting Tests and Writing Reports*

## Overview

Synthesizing and interpreting assessment information is the culmination of the assessment process. The assessment report communicates what has been learned about the student and makes recommendations based on the assess-ment results. This chapter is a discussion of how to synthesize and interpret assessment information and how to complete an effective written report.

## Chapter Objectives _____

After completing this chapter, you should be able to:

- Discuss the process of interpreting assessment results.
- Explain the general principles that guide the development of assessment reports.
- Describe the components of an assessment report.

- Explain considerations in sharing reports with the student and with family members.
- Discuss the use of computer-generated test results and reports.

## What Shapes Our Views

The interpretation of assessment results involves the practitioner in a series of analyses—in examining the assessment data, explaining the results, and clarifying the information. In interpreting results, the examiner focuses on the assessment questions to give meaning to the information. Interpretation begins with an examination of the student's overall performance and then moves to a consideration of each of the appropriately measured behaviors, skills, and abilities.

Interpreting data takes practice and skill. Cohen, Stern, and Balaban (1983) suggest the following questions: "Can we verify every statement we make? Do we have evidence for our hunches and our guesses?" (p. 202). The more you use a test or conduct an observation or complete an interview, the more you will come to understand the information that can be gathered and how it can be interpreted. One method of interpreting results is a process called hypothesis generation.

## Generating a Hypothesis

When interpreting the results of testing, we prefer the process described as hypothesis generation (Kaufman, 1979, 1994; McGrew, 1986, 1994) or integrative interpretation (Kamphaus, 1993). In test interpretation, a hypothesis is an explanation of a student's performance and behavior based on the collected assessment data.

As the examiner reviews the assessment information, several hypotheses will emerge. One hypothesis will relate to the referral questions; other hypotheses may relate to levels of achievement, behavior, cognitive ability, communication, development, functioning, motor development, or sensory functioning.

The examiner will use the test data (i.e., the results of the various assessment approaches, including standardized testing, curriculum-based assessment, performance-based assessment, observations, interviews, and so on) to support one or more hypotheses. For example, an examiner may integrate information obtained from interviews with teachers, therapists, support staff, the student, and family members with information obtained from behavioral observations of the student to support the determination of attention-deficit hyperactivity disorder.

Kaufman, discussing his approach to test interpretation, cautions examiners to remember that hypotheses "are not facts and may indeed prove to be artifacts" (Kaufman, 1979, p. 177). Hypotheses are informed assumptions; when evidence does not substantiate hypotheses further investigation is necessary. The test data may need reanalyzation, or the examiner may have to collect additional data to generate new or modified hypotheses.

## Examiner Bias

Examiner bias can arise in the interpretation of assessment results. Examiners need to be aware of the types of biases in order to identify and control them. Bias colors how the data will be viewed and interpreted.

Bentzen (1993) describes two levels of potential bias. At one level is the personal bias and perspective of the examiner; the examiner brings individual experiences, abilities, attitudes, and knowledge to the interpretation process. Examiners need to take precautions in not letting personal bias interfere with the careful, objective interpretation of information. The second level of bias is the result of formal training and includes bias shaped by theory, conceptual framework, or philosophy. These biases affect how you interpret a situation, event, or behavior.

## Using Professional Knowledge

To interpret test results, the examiner must understand the purpose of the test itself, how it is administered, and what the test scores mean. In our discussion of norm-referenced tests and standardization samples in Chapter 3, you learned that a standardized test can be administered to students with characteristics that are similar to the norm group and that the examiner can compare the student's score with those of the norm group. In interpreting test results, the examiner must consider the norm sample of a test instrument; if the characteristics of the student tested are not similar to those of the norm group, the examiner will need to explain how this affects the test scores. The test scores of students who have characteristics different from the norm sample cannot be compared with the test scores of the students who participated in the standardization of the instrument.

Examiners need to understand the test scores and be able to explain them to others. For example, an examiner may be called upon to explain the difference between a percentile rank and a percentage-correct score or to clarify misperceptions about a grade equivalent score or standard score.

In interpreting assessment information, the examiner must be a keen observer of behavior and of environmental conditions that adversely affect student performance. In previous chapters we examine the effects of the physical, learning, and social environments on performance. Observations of the environment and of the student will add valuable information. As the examiner synthesizes assessment results, the observations may corroborate information obtained during formal testing, or these observations may help to explain why a student's score was unexpectedly low.

Interpreting assessment information requires a wide range of knowledge concerning child and adolescent growth and development as well as disability. Examiners need professional knowledge of classroom curriculum and pedagogy, and a solid understanding of statistics is essential in interpreting test scores. Knowledge of special education, related services, state regulations, and federal law is essential in clarifying the information.

## Responding to Diversity

In previous chapters we discuss problems of test bias regarding students who come from diverse cultural, ethnic, racial and linguistic backgrounds, geographic regions of origin, and gender, disability, and economic groups. Examiners must be aware not only that standardized instruments but other assessment approaches can show bias. For example, in Chapter 7 we examine how portfolio assessments are, for the most part, biased toward students who attend school infrequently.

We know that the purpose for one of the assessment steps, determining eligibility, is to identify students with disabilities who need special education services. Lyman (1986) describes these instruments:

Any test that is worthwhile must discriminate; after all, this is just another way of saying that it will "reveal individual differences." But the intended discrimination should be on the basis of the trait being measured, not on the basis of racial or ethnic background. (pp. 7–8)

## General Principles for Report Writing

The following general principles guide the development of a well-written report.

### Organize the Information

Organize the information systematically. Present information in sections with appropriate headings. Discuss conclusions and recommendations at the end of the report; do not insert them in the body of the document.

### Relate Only the Facts

Report only factual information. Do not include unsubstantiated information. When including information from other sources, such as other assessment reports, mention the date and name of the sources.

### Include Only Essential Information

Write about the facts, but avoid extraneous information about the student or family. Although your report must be comprehensive, some information is not essential; you will need to make judgments about whether what you have learned is appropriate for inclusion. Use only information that contributes to the understanding of the student, the test results, and recommendations.

### Be Aware of Bias

Avoid generalizations that can bias the report. Be careful about stereotyping groups. Critically review your report before submitting it.

### Present Accurate Information

Make sure that the information is accurate. Review the information to check for accuracy. When calculating test scores on the test form, be sure to double-check your work. Some tests require scores of several different types, and it is easy to make errors converting from one type of test score to another. The examiner must always verify that the test scores were copied correctly from the test to the report. Be sure that there are no misinterpretations about performance due to inaccurate calculations or inaccurate copying.

### Include Any Reservations

Incorporate, and discuss fully, any reservations about the assessment process and its effect on the results. Reservations may include observations of the student that indicate the results are not accurate or do not reflect the student's best abilities. Record any interruptions or other disturbances in the environment that may have affected the results, and note the limitations in technical adequacy of the instrument(s) for students with characteristics that the norming sample does not represent.

### Avoid Technical Jargon

Use clear, understandable language. Avoid discussion of the formulas used to measure discrepancies or of the theoretical perspectives of various experts. Technical jargon can make the report confusing or ambiguous. How could the language in the following excerpt be simplified?

> Tony has dual diagnostic deficits that affect expressive and receptive language, articulation, internal regulation, and cognition. A coexisting diagnosis can be made of Attention-Deficit Hyperactive Disorder and mental retardation. This diagnosis is strongly suggested by biological maternal history of ethanol abuse, apparently during the gestational period and Tony's striking physiognomy.

### Write Clearly

Work to develop report-writing skills. Use the writing process to create a working draft. Reread and rewrite the working draft. Check the draft for grammatical mistakes and punctuation errors. Use the spell check feature of your word processing program. Avoid ambiguous language. Use a checklist like that found in Table 18.1 later in this chapter to ensure that you have included all the necessary information.

## Types of Assessment Reports

Assessment reports are written for a variety of purposes, and the information they contain varies accordingly. Reports are written to (1) summarize a series of observations and synthesize the observational data, (2) report student progress over a period of time, (3) describe the results of administering an individual test, and (4) integrate and interpret the results of a comprehensive assessment.

### Reports of Observations

A teacher customarily writes a report providing a synthesis of several observations conducted on a student. We have discussed the importance of conducting multiple observations to obtain an accurate sample of student behavior. The written report organizes the information the teacher collected from all the observations.

**How to Write an Observation Report.** Examiners should complete a written observation as soon as possible after the final observation. Observation reports include the following information:

1. *Student information:* Includes name, date of birth, age, grade, and teacher's name.
2. *Dates of observations.*
3. *Purpose(s) for conducting the observations:* The observations may focus on the environment

or on the student. Clearly state the purpose of the observations and define the events or behaviors in observable terms.

4. *Setting(s) in which the observations took place.*
5. *Description of the environments:* Includes the physical, learning, and social aspects.
6. *Behavioral observations:* Be sure to relate only observed information. Do not interpret or make judgments.
7. *Discussion:* Summarize your observations of the environment and the student's behavior. Include your interpretation of the assessment data.
8. *Recommendations:* State realistic suggestions for implementing progress or improvement.

The Snapshot about John Diamond on page 486 illustrates an observation report written by the special education consultant.

**How to Represent Information Graphically.** Graphs allow us to illustrate information not readily available in a text format or on a data sheet. Graphs permit the viewer to think about the substance of the data and encourage the eye to compare different data (Tufte, 1983). Graphically displayed data enhance understanding and serve to highlight findings that may be embedded in the observation forms and not apparent on examination of the forms (Nicolson and Shipstead, 1994). Two commonly used types of graphs are

1. *Pie charts:* Pie charts are most useful in displaying percentages of data when the examiner wants to illustrate parts of a whole.
2. *Bar graphs:* Bar graphs are most useful in displaying frequency counts or plotting trends over time.

Let's examine these two methods within the context of an assessment question: "During math class, how much time is Cindy actively engaged in math-related activities?" Math-related activities are defined here as looking at the teacher during the class lesson, working with paper and

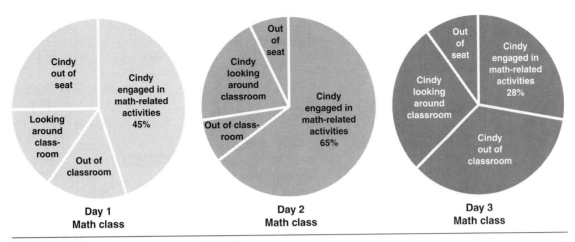

**FIGURE 18.1** *Data Presentation in Pie Charts*

pencil on math problems, and discussing solutions to the math problems with peers. The observer collected data over a period of three days. The data analysis indicated that Cindy engaged in several behaviors during the class period: she was out of her seat, out of the classroom, looking around the room, and engaged in math-related activities.

The three pie charts in Figure 18.1 allow comparison of Cindy's behavior on each day of the observation. A bar graph represents the same data as in Figure 18.2. The discussion in the assessment report could center on the types of teaching and learning strategies that were used on the different days or on the reasons why Cindy was out of her seat or out of the classroom. The pie chart allows us to see the whole period of time available for mathematics and how Cindy spent this time over the period observed.

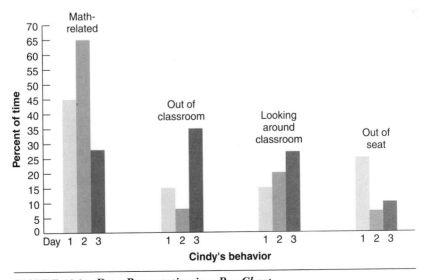

**FIGURE 18.2** *Data Presentation in a Bar Chart*

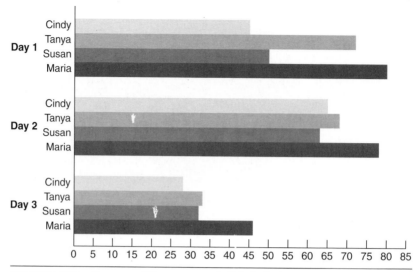

**FIGURE 18.3** *Percent of Engagement in Math-Related Activity for Four Students over Three Days*

The bar graph allows us to see the percentage of time Cindy was out of her seat, out of the classroom, looking around, and engaged in a math activity over the three-day period by activity. The discussion in the assessment report could compare Cindy's behaviors over the observation period. Which type of graph do you think best displays the data in answer to the observation question? (The answer is found at the end of the activities in Extending Learning.)

In earlier chapters we discuss the need to compare the target student with one or more other students about whom the teacher has no concern. Variations of bar graphs allow us to compare several students and provide additional information regarding whether or not the target student's (Cindy's) behavior is atypical (Figure 18.3).

## Progress Reports

Progress reports are a summary of the advances a student makes during a specific time period and provide a link to the IEP, which requires

---

**SNAPSHOT** ■ *Observation Report on John Diamond*

The special education consultant, Marilyn Fillbrick, was asked to observe an eighth-grade student, John, in his regular classroom. At the time, John was receiving speech therapy and had been referred to the school psychologist because the team was concerned with John's aggressive behavior. According to the eighth-grade teacher, "He is always in motion. He frequently hits and pushes other students, and he is verbally abusive."

Marilyn met with John's teacher to discuss John's problem behaviors more fully. The meeting helped to clarify the behaviors that were of concern and to plan the best time and place to conduct the observations. Marilyn decided to develop her own observation instrument based on an interval recording method described in Chapter 5.

After completing her observations, Marilyn wrote an observation report that summarized the

**SNAPSHOT** ■ *Continued*

findings. She also developed a graph to help explain the observation data. A copy of the graph (Figure 18.4) and one of her data sheets (Figure 18.5) that she developed to help explain her data follow her written report.

### Observation Report

*Name:* John Diamond

*Birth Date:* 9/21/xx

*Age:* 13 years, 2 months

*Grade:* 8

*Teacher:* Dara Hall

*Dates of Observations:* 11/1/xx; 11/4/xx; 11/8/xx

*Observer:* Marilyn Fillbrick

*Purpose of Observations:* The assessment team requested classroom observations because of concerns regarding John's behavior problems. Specific concerns include: his out-of-seat behavior, hitting and pushing other students, and verbally abusing others. The purpose of the observations was to determine the degree to which John actually engages in the behaviors of concern.

*Setting:* Students change classes for each subject. Three observations were conducted over a two-week period; John was observed in mathematics and language arts classes and during the lunch period. Each observation consisted of 30 minutes and took place between 9:00 and 11:00 a.m.

*Observations of the Environment:* The classrooms are designed for small group work with student desks clustered in groups of four. Students are not assigned a particular desk but are free to choose where to work. The classrooms consisted of 20–23 students with one teacher and occasional other support staff.

*Behavioral Observations:* Results of the observations indicate that John did indeed display many aggressive behaviors. John pushed and poked other students 5–6 times during each of the observations; less frequently (3–4 times each observation), he hit and swore at other students and occasionally (2 times each observation) swore at the teacher. These behaviors

usually occurred when students were changing classes.

At other times (5–6 times each observation), John joined the other students in laughter, volunteered answers, helped a student who was having difficulty with finding materials, and participated in activities willingly.

*Discussion:* John engages in pushing, hitting, and poking other students as well as swearing at others, including the teacher. These observations indicate that the teacher continually has to watch him closely, and frequently has to intervene on behalf of the other students.

John's problem behaviors are most apparent when he is listening without being able to be active, when the general noise level in the classroom begins to escalate, and when he is anticipating transition.

Aggression was especially high during transition, with no instances occurring during a spelling activity in which the teacher directed the whole class and each student was actively engaged. Few aggressive behaviors occurred during small group math manipulative activities. Both spelling and math were structured and required him to be more involved.

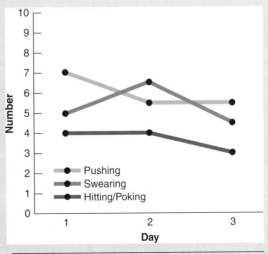

**FIGURE 18.4** *Teacher-Developed Graphs*

*(continued)*

**SNAPSHOT ■ Continued**

John appears to be a happy youngster, laughing and participating in activities willingly, but shows little self-control or regard for his effects on others.

*Recommendations:* John appears to benefit from structured learning activities that include active student participation. Classroom noise should be monitored, as this may have an adverse effect on his behavior. Positive behavior management strategies should be shared with his teacher and other support staff in the class room.

| Name: John | | | | | Date: November 1 |
|---|---|---|---|---|---|
| Two-minute interval | Behavior: p = push, h = hit, s = swear | **Total behaviors** | | | Comments Math class |
| | | p | h | s | |
| 00–02 | | | | | Teacher goes over assignment for following day. John asks questions to clarify. |
| 02–04 | | | | | |
| 04–06 | | || | | IIII | Class changes at 9:05 Behavior occurs during transition and in hallway. |
| 06–08 | | || | |||| | | Hits and pokes the boy behind him. |
| 08–10 | | | | | Other occurrences? —unable to follow John closely during this period. |
| 10–12 | | | | || | Language arts class begins at 9:12. |
| 12–14 | | | | | | Helps student find materials. |
| 14–16 | | | | | Volunteers to assist teacher. |
| 28–30 | | | | | |

**FIGURE 18.5    *Teacher-Developed Data Sheet***

periodic monitoring of the student's progress. Progress reports must relate information about the student with reference to these goals and intended outcomes of the IEP. Teachers can prepare these reports to accompany a report card at the end of the marking period or to provide an update of information to family and other team members. One example of a progress report is a checklist (Figure 18.6).

### Individual Test Reports

Individual test reports describe the test results and the examiner's interpretation of the student's performance. Usually, these reports are shared at the team meeting and become part of the student's permanent record. Individual reports of tests present a limited account of a student's performance, thus they may be combined later into a comprehensive assessment report to provide more complete information on the student.

Each member of the team who conducts an assessment of the student must complete a written test report. At the team meeting, reports by several examiners, such as the special education teacher, the school psychologist, the physical or occupational therapist, or the speech and language pathologist, are considered.

### Comprehensive Assessment Reports

A comprehensive assessment report is usually extensive; it summarizes what we know about the student and what we have learned from the results of a thorough assessment. Typically, a comprehensive report relies on the many sources of assessment information that we describe in this book.

### Writing the Report

Examiners should organize individual test reports and comprehensive test reports according to the following areas:

1. Identifying data
2. Reason for referral
3. Background information
4. Family involvement
5. Observations of the environment
6. Behavioral observations
7. Tests, interviews, and performance-based assessment
8. Discussion of the results
9. Summary
10. Recommendations

**FIGURE 18.6** *Progress Report*

| *Second Marking Period* | In Progress | Mastered |
|---|---|---|
| 1. Uses correct punctuation to end a sentence. | | × |
| 2. Uses correct form of *you're* and *your*. | × | |
| 3. Uses commas in a series correctly. | | × |
| 4. Correctly places apostrophe in contractions and possessives. | × | |
| 5. Uses correct form of *their*, *there*, and *they're*. | × | |
| 6. Uses correct form of adjectives. | × | |

Each area should be a separate section. Use appropriate subheadings to help organize the report, as suggested by the lists in the sections that follow.

### Identifying the Data

Information in the first section of the report identifies the student, the parents, the school, the test, and the examiner:

1. *About the student:* include the student's name, address, phone number, chronological age in years and months, birth date, and gender.
2. *About the family:* include the names and addresses of family members.
3. *About the school:* include the student's grade level, school's name, address, phone number, director or principal's name, and teacher's name.
4. *About the testing:* include the name of the examiner, the date of testing, and the date the report was written.

School records, the referral form, interviews with family members or teachers, records of administered tests, and so forth are standard sources for this information.

### Reason for Referral

The second section contains a summary of the reasons for referral and the name of the person who initiated the referral. Throughout the report, be sure to directly address the reasons for referral and make sure the conclusions and recommendations refer to them. As the report develops, one of its central themes will be the grounds for the referral and the extent to which the testing addressed these issues. Obtain this information from the referral form and from interviews with family members, teachers, and staff.

### Background Information

Briefly summarize information about the student's background—the student's education, family history, medical care, and previous assessment results.

Medical history can include a description of any unusual medical problems, diagnoses, extended hospital stays, continuing medical care, general health, and results of vision and hearing testing. Some students have experienced early and prolonged medical interventions; some of these students may have had extended hospital stays and received extensive care for genetic abnormalities or other conditions. Their medical folders can be quite lengthy, and the examiner will need to judge which information is pertinent to the reason for referral. Extensive discussion of a student's medical history may bias the reader to think that the child has a severe disability or may be unusually difficult to manage.

Facts such as dates of attendance, regularity of attendance, type of placement or services in place, performance, interventions tried, and results of previous educational testing is available from school records, interviews, and home visits. A summary of child care experiences, depending on the age of the student, is also important.

Details of familial and/or cultural background can be useful, but use this type of information carefully and judiciously and only when it is relevant and helps to explain the behavior of the student or the results of testing. Knowledge about the family and cultural background is customarily obtained from interviews with the student, family members, teachers, and other professionals, and through a home visit.

### Family Involvement

As members of the assessment team, parents can assist in identifying strengths and needs of their child and in gathering information by keeping logs, checklists, and other written documents. They also make observations or collect information by tape-recording or videotaping their child. In addition, family members contribute description and understanding through the interview process. Note the information family members collect or contribute in the written report.

## Observations of the Environment

The description of the classroom environment includes the physical setting and the learning and social environments. In several previous chapters we discuss important environmental factors and suggest ways to gather information about these aspects of the classroom.

## Behavioral Observations

The report includes a description of the student's behavior during testing. The examiner will want to observe whether the student was cooperative, distractible, attentive, tired, or shy, or exhibited other types of behavior. How did the student approach the testing situation? What was the student's behavior at the beginning of the testing? During the testing? At the end? This section reports any observations conducted in the classroom, playground, cafeteria, or other setting.

As Chapter 5 discusses, systematic observations can be an important source of data. Methodical observations help us to understand the student's behavior and learning strategies and can also inform us about intervention strategies. Nevertheless, observations about behavior in the testing situation may not be generalizable to other settings. Testing assesses a narrow sample of behavior. To a certain extent, the testing situation is artificial, and examiners must consider this when interpreting results and drawing conclusions about a student's behavior (Sattler, 2001). A student's behavior can vary in different settings and with different examiners.

In writing the report, use the following list of behaviors as a starting point for discussion (Sattler, 2001):

- Physical appearance
- Reactions to test session and to the examiner
- General behavior
- Typical mode of relating to the examiner
- Language style
- General response style
- Response to failures
- Response to successes
- Response to encouragement
- Activity level
- Attitude toward self
- Attitude toward the examiner and the testing process
- Visual-motor ability
- Unusual habits, mannerisms, or verbalizations
- Examiner's reaction to the student (p. 728)

## Tests, Interviews, and Performance-Based Assessment

The report includes a list of the tests and assessments, both formal and informal, and the interviews that teachers and others conducted to collect the assessment data.

## Discussion of Results

In listing the results of the assessment instruments, use the same types of scores throughout the section. Standard scores, percentiles, or stanines are preferable. You may report two or more types of scores, such as standard scores and percentiles. Always include the confidence intervals when reporting standard scores. Some examiners like to report scores in a table format within the discussion of the results.

This section of the report includes the interpretation of the assessment results. Include hypothesis generation, discussed earlier in this chapter, in the results section. Analyze each test separately, and then synthesize the results. The following steps for test interpretation are adapted from the works of Kamphaus (1993), Kaufman (1979, 1994), and McGrew (1986, 1994):

*Step 1:* Interpret overall performance. Describe the overall performance of the student on the tests, and supply an interpretation of the full-scale or total score performances.

*Step 2:* Determine relative strengths and needs in each area tested. Make a list of the subtests in each test that represent relative strengths and relative weaknesses. Determine the abilities that each of the subtests represent.

*Step 3:* Compare the subtests on all the tests. Consider each subtest and the abilities it measures. Compare the shared abilities across the test data. If relative strengths and weaknesses do not emerge across the data, then interpret unique abilities.

*Step 4:* Integrate the relative strengths and needs. Identify relative strengths and weaknesses by comparing all the test data, including the results of formal and informal testing, interviews, observations, and background information about the student.

## Summary

This section should be brief. Summarize the major points that have been discussed and synthesize the results. Report the current level of functioning and indicate areas of relative strength and need. Answer the referral questions. Restate the themes that have emerged.

## Recommendations

An assessment is conducted chiefly to answer the referral questions about the student and to develop recommendations. The recommendations should logically stem from the information in the assessment report. Suggest realistic, practical recommendations for implementation. Develop recommendations for the student in a variety of settings, including school, home, and community. Do not include specific goals and objectives in the assessment report; these are to be written in the IEP or IFSP during the team meeting. The following Snapshot about Gina illustrates an example of a comprehensive assessment report.

## Evaluating the Report

Writing an assessment report is an important way to communicate test findings. A report helps you to organize the results of testing systematically, to analyze a student's performance, and to make recommendations. You must write the reports clearly using correct grammar and spelling. Table 18.1 on page 496 illustrates a checklist for use when reviewing the adequacy of assessment reports.

## Sharing Assessment Results with Others

### Family Members

Share assessment results and recommendations with family members as soon as possible after you have completed the report. Look over the test results and make sure that you can explain the test scores. You will want to be careful that your words are not misunderstood, as family members may be very anxious about the assessment outcome. It is good practice to plan the topics you will be covering and what you want to say. Using descriptive terms to interpret test scores is helpful for parents and other team members. Lyman (1986) suggests the following scale:

## SNAPSHOT ■ *Gina's Comprehensive Assessment Report*

Larry Kahn is one of the special education consultants for the Allen School District. He recently completed a comprehensive assessment of Gina A., a first-grade student. Gina was referred to the assessment team by her teacher, Maria Gordon, who was troubled about her high level of activity and her lack of skills, among other concerns. The assessment report follows:

### Office of Special Services
14 Main Street
Allen, _____
Telephone: 200-299-2000

Name:  Gina A.

Address:  1 Hill Road
Allen, _____
Birth Date:  March 4, xxxx

Age:  7 years, 2 months

Sex:  female

Foster Parent:  C. B.

Address:  1 Hill Road
Allen, ____
Telephone:  xxx-xxx-xxxx

Date:  May 10, xxxx

Date of testing:  May 6, xxxx

Examiner:  L. A. Kahn

School:  Allen Elementary School

Principal:  L. Lindly

Teacher:  M. Gordon

Grade:  1

*Reason for Referral*
Gina was referred by her teacher because of problems of extreme activity within the classroom, developmental concerns, and a history of physical abuse.

*Background Information*
An evaluation by the E. C. Medical Center on 2/23/xx stated that Gina presented evidence of fetal alcohol syndrome. In at least four or five evaluations over the years, this child was identified as having a mild developmental delay. Efforts to secure early intervention services have been made off and on since infancy. However, because Gina's biological mother moved frequently, Gina received limited services. Dr. Jones on 10/10/xx indicated a *Wechsler (WISC–III)* score of 62 and "functioning well below her chronological age in language, cognitive, and motor skills areas."

Gina has been in foster care since the age of four, when she was exposed to inappropriate sexual behaviors at home, neglect, and abuse. Her biological mother, who has a history of physical and sexual abuse, is completing a prison sentence. Her brother, Paul, is living with a paternal grand-mother. Her father has infrequent contact with the family. Her foster care family wants to help Gina, and the family has been very involved in the assessment process.

*Family Involvement*
Mr. and Mrs. B., Gina's foster family, have been in frequent contact with the assessment team. Several team members visited the home, where Mr. and Mrs. B. shared their concerns about Gina and volunteered to participate with the team in identifying Gina's strengths and needs.

*Observations of the Environment*
Gina is currently in an inclusive first grade, that is, the classroom includes some children who have disabilities and some children who do not. There are 18 children in the classroom, with a teacher and an aide. In addition, an occupational therapist and a speech and language pathologist work with some of the children in the classroom on a weekly basis. The therapists are available to consult with the teacher during a weekly planning time.

The classroom is divided into four learning centers: math, science, reading, and community studies. There is much activity in the room as the

*(continued)*

children, teacher, aide, and related service personnel move about. Children's pictures and drawings cover the walls. The room appears to be stimulating and busy.

*Behavior Observations*

Informal testing and achievement testing were begun in a quiet corner of the classroom so that Gina could get used to the examiner before going to the examiner's office for further testing. The child was very reluctant to participate in the testing, and her behavior was consistently negative during the testing session. Gina repeatedly questioned why she was being asked to complete test items and several times she refused to try an item. Testing sessions were very brief because of her refusal to participate compounded by her short attention span. She could attend to a task for a few seconds but then was distracted by pictures on the wall, sounds from the radiator, and other background noise. She had to be coaxed to focus on the tasks. She was very distracted by all the test materials and touched everything throughout the session.

*Tests and Interviews*

The following tests were administered: *Kaufman Assessment Battery for Children (K–ABC), Peabody Picture Vocabulary Test–III,* and the *Child Behavior Checklist.* Gina was observed three different times in her classroom. Interviews were conducted with Gina's foster parent and with her teacher.

*Discussion of Results*

On the *Kaufman Assessment Battery for Children* Gina's mental processing composite score was a percentile rank of 2; the achievement score was a percentile rank of 1. Relative strengths on the cognitive and achievement batteries were Hand Movements (motor planning, perceptual organization) and Gestalt Closure (recall, alertness to the environment). Significant weaknesses on the cognitive and achievement batteries were Number Recall (short-term auditory memory, reproduction of a model), Riddles (word knowledge/recall), Word Order (verbal/auditory comprehension), Photo Series (visual sequencing, visual perceptual organization), Arithmetic (quantitative concepts, applied school-related skills, reasoning,

verbal comprehension), Reading/Decoding (applied school-related skills, early language development, long-term memory, reasoning).

On the *Peabody Picture Vocabulary Test–III,* Gina received a standard score of 45 with her true score following within the range of 45 to 57. The score indicates performance at the 1st percentile rank. Her performance remains consistent in terms of her overall standard score, indicating that her understanding of single words is commensurate with her cognitive ability.

On the *Child Behavior Checklist,* Gina scored in the high range of externalizing behaviors: attention problems, 80th percentile; delinquent behavior, 70th percentile; and aggressive behavior, 77th percentile.

Overall, it appears that Gina's short attention span and distractibility interfere with the formal testing. Observations confirmed that Gina performs somewhat better in the first-grade classroom than on the formal testing. However, when Gina's performance is compared with typical children in the kindergarten classroom, she performs well below her age peers. Classroom observations also indicate that Gina is reluctant to comply with requests made by her teacher and that she rarely cooperates with other children. She has a constant need for limit setting.

*Summary*

Gina is a child who has been diagnosed as having fetal alcohol syndrome. The results of formal testing, observations, and interviews indicate that she has a developmental delay, has a short attention span, is distractible, and has many negative behaviors. Her concept and language development are well below that of her age peers.

*Recommendations*

Gina is certainly in need of special education services to address her broad-based developmental delays. She will need intensive intervention services, consistent setting of limits, expectations for more age-appropriate behavior, and an environment with a great deal of structure.

Counseling and behavior management strategies should be offered to the foster family to help them deal with the negative behaviors, attention span, and distractibility.

SNAPSHOT ■ *Continued*

After completing the written report, Larry contacted Gina's foster parents to arrange for a convenient time to share the report with them. He wanted an opportunity to go over the report prior to the team meeting to allow the family an opportunity to ask questions and to discuss specific areas in more detail. During Gina's team meeting he will present the results and recommendations contained in the report, then file a copy of the report in the office of student records.

| Percentile ranks | Descriptive terms |
|---|---|
| 96 or above | Very high; superior |
| 85–95 | High; excellent |
| 75–85 | Above average; good |
| 25–75 | About average; satisfactory or fair |
| 15–25 | Below average; fair or slightly weak |
| 05–15 | Low; weak |
| 5 or below | Very low; very weak (p. 136) |

***The Family Educational Rights and Privacy Act.*** In Chapter 1 we discuss the Family Educational Rights and Privacy Act (also known as the Buckley amendment). The Buckley amendment allows families access to their records held at any educational agency that accepts federal money, including a public school. Family members have a right to all assessment information, and you should provide a copy of the report to the family members that they can take with them, as is their choice.

The Buckley amendment also protects students and families from the illicit sharing of

*Once an examiner completes the assessment, she meets with the student to explain the overall results.*

**TABLE 18.1**   *A Checklist for Evaluating an Assessment Report*

| Report Section | Yes | No |
|---|---|---|
| **A.** Identifying Information | | |
|     **1.** Is the information complete? | _____ | _____ |
|     **2.** Is the information accurate? | _____ | _____ |
| **B.** Reason for Referral | | |
|     **1.** Is the reason for referral clearly described? | _____ | _____ |
|     **2.** Is the source of the referral included? | _____ | _____ |
|     **3.** Does the reason for referral provide a reason for conducting the assessment? | _____ | _____ |
| **C.** Background Information | | |
|     **1.** Is this section complete? | _____ | _____ |
|     **2.** Are any of the descriptions vague? | _____ | _____ |
|     **3.** Can some information be omitted? | _____ | _____ |
| **D.** Behavioral Observations | | |
|     **1.** Are the observations clearly described? | _____ | _____ |
|     **2.** Are any of the descriptions vague? | _____ | _____ |
|     **3.** Does this section help the reader to visualize the student's behavior? | _____ | _____ |
| **E.** Assessment Approaches Used | | |
|     **1.** Are the sources of information identified? | _____ | _____ |
| **F.** Discussion of Results | | |
|     **1.** Does the discussion relate to the referral questions? | _____ | _____ |
|     **2.** Is this section organized around themes? | _____ | _____ |
|     **3.** Are the themes discussed separately, including references to appropriate tests and assessment procedures? | _____ | _____ |
|     **4.** Are strengths and needs described? | _____ | _____ |
| **G.** Summary | | |
|     **1.** Does this section restate the major themes and how the testing addressed the reasons for referral? | _____ | _____ |
|     **2.** Is this section too long? | _____ | _____ |
| **H.** Recommendations | | |
|     **1.** Do the recommendations logically follow from the rest of the report? | _____ | _____ |
|     **2.** Can the recommendations be implemented? | _____ | _____ |
|     **3.** Are recommendations for a variety of settings included? | _____ | _____ |
|     **4.** Are the recommendations understandable? | _____ | _____ |
| **I.** General Evaluation | | |
|     **1.** Is the writing clear? | _____ | _____ |
|     **2.** Has the report been proofread? | _____ | _____ |
|     **3.** Have the spelling, grammar, and punctuation been checked? | _____ | _____ |
|     **4.** Are the sections of the report identifiable? | _____ | _____ |
|     **5.** Has technical language been minimized? | _____ | _____ |
|     **6.** Is there any bias? | _____ | _____ |

assessment information. Before the school can release assessment information to other agencies or individuals outside of the school system, the parent must sign a written consent form. The consent form specifies which records to release, to whom, and the reason for the release. A copy of the records to be released must be sent to the student's parents.

## The Student

Students usually are anxious to know, "How did I do?" When students pose this question during the test, the examiner should offer a neutral response. For example, "I can see that you are trying hard."

Upon completion of the assessment the student may ask or expect you to explain some of the general results, depending on the age of the student, the student's interest in the testing situation, and your knowledge of the student. In some instances, your explanation may need to be a delicate balance between not discouraging the student on the one hand and helping the

older student accept certain limitations and appreciate what can be accomplished on the other. Thus, you might say, "You may have to study harder and longer than some boys and girls do to get good grades" (Lyman, 1986, p. 135).

## Test Software

Test publishers frequently offer test software that not only computes test scores but also generates reports. Table 18.2 provides a software review checklist for evaluating test scoring and computer-generated reports. For most computer scoring programs, the examiner enters the identifying information and the raw scores. Raw scores are computed, and the results can be printed in a variety of formats (Figure 18.7).

Test-scoring software and computer-generated reports help minimize scoring and computation errors and can be helpful in producing an individual test report. Select and use these programs carefully.

Since most of these programs yield a report based on a single test, they do not integrate

---

**TABLE 18.2    *Considerations for Evaluating Test-Scoring and Report Software***

1. Name of software:
2. System requirements:
3. Ease of use:

   Is program easily installed and user friendly?

   Is there a telephone hotline?

   Is the documentation easy to use?
4. Does the program allow information to be entered by a scanner?
5. Does the program allow cross-referencing:

   To student's IEP?
6. What test scores does the program yield?

       Standard scores        Stanines        Percentiles        Other
7. Does the program generate confidence intervals (with standard scores)?
8. Quality of the report:

   Does the report contain technical jargon?

   Does the report contain any generalizations that may bias the report?

**FIGURE 18.7**    *Example of a Computerized Scoring Program*

## Compuscore Version 1.1b
## Summary and Score Report

| | | | |
|---|---|---|---|
| **Name:** | T1.1B, Chris | **School:** | Stevenson |
| **Date of Birth:** | 08/07/19xx | **Teacher:** | Garrett |
| **Age:** | 11 years, 1 month | **Grade:** | 5.0 |
| **Sex:** | Male | | |
| **Date of Testing:** | 09/14/xxxx | **Examiner:** | Ernest |

*Tests Administered:* Chris was administered a set of tests from the *WJ® III Tests of Cognitive Abilities* and from the *WJ® III Tests of Achievement*. Because these two batteries are co-normed, direct comparisons can be made among Chris's Cognitive and achievement scores. These comparisons help determine the presence and significance of any strengths and weaknesses among his abilities.

*Table of Scores: Woodcock-Johnson® III Tests of Cognitive Abilities* and *Tests of Achievement*. Norms based on grade 5.0.

| Cluster/Test | Raw | GE | Easy to Diff | | RPI | PR | SS (68% Band) |
|---|---|---|---|---|---|---|---|
| GIA (Ext) | — | 4.8 | 2.7 | 7.7 | 89/90 | 47 | 99  (97–101) |
| Verbal Ability (Ext) | — | 8.8 | 6.4 | 12.1 | 98/90 | 93 | 122 (117–127) |
| Thinking Ability (Ext) | — | 4.5 | 1.9 | 10.2 | 89/90 | 44 | 98  (95–100) |
| Cog Efficiency (Ext) | — | 3.0 | 2.2 | 4.1 | 59/90 | 12 | 82  (78–86) |
| Comp-Knowledge Gc) | — | 8.8 | 6.4 | 12.1 | 98/90 | 93 | 122 (117–127) |
| L-T Retrieval (Glr) | — | 2.0 | K.3 | 8.1 | 80/90 | 7 | 77  (73–82) |
| Vis-Spatial Think (Gv) | — | 14.9 | 5.5 | >18.0 | 97/90 | 91 | 120 (114–125) |
| Auditory Process (Ga | — | 1.0 | K.1 | 3.2 | 67/90 | 8 | 79  (74–84) |
| Fluid Reasoning (Gf) | — | 6.3 | 3.9 | 9.9 | 94/90 | 63 | 105 (101–109) |
| Process Speed (Gs) | — | 5.5 | 4.4 | 6.8 | 93/90 | 61 | 104 (100–108) |
| Short-Term Mem (Gsm) | — | K.8 | K.1 | 1.5 | 13/90 | 2 | 68  (63–73) |
| Phonemic Aware | — | K.3 | <K.0 | 1.8 | 54/90 | 3 | 71  (65–76) |
| Phonemic Aware III | — | K.9 | K.1 | 2.1 | 49/90 | 2 | 69  (65–73) |
| Working Memory | — | 1.8 | 1.0 | 2.7 | 35/90 | 6 | 76  (72–81) |
| Broad Attention | — | 2.8 | 1.7 | 4.5 | 70/90 | 14 | 83  (80–87) |
| Cognitive Fluency | — | 6.2 | 4.1 | 8.7 | 94/90 | 67 | 107 (104–109) |
| Exec Processes | — | 5.8 | 3.4 | 9.5 | 92/90 | 62 | 105 (102–108) |
| Knowledge | — | 9.4 | 7.1 | 12.9 | 99/90 | 96 | 126 (122–131) |
| Oral Language (Ext) | — | 6.6 | 3.8 | 11.0 | 94/90 | 70 | 108 (104–112) |
| Oral Expression | — | 7.8 | 4.4 | 12.9 | 96/90 | 78 | 112 (107–117) |
| Listening Comp | — | 5.5 | 3.4 | 9.5 | 92/90 | 56 | 102 (98–107) |
| Total Achievement | — | 3.6 | 2.8 | 4.6 | 67/90 | 22 | 88  (87–90) |
| Broad Reading | — | 2.8 | 2.4 | 3.3 | 24/90 | 8 | 79  (77–81) |
| Broad Math | — | 6.6 | 5.0 | 8.8 | 96/90 | 84 | 115 (111–118) |
| Broad Written Lang | — | 2.7 | 1.9 | 3.7 | 51/90 | 8 | 79  (76–82) |

**FIGURE 18.7**   *Continued*

| Cluster/Test | Raw | GE | Easy to Diff | | RPI | PR | SS (68% Band) | |
|---|---|---|---|---|---|---|---|---|
| Basic Reading Skills | — | 2.2 | 1.9 | 2.5 | 5/90 | 4 | 74 | (71–76) |
| Reading Comp | — | 3.9 | 2.8 | 5.8 | 82/90 | 34 | 94 | (91–97) |
| Math Calc Skills | — | 5.7 | 4.2 | 7.8 | 93/90 | 68 | 107 | (102–112) |
| Math Reasoning | — | 7.2 | 5.7 | 9.7 | 98/90 | 87 | 117 | (113–121) |
| Basic Writing Skills | — | 2.2 | 1.7 | 2.8 | 17/90 | 4 | 74 | (70–77) |
| Written Expression | — | 4.0 | 2.7 | 5.8 | 82/90 | 30 | 92 | (88–97) |
| Academic Skills | — | 2.7 | 2.3 | 3.2 | 19/90 | 4 | 74 | (71–76) |
| Academic Fluency | — | 3.9 | 3.0 | 5.0 | 75/90 | 27 | 91 | (89–93) |
| Academic Apps | — | 5.5 | 3.9 | 8.2 | 94/90 | 61 | 104 | (100–109) |
| Academic Knowledge | — | 9.3 | 7.3 | 12.5 | 99/90 | 95 | 125 | (120–131) |

*Source:* Copyright © 2001. From the *Woodcock-Johnson*® *III*. Reprinted with permission of The Riverside Company. All rights reserved.

information from other sources, such as additional assessments, observations and interviews. Perhaps, more important, computer-generated reports do not provide the quality of interpretation that an experienced professional, using a variety of sources, can produce.

## Preferred Practices

Interpreting and writing assessment reports takes practice and a solid base of professional knowledge. Beginning teachers should have the opportunity to work with a mentor during the assessment process. A mentorship must include time to discuss interpretations of assessment information and to review and examine drafts of the assessment report.

Care needs to be taken when interpreting low scores. We know that students often live up—or down—to our expectations. The report that we share with family members and later file in the student's records can have an impact on how the family and teachers perceive the student in years to come.

The role of technology in assessment continues to evolve and will provide many exciting options in the future. We will need to keep abreast of these new developments and be prepared to learn new skills. The use of technology in interpreting and reporting assessment information may offer different promises tomorrow. Our challenge will be to use both our skills as professionals and our skills as thoughtful human beings to determine what is appropriate and what is not.

## Extending Learning

1. Working with others in a small group, prepare an explanation of the purposes of assessment reports. Exchange papers with another group and compare your work.

2. Discuss how the hypothesis generation approach can be useful in interpreting test performance.

3. Make plans to conduct a series of observations in a classroom. Working with a small group of students, identify the purpose of your observations and what you will be observing. You may want to refer to Chapter 5 for the steps in planning an observation. After you have completed the observations, write an observation report. Be sure to keep your original data collection forms. Share your report with others in your group. Could you enhance the information in your report? How could you display your observation data graphically? Use your small group to discuss ways to represent the data.

4. Use the checklist for evaluating an assessment report to critique Larry Kahn's report on Gina. Can you make any suggestions for improvement?

5. Obtain a computer program related to testing. Using the criteria this chapter presents, evaluate the usefulness of this program. What additional criteria would you add to our list?

(Answer to Cindy's math class observation data from page 485: The pie chart is the best way to display data in answer to the observation question because it allows the viewer to see how Cindy spends her time during the entire math class. If the observation question had been concerned with increasing or decreasing a behavior, then the bar graph would have been the best choice.)

## References

Bentzen, W. R. (1993). *A guide to observing and recording behavior.* 2d ed. Albany, NY: Delmar.

Cohen, D. H., V. Stern, and N. Balaban (1983). *Observing and recording behavior of young children.* 3d ed. New York: Teachers College Press.

Kamphaus, R. W. (1993). *Clinical assessment of children's intelligence.* Boston: Allyn & Bacon.

Kaufman, A. (1979). *Intelligent testing with the WISC–R.* New York: Wiley.

Kaufman, A. (1994). *Intelligent testing with the WISC–III.* New York: Wiley.

Lyman, H. B. (1986). *Test scores and what they mean.* 4th ed. Englewood Cliffs, NJ: Prentice-Hall.

McGrew, K. S. (1986). *Clinical interpretation of the Woodcock-Johnson tests of cognitive ability.* Orlando, FL: Grune & Stratton.

McGrew, K. S. (1994). *Clinical interpretation of the Woodcock-Johnson tests of cognitive ability–revised.* Boston: Allyn & Bacon.

Nicolson, S., and S. G. Shipstead (1994). *Through the looking glass.* New York: Merrill.

Sattler, J. (2001). *Assessment of children.* 4th ed. La Mesa, CA: Jerome M. Sattler.

Tufte, E. R. (1983). *The visual display of quantitative information.* Cheshire, CT: Graphics Press.

# 19

## *Implementing Program Evaluation*

## Overview

**Program evaluation** is a critical aspect of our work with students and their families. In this chapter we explore the evaluation process at three different programmatic levels. First, we examine ways of gathering, on an ongoing basis, information about the student. This, you will recall, is the monitoring step. We will need to evaluate and document advancement toward the goals and objectives developed in the IEP. As a result of monitoring a student's progress, we

often decide to make changes in instruction and in the services. In a review of the literature, Gallagher and Desimone (1995) found that the process of monitoring IEPs is largely neglected. This is a disturbing finding, given the critical need to carefully review services as they are being provided and the lost opportunity to make necessary changes when they are identified during the monitoring process.

At another level, we want to evaluate the student's overall program after a period of time. This level is the evaluation step in the assessment process and is conducted annually for students with IEPs. Does the student continue to need special education services?

Third, we should evaluate the services that our school or agency offers. We can gather information from several different sources for this kind of inquiry. Teachers can provide administrators with information regarding work conditions, equipment needs, or training priorities. Many programs that have a high staff turnover can gain valuable feedback through regular program evaluation. We will want to gather information from parents or other family members. Are they satisfied with their child's education program? Do they feel that the teachers are responsive to their questions and concerns? Are they involved in the process of making educational decisions? We can also aggregate information about the progress of groups of students in order to examine a program's success and benefits. If the program is funded by public monies, then periodic evaluations are necessary to demonstrate accountability for funds expended.

## Chapter Objectives

After completing this chapter, you should be able to:

- Define the term *evaluation* and describe a rationale for conducting evaluations.
- Compare and contrast different models of evaluation.
- Contrast the process of review and evaluation of the IFSP and an IEP.
- Describe important areas to address in conducting program evaluation.

## Introduction to Evaluation

Evaluation is a process that we all undertake frequently, especially as college and university students. We compare instructors, "Dr. DiMatina is so much more interesting than Dr. Doyle." We rate the exams, "That exam was terrible—it didn't cover what I had studied." Or we measure classroom learning activities: "That small-group exercise in class really helped me understand the different group dynamics involved in teamwork."

In terms of an overall course evaluation, we could provide our instructor with several different types of information. We could provide feedback on lectures: Are they interesting? Are they delivered too quickly? Or on the classroom climate, both physical and social: Is it too cold? Is the seating comfortable? Is there a feeling of support and encouragement? Or on the assignments: Are there too many? Do they relate to the course objectives stated in the syllabus? The results of our evaluation will be helpful to our instructor. Perhaps some changes will be made before the next term!

There are many different ways of "evaluating." In fact, there are many different definitions of **evaluation.** We will use the definition developed by Smith and Glass (1987), which states that evaluation is the process of establishing a value judgment based on the collection of actual data.

The Joint Committee on Standards for Education Evaluation, which includes individuals representing the major educational organizations, has published a list of standards for designing and implementing evaluations of educational programs. According to the Joint Committee (1994), a good evaluation must satisfy four important criteria.

- *Utility:* An evaluation should be informative and useful as well as timely.
- *Feasibility:* An evaluation should be appropriate to the setting and cost-effective.

- *Propriety:* An evaluation should protect the rights of individuals affected by the evaluation.
- *Accuracy:* The evaluation instrument should be valid and reliable.

The field of evaluation has its own terms for the individuals who participate in the evaluation process. **Stakeholders** are individuals who are interested in the results of the evaluation. An evaluation of the effectiveness of the program at Wentworth School will have several different groups, or stakeholders, who are interested in the findings. The teachers, therapists, and other staff at the school will want to know the results of the evaluation, as will the parents and administrators. On the other hand, an evaluation of the cost-effectiveness of the same program may be of primary interest to the school board members and administrators.

An individual with a background in research design, measurement, and evaluation should conduct the evaluation. The person may be an **internal evaluator,** such as a teacher or administrator who is trained in these skills, or from the outside, an **external evaluator** who is hired specifically for the purpose of completing the evaluation. There are advantages as well as disadvantages in using an inside or outside evaluator. Which of the following aspects do you consider to be an advantage in hiring an inside evaluator? an outside evaluator? (The answer is found at the end of the section on Extending Learning.)

- No bias
- Knowledge of special education programs
- Time to complete evaluation
- Cost savings
- Knowledge of questions to ask
- Knowledge of effective strategies for evaluation

The client who has requested the evaluation hires the evaluator. The client may be one person, such as the administrator of the program, or the client may be a group of people,

such as an advisory board, parent group, or state education department.

## When Does Evaluation Happen?

### Formative Evaluation

An evaluation that is ongoing during the period of program implementation is called a **formative evaluation.** Formative evaluation is very useful to teachers and therapists who are providing direct services because, by examining the data, they can make adjustments and changes before the end of the program cycle. This process is seen in Figure 19.1.

In this example, practitioners conduct an evaluation to monitor the student's progress throughout the program year. If the data indicate a need to adjust the program substantially from what the education program describes, they must call an IEP team meeting and parents must approve these changes.

### Summative Evaluation

An evaluation that is completed at the end of the cycle is called a **summative evaluation.** Summative evaluations can be completed on an individual student's program plan. For example, the

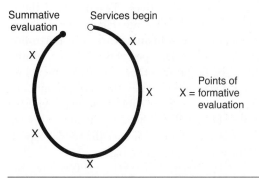

**FIGURE 19.1** *Evaluation as an Ongoing Process*

*Source:* From Cohen, Libby G., and Loraine J. Spenciner, *Assessment of Young Children.* Copyright © 1994. White Plains, NY: Longman Publishers. Reprinted/adapted by permission by Allyn & Bacon.

IEP team completes a summative evaluation during the annual review of the IEP.

Educators and others can conduct summative evaluations on entire programs, too. Depending on the focus, these evaluations provide administrators with a variety of information, including accountability and cost-effective data, parent or staff satisfaction data, or program effectiveness data.

## What Shapes Our Views

One of the most well-known models for evaluating special education services was developed by Ralph Tyler, one of the founders of educational evaluation. This model—called objectives-based evaluation—has long been in use by teachers and administrators in special education in several different ways:

1. to evaluate a student's ongoing progress toward the objectives described in the IEP;
2. to evaluate the student's program at the end of a time period or unit of study; or
3. to evaluate the overall program of the school.

The first step in conducting an *objectives-based evaluation* begins with identifying the set of objectives for measurement. The next step is to identify or develop the procedures or instruments to assess these objectives. Teachers and therapists who are monitoring IEP progress collect products of the student's work, use portfolios, make periodic videotapes of the student, administer tests, or develop their own instruments for measuring progress. They then collect and analyze products and test data to ascertain whether or not the objectives have been met. This approach is a recurring sequence that needs repeating on a regular, ongoing basis.

Dick, Carey, and Carey (2000) have described a similar model, which stresses the identification of student skills and the collection of data in order to revise instruction. The various steps in using an objectives-based model are seen in Figure 19.2.

## Planning an Evaluation of a Specific Student's Program

Teachers and other professionals who provide special education and related services must evaluate the education program periodically. IDEA states that the IEP and IFSP must be re-evaluated at least once a year. In addition, families receiving services under an IFSP must receive a *review* of the plan at least every six months, or more often if appropriate, based on child or family needs. This review is important because services that the IEP team originally identified during the team meeting may need alterations or adjustments. (A note about terminology: We will be using the term *review* to address the process of examining the IEP and IFSP and the term *monitor* to address the ongoing process undertaken by teachers and therapists for evaluating a student's daily or weekly progress.)

### Steps to Reviewing and Evaluating the IFSP for Young Children

***Step 1: Identifying Outcomes.*** In Chapter 1 we discuss the fact that IFSPs are written with outcome statements, rather than goals, and in Chapter 2 we explain how outcome statements are developed during the early childhood team meeting. IFSP outcome statements derive from family concerns, resources, and priorities as they relate to the child's development or family life that is related to the developing child. Strategies and activities follow outcome statements and answer the following questions:

Who will do what?

When will they do it?

How will we know if there is progress?

***Step 2: Agreeing on Evaluation Criteria.*** The team will need to decide on the criteria for evaluating the outcome statements. How will we know if we have achieved the outcome statement? Not only should family members identify

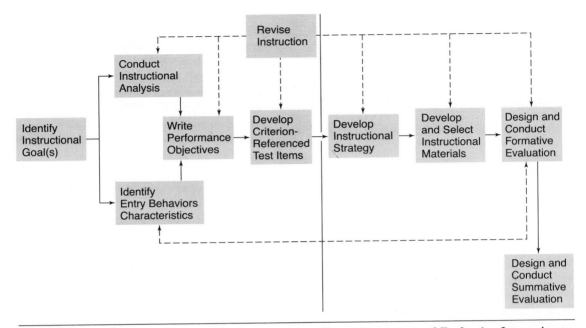

**FIGURE 19.2** *The Dick and Carey Systems Approach Model for Designing and Evaluating Instruction*

*Source:* From Walter Dick, Lou Carey, and James O. Carey, *The Systematic Design of Instruction,* 5th ed. Copyright © 2001 by Allyn & Bacon. Reprinted by permission.

the outcomes of the intervention services, but they should define how to measure the success of the outcome (Kramer, McGonigel, and Kaufman, 1991).

### Step 3: Meeting Time Lines: IFSP Review and Evaluation.

The team member who is acting as service coordinator is responsible for ensuring that the family receives a review of the IFSP every six months. The purpose of the review is to determine the degree of progress toward achieving the outcomes and to decide whether modifications or revisions are necessary.

The family service coordinator is also responsible for ensuring that an IFSP evaluation occurs at least once a year. The purpose of the reevaluation is to review the outcomes and current information, to revise outcomes, if necessary, and to write a new IFSP. How does all of this work? In the Snapshot about the Fandetti team, we can sit in on the last few minutes of a

team that is planning early intervention services for 3-year-old Brian, a little boy with Down syndrome.

## Steps to Monitoring and Evaluating the IEP

### Step 1: Identifying Annual Goals and Evaluation Criteria.

The team writes measurable annual goals for each area in which the student will receive services. These goals need to describe gains that are reasonably achievable during the program year. The team should also explain evaluation procedures for these goals. Examples of an annual goal might be:

> *Written language:* By June, Raymond will demonstrate improvement in written language by his ability to write a three-paragraph story with 90 percent accuracy in grammar.

or

## SNAPSHOT ■ *The Fandetti Early Childhood Team*

The four members of the team are seated around the Fandetti's living room floor. Jane Skinner, the early intervention specialist and family service coordinator, is taking notes as Joe Lewis, the speech therapist, summarizes the team members' observations. Marie Fandetti, Brian's mother, smiles as Paula Roix, the preschool teacher, describes Brian's creative use of gestures and sounds. Mrs. Fandetti states that she would like to know what Brian is trying to tell her. From their discussion the following outcome is defined:

Brian will increase his attempts in using language in order to make his needs known and to communicate with others.

As the outcomes for services are defined, Jane asks Mrs. Fandetti if she would be willing to assist in the review process by observing and noting Brian's attempts at communication. The team decides to review Brian's progress every three months.

*Adaptive:* Alexandra will eat lunch independently in the school cafeteria by the end of the program year.

### Step 2: Identifying Short-Term Objectives and Evaluation Criteria.

Written statements of specific objectives, or benchmarks, help the student meet the annual goal. These statements must be written so that a teacher can readily identify whether or not the student is meeting objectives. Objectives that are written in this manner are called *behavioral objectives* because they describe a student's behavior and are not left to a chance interpretation.

Objectives include criteria for determining whether the student has achieved the objective; what the evaluation procedures are; and when the team will review the objective. Thus, objectives have the following components:

1. they describe the behavior in observable terms;
2. they state the criteria for successful performance;
3. they describe the method of evaluating the behavior;
4. they indicate the time period for review.

There are many different styles used in writing objectives. The following examples illustrate two different styles of writing objectives with criteria for evaluation.

Given ten computational problems in mathematics (sums to 10) and a set of manipulatives (e.g., blocks or sticks), Robin will calculate the correct answer with 100 percent accuracy as measured by teacher observation. To be reviewed: June 2xxx.

By June, Robin will compute correctly ten mathematical problems (sums to 10) using a calculator as measured by the *BRIGANCE® Comprehensive Inventory of Basic Skills.*

### Step 3: Monitoring Progress.

Teachers and others should monitor a student's progress on an ongoing basis. Teachers and therapists will want to review objectives each marking period, or sooner, in order to monitor progress. Some of the questions to ask include: Is the student making progress toward this objective? Is this objective still appropriate, or have conditions changed? This provides an opportunity to make adjustments, if necessary. Best practice dictates that parents receive a copy of the review.

Graphing is an excellent way of monitoring progress, and there are many different types and formats. Figure 19.3 illustrates a graph of a student's progress in decreasing undesirable behaviors. The teacher observed the frequency of a student's verbal outbursts during homeroom period for one week and recorded them as baseline data. The following week, the teacher began an intervention program and observed and recorded the number of undesirable behaviors for

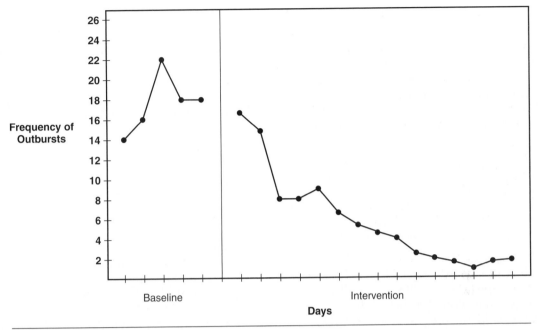

**FIGURE 19.3** *Charting a Student's Daily Progress*

*Source:* From *A Practical Guide to Solving Preschool Behavior Problems* by Eva L. Essa, Ph.D. Delmar Publishers Inc., Albany, NY; copyright 1990.

each day over the next three weeks. The procedure provides information to the teacher regarding the effectiveness of the intervention and allows continuous monitoring of the student's behaviors, presenting a profile of progress over a time. One of the disadvantages to graphing is that the adult must find time to record the information.

Students may take responsibility for graphing their progress. In fact, students can increase their independence by being able to record their own behavior through self-monitoring. Even preschool children with disabilities have increased appropriate behaviors through self-monitoring (Sainato, Strain, Lefebvre, and Rapp, 1990). McGinnis and Goldstein (1997) describe a method for helping elementary children and older adolescents with behavior problems in which students use a self-scoring cue card (Figure 19.4).

**FIGURE 19.4** *Student Cue Card*

**Staying Out of Fights**

❐ **1.** Stop and count to 10.

❐ **2.** Decide what your problem is.

❐ **3.** Think about your choices:

   Walk away.

   Talk to the person.

   Ask someone for help.

❐ **4.** Act out your best choice.

How did I do?

*Source: Skillstreaming the Elementary School Child: New Strategies and Perspectives for Teaching Prosocial Skills* (rev. ed., p. 216) by E. McGinnis and A. P. Goldstein, 1997, Champaign, IL: Research Press. Copyright 1997 by the authors. Reprinted by permission.

Self-monitoring techniques help students with disabilities increase opportunities for success in regular classroom settings. Dunlap, Dunlap, Koegel, and Koegel (1991) describe several examples of using self-monitoring for increasing on-task time, increasing responsivity to questions for a child with autism, and increasing accuracy on subtraction problems.

*Step 4: Evaluation.*    IDEA states that the IEP team must review existing evaluation data. On the basis of the review and input from the student's parents, the team identifies what additional data is needed. During this reevaluation, the team will consider whether the student continues to need services, what the present level of performance and educational needs of the student are, and whether the student needs changes in the type of services or in the amount of service time.

## Responding to Diversity

Evaluations that include family members have to be responsive to family diversity. To encourage family participation, you will need to consider the following questions: What family members should I contact? What are the preferences for communication? Should I send written materials? If so, are there alternative formats (such as braille) or translations that will be necessary?

Design evaluation procedures and the evaluation questions so as to encourage family members to contribute information. The Snapshot about Iliana Hernandez illustrates a case in point.

## Planning an Evaluation of a Program

### Identifying the Focus

An evaluation of an overall program, such as providing special education transition services to students in high school or a specialized reading program for students with disabilities, generates much useful information to advisory boards, administrators, staff, and parents. A program evaluation focuses on four general categories (Gall, Borg, and Gall, 1996). These include:

**1.** *Program goals:* What are the goals of the program? Does the program achieve the goals through the various services and activities? A goal is the purpose that the program attempts to achieve. Some programs may have goals that are very specific; other programs may have more general goals. However, goals are critical to the worth of the program.

**2.** *Program resources:* What are the program resources? Are they sufficient to meet the program goal(s)? Program resources may include a variety of areas, such as personnel,

**SNAPSHOT ■** *Iliana Hernandez*

Iliana Hernandez (1996) talks about her work with parents.

"I don't look Hispanic, but I am 100 percent, born in Cuba of Spanish descent. . . . I helped found Parent to Parent of Miami. My first attempt inviting parents to a Spanish-speaking meeting was a translated flyer. Guess what happened? Nobody showed up. That's when I said, 'Well, if I want to start helping my people, I have to know my people. . . . We needed more than language. We needed cultural understanding.'

"For instance, something I realized is the impact of the grandmother. There is nothing more powerful in a Hispanic family than the grandmothers. That old lady is the one who sets the rules of the house.

"Another thing that works well with Hispanic families is one-to-one support. We work more effectively on a personal basis. We hate papers. Parents tell me, 'I don't want to read it. I want you to tell me what you have for me. . . .'" (p. 6)

volunteers, transportation, materials, equipment, and space.

**3.** *Program procedures:* What procedures does the program use to achieve its goal(s)? Procedures may include teaching techniques and strategies or arrangements of the environment.

**4.** *Program management:* How does the program monitor resources and procedure? Is the management as efficient as it can be?

The program director, the administrator, or a staff meeting discussion usually determine the focus of the evaluation, although an advisory board or staff members could voice common concerns. These individuals, in consultation with the evaluator, will determine the evaluation procedures. For example, a special education director is interested in evaluating the efficiency and cost-effectiveness of special education services in the school district. However, more often than not, several different areas of concern or global questions regarding the program may have arisen. The director must decide which area needs evaluating.

## Developing a Needs Assessment Questionnaire

Sometimes administrators need assistance in specifying an area for evaluation. An informal survey or needs assessment questionnaire is an excellent way of identifying the area(s) of greatest need. There are several considerations in developing a questionnaire.

- Keep questionnaires fairly short and state questions simply.
- Incorporate items that can be checked and are easy to complete.
- Include some open-ended questions which allow individuals to respond to areas that you may have overlooked.
- People are much more likely to fill in and return questionnaires that are brief and easy to complete. Remember, a key issue in evaluation is obtaining as many responses as possible from all the relevant parties.

The design and development of questionnaires is beyond the scope of this book. We encourage the interested reader to refer to resources specific to the development of questionnaires and surveys.

In the Snapshot about the Waverly School District, Laurel Fuller, the special education director, conducted a needs assessment to determine a schedule of in-service training. Laurel wanted to identify the content areas that would be most beneficial to the teachers. This needs assessment solicited input from all the teachers and prioritized training needs.

---

**SNAPSHOT** ■ *An Informal Method for Identifying Needs at the Waverly School District*

The faculty at the Waverly School District used the following steps to identify and prioritize their needs. Laurel Fuller, special education director, solicited input from teachers and teaching assistants at a districtwide meeting by distributing sheets of paper and asking the educators to identify four areas that they felt needed attention and to number them in order of priority. The papers were collected and priorities were assigned points from 4 to 1. (The highest number was assigned to the first priority listed.) The total number of points was then calculated for each of the items listed and the top-priority item was identified. Through this informal needs assessment, Dr. Fuller was able to utilize information solicited from each member of the staff.

## Identifying the Informants

There are a number of individuals, or informants, who may provide information, including students, parents and other family members, teachers and support staff, administrators, and community members. When deciding whom to include in completing the evaluation, consider the questions that the program evaluation will need to answer. Generally speaking, program evaluations should include information from the consumers of services.

## Collecting Information

You can collect evaluation data in a variety of ways depending on the evaluation model you adopt. Hassel (1998) developed a comprehensive evaluation instrument to help school personnel gather information about efforts toward school reform. Using a rating scale format, teachers, administrators, and other school staff assess a variety of areas including assessment, curriculum, and instruction (Figure 19.5). This instrument collects both quantitative and qualitative data.

*Quantitative Data.* **Quantitative data** are information that can be assigned a number or score. Program evaluations often include pretest and posttest scores. Data collection includes the use of surveys or questionnaires on which individuals rate different statements. Family members as well as teachers and students can complete surveys and rating scales. The rating forms the basis of quantitative data. Quantitative data provides statistical information and analyses.

*Qualitative Data.* **Qualitative data** are descriptive rather than numeric. Interviews, discussions, observations, written answers, or students' work are the sources for qualitative data. Products that students have produced from work and play activities and video- and audiotape

*A program evaluator analyzes both quantitative and qualitative data.*

**FIGURE 19.5**  *An Instrument for Evaluating the School Program*

## Part II: The Current State of Our School's Program *(continued)*

| Methods and Strategies: Assessment | Judgment | | | Details and Evidence |
|---|---|---|---|---|
| | Low | High | Don't know | |
| How well does your school assess student learning? | 1 | 2 | 3 | 4 | |
| To what extent is assessment quality consistent across subjects, grade levels, and student groups? | 1 | 2 | 3 | 4 | |
| To what extent does your school use student assessment to help teachers change their practice? | 1 | 2 | 3 | 4 | |
| To what extent is student assessment aligned with curriculum and instruction in your school? | 1 | 2 | 3 | 4 | |
| How supportive is school staff of student assessment processes? | 1 | 2 | 3 | 4 | |
| To what extent is support for your school's student assessment process consistent across school staff? | 1 | 2 | 3 | 4 | |
| **Methods and Strategies: Instruction** | | | | |
| How effective is instruction in your school? | 1 | 2 | 3 | 4 | |
| To what extent is instructional quality consistent across subjects, grade levels, teachers, and student groups | 1 | 2 | 3 | 4 | |
| To what extent are instructional methods based on best-practices research? | 1 | 2 | 3 | 4 | |
| How well do instructional strategies meet the needs of specific student populations (at-risk, disabled, or LEP students)? | 1 | 2 | 3 | 4 | |
| To what extent is instruction aligned with curriculum in your school? | 1 | 2 | 3 | 4 | |
| To what extent is technology integrated into your school's instruction? | 1 | 2 | 3 | 4 | |
| How effective is technology as an instructional tool in engaging students in learning? | 1 | 2 | 3 | 4 | |
| To what extent is the use of technology consistent across subject, grade level, and student group? | 1 | 2 | 3 | 4 | |

*(continued)*

**FIGURE 19.5**  *Continued*

**Part I: Our Students**

| Students' Learning and Accomplishments | Low | High | Don't know | Details and Evidence |
|---|---|---|---|---|
| | | Judgment | | Details and Evidence |
| What proportion of your students meet your school's learning standards? | 1 | 2 | 3 4 | |
| To what extent is the proportion meeting your school's standards consistent across subjects, grade levels, and student groups? | 1 | 2 | 3 4 | |
| How successful are specific student populations (at-risk, disabled, or LEP) in their learning? | 1 | 2 | 3 4 | |
| What proportion of your students meet your school's standards for attendance and in-school behavior? | 1 | 2 | 3 4 | |
| To what extent are these proportions consistent across grade levels and student groups? | 1 | 2 | 3 4 | |
| To what extent are your students engaged in and excited about learning? | 1 | 2 | 3 4 | |
| To what extent is students' engagement in learning consistent across subjects, grade levels, and student groups? | 1 | 2 | 3 4 | |

*Source:* Copyright © 1998 by the North Central Regional Educational Laboratory. All Rights Reserved. Available: http://www.ncrel.org/csri/tools/makegood/makegoodp7.html.

recordings are all examples of qualitative data. Products of the program such as newsletters or monthly calendars of activities are also good sources. Anecdotal and running records as well as specimen records are other excellent sources. Although qualitative data are more difficult to synthesize, this type of data often provides helpful and, sometimes, unexpected findings.

*Focus Groups.*    **Focus groups** also provide an informal way of collecting information. Focus groups can be small gatherings of individuals

from similar constituencies or from different backgrounds, and the group may respond to specific questions or simply offer informal feedback to the group facilitator regarding the program.

A parent focus group can involve several family units; individual members may include mothers, fathers, grandparents, aunts, and other important individuals. Some groups include a deliberate mix of family members to encourage dialogue. Usually, families prefer focus groups because of their informal nature. Group interaction can often determine preferences and satisfaction with programs and services.

***Teacher-Developed Program Evaluation Instruments.*** Teachers and administrators often develop their own forms, tailored to meet the needs of the evaluation. Figure 19.6 illustrates a teacher-developed form that focused on the school's IEP team process. The IEP team developed this form as the result of a schoolwide effort to increase home-school partnerships. During the school-wide meeting of all teachers, the special education staff decided to look at the IEP process. Some of the questions that they wanted to answer included: Do parents feel welcome at the IEP team meetings? Do parents feel that we value their contributions? Are there areas where we could improve?

### Costs Involved

The final step in planning an evaluation is examining the costs involved. Typical cost items are consultant fees, including mileage, lodging, and meals; telephone; postage; computer time, including graphics production and supplies; copying; and so on.

Of course, costs do not only have to do with money. Other cost considerations include: How much time is involved? How much staff time do we need to allocate? Will we incur additional costs of staffing substitutes? What are the potential "costs" in terms of psycho-social issues to the staff? to the students? to the parents and other family members?

## Issues in Designing and Conducting Evaluations

In planning locally developed program evaluations, teachers and administrators must carefully consider the best methods for collecting evaluation information. In Figure 19.6 the teachers and administrators were interested in

---

**FIGURE 19.6** *A Teacher-Developed Form: Parent Satisfaction with the IEP Team Process*

| Question | Please circle the appropriate number: 1 = always, 2 = usually, 3 = sometimes, 4 = rarely. | | | | Additional Comments |
|---|---|---|---|---|---|
| 1. Were you given adequate notice of the team meeting? | 1 | 2 | 3 | 4 | |
| 2. Did you feel welcome at the team meeting? | 1 | 2 | 3 | 4 | |
| 3. Did you feel that other team members were interested in your comments during the meeting? | 1 | 2 | 3 | 4 | |
| 4. Did you feel that your questions or concerns were addressed adequately during the meeting? | 1 | 2 | 3 | 4 | |
| 5. Did you feel satisfied with the outcome of the team meeting? | 1 | 2 | 3 | 4 | |

gathering information about parents' feelings regarding the team process. Notice that items in the questionnaire are worded so as to gather information from the individual's perception.

In another school the special education administrator and teachers needed to know if the transition program at the high school was successful. The evaluation plan was to examine student test scores and to survey parents and students. Several school faculty members volunteered to work with the administrator in developing a draft student questionnaire (Figure 19.7).

After reading the draft, one of the teachers made the observation that there is only one question in this survey worded appropriately to gather information from the students' perspective. Which question is this? Instead of a survey, what are alternative ways to gather information regarding some of the other questions? Would these ways be advantageous? Why?

## Participating in an Evaluation of Your Program by Others

IDEA provides for the regular evaluation of local educational agencies, such as public schools, that serve students with disabilities. In fact, each state department of education in the United States must submit a plan to Washington that includes, in part, a description of their plan for evaluation. This plan must assess the effectiveness of a sample of programs in the state that are serving individuals with disabilities. The state evaluation must also address the effectiveness of the IEPs for individual students as well as the overall effectiveness of their program. The Snapshot of

---

**FIGURE 19.7**   *The First Draft of an Evaluation Form*

**Section I. (Organization)**
1.  I write down the due date of my assignments.
    _____always _____usually _____sometimes _____never
2.  I use the Study Skills Outline to plan my week.
    _____always _____usually _____sometimes _____never
3.  I remember to bring home the materials needed to finish my homework.
    _____always _____usually _____sometimes _____never

**Section II. (Survival Skills)**
4.  I can locate information in an appliance manual (for example a manual for a VCR).
    _____always _____usually _____sometimes _____never
5.  I can use my calculator to compute the correct amount of money at the shopping center.
    _____always _____usually _____sometimes _____never
6.  I can use a computer to search for information.
    _____always _____usually _____sometimes _____never

**Section III. (School/Work)**
7.  I feel that this job allows me to practice my skills.
    _____always _____usually _____sometimes _____never

**SNAPSHOT ■** *Evaluating Special Education Services at Sandy Brook Public School*

Three months ago, Josh Liebermann, the Director of Special Education Services at Sandy Brook Public School, received a form letter from the State Department of Education. The letter described the federal requirement that each local education agency that receives federal monies for the education of students with disabilities must be evaluated periodically by members of the State Education Department Program Review Team. Josh scanned the names of the individuals who were on the Department of Education team. There were four people who would be arriving: two consultants from the state education department, a special education director from a nearby school district, and an administrator from a school district in the southern part of the state. The letter described a tentative schedule for the visit and the items that the team would like to review.

The letter contained a clear description of what the team would need. They wanted to review several different IEPs, and they wanted to talk with several of the parents as well as teachers in the building. Later, the team would send a report summarizing their findings and recommendations for improvement, if necessary.

Sandy Brook Public School illustrates one way staff in a state department of education can choose to conduct their evaluation.

## Preferred Practices

Program evaluation must be a routine aspect of all programs. Evaluations must address the needs of different levels: from the student's (and family's) perspective and from the perspective of the overall program. The most useful program evaluations include data from a variety of sources and it is both quantitative and qualitative data. When conducting analyses of quantitative data, always use caution in interpreting scores that reflect change.

As funding continues to be an issue in the types of services that are offered, programs will be under more and more pressure to demonstrate effectiveness and accountability. Implementing program evaluation is an important component in the assessment process and should not be left to chance or excess funding at the end of a program cycle. As our field continues to grow and develop, we will need to continue the search for adequate methods and approaches with which to measure our work with students and their families.

## Extending Learning

1. Describe the different levels of program evaluation.
2. What are the federal requirements for evaluating the IFSP? the IEP?
3. Research other models of evaluation. For example, you might look at consumer-oriented or naturalistic models.
4. Make an appointment to talk to the special education administrator at your local school. How are special services evaluated?
5. You are interviewing for a job as special education teacher at the Riley School. The assistant principal asks you, "How would you monitor and evaluate progress of students in your program?" Prepare a response to the question.

(Answer to question on p. 503: Which of the following aspects are considered to be an advantage in hiring an outside evaluator? an inside evaluator?

Advantages to hiring an outside evaluator are that the person is nonbiased, knows the type of evaluation questions to ask, and has the time to complete the evaluation. On the other hand, the cost of using someone "in-house," an inside evaluator, will be less; and there is an assurance that the individual has a knowledge of special education programs.)

## References

Cohen, L. G., and L. J. Spenciner (1994). *Assessment of young children.* White Plains, NY: Longman.

Dick, W., L. Carey, and J. O. Carey (2000). *The systematic design of instruction.* New York: Allyn & Bacon.

Dunlap, L. K., G. Dunlap, L. K. Koegel, and R. L. Koegel (1991). Using self-monitoring to increase independence. *Teaching Exceptional Children* 23(3): 17–22.

Gall, M. D., W. R. Borg, and J. P. Gall (1996). *Educational research an introduction.* 6th ed. New York: Longman.

Gallagher, J., and L. Desimone (1995). Lessons learned from implementation of the IEP: Applications to the IFSP. *Topics in Early Childhood Special Education* 15(30): 353–378.

Hassel, B. (1998). *Comprehensive school reform: Making good choices.* Oak Brook, IL: North Central Regional Educational Laboratory.

Hernandez, I. (1996). Reaching underserved populations. *Families and Disabilities Newsletter* 7(1): 6.

Joint Committee on Standards for Educational Evaluation (1994). *The program evaluation standards.* 2nd ed. Thousand Oaks, CA: Sage.

Kramer, S., M. J. McGonigel, and R. K. Kaufman (1991). Developing the IFSP: Outcomes, strategies, activities, and services. In *Guidelines and recommended practices for the individualized family service plan*, ed. M. J. McGonigel, R. K. Kaufman, and B. H. Johnson, 57–66. Bethesda, MD: Association for the Care of Children's Health.

McGinnis, E., and A. P. Goldstein (1997). *Skillstreaming the elementary school child: New strategies and perspectives for teaching prosocial skills.* Rev. ed. Champaign, IL: Research Press.

North Central Regional Educational Laboratory (1998). *Comprehensive school reform: Making good choices.* Retrieved June 15, 2001. Available http://www.ncrel.org/csri/tools/makegood/makegoodp7.html.

Sainato, D. M., P. S. Strain, D. Lefebvre, and N. Rapp (1990). Effects of self-evaluation on the independent work skills of preschool children with disabilities. *Exceptional Children* 56(4): 540–549.

Smith, M. L., and G. V. Glass (1987). *Research and evaluation in education and the social sciences.* Englewood Cliffs, NJ: Prentice-Hall.

# Glossary

**ACCOMMODATIONS**  Changes to the education program that do not substantially alter the instructional level, the content of the curriculum, or the assessment criteria.

**ACHIEVEMENT TESTING**  The assessment of past learning.

**ADAPTIVE BEHAVIOR**  Refers to "the quality of everyday performance in coping with environmental demands" (Grossman, 1983, p. 42).

**ADAPTIVE DEVELOPMENT**  The young child's self-help skills, such as dressing, toileting, and grooming.

**ADAPTIVE SKILLS**  An individual's general competence in coping with the everyday demands of the environment. These skills include communication, self-care, home living, social skills, community use, self-direction, health and safety, functional academics, leisure, and work (American Association on Mental Retardation, 1992).

**ADVENTITIOUS VISUAL IMPAIRMENTS**  Conditions affecting sight that develop during childhood as the result of heredity, accident, or disease.

**ALTERNATE ASSESSMENTS**  Assessments that are aligned with the curriculum standards, which are used with all students, that enable students with severe or significant disabilities to participate in general large-scale assessments.

**ALTERNATE FORM RELIABILITY**  An estimate of the correlation of scores between two forms of the same test.

**ANALYTIC SCORING**  A type of scoring in which an independent score is reported for each area of the scoring rubric. This type of scoring provides diagnostic information. Individual scores indicate areas of strengths and areas that need improvement.

**ANCHOR PAPERS**  Student papers that represent writing at different levels of performance.

**ANECDOTAL RECORD**  A brief narrative description of an event or events that the observer felt was important to record.

**ASSESSMENT**  An evaluation process that includes observing, collecting, recording, and interpreting information to answer questions and make legal and instructional decisions about students.

**ASSESSMENT APPROACH**  A term used to describe the way information is collected for making an educational decision.

**ASSISTANCE TEAM**  A school-based team that consists of both regular and special education teachers who work together to solve problems and to offer suggestions to other teachers before the student is referred to the IEP team. This team may be known by other terms, such as **student assistance team, teacher assistance team,** or **intervention assistance team.**

**AUDIOGRAM**  A graph that traces the intensity of sounds detected at five different frequencies.

**AUGMENTATIVE/ALTERNATIVE COMMUNICATION (AAC)**  A method or device used by a person with a communication disability in order to communicate.

**AUTHENTIC ASSESSMENT**  The student completes or demonstrates knowledge, skills, or behavior in a real-life context; real-world standards are used to measure the student's knowledge, skills, or behavior.

**BASAL LEVEL**  The point below which the examiner assumes that the student could obtain all correct responses and at which the examiner begins testing.

**BENCHMARKS**  Examples of student work that illustrate each scoring level on the assessment scale.

**CATEGORY RECORDING**  A system of recording behavior by discrete groupings.

**CEILING LEVEL**  The point above which the examiner assumes that the student would obtain all incorrect responses if the testing were to continue and the point at which the examiner stops testing.

**CHECKLIST**  A list of characteristics or behaviors arranged in a consistent manner that allows the evaluator to record the presence or absence of individual characteristics, events, or behaviors.

**CHILD FIND**  A series of activities that increase public awareness and provide information about screening, programs, and early intervention or special education services. These services and activities help in locating children with special needs.

**COLLABORATING** A process that involves a commitment to work cooperatively with others to address common interests and issues.

**CONCURRENT VALIDITY** The extent to which two different tests administered at about the same time correlate with each other.

**CONDUCTIVE HEARING LOSS** Hearing loss that is due to some barrier to the sound waves that travel from the outer ear to the inner ear.

**CONFERENCING** A process conducted by two or more individuals for the purpose of sharing information, concerns, and ideas regarding common issues.

**CONFIDENCE INTERVAL** The range within which the true score can be found; frequently called the band of error or confidence level.

**CONGENITAL VISUAL IMPAIRMENTS** Conditions affecting sight that develop during the prenatal period or result from events during the birth process.

**CONSEQUENTIAL VALIDITY** The extent to which an assessment instrument promotes the intended consequences.

**CONSTRUCT VALIDITY** The extent to which a test measures a particular construct or concept.

**CONTENT VALIDITY** The extent to which the test items reflect the content it is designed to cover.

**CORRELATION** The extent to which two or more scores vary together.

**CORRELATION COEFFICIENT** A statistical technique for determining the direction and strength of the relationship between scores or among groups of scores.

**CRITERION-REFERENCED TEST (CRT)** A test that measures a student's test performance with respect to a well-defined content domain.

**CRITERION-RELATED VALIDITY** The extent that test scores obtained on one test or another measure are related to scores obtained on another test or another outcome.

**CRITICAL PERIODS** An interval of time in which the child is most responsive. If the individual has little or no opportunity to develop the skill or behavior during this period, the individual may have difficulty in doing so later on.

**CURRICULUM-BASED ASSESSMENT (CBA)** A broad approach to linking instruction with assessment.

**CURRICULUM BASED MEASUREMENT (CBM)** A type of curriculum-based assessment that emphasizes repeated, direct measurement of student performance.

**CURRICULUM-BASED VOCATIONAL ASSESSMENT (CBVA)** A type of curriculum-based assessment used in planning and developing vocational educational opportunities for students with disabilities.

**CUT SCORES** A prespecified score established in order to select or classify students for special education or labeling.

**DEAFNESS** A condition in which an individual is unable to hear and comprehend speech without visual cues, such as signing or speech reading.

**DERIVED SCORES** The result of transforming raw scores to other types of scores.

**DESCRIPTORS** Written descriptions used in a rating scale or in a rubric to explain and provide more detail about each of the levels of achievement.

**DETERMINING ELIGIBILITY** A process used to determine if a student meets the eligibility criteria for services according to federal and state definitions. Determining eligibility represents Step 3 of the assessment process.

**DEVELOPMENTAL DELAY** A delay in one or more of the following areas of development: physical, including fine and gross motor; cognitive; communication; social or emotional; or adaptive development. The term is used to identify infants and toddlers so that they can receive early intervention services without being labeled for a specific disability. IDEA states that, at the discretion of an individual state, the term *developmental delay* may be used with children ages 3 through 9 so that young children can receive special education services without being labeled for a specific disability category.

**DEVELOPMENTAL DOMAIN** Areas associated with the young child's general development. These areas include: physical, cognitive, communication, social, emotional, and adaptive development.

**DEVELOPMENTAL SCORES** Raw scores that have been transformed to reflect the average performance at age and grade levels.

**DEVELOPMENTAL QUOTIENT** An estimate of the rate of development.

**DEVIATION IQ SCORES** A standard score with a mean of 100 and a standard deviation of 15 or 16.

**DISTANCE VISUAL ACUITY** Part of a comprehensive eye exam, distance visual acuity measures sharpness of vision at 20 feet distance.

**DIRECT OBSERVATION** The systematic process of gathering information by looking at students and their environments.

**DOMAIN** A specific range of test items.

**DUE PROCESS** A set of safeguards to be followed during the assessment process and the delivery of services described in IDEA. Due process ensures that the rights of families and their children are not violated.

**DURATION RECORDING**  A method of recording that measures the length of time a specific event or behavior persists.

**EARLY CHILDHOOD TEAM**  A team that consists of the parents, the family service coordinator, and representatives of various disciplines who assess and implement early intervention services. The team makes decisions regarding eligibility and services for children birth through age 2 and, in some states, for children ages 3 to 5.

**EQUITY**  Refers to assessment that is approached in a fair, impartial, and just manner.

**ERROR ANALYSIS**  A technique that identifies patterns of errors in students' work.

**EVALUATION**  The process of establishing a value judgment based on the collection of actual data (Smith and Glass, 1987).

**EVENT RECORDING**  The recording of a behavior each time it occurs during an observation period; also called frequency recording.

**EXPANSION**  A restatement of the student's verbal language that adds words or more complex phrases.

**EXPRESSIVE LANGUAGE**  The ability to use language to communicate information, thoughts, feelings, and ideas.

**EXHIBITION**  A display of a student's work that demonstrates knowledge, abilities, skills, and attitudes.

**EXTERNAL EVALUATOR**  A person with a background in research design, measurement, and evaluation who is hired specifically for the purpose of completing an evaluation.

**EXTERNALIZING BEHAVIORS**  A broad array of behaviors directed outward that include disruptive and antisocial behaviors.

**EXTRAPOLATION**  The process of estimating the performance of students outside the ages and grades of the normative sample.

**FALSE NEGATIVE**  The type of error that is made when a student is not referred by the screening but should have been.

**FALSE POSITIVE**  The type of error that is made when a student is referred by the screening but should not have been.

**FAMILY**  A unit of two or more individuals who may or may not be related but who have extended commitments to each other.

**FAMILY-DIRECTED ASSESSMENT**  A type of assessment that focuses on information family members choose to share with other team members regarding family resources, priorities, and concerns. Family-directed assessment relates to children ages birth through 2 and, in some states, to children ages 3 to 5.

**FAMILY EDUCATIONAL RIGHTS AND PRIVACY ACT (FERPA)**  The Family Rights and Privacy Act (PL 93–380) states that no educational agency may release student information without written consent from the student's parents. FERPA also gives the family the right to review all records kept on their child as well as the right to challenge any of the information within the records.

**FAMILY-FOCUSED PHILOSOPHY**  This approach to working with families emphasizes the importance of enabling family members to mobilize their own resources in order to promote child and family functioning.

**FOCUS GROUPS**  Small gatherings of individuals from similar constituencies or from different backgrounds who respond to specific questions or provide informal feedback to the group facilitator. Focus groups can be used to evaluate the overall effectiveness of a school program.

**FORMATIVE EVALUATION**  An evaluation that is ongoing during the period of program implementation.

**FREE APPROPRIATE PUBLIC EDUCATION (FAPE)**  A term that refers to one of the rights guaranteed to children and youth with disabilities under IDEA.

**FREQUENCY DISTRIBUTION**  A way of organizing test scores based on how often they occur.

**FUNCTIONAL BEHAVIORAL ASSESSMENT**  A systematic process of gathering information that identifies the causes of and interventions for addressing problem behaviors.

**FUNCTIONAL VISION**  A term that refers to an individual's ability to use vision to complete everyday tasks.

**FUNCTIONAL VISION ASSESSMENT**  A systematic process of gathering information by a trained teacher of students with visual impairments, or similarly trained professional, to determine the extent of a student's use of residual vision.

**GRAPHEME**  The written equivalent of a phoneme.

**GRAPHOPHONICS**  Knowledge of letters and their associated sounds.

**HEARING IMPAIRMENT**  A blanket term that covers all types of hearing loss.

**HOLISTIC SCORING**  A type of scoring in which the teacher assigns a single score based on a scoring rubric. This type of scoring lacks the depth of information found in analytic scoring; however, it may be easier to design and conduct than analytic scoring.

**HYPERTONIC** Indicates muscles that are constantly tensed or stretched.

**HYPOTONIC** Indicates muscles that have too little tone and appear limp.

**INDIVIDUALS WITH DISABILITIES EDUCATION ACT (IDEA)** A federal law that focuses on the education of children and youth with disabilities. IDEA mandates specific requirements relating to the assessment process that teachers and test examiners must know and understand.

**INDIVIDUALIZED EDUCATION PROGRAM (IEP)** IDEA mandates that all students with disabilities ages 3 through 21 have an individualized education program (IEP). This written plan specifies the special education and related services that must be provided.

**INDIVIDUALIZED FAMILY SERVICE PLAN (IFSP)** IDEA mandates that all young children (birth through 2 years) and their families have an individualized family service plan (IFSP). Children ages 3 to 5 may receive services provided by an IFSP or an IEP. The IFSP is a written document that specifies the plan for services and is guided by the family's concerns, priorities, and resources.

**IEP TEAM** A multidisciplinary team consisting of the parents, school personnel, and, when possible, the student, that has the responsibility to make decisions regarding assessment procedures as defined by IDEA. This team may be known as the **special services team** or other term as defined by state regulation.

**INFORMANT** An individual who knows a student well and who can provide information about that student.

**INNER LANGUAGE** The language used during thinking, planning, and other mental processes.

**INTENSITY RECORDING** A measure of the strength of a behavior.

**INTERNAL CONSISTENCY RELIABILITY** An estimate of the homogeneity or interrelatedness of responses to test items.

**INTERNAL EVALUATOR** A person such as a teacher or administrator employed by the school who is trained in research design, measurement, and evaluation and who conducts and completes an evaluation.

**INTERNALIZING BEHAVIORS** Behaviors that are inner-directed and include social withdrawal, anxious or inhibited behaviors, or somatic problems.

**INTERPOLATION** The process of estimating the scores of students within the ages and grades of the norming sample.

**INTERSCORER/INTERRATER/INTEROBSERVER RELIABILITY** An estimate of the extent to which two or more scorers, observers, or raters agree on how to score a test or how to observe behaviors.

**INTERVAL RECORDING** A recording of specific events or behaviors during a prespecified time interval.

**INTERVAL SCALE** A scale in which the items are the same distance apart; the scale does not have an absolute zero.

**INTERVENTION ASSISTANCE TEAM** *See* **assistance team.**

**ITEM RESPONSE THEORY (IRT)** A conceptualization that involves a statistical calculation to determine how well the instrument differentiates between individuals at various levels of ability or characteristics that are measured.

**LANGUAGE DISORDER** A difficulty or inability in decoding or encoding the set of symbols used in language or an inability to effectively use inner language. *See* also **speech disorder.**

**LANGUAGE DOMINANCE** An individual's preferred language.

**LANGUAGE PROBE** A diagnostic technique in which instruction is modified to elicit specific information about a student's receptive or expressive language.

**LANGUAGE PROFICIENCY** An individual's level of expertise in a language.

**LANGUAGE SAMPLE** A recording of a student's oral language that yields information regarding vocabulary, syntax, semantics, articulation, and the ability to use language in functional ways.

**LATENCY RECORDING** A measure of the amount of time elapsed between a behavior or event (or request to begin the behavior) and the beginning of the prespecified behavior.

**LIKERT SCALE** A type of measurement that allows the evaluator to indicate extent of agreement with each statement on the assessment instrument. The statements are assigned a numerical value such as 1 to 5 or 1 to 7, with a rating of 1 being the lowest.

**MALADAPTIVE BEHAVIORS** Behaviors that include antisocial behaviors, aggression, withdrawal behavior, delayed social skills, and difficulties with interpersonal relationships.

**MEAN** The average score.

**MEAN LENGTH OF UTTERANCE (MLU)** Refers to the average number of individual units of meaning that the student expresses using phrases or sentences during the observation period. MLU can be used to assess amount of spoken language.

**MEDIAN**    The point on a scale above which and below which 50 percent of the cases occur. A point or score that separates the top 50 percent of students who took the test from the bottom 50 percent of students.

**MISCUES**    Patterns of errors. According to Goodman (1984, 1989) these are "natural" errors rather than mistakes.

**MIXED HEARING LOSS**    A hearing loss that results from damage to the inner ear and auditory nerve combined with the inability to hear sounds below a certain decibel level.

**MOBILITY**    The ability to move safely and efficiently from one place to another.

**MODE**    The score that occurs most often in a group of scores. The mode is the most commonly occurring test score.

**MODIFICATIONS**    Changes or adaptations made to the education program that alter the level, content, and or assessment criteria.

**MONITORING INDIVIDUAL PROGRESS**    A process used to determine if the student is making progress by examining the student's work, accomplishments, and achievements. Monitoring individual progress represents Step 5 of the assessment process.

**MORPHEME**    The single unit of letters that comprise a unit of meaning. A morpheme may be a whole word, prefix, or a suffix.

**MORPHOLOGY**    The study of the single units of letters that represent a unit of meaning.

**MULTIDISCIPLINARY TEAM**    Professionals from two or more disciplines or professions who are involved in the provision of integrated and coordinated services including assessment activities.

**MUSCLE TONE**    The amount of tension that is present in a resting muscle.

**NEAR VISUAL ACUITY**    A measure of near vision, usually given in inches, meters, or Jaeger chart numbers. Near visual acuity is part of a comprehensive eye exam.

**NEURODEVELOPMENTAL TREATMENT (NDT)**    A treatment approach that facilitates a child's normal, natural movement that allows a child to experience that feeling through typical activities.

**NOMINAL SCALE**    The items on the scale represent names; the values assigned to the names do not have any innate meaning or value.

**NORMAL CURVE**    A symmetrical bell-shaped curve.

**NORMAL CURVE EQUIVALENT (NCE)**    A standard score with a mean of 50 and a standard deviation of 21.06.

**NORM-REFERENCED TEST**    A test that compares a student's test performance with that of similar students who have taken the same test.

**NORMS**    The scores obtained by the standardization sample; the scores to which students are compared when they are administered a test.

**OBTAINED SCORE**    The score that an individual receives on a test.

**ORDINAL SCALE**    The items on the scale are listed in rank order.

**ORIENTATION**    The process that an individual with a visual impairment uses to establish one's position in the environment by using the other senses.

**OTOLOGIST/OTOLARYNGOLOGIST**    A physician who specializes in disorders of the ear.

**OUTCOME-ORIENTED PROCESS**    A process in which the focus is on the attainment of prespecified performance objectives.

**OUT-OF-LEVEL TESTING**    Students in one grade level are assessed with tests that are designed for students in another grade level.

**PARESIS**    A muscle weakness.

**PERCENTAGE DURATION RATE**    A term that refers to the percentage of time a behavior or event occurs.

**PERCENTAGE SCORE**    The percent of test items that were answered correctly.

**PERCENTILE RANK**    The point in a distribution at or below which the scores of a given percentage of students fall.

**PERFORMANCE-BASED ASSESSMENT**    The demonstration of knowledge, skills, or behavior.

**PHONEME**    The smallest unit of sound that has meaning in a language.

**PHONOLOGY**    The study of speech sounds.

**POPULATION**    The large group from which the sample of individuals is selected and to which individual comparisons are made regarding test performance.

**PORTFOLIO**    A systematic collection of a student's work, assembled over a period of time, that demonstrates the student's efforts, progress, and achievement.

**PRAGMATICS**    The study of the use of language in social situations.

**PREDICTIVE VALIDITY**    The extent to which one measure predicts later performance or behavior.

**PREREFERRAL**    A process in which questions and concerns about a student are raised and discussed. The law does not require a prereferral procedure and not all schools have a prereferral process.

**PROBE**   A diagnostic technique that modifies instruction in order to determine whether an instructional strategy is effective.

**PROGRAM EVALUATION**   A process used to assess (1) the progress the student has made in the individualized education program and (2) the overall quality of the school program. Evaluating the program represents Step 6 in the assessment process.

**PROGRAM PLANNING**   The process of determining the student's current level of functioning and planning the instructional program. Program planning is Step 4 of the assessment process.

**QUALITATIVE DATA**   Information that is descriptive rather than numeric.

**QUANTITATIVE DATA**   Information that can be assigned a number or score.

**QUESTIONNAIRE**   A set of questions designed to gather information.

**RATING SCALE**   A measure that helps answer questions about the learning environment or about one or more students.

**RATIO SCALE**   The items on the scale are the same distance apart; the scale does have an absolute zero.

**RAW SCORES**   The number of items correct without adjustment for guessing.

**REFERRAL**   A process in which questions and concerns about a student are raised and referred to the IEP team. The referral may come from a teacher, parent, or the student. Referral represents Step 2 of the assessment process.

**RELIABILITY**   Indicates the consistency or stability of test performance. The 1999 edition of *Standards for Educational and Psychological Testing* describes reliability and provides a departure from more traditional thinking about reliability. In this edition, reliability refers to the "scoring procedure that enables the examiner to quantify, evaluate, and interpret behavior or work samples. Reliability refers to the consistency of such measurements when the testing procedure is repeated on a population of individuals or groups" (p. 25).

**RECEPTIVE LANGUAGE**   The ability to understand spoken language.

**RUBRIC**   An assessment scale that identifies the area(s) of performance and defines various levels of achievement.

**RUNNING RECORD**   A description of the events that is written as the events occur.

**SAMPLE**   A subgroup of a large group that is representative of the large group. This subgroup is the group that is actually tested.

**SCATTER PLOT**   A type of interval recording form that the observer uses to record single behaviors or a series of behaviors during the observation period.

**SCHEMA**   An "interlocking knowledge network" (Rhodes and Shanklin, 1993, p. 151).

**SCREENING**   A process used to identify students who may have a disability and who will be referred for further assessment. Screening is Step 1 of the assessment process.

**SEMANTICS**   The study of word meanings.

**SENSORINEURAL HEARING LOSS**   A hearing loss that results from problems with the inner ear or auditory nerve.

**SENSORY INTEGRATION**   A treatment approach that assists the brain in organizing and interpreting everyday sensory experiences including touch, movement, body awareness, sight, sound, and the pull of gravity.

**SHAPING**   A term that refers to reinforcing successive approximations of the target or goal behavior. In reference to the development of language, the verbal response is reinforced as the sound or word being produced more and more closely approximates the sound or word in the language.

**SKEWED DISTRIBUTION**   A curve in which most of the scores are at the low end or the high end of the curve.

**SPECIAL SERVICES TEAM**   *See* **IEP team.**

**SPEECH**   The production of oral language for the purpose of expression.

**SPEECH DISORDER**   A speech disorder refers to a difficulty in articulation, such as the way words are pronounced; the fluency of speech, including rate and rhythm; and the pitch, volume, and quality of the voice.

**SPLIT-HALF RELIABILITY**   An estimate of the correlation of scores between two halves of a test.

**STAKEHOLDERS**   Individuals who are interested in the results of the evaluation.

**STANDARD DEVIATION (SD)**   A measure of the degree to which various scores deviate from the mean, or average score.

**STANDARD ERROR OF MEASUREMENT (SEM)**   The amount of error associated with individual test scores, test items, item samples, and test times.

**STANDARDIZATION SAMPLE**   The individuals who are actually tested during the process of test development.

**STANDARDIZED TEST**   A test in which the administration, scoring, and interpretation procedures are prescribed in the test manual and must be strictly followed. A standardized test is usually norm referenced.

**STANDARD SCORES**  Raw scores that have been transformed so that they have the same mean and the same standard deviation.

**STANINE**  A type of standard score that has a mean of 5 and a standard deviation of 2; a distribution of scores can be divided into 9 stanines.

**STUDENT ASSISTANCE TEAM**  *See* **assistance team.**

**SUMMATIVE EVALUATION**  An evaluation that is completed at the end of a cycle or program year.

**SUPPORTS**  "Resources and strategies that promote the interests and causes of individuals with or without disabilities; that enable them to access resources, information, and relationships inherent within integrated work and living environments; and that result in their enhanced interdependence/intradependence, productivity, community integration, and satisfaction" (American Association on Mental Retardation, 1992, p. 101).

**SYNTAX**  A system of rules that dictates how words are combined into meaningful phrases and sentences.

**TARGET BEHAVIOR**  A behavior that is acquired or eliminated by manipulating the antecedents and consequences.

**TASK ANALYSIS**  The division of a skill into small, discrete, sequential steps.

**TEACHER ASSISTANCE TEAM**  *See* **assistance team.**

**TESTING**  Administering a set of questions to an individual or group in order to determine knowledge or skills. Results are reported in one or more types of scores.

**TEST-RETEST RELIABILITY**  An estimate of the correlation between scores when the same test is administered two times.

**TRANSITION**  Moving from one system of services to another.

**TRANSITION SERVICES**  A coordinated set of activities for a student, designed within an outcome-oriented process, that promotes movement from school to post-school activities, including postsecondary education, vocational training, integrated employment (including supported employment), continuing and adult education, adult services, independent living, and community participation.

**TREMORS**  Problems in muscle control that appear as jerky involuntary movements of the arms and legs.

**TRIANGULATION**  Conclusions about student performance that are based on multiple sources of information.

**TRUE SCORE**  The score an individual would obtain on a test if there were no measurement errors.

**VALIDITY**  The extent to which a test measures what it says it measures.

**VISUAL IMPAIRMENT**  A loss in one or more of the areas of visual functioning, including near and distance acuity, visual field, or color vision.

**YOUNG CHILDREN**  Children ages birth through age 8.

# Index

# *Photo Credits*

544